DATA STRUCTURES

[Concepts and Implementation]

Anuradha A. Puntambekar

M.E. (Computer)

Formerly Assistant Professor in

P.E.S. Modern College of Engineering,

Pune

TECHNICAL PUBLICATIONS

SINCE 1993

An Up-Thrust for Knowledge

DATA STRUCTURES

First Edition : December 2020

Published by :

TECHNICAL PUBLICATIONS
SINCE 1993 An Up-Thrust for Knowledge

Amit Residency, Office No.1, 412, Shaniwar Peth, Pune - 411030, M.S. INDIA
Ph.: +91-020-24495496/97, Email : sales@technicalpublications.org
Website : www.technicalpublications.org

ISBN 978-93-332-2391-1

9789333223911

PREFACE

The importance of **Data Structures** is well known in various engineering fields. Overwhelming response to my books on various subjects inspired me to write this book. The book is structured to cover the key aspects of the subject **Data Structures.**

The book uses plain, lucid language to explain fundamentals of this subject. The book provides logical method of explaining various complicated concepts and stepwise methods to explain the important topics. Each chapter is well supported with necessary illustrations, practical examples and solved problems. All the chapters in the book are arranged in a proper sequence that permits each topic to build upon earlier studies. All care has been taken to make students comfortable in understanding the basic concepts of the subject.

Representative questions have been added at the end of each section to help the students in picking important points from that section.

The book not only covers the entire scope of the subject but explains the philosophy of the subject. This makes the understanding of this subject more clear and makes it more interesting. The book will be very useful not only to the students but also to the subject teachers. The students have to omit nothing and possibly have to cover nothing more.

I wish to express my profound thanks to all those who helped in making this book a reality. Much needed moral support and encouragement is provided on numerous occasions by my whole family. I wish to thank the **Publisher** and the entire team of **Technical Publications** who have taken immense pain to get this book in time with quality printing.

Any suggestion for the improvement of the book will be acknowledged and well appreciated.

Author
A.A. Puntambekar

Dedicated to God.

SYLLABUS

1. Introduction to Data Structure

Data management concepts, Data types - primitive and non-primitive, Performance analysis and measurement (Time and space analysis of algorithms - Average, best and worst case analysis), Types of data structures - Linear and non linear data structures. **(Chapter - 1)**

2. Linear Data Structure

Array : Representation of arrays, Applications of arrays, Sparse matrix and its representation.

Stack : Stack-Definitions and concepts, Operations on stacks, Applications of stacks, Polish expression, Reverse polish expression and their compilation, Recursion, Tower of Hanoi.

Queue : Representation of queue, Operations on queue, Circular queue, Priority queue, Array representation of priority queue, Double ended queue, Applications of queue.

Linked list : Singly linked list, Doubly linked list, Circular linked list, Linked implementation of stack, Linked implementation of queue, Applications of linked list. **(Chapters - 2, 3, 4, 5)**

3. Nonlinear Data Structure

Tree-definitions and concepts, Representation of binary tree, Binary tree traversal (Inorder, Postorder, Preorder), Threaded binary tree, Binary search trees, Conversion of general trees to binary trees, Applications of trees - Some balanced tree mechanism, e.g. AVL trees, 2-3 trees, Height balanced, Weight balance. Graph-matrix representation of graphs, Elementary graph operations, (Breadth first search, Depth first search, Spanning trees, Shortest path, Minimal spanning tree). **(Chapters - 6, 7)**

4. Hashing and File Structures

Hashing : The symbol table, Hashing functions, Collision resolution techniques.

File structure : Concepts of fields, Records and files, Sequential, Indexed and relative / random file organization, Indexing structure for index files, Hashing for direct files, Multi-key file organization and access methods. **(Chapters - 8, 9)**

5. Sorting and Searching

Sorting - Bubble sort, Selection sort, Quick sort, Merge sort searching - Sequential search and binary search. **(Chapter - 10)**

List of Practical

At least 10 practical should be performed by students using programming language.

1. Introduction to pointers. Call by Value and Call by reference.
2. Introduction to Dynamic Memory Allocation. DMA functions malloc(), calloc(), free() etc.
3. Implement a program for stack that performs following operations using array.

   (a) PUSH (b) POP (c) PEEP (d) CHANGE (e) DISPLAY
4. Implement a program to convert infix notation to postfix notation using stack.
5. Write a program to implement QUEUE using arrays that performs following operations (a) INSERT (b) DELETE (c) DISPLAY
6. Write a program to implement Circular Queue using arrays that performs following operations. (a) INSERT (b) DELETE (c) DISPLAY
7. Write a menu driven program to implement following operations on the singly linked list.

   (a) Insert a node at the front of the linked list.

   (b) Insert a node at the end of the linked list.

   (c) Insert a node such that linked list is in ascending order.(according to info. Field)

   (d) Delete a first node of the linked list.

   (e) Delete a node before specified position.

   (f) Delete a node after specified position.
8. Write a program to implement stack using linked list.
9. Write a program to implement queue using linked list.
10. Write a program to implement following operations on the doubly linked list.

    (a) Insert a node at the front of the linked list.

    (b) Insert a node at the end of the linked list.

    (c) Delete a last node of the linked list.

    (d) Delete a node before specified position.
11. Write a program to implement following operations on the circular linked list.

    (a) Insert a node at the end of the linked list.

    (b) Insert a node before specified position.

    (c) Delete a first node of the linked list.

    (d) Delete a node after specified position.
12. Write a program which create binary search tree.
13. Implement recursive and non-recursive tree traversing methods inorder, preorder and post-order traversal.
14. Write a program to implement Queue Sort
15. Write a program to implement Merge Sort
16. Write a program to implement Bubble Sort
17. Write a program to implement Binary Search.

TABLE OF CONTENTS

Data Structures Laboratory (L - 1) to (L - 10)

1 Introduction to Data Structures

Syllabus

Data management concepts, Data types - primitive and non-primitive, Performance analysis and measurement (Time and space analysis of algorithms-average, Best and worst case analysis), Types of data structures - Linear and non linear data structures.

Contents

1.1 Data Management Concepts

The Concept of data management deals with collection of data, data organization in appropriate data structures and use of appropriate algorithm for implementation.

1.1.1 Data

- Data is a collection of information but it is in **raw form**.
- When data is processed it becomes **information**.
- Data can be a number, symbol, character or any kind of information.
- The logical and meaningful form of data is called **information**.
- Data is plural and datum is singular form.
- A data type is a term which to the kind of data a specific variable may hold in programming language. For example in C there the data types are int,float,char,double etc.
- Generally a programming language supports a set of built in data types and allows the user to define a new type those are called user defined data types. So there are two types of data types -

1. **Built in data type :** Such as int, float, char, double which are defined by programming language itself.
2. **User defined data type :** Using the set of built in data types user can define his own data type.

For example :

```
typedef struct student
{
        int roll;
        char name;
}s;
s s1;
```

s is tag for user defined data type which defines the structure student and s1 is variable of data type s.

1.1.2 Data Object

- Data object is a term that refers to a set of elements such a set may be finite or infinite.
- For example - consider a set of students studying in second year of computer engineering.
- It is a finite set, whereas set of natural numbers is an infinite set.

1.1.3 Data Structure

- The combination which describes the set of elements together with the description of all legal operations is termed as data structure. In other words data structure will tell us which are the elements required as well as the legal operations on those set of elements.
- **For example :**
- Consider the set of elements as integer, and the operations on integer are addition, subtraction, multiplication, division etc. Therefore the data object - integer along with description of these operation will be a data structure.

The standard way of defining data structure is as follows -

- **Definition :**

A data structure is a set of domains D, a set of functions F and set of axioms A.

This triple (D, F, A) denotes the data structure d. Where D is the domain.

1.1.4 Abstract Data Type

- The abstract data type is a triple of D - set of domains, F - set of functions, A - axioms in which only what is to be done is mentioned but how is to be done is not mentioned.
- In ADT, all the implementation details are hidden. In short

ADT = Type + Function names + Behavior of each function

We will discuss in further chapters how the ADT can be written

1.1.5 Example of ADT

- The abstract data type consists of following things
  1. Data used along with its data type.
  2. Declaration of functions which specify only the purpose. That means "What is to be done" in particular function has to be mentioned but "how is to be done" must be hidden.
  3. Behaviour of function can be specified with the help of data and functions together.
- Thus ADT allows programmer **to hide the implementation details**. Hence it is called **abstract**. For example : If we want to write ADT for a set of integers, then we will use following method

```
AbstractDataType Set {
Instances : Set is a collection of integer type of elements.
Preconditions : none
Operations :
1. Store ( ) : This operation is for storing the integer element in a set.
2. Retrieve ( ) : This operation is for retrieving the desired element from the given
   set.
3. Display ( ) : This operation is for displaying the contents of set.
}
```

- There is a specific method using which an ADT can be written. We begin with keyword **AbstractDataType** which is then followed by name of the data structure for which we want to write an ADT. In above given example we have taken **Set** data structure.
- Then inside a pair of curly brackets ADT must be written.
- We must first write **instances** in which the basic idea about the corresponding data structure must be given. Generally in this section definition of corresponding data structure is given.
- Using **Preconditions** or **Postconditions** we can mention specific conditions that must be satisfied before or after execution of corresponding function.

1.2 Data Types

GTU : CE, Dec.- 03, IT, Dec.-05, Winter-17

- The data type represents the type of data.
- The data type can be numeric or character type.
- It is categorized into two groups - primitive and non primitive.
- Any variable in C can be declared as,

Data_type Variable_name

First of all, let us get introduced with the basic four data types.

1. Integer Data Type :

This data type is used to have the integer value in a variable. The value should not contain any fractional data.

For example

int a;
a=5; is allowed but
a=5.0 is not allowed.

Here a is a variable name which can store integer data.

2. Float Data Type :

This data type is used to store the real values in a variable. The value may contain some fractional data.

For example

```
        float a;
        a=5; is allowed but
             it will be interpreted as
        a=5.0
             similarly
        float val;
        val=3.79 is perfectly allowed.
```

3. Character Data Type :

This data type is used to have some text or alphabetical information in a variable.

For example

If one needs to store the status as T or F, then we will use the variable which is of character type which is denoted by char.

```
        char status;
        status='T';
```

Note that the character is always written within single quotes.

4. Double Data Type :

This data type is used to store the numeric information in the variable. This data type is mainly meant for the real values. It is same as of float data type but the capacity of this data type is larger than the float data type.

For example

```
    double val;
```

To summarize everything -

Name	Format specification	Memory requirement	Range
int	%d	2 bytes	- 128 to 127
float	%f	4 bytes	- 32,768 to 32,767
char	%c	1 byte	3.4e - 38 to 3.4e+38
double	%lf	8 bytes	1.7e - 308 to 1.7e+308

Note that the C language is a case-sensitive and everything should be written in lower case in C. But one can give the variable name in capital letters. Similarly every statement in C should be terminated by ; (semicolon), which is known as terminating symbol.

Validity of variable names

- In C, the identifier should have appropriate names. Following are the **rules** which should be followed while deciding the variable names
  1) The variable name is a collection of alphanumeric characters in which the first letter should be an alphabet and should not be digit or any special character.
  2) Special characters are not allowed in the variable name except underscore.
  3) The variable name is case sensitive. A variable name can be in capital letters. But variable **d** and variable **D** are two different variables.
  4) The length of the variable name can be any but only first 31 characters are recognised.
  5) The keywords are not valid variable names.
  6) Blank spaces or special characters, commas, use of quotes "or' are not allowed in the variable name.
  7) Arithmatic operators should not be used in the variable names.
- **For example**

Count,tax_id,INDEX,Xyz,brick01

The invalid variable names are

_file,char,#id,1A,valid name

- The variable names should be informative. It should describe the purpose of it by its name.
- **For example :** int count,sum ;
- The variable name count itself indicates that it is used to store the value of some counting, similarly sum is a variable which stores the sum of some numbers.
- Instead of using lengthy variable names make use of underscores in between.

For example, using **employee_id** is more suitable than **employeeid**

Key Point *Data type means type of data.*

1.2.1 Primitive and Non Primitive

- The primitive data types are the fundamental data types. The non primitive data types can be built using primitive data types.
- Examples of Primitive data types are: In C language the primitive data types are int, float, double, char.
- The non-primitive data types are user defined data types.
- Examples of non-primitive data types are : In C language the non primitive data types are structure, union and enumerated data types.

Examples :

Primitive Data Types	Non-primitive Data Types
int count; float average; char choice;	typedef struct student { int roll_no; float marks; } S; S S1

Example 1.2.1 *A communications network is represented by graph. Each node represents a communication line and each edge indicate the presence of interconnection between the lines. Which traversal technique can be used to find breakdown in line ? Explain.*

GTU : Winter-17, Marks 4

Solution : • The Breadth First Traversal technique of graph can be used to find breakdown in line.

- The Breadth First Traversal (BFS) starts from any desired node and start finding all neighboring nodes or adjacent nodes.
- Thus using BFS one can reach to all the nodes.
- If the neighboring node is not found then that indicates the broken link, in communication network.

Review Questions

1. *Explain primitive and non-primitive data structure and give the example of them.*

   GTU : CE, Dec.-03, Marks 4

2. *Define data type. Narrate importance of abstract datatype with suitable example.*

   GTU : IT, Dec.-05, Marks 4

1.3 Algorithms

- An algorithm is a finite set of instructions for performing a particular task. The instructions are nothing but the statements in simple English language.
- **Example :**

Let us take a very simple example of an algorithm which adds the two numbers and store the result in a third variable.

Step 1 : Start.

Step 2 : Read the first number is variable 'a'.

Step 3 : Read the second number in variable 'b'.

Step 4 : Perform the addition of both the numbers i.e. and store the result in variable 'c'.

Step 5 : Print the value of 'c' as a result of addition.

Step 6 : Stop.

Only defining an algorithm is again not useful. Here are some characteristics of algorithm.

1.3.1 Characteristics of Algorithm

1. Each algorithm is supplied with zero or more external quantities.

   Here supplying external quantities means giving input to the algorithm.
2. Each algorithm must produce at least one quantity.

   Production of at least one quantity means there should be some output.
3. Each algorithm should have **definiteness** i.e. each instruction must be clear and unambiguous.
4. Each algorithm should have **finiteness** i.e. if we trace out the instructions of an algorithm, then for all cases the algorithm will terminate after finite number of steps.
5. Each algorithm should have **effectiveness** i.e. every instruction must be sufficiently basic that it can in principal be carried out by a person using only pencil and paper. Moreover each instruction of an algorithm must also be feasible.

Review Question

1. *What do you understand by the term algorithm ? Describe the characteristics of an algorithm.*

1.4 Performance Analysis and Measurement

GTU : May-05, 07, 09, 12, IT, Dec.-05, 06, Winter-14,17, Summer-17

The efficiency of an algorithm can be decided by measuring the performance of an algorithm. We can measure the performance of an algorithm by computing **two factors**.

1. Amount of **time** required by an algorithm to execute.
2. Amount of **storage** required by an algorithm.

This is popularly known as **time complexity** and **space complexity** of an algorithm.

1.4.1 Time Complexity

- Time complexity is the amount of time taken by the program for execution. As it is difficult to measure the time complexity in terms of clock units, we will measure the time complexity using the **frequency count**.

- **Frequency count -** The efficiency of a program is measured by inserting a counter in the algorithm in order to count the number of times the basic operation is executed. This is a straightforward method of measuring the time complexity of the program.

Example 1.4.1 *Consider following piece of code for obtaining the frequency count -*

```
void display()
  {
    int a,b,c;
    a = 10;
    b = 20;
    c = a+b;
    printf("%d",c);
  }
```

Solution :

Code	Frequency count
a = 10	1
b = 20	1
c = a + b	1
printf("%d", c)	1
Total	**4**

Explanation :

In above code, the statements such as assignment statements, input and output statements or if statements execute for once. Hence the frequency count of such statement is considered as 1. Therefore we get the frequency count as 4 in above case.

Example 1.4.2 *Find the frequency count of :*

```
i) for (i = 1; i < = n; i ++)
   for (j = 1; j < = i; j ++)
                  x = x + 1;

ii) i = 1;
   while (i < = n)
  {    x = x + 1;
         i = i + 1;
   }
```

GTU : May-05, Marks 6

Solution : i) The frequency count can be computed as follows -

Statement	Frequency count
i = 1	1
i < = n	n + 1
i + +	n
j = 1	n
j < = i	n (n + 1)
j + +	n · n
x = x + 1	n · n
Total	$3n^2 + 4n + 2$

ii)

Statement	Frequency count
i = 1	1
i < = n	n + 1
x = x + 1	n
i = i + 1	n
Total	**3n + 2**

Example 1.4.3 *Find the frequency count of :*

```
i) for (i = 1; i < = n; i ++)
     for (j = 1; j < = n; j ++)
        a = a + 2;
ii) i = 1
  do
   {
      x = x + 2;
      i ++;
   } while ( i < = n );
```

GTU : May-05, Marks 6

Solution : i)

Statement	Frequency count
i = 1	1
i < = n	n + 1
i + +	n
j = 1	n
j < = n	n (n + 1)
j + +	n · n
a = a + 2	n · n
Total	**$3n^2 + 4n + 2$**

ii)

Statement	Frequency count
i = 1	1
x = x + 2	n
i + +	n
i < = n	n
Total	**3n + 1**

Example 1.4.4 *Determine the frequency count for each statement in the following piece of code. Obtain its time complexity in terms of 'n'.*

```
for (i = 1; i < = n; i ++)
   for (j = 1; j < = i; j ++)
      for (k = 1; k < = j; k + +)
      x =  x + 1;
```

GTU : May-07, Marks 6

Solution :

Statement	Frequency count
i = 1	1
i < = n	n + 1
i + +	n
j = 1	n
j < = i	n (n + 1)
j + +	n · n
k = 1	n · n · n

k < = j	n · n · (n + 1)
k + +	n · n · n
x = x + 1	n · n · n
Total	$\mathbf{4n^3 + 3n^2 + 3n + 2}$

The higher order degree is considered. Therefore time complexity = **O (n^3)**

Example 1.4.5 *Determine the frequency count of each statement in the following piece of code. Obtain its time complexity in terms of 'n' :*

```
for (i = 1; i < = n; i ++)
 for (j = 1; j < = n; j ++)
{
         C[i] [j] = 0;
         for (k = 1; k < = n; k ++ )
      C[i] [j] = C[i] [j] + a[i] [k] * b[k] [j].
}
```

GTU : May-09, Marks 6

Solution :

Statement	Frequency count
i = 1	1
i < = n	n + 1
i + +	n
j = 1	n
j < = n	n (n + 1)
j + +	n · n
C[i] [j] = 0	n · n
k = 1	n · n
k < = n	n · n · (n + 1)
k + +	n · n · n
C[i] [j] = C[i] [j] + a[i] [k] * b [k] [j];	n · n · n
Total	$\mathbf{3n^3 + 5n^2 + 4n + 2}$

For finding the time complexity, we must neglect all the constants and only order of magnitude is considered. The highest degree in above polynomial is **3**. Hence time complexity in terms of n is **O(n^3)**.

Example 1.4.6 *Write an algorithm for finding average of given numbers. Calculate time complexity.* **GTU : Summer-17, Marks 3**

Solution :

```
Algorithm  Avg (a, n)
{
        Sum : = 0.0
        for i : = 1 to n do
                read (a[i]);
        for i = 1 to n do
        sum : = Sum + a[i]
        avg : = Sum/n;
        print (avg);
}
```

Time complexity is O (n).

Example 1.4.7 *Write an algorithm for calculating square of the number for all the prime numbers ranging between 1 to n. Perform time and space analysis.* **GTU : Winter-17, Marks 4**

Solution :

```
void Prime_Square()
{
        int num,i,count,n,sq;
        printf("Enter value of n: ");
        scanf("%d",&n);
        for(num = 1;num<=n;num++)
        {
                count = 0;
                for(i=2;i<=num/2;i++)
                {
                        if(num%i==0)
                        {
                                count++;
                                break;
                        }
                }
                if(count==0 && num!= 1)
                {
                        sq=num*num;
                        printf("The prime number is %d and its square is %d",num,sq);
                }
        }
}
The worst case time complexity of this algorithm is O(n^2)
```

1.4.2 Space Complexity

- The space complexity can be defined as amount of memory required by an algorithm to run.
- To compute the space complexity we use two factors : **Constant and instance characteristics**. The space requirement S(p) can be given as

$$S(p) = C + Sp$$

where **C** is a constant i.e. fixed part and it denotes the space of inputs and outputs. This space is an amount of space taken by instruction, variables and identifiers. And **Sp** is a space dependent upon instance characteristics. This is a variable part whose space requirement depends on particular problem instance.

- There are two types of components that contribute to the space complexity - **Fixed part** and **variable part**.
- The **fixed part** includes space for
  i) Instructions
  ii) Variables
  iii) Array size
  iv) Space for constants
- The **variable part** includes space for
  - The variables whose size is dependent upon the particular problem instance being solved. The control statements (such as for, do, while, choice) are used to solve such instances.
  - Recursion stack for handling recursive call.

Consider an example of algorithm to compute the space complexity.

Example 1.4.8 *Compute the space complexity for the code fragment*

```
Algorithm Sum(a,n)
{
    s : = 0.0 ;
        for i : = 1 to n do
            s : = s + a[i] ;
            return s
}
```

Solution : In the given code we require space for

s : = 0 ← **Requires 1 unit of Space**

for i : = 1 to n ← **Requires n unit of Space**

s : = s + a[i] ; ← **Requires n unit of Space**

returns ; ← **Requires 1 unit of Space**

Thus total 2n+2 units of space is required. If we neglect the constants of this equation and if consider only the order of magnitude then the space complexity is denoted using Big Oh notation as O(n)

Example 1.4.9 *Define time complexity and space complexity. Calculate time complexity for given expression*

```
for (k = 0 ; k < n ; k++)
{
        rows [k] = 0 ;
        for (j = 0 ; j < n ; j++)
        {
                rows [k] = rows [k] + matrix [k] [j] ;
                total = total + matrix [k] [j] ;
        }
}
```

GTU : May-12, Marks 4

Solution : Refer sections 1.4.1 and 1.4.2 for definitions.

Code	Frequency Count
k = 0	1
k < n	n+1
k++	n+1
rows [k] = 0	n
for (j=0 ...)	n(n+1)
rows [k] = ...	n(n)
total = ...	n(n)

The frequency count will be $3n^2 + 4n + 3$. Just by considering the order of magnitude we can express the time complexity in terms of big oh notation as $O(n^2)$. As it requires two dimensional array the space complexity is $O(n^2)$.

Review Questions

1. *Explain time and space complexity with example.*

   GTU : IT, Dec.-05, Marks 4; IT, Dec.-06, Marks 6

2. *Write short note on performance analysis and performance measurement of an algorithm.*

   GTU : Winter-14, Marks 7

1.5 Average Best and Worst Case Analysis

GTU : Winter-18

If an algorithm takes minimum amount of time to run to completion for a specific set of input then it is called **best case** time complexity.

For example : While searching a particular element by using sequential search we get the desired element at first place itself then it is called best case time complexity.

If an algorithm takes maximum amount of time to run to completion for a specific set of input then it is called **worst case** time complexity.

For example : While searching an element by using linear searching method if desired element is placed at the end of the list then we get worst time complexity.

The time complexity that we get for certain set of inputs is as a average same. Then for corresponding input such a time complexity is called **average case** time complexity.

Consider the following algorithm

```
Void seq search()
{
        for (i = 0; i<n; i++)
        {
                if(a[i] ==key)
                return i;
        }
}
```

Best case time complexity

Best case time complexity is a time complexity when an algorithm runs for short time. In above searching algorithm the element **key** is searched from the list of **n** elements. If the **key** element is present at first location in the list(a[0...n–1]) then algorithm runs for a very short time and thereby we will get the best case time complexity. We can denote the best case time complexity as

$$C_{best} = 1$$

Worst case time complexity

Worst case time complexity is a time complexity when algorithm runs for a longest time. In above searching algorithm the element **key** is searched from the list of **n** elements. If the **key** element is present at n^{th} location then clearly the algorithm will run for longest time and thereby we will get the worst case time complexity. We can denote the worst case time complexity as

$$C_{worst} = n$$

The algorithm guarantees that for any instance of input which is of size n, the running time will not exceed $C_{worst}(n)$. Hence the worst case time complexity gives important information about the efficiency of algorithm.

Average case time complexity

This type of complexity gives information about the behaviour of an algorithm on specific or random input. Let us understand some terminologies that are required for computing average case time complexity.

Let the algorithm is for sequential search and

P be a probability of getting successful search.

n is the total number of elements in the list.

The first match of the element will occur at i^{th} location. Hence probability of occurring first match is P/n for every i^{th} element.

The probability of getting unsuccessful search is (1 – P).

Now, we can find average case time complexity $C_{avg}(n)$ as -

$$C_{avg}(n) = \text{Probability of successful search (for elements 1 to n in the list)} + \text{Probability of unsuccessful search}$$

$$C_{avg}(n) = \left[1 \cdot \frac{P}{n} + 2 \cdot \frac{P}{n} + \ldots + i \cdot \frac{P}{n}\right] + n \cdot (1-P)$$

There may be n elements at which chances of 'not getting element' are possible. Hence n.(1 – P)

$$= \frac{P}{n}[1+2+\ldots+i\ldots n] + n(1-P)$$

$$= \frac{P}{n}\frac{n(n+1)}{2} + n(1-P)$$

$$C_{avg}(n) = \frac{P(n+1)}{2} + n(1-P)$$

Thus we can obtain the general formula for computing average case time complexity.

Suppose if P = 0 that means there is no successful search i.e. we have scanned the entire list of n elements and still we do not found the desired element in the list then in such a situation,

$$C_{avg}(n) = 0\,(n+1)/2 + n\,(1-0)$$

$$C_{avg}(n) = n$$

Thus the average case running time complexity becomes equal to n.

Suppose if P = 1 i.e. we get a successful search then

$$C_{avg}(n) = 1\,(n+1)/2 + n\,(1-1)$$

$$C_{avg}(n) = (n + 1)/2$$

That means the algorithm scans about half of the elements from the list.

For calculating average case time complexity we have to consider probability of getting success of the operation. And any operation in the algorithm is heavily dependent on input elements. Thus computing average case time complexity is difficult than computing worst case and best case time complexities.

Review Question

1. *Explain average case timing analysis for search algorithm.* **GTU : Winter-18, Marks 4**

1.6 Types of Data Structures

GTU : IT, Dec.-05, 06, CE, Nov.-05, Dec.-06, May-12, Summer-13, 18

Organizing data in proper manner makes the program development an efficient process. For many applications, choosing a proper data structure is an important decision. Basically data can be organized in various categories which is as given in Fig. 1.6.1.

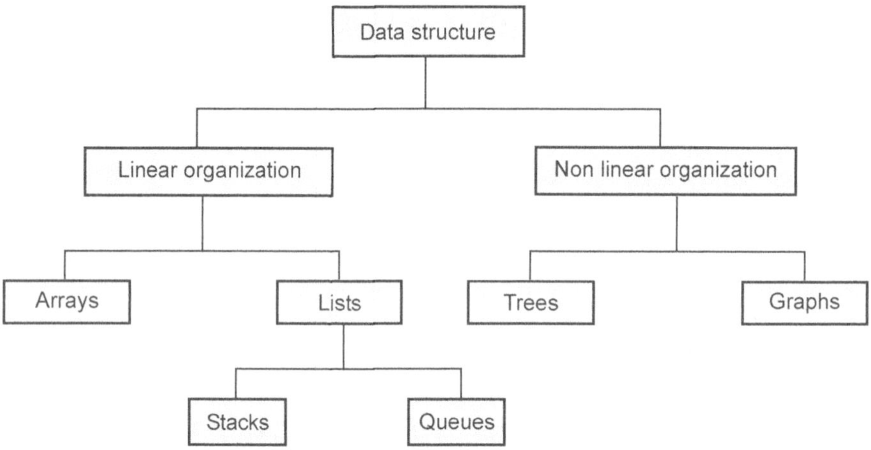

Fig. 1.6.1 Elementary data organization

Difference between Data Type and Data Structure

Sr. No.	Data structure	Data type
1.	A data structure is an abstract description of a way of organizing data to allow certain operations on it to be performed efficiently.	Data type represents the basic type of the data.
2.	Data structures can be reduced.	The data type can not be reduced.

3.	Data structure is formed using data types.	Data types are the primitive types.
4.	Example : Array, Linked List, Stack, Queues	Example : **int, char, double, float** and so on. The **struct** is an extended type which contains members of various data types.

Role of Data Structure in Problem Solving

The data structure is used for modelling the problem. That means, we can apply some algorithm on the data structure to solve particular problem.

For instance : If we want to perform addition of two polynomials then first of all we need to build a data structure for storing the polynomial. We can use either a two dimensional array or we can use an array of structure to store coefficient and exponent values of each term of polynomial. Similarly we can make use of dynamic data structure like linked list for representing the polynomial. And then accordingly appropriate algorithm can be applied on the polynomial data structure to perform addition operation. Thus for solving any problem data structure along with appropriate algorithm is required.

1.6.1 Linear Data Structure

Linear data structures are the data structures in which data is arranged in a list or in a straight sequence.

For example : arrays, list

1.6.2 Non Linear Data Structure

Non linear data structures are the data structures in which data may be arranged in hierarchical manner.

For example : trees, graphs.

Example 1.6.1 *What is primitive data structure ? Is pointer primitive data structure ?*

GTU : IT, Dec.-05, Marks 4

Solution : Primitive data structure is a basic data structure which operates on basic data types or machine instructions.

Pointer is a primitive data structure.

Review Questions

1. *What is the difference between data type and data structure ? What role data structure plays in problem solving ?* **GTU : CE, Nov.-05, Marks 6**
2. *Explain the classification of data structure.* **GTU : IT, Dec.-06, Marks 4**

3. *Explain difference between linear and non linear data structures with example.*
GTU : CE, Dec.-06, Marks 6

4. *What is data structure ? Explain linear and non linear data structure with example*
GTU : May-12, Marks 3, Summer-13, Marks 7

5. *Differentiate between linear and non linear data structures.* **GTU : Summer-18, Marks 3**

1.7 Oral Questions and Answers

Q.1 What is the difference between data and information ?

Ans. : Data is a collection of information but it is in raw form. The logical and meaningful form of data is called information.

Q.2 List out the types of data type.

Ans. : There are two type of data types - i) Built in data type and ii) User defined data type.

Q.3 Define the term Data structure. **GTU : Winter-15**

Ans. : The combination which describes the set of elements together with the description of all legal operations is termed as data structure.

Q.4 What is abstract data type ?

Ans. : The abstract data type is a triple of D - set of domains, F - set of functions and A - axioms in which only what is to be done is mentioned but how is to be done is not mentioned.

In ADT the implementation details are hidden.

ADT= Data type + Function names + Behavior of each function.

Q.5 State the advantages of abstract data type.

Ans. : Following are some advantages of abstract data type -

1. Abstract data type is useful for representing all possible operations of the data structure.
2. The implementation details can be hidden in ADT.
3. The implementation details can be changed later on during maintenance and bug fixing when the ADT is available.
4. ADT helps to define the program definition in general form.

Q.6 List out the areas in which data structures are applied extensively.

Ans. : Following are the areas in which the data structures are applied extensively.

1. Operating system - The data structures like priority queues are used for scheduling the jobs in the operating system.

2. Compiler design - The tree data structure is used in parsing the source program. Stack data structure is used in handling the recursive calls.
3. Database management system - The file data structure is used in database management systems. Sorting and searching techniques can be applied on these data in the file.

Q.7 Distinguish between linear and non linear data structure.

Ans. : The linear data structure is a kind of data structure in which the elements are arranged linearly, whereas non linear data structure is a kind of data structure in which the elements are not arranged in linear fashion.

Examples of linear data structure are - Linked list, stacks and queues

Examples of non linear data structure are - Trees and Graphs

Q.8 List out the measures of efficiency of program.

Ans. : Time complexity and space complexity are the two measures used for computing the efficiency of a program.

Q.9 Define the term time complexity. GTU : Summer-16, Winter-16

Ans. : The amount of time required by the program to execute is called time complexity.

Q.10 Define the term space complexity. GTU : Summer-16

Ans. : The amount of space required by the program to execute is called space complexity.

Q.11 What is the role of data structure in problem solving ?

Ans. : The data structure is used for modelling the problem. That means, we can apply some algorithm on the data structure to solve particular problem.

Q.12 Define primitive data structure. GTU : Summer-16, Winter-16

Ans. : Primitive data structure is a basic data structure which operates on basic data types or machine instructions. For example - ineger, float are primitive data structure is C.

Q.13 Is pointer primitive data structure ?

Ans. : Yes Pointer is a primitive data structure.

Q.14 What is unit used to measure the time factor for determining the efficiency of a program ?

Ans. : The number of statements executed is used to measure the time factor for determining the efficiency of a program.

Q.15 Define data structure. GTU : Winter-15

Ans. : **Data structure :** The combination which describes the set of elements together with the description of all legal operations is termed as data structure.

Q.16 Non-primitive data structure. GTU : Winter-16

Ans. : The non-primitive data types are user defined data types.

Examples of non-primitive data types are : In C language the non primitive data types are structure, union and enumerated data types.

Q.17 Linear data structure. GTU : Winter-16

Ans. : Linear data structures are the data structures in which data is arranged in a list or in a straight sequence.

For example : arrays, list

Q.18 Non-linear data structure. GTU : Winter-16

Ans. : Non linear data structures are the data structures in which data may be arranged in hierarchical manner.

For example : trees, graphs.

Q.19 Arithmetic expression evaluation is an explanation of which data structure ? GTU : Summer-17

Ans. : Arithmetic expression evaluation is an explanation of stack data structure.

❑❑❑

2 Array

Syllabus

Representation of arrays, Applications of arrays, Sparse matrix and its representation.

Contents

2.1 Concept of Array as Sequential Representation

Definition : Array is a consecutive set of memory locations.

We define array as a **set of pair-index and the value**. Also as a **data structure**. The basic operations of an array are only two. One operation is **storing** of data at desired location or index and the other one is **retrieving** of data from desired location (index).

Advantages of sequential organization of data structure

1. Elements can be retrieved or stored very efficiently in sequential organization with the help of index or memory location.
2. All the elements are stored at continuous memory locations. Hence searching of element from sequential organization is easy.

Disadvantages of sequential organization of data structure

1. Insertion and deletion of elements becomes complicated due to sequential nature.
2. For storing the data large continuous free block of memory is required.
3. Memory fragmentation occurs if we remove the elements randomly.

2.2 Representation of Arrays

GTU : CE, Dec.-06, Winter 13, Marks 7

- The arrays may be of any data type such as int, char, float or double.
- The **syntax** of declaring an array is

data_type name_of_array [size] ;

For example, int a [10]; double b[10] [10];

Here 'a' is the name of the array inside the square bracket size of the array is given. This array is of integer type i.e. all the elements are of integer type in array 'a'. Similarly arrays may be of user defined type, called as array of structure C supports both one dimensional and multidimensional arrays.

One dimensional array :

The one dimensional array 'a' is declared as int a[10];

Two dimensional array :

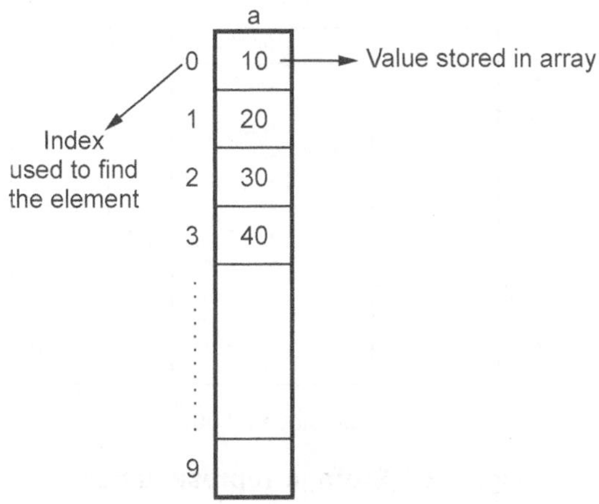

If we declare a two dimensional array as

```
int a[10] [3];
```

Then it will look like this -

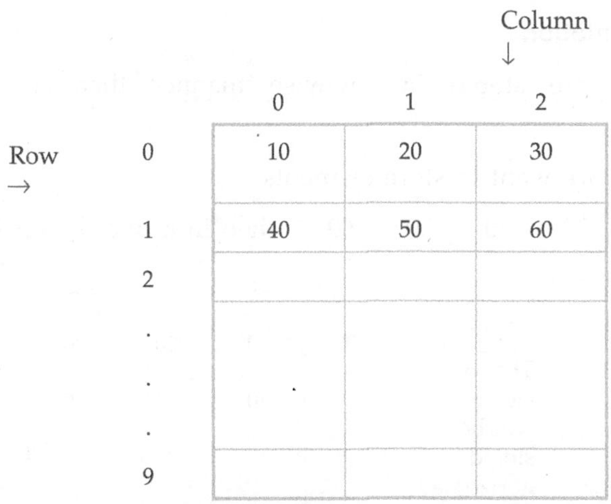

The two dimensional array should be in row-column form. We will also see another form of array using structure.

For example :

```
struct emp
{
        int no;
        char name;
        float salary;
}employee[100];
```

The elements of a two dimensional array may be arranged either in **rowwise** or **columnwise.** Thus the two dimensional array is the **matrix representation.** A

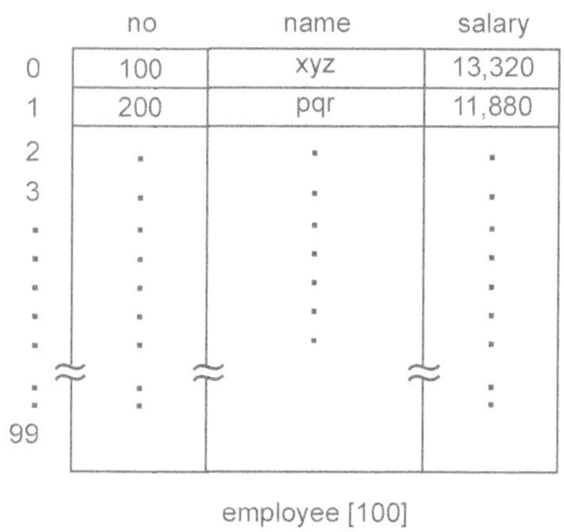

Fig. 2.2.1 Storage representation

representation in which elements are arranged rowwise is called **row major representation** and a representation in which elements are arranged columnwise is termed as **column major representation.**

Row major representation

If the elements are stored in rowwise manner then it is called row major representation.

For example : If we want to store elements

10 20 30 40 50 60 then in a two dimensional array

The ⇒ elements will be stored horizontally

	0	1	2
0	10	20	30
1	40	50	60
.			
.			
.			
9			

To access any element in two dimensional array we must specify both its row number and column number. That is why we need two variables which act as row index and column index.

Column major representation

If elements are stored in columnwise manner then it is called column major representation.

For example : If we want to store elements

10 20 30 40 50 60 then the elements will be filled up by columnwise manner as follows (consider array a[3] [2]).

	0	1
0	10	40
1	20	50
2	30	60

Each element is occupied at successive locations if the element is of integer type then 2 bytes of memory will be allocated, if it is of floating type then 4 bytes of memory will be allocated and so on.

For example :

int a [3] [2] = { {10, 20}

{30, 40}

{50, 60} }

Then in row major matrix

a[0][0]	a[0][1]	a[1][0]	a[1][1]	a[2][0]	a[2][1]	
10	20	30	40	50	60	...
100	102	104	106	108	110	

And in column major matrix

a[0][0]	a[1][0]	a[2][0]	a[0][1]	a[1][1]	a[2][1]	
10	30	50	20	40	60	...
100	102	104	106	108	110	

Here each element occupies 2 bytes of memory base address will be 100.

Address calculation for any element will be as follows.

In row major matrix, the element a[i] [j] will be at

base address + (col_index * total number of rows + row_index) * element_size.

In column major matrix, the element at a[i] [j] will be at

base address + (row_index * total number of columns + column_index) * element.

In C normally the row major representation is used.

Example 2.2.1 *Consider integer array int arr[3][4] declared in 'C' program. If the base address is 1050, find the address of the element arr[2][3] with row major and column major representation of array.*

Solution : Row major representation

The element a[i][j] will be at

a[i][j] = base address + (col_index*total number of rows + row_index)*element_size

= (base address + (j*row_size + i)*element_size)

When i = 2 and j = 3, element_size = int occupies 2 bytes of memory hence it is 2.

Total number of rows = 3

a[2][3] = 1050 + (3*3 + 2)*2

= 1050 + 22

a[2][3] = 1072

Column major representation

The element a[i][j] will be at

a[i][j] = base address + (row_index*total number of columns + col_index)*element_size

= (base address + (i*col_size + j)*element_size)

When i = 2 and j = 3 ,element_size = int occupies 2 bytes of memory hence it is 2

total number of columns = 4

a[2][3] = 1050 + (2*4 + 3)*2

= 1050 + 22

a[2][3] = 1072

Example 2.2.2 *Consider integer array int arr[4][5] declared in 'C' program. If the base address is 1020, find the address of the element arr[3][4] with row major and column major representation of array.*

Solution : Row major representation

The element a[i][j] will be at

a[i][j] = base address + (col_index*total number of rows + row_index)*element_size

= (base address + (j*row_size + i)*element_size)

When i = 3 and j = 4 ,element_size = int occupies 2 bytes of memory hence it is 2 total number of rows = 4

a[3][4] = 1020 + (4*4+3)*2

= 1020 + 38

a[3][4] = 1058

Column major representation

The element a[i][j] will be at

a[i][j] = base address + (row_index*total number of columns + col_index)*element_size

= (base address + (i*col_size+j)*element_size)

When i = 3 and j = 4, element_size=int occupies 2 bytes of memory hence it is 2

Total number of columns = 5

a[3][4] = 1020+(3*5 + 4)*2

= 1020 + 38

a[2][3] = 1058

Multidimensional array

The multidimensional array is similar to the two dimensional array with multiple dimensions. For example : Here is 3-D array.

a[3] [2] [3] = { { { 1, 2, 3 }, { 4, 5, 6 } },

{ { 7, 8, 9 }, { 10, 11, 12 } },

{ { 13, 14, 15 }, { 16, 17, 18 }

}

We can represent it graphically as

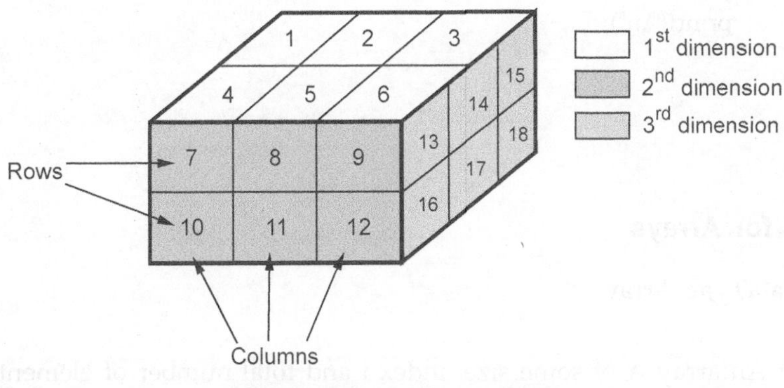

Fig. 2.2.2 Dimensional array

Program

```
/*
This program is for storing and retrieving the elements in a 3-D
array
*/
#include<stdio.h>
#include<conio.h>
void main ( )
{
        int a [3] [2] [3];
        int i, j, k;
        Clrscr ( );
        printf ("\n Enter the elements");
        for (i=0; i<3; i++)
        {
            for (j=0; j<2; j++)
            {
                for (k=0; k<3; k++)
                {
                    scanf ("%d", &a[i][j][k]);
                }
            }
        }
        printf ("\n Printing the elements \n");
        for    (i=0; i<3; i++)
            {
            for (j=0; j<2; j++)
            {
            for (k=0; k<3; k++)
                {
                    printf("%d", a[i][j][k]);
                }
            printf ("\n");
            }
            printf("\n");
        }
    }
    getch();
}
```

2.2.1 ADT for Arrays

AbstractDataType Array

{

Instances : An array A of some size, index i and total number of elements in the array n.

Operations :

store () - This operation stores the desired elements at each successive location.

display () - This operation displays the elements of the array.

}

Review Questions

1. *Attempt - Storage representation of three dimensional array.* **CE, Dec.-06, Marks 4**
2. *Explain multi dimensional array. How it is stored in memory ?* **Winter 13, Marks 5**
3. *Explain the Arrays as ADT.*

2.3 Basic Operations on Arrays

There are two basic operations which can be performed on arrays and those are

1. Storing the elements in an array.
2. Retrieval of elements from an array.

Basic operations in one dimensional arrays -

```
int i, n, a[10];
printf ("\n How many elements
        to store?");
scanf("%d", &n);
printf ("\n Now store the
        elements");
for (i=0; i<n; i++)
scanf ("%d", &a[i]);
printf("The elements are
        .....");
for (i=0; i<n; i++)
printf("%d", a[i]);
```

Execute for O(n) time

O(n) time

For example

n = 5

0	1	2	3	4
10	20	30	40	50

a [5]

i varies from 0 to 4.
Each time i gets increment

10 20 30 40 50

In the above 'C' code the for loop is used to store the elements in an array. By this from location 0 to n–1 the elements will be stored. Similarly, for retrieval of elements again a for loop is used.

Analysis : The above code takes **O(n)** time.

Basic operations in two dimensional array -

```
int i,m,n a[10][3]
printf ("How many rows and
                    columns?");
scanf ("%d %d",&m,&n);
```

```
printf("Now store the
        elements");
for(i=0;i<m;i++)
for (j=0; j<n, j++)
scanf ("%d", & a [i][j]);
printf ("The Elements are ");
for (i=0 ; i<m ; i++)
for  (j=0 ; j<n ; j++)
printf ("%d", a[i][j]);
```

$O(n^2)$ time

For example

m = 2, n = 3

	j = 0	j = 1	j = 2
i = 0	10	20	30
i = 1	40	50	60

a [2] [3]

The elements are

10 20 30 40 50 60

Usually elements in an array are to be stored from **0th location.**

Analysis : The above code takes overall **$O(n)^2$** time.

2.4 Applications of Arrays

Following are some typical applications of arrays -

1. **Ordered list** can be represented using arrays. The order list is useful for polynomial representation, addition and multiplication of two **polynomials.**
2. The arrays are also used for representing some sequential data structures such as **stacks** and **queues.**
3. Arrays are used to represent **sparse matrices.**

Review Question

1. *Enlist the basic applications of arrays*

2.5 Sparse Matrix and Its Representation

GTU : CE, Dec.-05, Summer-13, Marks 5

Matrices play a very important role in solving many interesting problems in various scientific and engineering applications. It is therefore necessary for us to design efficient representation for matrices. Normally **matrices** are represented in a **two dimensional array**. In a matrix, if there are m rows and n columns then the space required to store the numbers will be $m \times n \times s$ where s is the number of bytes required to store the value. Suppose, there are 10 rows and 10 columns and we have to store the integer values then the space complexity will be bytes.

$$10 \times 10 \times 2 \;=\; 200 \text{ bytes}$$

Here 2 bytes are required to store an integer value and time complexity will be $O(n^2)$, because the operations that are carried out on matrices need to scan the matrices one row at a time and individual columns in that row, results in use of two nested loops.

It is observed that, many times we deal with matrix of size $m \times n$ and values of m and n are reasonably higher and only a few elements are non zero. Such matrices are called sparse matrices.

In other words **a sparse matrix is that matrix which has a very few non zero elements,** as compared to the size $m \times n$ of the matrix.

For example - if the matrix is of size 100×100 and only 10 elements are non zero. Then for accessing these 10 elements one has to make 10000 times scan. Also only 10 spaces will be with non-zero elements remaining spaces of matrix will be filled with zeros only. i.e. we have to allocate the memory of $100 \times 100 \times 2 = 20000$.

The concept of sparse matrix has therefore came forward in computer science to investigate that representation which will store only non-zero elements of the matrix and still carryout the operations quite efficiently. Now, we will discuss such a efficient representation of sparse matrix.

2.5.1 Representation of Sparse Matrix

- The representation of sparse matrix will be a **triplet** only. In the sense that basically the sparse matrix means very few non-zero elements having in it. Rest of the spaces are having the values zero which are basically useless values or simply empty values. So in this efficient representation we will consider **all the non-zero** values along with their positions.
- In a row wise representation of sparse matrix (Sparse matrix is two dimensional matrix) the 0th row will store total rows of the matrix, total columns of the matrix, and total non-zero values.
- For example - Suppose a matrix is 6×7 and number of non zero terms are say 8. In our sparse matrix representation the matrix will be stored as shown below -

Index	Row No.	Col. No.	Value
0	6	7	8
1	0	6	– 10
2	1	0	55
3	2	5	– 23
4	3	1	67
5	3	6	88
6	4	3	14
7	4	4	– 28
8	5	0	99

Table 2.5.1 Sparse-Matrix representation

- In above representation, the total number of rows and columns of the matrix (6×7) are given in 0th row. Also total number of non-zero elements are given in 0th row of value column i.e. 8.
- Here the above array is say named "Sparse". Then

  Sparse [0][0] = 6

  Sparse [0][1] = 7

  Sparse [0][2] = 8

  Sparse [1][0] = 0

  Sparse [1][1] = 6

  Sparse [1][2] = – 10 and so on.
- In our normal representation of the matrix this will take 6 × 7 × 2 = 84 bytes space, assuming an integer needs two bytes of memory.
- In above representation (total number of non zero values + 1) × 3 × 2. If integer values are stores. So it will be (8 + 1) × 3 × 2 = 54 bytes. Clearly in first representation 30 bytes is unused space, which we are saving in the representaion shown above. Thus we will now make use of above representation in our program to make it space efficient program!

2.5.2 Transpose of Sparse Matrix

We will now discuss the algorithm for performing transpose of sparse matrix.

For eg :

Index	Row No.	Col. No.	Value
0	6	7	8
1	0	6	- 10
2	1	0	55
3	2	5	- 23
4	3	1	67
5	3	6	88
6	4	3	14
7	4	4	- 28
8	5	0	99

will become

Index	Row No.	Col. No.	Value
0	7	6	8
1	0	1	55
2	0	5	99
3	1	3	67
4	3	4	14
5	4	4	– 28
6	5	2	– 23
7	6	0	– 10
8	6	3	88

If you observe the transposed matrix you will notice one thing that we have transposed the original matrix not simply by interchanging rows and columns but we have maintained the rows in sorted order. If we interchange row to col and col to row and then sort the sparse matrix then it will involve lot of movement of data and will be costlier. To overcome this problem, what we will do is we will find all elements in the first column and store them in first row, find all the elements from second column store them in second row and so on. As the originally the sequence is sorted row wise we will be able to locate the elements in correct columnwise order. Now let us see the C program for the transpose.

C Program :

C program followed by discussion of time complexity.

```
/*************************************************************
    Program to read a sparse matrix of size m x n
    and to provide transpose of the sparse matrix
*************************************************************/
/* List of include files */

#include <stdio.h>
#include <conio.h>
#include <process.h>
#include <stdlib.h>

/* List of defined constants */
```

```
#define size 30

void main ( )
{
      /* Local declarations */
      void create(int s[10][3]);
      void show(int s[10][3]);
      void transp(int s1[10][3],int s2[10][3]);
      int s1[size+1][3],s2[size+1][3] ;

      clrscr();
      create(s1) ;
      show ( s1 );
      getch();
      transp( s1, s2 );
      show ( s2 );
      getch();
      exit(0);
}
/*
------------------------------------------------------------
      Function create to read the nonzero elements of
      the given sparse matrix
------------------------------------------------------------
*/
void create ( int s1[][3]  )
{
/* Local Declarations */
      int n, m, terms;
      int i, row, col, val ;
      printf("Enter Number of Rows and Columns of a matrix :");
      scanf("%d%d", &n, &m);
      printf("Enter Number of non-zero terms in the matrix:");
      scanf("%d", &terms);
      if ( terms > size )
      {
            printf("Error: Maximum terms should be 0 to %d\n",size);
            getch();
            exit(1);
      }
      s1[0][0] = n;
      s1[0][1] = m;
      s1[0][2] = terms;
      for ( i = 1; i <= terms; i++)
```

```
	{
		printf("Enter the Row, Column and value of next  nonzero term\n");
		scanf("%d%d%d", &row, &col, &val);
		if ( row > n )
		{
			printf("Error: Maximum Row No. should be %d\n", n);
			getch();
			exit(1);
		}
		if ( col > m )
		{
			printf("Error: Maximum Column No. should be%d\n",m);
			  getch();
			  exit(1);
		}
		s1[i][0] = row;
		s1[i][1] = col;
		s1[i][2] = val;
	}
}
/*----------------End of Create Function-----------------*/
/*
	Function show to print the nonzero elements of
	the given sparse matrix

*/
void show (int s[][3] )
{
	/* Local Declarations */
	int i;
	printf("The details of the given sparse matrix are as follows\n");
	printf("Number of Rows  : %d\n", s[0][0]);
	printf("Number of Cols  : %d\n", s[0][1]);
	printf("Number of Terms : %d\n", s[0][2]);
	printf("\nThe nonzero terms of the matrix are as follows\n");
	printf("\n Row No\tColNo\tValue\n");
	for ( i =0; i <= s[0][2]; i++ )
	{
	  printf("%5d\t%5d\t%5d\n", s[i][0], s[i][1],s[i][2]);
	}
}
/*-------------------End Of show Function-----------------*/
```

```
/*
	Function to transp the given sparse matrix.
	This is the function containing the major logic
	of the program
*/
void transp (int s1[size+1][3],int s2[size+1][3] )
{
	/* Local Declarations */

	int  nxt,c, row, col,Term, val ;
	int    n, m, terms ;
	/* Read Number of rows, columns and terms of given matrix */
	n     = s1[0][0] ;
	m     = s1[0][1] ;
	terms = s1[0][2] ;

	/* Interchange Number of rows with number of columns */

	s2[0][0] = m;
	s2[0][1] = n;
	s2[0][2] = terms;
	if ( terms > 1 ) /* if nonzero matrix then */
	{
		nxt = 1 ; /* Gives next position in the transposed matrix */
		/* Do the transpose columnwise */
		for ( c = 0; c <= m ; c ++ )
		{
	/* for each column scan all the terms for a term in that column */
			for ( Term = 1; Term <= terms; Term ++)
			{
				if ( s1[Term][1] == c )
				{
				 /* Interchange Row and Column */
				s2[nxt][0] = s1[Term][1];
				s2[nxt][1] = s1[Term][0];
```

```
                s2[nxt][2] = s1[Term][2];
                nxt ++;
               }
            }
           }
      }
   }
/**************** End of the Program *********************/
```

Output

```
Enter Number of Rows and Columns of a matrix :3 3
Enter Number of non-zero terms in the matrix :4
Enter the Row, Column and value of next nonzero term
0 0 10
Enter the Row, Column and value of next nonzero term
0 2 20
Enter the Row, Column and value of next nonzero term
1 1 30
Enter the Row, Column and value of next nonzero term
2 1 40
The details of the given sparse matrix are as follows
Number of Rows  : 3
Number of Cols  : 3
Number of Terms : 4

The nonzero terms of the matrix are as follows

     RowNo      ColNo      Value
       3          3          4
       0          0         10

       0          2         20
       1          1         30
       2          1         40

Number of Cols  : 3
Number of Terms : 4

The nonzero terms of the matrix are as follows

     Row No       ColNo        Value
     3            3            4
     0            0            10
     0            2            20
     1            1            30
```

```
2           1           40

The details of the given sparse matrix are as follows
Number of Rows  : 3
Number of Cols   : 3
Number of Terms: 4

The nonzero terms of the matrix are as follows
  RowNo  ColNo  Value
  3       3      4
  0       0      10
  1       1      30
  1       2      40
  2       0      20
```

Logic for simple transpose of sparse matrix

In above 'C' program we are creating a sparse matrix, printing it as well as we are performing a simple tranpose on the given matrix and storing the result in matrix.

For example : s1 will be

Row	Col	Val
3	3	4
0	0	1
1	0	2
2	0	3
3	1	4

Operate 0th row separately interchange row and col and put them in s_2 array at 0th row of it and copy the val to as it is so now will look like this -

s2	Row	Col	Val
0th	3	3	4

Now, in our program we have set nxt = 1 and we start with a for loop in which C = 0 to m. Let's execute it for our example.

nxt = 1

C = 0

Inside it again one more loop is there for scanning all the terms.

so it will be

nxt = 1

C = 0

Term = 1

We are comparing

	3	3	9
→	0	[0]	1
	1	0	2
	2	0	3
	3	1	4

is $\overset{?}{=}$ 0
if so interchange
row and col

so it will be

	3	3	9
	0	0	1
s1 is →	1	[0]	2
	2	0	3
	3	1	4

is $\overset{?}{=}$ 0
if so interchange
row and col

s2 will be

3	3	9
0	0	1
0	1	2
2	0	3
3	1	4

s1

	3	3	9
	0	0	1
	1	0	2
→	2	[0]	3
	3	1	4

it $\overset{?}{=}$ 0
interchange

s2

3	3	9
0	0	1
0	1	2
–	–	–
–	–	–

It will be

s1

3	3	9
0	0	1
1	0	2
2	0	3
→ 3	1	4

$\text{if} \overset{?}{=} 0$

if No – skip it

s2

3	3	9
0	0	1
0	1	2
0	2	3
–	–	–

Now increment C by 1 search for the col value as 1 and if found interchange row and col.

s1

3	3	9
0	0	1
1	0	2
2	0	3
→ 3	[1]	4

s2

3	3	9
0	0	1
0	1	2
0	2	3
–	–	–

Finally

s1

3	3	9
0	0	1
1	0	2
2	0	3
3	1	4

s2

3	3	9
0	0	1
0	1	2
0	2	3
1	3	4

Time complexity of simple transpose :

In the above program clearcut there are two nested for loops. So frequency count will be m × Term. In generalized words the frequency count will be n^2 for the above program. So we can say time complexity of simple transpose is **O(n^2)**.

2.5.3 Addition of Two Sparse Matrices

Actually all the operations which are possible on simple matrix are all possible on sparse matrix. Frankly speaking sparse matrix is nothing but a different style of representing the original matrix which has many zeros into it. One thing you will observe in addition of sparse matrix logic is that the logic for this program is same as addition of two polynomials. Let us see the algorithm.

Algorithm :

1. Start
2. Read the two sparse matrices say s1 and s2 respectively.
3. The index for s1 and s2 will be i and j respectively. Non zero elements are n1 and n2 for s1 and s2.
4. The k index will be for sparse matrix s3 which will store the addition of two matrices.
5. If s1 [0][0] > s2 [0][0] i.e. total number of rows then

   s3 [0][0] = s1 [0][0]

else

   s3 [0][0] = s2 [0][0]

   Similarly check in s1 and s2 the value of total number of columns which ever value is greater transfer it to s3.

   Set i = 1, j = 1, k = 1.
6. When i < n1 and j < n2.
7. a) If row values of s1 and s2 are same then check also column values are same, if so add the non-zero values of s1 and s2 and store them in s3, increment i, j, k by 1.

   b) Otherwise if colno of s1 is less than colno of s2 copy the row, col and nonzero value of s1 to s3. Increment i and k by 1.

   c) Otherwise copy the row, col and non-zero value of s2 to s3. Increment j and k by 1.
8. When rowno of s1 is less than s2 copy row, col and non-zero element of s1 to s3. Increment i and k by 1.
9. When rowno of s2 is less than s1 copy row, col and non-zero element of s2 to s3. Increment j, k by 1. Repeat step 6 to 9 till condition is true.
10. Finally whatever k value that will be total number of non-zero values in SP3 matrix.

∴ SP3 [0][2] = k

11. Print SP3 as a result.

12. Stop.

```
/*************************************************************
    Program to read a sparse matrix of size m x n
    and to perform the addition of two sparse matrices

*************************************************************/
/* List of include files */

#include <stdio.h>
#include <conio.h>
#include <process.h>
#include <stdlib.h>
#define size 10


void main ( )
{
    /* Local declarations */
    void create(int s[10][3]);
    void display(int s[10][3]);
    void add(int s1[10][3],int s2[10][3],int s3[10][3]);
    int s1[10][3],s2[10][3],s3[10][3];
    clrscr();
    create(s1) ;
    display (s1);
    getch();
    create(s2);
    display (s2);
    printf("\n The addition is \n");
    add(s1,s2,s3);
    display(s3);
    getch();
    exit(0);
}

void create(int s[][3] )
{
    /* Local Declarations */
    int n, m, terms;
    int i, row, col, val ;
    printf("Enter Number of Rows and Columns of a matrix :");
    scanf("%d%d", &n, &m);
    printf("Enter Number of non-zero terms in the matrix:");
```

```
        scanf("%d", &terms);
        if ( terms > size )
        {
                printf("Error: Maximum terms should be 0 to %d \n",size);
                getch();
                exit(1);
        }
        s[0][0] = n;
        s[0][1] = m;
        s[0][2] = terms;
        for ( i = 1; i <= terms; i++)
        {
                printf("Enter the Row, Column and value of next nonzero term\n");
                scanf("%d%d%d", &row, &col, &val);
                if ( row > n )
                {
                        printf("Error: Maximum Row No.should be %d\n",n);
                        getch();
                        exit(1);
                }
                if ( col > m )
                {
                        printf("Error: Maximum Column No. should be%d\n",m);
                        getch();
                        exit(1);
                }
                s[i][0] = row;
                s[i][1] = col;
                s[i][2] = val;
        }
}
void display(int s[][3])
{
        /* Local Declarations */
        int i;
        printf("The details of the given sparse matrix are as follows\n");
        printf("Number of Rows  : %d\n", s[0][0]);
        printf("Number of Cols  : %d\n", s[0][1]);
        printf("Number of Terms : %d\n", s[0][2]);
        printf("\nThe nonzero terms of the matrix are as follows\n");
        printf("\n Row No\tColNo\tValue\n");
        for ( i =0; i <= s[0][2]; i++ )
        {
          printf("%5d\t%5d\t%5d\n", s[i][0], s[i][1],s[i][2]);
        }
}
```

```
void add(int s1[10][3],int s2[10][3],int s3[10][3])
{
 int i,j,k;
 i=1;j=1;k=1;
 if((s1[0][0]==s2[0][0])&&(s1[0][1]==s2[0][1]))
 {
  s3[0][0]=s1[0][0];
  s3[0][1]=s1[0][1];
  while( (i<=s1[0][2])&&(j<=s2[0][2]))//traversing thru all the terms
  {
   if(s1[i][0]==s2[j][0])
   {        <------ row numbers from both matrices are same
    if(s1[i][1]==s2[j][1])<------ column numbers from both matrices are same
    {
      s3[k][2]=s1[i][2]+s2[j][2];
      s3[k][1]=s1[i][1];
      s3[k][0]=s1[i][0];
      i++;
      j++;
      k++;
    }
    else if(s1[i][1]<s2[j][1])
    {
      s3[k][2]=s1[i][2];
      s3[k][1]=s1[i][1];
      s3[k][0]=s1[i][0];
      i++;
      k++;
    }
    else
    {
      s3[k][2]=s2[j][2];
      s3[k][1]=s2[j][1];
      s3[k][0]=s2[j][0];
      j++;
      k++;
    }
   }//end of 0 if
   else if(s1[i][0]<s2[j][0])
   {
    s3[k][2]=s1[i][2];
    s3[k][1]=s1[i][1];
    s3[k][0]=s1[i][0];
    i++;
    k++;
   }
   else
```

```
  {
   s3[k][2]=s2[j][2];
   s3[k][1]=s2[j][1];
   s3[k][0]=s2[j][0];
   j++;
   k++;
  }
 }//end of while
 //copying remaing terms
 while(i<=s1[0][2])
 {
  s3[k][2]=s1[i][2];
  s3[k][1]=s1[i][1];
  s3[k][0]=s1[i][0];
  i++;
  k++;
 }
 while(j<=s2[0][2])
 {
  s3[k][2]=s2[j][2];
  s3[k][1]=s2[j][1];
  s3[k][0]=s2[j][0];
  j++;
  k++;
 }
 s3[0][2]=k-1;
}
else
      printf("\n Addition is not possible");
}
```

Output

```
Enter Number of Rows and Columns of a matrix :2 2
Enter Number of non-zero terms in the matrix:3
Enter the Row, Column and value of next nonzero term
1 1 10
Enter the Row, Column and value of next nonzero term
1 2 20
Enter the Row, Column and value of next nonzero term
2 1 30
The details of the given sparse matrix are as follows
Number of Rows  : 2
Number of Cols  : 2
Number of Terms : 3
```

```
The nonzero terms of the matrix are as follows

 Row No ColNo  Value
 2      2      3
 1      1      10
 1      2      20
 2      1      30
Enter Number of Rows and Columns of a matrix :2 2
Enter Number of non-zero terms in the matrix:2
Enter the Row, Column and value of next nonzero term
2 1 5
Enter the Row, Column and value of next nonzero term
2 2 40
The details of the given sparse matrix are as follows
Number of Rows  : 2
Number of Cols  : 2
Number of Terms : 2

The nonzero terms of the matrix are as follows

 Row No  ColNo    Value
   2       2        2
   2       1        5
   2       2        40

 The addition is
The details of the given sparse matrix are as follows
Number of Rows  : 2
Number of Cols  : 2
Number of Terms : 4

The nonzero terms of the matrix are as follows

 Row No   ColNo    Value
   2        2        4
   1        1        10
   1        2        20
   2        1        35
   2        2        40
```

Review Qustions

1. *Attempt - Sparse matrix and its use.* **CE, Dec.-05, Marks 4**
2. *Define sparse matrix. Briefly explain representation of sparse matrix with the help of link list and array.* **Summer-13, Marks 7**

2.7 Oral Questions and Answers

Q.1 Define array.

Ans. : Array is a consecutive set of memory locations.

Q.2 List various operations used in arrays.

Ans. :

1. Creation of array
2. Storing the values in array
3. Retrieving the desired value from array
4. Deletion of element from an array

Q.3 List out two advantages of arrays.

Ans. :

1. Elements can be retrieved or stored very efficiently in sequential organization with the help of index or memory location.
2. All the elements are stored at continuous memory locations. Hence searching of element from sequential organization is easy.

Q.4 List out two drawbacks of arrays.

Ans. :

1. Insertion and deletion of elements becomes complicated due to sequential nature.
2. For storing the data large continuous free block of memory is required.

Q.5 What is row-major and column-major representations ?

Ans. : When the elements of a two dimensional array are arranged either in row-wise manner then it is called **row major representation.**

When the elements of a two dimensional array are arranged in column-wise manner then it is called **column major representation.**

Q.6 Name two data structure that can be constructed using arrays.

Ans. : Stack and queues are constructed using arrays.

Q.7 What is sparse matrix ?

Ans. : Sparse matrix is a kind of matrix in which there are very few non zero elements.

Q.8 What is the use of arrays.

Ans. : Array is a collection of elements of similar data type. Hence multiple applications that require multiple data of same data type and are represented by a single name, make use of arrays. For example the names of 10 students can be stored in an array of character data type.

Q.9 Array subscript in C always start at ________.

Ans. : 0

Q.10 If arr is two dimensional array of 5 rows and 7 columns , then arr[3] logically points to ____ a. fourth row b. third row c. fourth column d third column.

Ans. : fourth row.

Q.11 What is traversing of an array ?

Ans. : Traversing of an array means visiting each element of an array linearly from left to right.

Q.12 Write an algorithm for performing addition of two matrices.

Ans. : Algorithm Add(a,b,n)

```
{
 for i1 to n do
    for j1 to n do
      c[i][j] 0
   for k 1 to n do
      c[i][j]a[i][j]+b[i][j]
}
```

Q.13 Explain how to initialize single dimensional array ?

Ans. : The array can be initialized as follows -

Method 1 : int a[]={1,2,3,4,5};

Method 2 :

```
int a[5];
printf("\n Enter five elements in an array");
for(i=0;i<5;i++)
      scanf("%d",&a[i]);
```

Q.14 What is base address in arrays ?

Ans. : The base address is the address of the first element of an array. Normally address of a[0][0] is base address. Sometimes simply the name of the array is also used to refer the base address.

Q.15 How many dimension of an array are required to perform matrix operations ?

Ans. : The two dimensional array is required to perform the matrix operations.

❑❑❑

3 Stack

Syllabus

Stact-definitions and Concepts, Operations on stacks, Applications of stacks, Polish expression, Reverse polish expression and their compilation, Recursion, Tower of Hanoi.

Contents

3.1 Definition and Concepts

Definition :

> A stack is an ordered list in which all insertions and deletions are made at one end, called the top.

If we have to make stack of elements 10, 20, 30, 40, 50, 60 then 10 will be the bottommost element and 60 will be the topmost element in the stack. A stack is shown in Fig. 3.1.1.

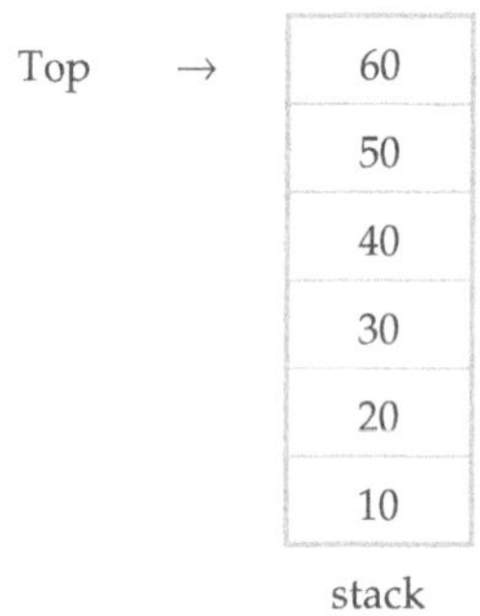

Fig. 3.1.1 Representation of stack

Example

The typical example can be a stack of coins. The coins can be arranged one on another, when we add a new coin it is always placed on the previous coin and while removing the coin the recently placed coin can be removed. The example resembles the concept of stack exactly!

3.2 Operations on Stack

The operations are as follows :

1. Create a stack.
2. Insert an element on to the stack.
3. Delete an element from the stack.
4. Check which element is at the top of the stack.
5. Check whether a stack is empty or not.

The create function creates a stack in the memory. Creation of stack can be either arrays or linked list. The insert function inserts a new element at the top of the stack, where as the delete function removes that element which is at the top of the stack.

Key Point *Stack is LIFO : Last In First Out data structure.*

3.3 Representation of Stack using Arrays

GTU : Dec.-10, May-11, Winter-12,14,15,17, Summer-13,14,17,18, Marks 7

There are two ways for declaration stack -

Declaration 1 :

```
#define size 100
int stack[size], top = -1;
```

In the above declaration stack is nothing but an array of integers. And most recent index of that array will act as a top.

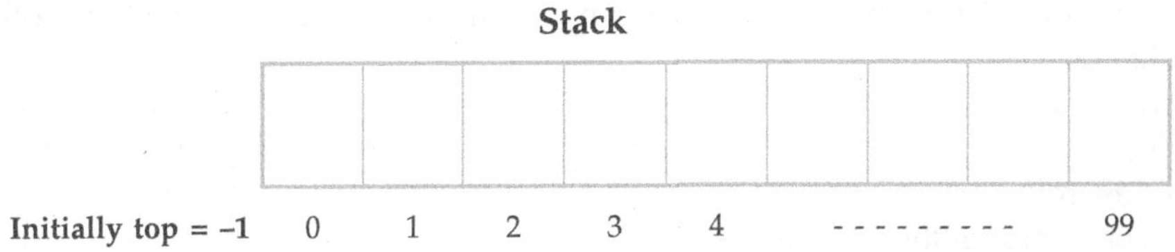

Fig. 3.3.1 Stack using one dimension array

The stack is of the size 100. As we insert the numbers, the top will get incremented. The elements will be placed from 0th position in the stack. At the most we can store 100 elements in the stack, so at the most last element can be at (size –1) position, i.e., at index 99.

Declaration 2 :

```
#define size 10
struct stack {
        int s[size];
        int top;
    }st;
```

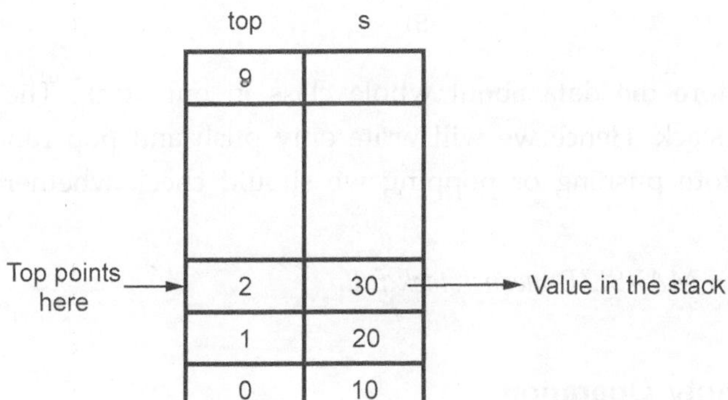

Fig. 3.3.2 Stack using structure

In the above declaration stack is declared as a structure.

Now compare declaration 1 and 2. Both are for stack declaration only. But the second declaration will always preferred. Why ? Because in the second declaration we have used a structure for stack elements and top. By this we are binding or co-relating top variable with stack elements. Thus top and stack are associated with each other by putting them together in a structure. The stack can be passed to the function by simply passing the structure variable.

We will make use of the second method of representing the stack in our program.

The stack can also be used in the databases. For example if we want to store marks of all the students of fourth semester we can declare a structure of stack as follows.

```
# define size 60
typedef struct student
    {
        int roll_no;
        char name[30];
        float marks;
    }stud;
    stud s1[size];
    int top = -1;
```

The above stack will look like this.

	roll_no	name	marks
59			
⋮			
top = 3 →	40	Mita	66
2	30	Rita	91
1	20	Geeta	88.3
0	10	Seeta	76.5

S1

Thus we can store the data about whole class in our stack. The above declaration means creation of stack. Hence we will write only push and pop function to implement the stack. And before pushing or popping we should check whether stack is empty or full.

Key Point *If top = MAXSIZE means stack full.*

3.3.1 Stack Empty Operation

Initially stack is empty. At that time the top should be initialized to – 1 or 0. If we set top to – 1 initially then the stack will contain the elements from 0th position and if we set top to 0 initially, the elements will be stored from 1st position, in the stack. Elements may be pushed onto the stack and there may be a case that all the elements are removed from the stack. Then the stack becomes empty. Thus whenever top reaches to – 1 we can say the stack is empty.

```
int stempty()
{
 if(st.top==-1)
  return 1;
 else
  return 0;
}
```

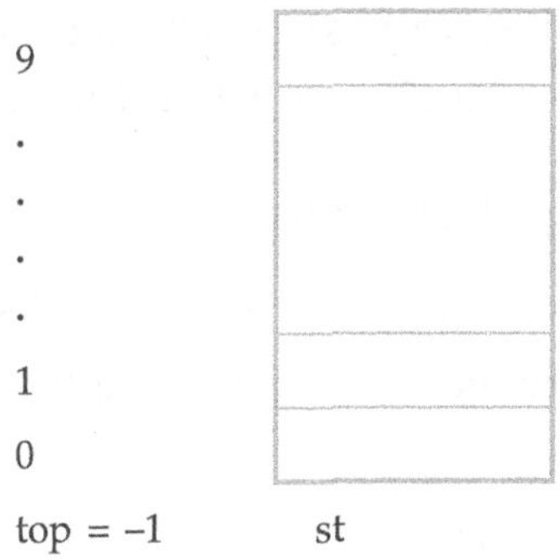

Fig. 3.3.3 Stack empty condition

Key Point *If top = – 1 means stack empty.*

3.3.2 Stack Full Operation

In the representation of stack using arrays, size of array means size of stack. As we go on inserting the elements the stack gets filled with the elements. So it is necessary before inserting the elements to check whether the stack is full or not. Stack full condition is achieved when stack reaches to maximum size of array.

```
int stfull()
{
 if(st.top>=size-1)
  return 1;
 else
  return 0;
}
```

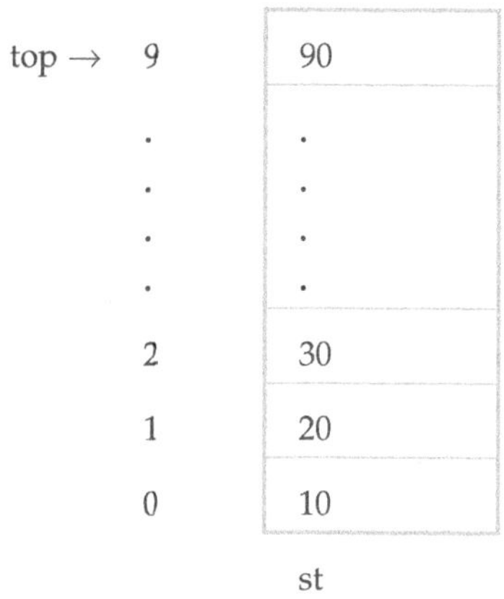

Fig. 3.3.4 Stack full condition

Thus stfull is a Boolean function if stack is full it returns 1 otherwise it returns 0.

3.3.3 The 'Push' and 'Pop' Functions

We will now discuss the two important functions which are carried out on a stack. Push is a function which inserts new element at the top of the stack. The function is as follows. .

```
void push(int item)
{
 st.top++;
 st.s[st.top] =item;
}
```

Note that the push function takes the parameter item which is actually the element which we want to insert into the stack - means we are pushing the element onto the stack. In the function we have checked whether the stack is full or not, if the stack is not full then only the insertion of the element can be achieved by means of push operation.

Now let us discuss the operation pop, which deletes the element at the top of the stack. The function pop is as given below.

Note that always top element can be deleted.

```
int pop()
{
 int item;
 item = st.s[st.top];
 st.top – –;
 return(item);
}
```

In the choice of pop- it invokes the function 'stempty' to determine whether the stack is empty or not. If it is empty, then the function generates an error as stack underflow! If not, then pop function returns the element which is at the top of the stack. The value at the top is stored in some variable as item and it then decrements the value of the top, which now points to the element which is just under the element being retrieved from the stack. Finally it returns the value of the element stored in the variable item. Note that this is what called as logical deletion and not a physical deletion, i.e. even when we decrement the top, the element just retrieved from the stack remains there itself, but it no longer belongs to the stack. Any subsequent push will overwrite this element.

The push operation can be shown by following Fig. 3.3.5.

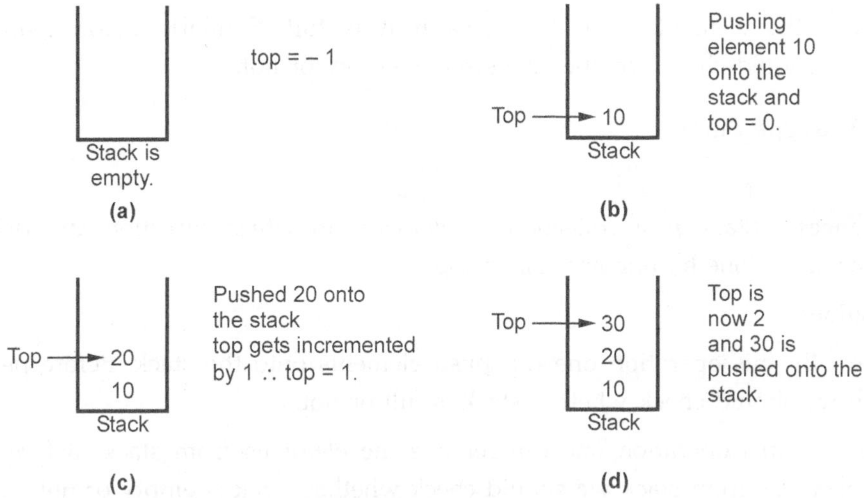

Fig. 3.3.5 Performing push operation

The pop operation can be shown by following Fig. 3.3.6.

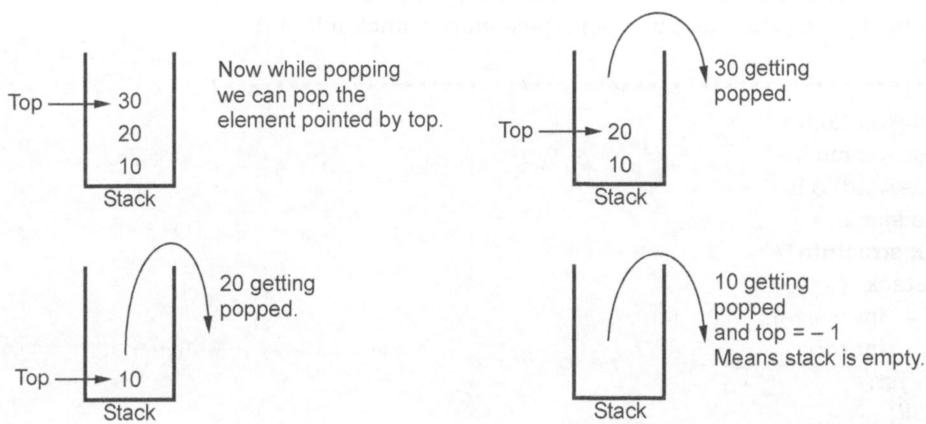

Fig. 3.3.6 Performing pop operation

Key Point *If stack is empty, then we cannot pop and if stack is full we cannot push.*

3.3.4 ADT for Stack

The stack is a data structure which posses the **LIFO property**. When we declare the structure for stack at that time it gets created. There is no need to write separate function for creation of stack. We can perform push and pop operations on the stack. Before pushing the elements it is necessary to check whether stack is full or not. We cannot push the elements onto the stack if it is full. Similarly before popping the elements we should check whether the stack is empty or not.

AbstractDataType Stack

{

Instances : Stack is a collection of elements in which insertion and deletion of elements is done by one end called top.

Operations

1. **Push :** By this operation one can push elements onto the stack. Before performing push we should check whether stack is full or not.
2. **Pop :** By this operation one can remove the elements from stack. Before popping the elements from stack we should check whether stack is empty or not.

}

'C' Program

```
/**************************************************************
Program for  implementing a stack using arrays.It involves
various operations such as push,pop,stack empty,stack full and
display.
**************************************************************/
#include<stdio.h>
#include<conio.h>
#include<stdlib.h>
#define size 5
/* stack structure*/
struct stack {
            int s[size];
            int top;
         }st;
int stfull()
{
 if(st.top>=size-1)
return 1;
 else
```

```
 return 0;
}
void push(int item)
{
 st.top++;
 st.s[st.top] =item;
}
int stempty()
{
 if(st.top==-1)
  return 1;
 else
  return 0;
}
int pop()
{
 int item;
 item=st.s[st.top];
 st.top--;
 return(item);
}
void display()
{
 int i;
 if(stempty())
   printf("\n Stack Is Empty!");
 else
 {
  for(i=st.top;i>=0;i--)        <-- Displaying stack from top to bottom
  printf("\n%d",st.s[i]);
 }
}
void main(void)
{
int item,choice;
char ans;
st.top=-1;
clrscr();
printf("\n\t\t Implementation Of Stack");
do
{
 printf("\n Main Menu");
 printf("\n1.Push\n2.Pop\n3.Display\n4.exit");
 printf("\n Enter Your Choice");
 scanf("%d",&choice);
 switch(choice)
 {
```

```
case 1:printf("\n Enter The item to be pushed");
          scanf("%d",&item);
          if(stfull())
           printf("\n Stack is Full!");
          else
           push(item);
         break;
case 2:if(stempty())
         printf("\n Empty stack!Underflow !!");
    else
     {
      item=pop();
      printf("\n The popped element is %d",item);
     }
     break;
case 3:display();
        break;
case 4:exit(0);
}
printf("\n Do You want To Continue?");
ans=getche();
}while(ans =='Y' ||ans =='y');
getch();
}
/******************** End Of Program ************************/
```

Before pushing we should check stack full condition.

Before popping we should check for stack empty condition.

Output

```
            Implementation of Stack
Main Menu
1. Push
2. Pop
3. Display
4. Exit
Enter Your Choice 1
Enter The item to be pushed 10
Do You want To Continue?y
Main Menu
1. Push
2. Pop
3. Display
4. Exit
Enter Your Choice 1
Enter The item to be pushed 20
Do You want To Continue?
Do You want To Continue?y
Main Menu
1. Push
2. Pop
```

```
3. Display
4. Exit
 Enter Your Choice 3
20
10
 Do You want To Continue?y
 Main Menu
1. Push
2. Pop
3. Display
4. Exit
 Enter Your Choice 2
 The popped element is 20
 Do You want To Continue?y
 Main Menu
1. Push
2. Pop
3. Display
4. Exit
 Enter Your Choice 2
 The popped element is 10
 Do You want To Continue?y
 Main Menu
1. Push
2. Pop
3. Display
4. Exit
 Enter Your Choice 2
 Empty stack!Underflow !!
 Do You want To Continue?n
```

Example 3.3.1 *Write an algorithm to change the ith value of stack to value X.*

GTU : Dec.-10, Marks 5

Solution : Algorithm

1. Pop the contents of stack until the ith element is obtained.
2. Store the popped contents to an array a.
3. Change the value of ith element by X.
4. Push the modified element onto the stack.
5. Read the array one element at a time and push it onto the stack. Repeat this step for all the elements of array.

Example 3.3.2 *Write an algorithm to return the value of ith element from top of the stack.*

GTU : Summer-17, Marks 3

Solution :

```
void get_element (int i)
{
        int item;
        for (j = top; j > = i; j - -)
        item = stack [j];
        return item;         // i^th element
}
```

Example 3.3.3 *i) In which case insertion and delection cannot be performed in stack ?*

ii) How stack can be used to recognize strings aca, bcb, abcba, bacab, abbcbba ? Show the trace of contents of stack for recognizing the string abcba. **GTU : Winter-17, Marks 7**

Solution :

i) If stack is full then insertion operation is not possible. Similarly if the stack is empty then delection operation is not possible.

ii) Following algorithm is used to recognize the strings aca, bcb, abcba, bacab, abbcbba -

1) Read a or b and push it onto the stock.
2) Repeat step (1) until you read c.
3) Just read c and move on to read next character.
4) If we read 'a' then POP single character from the stack. If the popped character is not 'a' then display message "string can not be recognized". Similarly if we read 'b' POP single character from the stack. If the popped character is not 'b' then display message "string can not be recognized".
5) Finally if there is no character to read and stack is also empty then display message "string can be recognized".

Example 3.3.4 *Consider the stack S of characters where S is allocated 8 memory cells*

S : A, C, D, F, K, _, _, _

Describe the stack as the following operations take place.

Pop(), Pop(), Push(L), Push(P), Pop(), Push(R), Push(S), Pop(). **GTU : Summer-18, Marks 4**

Solution :

Step 1 : Initially stack will be

Step 2 : Pop()

K will be popped.

Step 3 : Pop()

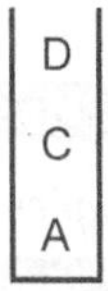

Stack

F will be popped.

Step 4 : Push(L)

Stack

Step 5 : Push(P)

Step 6 : Pop()

Popped element is P.

Step 7 : Push(R)

Step 8 : Push(S)

Step 9 : Pop()

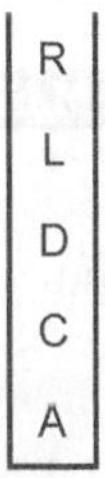

The S will be popped off.

Difference between Pop and Peep is : Pop gets and value of topmost data item from the stack and decrement top by 1. Whereas, Peep only get the value of topmost data item from the stack but don't decrement top by 1.

Review Questions

1. *Explain PUSH and POP operations of the stack with algorithm*
GTU : May-11, Marks 3, Winter-12, Marks 7
2. *Write an algorithm for stack operations Push, Pop, and Empty. Assume stack is implemented using arrays.* **GTU : Summer-13, Marks 7**
3. *Differentiate Peep() and Pop() functions* **GTU : Summer-14, Marks 3**
4. *What is stack ? List out different operations of it and write algorithm for any two operations.*
GTU : Winter-14, Marks 7
5. *Write a C program to implement a stack with all necessary overflow and underflow checks using array.* **GTU : Winter-15, Marks 7**
6. *Write an algorithm for inserting an element in a stack, removing an element from stack.*
GTU : Summer-17, Marks 4
7. *Write algorithm for push and pop operations on a stack.* **GTU : Winter-18, Marks 7**

3.4 Applications of Stack

GTU : Dec.-05, May-12, Winter-15,16, Summer-15,16, Marks 7

Various applications of stack are

1. Expression conversion.
2. Expression evaluation.
3. Parsing well formed parenthesis.
4. Decimal to binary conversion.
5. Reversing a string.
6. Storing function calls.

Example 3.4.1 *Write an algorithm to reverse a string of characters using stack.*

GTU : Summer-15, Marks 7

Solution : Algorithm

Step 1 : Read each character of the string from left to right and push it onto the stack.

Step 2 : Repeat step 1 until string does not get terminated.

Step 3 : Now pop each character from the stack and store it in an array say a[ ].

Step 4 : Repeat step 3 until stack does not get empty.

Step 5 : Print array a [ ] as a reversed string.

C code

```
i = 0, j = 0 ;
While (string [i] ! = '\0' ) // step 1 and step 2
{
      push (string [ i ]);
      i++;
```

```
}
While ( ! stempty () ) // step 3 and step 4
{
a[j] = pop ( );
j++;
}
a[j] = '10';
For  (1 = 0; i < j; i ++)
printf ("%C", a[j] );
```

Example 3.4.2 *Write an algorithm to check if an expression has balaced parenthesis using stack.* **GTU : Winter-15, Marks 3**

Solution :

Step 1 : Create a stack of characters. Initially it is empty.

Step 2 : Read the given expression from left to right one character at a time.

Step 3 : a) If the current character is ' (' then push it onto the stack

b) If the current character is ') ' then POP from the stack.

If popped character is ' (' then the expression has balaced parenthesis otherwise "It is not with balanced parenthesis".

Step 4 : After complete traversal, if the stack is empty then "Expression is with balaced parenthesis" otherwise "It is not with balaced parenthesis"

Review Questions

1. *What are the applications of stack ?* **GTU : Dec.-05, Marks 4, May-12, Marks 7**
2. *Write an algorithm to reverse a string using stack.* **GTU : Summer-16, Marks 4**
3. *Enlist and briefly explain various applications of stack.* **GTU : Winter-16, Marks 3**

3.5 Expressions

GTU : Nov-06, May-12, Summer-13,14,18, Winter-13,14,16,17,18, Marks 7

There are three types of expressions-

1. Infix Expression 2. Postfix Expression 3. Prefix Expression

1. Infix Expression :

In this type of expressions the arrangement of operands and operator is as follows.

Infix expression = operand1 operator operand2

For example 1. (a+b) 2. (a+b) * (c – d)

3. (a+b/e) * (d+f)

Parenthesis can be used in these expressions infix expression are the most natural way of representing the expressions.

2. Postfix Expression (Reverse Polish Notation) :

In this type of expressions the arrangement of operands and operator is as follows.

Postfix expression = operand1 operand2 operator

For example

1. ab+
2. ab + cd – *
3. ab + e / df + *

In postfix expression there is no parenthesis used. All the corresponding operands come first and then operator can be placed.

3. Prefix Expression (Polish Notation) :

In prefix expression the arrangement of operands and operators is as follows.

Prefix expression = operator operand1 operand2

For example

1. + ab
2. * + ab – cd
3. * / + abe + df

In prefix expression, there is no parenthesis used. All the corresponding operators come first and then operands are arranged.

3.5.1 Conversion of Infix Expression to Postfix

Algorithm

1. Read the infix expression from left to right one character at a time.
2. Initially push $ onto the stack. For $ in stack set priority as – 1.

   If input symbol read is '(' then push it onto the stack.
3. If the input symbol read is an operand then place it in postfix expression.
4. If the input symbol read is operator then

a) Check if priority of operator in stack is greater than the priority of incoming (or input read) operator then pop that operator from stack and place it in the postfix expression. Repeat step 4(a) till we get the operator in the stack which has greater priority than the incoming operator.

b) Otherwise push the operator being read, onto the stack.

c) If we read input operator as ')' then pop all the operators until we get "(" and append popped operators to postfix expression. Finally just pop "("

5. Finally pop the remaining contents, from the stack until stack becomes empty, append them to postfix expression.

6. Print the postfix expression as a result.

The priorities of different operators when they are in stack will be called as **instack** priorities. And the priorities of different operator when then are from input will be called as **incoming priorities**. These priorities are as given below.

Operator	Instack priority	Incoming priority
+ or −	2	1
* or /	4	3
∧ for any exponential operator	5	6
(	0	9
Operand	8	7
)	NA	0

Example 3.5.1 $A * B + C \$$.

Solution :

Input	Stack	Output
none	empty	none
A	empty	A
*	*	A
B	*	AB
+	Pop * and Push	AB*
C	+	AB*C
$	Empty	AB*C +

Example 3.5.2 *Convert the following infix expression to the postfix expression. Show stack traces. i) A/B$C+D*E/F-G+H ii) (A+B)*D+E/(F+G*D)+C.*

GTU : Summer-13, Marks 7

Solution : i)

Expression	Current Symbol	Action Taken	Stack	Output
A/B$C+D*E/F-G+H	Initial State		Empty	-
/B$C+D*E/F-G+H	A	Print A	Empty	A
B$C+D*E/F-G+H	/	Push /	/	A
$C+D*E/F-G+H	B	Print B	/	AB
C+D*E/F-G+H	$	Push $	/$	AB
+D*E/F-G+H	C	Print C	/$	ABC
D*E/F-G+H	+	Pop $, print it. Then Pop/print it. Then Push +	+	ABC$/
*E/F-G+H	D	Print D	+	ABC$/D
E/F-G+H	*	Push *	+*	ABC$/D
/F-G+H	*	Print E	+*	ABC$/DE
F-G+H	/	Pop * print it. Then Push /	+/	ABC$/DE*
-G+H	/	Print F	+/	ABC$/DE*F
G+H	-	Pop /, print it. Then pop + print it. Then push -	-	ABC$/DE*F/+
+H	G	Print G	-	ABC$/DE*F/+G
H	+	Pop -, print it. Then Push +	+	ABC$/DE*F/+G-
	H	Print H	+	ABC$/DE*F/+G-H
		Pop +, print it. Then Print complete string as an output	empty	**ABC$/DE*F/+G-H+**

ii)

Expression	Current Symbol	Action Taken	Stack	Output
(A+B)*D+E/(F+G*D)+C	Initial State		Empty	-
(A+B)*D+E/(F+G*D)+C	(	Push (	(	
+B)*D+E/(F+G*D)+C	A	Print A	(	A
B)*D+E/(F+G*D)+C	+	Push +	(+	A
)*D+E/(F+G*D)+C	B	Print B	(+	AB
*D+E/(F+G*D)+C	)	Pop all the stack contents and print them except (		AB+
D+E/(F+G*D)+C	*	Push	*	AB+
+E/(F+G*D)+C	D	Print D	*	AB+D
E/(F+G*D)+C	+	Pop *, print it. Then push +	+	AB+D*
E/(F+G*D)+C	E	Print E	+	AB+D*E
(F+G*D)+C	/	Push /	+/	AB+D*E
F+G*D)+C	(	Push (	+/(	AB+D*E
+G*D)+C	F	Print F	+/(	AB+D*EF
G*D)+C	+	Push +.	+/(+	AB+D*EF
*D)+C	G	Print G	+/(+	AB+D*EFG
D)+C	*	Push *	+/(+*	AB+D*EFG
)+C	D	Print D	+/(+*	AB+D*EFGD
+C	)	Pop all the contents until (. Print them.	+/	AB+D*EFGD*+
C	+	Pop /, print it. Pop + print it. then push +	+	AB+D*EFGD*+/+
	C	Print C	+	AB+D*EFGD*+/+C
		Pop the + from the stack and print		AB+D*EFGD*+/+C+
		Print the output		**AB+D*EFGD*+/+C+**

Example 3.5.3 *Convert following infix expression into postfix expression. Show each Step A+B^C^D-E*F/G* **GTU : Winter-13, Marks 7**

Solution :

Expression	Current Symbol	Action Taken	Stack	Output
A+B^C^D-E*F/G	Initial State		Empty	
+B^C^D-E*F/G	A	Print A	Empty	A
B^C^D-E*F/G	+	push +	+	A
^C^D-E*F/G	B	Print B	+	AB
C^D-E*F/G	^	Push ^	+^	AB
^D-E*F/G	C	Print C	+^	ABC
D-E*F/G	^	Push ^	+^^	ABC
-E*F/G	D	Print D	+^^	ABCD
E*F/G	-	Pop ^, print it. Then Pop ^ print it. Then Pop +, print it. Then push -	-	ABCD^^+
*F/G	E	Print E	-	ABCD^^+E
F/G	*	Push *	-*	ABCD^^+E
/G	F	Print F	-*	ABCD^^+EF
G	/	Pop *, print it. Then push /	-/	ABCD^^+EF*
	G	Print G	-/	ABCD^^+EF*G
		Pop / and print it. Pop - and print it	empty	ABCD^^+EF*G/-
		Print the output	empty	**ABCD^^+EF*G/-**

Example 3.5.4 *Convert A+(B*C-(D/E^F)*G) infix expression into postfix format showing stack status after every step in tabular form.* **GTU : Winter-14, Marks 7**

Solution :

Expression	Current Symbol	Action Taken	Stack	Output
A+(B*C-(D/E^F)*G)	Initial State		Empty	
+(B*C-(D/E^F)*G)	A	Print A	Empty	A
(B*C-(D/E^F)*G)	+	Push +	+	A

B*C-(D/E^F)*G)	(	Push (	+ (	A
*C-(D/E^F)*G)	B	Print B	+(	AB
C-(D/E^F)*G)	*	Push *	+(*	AB
-(D/E^F)*G)	C	Print C	+(*	ABC
(D/E^F)*G)	-	Pop * print then push -	+(-	ABC*
D/E^F)*G)	(	Push (	+(-(	ABC*
/E^F)*G)	D	Print D	+(-(	ABC*D
E^F)*G)	/	Push /	+(-(/	ABC*D
^F)*G)	E	Print E	+(-(/	ABC*DE
F)*G)	^	Push ^	+(-(/^	ABC*DE
)*G)	F	Print F	+(-(/^	ABC*DEF
*G)	)	Pop ^ print, then pop / print, then pop (	+(-	ABC*DEF^/
G)	*	Push *	+(-*	ABC*DEF^/
)	G	Print G	+(-*	ABC*DEF^/G
	)	Pop * print, then pop - print, then pop (	+	ABC*DEF^/G*-
		Pop +, print	Empty	**ABC*DEF^/G*-+**

Thus the equivalent postfix expression is **ABC*DEF^/G*-+**

Example 3.5.5 *Convert the following infix expression into postfix.*

*A + B – C * D * E $ F $ G* **GTU : Winter-16, Marks 3**

Solution :

Expression	Current Symbol	Action Taken	Stack	Output
A+B-C*D*EFG	Initial State		Empty	-
+B-C*D*EFG	A	Print A		A
B-C*D*EFG	+	Push +	+	A

-C*D*EFG	B	Print B	+	AB
C*D*EFG	-	Pop +, print then push -	-	AB+
*D*EFG	C	Print C	-	AB+C
D*EFG	*	Push *	-*	AB+C
*EFG	D	Print D	- *	AB+CD
EFG	*	Pop *, print it. Then push *	-*	AB+CD*
FG	E	Print E	-*	AB+CD*E
F$G	$	Push $	-*$	AB+CD*E
$G	F	Print F	-*$	AB+CD*EF
G	$	push $	-*$$	AB+CD*EF
	G	Print G	-*$$	AB+CD*EFG
		Pop the contents of stack and print it.		AB+CD*EFG$$*-

The resultant postfix expression is **AB+CD*EFG$$*-**

Example 3.5.6 *i) Convert a+b*c-d/e*h to postfix.*

ii) Convert ((a+b^c^d)(e+f/d)) to postfix.*

iii) Which stack operations are needed for performing conversion from infix to postfix ? Write the algorithm. **GTU : Winter-17, Marks 7**

Solution :

i) Conversion of a+b*c-d/e*h to postfix

Expression	Current Symbol	Action Taken	Stack	Output
+b*c-d/e*h	a	Print a	empty	a
b*c-d/e*h	+	Push +	+	a
*c-d/e*h	b	Print b	+	ab
c-d/e*h	*	Push *	+*	ab
-d/e*h	c	Print c	+*	abc
d/e*h	-	Pop *, Print. Pop +, Print. Then Push -	-	abc*+
/e*h	d	Print d	-	abc*+d
e*h	/	Push /	-/	abc*+d

*h	e	Print e	-/	abc*+de
h	*	Pop /, Print. Then Push *	-*	abc*+de/
	h	print h	-*	abc*+de/
	none	Pop all the contents of stack and print	empty	**abc*+de/*-**

The postfix expression is **abc*+de/*-**

ii) Conversion of ((a+b^c^d)*(e+f/d)) to postfix

Expression	Current Symbol	Action Taken	Stack	Output
(a+b^c^d)*(e+f/d))	(	Push (	(	
a+b^c^d)*(e+f/d))	(	Push (	((	
+b^c^d)*(e+f/d))	a	Print a	((	a
b^c^d)*(e+f/d))	+	Push +	((+	a
^c^d)*(e+f/d))	b	Print b	((+	ab
c^d)*(e+f/d))	^	Push ^	((+^	ab
^d)*(e+f/d))	c	Print c	((+^	abc
d)*(e+f/d))	^	Push ^	((+^^	abc
)*(e+f/d))	d	Print d	((+^^	abcd
*(e+f/d))	)	Pop all the contents until (is read. Pop (.	(	abcd^^+
(e+f/d))	*	Push *	(*	abcd^^+
e+f/d))	(	Push (	(*(	abcd^^+
+f/d))	e	Print e	(*(	abcd^^+e
f/d))	+	Push +	(*(+	abcd^^+e
/d))	f	Print f	(*(+	abcd^^+ef
d))	/	Push /	(*(+/	abcd^^+ef
))	d	Print d	(*(+/	abcd^^+efd
)	)	Pop all the contents until (is read. Pop (.	(*	abcd^^+efd/+
	)	Pop *, print. Pop (		**abcd^^+efd/+***

The postfix expression is **abcd^^+efd/+***

iii) The push and pop operations are needed to convert infix to postfix. For algorithm refer section 3.5.1.

Example 3.5.7 *Write algorithm to convert an infix expression to postfix expression. Show the working of the algorithm for the following expression A-B*C/D$E-(F*G).*

GTU : Summer-18, Marks 7

Solution :

Expression	Current Symbol	Action Taken	Stack	Output
A-B*C/D$E-(F*G)	A	Print A	Empty	A
B*C/D$E-(F*G)	B	Print B	Empty	AB
*C/D$E-(F*G)	*	Push *	*	AB
C/D$E-(F*G)	C	Print C	*	ABC
/D$E-(F*G)	/	Pop *, Print *, Push /	/	ABC*
D$E-(F*G)	D	Print D	/	ABC*D
$E-(F*G)	$	Push $	/$	ABC*D
E-(F*G)	E	Print E	/$	ABC*DE
-(F*G)	-	Pop $, Print, pop /, print, Push -	-	ABC*DE$/-
(F*G)	(	Push (	-(	ABC*DE$/-
F*G)	F	Print F	-(	ABC*DE$/-F
*G)	*	Push *	-(*	ABC*DE$/-F
G)	G	Print G	-(*	ABC*DE$/-FG
)	)	Pop *, print, Pop (, pop - print	Empty	ABC*DE$/-FG*-

The postfix expression is **ABC*DE$/-FG*** -

Example 3.5.8 *Convert infix expression A^B*C-D+E/F/(G+H) into postfix expression using stack.* **GTU : Winter-18, Marks 3**

Solution :

Expression	Current Symbol	Action Taken	Stack	Output
A^B*C-D+E/F/(G+H)	A	Print A	empty	A
^ B*C-D+E/F/(G+H)	^	Push ^	^	A
B*C-D+E/F/(G+H)	B	Print B	^	AB
* C-D+E/F/(G+H)	*	Pop ^, print, Push *	*	AB^
C-D+E/F/(G+H)	C	Print C	*	AB^C
- D+E/F/(G+H)	-	Pop *, print, push -	-	AB^C*
D+E/F/(G+H)	D	Print D	-	AB^C*D
+ E/F/(G+H)	+	Pop -, print, Push +	+	AB^C*D-
E/F/(G+H)	E	Print E	+	AB^C*D-E
/ F/(G+H)	/	Push /	+/	AB^C*D-E
F/ (G + H)	F	Print F	+/	AB^C*D-EF
/ (G + H)	/	Pop /, print. Push /	+/	AB^C*D-EF/
(G + H)	(	Push (	+/(	AB^C*D-EF/
G +H)	G	Print G	+/(	AB^C*D-EF/G
+ H)	+	Push +	+/(+	AB^C*D-EF/G
H)	H	Print H	+/(+	AB^C*D-EF/GH
)	)	Pop +, print, pop (. Pop / print, pop +, print	empty	AB^C*D-EF/GH+/+

The postfix expression is **AB^C* D – EF / GH + / +**

C Program

```
/*********************************************************************
Program for converting infix expression to postfix form
*********************************************************************/
#include<stdio.h>
#include<conio.h>
struct stack
{
	char s[30];
	int top;
}st;
void main()
{
	char infix[30];
	void intopost(char infix[30]);
	clrscr();
	printf("\n Enter the infix expression ");
	scanf("%s",infix);
	intopost(infix);
	getch();
}
void intopost(char infix[30])
{
 st.top=-1;
 st.top=st.top+1;
 st.s[st.top]='$';
 char postfix[30];
 int i,j;
 char ch;
 int instack(char ch);
 int incoming(char ch);
 void push(char item);
 char pop();
 j=0;
 for(i=0;infix[i]!='\0';i++)
 {
	ch=infix[i];
	while(instack(st.s[st.top])>incoming(ch))
	{
	 postfix[j]=pop();
	 j++;
	}
	if(instack(st.s[st.top])!=incoming(ch))
		push(ch);
	else
	 pop();
 }
 while((ch=pop())!='$')
 {
	postfix[j]=ch;
```

```
        j++;
  }
        postfix[j]='\0';
        printf("\n The postfix expression is =>%s",postfix);
}
int instack(char ch)
{
        int priority;
        switch(ch)
        {
                case '+':
                case '-': priority=2;
                                break;
                case '*':
                case '/': priority=4;
                                break;
                case '^': priority=5;
                                break;
                case '(': priority=0;
                                break;
                case '$': priority=-1;
                                break;
                default:  priority=8;
        }
        return priority;
}
int incoming(char ch)
{
        int priority;
        switch(ch)
        {
                case '+':
                case '-': priority=1;
                                break;
                case '*':
                case '/': priority=3;
                                break;
                case '^': priority=6;
                                break;
                case '(': priority=9;
                                break;
                case ')': priority=0;
                                break;
                default:  priority=7;

        }
        return priority;
}
void push(char item)
{
 st.top++;
 st.s[st.top]=item;
```

```
}
char pop()
{
      char e;
      e=st.s[st.top];
      st.top--;
      return e;
}
```

Output

```
Enter the infix expression (a+b)*(c/d)

The postfix expression is =>ab+cd/*
```

Review Question

1. *Write a 'C' progam or an algorithm to convert infix expression without parenthesis to postfix expression.* **GTU : Winter-14, 18, Marks 7**

3.5.2 Conversion of Infix to Prefix

Algorithm

1. Reverse the infix expression.
2. Read this reversed expression from left to right one character at a time.
3. Initially push $ onto the stack. If $ is there in stack then set the priority to be – 1. If ')' is read, then push it onto the stack.
4. If input symbol being read is operand then place it in prefix expression.
5. If input symbol read is operator then
   a) Check if priority of operator in stack is greater than priority of incoming (or input) operator then pop that operator from stack and place it in prefix expression. Repeat step 5(a) till we get the operator in the stack which has greater priority than incoming operator.
   b) Otherwise push the operator being read.
   c) If we read "(" as input symbol then pop all the operators until we get ")" and append popped operators to prefix expression.
6. Finally pop the remaining contents of stack and append them to prefix expression.
7. Reverse the obtained prefix expression and print it as result.

The instack and incoming priorities of operators are defined as below -

Operator	Instack priority	Incoming priority
)	0	9
+ or –	1	2
* or /	3	4

^	6	5
$	– 1	
Operands	8	7
(	NA	0

For example : Convert the infix expression (a + b) * (c – d) into equivalent prefix form.

Step 1 :

(a + b) * (c – d) must be reversed first. So we get) d – c (*) b + a (. Now we will read each character from left to right one at a time.

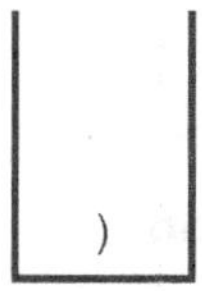

) d – c (*) b + a (
↑

Operator) is read push it onto the stack

Step 2 :

) d – c (*) b +a (
↑

Operand is read
∴ append it in prefix expression

Prefix = d

Step 3 :

) d – c (*) b + a (
↑

Push it onto the stack

Prefix = d

Step 4 :

) d – c (*) b + a (
↑

Operand is read
∴append it to prefix

Prefix = dc

Step 5 :

) d – c (*) b + a (
↑

POP all the contents until we get) and append them to prefix

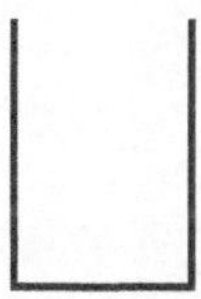

Prefix = dc –

Step 6 :

) d – c (*) b + a (
↑ (at *)

Push * onto the stack.

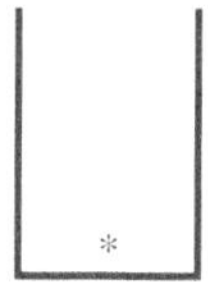

Prefix = dc –

Step 7 :

) d – c (*) b + a (
↑ (at))

Push) onto the stack

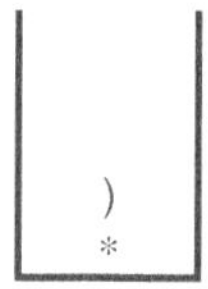

Prefix = dc –

Step 8 :

) d – c (*) b + a (
↑ (at b)

Operand is read ∴append it to prefix

Prefix = dc – b

Step 9 :

) d – c (*) b + a (
↑ (at +)

Push + onto the stack

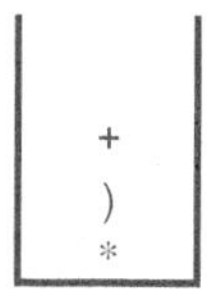

Prefix = dc – b

Step 10 :

) d – c (*) b + a (
↑ (at a)

Operand is read ∴append it to

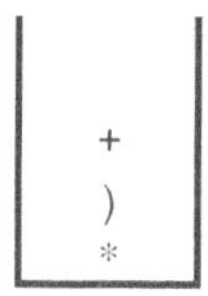

Prefix = dc – ba

Step 11 :

) d – c (*) b + a (
↑ (at ()

POP all the contents until we get ')' and append them to prefix, except (symbol. Finally pop everything and append it to prefix.

Prefix = dc – ba + *

Step 12 :

Now reverse the prefix expression. It will be * **+ ab – cd**. Print it as a result.

Example 3.5.9 *Translate the following into Polish notation and trace the content of the stack.*

*A-(B/C+(D%E*F)/G)*H.* **GTU : Summer-14, Marks 7**

Solution :

Step 1 : Reverse the infix expression.

H*)G/)F*E%D(+C/B(-A

Step 2 : Make every) and (as (and).

H*(G/(F*E%D)+C/B)-A

Step 3 : Convert the expression to postfix form

Expression	Current Symbol	Action Taken	Stack	Output
H*(G/(F*E%D)+C/B)-A	Initial State		Empty	-
*(G/(F*E%D)+C/B)-A	H	Print H		H
(G/(F*E%D)+C/B)-A	*	Push *	*	H
G/(F*E%D)+C/B)-A	(	Push (	*(	H
/(F*E%D)+C/B)-A	G	Print G	*(	HG
(F*E%D)+C/B)-A	/	Push /	*(/	HG
F*E%D)+C/B)-A	(	Push (	*(/(	HG
*E%D)+C/B)-A	F	Print F	*(/(	HGF
E%D)+C/B)-A	*	Push *	*(/(*	HGF
%D)+C/B)-A	E	Print E	*(/(*	HGFE
D)+C/B)-A	%	Push %	*(/(*%	HGFE
)+C/B)-A	D	Print D	*(/(*%	HGFED
+C/B)-A	)	Pop % and * and print. Pop (	*(/	HGFED%*
C/B)-A	+	Pop /, print it. Then push +.	*(+	HGFED%*/
/B)-A	C	Print C	*(+	HGFED%*/C
B)-A	/	Push /	*(+/	HGFED%*/C
)-A	B	Print B	*(+/	HGFED%*/CB

-A	)	Pop / print it, then + print it. Then pop (	*	HGFED%*/CB/+
A	-	Pop * print it then push -	-	HGFED%*/CB/+*
	A	Print A	-	HGFED%*/CB/+*A
		Pop -	empty	HGFED%*/CB/+*A-

Now reverse the string HGFED%*/CB/+*A- and then **-A*+/BC/*%DEFGH** will be the polish notation.

Example 3.5.10 *What is prefix notation ? Convert the following infix expression into prefix.*

$A + B - C * D * E \$ F \$ G$ **GTU : Winter-16, Marks 4**

Ans. :

Prefix Notation : Refer section 3.5

Step 1 : Reverse the infix expression

GFE*D*C-B+A

Step 2 : Convert expression to postfix form

Expression	Current Symbol	Action Taken	Stack	Output
GFE*D*C-B+A	Initial State		Empty	-
FE*D*C-B+A	G	Print G		G
F$E*D*C-B+A	$	Push $	$	G
$E*D*C-B+A	F	Print F	$	G F
E*D*C-B+A	$	push $	$$	GF
*D*C-B+A	E	Print E	$$	GFE
D*C-B+A	*	Pop $, print. Pop $, print Then push *	*	GFE$$
*C-B+A	D	Print D	*	GFE$$D
C-B+A	*	Pop *, print. Then push *	*	GFE$$D*
-B+A	C	Print C	*	GFE$$D*C

B+A	-	Pop *, print it. Then push -	-	GFE$$D*C*
+A	B	Print B	-	GFE$$D*C*B
A	+	Pop -, print it. Then push +	+	GFE$$D*C*B-
	A	Print A	+	GFE$$D*C*B-A
		Pop the contents of stack and print	Empty	GFE$$D*C*B-A +

Step 3 : Now reverse the output obtained in above table . It is

+A-B*C*D$$EFG

This is the equivalent prefix expression.

Review Question

1. *Write an algorithm to convert infix to postfix expression and explain with example.*

GTU : Nov-06, Marks 6, May-12, Marks 5, Summer-14, Marks 7

3.6 Reverse Polish Compilation

GTU : May-12, Winter-12,15,18, Summer-13,14,15,16,17, Marks 7

Algorithm for evaluation of postfix

1. Read the postfix expression from left to right.
2. If the input symbol read is an operand then push it onto the stack.
3. If the operator is read POP two operands and perform arithmetic operations if operator is

+	then result = operand 1 + operand 2
–	then result = operand 1 – operand 2
*	then result = operand 1 * operand 2
/	then result = operand 1 / operand 2

4. Push the result onto the stack.
5. Repeat steps 1-4 till the postfix expression is not over.

For example : Consider postfix expression -

AB + C – BA + C $ – for A = 1, B = 2 and C = 3

Now as per the algorithm of postfix expression evaluation, we scan the input from left to right. If operand comes we push them onto the stack and if we read any operator, we must pop two operands and perform the operation using that operator. Here $ is taken as exponential operator.

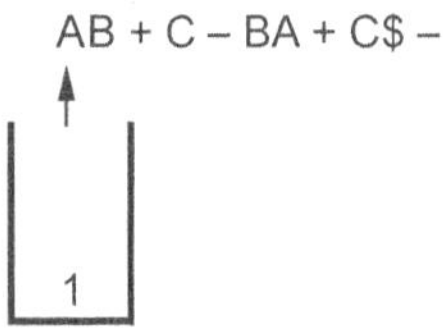

As A = 1, push 1

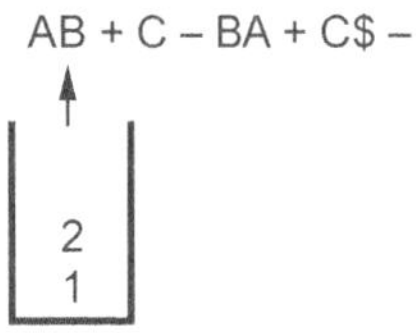

As B = 2, push 2

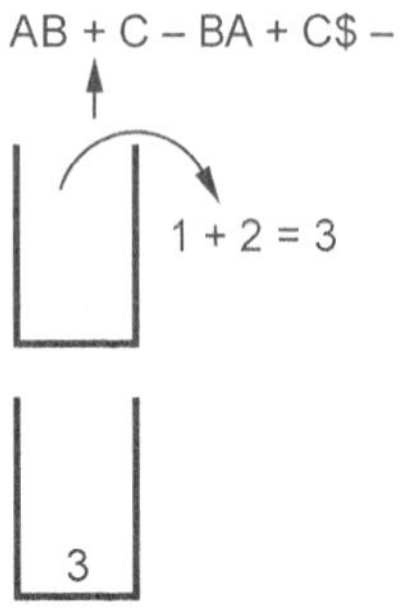

POP two operands and perform addition of 1 and 2. Then push the result onto the stack.

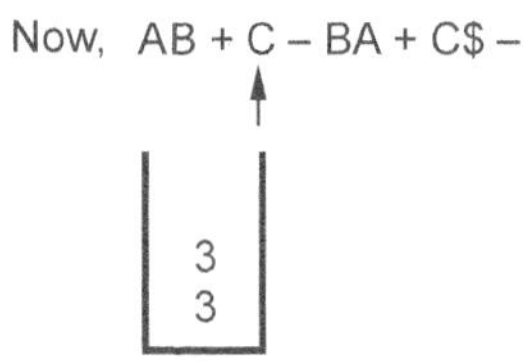

As C = 3, push 3 onto the stack.

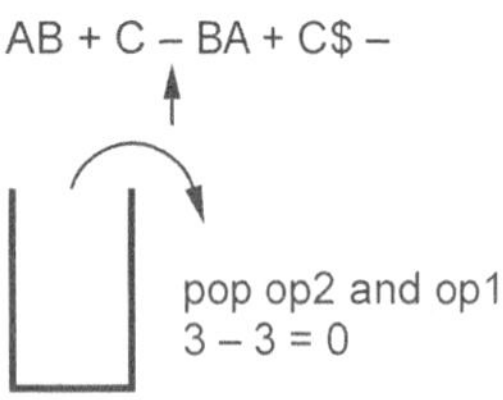

Perform subtraction.

Then push the result onto the stack.

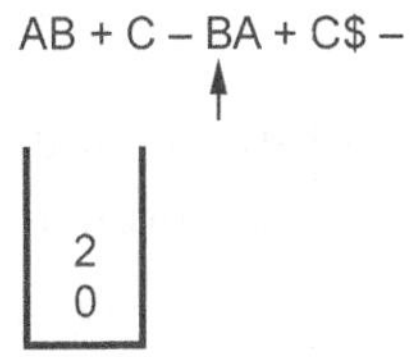

Push B = 2.

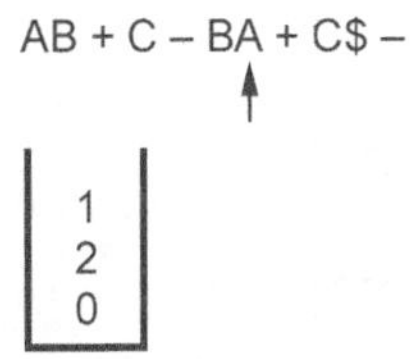

Push A = 1.

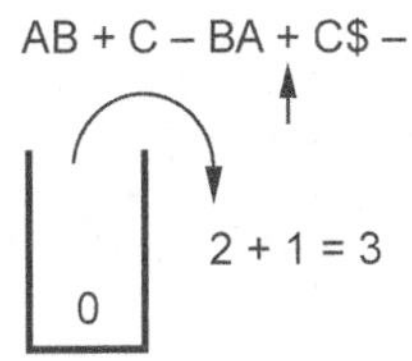

As operator comes perform operation by popping two operands.

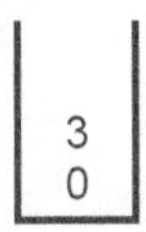

Then push the result onto the stack.

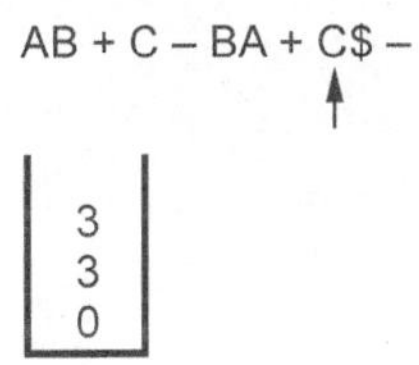

Push C = 3 onto the stack.

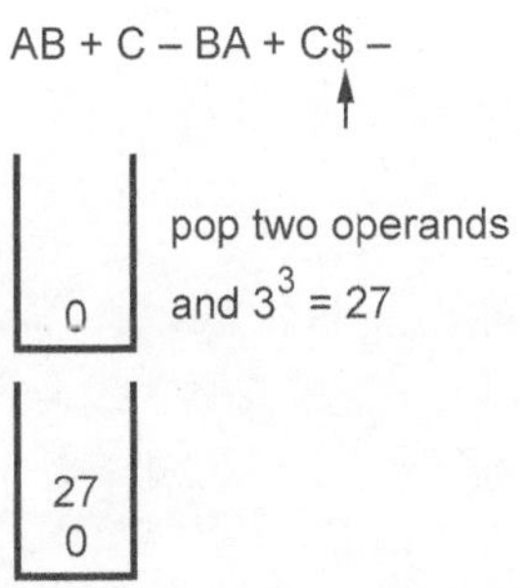

Then push the computed result.

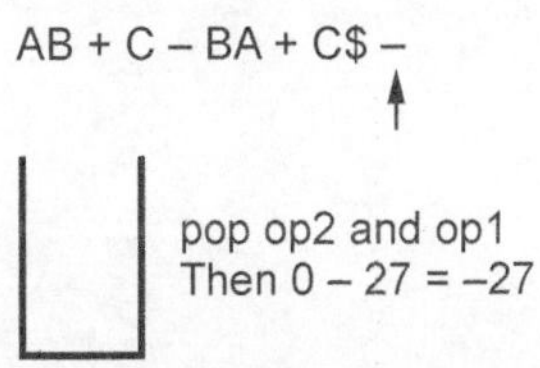

Perform the subtraction.

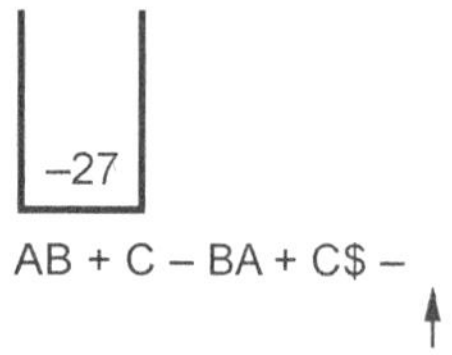

Now since there is no further input we should pop the contents of stack and print it as a result of evaluation.

Hence output will be – 27.

'C' Program

```
/**************************************************************
	Program to evaluate a given postfix expression.
**************************************************************/
#include<stdio.h>
#include<conio.h>
#include<stdlib.h>
#include<string.h>
#include<math.h>
#define size 80

/*declaration of stack data structure*/
struct stack
{	double	s[size];
	int top;
}st;
/*-----------------------------------------------------------
	The main function
	Input : None
	Output: None
	Parameter Passing Method :None
	Called By : OS
	Calls :post()
-------------------------------------------------------------
*/
void main ( )
{
	char exp[size];
	int	len;
	double Result;
	double post();
	clrscr();
	printf("Enter the postfix Expression\n");
	scanf("%s",exp);
	len = strlen(exp);
	exp[len] = '$'; /* Append $ at the end as a endmarker*/
	Result = post(exp);
	printf("The Value of the expression is %f\n", Result);
	getch();
```

```
    exit(0);
}

/*-------------------------------------------------------------
 The post function which is for evaluating postfix expression
 Input : A post Expression of single digit operand
 Output: Resultant value after evaluating the expression
 Parameter Passing Method :By reference
 Called By : main()
 Calls :push(), pop()
------------------------------------------------------------
*/
double  post(char exp[])
{
    char  ch,*type;
    double  result, val, op1, op2;
    void push(double);
    double pop();
    int i;
    st.top = 0;
    i=0;
    ch = exp[i];
    while ( ch != '$' )
    {
        if ( ch >= '0' && ch <= '9')
        type ="operand";
        else if ( ch == '+'|| ch == '-'||
         ch == '*'|| ch == '/' ||
         ch == '^' )
        type="operator";
        if( strcmp(type,"operand")==0)/*if the character is operand*/
        {
        val = ch - 48;
        push( val);
        }
        else
            if (strcmp(type,"operator")==0)/*if it is operator*/
    {
         op2 = pop();
         op1 = pop();
         switch(ch)
     {
        case '+' : result = op1 + op2;
         break;
        case '–' : result = op1 – op2;
        break;
        case '*' : result = op1 * op2;
        break;
```

The characters '0', '1', ... '9' will be converted to their values, so that they will perform arithmetic operation.

Popping two operands to perform arithmetic operation

```
        case '/' : result = op1 / op2;
        break;
        case '^' : result = pow(op1,op2);
        break;
    }/* switch */                    Finally result will be
    push(result);                    pushed onto the stack.
    }
        i++;
        ch=exp[i];
    } /* while */
    result = pop(); /*pop the result*/
    return(result);
}
/*
-----------------------------------------------------------------
    The push function
    Input : A value to be pushed on global stack
    Output: None, modifies global stack and its top
    Parameter Passing Method :By Value
    Called By : Post()
    Calls :none
-----------------------------------------------------------------
*/
void push(double val)
{
    if ( st.top+1 >= size )
        printf("\nStack is Full\n");
    st.top++;
    st.s[st.top] = val;
}
/*---------------------------------------------------------------
    The pop function
    Input : None, uses global stack and top
    Output: Returns the value on top of stack
    Parameter Passing Method :None
    Called By : post()
    Calls :none
-----------------------------------------------------------------
*/
```

```
double pop()
{
        double val;
        if ( st.top == -1 )
                printf("\nStack is Empty\n");
        val = st.s[st.top];
        st.top- -;
        return(val);
}
```

Output

```
Enter the postfix Expression
12+34*+
The Value of the expression is 15.0000
```

Logic of evaluation of postfix expression [Refer the above program]

Let us take some example of postfix expression and try to evaluate it

123+*

Step 1 : Assume the array exp [ ] contains the input

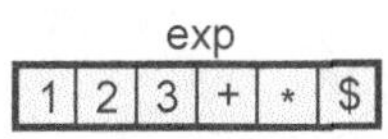

The $ symbol is used as an end marker. Read from first element of the array if it is **operand** push it onto the stack.

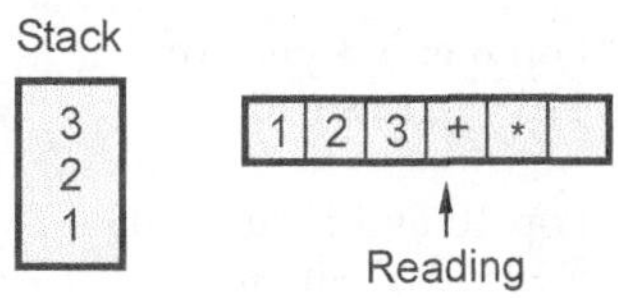

Step 2 : If the operator is read pop two operands

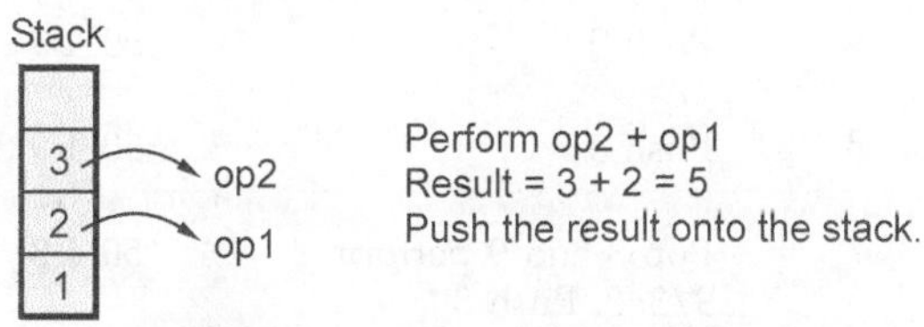

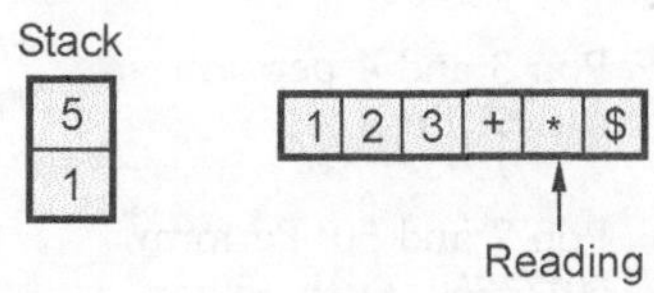

Step 3 : Again pop two operands and perform the operation.

Step 4 :

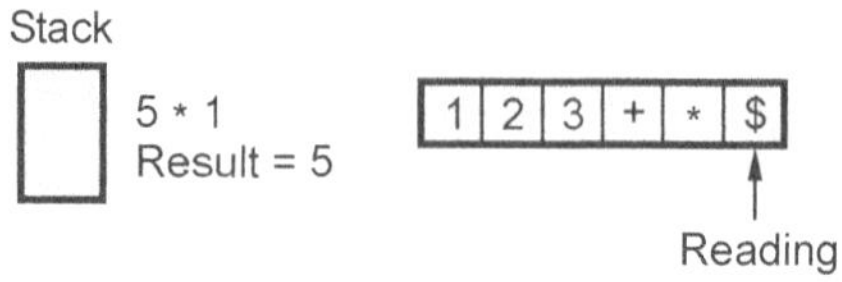

At this point the stack is empty and the input is read as $. So here stop the evaluation procedure and return the result = 5.

Example 3.6.1 *Find the value of following postfix expression using stack trace*

i) 5 4 6 + 4 9 3 /+*   ii) 3 5 * 6 2 / +*   **GTU : Winter-12, Marks 7**

Solution : i)

Expression	Current Symbol	Action Taken	Stack	Output
5 4 6 + * 4 9 3 / + *	Initial State		empty	-
4 6 + * 4 9 3 / + *	5	Push 5	5	-
6 + * 4 9 3 / + *	4	Push 4	5 4	-
+ * 4 9 3 / + *	6	Push 6	5 4 6	-
* 4 9 3 / + *	+	Pop 6 and 4 perform 4+6=10. Push 10	5 10	-
4 9 3 / + *	*	Pop 10 and 5 perform 5*10=50. Push 50	50	-
9 3 / + *	4	Push 4	50 4	-
3 / + *	9	Push 9	50 4 9	-
/ + *	3	Push 3	50 4 9 3	-
+ *	/	Pop 3 and 9 perform 9/3=3. Push 3	50 4 3	-
*	+	Pop 3 and 4 perform 4+3=7. Push 7	50 7	-
	*	Pop 7 and 50. Perform 50*7=350. Push 350	350	-
		Pop 350 and print the result	empty	**350**

ii)

Expression	Current Symbol	Action Taken	Stack	Output
35*62/+	Initial State		empty	-
5*62/+	3	Push 3	3	
*62/+	5	Push 5	3 5	
62/+	*	Pop 5 and 3 perform 3*5=15. Push 15	15	
2/+	6	Push 6	15 6	
/+	2	Push 2	15 6 2	
+	/	Pop 2 and 6. Perform 6/2=3. Push 3 onto the stack	15 3	
	+	Pop 3 and 15. Perform 15+3=18. Push 18 onto the stack.	18	
		Pop 18 and print the result	empty	18

Example 3.6.2 *Evaluate the following postfix expression using stack*

*AB+CD/*GH*+ where A=2, B=4, C=6, D=3, G=8, H=7* **GTU : Summer-14, Marks 4**

Solution :

Step 1 : We will replace the A, B, C and D with their given values and form the postfix expression for evaluation.

Expression	Current Symbol	Action Taken	Stack	Output
24+63/*87*+	Initial State		empty	-
4+63/*87*+	2	Push 2	2	
+63/*87*+	4	Push 4	2 4	
63/*87*+	+	Pop 4 and then 2 and perform 2+4=6. Push 6	6	
3/*87*+	6	Push 6	6 6	
/*87*+	3	Push 3	6 6 3	

87+	/	Pop 3 and 6 . Perform 6/3=2. Push 2	6 2	
87*+	*	Pop 2 and 6. Perform 6*2=12. Push 12	12	
7*+	8	Push 8	12 8	
*+	7	Push 7	12 8 7	
+	*	Pop 7 and 8. Perform 8*7=56. Push 56	12 56	
	+	Pop 56 and 12. Perform 12+56=68. Push 68	68	
		Pop 68 and print the result	empty	**68**

Example 3.6.3 *Evaluate following prefix expression.*

*+*AB–C+C*BA (A = 4, B = 8, C = 12)* **GTU : May-12, Marks 3**

Solution : $+(*AB)-C+C*BA$

$$= +(4*8)-C+C*BA$$

$$= +32-C+C(*BA)$$

$$= +32-C+C(8*12)$$

$$= +32-C(+C96)$$

$$= +32-C(12+96)$$

$$= +32(-C108)$$

$$= +32(-12+108)$$

$$= (32+-96)$$

$$= \mathbf{-64}$$

Example 3.6.4 *Convert (A+B) * C - D ∧ E ∧ (F * G) infix expression into prefix format showing stack status after every step in tabular form.* **GTU : Summer-15, Marks 7**

Solution :

Step 1 : Reverse the infix expression.

) G * F (∧ E ∧ D – C *) B + A (

Step 2 : Make every) as (. And (as)

(G * F) ∧ E ∧ D – C * (B + A)

Step 3 : Convert the expression into postfix form.

Expression	Current Symbol	Action Taken	Stack	Output
(G * F) ∧ E ∧ D – C * (B + A)	Initial state		empty	
G * F) ∧ E ∧ D – C * (B + A)	(	push	(	
* F) ∧ E ∧ D – C * (B + A)	G	print G	(	G
F) ∧ E ∧ D – C * (B + A)	*	push	(*	G
) ∧ E ∧ D – C * (B + A)	F	print F	(*	
∧ E ∧ D – C * (B + A)	)	pop *, print. pop (.		*
E ∧ D – C * (B + A)	∧	push	∧	*
∧ D – C * (B + A)	E	print E	∧	* E
D – C * (B + A)	∧	push ∧	∧	* E
– C * (B + A)	D	Print D	∧ ∧	GF * ED
C * (B + A)	–	pop ∧, print pop ∧, print push -	–	GF * ED ∧∧
* (B + A)	C	print C	–	GF * ED ∧∧ C
(B + A)	*	push *	–*	GF * ED ∧∧ C
B + A)	(	push (	–* (	GF * ED ∧∧ C
+ A)	B	print B	–* (	GF * ED ∧∧ C B
A)	+	push +	–* (+	GF * ED ∧∧ C B
)	A	print A	–* (+	GF * ED ∧∧ C BA
	)	pop +, print pop (. pop * , print pop – , print	empty	GF * ED ∧∧ C BA+ * –

Step 4 : Now reverse the output expression obtained in above table.

– * + A B C ∧ ∧ D E * F G

This is the required prefix expression.

Example 3.6.5 *What is post fix notation? What are its advantages ? Convert the following infix expression to postfix.*

*A $ B – C * D + E $ F / G* **GTU : Winter-15, Marks 4**

Solution : Postfix Notation : The form in which the operands appear before operator are called postfix notation.

For example : (a + b) is an infix expression and **ab+** is post Fix expression. The post Fix form is used for evaluation of expression.

Expression	Current Symbol read	Action Taken	Stack	Output
A $ B – C * D + E $ F/G	A	print A	empty	A
$ B – C * D + E $ F/G	$	push $	$	A
B – C * D + E $ F/G	B	print B	$	AB
– C * D + E $ F/G	–	pop $, print. Then push -	–	AB$
C * D + E $ F/G	C	print C	–	AB$C
* D + E $ F/G	*	push *		AB$C
D + E $ F/G	D	print	– *	AB$CD
+ E $ F/G	+	pop *, print then pop– , print. Then push +	+	AB$CD* –
E $ F/G	. E	print	+	AB$CD* – E
$ F/G	$	push $	+ $	AB$CD* – E
F/G	F	Print	+ $	AB$CD* – E F
/G	/	pop $, print then push/	+ /	AB$CD* – E F $
G	G	print G	+ /	AB$CD* – E F $ G
end of input		Pop / , print pop + , print	empty	AB$CD* – E F $ G / +

The postfix expression is **A B $ C D * – E F $ G / +**

Example 3.6.6 *Evaluate the following postfix expression using a stack. Show the stack contents*

*A B * C D $ – E F / G / +*

A = 5, B = 2, C = 3, D = 2, E = 8, F = 2 and G = 2. **GTU : Winter-15, Marks 3**

Solution : We will replace A, B, C, D, E, F, G with their values.

Expression	Current Symbol read	Action Taken	Stack
5 2 * 3 2 $ − 8 2 / 2 / +	Initial State		empty
2 * 3 2 $ − 8 2 / 2 / +	5	push 5	5
* 3 2 $ − 8 2 / 2 / +	2	push 2	5 2
3 2 $ − 8 2 / 2 / +	*	pop 2, pop 5. Perform $5 \times 2 = 10$. push 10	10
2 $ − 8 2 / 2 / +	3	push 3	10 3
$ − 8 2 / 2 / +	2	push 2	10 3 2
− 8 2 / 2 / +	$	pop 2, pop 3 perform $3^2 = 9$. push 9	10 9
8 2 / 2 / +	−	pop 9, pop 10 perform 10 − 9 = 1 push 1	1
2 / 2 / +	8	push 8	1 8
/ 2 / +	2	push 2	1 8 2
2 / +	/	pop2, pop 8. Perform 8/2 = 4 Push 4.	1 4
/ +	2	push 2	1 4 2
+	/	pop 2, pop 4. Perform 4/2 = 2 push 2	1 2
	+	pop 2, pop 1. Perform 1 + 2 = 3 push 3	3
		Pop 3 and print as output	empty

The result of evaluation is 3.

Example 3.6.7 *Evaluate the following postfix expression using a stack.*

*a) 9 3 4 * 8 + 4 / - b) 5 6 2 + * 1 2 4 / - +* **GTU : Summer-16, Marks 3**

Solution : i)

Expression	Current Symbol	Action Taken	Stack	Output
9 3 4 * 8 + 4 / -	Initial Step		Empty	-
3 4 * 8 + 4 / -	9	Push 9	9	-
4 * 8 + 4 / -	3	Push 3	9 3	-
* 8 + 4 / -	4	Push 4	9 3 4	-
8 + 4 / -	*	Pop 4 as op2, then pop 3 as op1 perform op1*op2 i.e. 3*4=12. Push 12	9 12	-
+ 4 / -	8	Push 8	9 12 8	-
4 / -	+	Pop 8 as op2 and 12 as op1. Perform op1+op2 i.e. 12+8=20. Push 20.	9 20	-
/ -	4	Push 4	9 20 4	-
-	/	Pop 4 as op2 and 20 as op1. Perform op1/op2 i.e. 20/4=5. Push 5.	9 5	-
	-	Pop 5 as op2 and 9 as op1. Perform op1-op2 i.e. 9-5=4. Push 4.	4	-
End of Input		Pop the stack content and display it as output.	Empty	4

The result of evaluation is **4**

ii)

Expression	Current Symbol	Action Taken	Stack	Output
5 6 2 + * 1 2 4 / - +	Initial Step		Empty	-
6 2 + * 1 2 4 / - +	5	Push 5	5	-
2 + * 1 2 4 / - +	6	Push 6	5 6	-
+ * 1 2 4 / - +	2	Push 2	5 6 2	-
* 1 2 4 / - +	+	Pop 2 as op2 and 6 as op1. Perform op1+op2 i.e. 6+2=8. Push 8.	5 8	-

1 2 4 / - +	*	Pop 8 as op2 and 5 as op1. Perform op1*op2 i.e. 5+8=40. Push 40.	40	-
2 4 / - +	1	Push 1	40 1	-
4 / - +	2	Push 2	40 1 2	-
/ - +	4	Push 4	40 1 2 4	-
- +	/	Pop 4 as op2 and 2 as op1. Perform op1/op2 i.e. 2/4=0. Push 0.	40 1 0	-
+	-	Pop 0 as op2 and 1 as op1. Perform op1-op2 i.e. 1-0=1. Push 1.	40 1	-
	+	Pop 1 as op2 and 40 as op1. Perform op1+op2 i.e. 40+1=41. Push 41.	41	-
End of input		Pop the content of stack and display as output	41	41

The result of evaluation is 41

Example 3.6.8 *Evaluate the following postfix expression using stack. Show the steps 2$3+5*2$2-12$6.* **GTU : Summer-18, Winter-18, Marks 3**

Solution :

Expression	Current Symbol	Action Taken	Stack	Output
623 + – 382/ + * 2 $ 3 +	Initial step		Empty	-
23 + – 382/ + * 2 $ 3 +	6	Push 6	6	-
3 + – 382/ + * 2 $ 3 +	2	Push 2	6 2	-
3 + – 382/ + * 2 $ 3 +	3	Push 3	6 2 3	-
+ – 382/ + * 2 $ 3 +	+	Pop 3, as op2, pop2 as op1 perform op1 + op2 i.e. 3 + 2 = 5 push 5	6 5	
– 382/ + * 2 $ 3 +	–	Pop 5 as op2, pop 6 as op1. Perform 6 – 5 = 1. push 1	1	
382/ + * 2 $ 3 +	3	Push 3	1 3	

82/ + * 2 $ 3 +	8	Push 8	1 3 8	-
2/ + * 2 $ 3 +	2	Push 2	1 3 8 2	-
/ + * 2 $ 3 +	/	Pop 2 as op2, pop 8 as op1 8/2 = 4 push 4	1 3 4	
+ * 2 $ 3 +	+	Pop 4 as op2, pop 3 as op1 3 + 4 = 7 push 7	1 7	-
* 2 $ 3 +	*	Pop 7 as op2, pop 1 as op1. Perform 1 * 7 = 7 push 7	7	-
2 $ 3 +	2	Push	7 2	-
$ 3 +	$	Pop 2 as op2, pop 7 as op1. perform 7 $ 2 = 49 push 49	49	-
3 +	$	Push 3	49 3	-
+	+	Pop 3 as op2, pop 49 as OP1. 49 + 3 = 51 push 51	51	-
End of input		Pop 51 and print	Empty	51

The result of evaluation is **51.**

Advantage of postfix expression over infix expression

1. Any expression can be denoted without using parenthesis.
2. It is convenient to evaluate postfix expression using stack.
3. Infix expression needs the precedence to evaluate the expression. Postfix expression eliminates this nuisance.

Review Question

1. *What is the advantage of postfix expression over infix expression? Write an algorithm of postfix evaluation* **GTU : Summer-13, Marks 7**

3.7 Recursion

GTU : Dec.-05, Summer-15, Winter-18, Marks 6

> **Definition :** *Recursion is a programming technique in which the function calls itself repeatedly for some input.*

3.7.1 Factorial Function

One can define the factorial of some number n as a product of all the integers from n to 1.

For example, if the 5 factorial has to be calculated then, it will be = 5*4*3*2*1 =120.

Similarly 3! = 3*2*1 = 6 and the 0! = 1. The exclamation mark is used to denote the factorial. We may write the definition of factorial function as -

$$n! = 1 \text{ if } n==0$$

Otherwise, $$n! = n*(n-1)*(n-2)*\ldots*1 \text{ if } n>0$$

If the value of n is any of the 0, 1, 2, 3 or 4 then the definition will be -

$$0! = 1$$

$$1! = 1$$

$$2! = 2*1$$

$$3! = 3*2*1$$

$$4! = 4*3*2*1$$

Here we are presenting an algorithm that takes the input as value of n and returns the result of n!. There are two ways of doing this-

1. Iterative method 2. Recursive method

Algorithm for Factorial Function using Iterative Definition :

```
prod = 1;
x=n;
while(x>0)
{
prod = prod*x;
x – –;
}
return(prod);
```

Such an algorithm is called as an **iterative** algorithm because it calls explicit repetition of some process (in our example the process multiplication and decrementing x by 1) until certain condition is met (for example x>0).

Let us analyze the definition of factorial function.

The definition of factorial is

n! = 1 if n==0

Otherwise, n! = n*(n–1)*(n–2)*...*1 if n>0

This definition is called the **recursive definition** of the factorial function. This definition is called recursive because again and again the same procedure of multiplication is followed but with the different input and result is again multiplied with the next input. Let us see how the recursive definition of the factorial function is used to evaluate the 5!

Step 1 : 5! = 5*4!

Step 2 : 4! = 4*3!

Step 3 : 3! = 3*2!

Step 4 : 2! = 2*1!

Step 5 : 1! = 1*0!

Step 6 : 0! = 1.

Actually the step 6 is the only step which is giving the direct result. So to solve 5! we have to backtrack from step 6 to step 1, collecting the result from each step. Let us see how to do this.

Step 6′ : 0! =1

Step 5′ : 1! = 1* 0! = 1 from step 6′

Step 4′ : 2! = 2*1! = 2 from step 5′

Step 3′ : 3! = 3*2! = 6 from step 4′

Step 2′ : 4! = 4*3! = 24 from step 3′

Step 1′ : 5! = 5*4! = 120 from step 2′

Algorithm for Factorial Function using the Recursive Definition :

```
1. if(n==0)
2. fact =1;
3. else
   {
4. x=n–1;
5. y= value of x!;
6. fact = n* y ;
7. } /*else ends here */
```

Advantages

1. Recursive methods bring compactness in program.
2. There is no need of using programming constructs such as for, while, do-while.

Disadvantages

1. Memory utilization is more in recursive functions because all pending operations must be preserved.
2. Recursive methods are less efficient than iterative methods.
3. Recursive methods are complex to implement.

3.7.2 Properties of Recursive Definition

- The very essential property of recursive definition is that there should be **atleast one non recursive call,** because of which the procedure won't go in the infinite condition. Thus the nonrecursive exit will help a recursive procedure to terminate.

For example :

```
if(n==0)
        return 1;
is a non recursive
call for factorial
```

- Another property of recursive function is that any instant of **recursive definition** must **eventually reduce** to some manipulation. By this one can reach to the answer after certain number of steps.

Example : Factorial of a number

```
/************************************************************
Program for finding out the factorial for any given number.
************************************************************/
#include<stdio.h>
#include<stdlib.h>
#include<conio.h>

void main(void)
 {
  int n,f;
  int fact(int n);/*declaration*/
  clrscr();
  printf("\n\t\t Program For finding the  factorial of n");
   printf("\n\n Enter the number for finding the factorial: ");
   scanf("%d",&n);
   f=fact(n);/*call to function*/
   printf("\n the factorial of %d is %d",n,f);
   getch();
}
```

```
int fact(int n)
{
 int x,y;
 if(n<0)
 {
  printf("The negative parameter in the factorial function");
  exit(0);
 }
 if(n==0)
   return 1;
 x=n-1;
 y=fact(x);        /*recursive call*/
 return(n*y);
}
/****************** End Of Program **********************/
```

Output

```
Program For finding the  factorial of n
Enter the number for finding the factorial: 5
The factorial of 5 is 120
```

Example 3.7.1 *What is recursion ? Write a pseudo code in 'C' language to find the multiplication of two natural numbers.* **GTU : Winter-18, Marks 3**

Solution : Recursion - Refer section 3.7.

Recursive program for multiplication of two numbers

```
#include<stdio.h>
#include<conio.h>
void main()
{
      int a,b,result=0;
      int mul(int a,int b);
      clrscr();
      printf("\n Enter the values of a and b: ");
      scanf("%d%d",&a,&b);
      result=mul(a,b);
      printf("The multiplication is = %d",result);
      getch();
}
int mul(int a,int b)
{
      if(b==1)
            return a;
      else
```

```
        return(mul(a,b-1)+ a);
}
```

Output

```
Enter the values of a and b: 5 7
The multiplication is = 35
```

Review Questions

1. *What is recursion? Discuss its advantages and disadvantages.* **GTU : Dec.-05, Marks 6**
2. *Describe : Recursion.* **GTU : Summer-15, Marks 2**

3.8 Tower of Hanoi

GTU : Nov.-06, May-12, CE : Dec.-03, Marks 6

The problem is the "Towers of Hanoi". The initial setup is as shown in Fig. 3.8.1.

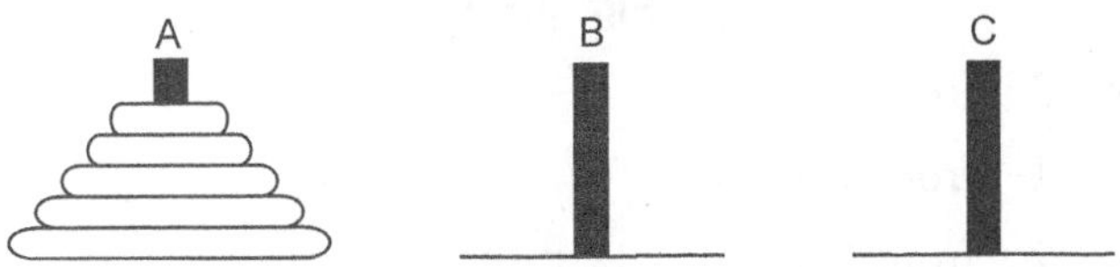

Fig. 3.8.1

There are three pegs named as A, B and C. The fire disks of different diameters are placed on peg A. The arrangement of the disks is such that every smaller disk is placed on the larger disk.

The problem of " Towers of Hanoi" states that move the five disks from peg A to Peg using peg B as a auxiliary.

The conditions are :

i) Only the top disk on any peg may be moved to any other peg.

ii) A larger disk should never rest on the smaller one.

The above problem is the classic example of recursion. The solution to this problem is very simple.

First of all let us number out the disks for our comfort.

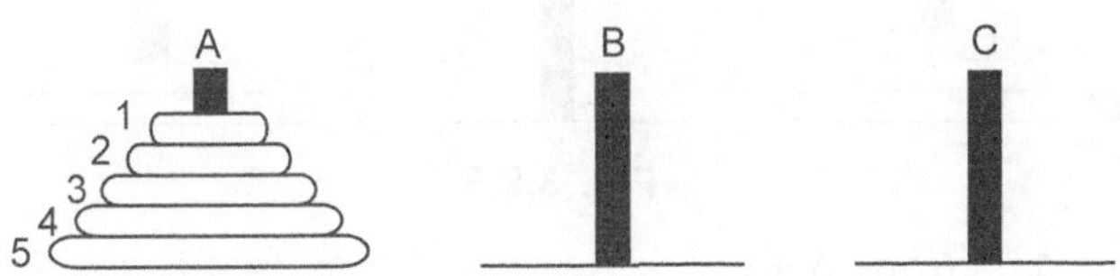

Fig. 3.8.2

The solution can be stated as

1. Move top n–1 disks from A to B using C as auxiliary.
2. Move the remaining disk from A to C.
3. Move the n–1 disks from B to C using A as auxiliary.

We can convert it to

move disk 1 from A to B.

move disk 2 from A to C.

move disk 1 from B to C.

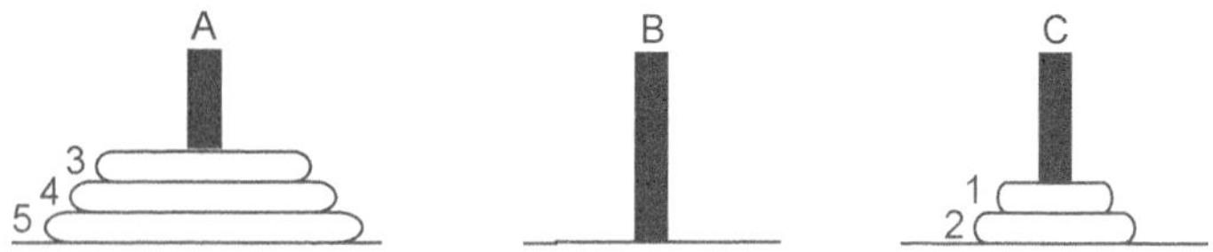

Fig. 3.8.3

move disk 3 from A to B

move disk 1 from C to A

move disk 2 from C to B

move disk 1 from A to B

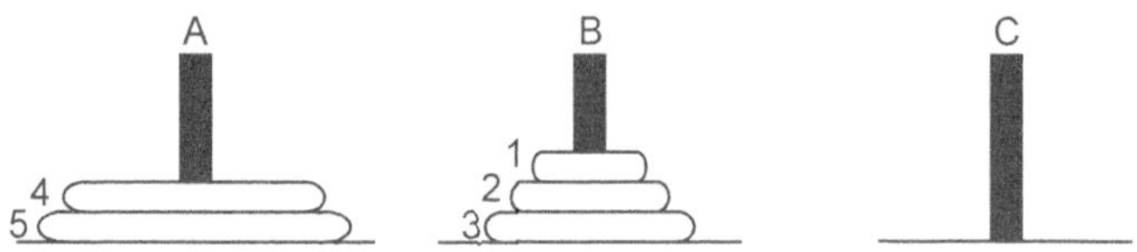

Fig. 3.8.4

move disk 4 from A to C

move disk 1 from B to C

move disk 2 from B to A

move disk 1 from C to A

move disk 3 from B to C

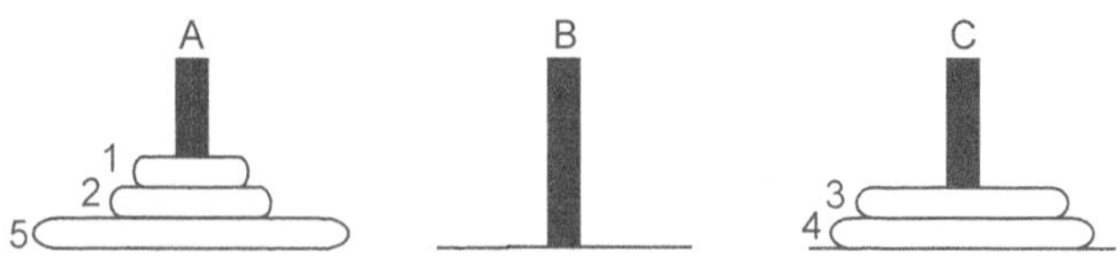

Fig. 3.8.5

move disk 1 from A to B

move disk 2 from A to C

move disk 1 from B to C

Thus actually we have moved n–1 disks from peg A to C. In the same way we can move the remaining disk from A to C.

'C' Program

```
/*************************************************************
Program For Towers of Hanoi. The input will be the number of disks for which the
program should operate.
*************************************************************/
#include<stdio.h>
#include<conio.h>
#include<stdlib.h>

void main(void)
{
 int n;
 void towers(int n,char from,char to,char aux);
 clrscr();
 printf("\n\t\t Program For Towers Of Hanoi");
 printf("\n\n Enter the total number of disks");
 scanf("%d",&n);
 towers(n,'A','C','B');
 getch();
}

void towers(int n,char from,char to,char aux)
{
 /*if only one disk has to be moved*/
 if(n==1)
 {
      printf("\n Move disk 1 from %c peg to %c
          peg",from,to);
      return;
 }
 /*move top n-1 disks from A to B using C*/
 towers(n-1,from,aux,to);
 printf("\n Move disk %d from %c peg to %c peg",n,from,to);
 /* move remaining disk from B to C using A*/
 towers(n-1,aux,to,from);
}
```

Output

```
               Program for Towers of Hanoi
Enter the total number of disks 4

Move disk 1 from A peg to B peg
Move disk 2 from A peg to C peg
Move disk 1 from B peg to C peg
Move disk 3 from A peg to B peg
Move disk 1 from C peg to A peg
Move disk 2 from C peg to B peg
Move disk 1 from A peg to B peg
Move disk 4 from A peg to C peg
Move disk 1 from B peg to C peg
Move disk 2 from B peg to A peg
Move disk 1 from C peg to A peg
Move disk 3 from B peg to C peg
Move disk 1 from A peg to B peg
Move disk 2 from A peg to C peg
Move disk 1 from B peg to C peg
```

Example 3.8.1 *Show the stack contents for 2 plates for tower of Hanoi problem.*

GTU : CE : Dec.-03, Marks 4

Solution : The algorithm for Tower of Hanoi problem will be -

1. Move top (n – 1) disks from A to B using C as auxiliary.
2. Move the remaining disk from A to C.
3. Move the (n – 1) disks from B to C using A as auxiliary.

Step 1 : Initially both the plates are stacked on peg A.

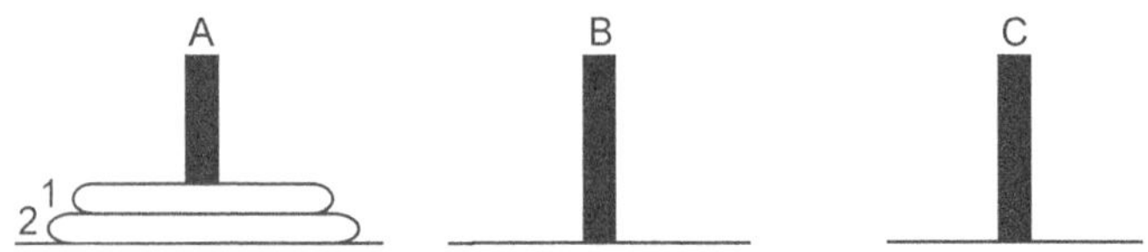

Fig. 3.8.6 Initial configuration

Step 2 : Now we will move (n – 1) i.e. 1 disk to peg B.

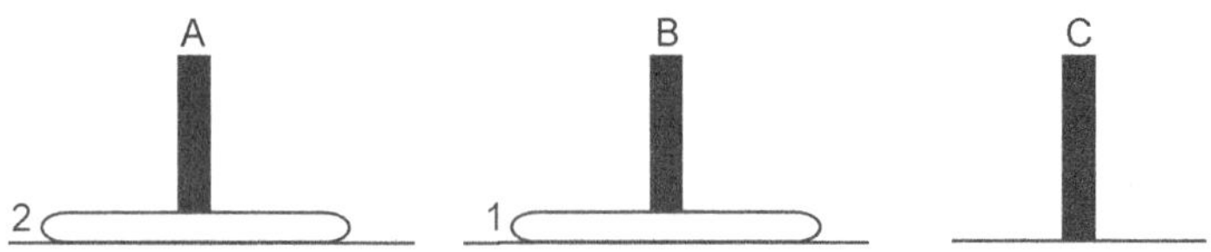

Fig. 3.8.7 Disk 1 moved to peg B from A

Step 3 : Move remaining disk i.e. disk 2 from peg A to peg C.

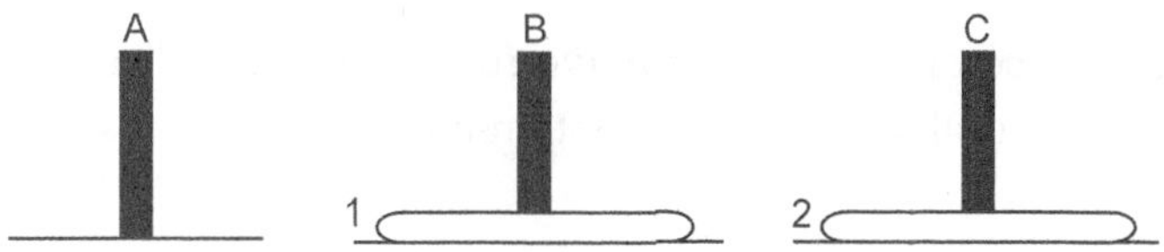

Fig. 3.8.8 Disk 2 from A to C

Step 4 : Move disk 1 from B to C.

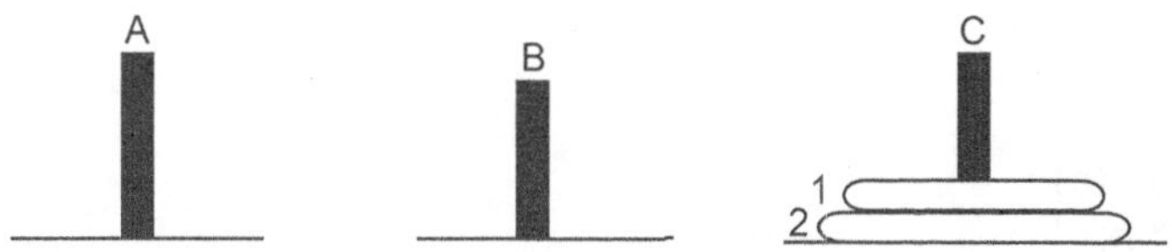

Fig. 3.8.9 Final configuration

Review Questions

1. *Explain Tower of Hanoi by using recursion* **GTU : Nov.-06, Marks 6**
2. *What is Tower of Hanoi ? Explain it with n = 3.* **GTU : May-12, Marks 4**

3.9 Iteration Vs Recursion

Sr. No.	Iteration	Recursion
1.	Iteration is a process of executing certain set of instructions repeatedly, without calling the self function.	Recursion is a process of executing certain set of instructions repeatedly by calling the self function repeatedly.
2.	The iterative functions are implemented with the help of for, while, do-while programming constructs.	Instead of making use of for, while, do-while the repetition in code execution is obtained by calling the same function again and again over some condition.
3.	The iterative methods are more efficient because of better execution speed.	The recursive methods are less efficient.
4.	Memory utilization by iteration is less.	Memory utilization is more in recursive functions.
5.	It is simple to implement.	Recursive methods are complex to implement.
6.	The lines of code is more when we use iteration.	Recursive methods bring compactness in the program.

3.10 Use of Stack in Recursive Functions

GTU : CE : Dec.-05, Winter-17, Marks 6

For illustrating the use of stack in recursive functions, we will consider an example of finding factorial. The recursive routine for obtaining factorial is as given below -

```
int fact (int num)
{
        int a, b;
        if (num = = 0)
                return 1 ;
                else
        {
                a = num – 1 ;
                b = fact (a) ;
                f = a * b;
                return f ;
        }
}
/* Call to the function */
ans = fact (4) ;
```

For the above recursive routine we will see the use of stack. For the stack the only principle idea is that – when there is a call to a function the values are pushed onto the stack and at the end of the function or at the return the stack is popped

Suppose we have num = 4. Then in function **fact** as num ! = 0 else part will be executed. We get

a = num – 1

a = 3

And a recursive call to fact (3) will be given. Thus internal stack stores

Next fact (2) will be invoked. Then

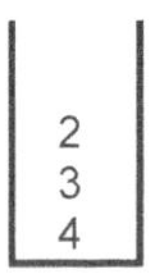

∵ a = num – 1

a = 3 – 1

b = fact (2)

Then,

∵ a = num – 1

a = 2 – 1

b = fact (1)

Now next as num = 0, we return the value 1.

∴ a = 1, b = 1, we return f = a ∗ b = 1 from function **fact**. Then 1 will be popped off.

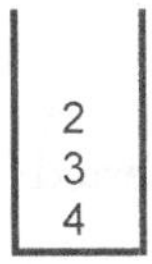

Now the top of the stack is the value of a

Then we get b = fact (2) = 1.

∴ f = a ∗ b = 2 ∗ 1 = 2 will be returned.

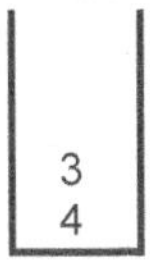

Here a = 3

Then b = fact (3)

b = 2

∴ f = a ∗ b = 6 will be returned.

The stack will be

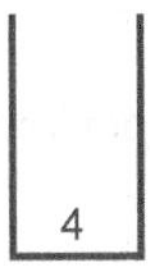

Here a = 4

Then b = fact (4)

= 6

∴ f = a ∗ b = 24 will be returned.

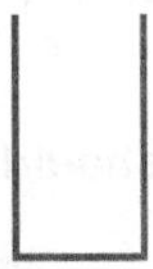

As now stack is empty. We return f = 24 from the function **fact**.

Review Questions

1. *How stack is useful in implementation of recursion ? Explain with the example of factorial.* **GTU : CE : Dec.-05, Marks 6**
2. *Write recursive algorithm for computing factorial. Which data structure can be used to implement this algorithm ?* **GTU : Winter-17, Marks 4**

3.11 Oral Questions and Answers

Q.1 Give an example that shows how a stack is used by a computer system ?

Ans. : In computer system the memory model consists of stack memory which stores types of variables that have a fixed lifetime. Stack is basically a section of RAM that grows and shrinks as the program runs. When you call a function, its parameters and any variables you have defined in that function (which are not static) are stored in the stack.

Q.2 Name the data structure which is also known as LIFO data structure.

Ans. : Stack.

Q.3 Define the term stack.

Ans. : Stack is a data structure in which the elements are inserted or deleted using only one end called top.

Q.4 Why stack is called LIFO ?

Ans. : LIFO stands for Last In First Out. The element to be inserted **last** is to be deleted **first.**

Q.5 List out the operations of stack.

Ans. :

1. Push operation is used to insert the element onto the stack.
2. Pop operation is used to delete the element from the stack.

Q.6 What is meant by underflow condition in a stack ?

Ans. : Underflow is a situation in which the pop operation is performed on the stack which is empty.

Q.7 What is meant by overflow condition in a stack ?

Ans. : The overflow is a situation in which the push operation is performed on the stack which is full.

Q.8 Assume that stack is implemented using arrays. What should be the value of top to check the empty and stack full conditions ?

Ans. : When the stack is empty then top must be equal to -1. When the stack becomes full then the top=Maximum size of array.

Q.9 Describe the situations in which push and pop operations are not possible.

Ans. : If the stack is empty then we can not perform pop operation. If stack is full then we can not perform push operation.

Q.10 What do you understand by polish notation ? Explain.

Ans. : This is also called as prefix notation. In this type of notation the operator followed by two operands. For example if (a+b)*c is a given expression then its polish notation will be *+ abc.

Q.11 What is a top pointer of a stack ?

Ans. : The top denotes the only one end of the stack from which the element can be inserted or deleted. When we push the element onto the stack, the top is incremented. When we pop the element from the stack the top is decremented.

Q.12 Write the postfix notation for following expression. (A+B)*C-(D-E)^F.

Ans. : Following steps can be followed for computing the postfix expression -

Step 1 : (AB+)*C-(D-E)^F

Step 2 : (AB+C*)-(D-E)^F

Step 3 : (AB+C*)-(DE-)^F

Step 4 : (AB+C*)-(DE-F^)

Step 5 : AB+C*DE-F^-

Q.13 List the applications of stack. **GTU : Summer-16**

Ans. : The stack can be used for -

1. Conversion of expression from one form to another. Various forms of expression are infix, prefix and postfix.
2. Evaluation of postfix expression.
3. Evaluation of recursive functions.
4. Reversing the string.
5. For checking the well formedness of parenthesis.

Q.14 List the characteristics of stacks.

Ans. :

1. Insertion and deletion can be made by one end only. Hence the element inserted last will be first one to come out. Hence sometimes it is called LIFO.
2. Stacks are useful for evaluating an expression.
3. Stacks can store the functions calls.

Q.15 Write the role of stack in function call.

Ans. : The stack is an useful data structure for handling the recursive function calls. When a recursive call is encountered, the status of call is pushed onto the stack. And at the return of the call the stack is popped off. Thus execution of recursive statements is done with the help of stack.

Q.16 What is Last-In-First-Out strategy ? Which data structure follows this strategy ?

Ans. : In the Last In First Out strategy we insert the element in the data structure lastly and while removing the elements from this data structure, the element which is inserted lastly will get removed first.

The stack data structure makes use of Last In First Out(LIFO) data structure.

Q.17 Write the steps to reverse the contents of the list with the help of stack data structure.

Ans. :

Step 1 : Read each element from the list and push it onto the stack.

Step 2 : Pop the element from the stack and store the popped element in a separate array.

Step 3 : Read the array completely from left to write. This will be the reversed list of the elements.

Q.18 ______ data structure is used in handling the recursive function.

Ans. : **Stack** data structure is used to handle the recursive function call.

Q.19 Name the data structure that can be used for checking the well formedness of parenthesis.

Ans. : The stack data structure is used for checking the well formedness of parenthesis.

Q.20 Write an algorithm used for checking the well formedness of parenthesis

Ans. :

1. If (parenthesis is read push it onto the stack.
2. When) is read then for each) parenthesis, pop single (parenthesis.
3. When the complete string is read, the stack should be empty.

Q.21 List operations performed on a stack. **GTU : Winter-15**

Ans. : **i) Push** - This operation is for pushing the element onto the stack.

ii) POP - This operation is for popping the element from the stack.

Q.22 Recursion. **GTU : Winter-16**

Ans. : Recursion is a programming technique in which the function calls itself repeatedly for some input.

Q.23 What is the reverse polish notation for infix expression a/b*c ? **GTU : Summer-17**

Ans. : ab / c*

❑❑❑

4 Queue

Syllabus

Representation of queue, Operations on queue, Circular queue, Priority queue, Array representation of priority queue, Double ended queue, Applications of queue.

Contents

4.1 Representation of Queue

GTU : Winter-18, Marks 4

Definition : The queue can be formally defined as ordered collection of elements that has two ends named as **front** and **rear**. From the front end one can delete the elements and from the rear end one can insert the elements.

For example :

The typical example can be a queue of people who are waiting for a city bus at the bus stop. Any new person is joining at one end of the queue, you can call it as the rear end. When the bus arrives the person at the other end first enters in the bus. You can call it as the front end of the queue.

Following Fig. 4.1.1 represents the queue of few elements.

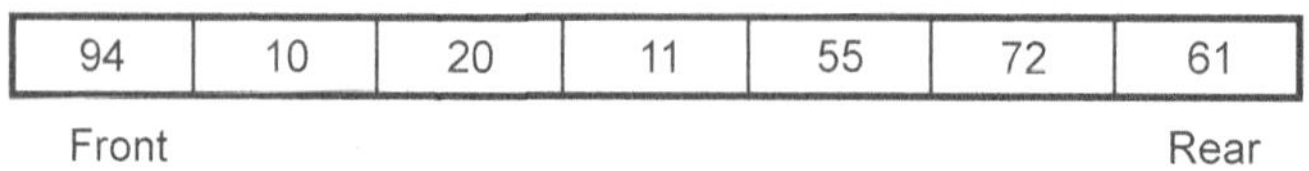

Fig. 4.1.1 Queue

Difference between Stack and Queue

Sr. No.	Stack	Queue
1.	The stack is a data structure in which the insertion and deletion of elements can be done by only one end.	The queue is a data structure in which insertion and deletion is carried out by two different ends.
2.	**For example** Insert 10, 20, 30, 40 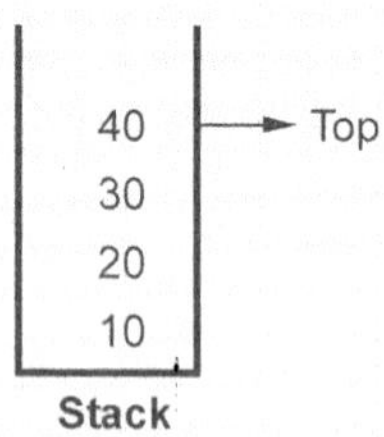 In stack the only one being used is called **top**.	**For example** Insert 10, 20, 30, 40  In queue there are two ends used; the end from which the element gets inserted is called **rear** and the element from which the element gets deleted is called **front**.
3.	The stack is called Last In First Out i.e. LIFO data structure, because in stack the last inserted element is always removed first.	The queue is called First In First Out i.e. FIFO data structure, because in queue the element which is inserted first gets removed first.

4.	Stack is useful data structure for expression conversion and evaluation, handing recursive function calls and for checking well formedness of parenthesis.	Queue is useful data structure for prioritizing jobs in operating system, for categorizing data and for simulations.

Review Question

1. *Differentiate between Stack and Queue.* **GTU : Winter-18, Marks 4**

4.2 Operations of Queue

GTU : CE : Dec.-06, Summer-15,18 Winter-16 Marks 7

AbstractDataType queue

{

Instance :

The queue is collection of elements in which the element can be inserted by one end called rear and elements get deleted from the end called front.

Operations

que_full ( ) - Checks whether queue is full or not.

que_empty ( ) - Checks whether queue is empty or not.

Q _ insert ( ) - Inserts the element in queue from rear end.

Q _ delete ( ) - Deletes the element from the queue by front end.

}

Thus the ADT for queue gives the abstract for what has to be implemented, which are the various operations on queue. But it never specifies how to implement those.

Let us see each operation one by one.

'C' representation of queue.

```
struct queue
{
    int que [size];
    int front;
    int rear;
} Q;
```

1. Insertion of element into the queue

The insertion of any element in the queue will always take place from the rear end.

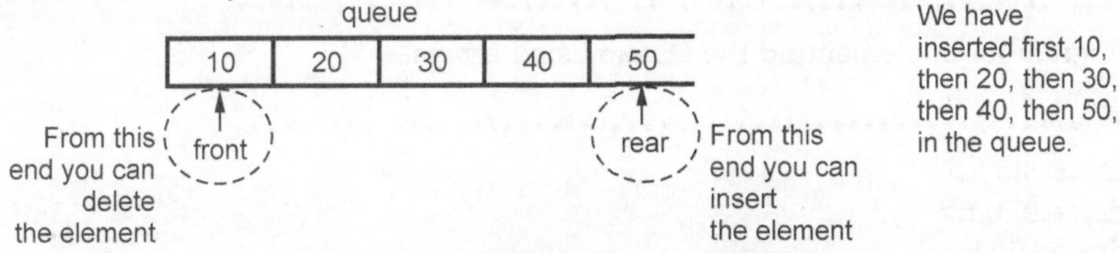

Fig. 4.2.1 Representing the insertion

Before performing insert operation you must check whether the queue is full or not. If the rear pointer is going beyond the maximum size of the queue then the queue overflow occurs.

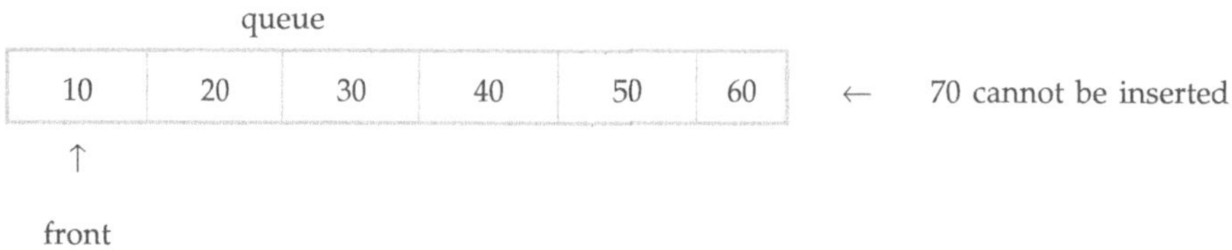

Fig. 4.2.2 Representing the queue overflow

2. Deletion of element from the queue

The deletion of any element in the queue takes place by the front end always.

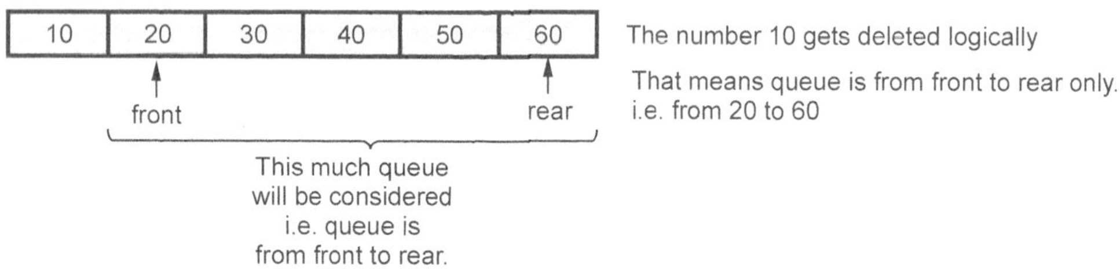

Fig. 4.2.3 Representing the deletion

Before performing any delete operation one must check whether the queue is empty or not. If the queue is empty, you cannot perform the deletion. The result of illegal attempt to delete an element from the empty queue is called the Queue Underflow condition.

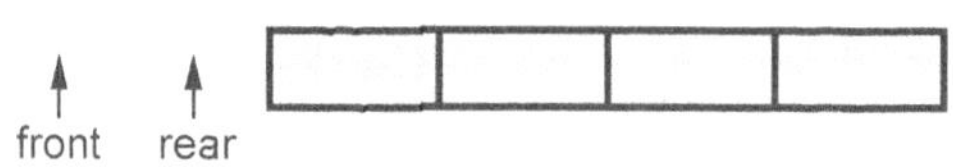

Fig. 4.2.4 Figure representing the queue underflow

Let us see the 'C' implementation of the queue.

'C' program

```
/*****************************************************************
    Program for implementing the Queue using arrays.

*****************************************************************/
#include<stdio.h>
#include<stdlib.h>
#include<conio.h>
```

```
#define size 5
struct queue
{
 int que[size];
 int front,rear;
}Q;
```

Queue data structure declared with array que [ ] , front and rear

```
 Qfull()
 {
 if(Q.rear >=size-1)
  return 1;
 else
  return 0;
}
```

If Queue exceeds the maximum size of the array then it returns 1 - means queue full is true otherwise 0 means queue full is false

```
int insert(int item)
{
 if(Q.front == -1)
  Q.front++;
 Q.que[++Q.rear] = item;
 return Q.rear;
}
```

This condition will occur initially when queue is empty when single element will be present then both front and rear points to the same

Always increment the rear pointer and place the element in the queue

```
int Qempty()
{
 if((Q.front == - 1) || (Q.front > Q.rear))
  return 1;
 else
  return 0;
}
```

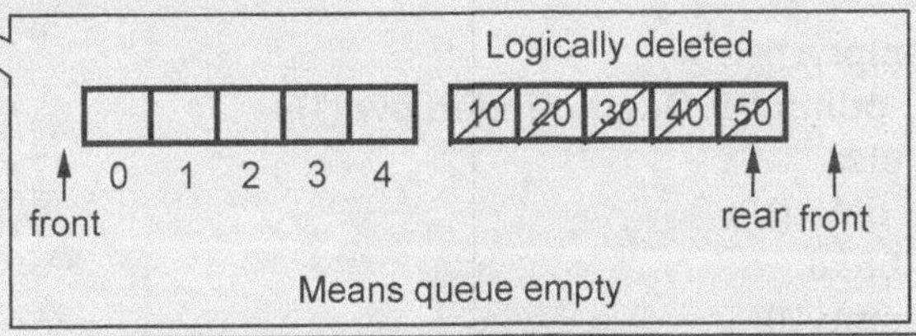


```
int delet()
{
 int item;

 item = Q.que[Q.front];
 Q.front++;
 printf("\n The deleted item is %d",item);
 return Q.front;
}
```

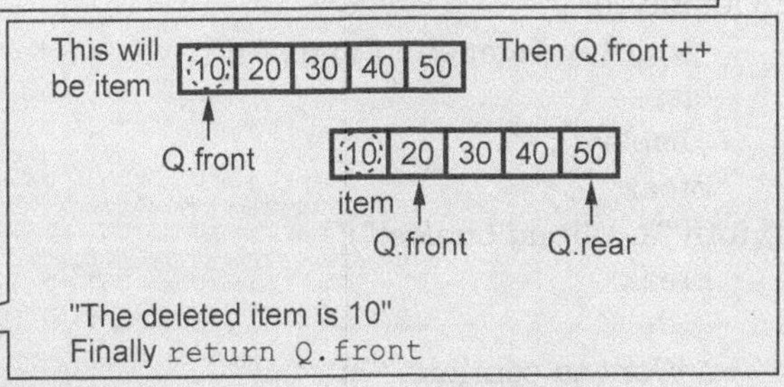


```
void display()
{
 int i;
 for(i=Q.front;i<=Q.rear;i++)
  printf("  %d",Q.que[i]);
```

Printing the queue from front to rear

```
}
void main(void)
{
 int choice,item;
 char ans;
 clrscr();
 Q.front = -1;  }
 Q.rear  = -1;  }     Initially
```

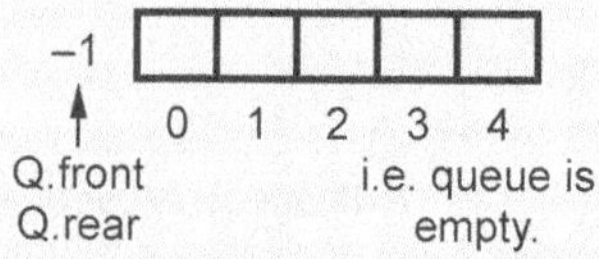


```
 do
 {
  printf("\n Main Menu");
  printf("\n1.Insert\n2.Delete\n3.Display");
  printf("\n Enter Your Choice");
  scanf("%d",&choice);
  switch(choice)
     {
     case 1:if(Qfull())        //checking for Queue overflow
                  printf("\n Can not insert the element");
            else
            {
                  printf("\n Enter The number to be inserted");
                  scanf("%d",&item);
                  insert(item);
            }
            break;
     case 2:if(Qempty())
                   printf("\n Queue Underflow!!");
                  else
                   delet();
                  break;
     case 3:if(Qempty())
                   printf("\nQueue Is Empty!");
                  else
                   display();
                  break;
     default:printf("\n Wrong choice!");
                  break;
     }
  printf("\n Do You Want to continue?");
  ans =getche();
  }while(ans =='Y'||ans =='y');
}
/********************** End Of Program ***********************/
```

Output

```
Main Menu
     1. Insert
     2. Delete
```

```
3. Display
 Enter Your Choice 1
 Enter The number to be inserted 10
 Do You Want to continue?y
 Main Menu
1. Insert
2. Delete
3. Display
 Enter Your Choice 1
 Enter The number to be inseted 20
 Do You Want to continue?y
 Main Menu
1. Insert
2. Delete
3. Display
 Enter Your Choice 3
  10  20
 Do You Want to continue?y
 Main Menu
1. Insert
2. Delete
3. Display
 Enter Your Choice 2
 The deleted item is 10
 Do You Want to continue?y
 Main Menu
1. Insert
2. Delete
3. Display
 Enter Your Choice 3
  20
 Do You Want to continue?n
```

Key Point *Always check queue full before insert operation and queue empty before delete operation.*

Analysis :

In above program each operation such as insert or delete will get executed only for once at a time. The worst case is that if we want to insert n elements in a queue then it requires **O(n)** time. Similarly if we want to delete n elements from the queue then it requires **O(n)** time. The display routine contains **for loop** which executes for front to rear values. Hence it takes **O(n)** time. Hence overall time complexity of above algorithm is **O(n)**.

Review Questions

1. *Explain insert and delete operation in simple queue.* **GTU : CE : Dec.-06, Marks 6**
2. *Write an algorithm to implement insert and delete operations in a simple queue.* **GTU : Summer-15, Marks 7**
3. *Write an algorithm to perform various operations (insert, delete and display) for simple queue.* **GTU : Winter-16, Marks 7**
4. *Write a program to implement queue and check for boundary conditions.* **GTU : Summer-18, Marks 7**

4.3 Circular Queue

GTU : CE : Dec.-03, 05, 06, Winter-14, 15, 16,18. Summer-14, 15, 16, 17 Marks 7

As we have seen, in case of linear queue the elements get deleted logically. This can be shown by following Fig. 4.3.1

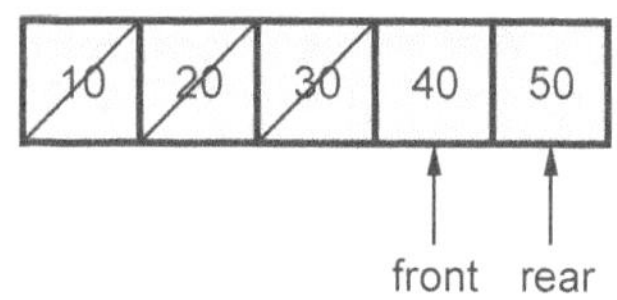

Fig. 4.3.1 Linear queue

We have deleted the elements 10, 20 and 30 means simply the front pointer is shifted ahead. We will consider a queue from front to rear always. And now if we try to insert any more element then it won't be possible as it is going to give "queue full !" message. Although there is a space of elements 10, 20 and 30 (these are deleted elements), we cannot utilize them because queue is nothing but a linear array !

Hence there is a concept called **circular queue**. The **main advantage of circular queue** is we can **utilize the space** of the queue fully. The circular queue is shown by following Fig. 4.3.2

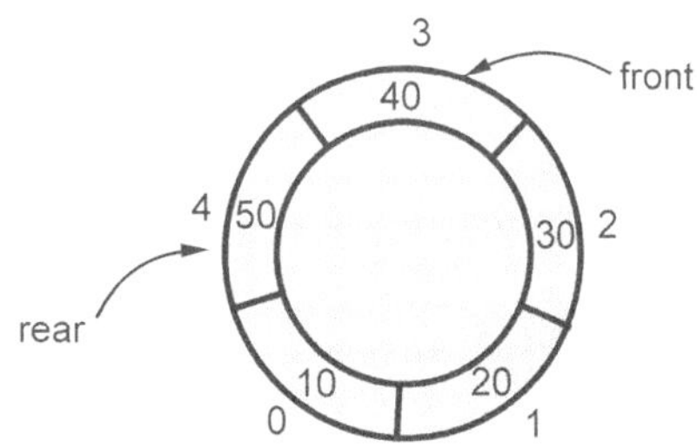

Fig. 4.3.2 Circular queue

Considering that the elements deleted are 10, 20 and 30.

There is a formula which has to be applied for setting the front and rear pointers, for a circular queue.

$$\text{rear} = (\text{rear} + 1) \ \% \ \text{size}$$
$$\text{front} = (\text{front} + 1) \ \% \ \text{size}$$

$$\begin{aligned} \text{rear} &= (\text{rear} + 1) \ \% \ \text{size} \\ &= (4 + 1) \ \% \ 5 \\ \text{rear} &= 0 \end{aligned}$$

So we can store the element 60 at 0th location similarly while deleting the element.

$$\text{front} = (\text{front} + 1) \ \% \ \text{size}$$
$$= (3 + 1) \ \% \ 5$$
$$\text{front} = 4$$

So delete the element at 4th location i.e. element 50.

Let us see the 'C' program now.

'C' program

```
/*************************************************************
Program For circular queue using arrays. It performs the basic
operations such as insertion, deletion of the elements by taking
care of queue Full and queue Empty conditions. The appropriate
display is for displaying the queue.
*************************************************************/
#include<stdio.h>
#include<conio.h>
#include<stdlib.h>
#define size 5
int queue[size];
int front=-1; /* queue initialization by front = - 1 and rear = 0*/
int rear =0;
int qFull()
{
 if(front==(rear+1)%size)
  return 1;
 else
 return 0;
}
```

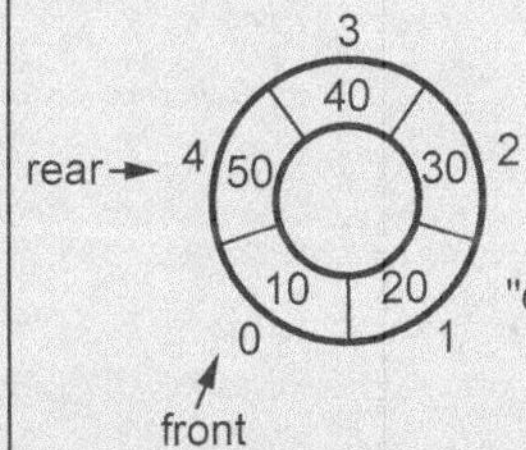

front = 0
rear = 4
i.e. front = (rear + 1)% size
= (4 + 1)%5
= 5%5
front = 0
"queue full condition"

```
int qEmpty()
{
 if(front ==-1)
  return 1;
 else
  return 0;
}
void add(int Item)
{
 if(qFull()) /* qFull() returns true value */
  printf("\n The circular Queue is full!");
 else
 {
  if(front ==-1)/* only one element in the queue */
  front=rear=0;
```

Note that before inserting any element in queue the Front = –1, that means queue is empty

```
else
 rear =(rear+1)%size;
 queue[rear]=Item;
 }
}
```

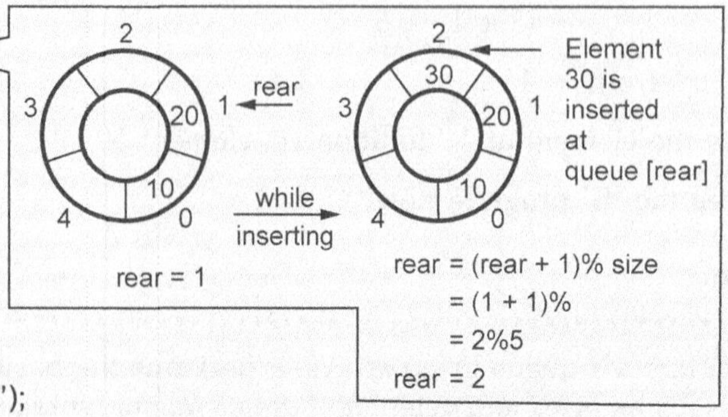


```
void delet()
{
 int Item;
 if(qEmpty())
  printf("\n Queue Is Empty!");
 else
 {
  Item=queue[front];
  if(front ==rear)
  {
       front=rear=-1;
  }
  else
       front =(front+1)%size;
  printf("\n The deleted item is %d",Item);
 }
}
```

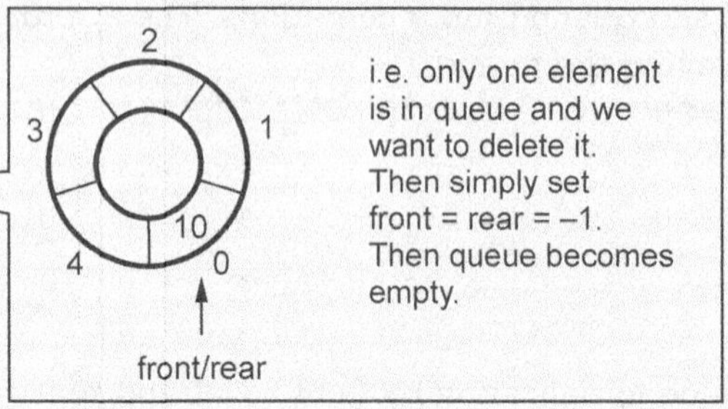


```
void display()
{
 int i;
 if(qEmpty())
 {
  printf("\nThe Queue Is Empty");
  return;
 }
 i=front;
 while(i!=rear)
 {
  printf("  %d",queue[i]);
  i=(i+1)%size;
 }
 printf("  %d",queue[i]);
}
void main(void)
{
 int choice,Item;
 char ans;
 clrscr();
 do
 {
```

While front does not reach to rear scan the elements and print them

```
  printf("\n Main Menu");
  printf("\n 1.Insert\n2.Delete\n3.Display");
  printf("\n Enter Your Choice");
  scanf("%d",&choice);
  switch(choice)
  {
   case 1:printf("\nEnter The element");
           scanf("%d",&Item);
           add(Item);
           break;
   case 2:delet();
           break;
   case 3:display();
           break;
   default:exit(0);
  }
  printf("\n Do u want to continue?");
  ans =getch();
}while(ans =='Y'||ans == 'y');
 getch();
}
/************************ End Of Main ***********************/
```

Example 4.3.1 *Consider the following queue, where queue is a circular queue having 6 memory cells. Front = 2, Rear = 4, Queue : _ , A, C, D, _ , _*

Describe queue as following operation take place :

F is added to the queue

Two letters are deleted

R is added to the queue

S is added to the queue

One letter is deleted.

Solution : Initially the queue will be,

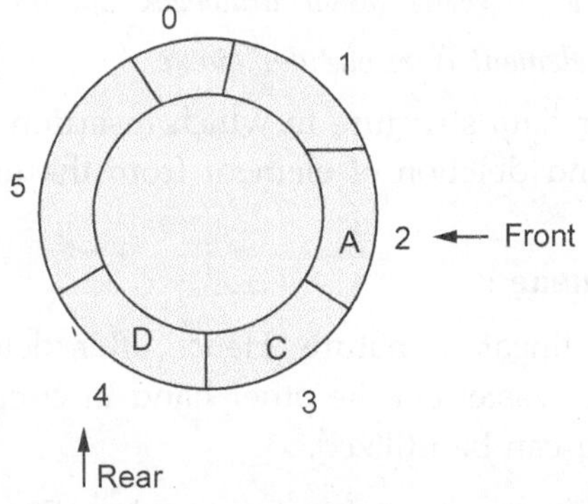

Step 1 : Insert F

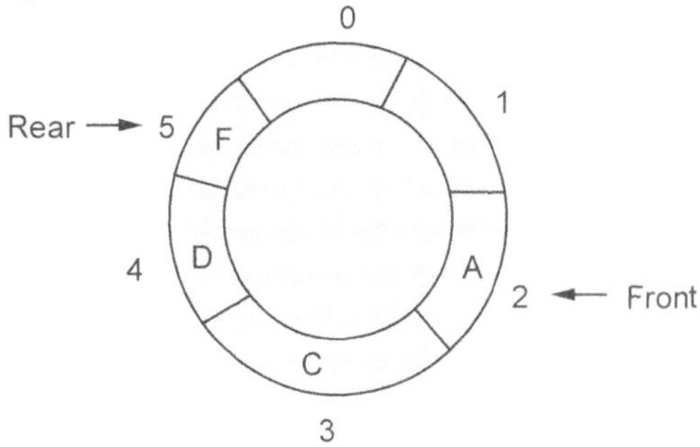

Step 2 : Delete two letters

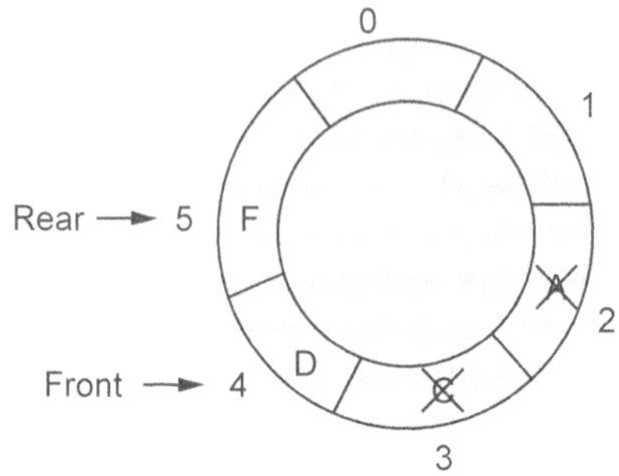

Step 3 : Insert R

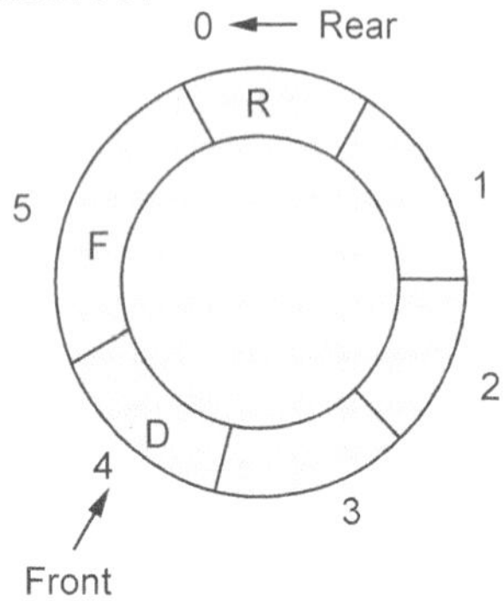

Step 4 : Insert S

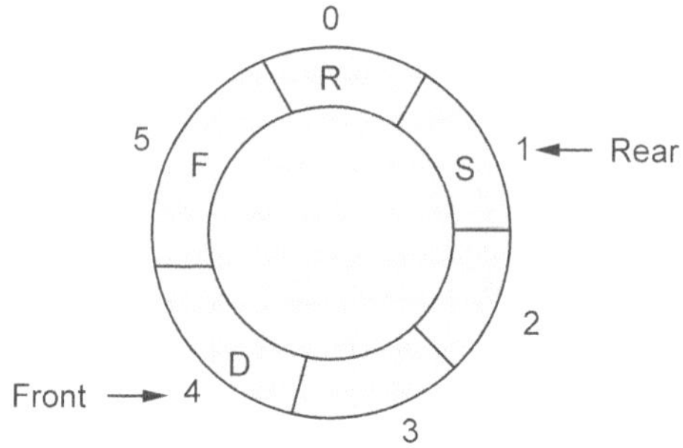

Step 5 : One letter is deleted

Rear = 1
Front = 5

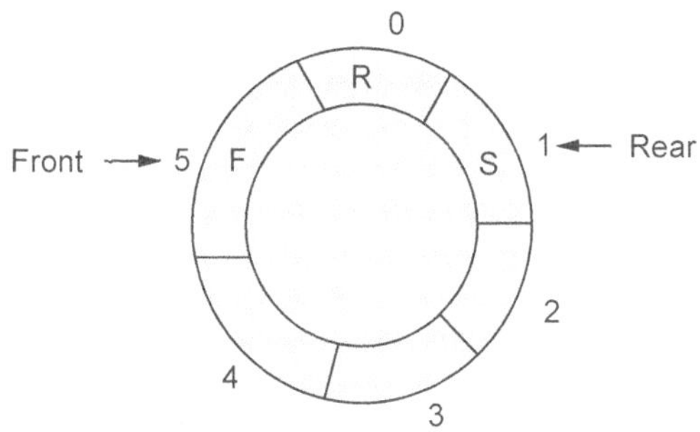

This is the final configuration.

Example 4.3.2 *What is queue ? Write down drawback of simple queue ? Also write an algorithm for deleting an element from circular queue.* **GTU : Winter14, Marks 7**

Solution : Queue is a linear data structure in which insertion of elements in the queue is from one end called **rear** and deletion of element from the other end called **front**. Refer Fig. 4.1.1.

Drawbacks of simple queue :

1. The simple queue is linear in nature. Hence after deletion of some element the corresponding space can go waste. On the other hand in circular queue the intermediate space that is left in between can be utilized.

2. It is possible to move from rear end to front end easily.

Deletion of element from circular queue

Refer C program in section 4.3.

Example 4.3.3 *Compare : Circular queue and linear queue.* **GTU : Summer-15, Marks 3**

Solution :

Circular Queue	Simple Queue
The circular queue is circular in nature having front and rear ends adjacent to each other.	Simple queue is linear in nature having boundry between front and rear.
In circular queue we can utilize the memory space effectively, because front and rear are adjacent to each other.	In simple queue there can be wastage of space as front and rear are away from each other.

Example 4.3.4 *Perform following operations in a circular queue of length 4 and give the front, Rear and size of the queue after each operation*

1) Insert A, B 2) Insert C 3) Delete 4) Insert D. 5) Insert E 6) Insert F) Delete

GTU : Winter-15, Marks 4

Solution :

Step 1 : Insert A, B

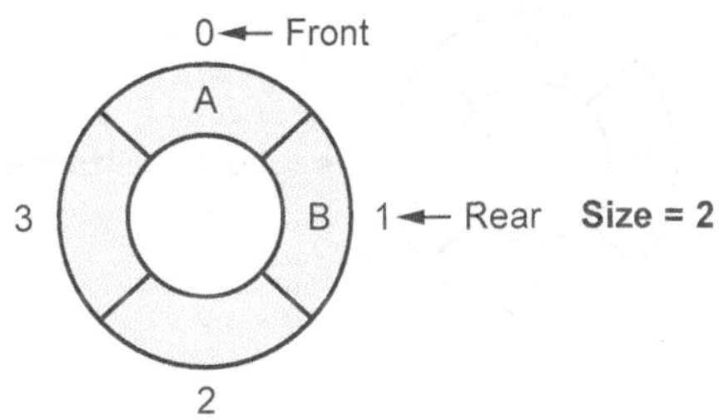

Step 2 : Insert C

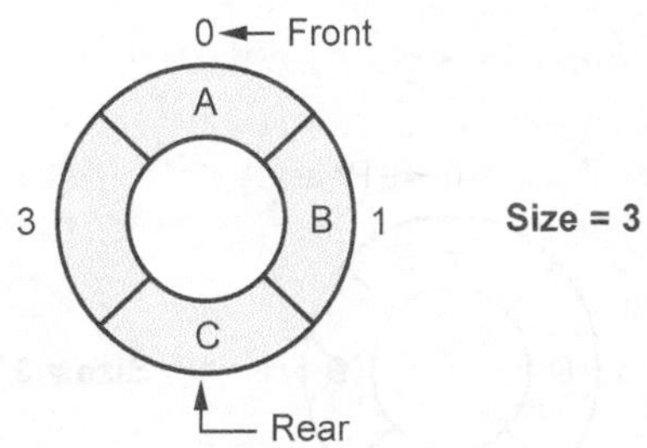

Step 3 : Delete

The element pointed by front pointer will be deleted.

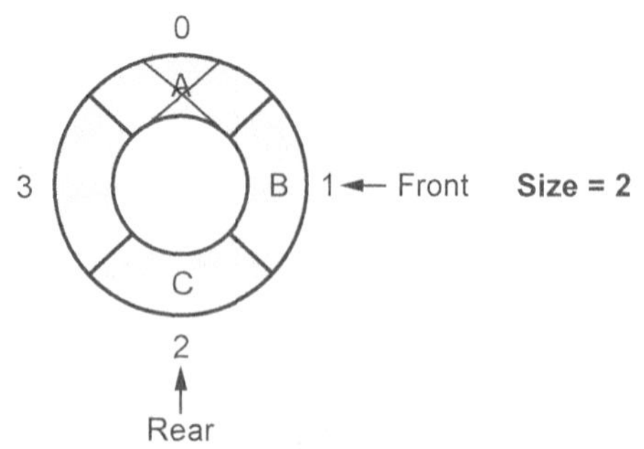

Step 4 : Insert D

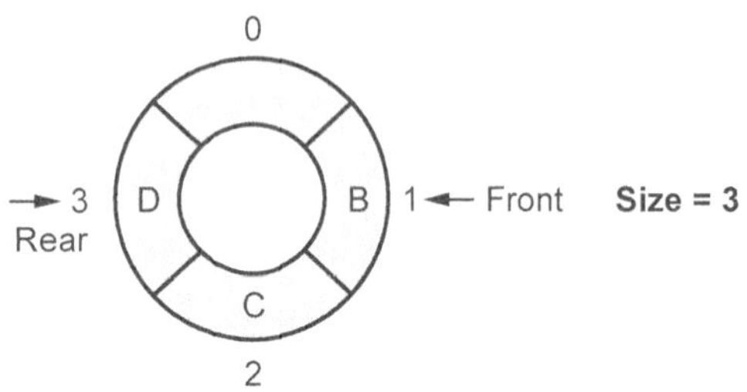

Step 5 : Insert E

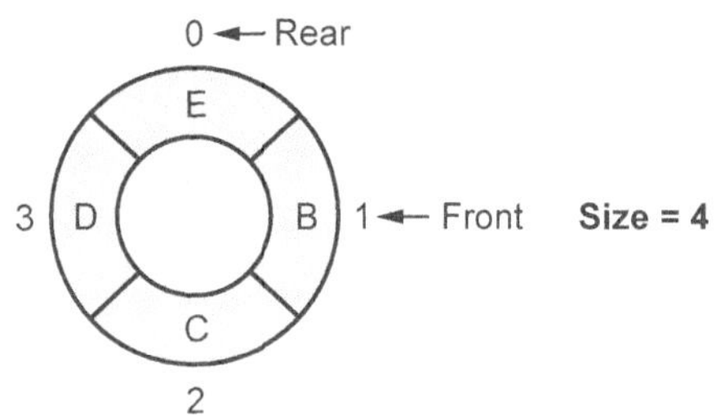

Step 6 : Insert F

It will display queue full message.

Step 7 : Delete

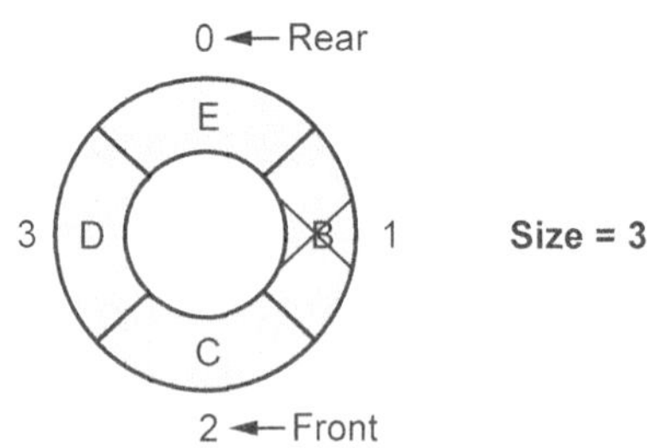

Example 4.3.5 *Consider an example where the size of the queue is four elements. Initially the queue is empty. It is required to insert symbols 'A', 'B' and 'C'. Delete 'A' and 'B' and insert 'D' and 'E'. Show the trace of the contents of the queue.*

GTU : Summer-17, Marks 7

Solution : Step 1 : Insert A, B and C.

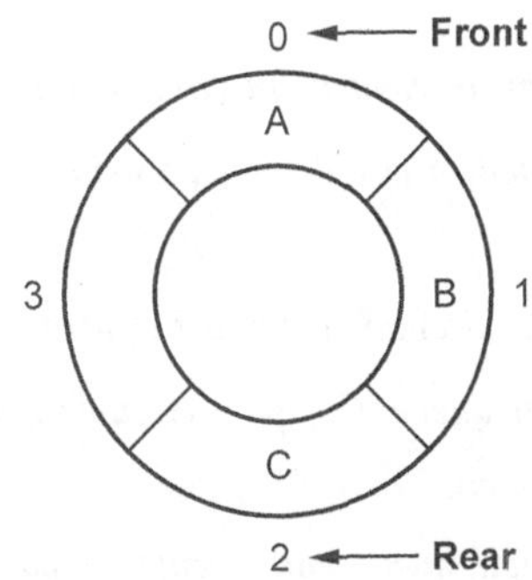

Step 2 : Delete A, B.

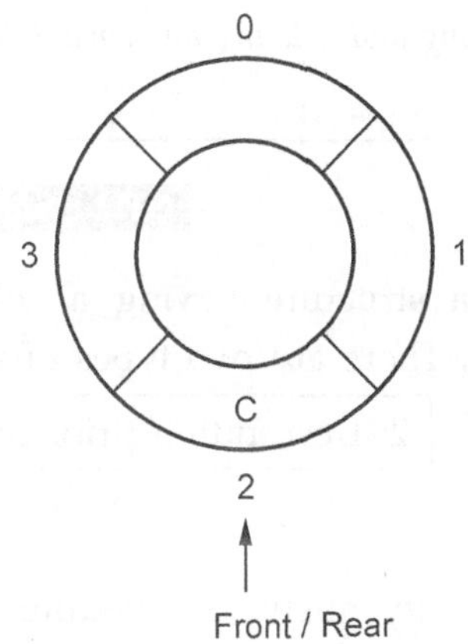

Step 3 : Insert D and E

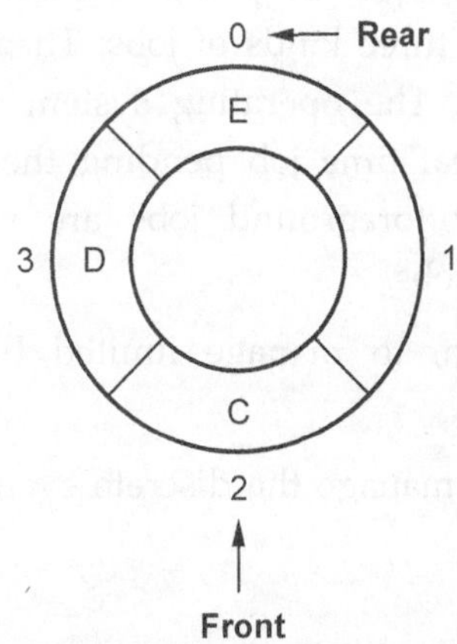

Review Questions

1. *Write an algorithm for inserting and deleting an element in circular queue.*
GTU : CE : Dec.-03, Marks 7, Dec.-05, 06, Winter-18, Marks 6
2. *Write user defined C function for inserting an element into circular queue.*
GTU : Winter-14, Marks 7
3. *Write a 'C' functions to insert an element in circular queue.* **GTU : Summer-15, Marks 4**
4. *Write a C program to implement a circular queue using array with all necessary overflow and underflow checks.* **GTU : Winter-15, Marks 7**
5. *Write a program to implement circular queue using array.* **GTU : Summer-16, Marks 7**
6. *Explain the concept of circular queue. Compare circular queue with simple queue.*
GTU : Summer-16, Marks 4
7. *Write differences between simple queue and circular queue. Write an algorithm for insert and delete operations for circular queue.* **GTU : Winter-16, Marks 7**
8. *Write an algorithm for inserting and deleting an element in a circular queue.*
GTU : Summer-17, Marks 7

4.4 Priority Queue

GTU : Summer-14, 15, Winter-18 Marks 2

The priority queue is a data structure having a collection of elements which are associated with specific ordering. There are two types of priority queues -

1. Ascending priority queue
2. Descending priority queue

Application of Priority Queue

1. The typical example of priority queue is scheduling the jobs in operating system. Typically operating system allocates priority to jobs. The jobs are placed in the queue and position of the job in priority queue determines their priority. In operating system there are three kinds of jobs. These are real time jobs, foreground jobs and background jobs. The operating system always schedules the real time jobs first. If there is no real time job pending then it schedules foreground jobs. Lastly if no real time or foreground jobs are pending then operating system schedules the background jobs.
2. In network communication, to manage limited bandwidth for transmission the priority queue is used.
3. In simulation modeling, to manage the discrete events the priority queue is used.

Types of Priority Queue

The elements in the priority queue have specific ordering. There are two types of priority queues -

1. Ascending Priority Queue - It is a collection of items in which the items can be inserted arbitarily but only smallest element can be removed.

2. Descending Priority Queue - It is a collection of items in which insertion of items can be in any order but only largest element can be removed.

In priority queue, the elements are arranged in any order and out of which only the smallest or largest element allowed to delete each time.

The implementation of priority queue can be done using arrays or linked list. The data structure heap is used to implement the priority queue effectively.

ADT for Priority Queue

Various operations that can be performed on priority queue are -

1. Insertion 2. Deletion 3. Display

Hence the ADT for priority queue is given as below -

Instances :

P_que[**MAX**] is a finite collection of elements associated with some priority.

Precondition :

The front and rear should be within the maximum size **MAX**.

Before insertion operation, whether the queue is full or not is checked.

Before any deletion operation, whether the queue is empty or not is checked.

Operations :

1. create() - The queue is created by declaring the data structure for it.
2. insert() - The element can be inserted in the queue.
3. delet() - If the priority queue is ascending priority queue then only smallest element is deleted each time. And if the priority queue is descending priority queue then only largest element is deleted each time.
4. display() - The elements of queue are displayed from front to rear.

Review Questions

1. *What are priority queues ? Explain its uses.* **GTU : Summer-14, Marks 2**
2. *Describe : Priority queue.* **GTU : Summer-15, Marks 2**
3. *Explain priority queue ?* **GTU : Winter-18, Marks 3**

4.5 Array Representation of Priority Queue **GTU : Summer-17, Winter-17**

The implementation of priority queue using arrays is as given below -

1. Insertion operation : While implementing the priority queue we will apply a simple logic. That is while inserting the element we will insert the element in the array at the proper position. For example, if the elements are placed in the queue as

9	12			
que[0]	que[1]	que[2]	que[3]	que[4]
front	rear			

And now if an element 8 is to be inserted in the queue then it will be at 0th location as -

8	9	12		
que[0]	que[1]	que[2]	que[3]	que[4]
front		rear		

If the next element comes as 11 then the queue will be -

8	9	11	12	
que[0]	que[1]	que[2]	que[3]	que[4]
front			rear	

The C function for this operation is as given below -

```
int insert(int que[SIZE],int rear,int front)
{
	int item,j;
	printf("\nEnter the element: ");
	scanf("%d",&item);
	if(front ==-1)
		front++;
	j=rear;
	while(j>=0 && item<que[j])
	{
	 que[j+1]=que[j];
	 j--;
	}
	que[j+1]=item;
	rear=rear+1;
	return rear;
}
```

2. Deletion operation

In the deletion operation we are simply removing the element at the front.

For example, if queue is created like this -

8	9	11	12	
que[0] front	que[1]	que[2]	que[3] rear	que[4]

Then the element at que[0] will be deleted first.

~~8~~	9	11	12	
~~que[0]~~	que[1] front	que[2]	que[3] rear	que[4]

and then new front will be que[1].

The deletion operation in C is as given below -

```
int delet(int que[SIZE],int front)
{
        int item;
        item=que[front];
        printf("\n The item deleted is %d",item);
        front++;
        return front;
}
```

The complete implementation of priority queue is as given below -

```
/**********************************************************
Program for implementing the ascending priority Queue
**********************************************************/
/*Header Files*/
#include<stdio.h>
#include<conio.h>
#define SIZE 5
void main(void)
{
        int rear,front,que[SIZE],choice;
        int Qfull(int rear),Qempty(int rear,int front);
        int insert(int que[SIZE],int rear,int front);
        int delet(int que[SIZE],int front);
        void display(int que[SIZE],int rear,int front);
        char ans;
        clrscr();
        front=0;
        rear=-1;
```

```
    do
    {
     clrscr();
     printf("\n\t\t Priority Queue\n");
     printf("\n Main Menu");
     printf("\n1.Insert\n2.Delete\n3.Display");
     printf("\n Enter Your Choice: ");
     scanf("%d",&choice);
     switch(choice)
     {
          case 1:if(Qfull(rear))
                        printf("\n Queue IS full");
                    else
                         rear=insert(que,rear,front);
                    break;
          case 2:if(Qempty(rear,front))
                          printf("\n Cannot delete element");
                    else
                          front=delet(que,front);
                    break;
          case 3:if(Qempty(rear,front))
                          printf("\n Queue is empty");
                    else
                         display(que,rear,front);
                         break;
     default:printf("\n Wrong choice");
               break;
     }
      printf("\n Do You Want TO continue?");
      ans =getche();
    }while(ans=='Y' ||ans=='y');
    getch();
}

int insert(int que[SIZE],int rear,int front)
{
    int item,j;
    printf("\nEnter the element: ");
    scanf("%d",&item);
    if(front ==-1)
         front++;
    j=rear;
    while(j>=0 && item<que[j])
    {
     que[j+1]=que[j];
     j--;
    }
```

```
        que[j+1]=item;
        rear=rear+1;
        return rear;
}
int Qfull(int rear)
{
 if(rear==SIZE-1)
         return 1;
 else
        return 0;
}

int delet(int que[SIZE],int front)
{
        int item;
        item=que[front];
        printf("\n The item deleted is %d",item);
        front++;
        return front;
}
Qempty(int rear,int front)
{
 if((front==-1)||(front>rear))
        return 1;
 else
        return 0;
}
void display(int que[SIZE],int rear,int front)
{
 int i;
 printf("\n The queue is:");
 for(i=front;i<=rear;i++)
 printf("  %d",que[i]);
}
```

Output

```
         Priority Queue

 Main Menu
1.Insert
2.Delete
3.Display
 Enter Your Choice: 1

Enter the element: 30

 Do You Want TO continue?
```

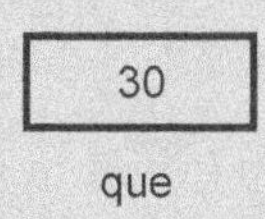

```
Priority Queue

Main Menu
1.Insert
2.Delete
3.Display
Enter Your Choice: 1
Enter the element: 10

Do You Want TO continue?
Priority Queue

Main Menu
1.Insert
2.Delete
3.Display
Enter Your Choice: 1

Enter the element: 20

Do You Want TO continue?

Priority Queue

Main Menu
1.Insert
2.Delete
3.Display
Enter Your Choice: 1

Enter the element: 50

Do You Want TO continue?

Priority Queue

Main Menu
1.Insert
2.Delete
3.Display
Enter Your Choice: 1

Enter the element: 40

Do You Want TO continue?
```

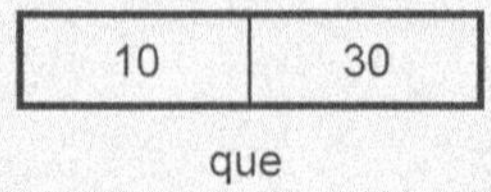

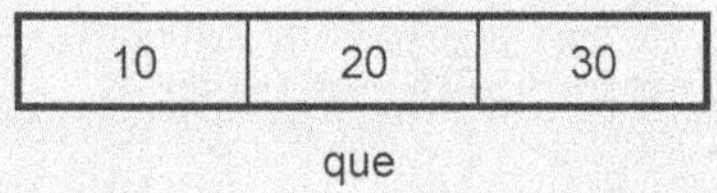

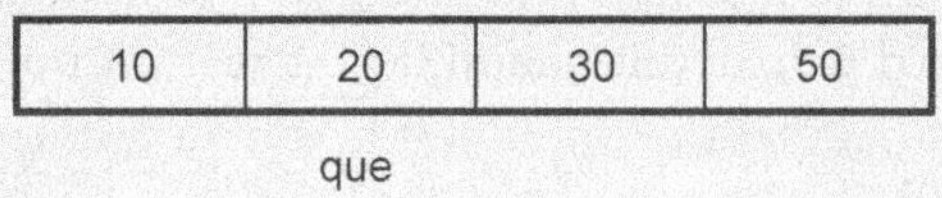

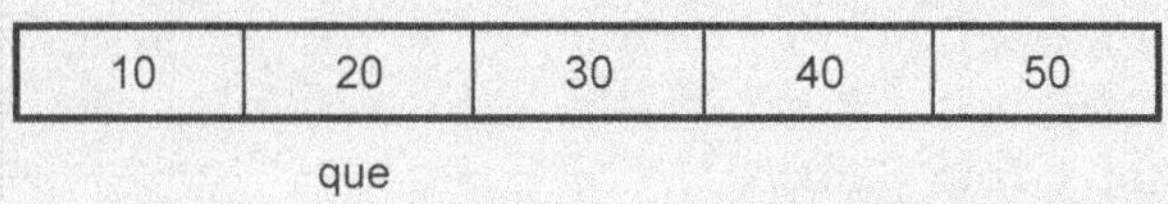

```
        Priority Queue

Main Menu
1.Insert
2.Delete
3.Display
Enter Your Choice: 3

The queue is:  10  20  30  40  50
Do You Want TO continue?

        Priority Queue

Main Menu
1.Insert
2.Delete
3.Display
Enter Your Choice: 2

The item deleted is 10
Do You Want TO continue?
```

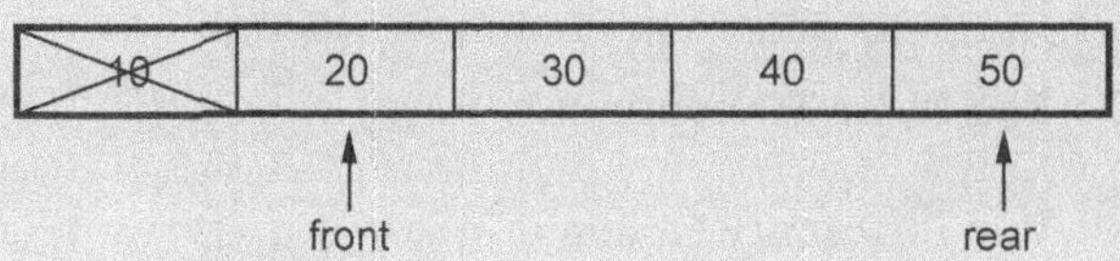


```
        Priority Queue

Main Menu
1.Insert
2.Delete
3.Display
Enter Your Choice: 2

The item deleted is 20
Do You Want TO continue?
```

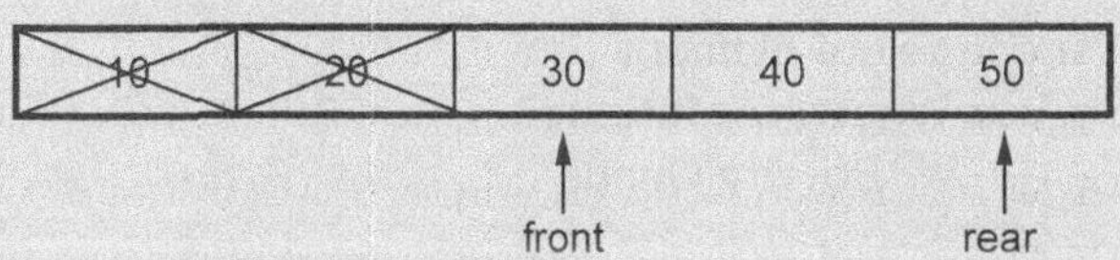


```
        Priority Queue

Main Menu
1.Insert
2.Delete
3.Display
Enter Your Choice: 2

The item deleted is 30
Do You Want TO continue?
```

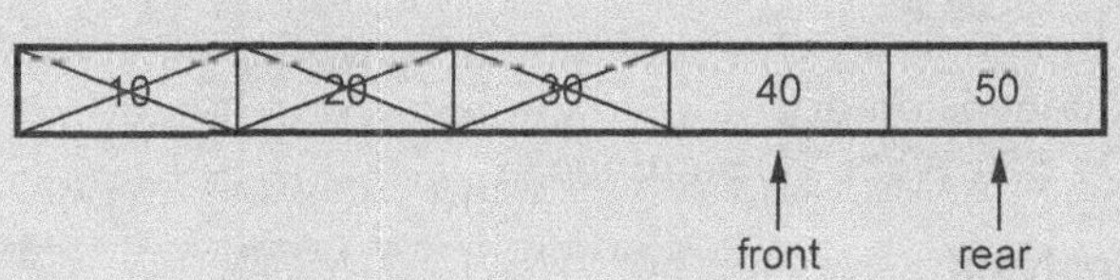


```
        Priority Queue

Main Menu
1.Insert
```

```
2.Delete
3.Display
 Enter Your Choice: 2

 The item deleted is 40
 Do You Want TO continue?
```

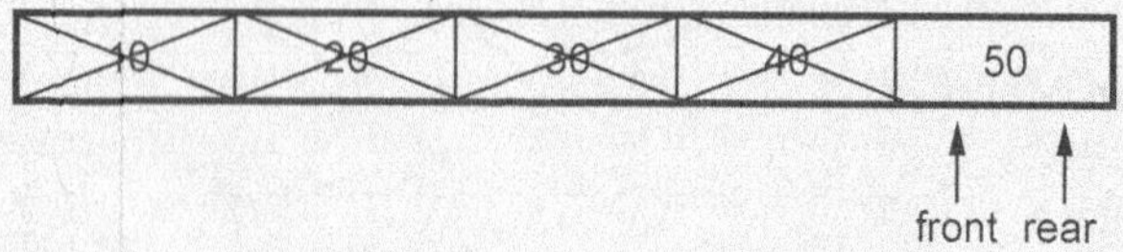


```
                Priority Queue

 Main Menu
 1.Insert
 2.Delete
 3.Display
 Enter Your Choice: 2

 The item deleted is 50
 Do You Want TO continue?
```

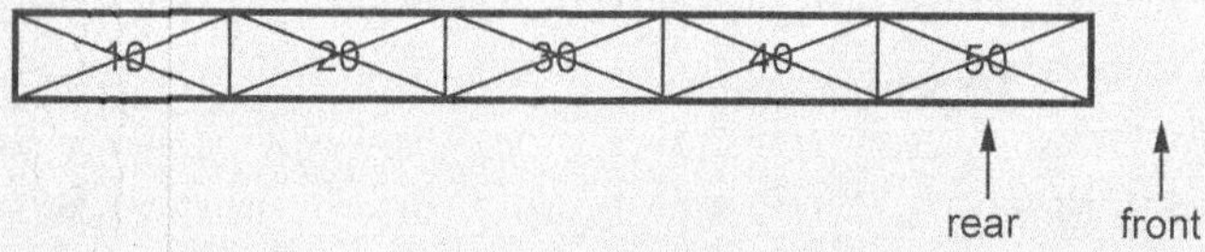


```
                Priority Queue

 Main Menu
 1.Insert
 2.Delete
 3.Display
 Enter Your Choice: 2

 Cannot delete element
 Do You Want TO continue?
                Priority Queue

 Main Menu
 1.Insert
 2.Delete
 3.Display
 Enter Your Choice: 3

 Queue is empty
 Do You Want TO continue?n
```

Analysis :

The above program contains insert, delete and display operation. If size of the queue n then each insert and delete operations will require **O(1)** time. Display will take O(n) time. Hence time complexity is **O(n)**.

Review Questions

1. *What is priority queue ? Explain the array representation of priority queue.* **GTU : Summer-17, Marks 7**
2. *How does priority queue work ?* **GTU : Winter-17, Marks 3**

4.6 Double Ended Queue **GTU : CE : Dec.-03, May-12, Summer-16, 18 Marks 7**

In a linear queue, the usual practice is for insertion of elements we use one end called rear and for deletion of elements we use another end called as front. But in the doubly ended queue we can make use of both the ends for insertion of the elements as well as we can use both the ends for deletion of the elements. That means it is possible to insert the elements by rear as well as by front. Similarly it is possible to delete the elements from front as well as from rear. Just see the following figure to understand the concept of doubly ended queue i.e. dequeue.

Definition : Doubly ended queue is a type of queue for which we can insert the elements from both front as well as rear. Similarly we can delete the element from both front and rear.

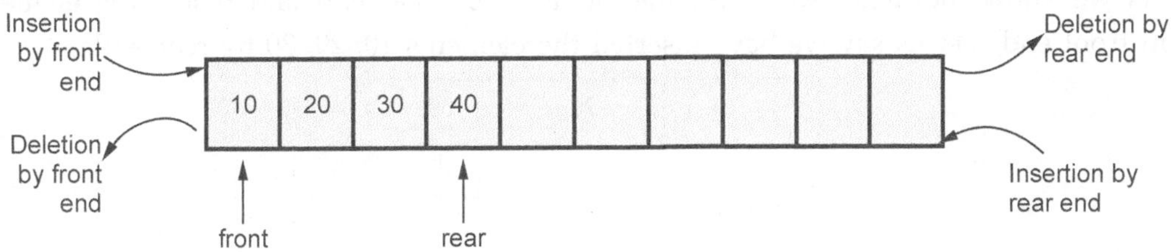

Fig. 4.6.1 Doubly ended queue

ADT for Dequeue

AbstractDataType Dequeue {

Instances :

Deq[MAX] is a finite collection of elements in which the element can be inserted from both the ends i.e rear and front. Similarly, the elements can be deleted from both the ends i.e. front and rear.

Precondition :

The front and rear should be within the maximum size MAX.

Before insertion operation, whether the queue is full or not is checked.

Before deletion operation, whether the queue is empty or not is checked.

Operations :

1. create() : The dequeue is created by declaring data structure for it.
2. insert_rear() : This operation is used for inserting the element from the rear end.
3. delete_front() : This operation is used for deleting the element from the front end.
4. insert_front() : This operation is used for inserting the element from the front end.
5. delete_rear() : This operation is used for deleting the element from the rear end.
6. display() : The elements of the queue can be displayed from front to rear.

}

In doubly ended queue we can use both the front and rear end for insertion and deletion operations. When we use only one end for inserting an element and both the ends for performing deletion operation then such a queue is called **input restricted queue**. Similarly, when we use only one end for deleting an element and both the ends for insertion of elements then such a queue is called **output restricted queue.**

As we know, normally we insert the elements by rear end and delete the elements from front end. Let us say we have inserted the elements 10, 20, 30 by rear end.

10	20	30
↑		↑
front		rear

Now if we wish to insert any element from front end then first we have to shift all the elements to the right.

For example if we want to insert 40 by front end then, the deque will be

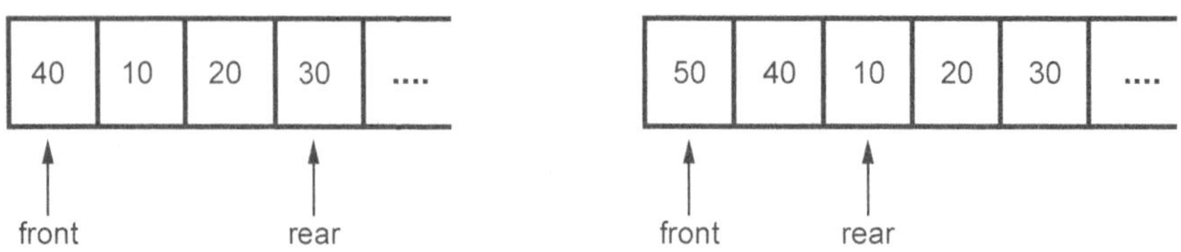

Inserted 40 in the queue by front end

Inserted 50 in the queue by front end

(a) Insertion by front end

(b) Deletion by rear end

Fig. 4.6.2 Operations on deque

We can place –1 for the element which has to be deleted.

Let us see the implementation of deque using arrays

```
/****************************************************************
        Program To implement Doubly ended queue using arrays

****************************************************************/
#include<stdio.h>
#include<conio.h>
#include<stdlib.h>
#define size 5
/*Data structure for deque*/
struct queue {
                int que[size];
                int front,rear;
                }Q;
int Qfull()
{
 if(Q.rear==size-1)
  return 1;
 else
  return 0;
}
int Qempty()
{
   if((Q.front>Q.rear)||(Q.front==-1&&Q.rear==-1))
        return 1;
   else
        return 0;
}
int insert_rear(int item)
{
 if(Q.front==-1&&Q.rear==-1)
 Q.front++;
 Q.que[++Q.rear]=item;
 return Q.rear;
```

```
}
int delete_front()
{
 int item;
 if(Q.front==-1)
 Q.front++;
 item=Q.que[Q.front];
 Q.que[Q.front]=-1;
 Q.front++;
 return item;
}
int insert_front(int item)
{
 int i,j;
 if(Q.front==-1)
 Q.front++;
 i=Q.front-1;
 while(i>=0)
 {
  Q.que[i+1]=Q.que[i];
  i--;
 }
 j=Q.rear;
 while(j>=Q.front)
 {
  Q.que[j+1]=Q.que[j];
  j--;
 }
 Q.rear++;
 Q.que[Q.front]=item;
 return Q.front;
}
int delete_rear()
{
 int item;
 item=Q.que[Q.rear];
 Q.que[Q.rear]=-1;/*logical deletion*/
 Q.rear--;
 return item;
}
void display()
{
 int i;
 printf("\n Straight Queue is:");
  for(i=Q.front;i<=Q.rear;i++)
  printf("  %d",Q.que[i]);
}
```

```
void main()
{
 int choice,i,item;
 char ans;
 ans='y';
 Q.front=-1;
 Q.rear=-1;
 for(i=0;i<size;i++)
  Q.que[i]=-1;
 clrscr();
 printf("\n\t\t Program For doubly ended queue using arrays");
 do
 {
 printf("\n1.insert by rear\n2.delete by front\n3.insert by front\n4.delete by rear");
 printf("\n5.display\n6.exit");
 printf("\n Enter Your choice");
 scanf("%d",&choice);
 switch(choice)
  {
  case 1:if(Qfull())
              printf("\n Doubly ended Queue is full");
             else
             {
              printf("\n Enter The item to be inserted");
              scanf("%d",&item);
              Q.rear=insert_rear(item);
             }
             break;
  case 2:if(Qempty())
              printf("\n Doubly ended Queue is Empty");
             else
             {
             item=delete_front();
            printf("\n The item deleted from queue is %d",item);
             }
             break;
  case 3:if(Qfull())
              printf("\n Doubly ended Queue is full");
             else
             {
              printf("\n Enter The item to be inserted");
              scanf("%d",&item);
              Q.front=insert_front(item);
             }
```

```
            break;
  case 4:if(Qempty())
             printf("\n Doubly ended Queue is Empty");
            else
            {
            item=delete_rear();
           printf("\n The item deleted from queue is %d",item);
            }
            break;
  case 5:display();
            break;
  case 6:exit(0);
  }
 printf("\n Do You Want To Continue?");
 ans=getch();
}while(ans=='y'||ans=='Y');
getch();
}
```

Output

```
Program For doubly ended queue using arrays
1. insert by rear
2. delete by front
3. insert by front
4. delete by rear
5. display
6. exit
Enter Your choice1
Enter The item to be inserted10
Do You Want To Continue?
1. insert by rear
2. delete by front
3. insert by front
4. delete by rear
5. display
6. exit
Enter Your choice 3
Enter The item to be inserted 20
Do You Want To Continue?
1. insert by rear
2. delete by front
3. insert by front
4. delete by rear
5. display
6. exit
Enter Your choice 5
Straight Queue is:  20  10
```

```
Do You Want To Continue?
1. insert by rear
2. delete by front
3. insert by front
4. delete by rear
5. display
6. exit
Enter Your choice4
The item deleted from queue is 10
Do You Want To Continue?
```

Review Questions

1. *Define and explain the following terms deque, priority queue.*
   GTU : CE : Dec.-03, Marks 2 + 2
2. *Write an algorithm for Double Ended Queue that insert an element at front end*
   GTU : May-12, Marks 7
3. *Explain double ended queue.* **GTU : Summer-16, Marks 3**
4. *Discuss the variations of a queue.* **GTU : Summer-18, Marks 4**

4.7 Applications of Queue

GTU : Dec.-05, 06, Winter-15, Summer-17, Winter-17 Marks 4

There are various applications of queues such as

1. Job Scheduling

In the operating system various programs are getting executed.

We will call these programs as jobs. In this process, some programs are in executing state. The state of these programs is called as 'running' state. Some programs which are not executing but they are in a position to get executed at any time such programs are in the 'ready' state. And there are certain programs which are neither in running state nor in ready state. Such programs are in a state called as blocked state.

The operating system maintains a queue of all such running state,ready state, blocked state programs. Thus use of queues help the operating system to schedule the jobs. The jobs which are in running state are removed after complete execution of each job, then the jobs which are in ready state change their state from ready to running and get entered in the queue for running state. Similarly the jobs which are in blocked state can change their state from blocked to ready state. These jobs then can be entered in the queue for ready state jobs. Thus every job changes its state and finally get executed. Refer Fig. 4.7.1 Thus queues are effectively used in the operating system for scheduling the jobs.

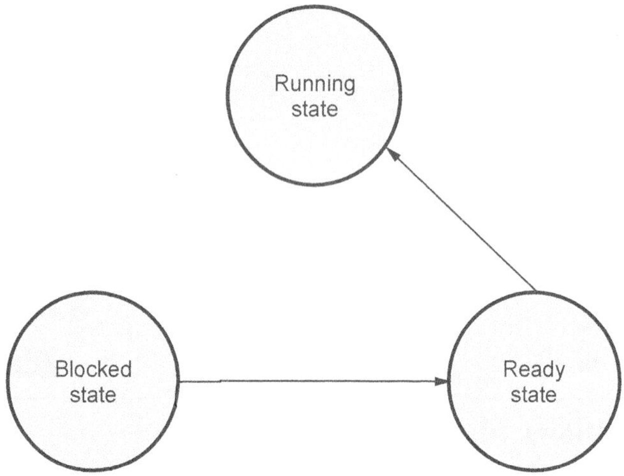

Jobs are changing their state of execution

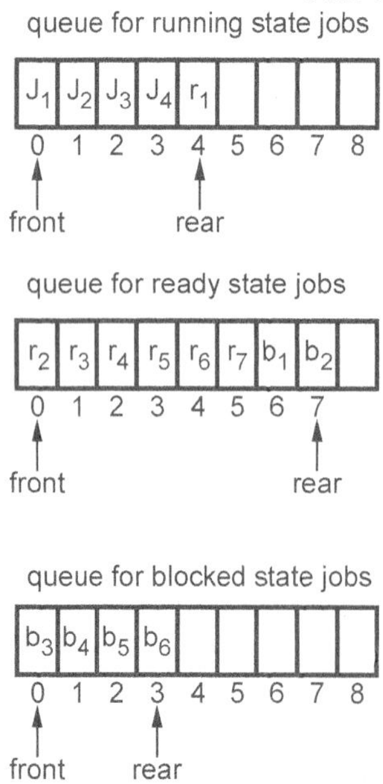

Fig. 4.7.1 Job scheduling in operating system

2. Categorizing Data

The queue can be used to categorize the data. The typical example for categorizing the data is our college library. The library has various sections in which the books from each stream are arranged. These sections are like multiple queues in which appropriate data (books) are stored. Thus categorization of data can be possible using multiple queues.

3. Josephus Problem

This is one of the applications of queue, in which the circular queue is being used. The statement is as follows -

"The situation is that the enemy is coming nearer and can attack a group of soldiers at any time and there is only one horse available for escape. The soldiers played a trick. They form a circle and pick up a number which is between 1 and m. The soldier is selected randomly to start with. Beginning with this selected soldier, they began counting clockwise around the circle. When the count reaches n then that corresponding soldier is removed from the circle. The count then begins from the next soldier. This process continues until 1 soldier is left. This single soldier takes the horse and summons help". The above described problem can be illustrated by following figure.

Assume that there are 5 soldiers.

Let, the number n = 3. We select randomly soldier number 5.

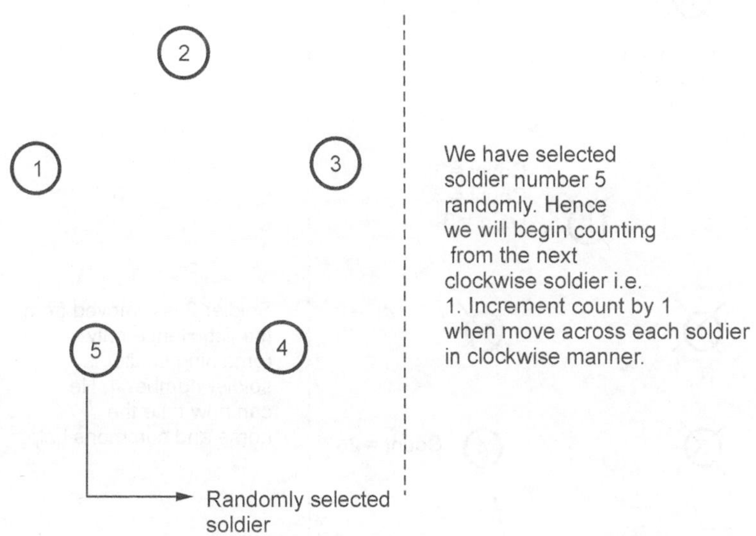

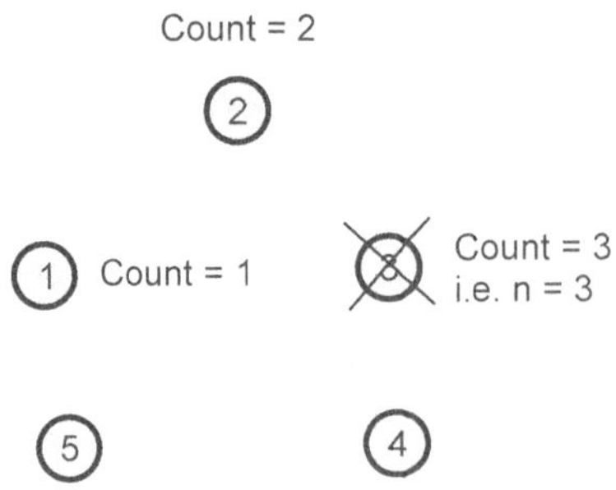

When count reaches to n = 3 remove that soldier from the list. Hence soldier number 3 is removed from list.

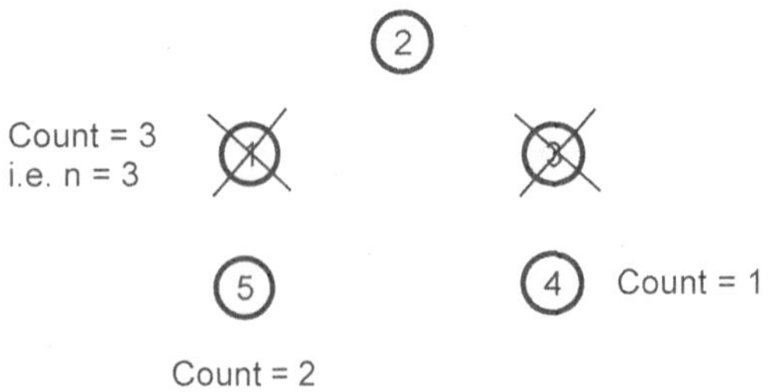

Again begin counting. Soldier 1 is removed from list.

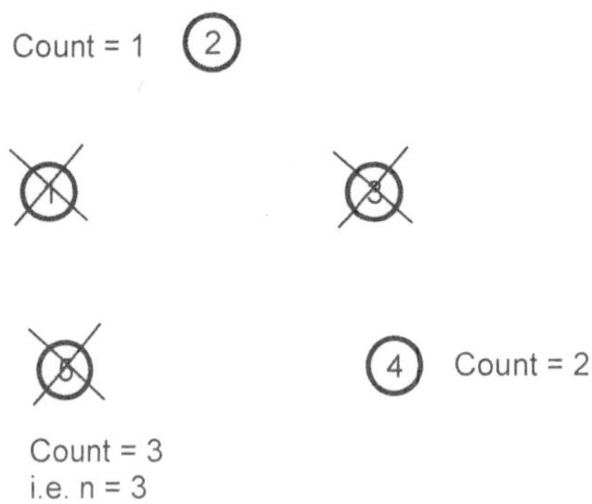

Soldier 5 is removed from list.

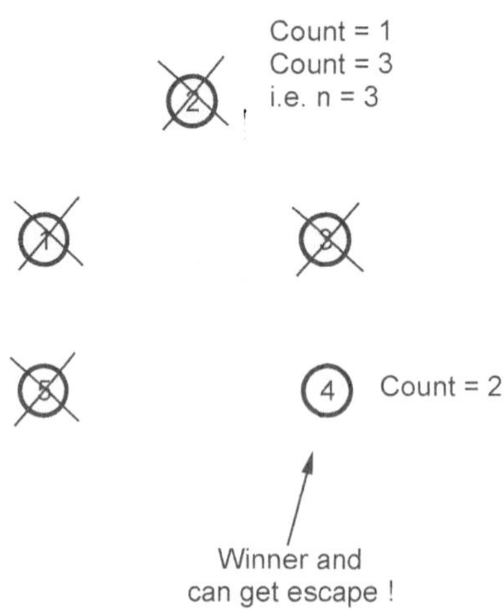

Soldier 2 is removed from the list. Hence only remaining soldier is soldier number 4. He can now take the horse and summons help.

Review Questions

1. *Attempt - Applications of queue.* **GTU : CE : Dec.-05, 06, Marks 4, Winter-15, Marks 3**
2. *Write and explain application of queue.* **GTU : Summer-17, Marks 3**
3. *Which data structure is used in a time sharing single central processing unit and one main memory computer system where many users share the system simultaneously ? How users are added for use of the system ?* **GTU : Winter-17, Marks 4**

4.8 Oral Questions and Answers

Q.1 What do the term FIFO means ? Explain.

Ans. : The FIFO stands for First In First Out. This property belongs to queue. That means the element inserted first in the queue will be the first to get deleted.

Q.2 What are the front and rear pointers of queue.

Ans. : The front end of the queue from which the element gets deleted is called front and the end from which the element is inserted in the queue is called rear.

Q.3 What is a circular queue ?

Ans. : Circular queue is a queue in which the front end is just adjacent to the rear end. The elements get arranged in circular manner.

Q.4 Write any four applications of queues.

Ans. :

1. In operating system for scheduling jobs, priority queues are used.
2. In Local Area Network (LAN) multiple computers share few printers. Then these printers accumulate jobs in a queue. Thus printers can process multiple print commands with the help of queues.

Q.5 How do you test for an empty queue ?

Ans. : Following is a C code which is used to test an empty queue :

```
if((Q.front==-1)||(Q.front>Q.rear))
        printf("\n The Queue is Empty!!");
else
        printf("\n The Queue is not Empty!!");
```

Q.6 What is the use of queue in operating system ?

Ans. : The queue is used for scheduling the jobs in operating system.

Q.7 What is the need for circular queue ?

Ans. : The circular queue is an useful data structure in which all the cells of the queue can be utilized. Secondly due to circular queue one can traverse to the first node from the last node very efficiently.

Q.8 What is the priority queue ?

Ans. : Priority queue is the queue data structure in which the elements are inserted in any order but the elements with high priority are deleted first.

Q.9 What are two types of priority queue ?

Ans. : The two types of priority queue are - 1. Ascending priority queue 2. Descending priority queue

Q.10 What is the major difference between stack and queue ?

Ans. : 1. The stack is a LIFO data structure while queue is a FIFO data structure. 2. In stack only one pointer i.e. top is used while in queue front and rear are the two pointers that are used.

Q.11 What is the application of priority queue ?

Ans. : Operating system allocates priority to jobs. The jobs are placed in the queue and position of the job in priority queue determines their priority. In operating system there are three kinds of jobs. These are real time jobs, foreground jobs and background jobs. The operating system always schedules the real time jobs first. If there is no real time job pending then it schedules foreground jobs. Lastly if no real time or foreground jobs are pending then operating system schedules the background jobs.

Q.12 What is ascending priority queue ?

Ans. : It is a collection of items in which the items can be inserted arbitarily but only smallest element can be removed.

Q.13 What is descending priority queue ?

Ans. : It is a collection of items in which insertion of items can be in any order but only largest element can be removed.

Q.14 What is dequeue ?

Ans. : Dequeue is a finite collection of elements in which the element can be inserted from both the ends i.e rear and front. Similarly, the elements can be deleted from both the ends i.e. front and rear.

Q.15 What is input restricted queue ?

Ans. : When we use only one end for inserting an element and both the ends for performing deletion operation then such a queue is called input restricted queue.

Q.16 What is output restricted queue ?

Ans. : when we use only one end for deleting an element and both the ends for insertion of elements then such a queue is called output restricted queue.

Q.17 Mention variations of the queue data structure. **GTU : Winter-15**

Ans. : Variations of queue data structure are i) Linear queue ii) Circular queue iii) Priority queue iv) Doubly ended queue.

Q.18 Is Queue a priority queue ? Justify. **GTU : Winter-15**

Ans. : The queue is not a priority queue because from the front end the deletion of element takes place and the element present at the front end only can be deleted irrespective of its priority.

Q.19 Define priority queue. **GTU : Summer-16, Winter-16**

Ans. : The priority queue is a data structure having a collection of elements which are associated with specific ordering.

Q.20 Double-ended queue. **GTU : Winter-16**

Ans. : Doubly ended queue is a queue in which insertion and deletion of elements is by both the rear and front end.

Q.21 How many stacks are needed to implement a queue. Consider the situation where no other data structure like arrays, linked list is available. **GTU : Summer-17**

Ans. : Two stacks are required to implement a queue.

i) Insert Queue operation

Just insert elements in stack 1. For example - Insert 10, 20, 30

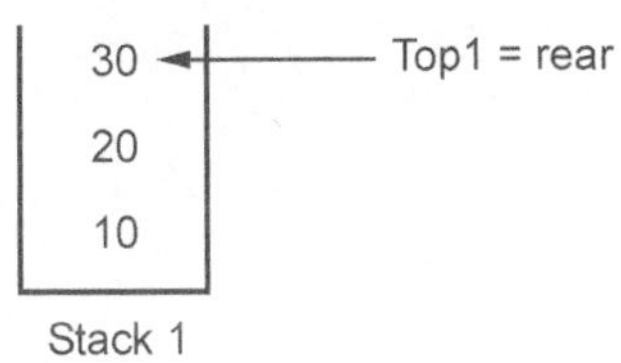

ii) Delete Queue Operation

a) POP element from stack 1 and push it onto the second stack.

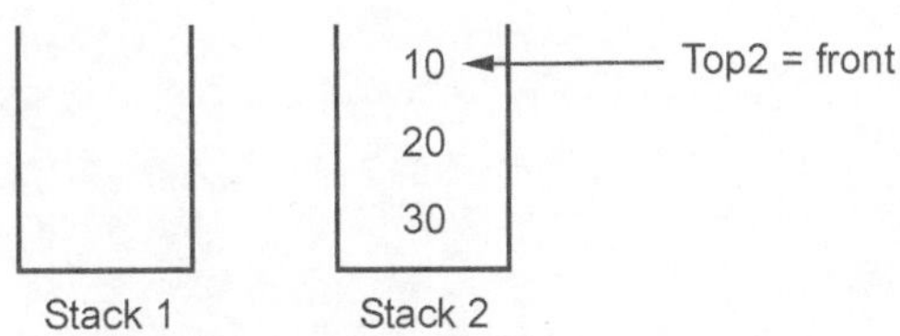

b) Now remove the top elements of stack 2.

Notes

5 Linked List

Syllabus

Singly linked list, Doubly linked list, Circular linked list, Linked implementation of stack, Linked implementation of queue, Applications of linked list.

Contents

5.1 Concept of Linked List

A linked list is a set of nodes where each node has two fields ' **data' and 'link'**. The 'data' field stores actual **piece of information** and 'link' field is used **to point to next node**. Basically 'link' field is nothing but address only.

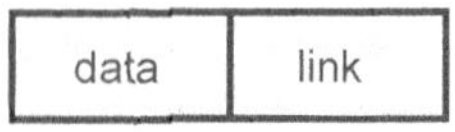

Fig. 5.1.1 Structure of node

Hence link list of integers 10, 20, 30, 40 is

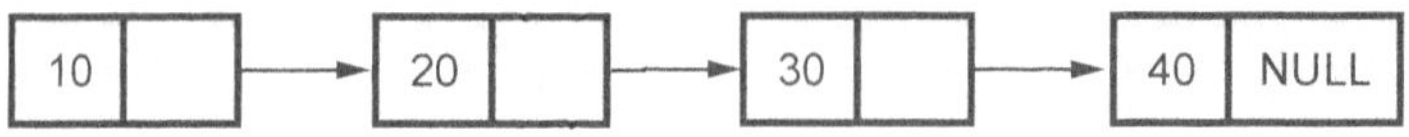

Fig. 5.1.2

Note that the 'link' field of last node consists of NULL which indicates end of list.

5.1.1 'C' Representation of Linked List

'C' structure

```
typedef struct node
{
      int data; /* data field */
      struct node * next; /* link field */
} SLL;
```

while declaring C structure for a linked list –

- Declare a structure in which two members are there i.e. data member and next pointer member.
- The **data** member can be character or integer or real kind of data depending upon the type of the information that the linked list is having.
- The **'next'** member is essentially of a pointer type. And the pointer should be of structure type. Because the **'next'** field holds the address of next node. And each node is basically a structure consisting of **'data'** and **'next'**.

Advantages of linked organization

1. In linked organization, insertion and deletion of elements can be efficiently done.
2. There is no wastage of memory. The memory can be allocated and deallocated as per requirement.

Disadvantages of linked organization

1. Linked organization does not support random or direct access.
2. Each data field should be supported by a link field to point to next node.

Key Point *The linked list is a collection of nodes. Each node consists of two fields: 'data' field and 'link' field.*

5.1.2 Linked List and Dynamic Memory Management

Before understanding how memory gets allocated dynamically, let us first understand the memory model

As shown in Fig. 5.1.3, C program uses the memory which is divided into three parts static area, local data and heap. The static area stores the global data. The stack is for local data area i.e for local variables and heap area is used to allocate and deallocate memory under program's control. Thus stack and heap area are the parts of dynamic memory management. Note that the stack and heap grow towards each other. Their areas are flexible.

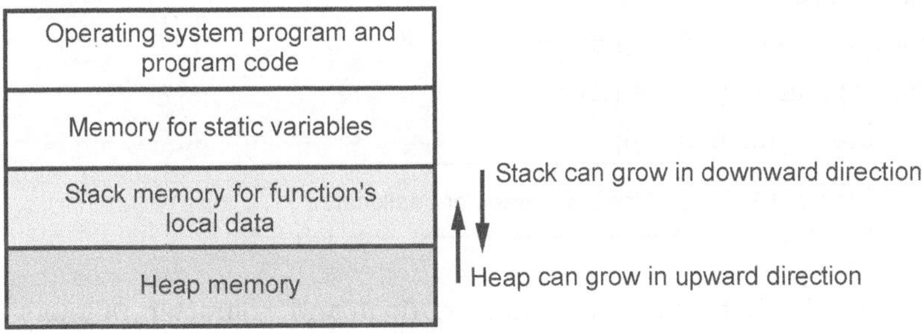

Fig. 5.1.3 Memory model

5.1.3 Dynamic Memory Allocation in 'C'

In computer world the two words 'static' and 'dynamic' have great importance. The static refers to an activity which is carried out at the time of compilation of a program and before execution of the program whereas dynamic means the activity carried out while the program is executed. Here we are going to see what is static and dynamic memory management. The static memory management means allocating/ deallocating of memory at compilation time while the word dynamic refers to allocation/deallocation of memory while program is running (after compilation). The advantage of dynamic memory management in handling the linked list is that we can create as many nodes as we desire and if some nodes are not required we can deallocate them. Such a deallocated memory can be reallocated for some other nodes. Thus the total memory utilization is possible.

5.1.4 Dynamic Memory Allocation in 'C'

In 'C' language for allocating the memory dynamically 'malloc' function is used we should include **alloc.h** file in our program to support malloc. Similarly for deallocating the memory 'free' function is used.

Examples of 'malloc' and 'free' functions :

Let us take a piece of 'C' code to understand how malloc works.

```
int *i;   → Pointer to integer variable
float *f; → Poiner to float variable
char *C;  → Pointer to character type variable
typedef struct student
{
      int roll_no;
      char name [10];
}s;                     Type casting done. Because by
                        default malloc returns void pointer
s *s1;
      i = (int*) malloc (size of (int));
      f = (float*) malloc (size of (float));
      C = (char*) malloc (size of (char));
     s1 = (s*) malloc (size of (s));
          free (i);     ← Memory is freed or deallocated
```

In above example, i, f and C are integer, float and character pointers respectively. Also s1 is the pointer to structure s. In malloc function one parameter is passed because syntax of malloc is

```
malloc (size)
```

Where the size means how many bytes has to be allocated ? The size can be obtained by the function 'sizeof' where syntax of size of is

```
sizeof (datatype)
```

Therefore in above 'C' code in malloc functions size of integer, float, char and even the structure is obtained to allocate those many bytes of memory. Even we are type casting the malloc functions. For example (int *) or (float *) or (char *) and so on. Type casting means conversion from one data type to other. This is because by default malloc returns the 'void pointer' and we are assigning these values to integer pointer or float pointer or character pointer or structure pointer. The first statement calls malloc with int as the parameter of the size of function. Suppose the machine on which we want to execute the program needs two bytes of memory for integer type of variable, then size of will return to bytes of memory, which is then passed on to malloc function, malloc then allocates two bytes of memory from memory buffer called heap. Since we are getting void pointer we are type casting it to an integer pointer this value will be assigned to left side variable which is integer pointer variable.

Similarly the last statement in above example is free function which deallocates the memory of integer pointer i. So two bytes memory gets freed.

Difference between malloc() and calloc()

Sr. No.	malloc()	calloc()
1.	Malloc takes only one element and that is size of the block to be allocated.	It takes two arguments the first one is number of items to be allocated say n and second argument is size of each item say s. The function thus allocates nXs bytes of memory from heap.
2.	Malloc does not initialize the contents of memory that is been allocated. That means after allocation of memory by using malloc function initially we may get garbage value.	The calloc initializes the memory after allocation. Thus it is safe to use calloc since all the locations will have the value 0 after allocation.

5.2 Singly Linked List

GTU : Dec.-10, May-11, Winter-13, 14, 15, 17, 18 Summer-15, 17, 18 Marks 7

1. Creation of linked list
2. Display of linked list
3. Insertion of any element in the linked list
4. Deletion of any element from the linked list
5. Searching of desired element in the linked list.

We will discuss each operation one by one -

1. Creation of linked list

```
node* create()
{
        node *temp, *New, *head;
        int  val, flag;
        char ans='y';
        node *get_node();
        temp = NULL ;
        flag = TRUE; /* flag to indicate whether a new node
                      is created for the first time or not */
```

```
    do
{
        printf("\nEnter the Element :");
        scanf("%d", &val);
        /* allocate new node */
        New =get_node();
        if ( New == NULL )
            printf("\nMemory is not allocated");
        New -> data  = val ;
        if (flag==TRUE) /* Executed only for the first
            time */

        {
            head = New;
            temp=head; /*head is a first node in the
            SLL*/
            flag = FALSE;
        }
        else
        {
            /* temp keeps track of the most recently
                created node */
            temp ->next = New;
            temp = New;
        }

    printf("\n Do you Want to enter more elements?(y/n)");
    ans=getche();
    }while(ans=='y');
    printf("\nThe Singly Linked List is created\n");
    getch();
    clrscr();
    return head;
}
node *get_node()
{
 node *temp;
 temp=( node *) malloc( sizeof(node) );
 temp->next=NULL;
 return temp;
}
```

Creation of linked list (logic explanation part)

Initially one variable flag is taken whose value is initialized to TRUE (i.e. 1). The purpose of flag is for making a check on creation of first node. That means if flag is TRUE then we have to create head node or first node of linked list. Naturally after creation of first node we will reset the flag (i.e. assign FALSE to flag). Consider that we have entered the Element value 10 initially then

Step 1 :

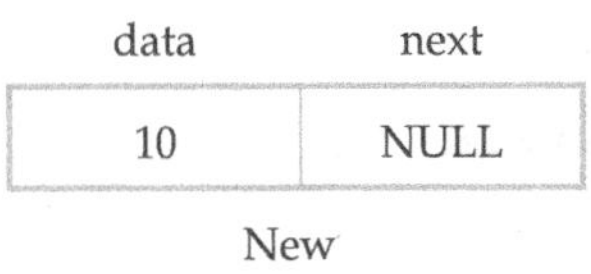


```
New = get_node ();
/* memory gets allocated for
New node */
New → data = Val;
/* value 10 will be put in data field of New */
```

Step 2 :

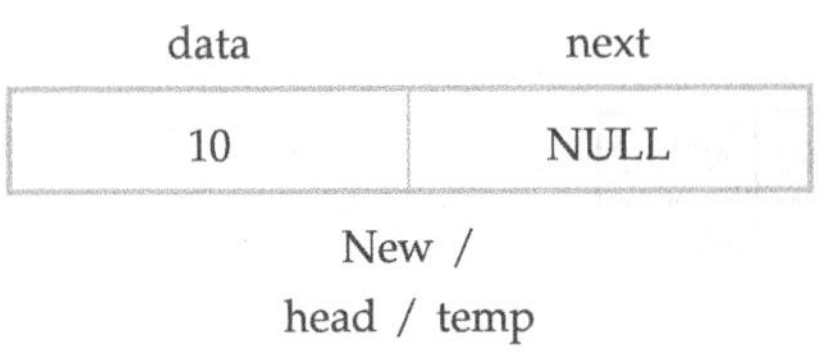


```
if (flag == TRUE)
{
head = New
temp = head;
/* We have also called this node as temp because
head's address will be preserved in 'head' and we can
change 'temp' node as per requirement */
flag = FALSE;
/* After creation of first node flag is reset */
}
```

Step 3 :

If **head** node of linked list is created we can further create a linked list by attaching the subsequent nodes. Suppose we want to insert a node with value 20 then

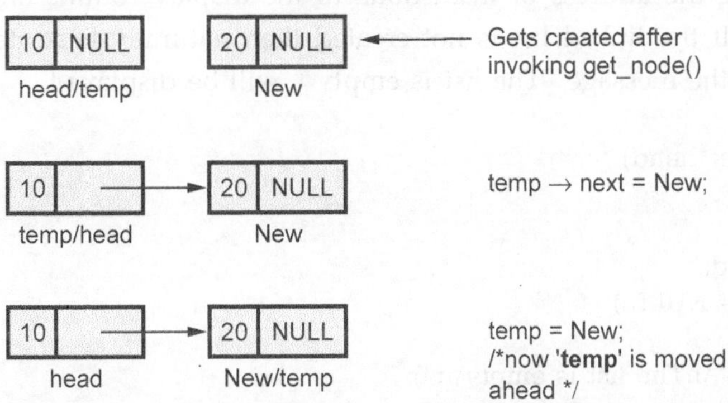

Step 4 :

If user wants to enter more elements then let say for value 30 the scenario will be

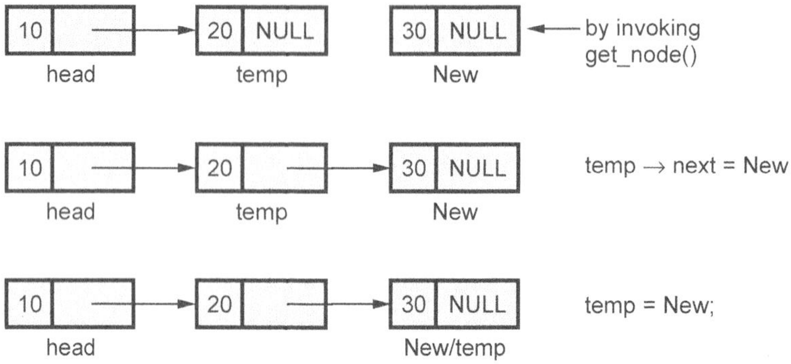

Then for value 40 -

Step 5 :

Next if we enter 40 then

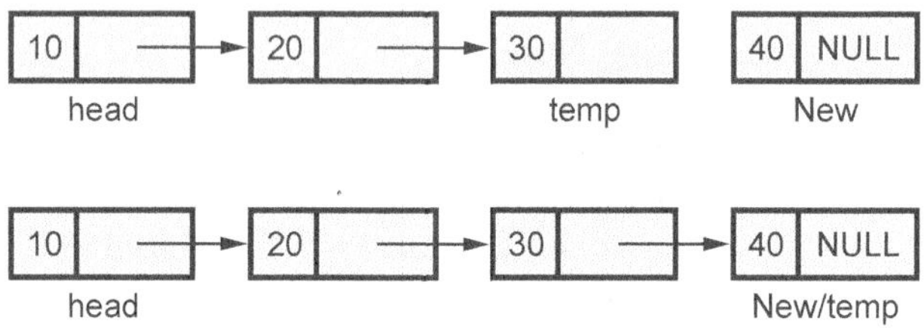

Next if we enter 50 then

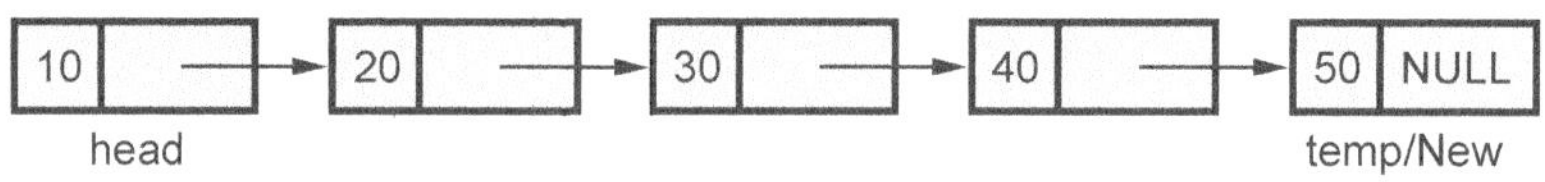

is the final linked list.

2. Display of linked list

We are passing the address of **head** node to the display routine and calling head as the **'temp'** node. If the linked list is not created then naturally head=temp node will be **NULL.** Therefore the message "The list is empty " will be displayed.

```
void display(node *head)
{
      node *temp ;
      temp = head;
      if ( temp == NULL )
      {
            printf("\nThe list is empty\n");
            getch();
```

```
        clrscr();
        return;
    }

    while ( temp != NULL )
    {
        printf(" %d -> ", temp->data );
        temp = temp -> next;
    }
    printf("NULL");
    getch();
    clrscr();
}
```

If we have created some linked list like this then -

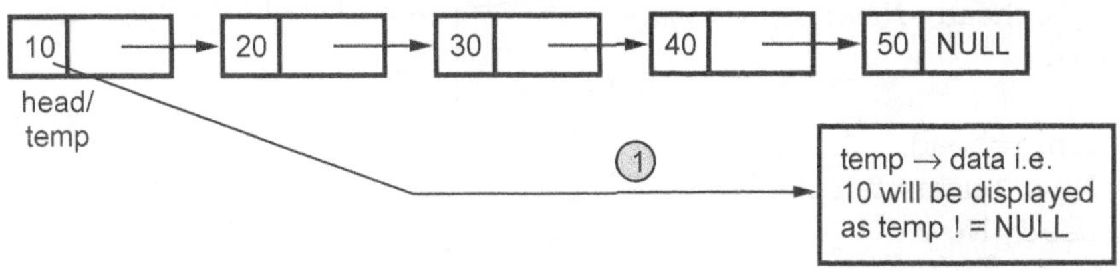

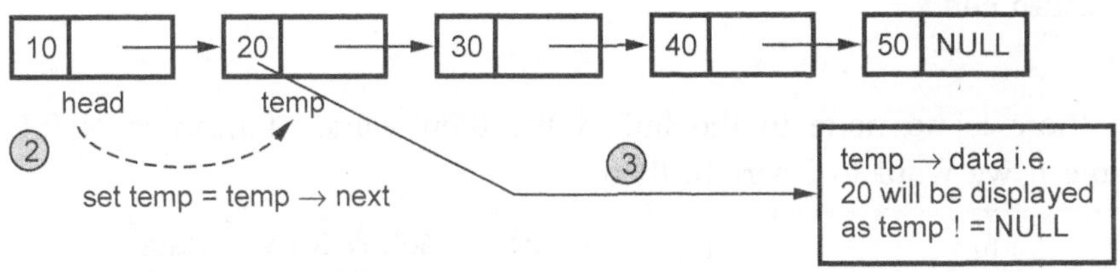

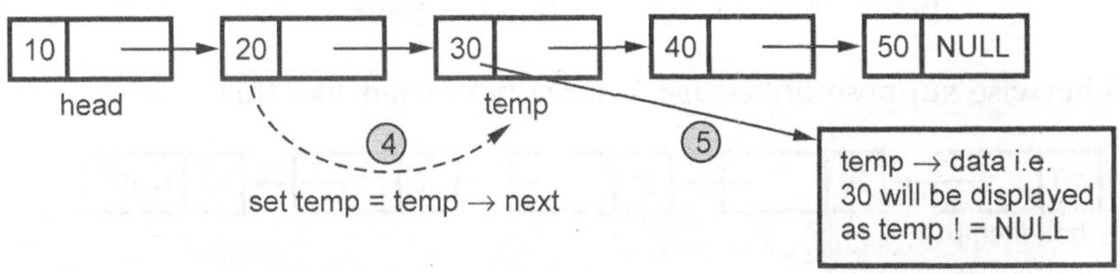

Continuing in this fashion we can display remaining nodes 40, 50. When

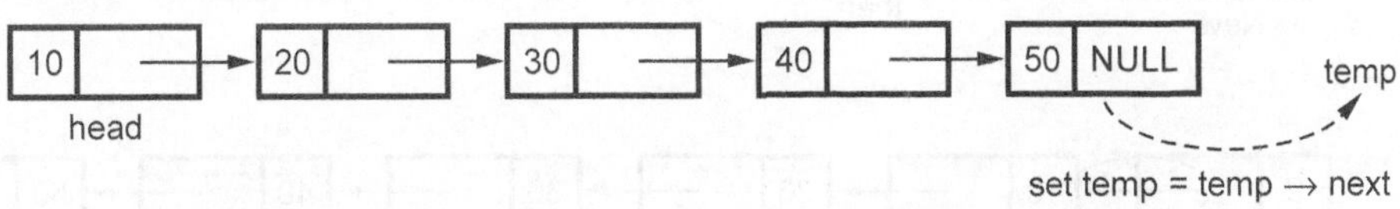

As now value of temp becomes NULL we will come out of **while** loop. As a result of such display routine we will get

10 → 20 → 30 → 40 → 50 → NULL

will be printed on console.

3. Insertion of any element at anywhere in the linked list

There are three possible cases when we want to insert an element in the linked list-

a) Insertion of a node as a head node

b) Insertion of a node as a last node

c) Insertion of a node after some node.

We will see the case a) first –

```
node *insert_head(node *head)
{
 node *New,*temp;
 New=get_node();
 printf("\n Enter The element which you want to insert");
 scanf("%d",&New->data);
 if(head==NULL)
        head=New;
 else
 {
  temp=head;
  New->next=temp;
  head=New;
 }
 return head;
}
```

No node in the linked list. i.e. when linked list is empty

If there is no node in the linked list then value of head is NULL. At that time if we want to insert 10 then

scanf ("%d", & New $\rightarrow$ data)
if (head == NULL)
head = New;

Otherwise suppose linked list is already created like this

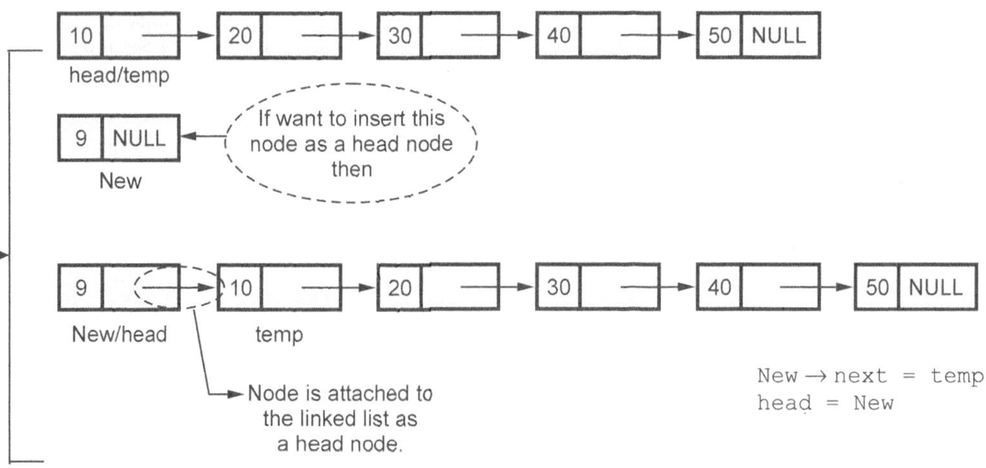

New $\rightarrow$ next = temp
head = New

Now we will insert a node at the end i.e. case b)

```
void insert_last(node *head)
{
  node *New,*temp;
  New=get_node();
  printf("\n Enter The element which you want to insert");
  scanf("%d",&New->data);
  if(head==NULL)
      head=New;
  else
  {
       temp=head;
       while(temp->next!=NULL)
         temp=temp->next;          /* Finding end of the linked list.
                                      Then temp will be a last node */
       temp->next=New;
       New->next=NULL;
       }
}
```

To attach a node at the end of linked list assume that we have already created a linked list like this -

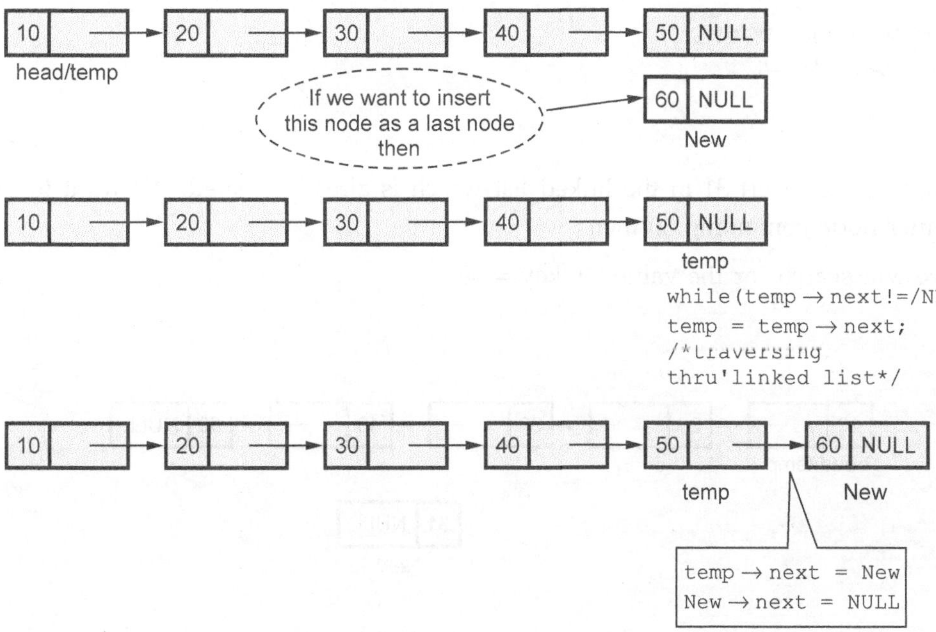

Now we will insert a new node after some node at intermediate position i.e. case c)

```
void insert_after(node *head)
{
 int key;
 node *New,*temp;
 New= get_node();
 printf("\n Enter The element which you want to insert");
 scanf("%d",&New->data);
 if(head==NULL)
 {
 head=New;
 }
 else
 {
  printf("\n Enter The element after which you want to insert the node");
  scanf("%d",&key);
  temp=head;
  do
  {
       if(temp->data==key)
       {
               New->next=temp->next;
               temp->next=New;
               return;
       }
 else
        temp=temp->next;
 }while(temp!=NULL);
}
}
```

If we want to insert 31 in the linked list which is already created. We want to insert this 31 after node containing 30 then

As we will search for the value 30, key = 30.

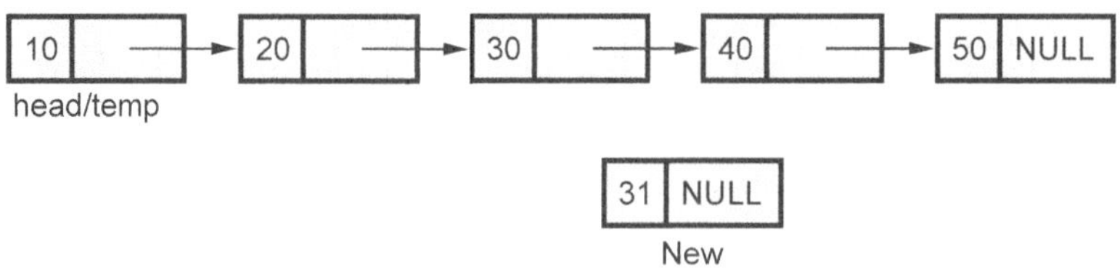

Then,

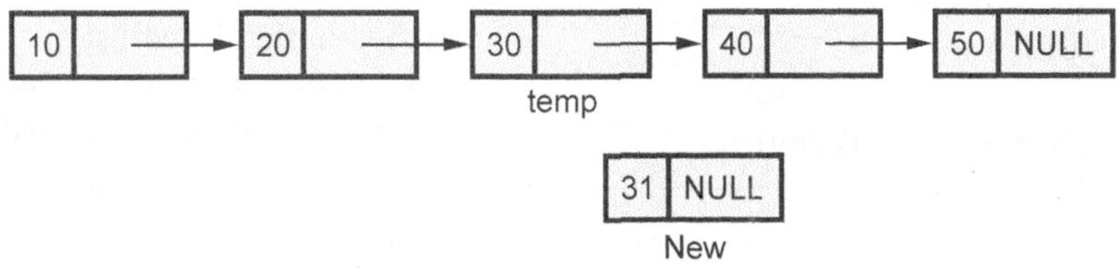

Thus desired node gets inserted at desired position.

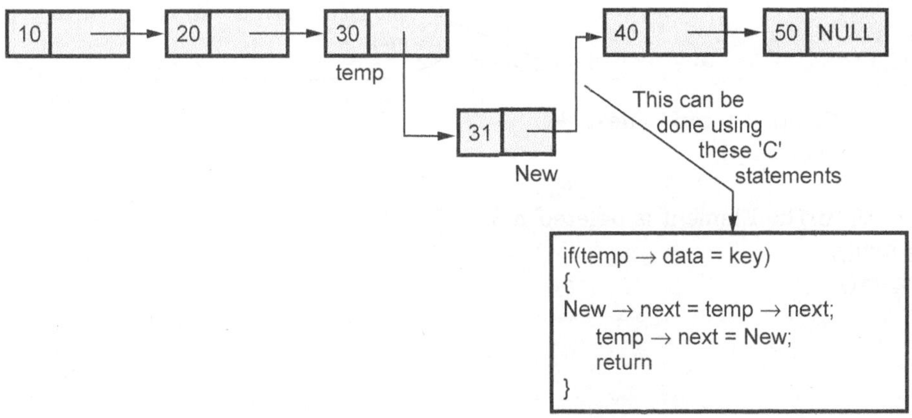

4. Deletion of any element from the linked list

```
void dele(node **head)
{
 node *temp,*prev ;
 int  key;
 temp = *head;
 if ( temp == NULL )
 {
        printf("\nThe list is empty\n");
        getch();
        clrscr();
        return ;
 }
```

Always check before deletion whether the linked list is empty or not. Because if the list is empty there is no point in performing deletion

```
clrscr();
printf("\nEnter the Element you want to delete: ");
scanf("%d", &key);
temp = search(*head,key);
if ( temp != NULL )
{
      prev = get_prev(*head,key);
      if ( prev != NULL )
      {
            prev -> next = temp->next;
            free (temp);

      }
      else
      {


            *head = temp ->next;
            free(temp);
      }
      printf("\nThe Element is deleted\n");
      getch();
      clrscr();
}
}
```

Firstly, Node to be deleted is searched in the linked list

Once the node to be deleted is found then get the previous node of that node in variable **prev**

If we want to delete head node then set adjacent node as a new head node and then deallocate the previous head node

Suppose we have

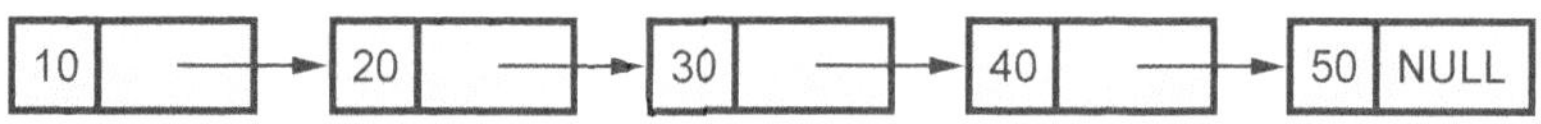

Suppose we want to delete node 30. Then we will search the node containing 30, using search (* head, key) routine. Mark the node to be deleted as **temp**. Then we will obtain previous node of **temp** using get_prev ( ) function. Mark previous node as **prev**

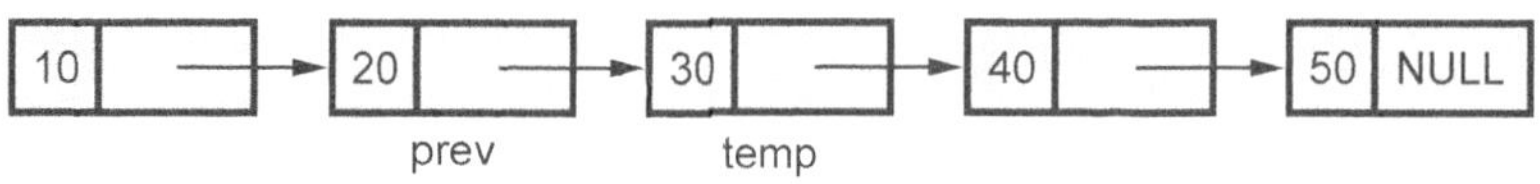

Then

```
prev → next = temp → next
```

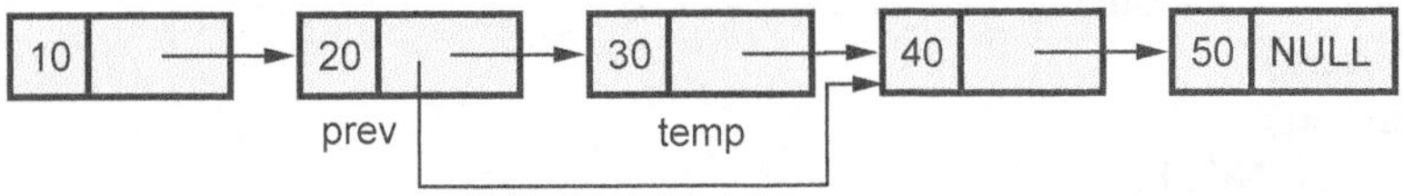

Now we will **free** the **temp** node using free function. Then the linked list will be -

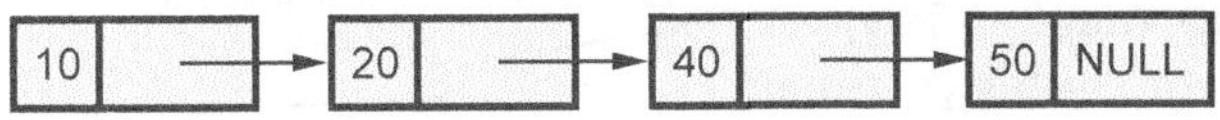

Another case is, if we want to delete a head node then -

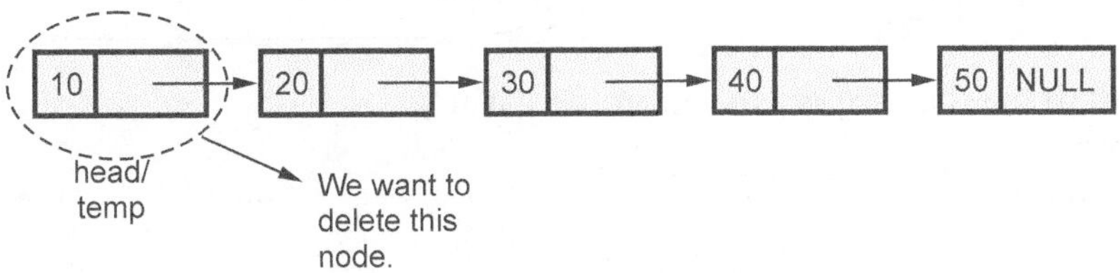

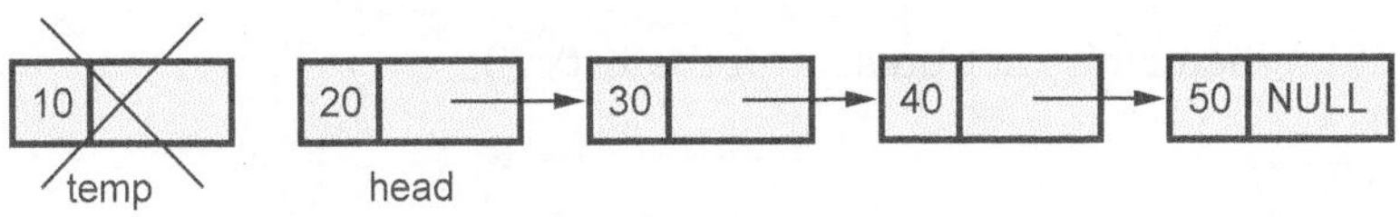

This can be done using following statements

```
*head = temp → next;
free (temp);
```

5. Searching of desired element in the linked list.

The search function is for searching the node containing desired value. We pass the head of the linked list to this routine so that the complete linked list can be searched from the beginning.

```
node *search(node *head, int key)
{
    node *temp;
    int found;
```

```
        temp = head;
        if ( temp == NULL )
        {
                printf("The Linked List is empty\n");
                getch();
                clrscr();
                return NULL;
        }
        found = FALSE;
        while ( temp != NULL && found==FALSE)
        {
                if ( temp->data != key)
                        temp = temp -> next;
                else
                        found = TRUE;
        }
        if ( found==TRUE )
        {
         printf("\nThe Element is present in the list\n");
         getch();
         return temp;
        }
        else

        {
         printf("The Element is not present in the list\n");
         getch();
         return NULL;
        }
}
```

Compare data at each node with the key value. If not matching then move to next node

If the node containing desired data is obtained in the linked list then **found** variable is set to **TRUE.**

Consider that we have created a linked list as

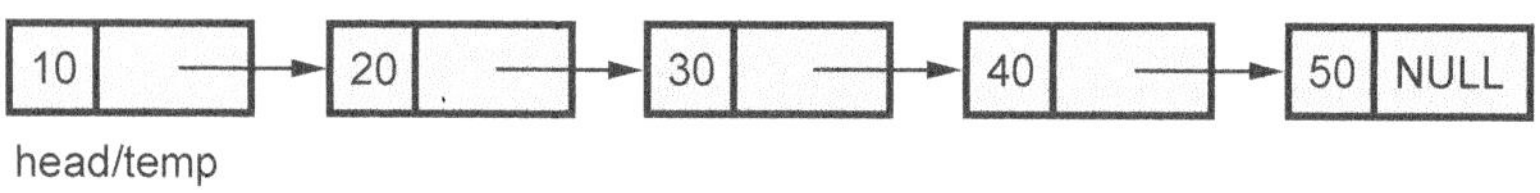

Suppose key = 30 i.e. we want a node conaining value 30 then compare **temp → data** and **key** value. If there is no match then we will mark next node as **temp**.

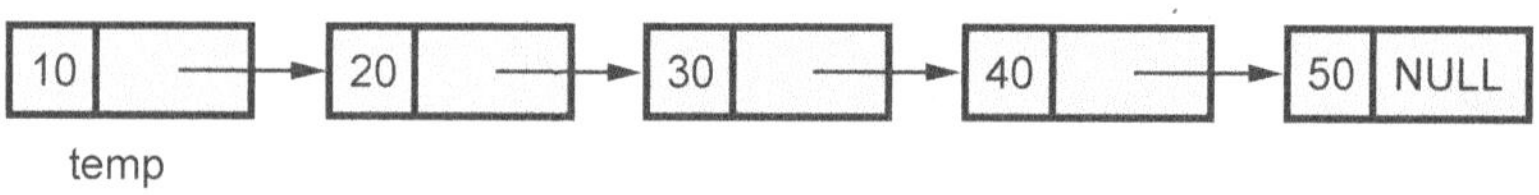

Is temp → data $\stackrel{?}{=}$ key No

Is temp → data $\stackrel{?}{=}$ key ⋯⋯▶ No

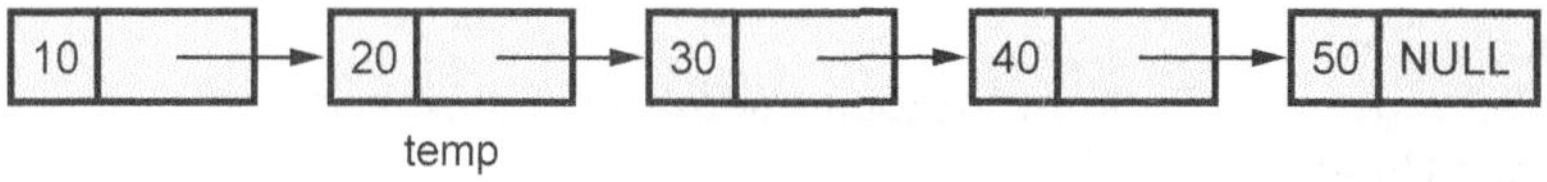

Is temp → data $\stackrel{?}{=}$ key ⋯⋯▶ Yes

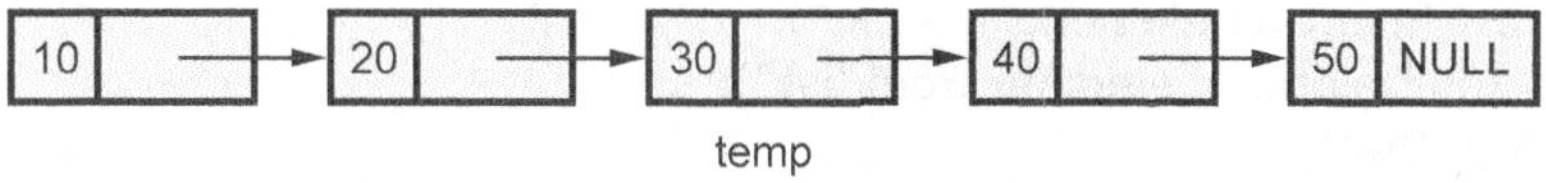

Hence print the message⋯▶ **"The Element is present in the list"**

Thus in search operation the entire list can be scanned in search of desired node. And still, if required node is not obtained then we have to print the message.

"The Element is not present in the list"

Let us see the complete program for it -

C Program :

```
/*************************************************************
Program to perform various operations such as creation, insertion, deletion, search and
display on singly link lists.
*************************************************************/
#include <stdio.h>
#include <conio.h>
#include <stdlib.h>
#define    TRUE     1
#define    FALSE    0

typedef struct SLL
{
      int data;
      struct SLL *next;
}node;

node *create();
void main()
{
      /* Local declarations */
      int choice, val;
      char ans;
      node *head;
      void display(node *);
      node *search(node *,int);
      node *insert(node *);
      void dele(node **);
      head = NULL;
```

```
    do
    {
     clrscr();
     printf("\nProgram to Perform Various operations on Linked List");
     printf("\n1.Create");
     printf("\n2.Display");
     printf("\n3.Search for an item");
     printf("\n4.Insert an element in a list");
      printf("\n5.Delete an element from list");
     printf("\n6.Quit");
     printf("\nEnter Your Choice ( 1-6) ");
     scanf("%d",&choice);
     switch( choice)
     {
       case 1:head = create();
              break;
       case 2:display(head);
              break;
       case 3:printf("Enter the element you want to search");
            scanf("%d", &val);
                search(head, val);
                break;
       case 4:head=insert(head);
              break;
       case 5:dele(&head);
              break;
      case 6:exit(0);
      default:clrscr();
              printf("Invalid Choice, Try again");
              getch();
     }
    }while(choice != 6);
}
node* create()
{

    node *temp, *New, *head;
    int  val, flag;
    char ans='y';
    node *get_node();
    temp = NULL ;
  flag = TRUE; /* flag to indicate whether a new node
                  is created for the first time or not */
    do
    {
```

```
            printf("\nEnter the Element :");
            scanf("%d", &val);
            /* allocate new node */
            New =get_node();
            if ( New == NULL )
                  printf("\nMemory is not allocated");
            New -> data  = val ;
            if (flag==TRUE) /* Executed only for the first
                  time */
            {
                  head = New;
                  temp=head; /*head is a first node in the
                  SLL*/
                  flag = FALSE;
            }
            else
            {
                  /* temp keeps track of the most recently
                        created node */
                  temp ->next = New;
                  temp = New;
            }
      printf("\n Do you Want to enter more elements?(y/n)");
      ans=getche();
      }while(ans=='y');
      printf("\nThe Singly Linked List is created\n");
      getch();
      clrscr();
      return head;
}
node *get_node()
{
 node *temp;
 temp=( node *) malloc( sizeof(node) );
 temp->next=NULL;
 return temp;
}
void  display(node *head)
{
      node *temp ;
      temp = head;
      if ( temp == NULL )
      {
            printf("\nThe list is empty\n");
            getch();
            clrscr();
            return;
```

```
        }
        while ( temp != NULL )
        {
                printf(" %d -> ", temp->data );
                temp = temp -> next;
        }
        printf("NULL");
        getch();
        clrscr();
}
node *search(node *head, int key)
{
 node *temp;
 int found;
 temp = head;
 if ( temp == NULL )
 {
  printf("The Linked List is empty\n");
  getch();
  clrscr();
  return NULL;
 }
 found = FALSE;
 while ( temp != NULL && found==FALSE)
 {
  if ( temp->data != key)
    temp = temp -> next;
  else
    found = TRUE;
 }
 if ( found==TRUE )
 {
    printf("\nThe Element is present in the list\n");
  getch();
  return temp;
 }
 else
 {
  printf("The Element is not present in the list\n");
  getch();
  return NULL;
 }
}
node *insert(node *head)
{
 int choice;
 node *insert_head(node *);
```

```
void insert_after(node *);
void insert_last(node *);
printf("\n 1. Insert a node as a head node");
printf("\n 2. Insert a node as a last node");
printf("\n 3. Insert a node at intermediate position in the linked list");
printf("\n Enter the your choice for insertion of node");
scanf("%d",&choice);
switch(choice)
{
case 1:head=insert_head(head);
        break;
case 2:insert_last(head);
        break;
case 3:insert_after(head);
        break;
}
return head;
}
/* Insertion of node at first position*/
node *insert_head(node *head)
{
 node *New,*temp;
 New=get_node();
 printf("\n Enter The element which you want to insert");
 scanf("%d",&New->data);
```

New head is returned from function **insert_head()**.

Hence we have to return the new head from the **insert** function to main

```
 if(head==NULL)
        head=New;
 else
 {
  temp=head;
  New->next=temp;
  head=New;
 }
 return head;
}
/*Insertion of node at last position*/
void insert_last(node *head)
{
 node *New,*temp;
 New=get_node();
 printf("\n Enter The element which you want to insert");
 scanf("%d",&New->data);

 if(head==NULL)
```

No node in the linked list. i.e. when linked list is empty.

```
        head=New;
  else
  {
        temp=head;
        while(temp->next!=NULL)
          temp=temp->next;
        temp->next=New;
        New->next=NULL;
       }
}
/*Insertion of node at intermediate position */
void insert_after(node *head)
{
 int key;
 node *New,*temp;
 New= get_node();
 printf("\n Enter The element which you want to insert");
 scanf("%d",&New->data);
 if(head==NULL)
 {
  head=New;
 }
 else
 {
  printf("\n Enter The element after which you want to insert the node");
  scanf("%d",&key);
    temp=head;
    do
    {
      if(temp->data==key)
      {
            New->next=temp->next;
            temp->next=New;
            return;
      }
    else
        temp=temp->next;
  }while(temp!=NULL);
 }
}
node*  get_prev(node *head, int val)
{
      node *temp, *prev ;
      int    flag;

      temp = head;
      if ( temp == NULL )
```

```
            return NULL;
      flag = FALSE;
      prev = NULL;
      while ( temp != NULL && !flag)
      {
            if ( temp->data != val)
            {
                  prev = temp;
                  temp = temp -> next;
            }
            else
                  flag = TRUE;
      }
      if ( flag )/*if flag is true*/
            return prev;
      else
            return NULL;
}

void dele(node **head)
{
      node *temp,*prev ;
      int  key;
      temp = *head;
      if ( temp == NULL )
      {
            printf("\nThe list is empty\n");
            getch();
            clrscr();
            return ;
      }
      clrscr();
      printf("\nEnter the Element you want to delete: ");
      scanf("%d", &key);
      temp = search(*head,key);
      if ( temp != NULL )
      {
            prev = get_prev(*head,key);
            if ( prev != NULL )
            {
                  prev -> next = temp->next;
                  free (temp);
            }
            else
            {
                  *head = temp ->next;
```

```
                free(temp);
            }
            printf("\nThe Element is deleted\n");
            getch();
            clrscr();
        }
}
```

Output

```
Program to Perform Various operations on Linked List
1.Create
2.Display
3.Search for an item
4.Insert an element in a list
5.Delete an element from list
6.Quit
Enter Your Choice ( 1-6) 1
Enter the Element :10
 Do you Want to enter more elements?(y/n)y
 Enter the Element :20
Do you Want to enter more elements?(y/n)y
Enter the Element :30
Do you Want to enter more elements?(y/n)y
Enter the Element :40
Do you Want to enter more elements?(y/n)y
Enter the Element :50
Do you Want to enter more elements?(y/n)n
The Singly Linked List is created
Program to Perform Various operations on Linked List
1.Create
2.Display
3.Search for an item
4.Insert an element in a list
5.Delete an element from list
6.Quit
Enter Your Choice ( 1-6) 2
10 ->  20 ->  30 ->  40 ->  50 -> NULL
```

Review Questions

1. *Consider singly linked storage structures. Write an algorithm which performs an insertion at the end of a linked linear list.* **GTU : Summer-17, Marks 3**
2. *Write an algorithm for insertion of node at last position in liner linked List.* **GTU : Winter-18, Marks 4**
3. *Write an algorithm for deletion of node in liner linked list.* **GTU : Winter-18, Marks 4**

5.2.1 Other Linked List Operations

In this section we will discuss various operations that can be performed on the linked list. For the sake of convenience we will discuss only functions performing these operations assuming that the list is already created. The **create()** and **display()** functions will be common to all these operations

1. Counting the nodes

```
void count()
{
 node *temp;
 int c=0;
 temp=head;
 if(temp==NULL)
 {
  printf("\n The list is empty");
  return;
 }
 while(temp!=NULL)/*visiting each node*/
 {
  c=c+1;/*c is for counting the node*/
  temp=temp->next;
 }
 printf("\nThe Total number of nodes are : %d",c);
 getch();
}
```

2. Reversing the linked list (This is done using three pointers)

```
void reverse ()
{
 node *temp1,*temp2,*temp3;
 temp1=head;
 if(temp1==NULL)
 {
  printf("\n The List is empty");
  getch();
 }
 else
 {
  temp2=NULL;
   while(temp1!=NULL)
   {
    temp3=temp2;
    temp2=temp1;
    temp1=temp1->next;
    temp2->next=temp3;
   }
   head=temp2;
```

```
 }
 printf("\n The List is REVERSED");
}
```

For example

Consider a linked list -

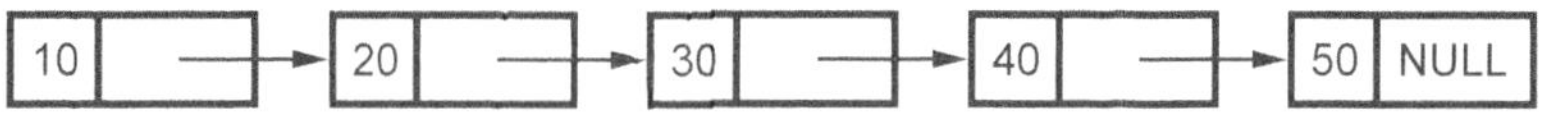

Step 1: As given in above algorithm initially

temp1 = head

temp2=temp3=NULL;

Step 2:

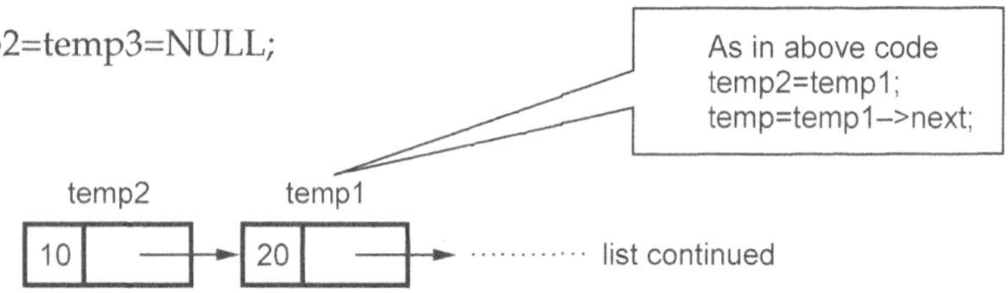

temp3=NULL

Step 3: For the statements

```
temp3=temp2;
temp2=temp1;
temp1=temp1->next;
```

we get the marking of nodes as -

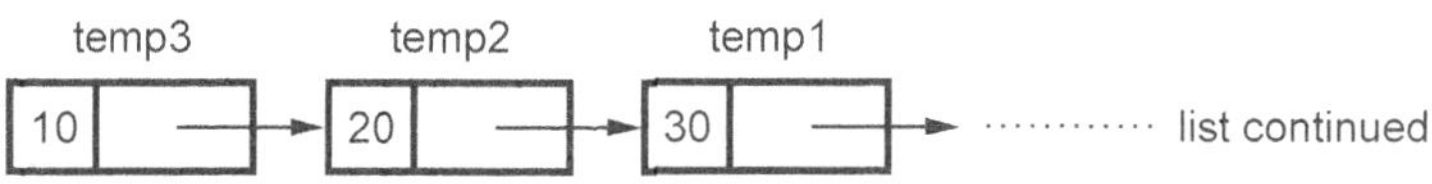

Step 4:

As

```
temp2->next=temp3
```

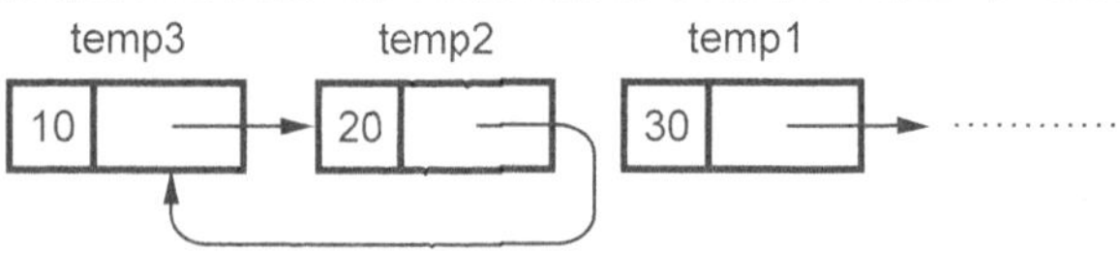

Step 5:

```
temp3=temp2;
temp2=temp1;
temp1=temp1->next;
temp2->next=temp3;
```

will give us -

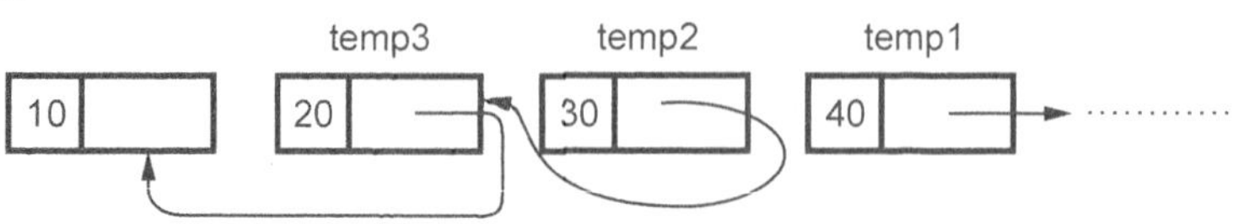

Step 6:

Continuing the steps

```
temp3=temp2;
temp2=temp1;
temp1=temp1->next;
temp2->next=temp3;
```

We get -

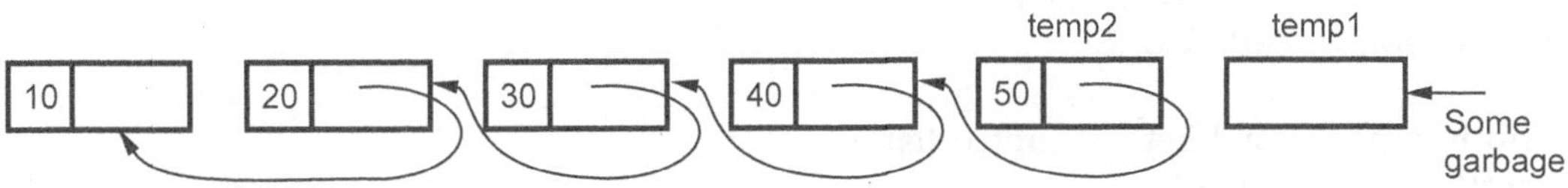

Step 7:

Finally set temp2 as head node. Hence the list becomes

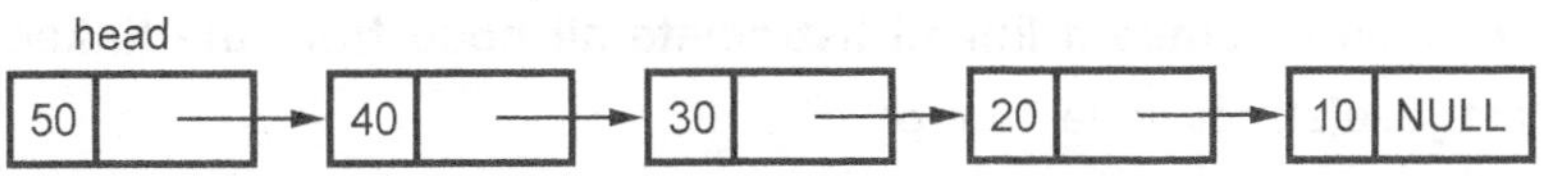

Thus the linked list gets reverse using three pointers

3. Concatenation of two linked list

```
void concat(node *head1,node *head2)
{
 node *temp1,*temp2;
 temp1=head1;
 temp2=head2;
 while(temp1->next!=NULL)
  temp1=temp1->next;/*searching end of first list*/
 temp1->next=temp2;/*attaching head of the second list*/
 printf("\n The concatenated list is ...\n");
 temp1=head1;
 while(temp1!=NULL)
 { /*printing the concatenated list*/
  printf(" %d",temp1->Data);
  temp1=temp1->next;
 }
}
```

4. Algorithm to copy one singly list to another

```
void copy(node *head1,node *head2)
{
 node *temp1,*temp2;
 temp1=head1;/*first non empty linked list*/
 head2=(node *)malloc(sizeof(node));
 temp2=head2;/*second empty linked list*/
```

```
 while(temp1!=NULL)/*while not end of first linked list*/
 {
  temp2->data=temp1->data;/*copy the content to other node*/
  temp2->next=(node *)malloc(sizeof(node));
  temp2=temp2->next;/* moving one node ahead */
  temp1=temp1->next;
 }
 temp2=NULL;/*set the next pointer of last node of second list to NULL*/
 printf("\n The list is copied \n");
 while(head2->next!=NULL)
 {
/*printing the second list i.e. copied list*/
  printf(" %d",head2->data);
  head2=head2->next;
 }
}
```

5. Recursive routine to erase a linked list(delete all node from the linked list)

```
struct node *list_free(struct node *temp)
{
 if(temp->next!=NULL)
 {
       temp1=temp->next;/*temp1 is declared globally*/
       temp->next=NULL;
       free(temp);
       list_free(temp1);/*recursive call*/
 }
 temp=NULL;
 return temp;
}
```

6. Sort the contents of singly linked list

```
node *Sort(node *head)
 {
  node *temp1,*temp2,*temp3,*current,*temp;
  void swap(node*,node*,node*);
  current=NULL;
  while(current!=head->next)
   {
   temp1=head;
   temp2=head->next;
   temp3=temp1;
   while(temp1!=current)
    {
    if(temp1->data>temp2->data)
     {
     if(temp1==head)//first node
```

```
      {
       swap(temp1,temp2,temp);
       head=temp2;
       temp3=head;
      }
      else
      {
       swap(temp1,temp2,temp);
       temp3->next=temp2;
       temp3=temp3->next;
      }
    }
    if(temp1->data<temp2->data)
    {
     temp3=temp1;
     temp1=temp1->next;
    }
    temp2=temp1->next;
    if(temp2==current)
     current=temp1;
  }
 }
 return head;
}

void swap(node *temp1,node *temp2,node *temp)
{
    temp=temp2->next;
    temp2->next=temp1;
    temp1->next=temp;
}
```

Example 5.2.1 *Write a C function to find the maximum element in the linked list.*

Solution :

```
void maxElement(node *root)
{
        node *temp;
        int Maxval;
        temp=root;
        Maxval=temp->data;
        while(temp!=NULL)
        {
                if(temp->data>Maxval)
                {
                        Maxval=temp->data;
                }
```

```
        temp=temp->next;
    }
    printf("\n Maximum Value is: %d",Maxval);
}
```

Example 5.2.2 *Write a C function to find the product of all the elements in the linked list.*

Solution :

```
void Product(node *root)
{
    node *temp;
    int p=1;
    temp=root;
    while(temp!=NULL)
    {
        p=p*temp->data;
        temp=temp->next;
    }
    printf("\n Product of all the elements: %d",p);
}
```

Example 5.2.3 *Write an algorithm to swap two nodes n and n + 1 in a singly linked list.*

GTU : Summer-18, Marks 4

Solution :

1. Enter the number n that denotes the node n.
2. Mark **Prev** to the previous node of n.
3. Traverse through the linked list from start to n^{th} node. Mark n^{th} node as **temp**.
4. Set (Prev→next) = (temp→next)
5. temp→next = (temp→next) → next
6. (Prev→next)→next = temp

For example n = 2

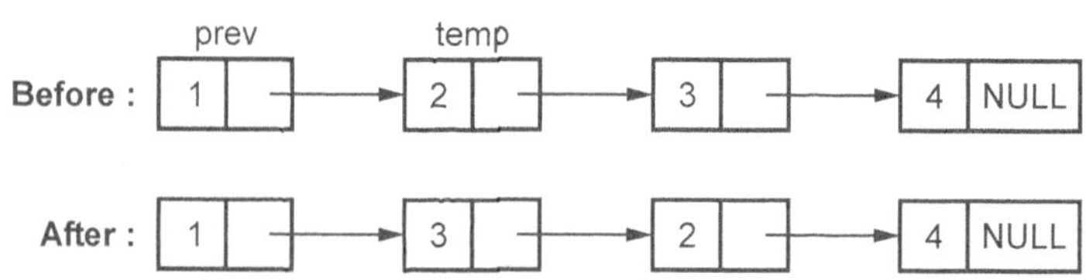

Review Questions

1. *Given a linked list whose typical node consists of an INFO and LINK field. Formulate an algorithm which will count the number of nodes in the list.* **GTU : Winter-17, Marks 7**

5.2.2 Difference between Linked List and Arrays

The comparison between linked list and arrays is as shown below -

Sr. No.	Linked List	Array
1.	The linked list is a collection of nodes and each node is having one data field and next link field. For example 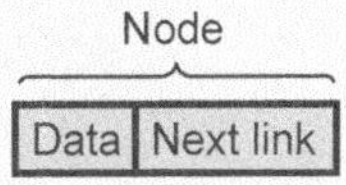	The array is a collection of similar types of data elements. In arrays the data is always stored at some index of the array. For example 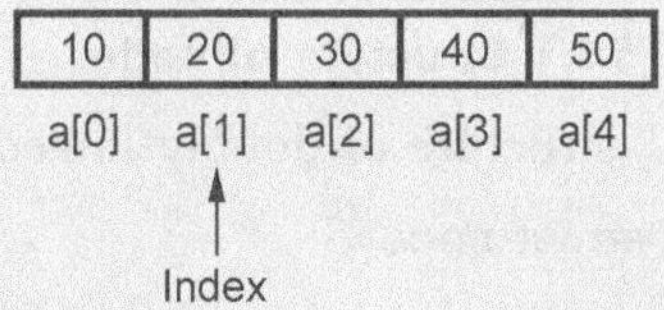
2.	Any element can be accessed by sequential access only.	Any element can be accessed randomly i.e. with the help of index of the array.
3.	Physically the data can be deleted.	Only logical deletion of the data is possible.
4.	Insertions and deletion of data is easy	Insertions and deletion of data is difficult.
5.	Memory allocation is dynamic. Hence developer can allocate as well as deallocate the memory. And so no wastage of memory is there.	The memory allocation is static. Hence once the fixed amount of size is declared then that much memory is allocated. Therefore there is a chance of either memory wastage or memory shortage.

Review Questions

1. *Write an algorithm to insert an element into a singly linked list.* **GTU : Dec.-10, Marks 4**
2. *Write a program to count the number of nodes in a linked list.* **GTU : May-11, Marks 4**
3. *Write an algorithm to "Insert a node at End" operation of singly linked list* **GTU : Winter-13, Marks 7**
4. *Write a 'C' functions to insert a node at beginning in singly linked list .* **GTU : Summer-15, Marks 4**
5. *Write a program to insert and delete an element after a given node in a singly linked list.* **GTU : Winter-15, Marks 7**
6. *Differentiate between arrays and linked list.* **GTU : Winter-15, Marks 4**
7. *Write down advantages of linked list over array and explain it in detail.* **GTU : Winter-14, Marks 7**

5.3 Doubly Linked List

GTU : Winter-12,14,15,16,17,18 Summer-14,15,16,18 CE : Dec.-03, 05,10,May-12, Marks 7

- The doubly linked list has two link fields.
- One link field is previous pointer and the other link field is that next pointer.
- The typical structure of each node in doubly linked list is like this.

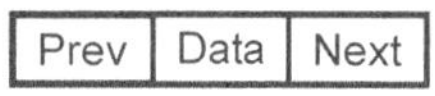

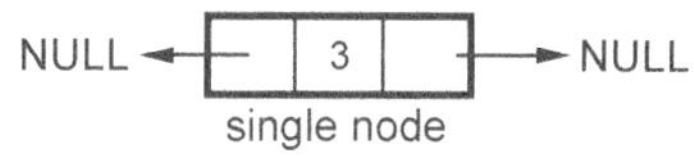

Fig. 5.3.1 Structure of node

- 'C' structure of doubly linked list :

```
typedef struct node
{
        int data;
        struct node *prev;
        struct node *next;
}dnode;
```

- The **linked representation** of a doubly linked list is

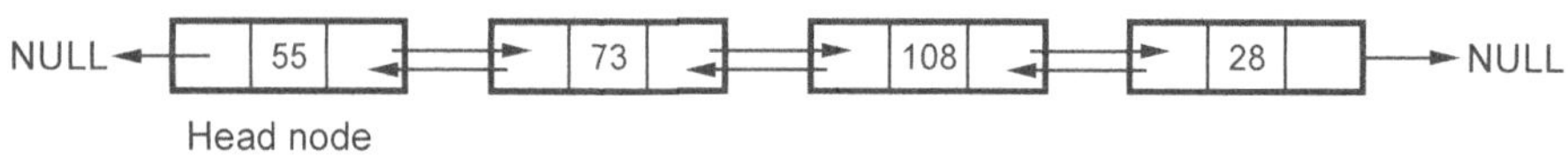

Thus the doubly linked list can traverse in both the directions, forward as well as backwards.

Now, there may be one question in your mind that how do the empty doubly circular linked lists look ? Here is the representation.

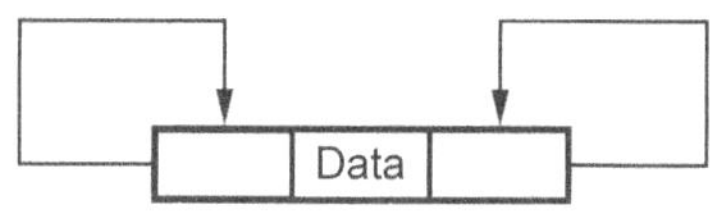

That means the prev and next pointers are pointing to the self node.

Logic for doubly linked list :

In doubly linked list there are following operations.

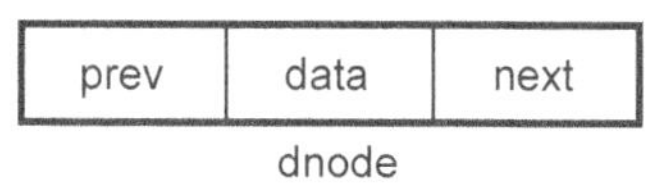

1) add 2) display 3) delete

Step 1 : Each node in doubly linked list will look like this

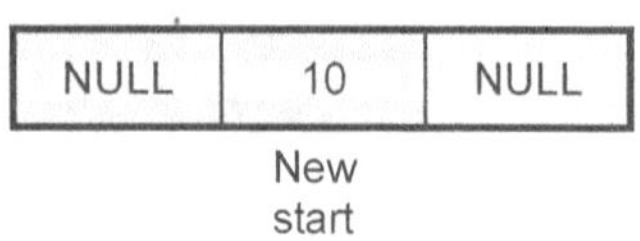

Step 2 : Set a new node as

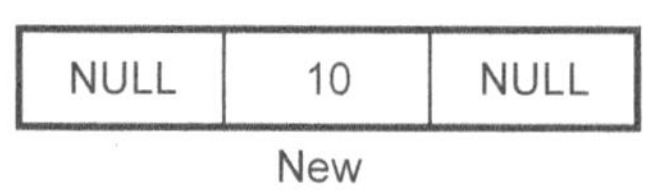

Initially a flag is taken to check whether it is a first node in variable first, as first = 0;

As soon as the very first node gets created we reset the first. i.e. first = 1;

Step 3 : For further addition of the nodes the New node is created.

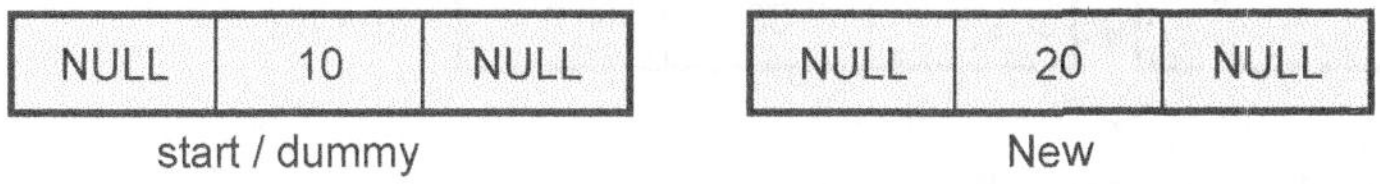

Step 4 : For further addition, the New node is created

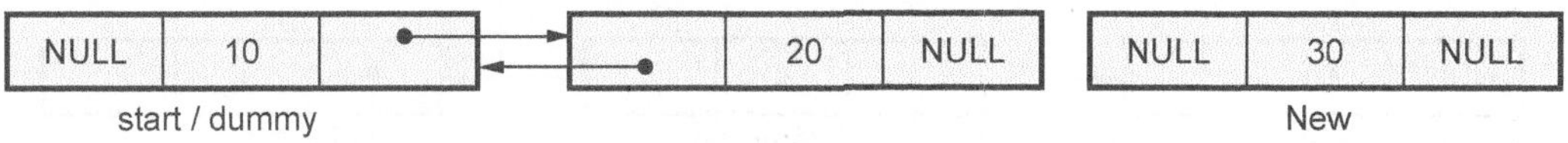

When $\quad$ dummy → next! = NULL

dummy $\quad$ = $\quad$ dummy → next

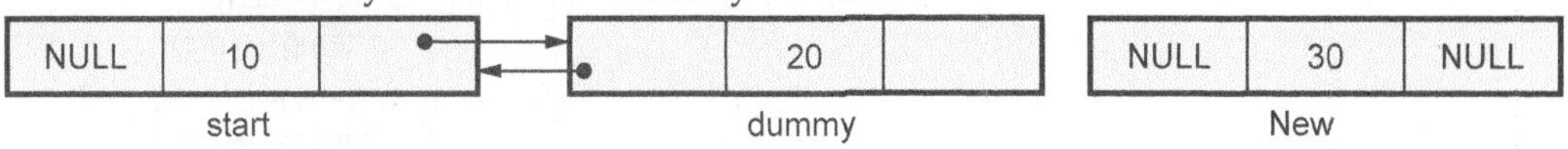

Then attach new node in the linked list.

Thus the doubly linked list can be created.

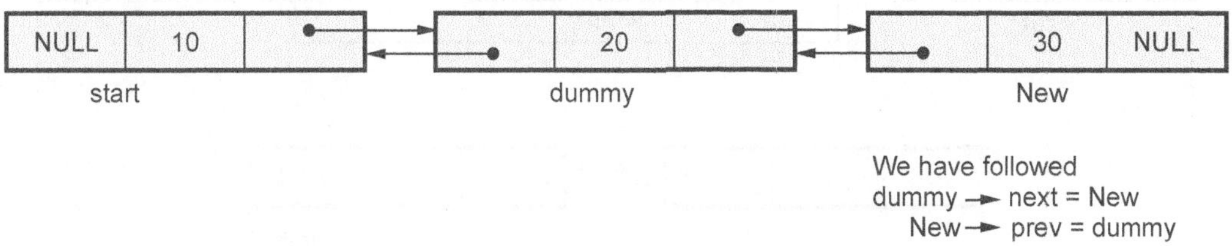

For deletion operation :

Step 1 : We assume the linked list as

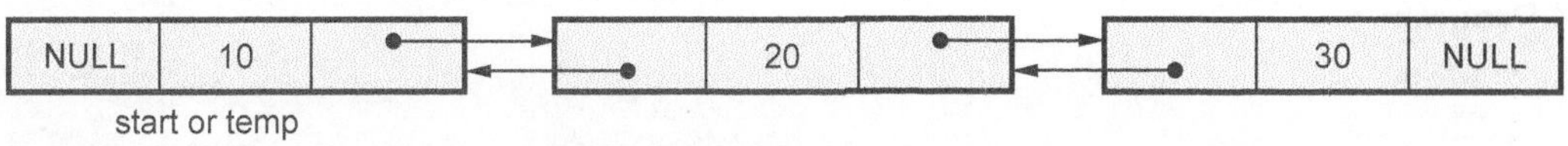

If the very first node has to be deleted, then

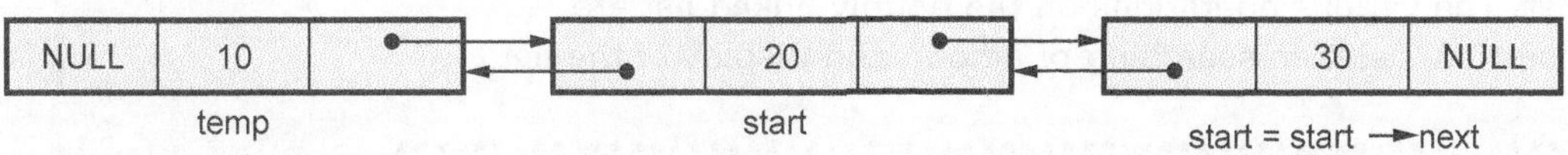

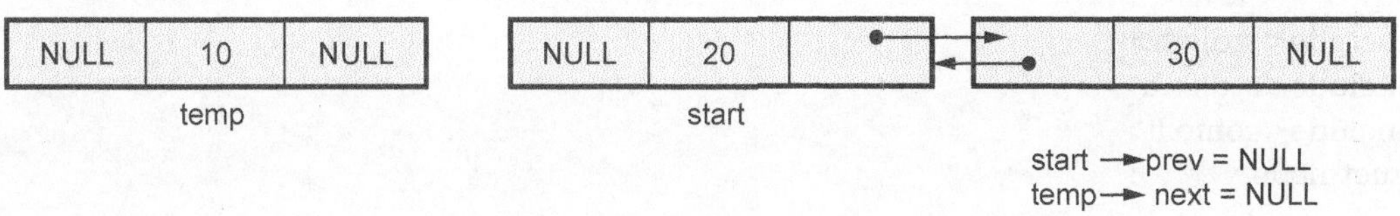

Step 2 : If we want to delete any node other than the first node then

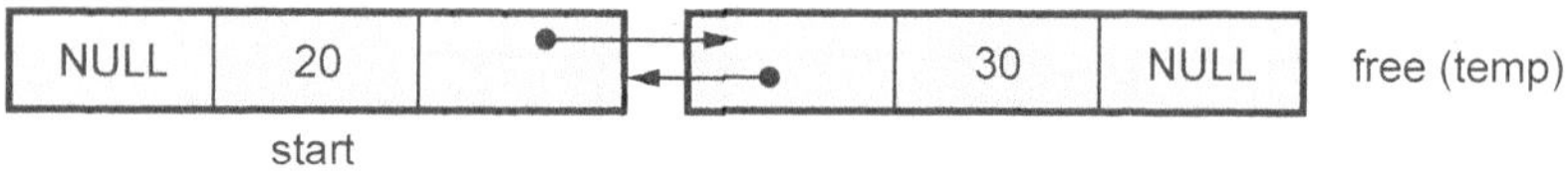

If we want to delete the node than 20 call it as temp node.

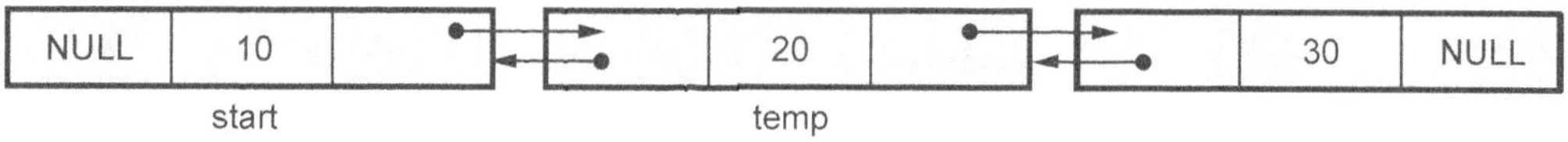

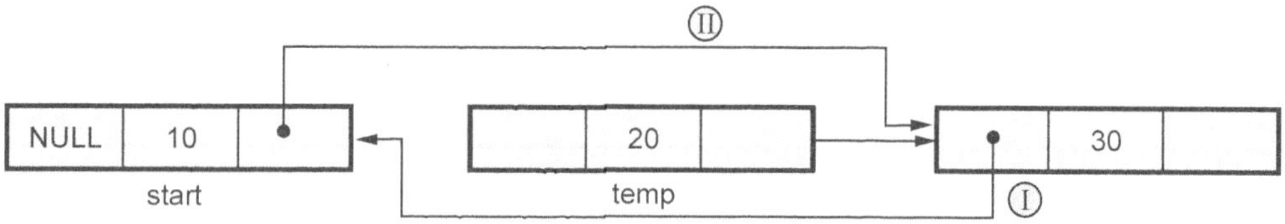

(I) (temp →next) →prev
= temp→ prev

(II) (temp→ prev)→ next
= temp → next

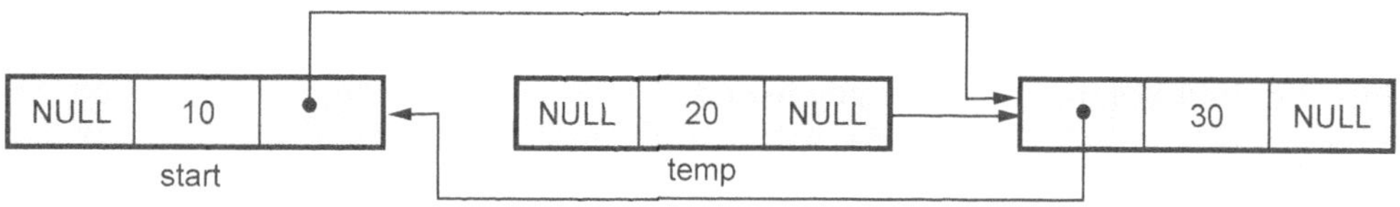

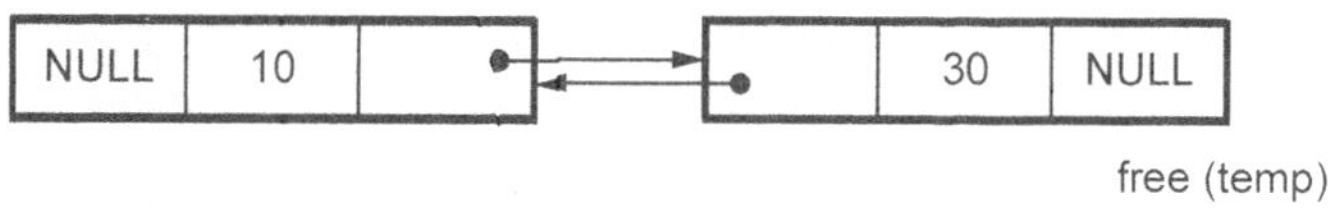

Thus the node 20 gets deleted!

- Based on this logic the C program can be written as follows -

'C' Program :

```
/*
******************************************************************
 Program Is To Perform Various Operations On a Doubly Linked
 List. The various operations on the doubly linked list are
 insertion, deletion,searching of a node and display of the list.

******************************************************************
*/
#include<stdio.h>
#include<stdlib.h>
#include<conio.h>
struct node
```

```
{
 int data;
 struct node *next,*prev;
}*New,*new1,*temp,*start,*dummy;

void add(void);
struct node *get_node();
void display(void);
void delet(void);
int find(int);
int first =1;
void main()
{
  char ans;
  int choice,num,found=0;
  start=NULL;
  do
  {
   clrscr();
   printf("\n \t   Program For Doubly Linked List     \n");
   printf("\n\n 1.Insertion Of Element \n\n");
   printf("2. Deletion Of element from the List\n\n");
   printf(" 3. Display Of Doubly Linked List\n\n");
   printf(" 4. Searching Of a Particular node
              in Doubly Linked List\n\n");
   printf(" 5.Exit");
   printf("\n Enter Your Choice");
   scanf("%d",&choice);
   switch(choice)
   {
       case 1 : add();
                 break;
       case 2 :delet();
                break;
       case 3 :display();
                break;
       case 4 :printf("\n Enter The number
                          which is to be searched");
                scanf("%d",&num);
                temp=start;
                while((temp!=NULL) && (found==0))
                  found=find(num);
                if(found)
                 printf("\n The number is present in the list");
                else
                 printf("\n The number is not present in the list");
                break;
```

```
      case 5:exit(0);
  }
  printf("\nDo you want to continue?\n");
  ans = getche();
  }while(ans == 'y' || ans == 'Y');
 getch();
}
void add(void)
{
 clrscr();
 New =get_node();
 printf("\n\n\n\tEnter the element\n");
 scanf("%d",&New->data);
 if(first ==1)/*insertion of starting node*/
 {
   start= New;
   first =0;
 }
 else
 {
  dummy=start;
  while(dummy->next != NULL)
  dummy=dummy->next;
  dummy->next=New;
  New->prev=dummy;
 }
}
struct node *get_node()
{
 new1=(node *) malloc(sizeof(struct node));
 new1->next = NULL;
 new1->prev=NULL;
 return(new1);
}
void display(void)
{
 clrscr();
 temp = start;
 if(temp == NULL)
   printf("\n The Doubly Linked List Is Empty\n");
 else
 {
  while(temp !=NULL)
  {
   printf("    %d =>    ",temp->data);
   temp = temp->next;
  }
```

```
 printf("NULL");
 }
 getch();
}
int find(int num)
{
       if (temp -> data == num )
        return(1);
       else
        temp=temp -> next;
       return 0;
}
void delet(void)
{
 int num,flag=0;
 int found;
 int last=0;
 clrscr();
 temp = start;
 if(temp == NULL)
  printf("\n\nSorry:DLL not created!\n");
 else
 {
  printf("Enter the number to be deleted ");
  scanf("%d",&num);

  while ((flag ==0 ) && (temp != NULL))
  {
       found=find(num);
       flag=found;
  }
  if (found==0)
        printf("\n Number not found ");
       else
       {
        if (temp==start)  /*deleting the start node*/
       {
       start=start->next;
       temp->next=NULL;
       start->prev=NULL;
       free(temp);
       getch();
       printf("\n The starting node is deleted");
       }
         else
       {
        if(temp->next==NULL)
```

```
        last=1;     /*keeping last flag for the last node*/
        else
        last=0;
      (temp -> next) -> prev=temp -> prev;
      ( temp -> prev) -> next=temp ->next;
      temp -> prev=NULL;
      temp -> next=NULL;
      free(temp);
      if(last)
      printf("\n The last node is deleted");
      else
      printf("\n The intermediate node is deleted");
      }
  }
 }
}
/****************** End Of The Program ********************/
```

Output

```
        Program For Doubly Linked List

 1. Insertion Of Element
 2. Deletion Of element from the List
 3. Display Of Doubly Linked List
 4. Searching Of a Particular node in Doubly Linked List
 5. Exit
 Enter Your Choice1
      Enter the element
11
Do you want to continue?
        Program For Doubly Linked List
 1. Insertion Of Element
 2. Deletion Of element from the List
 3. Display Of Doubly Linked List
 4. Searching Of a Particular node in Doubly Linked List
 5. Exit
 Enter Your Choice1
      Enter the element
22
Do you want to continue?
        Program For Doubly Linked List
 1. Insertion Of Element
 2. Deletion Of element from the List
 3. Display Of Doubly Linked List
 4. Searching Of a Particular node in Doubly Linked List
 5. Exit
```

```
 Enter Your Choice1
        Enter the element
33
Do you want to continue?
           Program For Doubly Linked List

 1. Insertion Of Element
 2. Deletion Of element from the List
 3. Display Of Doubly Linked List
 4. Searching Of a Particular node in Doubly Linked List
 5. Exit
 Enter Your Choice3
     11 =>        22 =>        33 =>    NULL
Do you want to continue?
           Program For Doubly Linked List
 1. Insertion Of Element
 2. Deletion Of element from the List
 3. Display Of Doubly Linked List
 4. Searching Of a Particular node in Doubly Linked List
 5. Exit
 Enter Your Choice4
 Enter The number which is to be searched22
 The number is present in the list
Do you want to continue?
           Program For Doubly Linked List
 1. Insertion Of Element
 2. Deletion Of element from the List
 3. Display Of Doubly Linked List
 4. Searching Of a Particular node in Doubly Linked List
 5. Exit
 Enter Your Choice4
 Enter The number which is to be searched99
 The number is not present in the list
Do you want to continue?
           Program For Doubly Linked List
 1. Insertion Of Element
 2. Deletion Of element from the List
 3. Display Of Doubly Linked List
 4. Searching Of a Particular node in Doubly Linked List
 5. Exit
 Enter Your Choice2
Enter the number to be deleted 22
 The intermediate node is deleted
Do you want to continue?
     11 =>        33 =>    NULL
Enter the number to be deleted 33
```

```
 The last node is deleted
Do you want to continue?
          Program For Doubly Linked List
 1. Insertion Of Element
 2. Deletion Of element from the List
 3. Display Of Doubly Linked List
 4. Searching Of a Particular node in Doubly Linked List
 5. Exit
 Enter Your Choice3
      11 =>    NULL
Do you want to continue?
n
```

Review Questions

1. *Write 'C' functions to implement DELETE_FIRST_NODE and TRAVERSE operations in doubly linked list.* **GTU : Summer-16, Marks 4**
2. *Write algorithm(s) to perform INSERT_FIRST (to insert a node at the first position) and REVERSE_TRAVERSE (to display the data in nodes in reverse order) operations in doubly linked list.* **GTU : Winter-16, Marks 4**
3. *What is the need of doubly linked linear list to the left of a specified node whose address is given by variable M. Give details of algorithm.* **GTU : Winter-17, Marks 7**
4. *List the advantages of a doubly linked list over singly linked list.* **GTU : Summer-18, Marks 3**
5. *Write an algorithm for insertion of a node in doubly linked list.* **GTU : Winter-18, Marks 4**
6. *Write an algorithm for deletion of a node in doubly linked list.* **GTU : Winter-18, Marks 4**

5.3.1 Comparison between Singly and Doubly Linked List

Sr. No.	Singly linked list	Doubly linked list
1.	Singly linked list is a collection of nodes and each node is having one data field and next link field. For example : 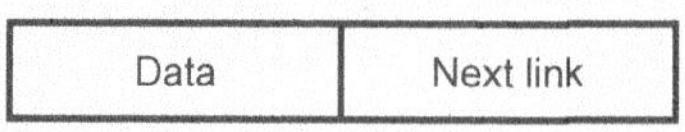	Doubly linked list is a collection of nodes and each node is having one data field, one previous link field and one next link field. For example : 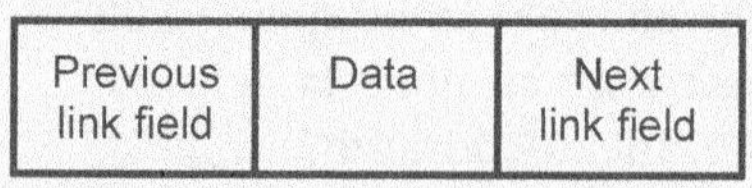
2.	The elements can be accessed using next link.	The elements can be accessed using both previous link as well as next link.

3.	No extra field is required; hence node takes less memory in SLL.	One field is required to store previous link hence node takes more memory in DLL.
4.	Less efficient access to elements.	More efficient access to elements.

Example 5.3.1 *What are the advantages of doubly linked list. Write a C function to find the maximum element from doubly linked list.* **GTU : Winter-12, Marks 7**

Solution : Each node of doubly linked list has two pointers- next node pointer and previous node pointer. Due to these two pointers the entire list can be scanned from left to right or from right to left.

The operations such as deletion of a node and searching of particular node become efficient.

```
void MaxNode(node *head)
{
  node *temp;
  temp=head;
  int maxelement=temp->data;//Assume first element as max element
  while(temp!=NULL)
  {
     if(temp->data>maxelement)
     {
          maxelement=temp->data;
     }
     temp=temp->next;
  }
}
```

Example 5.3.2 *Write a program in any programming language to concatenate two doubly linked lists.* **GTU : Summer-14, Marks 7**

Solution :

```
#include<stdio.h>
#include<stdlib.h>
#include<conio.h>
struct node
{
 int data;
 struct node *prev;
 struct node *next;
};

void main()
{
      char ch;
      int choice;
      struct node *head1,*head2,*head,*New,*temp;
      struct node *Create(void);
```

```
    void Display(struct node *);
    struct node *concat(struct node *, struct node *);
    head=NULL;
    head1=NULL;
    head2=NULL;
    do
    {
     printf(" 1. Creation  of Doubly Linked List \n\n");
     printf(" 2. Display of  List\n\n");
     printf(" 3. Concatenation of two lists \n\n");
     printf(" 4. Exit");
     printf("\n Enter Your Choice");
     scanf("%d",&choice);
     switch(choice)
     {
         case 1 :       printf("\n Create First DLL");
                          head1=Create();
                          printf("\n Create Second DLL");
                          head2=Create();
                          break;
         case 2 :     Display(head1);
                          Display(head2);
                          break;
         case 3 :     head=concat(head1,head2);
                          Display(head);
                          break;
         case 4 :     exit(0);
     }
     printf("\nDo you want to go to Main Menu?\n");
     ch = getch();
  }while(ch == 'y' || ch == 'Y');
}
struct node *Create()
{
  char ans;
  int flag=1;
  struct node *head,*New,*temp;
  struct node *get_node();
  clrscr();
  do
  {
     New = get_node();
     printf("\n\n\n\tEnter The Element\n");
     scanf("%d",&New->data);
     if(flag==1)   /*flag for setting the starting node*/
     {
         head = New;
```

```
            flag=0;/*reset flag*/
        }
        else            /* find last node in list */
        {
         temp=head;
         while (temp->next != NULL)/*finding the last node*/
                temp=temp->next; /*temp is a last node*/
         temp->next=New;
         New->prev=temp;
        }
        printf("\n Do you want to enter more nodes?");
        ans=getch();
        }while(ans=='y'||ans=='Y');
  return head;
}
struct node *get_node()
{
  struct node *New;
  New =(node *) malloc(sizeof(struct node));
  New->next = NULL;
  New->prev = NULL;
  return(New);/*created node is returned to calling
          function*/
}
void Display(struct node *head)
{
        struct node *temp;
        temp = head;
        if(temp == NULL)
         printf("\n Sorry ,The List Is Empty\n");
        else
        {
         while(temp!=NULL)
         {
          printf("%d\t",temp->data);
          temp=temp->next;
         }
        }
}
struct node *concat(node *head1,node *head2)
{
   struct node *temp;
   temp=head1;
   while(temp->next!=NULL)
    temp=temp->next;
   temp->next=head2;
   head2->prev=temp;
   return head1;
}
```

Review Questions

1. *Write a program to do following in a doubly linked list.*
   i) Print the node contents from right to left ii) Insert a node at the specified position.
   iii) Delete the node having value X. **GTU : CE : Dec.-03, Marks 9, Dec.-05, Marks 8**
2. *Write an algorithm to delete an element into a doubly linked list.*
   GTU : Dec.-10, Marks 4, Winter-14, Marks 7
3. *Write the difference between singly and doubly linked list.* **GTU : May-12, Marks 7**
4. *Write 'C' functions to : (1) insert a node at the end (2) delete a node from the beginning of a doubly linked list.* **GTU : Summer-15, Marks 7**
5. *Create a doubly circularly linked list and write a function to traverse it.*
   GTU : Winter-15, Marks 7

5.4 Circular Linked List

GTU : Dec.-03, 06, 10, May-11, 12, Summer-18, Winter-16 Marks 7

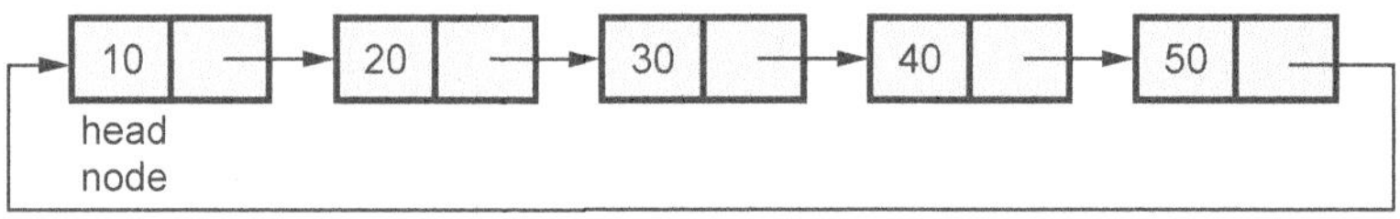

The circular linked list is as shown below -

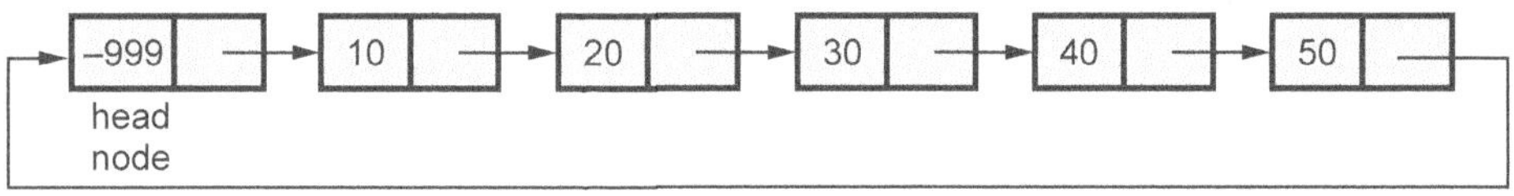

or

The Circular Linked List (CLL) is similar to singly linked list except that the last node's next pointer points to first node.

Various operations that can be performed on circular linked list are

1. Creation of circular linked list.
2. Insertion of a node in circular linked list.
3. Deletion of any node from linked list.
4. Display of circular linked list.

We will see each operation along with some example.

1. Creation of circular linked list

```
struct node *Create()
{
 char ans;
 int flag=1;
 struct node *head,*New,*temp;
 struct node *get_node();
 clrscr();
 do
```

```
New = get_node();
        printf("\n\n\n\tEnter The Element\n");
        scanf("%d",&New->data);
        if(flag==1)/*flag for setting the starting node*/
        {
                head = New;
                New->next=head;
                  flag=0;/*reset flag*/
        }
        else            /* find last node in list */
        {
         temp=head;
         while (temp->next != head)/*finding the last node*/
                temp=temp->next; /*temp is a last node*/
         temp->next=New;/*attaching the  node*/
         New->next=head; /*each time making the list
                    circular*/
        }
        printf("\n Do you want to enter more nodes?");
        ans=getch();
  }while(ans=='y'||ans=='Y');
  return head;
}
/* function used while allocating memory for a node*/
struct node *get_node()
{
 struct node *New;
 New =(node *) malloc(sizeof(struct node));
 New->next = NULL;
 return(New);/*created node is returned to calling function*/
}
```

Creating a single node in linked list

Initially we will allocate memory for **New** node using a function **get_node ( )** . There is one variable **flag** whose purpose is to check whether first node is created or not. That means flag is 1 (set) then first node is not created. Therefore after creation of first node we have to reset the flag (making flag = 0).

Initially

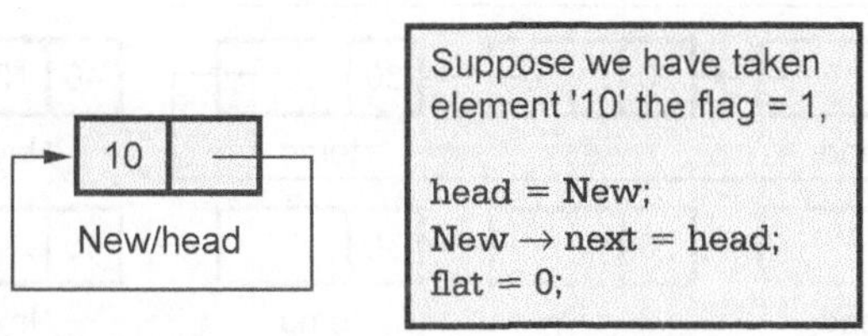

Here variable **head** indicates starting node.

Now as flag = 0, we can further create the nodes and attach them as follows.

When we have taken element '20'

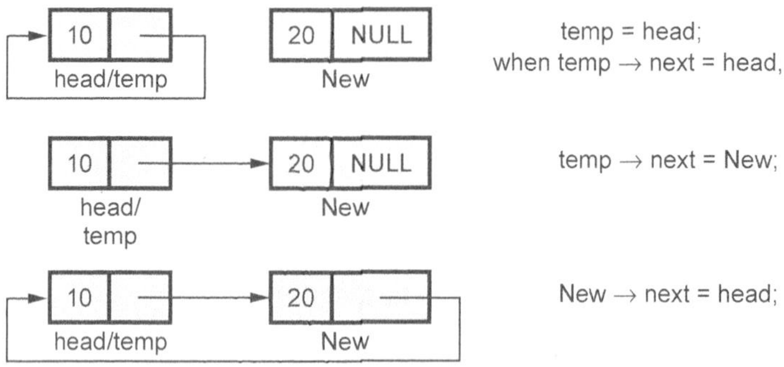

If we want to insert 30 then

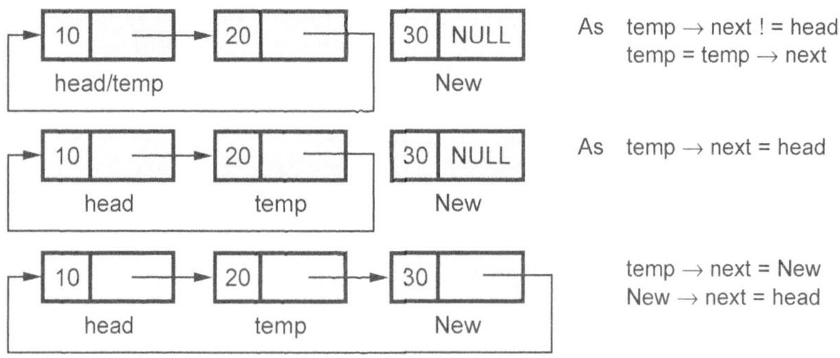

If we want to insert 40 then

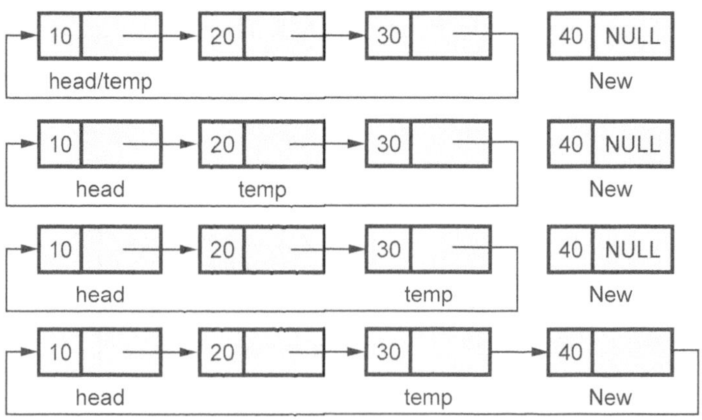

Thus we can create a circular linked list by inserting one more element 50. It is as shown below -

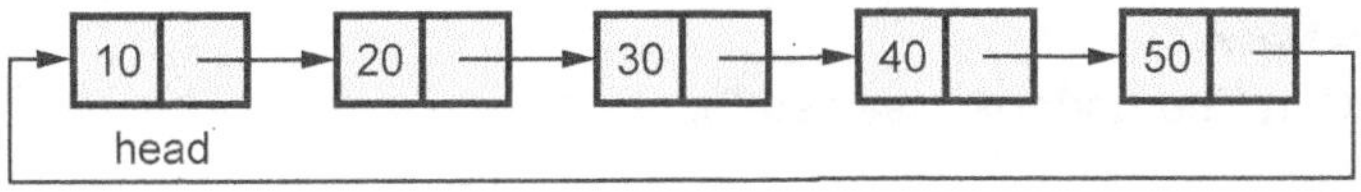

2. Display of circular linked list

```
void Display(struct node *head)
{
	struct node *temp;
	temp = head;
	if(temp == NULL)
	 printf("\n Sorry ,The List Is Empty\n");
	else
	{
	 do
	 {
		printf("%d\t",temp->data);
		temp = temp->next;
	 }while(temp != head);
	}
	getch();
}
```

3. Insertion of circular linked list

While inserting a node in the linked list, there are 3 cases -

a) inserting a node as a head node

b) inserting a node as a last node

c) inserting a node at intermediate position

The functions for these cases is as given below -

```
struct node *insert_head(struct node *head)
{
 struct node *get_node();
 struct node *New,*temp;
 New=get_node();
 printf("\n Enter The element which you want to insert ");
 scanf("%d",&New->data);
 if(head==NULL)
	head=New;
 else
{

		temp=head;
		while(temp->next!=head)
```

```
            temp=temp->next;
        temp->next=New;
        New->next=head;
        head=New;
        printf("\n The node is inserted!");
 }
 return head;
}
/*Insertion of node at last position*/
void insert_last(struct node *head)
{
    struct node *New,*temp;
    New=get_node();
    printf("\n Enter The element which you want to insert ");
    scanf("%d",&New->data);
    if(head==NULL)
        head=New;
    else
    {

         temp=head;
     while(temp->next!=head)
             temp=temp->next;
     temp->next=New;
     New->next=head;
     printf("\n The node is inserted!");
    }
}
void insert_after(struct node *head)
{
    int key;
    struct node *New,*temp;
    New= get_node();
    printf("\n Enter The element which you want to insert ");
    scanf("%d",&New->data);
    if(head==NULL)
    {
     head=New;
    }
    else

    {
     printf("\n Enter The element after which you want to insert the node ");
     scanf("%d",&key);
     temp=head;
     do
     {
```

```
            if(temp->data==key)
            {
                New->next=temp->next;
                temp->next=New;
                printf("\n The node is inserted");
                return;
            }
            else
                 temp=temp->next;
        }while(temp!=head);
    }
}
```

Suppose linked list is already created as -

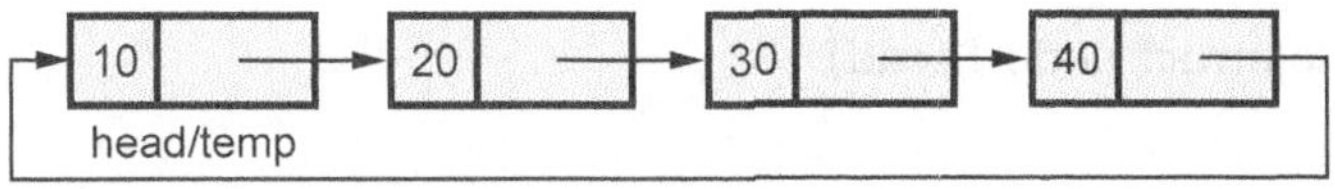

If we want to insert a **New** node as a head node then,

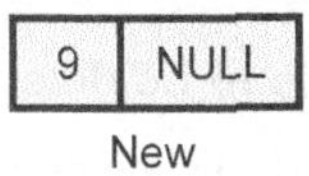

Then

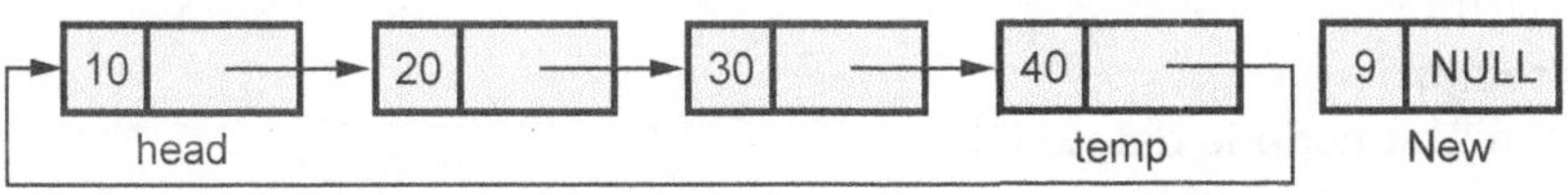

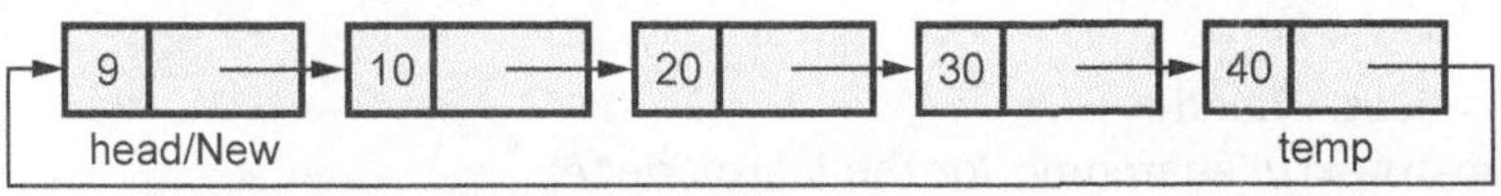

temp → next = New;
New → next = head;
head = New;

If we want to insert a New node as a last node consider a linked list

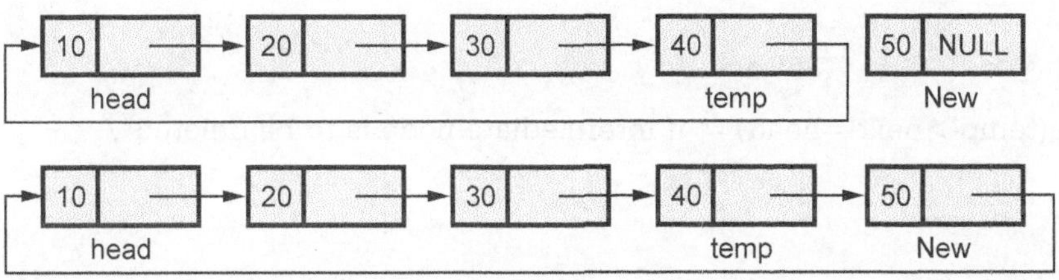

If we want to insert an element 35 after node 30 then

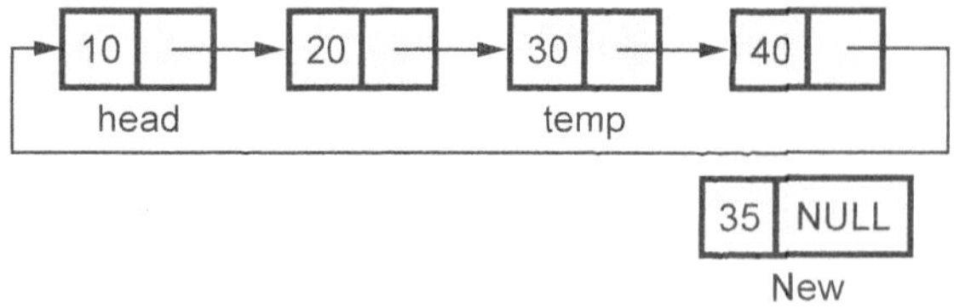

As key = 30
and temp → data = 30

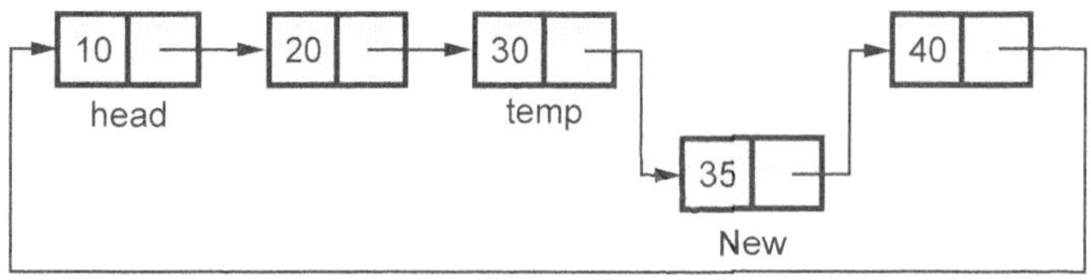

New → next = temp → next;
temp → next = New;

4. Deletion of any node

```
struct node *Delete(struct node *head)
{
 int key;
 struct node *temp,*temp1;
 printf("\n Enter the element which is to be deleted");
 scanf("%d",&key);
 temp=head;
if(temp->data==key)/*If header node is to be deleted*/
 {
        temp1=temp->next;
        if(temp1==temp)
```

If a single node is present in the list and we want to delete it

```
        {
               temp=NULL;
               head=temp;
               printf("\n The node is deleted");
        }
       else
        {
               while(temp->next!=head)
                 temp=temp->next;/*searching for the last node*/
               temp->next=temp1;
          head=temp1;/*new head*/
               printf("\n The node is deleted");
        }
 }
 else
 {
       while(temp->next!=head) /* if intermediate node is to be deleted*/
```

```
    {
      if((temp->next)->data==key)
      {
          temp1=temp->next;
          temp->next=temp1->next;
          temp1->next=NULL;
          free(temp1);
          printf("\n The node is deleted");
      }
      else
          temp=temp->next;


    }
}
return head;
}
```

> The previous node of the node to be deleted is searched.
> temp1 is the node to be deleted

Suppose we have created a linked list as

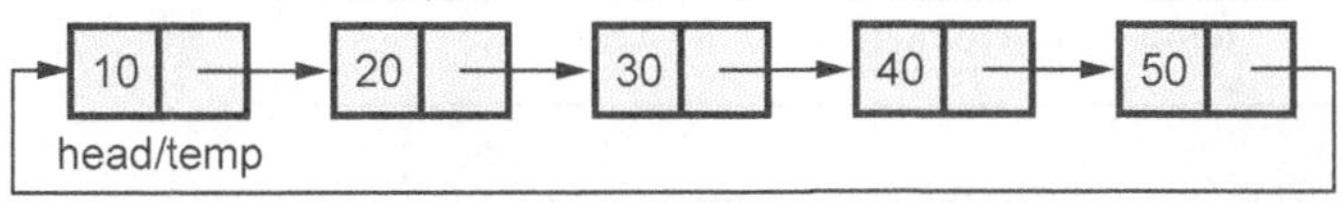

If we want to delete temp → data i.e. node 10 then,

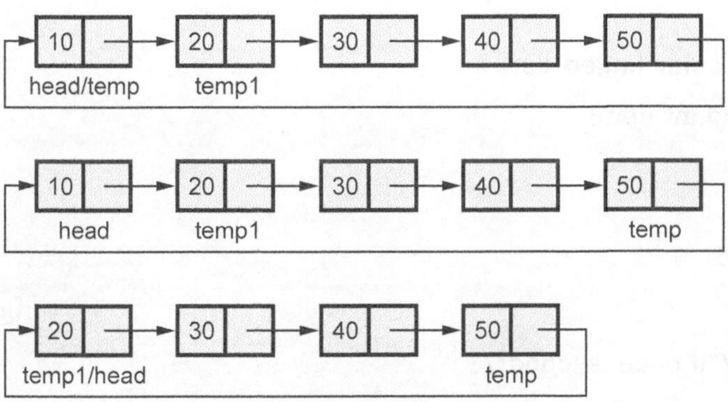

temp1 = temp → next;

while (temp → next ! head)
temp = temp → next;

temp → next = temp1;
head = temp1;

If we want to delete an intermediate node from a linked list which is given below

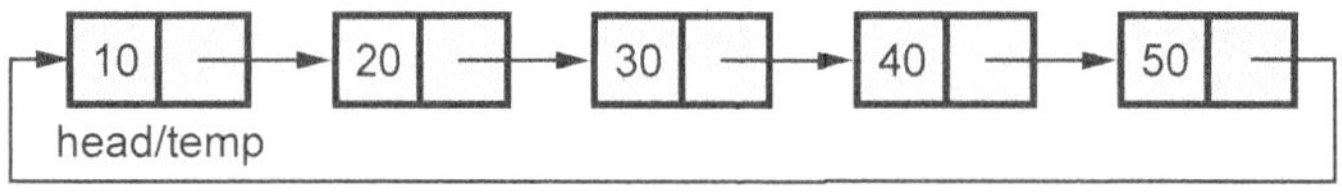

We want to delete node with '30' then

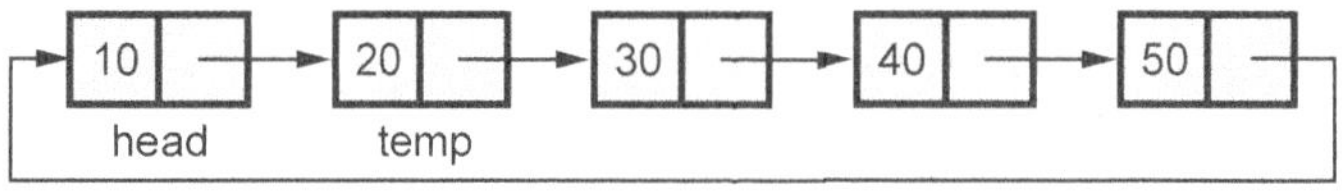

Key = 30
and
temp → next → data
= key, hence

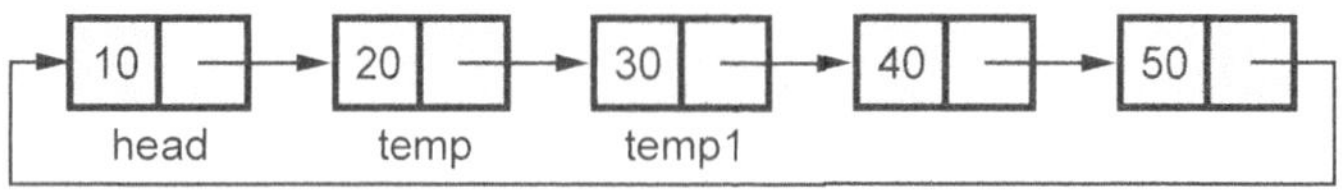

temp1 = temp → next;

Now

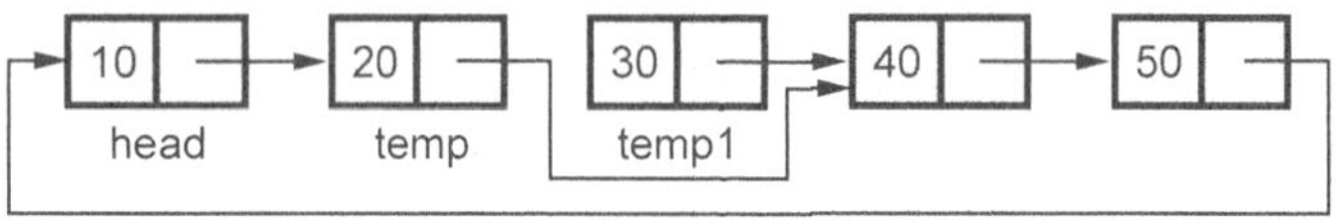

temp → next
= temp1 → next;

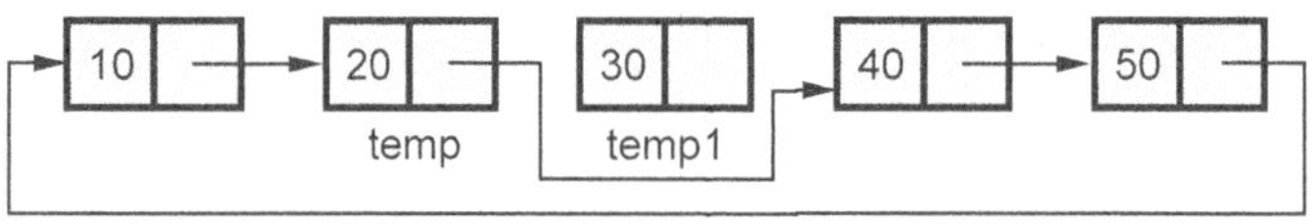

temp1 → next = NULL

Then free (temp1); / * to deallocate memory */

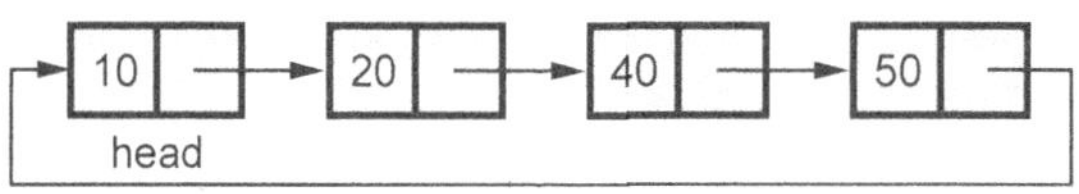

Thus node with value 30 is deleted from CLL.

The linked list can be -

5. Searching a node from circular linked list

```
struct node *Search(node *head,int num)
{
        struct node *temp;
        temp=head;
        while(temp->next!=head)
        {
         if(temp->data == num)
                    return temp;/*if node is found*/
         else
                    temp=temp->next;
        }
 return NULL;
}
```

while searching a node from circular linked list we go on comparing the data field of each node starting from the **head** node. If the node containing desired data is found we return the address of that node to calling function.

'C' Program

```
/*
***********************************************************
 Program To Perform The Various Operations On The Circular Linked List
***********************************************************
*/
#include<stdio.h>
#include<stdlib.h>
#include<conio.h>
struct node
{
 int data;
 struct node *next;
};

void main()
{
	char ch;
	int num,choice;
	struct node *head, *New,*temp;
	struct node *Create(void);
	void Display(struct node *);
	struct node *Insert(node *);
	struct node *Delete(struct node *);
	struct node *Search(struct node *,int);
	head=NULL;
	do
	{
	 clrscr();
	 printf("\n Program For Circular Linked List\n");
	 printf(" 1.Insertion of any node\n\n");
	 printf(" 2. Display of Circular List\n\n");
	 printf(" 3. Insertion of a node in Circular List\n\n");
	 printf(" 4. Deletion of any node \n\n");
	 printf(" 5. Searching a Particular Element in The  List\n\n");
	 printf(" 6.Exit");
	 printf("\n Enter Your Choice");
	 scanf("%d",&choice);
	 switch(choice)
	 {
		case 1 :head=Create();
			break;
```

```
        case 2 :Display(head);
                break;
        case 3:head=Insert(head);
                break;
        case 4:head=Delete(head);
                break;
        case 5:printf("\n Enter The Element Which Is To
        Be Searched ");
             scanf("%d",&num);
                temp=Search(head,num);
                if(temp!=NULL)
                  printf("\n The node is present");
                else
                  printf("\n The node is not present");
                break;
        case 6:exit(0);
    }
    printf("\nDo you want to go to Main Menu?\n");
    ch = getch();
}while(ch == 'y' || ch == 'Y');
}
struct node *Create()
{
char ans;
int flag=1;
struct node *head,*New,*temp;
struct node *get_node();
clrscr();
do
{
    New = get_node();
    printf("\n\n\n\tEnter The Element\n");
    scanf("%d",&New->data);
    if(flag==1)   /*flag for setting the starting node*/
    {
        head = New;
        New->next=head;  /*the circular list of a single node*/
        flag=0;/*reset flag*/
    }
    else            /* find last node in list */
    {
     temp=head;
     while (temp->next != head)/*finding the last node*/
         temp=temp->next; /*temp is a last node*/
     temp->next=New;
     New->next=head; /*each time making the list circular*/
    }
```

```
        printf("\n Do you want to enter more nodes?");
        ans=getch();
        }while(ans=='y'||ans=='Y');
 return head;
}

struct node *get_node()
{
 struct node *New;
 New =(node *) malloc(sizeof(struct node));
 New->next = NULL;
 return(New);/*created node is returned to calling function*/
}

void Display(struct node *head)
{
        struct node *temp;
        temp = head;
        if(temp == NULL)
         printf("\n Sorry ,The List Is Empty\n");
        else
        {
         do
         {
                printf("%d\t",temp->data);
                temp = temp->next;
         }while(temp != head);/*Circular linked list*/
         }
        getch();
}
struct node *Insert(node *head)
{
 int choice;
 struct node *insert_head(node *);
 void insert_after(struct node *);
 void insert_last(struct node *);
 printf("\n 1. Insert a node as a head node");
 printf("\n 2. Insert a node as a last node");
 printf("\n 3. Insert a node at intermediate position in the linked list");
 printf("\n Enter your choice for insertion of node");
 scanf("%d",&choice);
 switch(choice)
 {
  case 1:head=insert_head(head);
           break;
  case 2:insert_last(head);
          break;
```

```
  case 3:insert_after(head);
         break;
 }
 return head;
}

struct node *insert_head(struct node *head)
{
 struct node *get_node();
 struct node *New,*temp;
 New=get_node();
 printf("\n Enter The element which you want to insert ");
 scanf("%d",&New->data);
 if(head==NULL)
       head=New;
 else
 {
             temp=head;
             while(temp->next!=head)
                    temp=temp->next;
             temp->next=New;
             New->next=head;
             head=New;
             printf("\n The node is inserted!");
 }
 return head;
}
/*Insertion of node at last position*/
void insert_last(struct node *head)
{
       struct node *New,*temp;
       New=get_node();
       printf("\n Enter The element which you want to insert ");
       scanf("%d",&New->data);
       if(head==NULL)
             head=New;
       else
       {
        temp=head;
        while(temp->next!=head)
                    temp=temp->next;
        temp->next=New;
        New->next=head;
        printf("\n The node is inserted!");
       }
}
void insert_after(struct node *head)
```

```
{
 int key;
 struct node *New,*temp;
 New= get_node();
 printf("\n Enter The element which you want to insert ");
 scanf("%d",&New->data);
 if(head==NULL)
 {
    head=New;
 }
 else
 {
      printf("\n Enter The element after which you want to
    insert the node ");
      scanf("%d",&key);
      temp=head;
      do
      {
            if(temp->data==key)
            {
                  New->next=temp->next;
                  temp->next=New;
                  printf("\n The node is inserted");
                  return;
            }
            else
                   temp=temp->next;
    }while(temp!=head);
  }
}

struct node *Search(node *head,int num)
{
      struct node *temp;
      temp=head;
      while(temp->next!=head)
      {
       if(temp->data == num)
         return temp;/*if node is found*/
       else
         temp=temp->next;
      }
 return NULL;
}
struct node *Delete(struct node *head)
{
 int key;
```

```
struct node *temp,*temp1;
printf("\n Enter the element which is to be deleted");
scanf("%d",&key);
temp=head;
if(temp->data==key)/*If header node is to be deleted*/
{
    temp1=temp->next;
    if(temp1==temp)
 /*if single node is present in circular linked list
 and we want to delete it*/
    {
        temp=NULL;
        head=temp;
        printf("\n The node is deleted");
    }
    else /*otherwise*/
    {
     while(temp->next!=head)
       temp=temp->next;/*searching for the last node*/
        temp->next=temp1;
        head=temp1;/*new head*/
        printf("\n The node is deleted");
    }
}
else
{
    while(temp->next!=head) /* if intermediate node is to
                    be deleted*/
    {
    if((temp->next)->data==key)
    {
        temp1=temp->next;
        temp->next=temp1->next;
        temp1->next=NULL;
        free(temp1);
        printf("\n The node is deleted");
    }
    else
        temp=temp->next;
    }
}
return head;
}
```

Output

```
Program For Circular Linked List
 1. Insertion of any node
 2. Display of Circular List
```

```
3. Insertion of a node in Circular List
4. Deletion of any node
5. Searching a Particular Element in The  List
6. Exit
Enter Your Choice 1
     Enter The Element
10
Do you want to enter more nodes?
      Enter The Element
20
Do you want to enter more nodes?
      Enter The Element
30
Do you want to enter more nodes?
      Enter The Element
40
Do you want to enter more nodes?
Do you want to go to Main Menu?
Program For Circular Linked List
1. Insertion of any node
2. Display of Circular List
3. Insertion of a node in Circular List
4. Deletion of any node
5. Searching a Particular Element in The  List
6. Exit
Enter Your Choice 2
10      20      30      40
Do you want to go to Main Menu?
Program For Circular Linked List
1.Insertion of any node
2. Display of Circular List
3. Insertion of a node in Circular List
4. Deletion of any node
5. Searching a Particular Element in The  List
6.Exit
Enter Your Choice 3
1. Insert a node as a head node
2. Insert a node as a last node
3. Insert a node at intermediate position in the linked list
Enter your choice for insertion of node 3
Enter The element which you want to insert 33
Enter The element after which you want to insert the node 30
The node is inserted
Do you want to go to Main Menu?
Program For Circular Linked List
1. Insertion of any node
2. Display of Circular List
```

```
 3. Insertion of a node in Circular List
 4. Deletion of any node
 5. Searching a Particular Element in The  List
 6. Exit
 Enter Your Choice 2
10      20      30      33      40
 Program For Circular Linked List
 1. Insertion of any node
 2. Display of Circular List
 3. Insertion of a node in Circular List
 4. Deletion of any node
 5. Searching a Particular Element in The  List
 6. Exit
 Enter Your Choice 4
 Enter the element which is to be deleted 20
 The node is deleted
Do you want to go to Main Menu?
 Program For Circular Linked List
 1. Insertion of any node
 2. Display of Circular List
 3. Insertion of a node in Circular List
 4. Deletion of any node
 5. Searching a Particular Element in The  List
 6. Exit
 Enter Your Choice 2
10      30      33      40
Do you want to go to Main Menu?
 Program For Circular Linked List
 1. Insertion of any node
 2. Display of Circular List
 3. Insertion of a node in Circular List
 4. Deletion of any node
 5. Searching a Particular Element in The  List
 6. Exit
 Enter Your Choice 5
 Enter The Element Which Is To Be Searched 30
 The node is present
Do you want to go to Main Menu?
 Program For Circular Linked List
 1. Insertion of any node
 2. Display of Circular List
 3. Insertion of a node in Circular List
 4. Deletion of any node
 5. Searching a Particular Element in The  List
 6. Exit
 Enter Your Choice 5
 Enter The Element Which Is To Be Searched 101
```

```
The node is not present
Do you want to go to Main Menu?
Program For Circular Linked List
1. Insertion of any node
2. Display of Circular List
3. Insertion of a node in Circular List
4. Deletion of any node
5. Searching a Particular Element in The  List
6. Exit
Enter Your Choice 6
```

Advantages of Circular Linked List over Singly Linked List

In circular linked list the next pointer of last node points to the head node. Hence we can move from last node to the head node of the list very efficiently. Hence accessing of any node is much faster than singly linked list.

Example 5.4.1 *Write an algorithm for implementing : To concatenate two circularly linked list.* **GTU : Dec.-03, Marks 6**

Solution : The data structure for a node in circular linked list is -

```
typedef  struct cll
{
 int data;
 struct cll *next;
}node;
```

The function for concatenation of two CLL will be -

Algorithm

1. Create two circular linked lists. Let head1 will be the head node of first circular linked list and head2 will be the head node of second circular linked list.
2. For concatenating two CLL, traverse upto the end of first Circular linked list. Then attach the next pointer of the last node of first CLL to starting node of second list.
3. To make this joined list circular, attach the next pointer of last node of second list to head node of first list.
4. Display the concatenated circular linked list.

C function

```
node *concatenate(node *head1,node *head2)
{
 node *temp1,*temp2;
 temp1=head1;
 temp2=head2;
 while(temp1->next!=head1)
   temp1=temp1->next;/*finding last node of first list*/
 temp1->next=head2;/*attaching first list to second list*/
 /*finding last node of second list*/
 while(temp2->next!=head2)
   temp2=temp2->next;
 temp2->next=head1/*making the concatenated
                list circular */
 return head1;
}
```

Example 5.4.2 *Write an algorithm to count the number of nodes in a singly circularly linked list* **GTU : Summer-18, Marks 4**

Solution :

```
void count_nodes(struct node *head)
{
      struct node *temp;
      temp=head;
      count=0;
      if(temp==NULL)
            printf("\n The List is Empty");
      else
      {
            do
            {
                  count++;
                  temp=temp->next;
            }while(temp!=head);
      }
      printf("The total number of nodes are %d",count);
}
```

Review Questions

1. *Explain circular single linked list. Give algorithm for inserting an element in circular linked list* **GTU : Dec.-06, Marks 6**
2. *What is circular linked list ?* **GTU : Dec.-10, Marks 2**
3. *Write an advantage of linked list, doubly linked list and circular linked list.* **GTU : Dec.-10, May-11, Marks 4**

4. *Write an algorithm for inserting and deleting an element into circular linked list.* **GTU : May-12, Marks 7**

5. *Write 'C' functions to implement INSERT_FIRST (to insert a node at the first position), DELETE_FIRST (to delete a node from the first position), DELETE_LAST (delete a node from the last position) and TRAVERSE (to display the data in nodes) operations in circular linked list.* **GTU : Winter-16, Marks 7**

6. *Write a program to implement a circularly linked list.* **GTU : Summer-18, Marks 7**

5.5 Linked Implementation of Stack

GTU : Nov-06, Summer-16,17 Winter-16 Marks 8

Stack is a special case of list and therefore we can represent stack using arrays as well as using linked list. The advantage of implementing stack using linked list is that we need not have to worry about the size of the stack. Since we are using linked list as many elements we want to insert those many nodes can be created. And the nodes are dynamically getting created so there won't be getting any stack full condition.

The typical 'C' structure for linked stack can be

```
struct stack
{
      int data;
      struct stack  next;
}node;
```

Each node consists of data and the next field. Such a node will be inserted in the stack. Following figure represents stack using linked list.

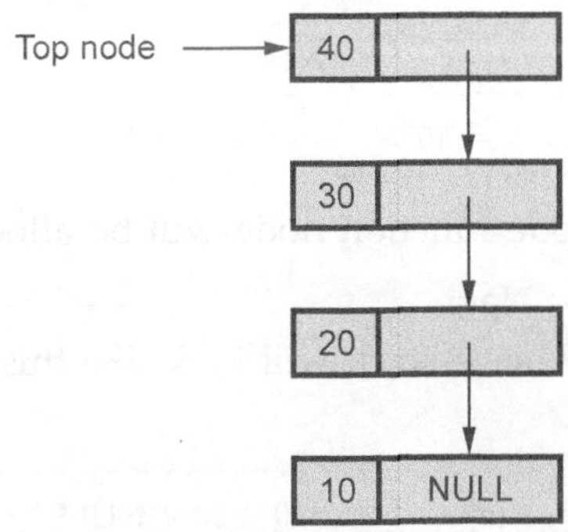

Fig. 5.5.1 Representing linked stack

There are various operations that can be performed on the linked stack. These operations are -

1. Push
2. Pop
3. Stack empty
4. Stack full

1. Push operation

The pseudo code for push operation as given below

```
void Push(int Item, node **top)
{
      node *New;
      node * get_node(int);

      New = get_node(Item);
      New -> next = *top;
   *top = New;
}

node * get_node( int item )
{
      node * temp;
      temp =(node *) malloc(sizeof(node) );
      if ( temp == NULL )
       printf("\nMemory Can not be allocated \n");
      temp -> data = item;


      temp -> next = NULL;
      return( temp);
}
```

The get_node() function is called to allocate the memory for the **New** node

For ex:

10	NULL

New/top

In the main function, when the item to be inserted is entered, a call to push function is given. In push function another function get_node is invoked to allocate the memory for a node as follows :

New

10	NULL

If item = 10, then by get node function node will be allocated.Then

*top = New

This is our new **top** node. Hence stack will look like this

New

top

10	NULL

If again **Push** function is called for pushing the value 20 then

New

20	NULL

top

20	NULL

This can be done using following statements -

```
New->next=*top;
top=New;
```

And we will get

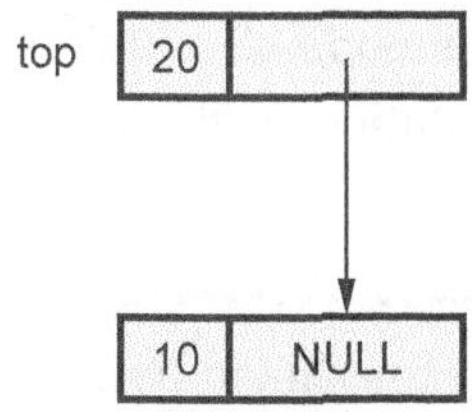

Fig. 5.5.2

When 30 is pushed then

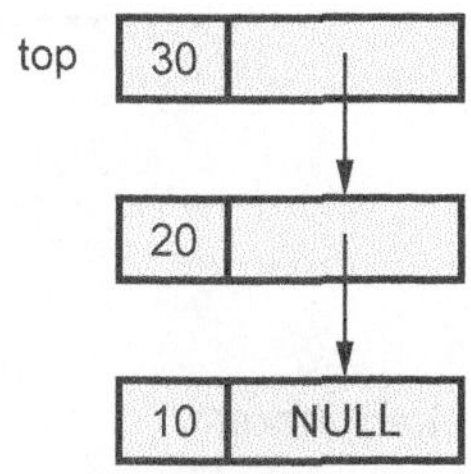

Fig. 5.5.3

Thus by pushing the items repeatedly we can create a stack using linked list.

2. Pop operation

```
int Pop(node **top)
{
    int     item;
    node *temp;
    item = (*top) ->data;
    temp = *top;
    *top = (*top) -> next;
    free(temp);
    return(item);
}
```

We want to delete top node hence to remember the data being deleted it is already stored as **item**.

Taking the address of **top** in **temp** node and assigning new **top** to next node

If stack is as follows -

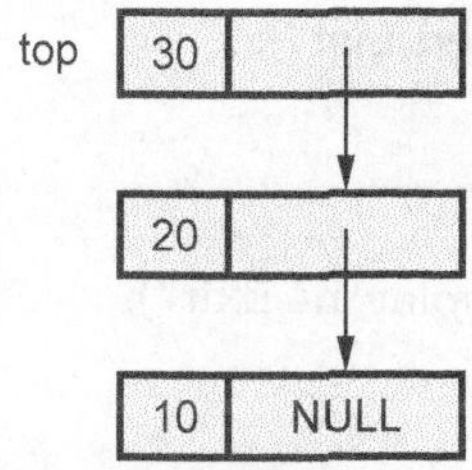

Fig. 5.5.4

If we write

```
item = *(top)->data                then item=30
temp=*top
*top=*top->next                         now top=20
free(temp);                  deallocating memory of node 30.That
                                    means node 30 is deleted.
```

Let us now see the 'C' implementation of it.

'C' Program

```
/**********************************************************
Program for creating the stack using the linked list.
Program performs all the operations such as push,pop and
display.It takes care of stack underflow condition.There cannot be stack full condition in
stack using linked list.
**********************************************************/
#include <stdio.h>
#include <conio.h>
#include <process.h>
#include <stdlib.h>
#include <alloc.h>
/*Declaration for data structure of linked stack*/
typedef struct stack
{
	int	data;
	struct stack *next;
}node;
void main ( )
{
	/* Local declarations */
	node *top;
	int data,item,choice;
	char ans,ch;
	void Push(int , node **);
	void Display(node **);
	int Pop(node **);
	int Sempty(node *);
	clrscr();
	top = NULL;
	printf("\n\t\t Stack Using Linked List");
	do
	{
	printf("\n\n The main menu");
	printf("\n1.Push\n2.Pop\n3.Display\n4.Exit");
	printf("\n Enter Your Choice");
	scanf("%d",&choice);
	switch(choice)
	{
```

```
        case 1:printf("\n Enter the data");
                    scanf("%d", &data);
                    Push(data,&top);
                    break;
        case 2:if(Sempty(top))   /*before popping the data
         whether stack is empty or not is checked*/
                    printf("\n stack underflow!");
              else
                 {
                    item = Pop(&top);
                    printf("\n The popped node is%d",item);
                 }
                    break;
     case 3:Display(&top);
 /*displays stack from top to bottom*/
             break;
         case 4:printf("\n Do You want To Quit?(y/n)");
                ch=getche();
                 if(ch=='y')
                   exit(0);
                else
                   break;
       }
       printf("\n Do you want to continue?");
       ans =getche();
      getch();
      clrscr();
  }while(ans =='Y' ||ans =='y');
 getch();
}
void Push(int Item, node **top)
{
      node *New;
      node * get_node(int);
      New = get_node(Item);
      New -> next = *top;
  *top = New;
}
node * get_node( int item )
{
      node * temp;
      temp =(node *) malloc(sizeof(node) );
      if ( temp == NULL )
       printf("\nMemory Can not be allocated \n");
      temp -> data = item;
      temp -> next = NULL;
```

```
        return( temp);
}
int Sempty(node *temp)
{
 if(temp ==NULL)
  return 1;
 else
  return 0;
}
int Pop(node **top)
{
        int     item;
        node *temp;
        item = (*top) ->data;
        temp = *top;
        *top = (*top) -> next;
        free(temp);
        return(item);
}
void Display(node **head )
{
        node *temp ;
        temp = *head;
        if(Sempty(temp))
         printf("\n The stack is empty!");
        else
        {
         while ( temp != NULL )
         {
          printf("%d\n",temp-> data);
          temp = temp -> next;
         }
        }
        getch();
}
```

Output

```
          Stack Using Linked List
 The main menu
1.Push
2.Pop
3.Display
4.Exit
 Enter Your Choice1
 Enter the data10
 Do you want to continue?y
 The main menu
1.Push
2.Pop
```

```
3.Display
4.Exit
 Enter Your Choice1
 Enter the data20
 Do you want to continue?y
 The main menu
1.Push
2.Pop
3.Display
4.Exit
 Enter Your Choice1
 Enter the data30
 Do you want to continue?y
 The main menu
1.Push
2.Pop
3.Display
4.Exit
 Enter Your Choice3
30
20
10
Do you want to continue?y
 The main menu
1.Push
2.Pop
3.Display
4.Exit
 Enter Your Choice2

 The popped node is30
Do you want to continue?y

 The main menu
1.Push
2.Pop
3.Display
4.Exit
 Enter Your Choice3
20
10
```

Review Questions

1. *Write a program to implement stack as a linked list.*

GTU : Nov-06, Marks 8; Summer-16, Marks 7

> 2. *Write a 'C' program to implement stack using linked list.* **GTU : Winter-16, Marks 7**
> 3. *Consider singly linked storage structures. Write an algorithm which inserts a node into a linked linear list in a stack like manner.* **GTU : Summer-17, Marks 3**

5.6 Linked Implementation of Queue

As we have seen that the queue can be implemented using arrays, it is possible to implement queues using linked list also. The main advantage in linked representation is that we need not have to worry about size of the queue. As in linked organization we can create as many nodes as we want so there will not be a queue full condition at all. The queue using linked list will be very much similar to a linked list. The only difference between the two is in queue, the leftmost node is called **front node** and the rightmost node is called **rear node**. And we cannot remove any arbitrary node from queue. We have to remove front node always :

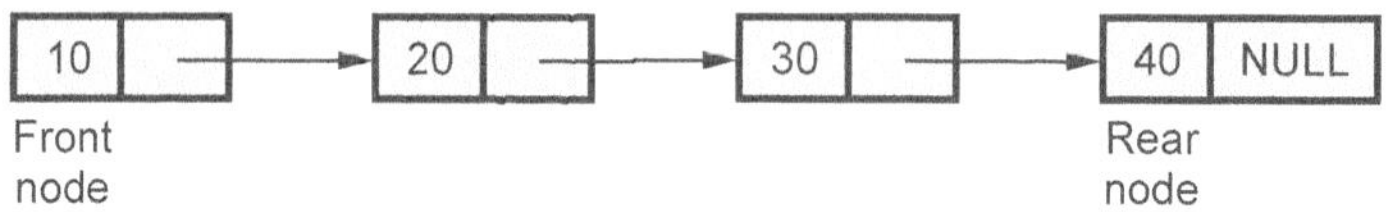

Fig. 5.6.1

The typical node structure will be

```
typedef struct node
    {
        int data;
        struct node  next;
    }Q;
```

Various operations that can be performed on queue are,

1. Insertion of a node in queue.
2. Deletion of node from the queue.
3. Checking whether queue is empty or not.
4. Display of a queue.

All these operations are implemented in following C program.

'C' Program

```
/*****************************************************
  Program For implementing the Queue using the linked list. The queue full condition
will never occur in this program.
*********************************************************/
#include<stdio.h>
#include<stdlib.h>
#include<conio.h>
/*Declaration of Linked Queue data structure*/
```

```
typedef struct node
{
 int data;
 struct node *next;
 }Q;
 Q *front,*rear;
void main(void)
{
 char ans;
 int choice;
 void insert();
 Q *delet();
 void display(Q *);
 front=NULL;
 rear= NULL;
 do
 {
     printf("\n\tProgram For Queue Using Linked List\n");
     printf("\n  Main Menu");
     printf("\n1.Insert\n2.Delete \n3.Display");
     printf("\n Enter Your Choice");
     scanf("%d",&choice);
     switch(choice)
     {
      case 1 : insert();
            break;
      case 2 :front =delet();
            break;
      case 3 :display(front);
            break;
     default: printf("\nYou have entered Wrong Choice\n");
            break;
  }
  printf("\nDo you want to continue?\n");
  flushall();
  ans = getch();
 }while(ans == 'y' || ans == 'Y');
 getch();
 clrscr();
}
Q *get_node(Q *temp)
{
 temp =(Q*) malloc(sizeof(Q));
 temp->next = NULL;
 return temp;
}
```

Queue is initialized to NULL in this way

Keeping track of front pointer

```
void insert()
{
 char ch;
 Q *temp;
 clrscr();
 temp =get_node(temp); /*allocates memory for temp node*/
 printf("\n\n\n\tInsert the element in the Queue\n");
 scanf("%d",&temp->data);

 if(front == NULL)/*creating first node*/
 {
  front= temp;
  rear=temp;
  }
  else /*attaching other nodes*/
   {
        rear->next=temp;
        rear=rear->next;
        }
}
```

Suppose if 10 is inse rted in queue

The node to be inserted is as temp node. We are attaching previous rear to temp and marking that temp as **rear**

```
int Qempty(Q *front)
{
 if(front==NULL)/*front is NULL means memory is not
              allocated to queue*/
  return 1;
 else
  return 0;
}
Q *delet()
{
  Q *temp;
  temp=front;
  if(Qempty(front))
  {
        printf("\n\n\t\tSorry!The Queue Is Empty\n");
        printf("\n Can not delete the element");
  }
  else
   {
         printf("\n\tThe deleted Element Is %d ",temp->data);
         front=front->next;/*deleting the front node*/
         temp->next=NULL;
         free(temp);
   }
 return front;
 }
void display(Q *front)
```

Qempty (front) function returns 1 (true). Hence queue is empty.

After delete operation, front is changed. Hence updated front pointer has to be returned from delete function.

```
{
 if(Qempty(front))
  printf("\n The Queue Is Empty\n");
 else
 {
  printf("\n\t The Display Of Queue Is \n ");
/*queue is displayed from front to rear*/
  for(;front !=rear->next;front=front->next)
       printf("\t%d ",front->data);
 }
 getch();
}
```

> Take the current front pointer and from **front** to **front! = rear->next** scan the queue each time by moving one node ahead.

Output

```
      Program For Queue Using Linked List
          Main Menu
      1.Insert
      2.Delete
      3.Display
       Enter Your Choice1

          Insert the element in the Queue
      10
      Do you want to continue?
    Program For Queue Using Linked List
            Main Menu
      1.Insert
      2.Delete
      3.Display
       Enter Your Choice1

           Insert the element in the Queue
      20
      Do you want to continue?
           Program For Queue Using Linked List
          Main Menu
      1.Insert
      2.Delete
      3.Display
       Enter Your Choice1
             Insert the element in the Queue
      30
      Do you want to continue?

             Program For Queue Using Linked List
                Main Menu
      1.Insert
      2.Delete
```

```
3.Display
 Enter Your Choice3

      The Display Of Queue Is
     10    20    30
Do you want to continue?.
       Program For Queue Using Linked List
           Main Menu
1.Insert
2.Delete
3.Display
 Enter Your Choice2

       The deleted Element Is 10
Do you want to continue?
       Program For Queue Using Linked List
   Main Menu
1.Insert
2.Delete
3.Display
 Enter Your Choice3

     The Display Of Queue Is
    20    30
Do you want to continue?
```

5.7 Applications of Linked List

Various applications of linked list are -

1. Representation of polynomial and performing various operations such as addition, multiplication and evaluation on it.
2. Performing addition of long positive integers.
3. Representing non integer and non homogeneous list.

These applications can be illustrated in detail with the help of examples and programs in the next subsequent sections.

Example 5.7.1 *Linked list application for Quadratic equation addition.*

Solution : The linked list is an useful data structure for representing quadratic equation. Any quadratic equation is in the form : $ax^2 + bx + c$. We can represent such an equation using 'C' structure as

```
struct Quad_Eq
{
     int coeff;
     int exp;
     struct Quad_Eq * next;
};
```

struct Quad_Eq * Eq1,* Eq2, * Eq3;

Graphically any quadratic equation can be represented using linked list as :

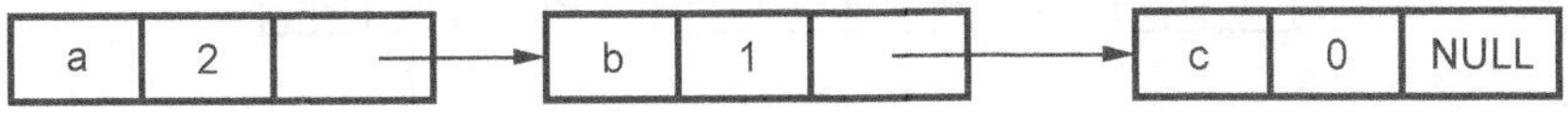

Representing $ax^2 + bx + c$

Consider, $Eq1 = 3x^2 + 2x + 5$

$Eq2 = 7x^2 + 3x + 8$

are two quadratic equations. Manually we can perform their addition as :

$$\begin{array}{rr} & 3x^2 + 2x + 5 \\ + & 7x^2 + 3x + 8 \\ \hline & 10x^2 + 5x + 13 \end{array}$$

Let us perform this addition using linked list as :

Step 1 :

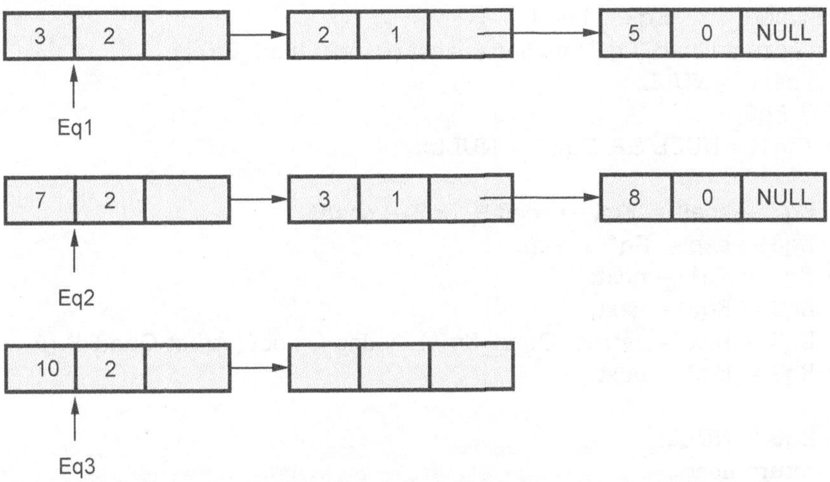

Step 2 :

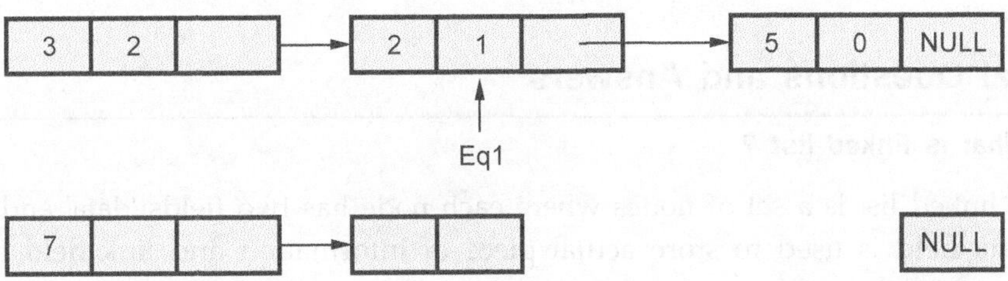

Step 3 :

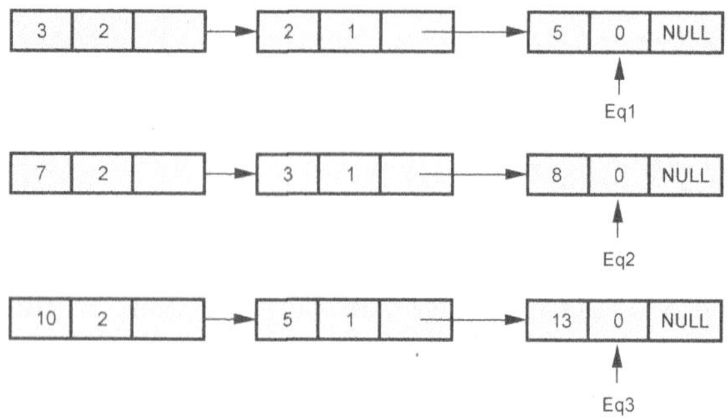

The 'C' code will be

```
struct Quad_Eq * addition (struct Quad_Eq * Eq1,
                           struct Quad_Eq * Eq2)
{
    struct Quad_Eq * Eq3, * head;
    Eq3 = (struct Quad_Eq *) malloc (sizeof (struct Quad_Eq));
    Eq3 → next = NULL;
    head = Eq3;
    while (Eq1!= NULL && Eq2 ! = NULL)
    {
        Eq3 → coeff = Eq1 → coeff + Eq2 → coeff;
        Eq3 → exp = Eq1 → exp;
        Eq1 = Eq1 → next;
        Eq2 = Eq2 → next;
        Eq3 → next = (struct Quad_Eq *) malloc (sizeof (struct Quad_Eq));
        Eq3 = Eq3 → next;
    }
        Eq3 = NULL;
        return head;
}
```

5.8 Oral Questions and Answers

Q.1 What is linked list ?

Ans. : A linked list is a set of nodes where each node has two fields 'data' and 'link'.

The data field is used to store actual piece of information and link field is used to store address of next node.

Q.2 What are the pitfalls encountered in singly linked list ?

Ans. : Following are the pitfalls encountered in singly linked list

1. The singly linked list has only forward pointer and no backward link is provided. Hence the traversing of the list is possible only in one direction. Backward traversing is not possible.

2. Insertion and deletion operations are less efficient because for inserting the element at desired position the list needs to be traversed. Similarly, traversing of the list is required for locating the element which needs to be deleted.

Q.3 Write down the steps to modify a node in linked lists.

Ans. :

1. Enter the position of the node which is to be modified.
2. Enter the new value for the node to be modified.
3. Search the corresponding node in the linked list.
4. Replace the original value of that node by a new value.
5. Display the message as "The node is modified".

Q.4 Differentiate between arrays and lists.

Ans. : In arrays any element can be accessed randomly with the help of index of array, whereas in lists any element can be accessed by sequential access only.

Insertions and deletions of data is difficult in arrays on the other hand insertion and deletion of data is easy in lists.

Q.5 State the properties of LIST abstract data type with suitable example.

Ans. : Various properties of LIST abstract data type are -

1. It is linear data structure in which the elements are arranged adjacent to each other.
2. It allows to store single variable polynomial.
3. If the LIST is implemented using dynamic memory then it is called linked list.

Example of LIST are - Stacks, Queues, Linked List.

Q.6 State the advantages of circular lists over doubly linked list.

Ans. : In circular list the next pointer of last node points to head node, whereas in doubly linked list each node has two pointers : One previous pointer and another is next pointer. The main advantage of circular list over doubly linked list is that with the help of single pointer field we can access head node quickly. Hence some amount of memory get saved because in circular list only one pointer field is reserved.

Q.7 What are the advantages of doubly linked list over singly linked list ?

Ans. : The doubly linked list has two pointer fields. One field is previous link field and another is next link field.

Because of these two pointer fields we can access any node efficiently whereas in singly linked list only one pointer field is there which stores forward pointer, which makes accessing of any node difficult one.

Q.8 Why is linked list used for polynomial arithmetic ?

Ans. : Following are the reasons for which linked list is used for polynomial arithmetic -

i) We can have separate coefficient and exponent fields for representing each term of polynomial. Hence there is no limit for exponent. We can have any number as an exponent.

ii) The arithmetic operation on any polynomial of arbitrary length is possible using linked list.

Q.9 What is the advantage of linked list over arrays ?

Ans. : The linked list makes use of the dynamic memory allocation. Hence the user can allocate or de allocate the memory as per his requirements. On the other hand, the array makes use of the static memory location. Hence there are chances of wastage of the memory or shortage of memory for allocation.

Q.10 What is circular linked list ?

Ans. : The circular linked list is a kind of linked list in which the last node is connected to the first node or head node of the linked list.

Q.11 What is the basic purpose of header of the linked list. GTU : Summer-18, Marks 3

Ans. : The header node is the very first node of the linked list. Sometimes a dummy value such as – 999 is stored in the data field of header node.

This node is useful for getting the starting address of the linked list. As there is only a forward link present in the linked list, for accessing the entire linked list it is necessary to obtain the starting address of the linked list.

Q.12 Should arrays or linked lists be used for the following type of applications. Justify your answer. a) Many search operations in sorted list. b) Many search operations in unsorted list.

Ans. :

a) If the list is sorted then using linked list the desired element can be searched, simply by moving forward using 'next' pointer.

b) If a list is not sorted then using arrays the desired element can be searched. The arrays facilitates the access to random element.

Q.13 Which operation will be efficient due to doubly linked list. Why ?

Ans. : Deletion operation becomes efficient due to doubly linked list. The deletion operation required to keep track of the previous node of the node being deleted. Due to previous pointer we can easily obtain the address of previous node.

Q.14 Name the functions (in C) used for allocation and de-allocation of a node.

Ans. : The malloc () is used for allocation of a node and free() is used for de-allocation operation.

Q.15 Explain the term dynamic memory.

Ans. : The dynamic memory allocation means one can allocate the memory of required size and deallocate it whenever required. So that free memory can be utilized further.

Q.16 Write a routine to display all the elements in the linked list.

Ans. :

```
void display(node *head)
{
    Node *temp
    temp=head;
    while(temp!=NULL)
    {
        printf("%d",temp->data);
        temp=temp->next;
    }
}
```

Q.17 Write a routine to count the number of nodes on a linked list.

Ans. :

```
void display(node *head)
{
    Node *temp
    temp=head;
    count=0;
    while(temp!=NULL)
    {
        count++;
        temp=temp->next;
    }
    printf("%d",count);
}
```

Q.18 Write a C function to find the product of all the elements in a linked list.

Ans. :

```
void Product(node *root)
{
    node *temp;
    int p=1;
    temp=root;
    while(temp!=NULL)
    {
        p=p*temp->data;
        temp=temp->next;
    }
    printf("\n Product of all the elements: %d",p);
}
```

Q.19 Mention one operation for which use of doubly linked list is preferred over the singly linked list. **GTU : Winter-15**

Ans. : For deletion operation doubly linked list is preferred over singly linked list. Due to doubly linked list it becomes easy to keep track of previous node.

Q.20 Write an algorithm/steps to traverse a singly linked list. **GTU : Winter-15**

Ans. : Algorithm Traverse (node *head)

```
{
    temp = head;
    // Now temp is the very first node
     while (temp → next ! = NULL)
    {
    // display the data at current node
      printf ("%d", temp → data);
      temp = temp → next; // move to
                              // next node
    }
     printf("%d", temp → data); //display
                                 //the last node
    }
```

Q.21 What is a header node and what is its use ? **GTU : Winter-15**

Ans. : Header node is the first node of the linked list. This node is used for holding the starting address of the linked list.

Q.22 Write 'C' structure of singly linked list. **GTU : Summer-16**

Ans. :

```
typedef struct node
{
    int data; /* data field */
    struct node * next; /* link field */
} SLL;
```

Q. 23 Circular linked list. **GTU : Winter-16**

Ans. : The Circular Linked List (CLL) is similar to singly linked list except that the last node's next pointer points to first node.

Q.24 What does the following function do for a given Linked List with first node as head ?

```
void fun1 (struct node* head)
{
if (head == NULL)
return;
fun1(head->next);
printf("%d", head->data);
}
```

GTU : Summer-17

Ans. : The given function displays value of every node in the linked list.

❑❑❑

6 Non Linear Data Structures : Trees

Syllabus

Tree-definitions and concepts, Representation of binary tree, Binary tree traversal (Inorder, Postorder, Preorder), Threaded binary tree, Binary search trees, Conversion of general trees to binary trees, Applications of trees - Some balanced tree mechanism, e.g. AVL trees, 2-3 trees, Height balanced, Weight balance.

Contents

6.1 Definition and Concepts

GTU : Dec.-05, 06, Marks 6

A tree is a finite set of one or more nodes such that -

i) There is a specially designated node called **root**.

ii) The remaining nodes are partitioned into n > = 0 disjoint sets $T_1, T_2, T_3 \ldots T_n$ where $T_1, T_2, T_3, \ldots T_n$ are called the subtrees of the root.

The concept of tree is represented by following Fig. 6.1.1

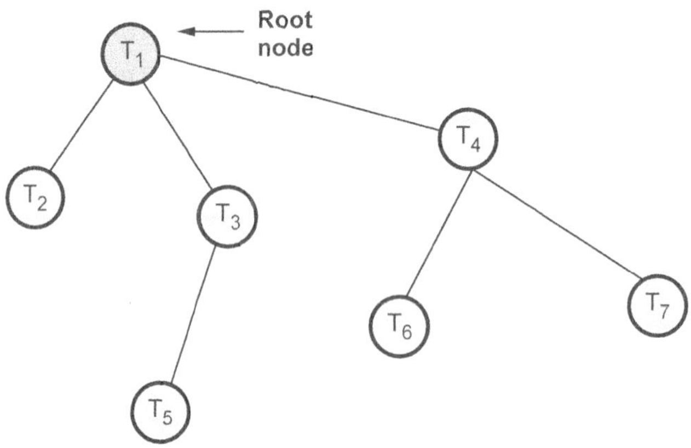

Fig. 6.1.1 Tree

6.1.1 Basic Terminologies

Let us get introduced with some of the definitions or terms which are normally used.

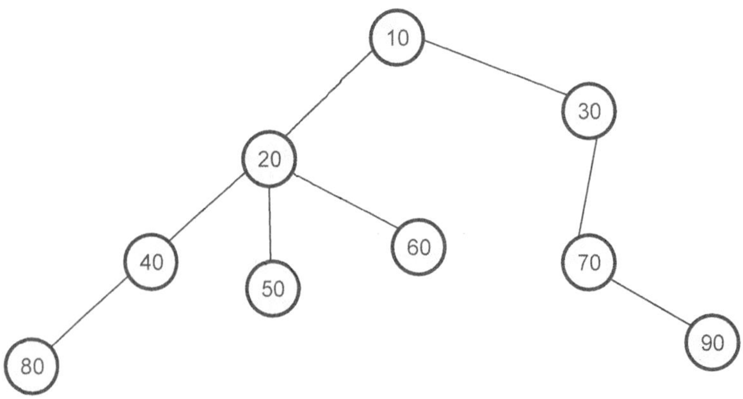

Fig. 6.1.2 Tree

From Fig. 6.1.2,

1. Root

Root is a unique node in the tree to which further subtrees are attached. For above given tree, node 10 is a root node.

2. Parent node

The node having further subbranches is called parent node. In Fig. 6.1.3 the 20 is parent node of 40, 50 and 60.

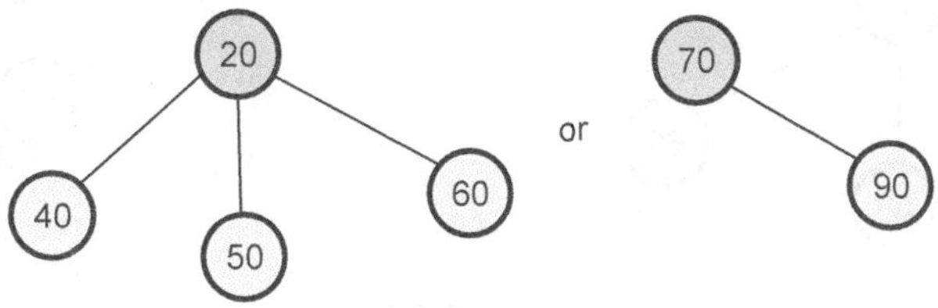

Fig. 6.1.3

3. Child nodes

The child nodes in above given tree are marked as shown below.

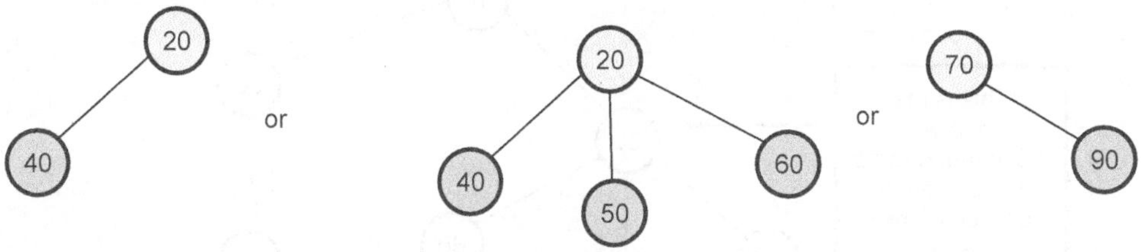

Fig. 6.1.4

4. Leaves

These are the terminal nodes of the tree.

For example :

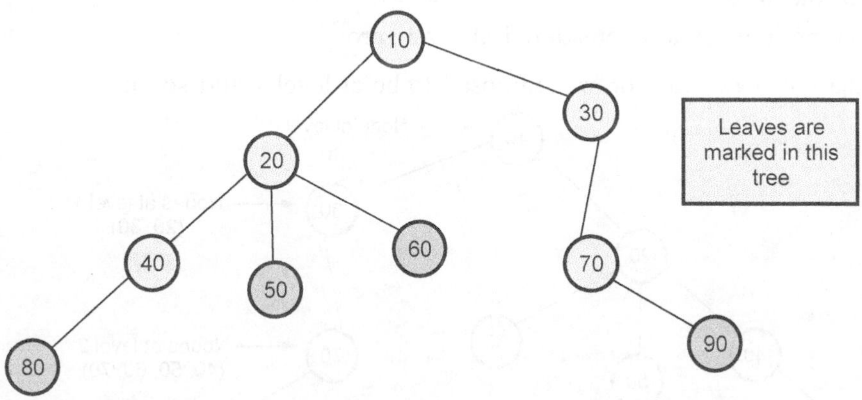

Fig. 6.1.5

5. Degree of the node

The total number of subtrees attached to that node is called the degree of a node.

For example :

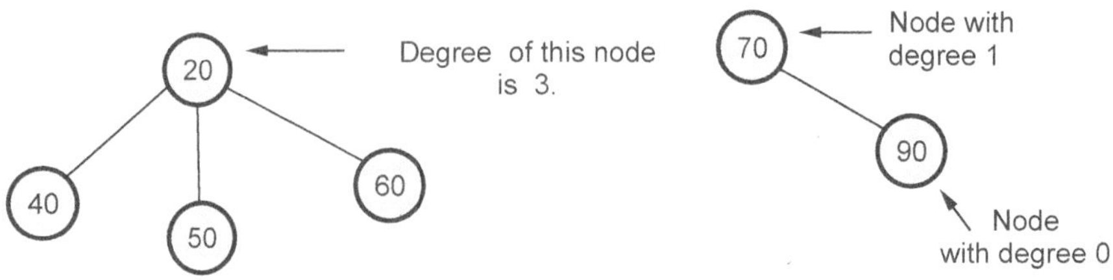

Fig. 6.1.6

6. Degree of tree

The maximum degree in the tree is degree of tree.

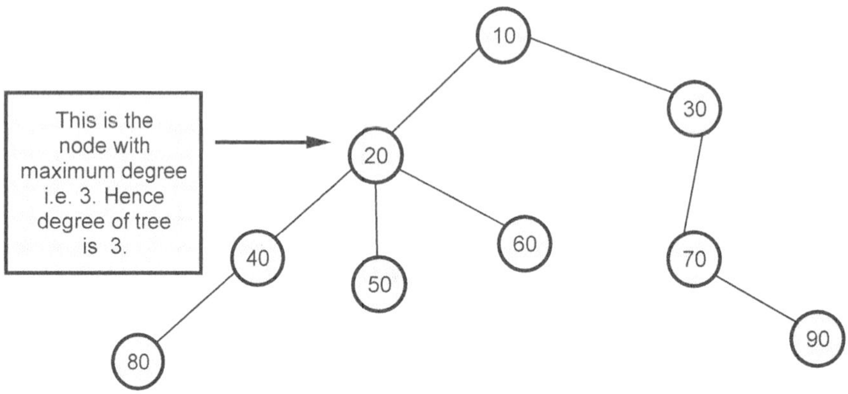

Fig. 6.1.7

7. Level of the tree

The root node is always considered at level zero.

The adjacent nodes to root are supposed to be at level 1 and so on.

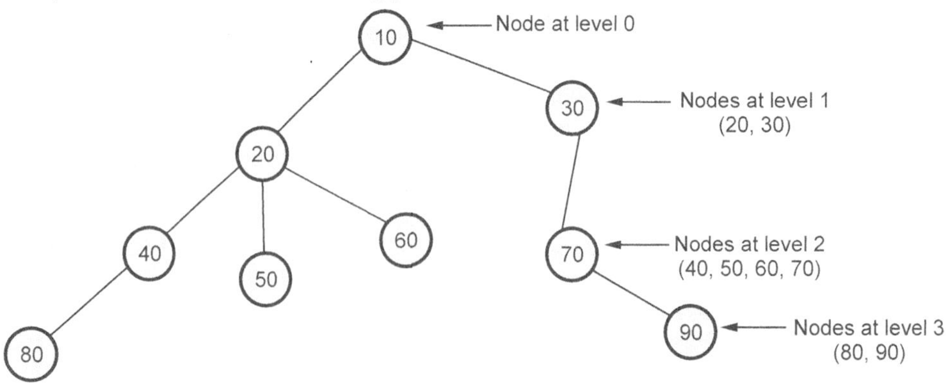

Fig. 6.1.8

8. Height of the tree

GTU : Summer-15, Mark 1

The maximum level is the height of the tree. In Fig. 6.1.8 the height of tree is 3. Sometimes height of the tree is also called **depth** of tree.

9. Predecessor or Ancestor

GTU : Summer-15, Mark 1

While displaying the tree, if some particular node occurs previous to some other node then that node is called **predecessor** of the other node.

For example : While displaying the tree in Fig. 6.1.8 if we read node 20 first and then if we read node 40, then 20 is a predecessor of 40.

10. Successor

Successor is a node which occurs next to some node.

For example : While displaying tree in Fig. 6.1.8 if we read node 60 after reading node 20 then 60 is called successor of 20.

11. Internal and external nodes

Leaf node means a node having no child node. As leaf nodes are not having further links, we call leaf nodes **external nodes** and non-leaf nodes are called **internal nodes.**

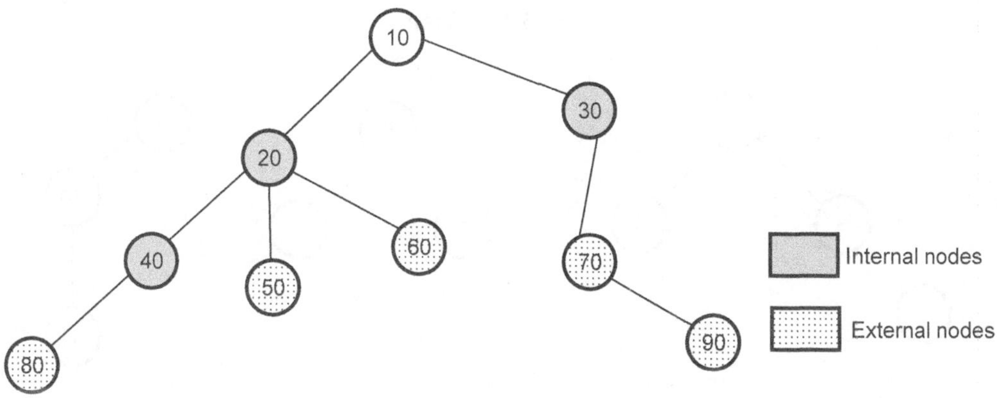

Fig. 6.1.9

12. Sibling

GTU : Summer-15, Mark 1

The nodes with common parent are called siblings or brothers.

For example :

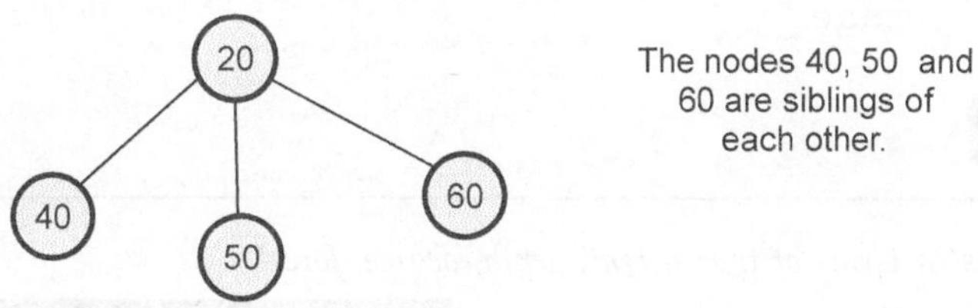

Fig. 6.1.10

13. Forest

Forest is a collection of disjoint trees. From a given tree if we remove its root then we get a forest.

For example :

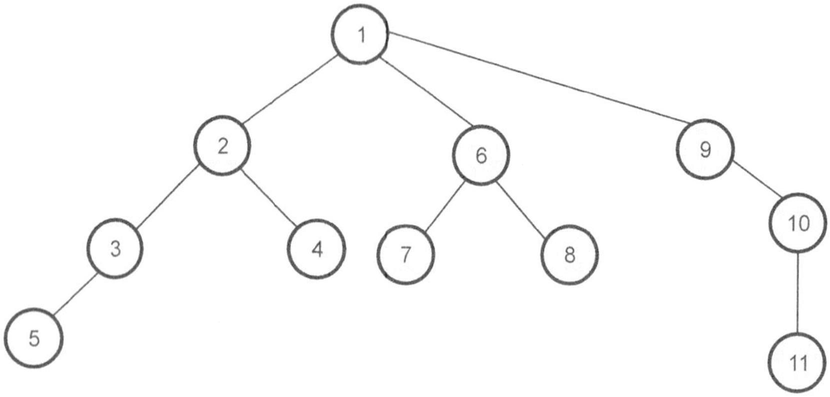

Fig. 6.1.11 Tree

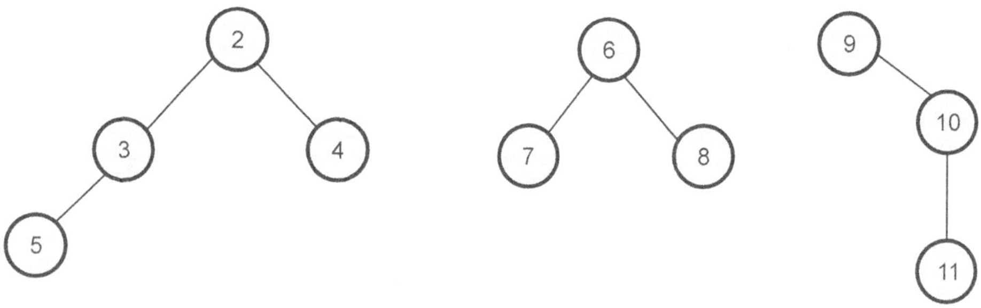

Fig. 6.1.12 Forest

6.1.2 Need for Nonlinear Data Structure

There are some **complex applications** for which use of linear data structure is not possible. For example : Trees, General trees, graphs, multi-link polynomials are some structure which are hard to represent using linear data structure. Hence there is a need for nonlinear data structure.

Review Question

1. *Explain terms in terms of tree: height, depth, degree, forest*

GTU : Dec.-05, Marks 4, Dec.-06, Marks 6

6.2 Concept of Binary Trees

GTU : Dec.-05, Summer-14, Winter-15, Marks 3

In the trees, we can have any number of child nodes to a parent node. But if we impose some restriction on number of child nodes i.e. if we allow at the most two children nodes then that type of tree is called binary tree. Let us formally define binary trees.

> **Definition of a binary tree :** *A binary tree is a finite set of nodes which is either empty or consists of a root and two disjoint binary trees called the left subtree and right subtree.*

The binary tree can be as shown below.

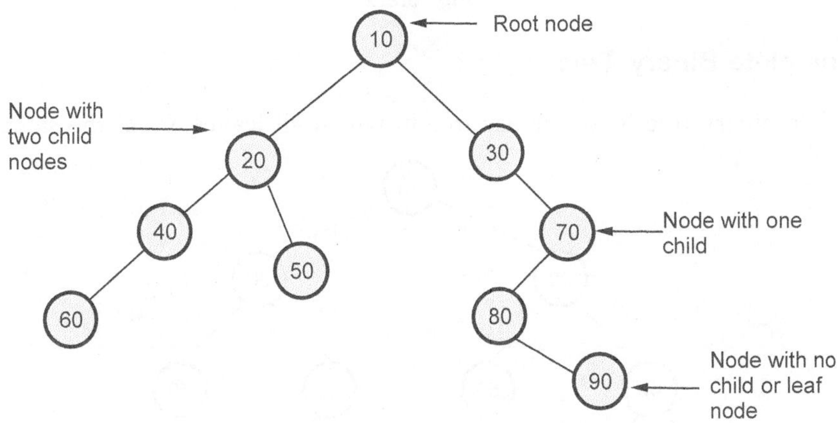

Fig. 6.2.1 Binary tree

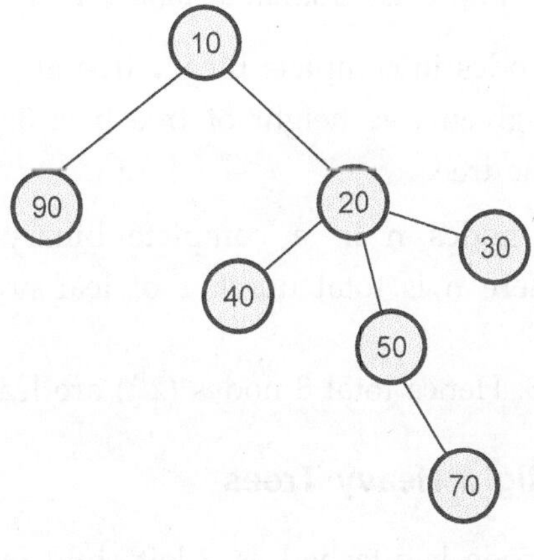

Fig. 6.2.2 Not a binary tree

6.2.1 Full Binary Tree (Strictly Binary Tree)

A full binary tree is a tree in which every node has zero or two children.

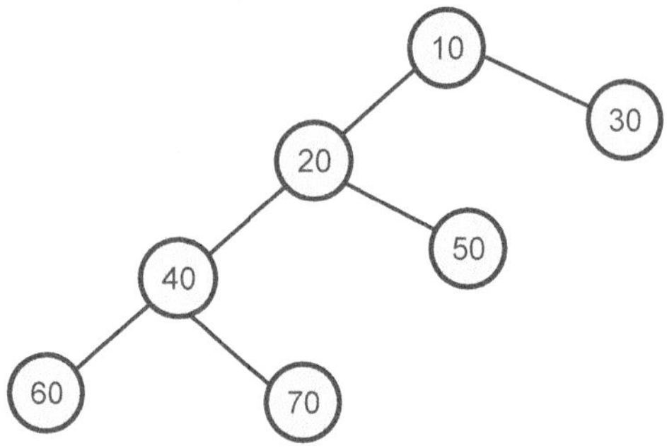

Fig. 6.2.3

6.2.2 Complete Binary Tree

A complete binary tree is full binary tree in which all leaves are at the same depth.

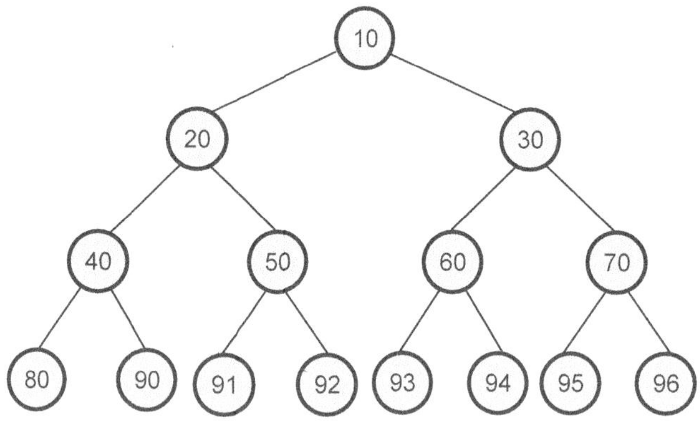

Fig. 6.2.4 Complete binary tree

- The total number of nodes in complete binary tree are $2^{h+1}-1$ where h is a height of the tree. In above given tree height of tree h is 3. Hence there are $2^{3+1}-1 = 2^4-1 = 15$ nodes in the tree.
- The number of leaf nodes n in a complete binary tree can be found using formula : $n = 2^h$ where n is total number of leaf nodes and h is the height of binary tree.

In above given tree h = 3. Hence total 8 nodes (2^h) are leaf nodes.

6.2.3 Left Heavy and Right Heavy Trees

The tree in which each node is attached as a left child of parent node then it is **left heavy tree**. The tree in which each node is attached as a right child of parent node then it is called **right heavy tree**.

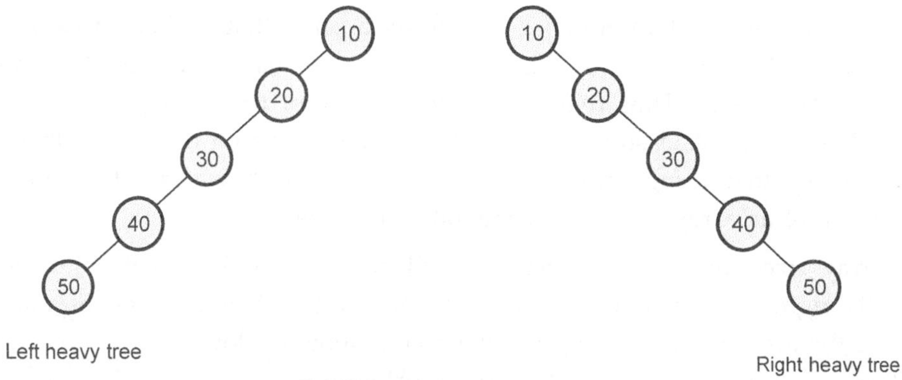

Fig. 6.2.5 Heavy trees

Review Questions

1. *What is complete binary tree? Is binary tree directed or undirected. ?* **GTU : Dec.-05, Marks 3**
2. *Define complete binary tree and full binary tree* **GTU : Summer-14, Marks 2**
3. *Define complete binary tree and almost complete binary tree.* **GTU : Winter-15, Marks 3**

6.3 Representation of Binary Tree

GTU : Winter-17, Marks 3

There are two ways of representing the binary tree.

1. Sequential representation

2. Linked representation.

Let us see these representations one by one.

1. Sequential representation of binary trees or array representation

Each node is sequentially arranged from top to bottom and from left to right. Let us understand this matter by numbering each node. The numbering will start from root node and then remaining nodes will give ever increasing numbers in level wise direction. The nodes on the same level will be numbered from left to right. The numbering will be as shown below.

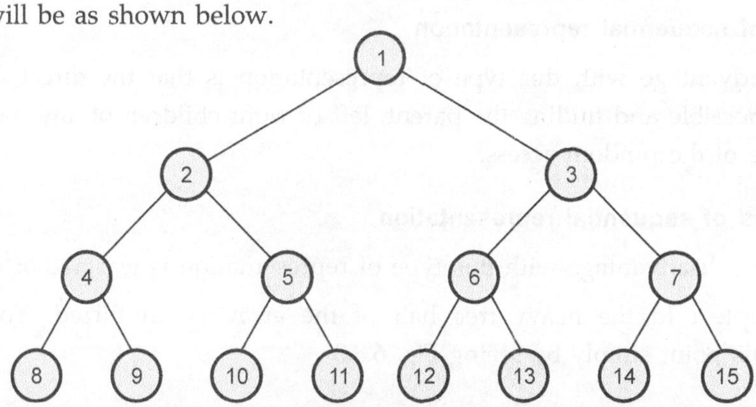

Fig. 6.3.1

Now, observe Fig. 6.3.1 carefully. You will get a point that a binary tree of depth **n** having $\mathbf{2^n-1}$ number of nodes. In Fig. 6.3.1 the tree is having the depth 4 and total number of nodes are 15. Thus remember that in a binary tree of depth n there will be maximum 2^n-1 nodes. And so if we know the maximum depth of the tree then we can represent binary tree using arrays data structure. Because we can then predict the maximum size of an array that can accommodate the tree.

Thus array size can be >= n. The root will be at index 0. Its left child will be at index 1, its right child will be at index 2 and so on. Another way of placing the elements in the array is by applying the formula as shown below.

- When n = 0 the root node will placed at 0th location.
- Parent(n) = floor(n–1)/2.
- Left(n) = (2n+1).
- Right(n) = (2n+2).

where n > 0

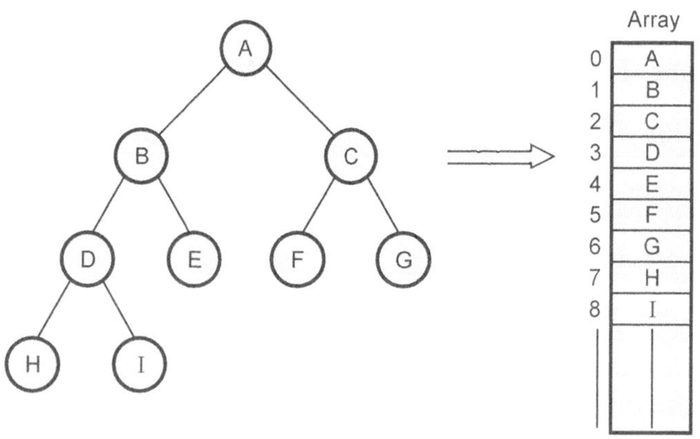

Root = A = Index 0.

Left child of A i.e. n = 0.
∴ B will be at location.
Similarly right child of
A is C.

∴ C will be at $2 \times 0 + 2 = 2^{nd}$ location

I is at 8th location
2n + 2 = 8
2n = 6
n = 3

That means parent of I is at 3rd location and i.e. D.

Fig. 6.3.2 Sequential representation of a tree

Advantages of sequential representation

The only advantage with this type of representation is that the direct access to any node can be possible and finding the parent, left or right children of any particular node is fast because of the random access.

Disadvantages of sequential representation

1. The major disadvantage with this type of representation is wastage of memory.

For example : In the heavy tree half of the array is unutilized. You can easily understand this point simply by seeing Fig. 6.3.3

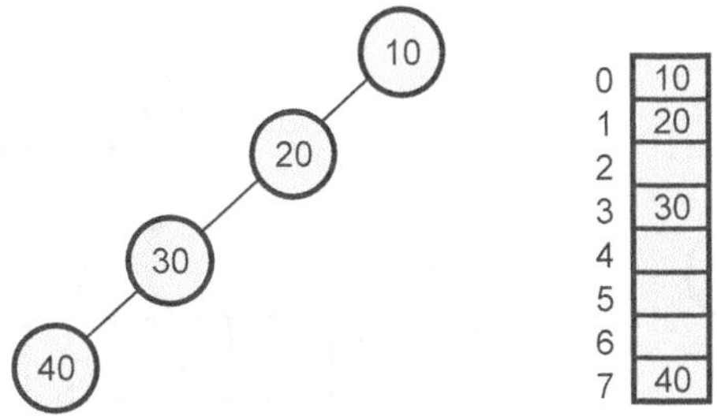

Fig. 6.3.3 Storing a tree in an array

2. In this type of representation the maximum depth of the tree has to be fixed because we have already decided the array size. If we choose the array size quite larger than the depth of the tree, then it will be wastage of the memory. And if we choose array size lesser than the depth of the tree then we will be unable to represent some part of the tree.
3. The insertions and deletion of any node in the tree will be costlier as other nodes have to be adjusted at appropriate positions so that the meaning of binary tree can be preserved.

As these drawbacks are there with this sequential type of representation, we will search for more flexible representation. So instead of array we will make use of linked list to represent the tree.

2. Linked representation or node representation of binary trees

In binary tree each node will have left child, right child and data field.

Left child	Data	Right child

The left child is nothing but the left link which points to some address of left subtree whereas right child is also a right link which points to some address of right subtree. And the data field gives the information about the node. Let us see the 'C' structure of the node in a binary tree.

```
typedef struct node
{
 int data;
 struct node *left;
 struct node *right;
}bin;
```

The tree with Linked representation is as shown below.

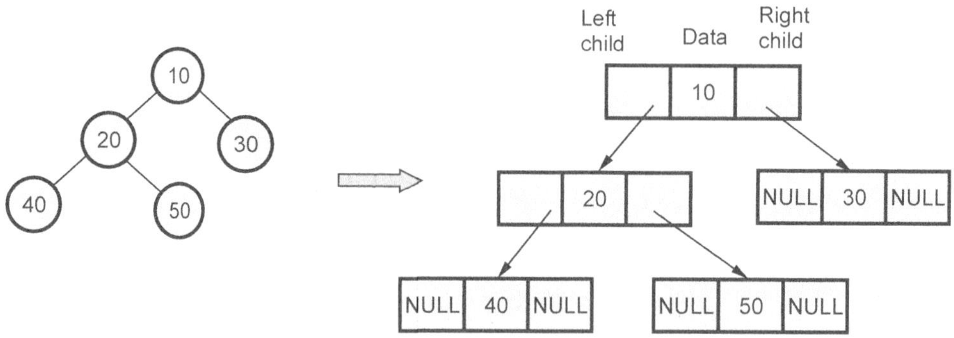

Fig. 6.3.4 Linked representation of tree

Advantages of linked representation

1. This representation is superior to our array representation as there is no wastage of memory. And so there is no need to have prior knowledge of depth of the tree. Using dynamic memory concept one can create as many memory (nodes) as required. By chance if some nodes are unutilized one can delete the nodes by making the address free.
2. Insertions and deletions which are the most common operations can be done without moving the other nodes.

Disadvantages of linked representation

1. This representation does not provide direct access to a node and special algorithms are required.
2. This representation needs additional space in each node for storing the left and right sub-trees.

Review Question

1. *How directed tree can be represented ?* **GTU : Winter-17, Marks 3**

6.4 Binary Tree Traversal

GTU : CE : Dec.-03, Winter-12, 15, 16, Summer-14, 16, 18, Dec.-05, 06, Marks 7

Traversing the tree means visiting each node exactly once. Basically there are six ways to traverse a tree. For these traversals we will use some notations as follows :

L means move to the Left child.

R means move to the the Right child.

D means the root/parent node.

Now, with this L, R, D one can have six different combinations of L,R,D nodes.

Such as LDR, LRD, DLR, DRL, RLD, RDL. But from computing point of view we will have three different ways of traversing a tree. Those three combinations will be LDR, DLR, LRD.Those are called Inorder, Preorder and Postorder traversals.

1. Inorder Traversal :

C-B-A-D-E is the inorder traversal i.e. first we go towards the leftmost node i.e C so print that node C. Then go back to the node B and print B. Then root node A then move towards the right subtree print D and finally E. Thus we are following the tracing sequence of LDR. This type of traversal is called inorder traversal. The basic principle is to traverse left subtree then root and then the right subtree.

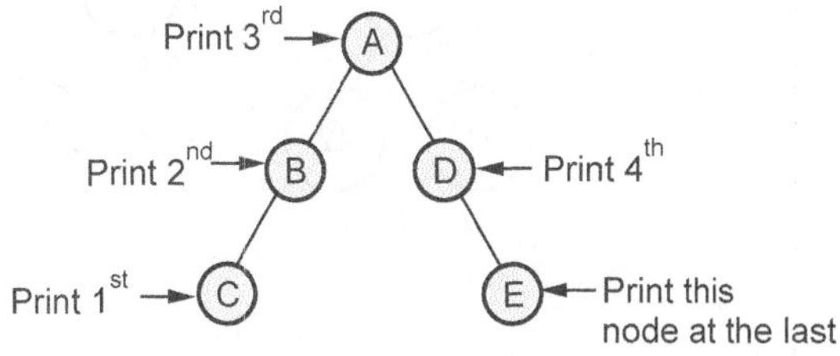

Fig. 6.4.1 Inorder traversal

2. Preorder Traversal :

A-B-C-D-E is the preorder traversal of the Fig. 6.4.2 We are following DLR path i.e data at the root node will be printed first then we move on the left subtree and go on printing the data till we reach to the leftmost node. Print the data at that node and then move to the right subtree. Follow the same DLR principle at each subtree and go on printing the data accordingly.

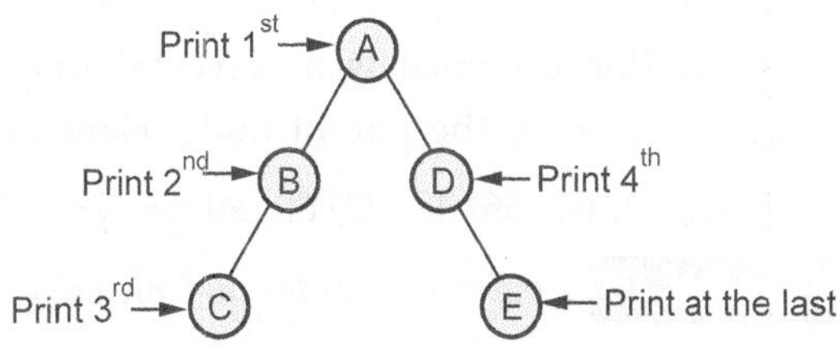

Fig. 6.4.2 Preorder traversal

3. Postorder Traversal :

From Fig. 6.4.3 the postorder sequence is C-D-B-E-A. In the postorder traversal we are following the LRD principle i.e. move to the leftmost node check if right subtree is there or not if not then print the leftmost node, if right subtree is there move towards the rightmost node. The key idea here is that at each subtree we are following the LRD principle and print the data accordingly.

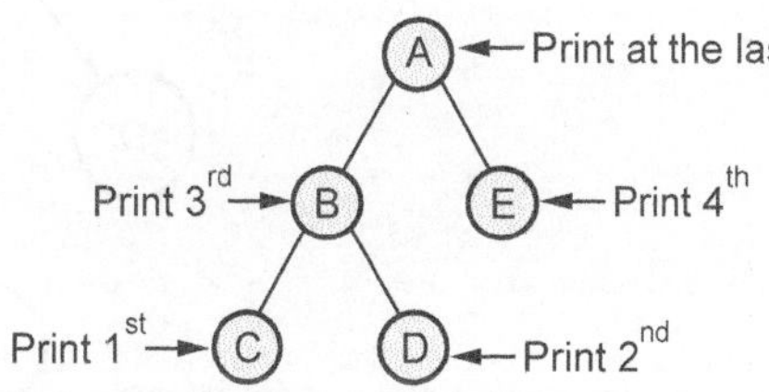

Fig. 6.4.3 Postorder traversal

Example 6.4.1 *Tree traversal for following tree.* **GTU : CE : Dec.-03, Marks 3**

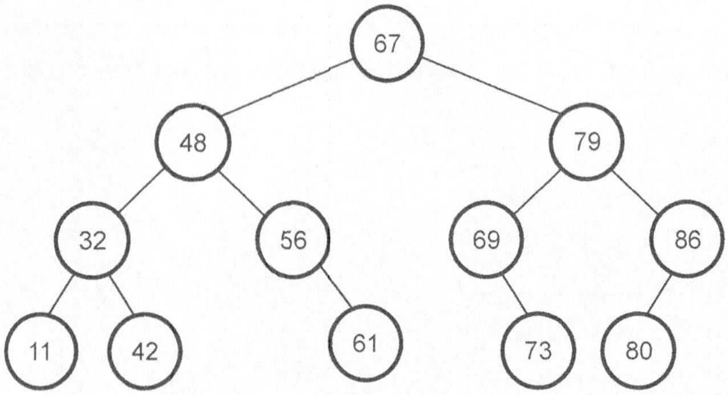

Solution : Inorder traversal is a traversal in which we travel left subtree then parent node and then right subtree. The inorder traversal of given tree will be

11, 32, 42, 48, 56, 61, 69, 73, 79, 80, 86

Preorder traversal is a traversal in which we travel the parent node first, then left subtree and then right subtree. The preorder traversal of given tree will be

67, 48, 32, 11, 42, 56, 61, 79, 69, 73, 86, 80

Postorder traversal is a traversal in which we travel the left subtree, then right subtree and then the parent node. Hence postorder traversal will be

11, 42, 32, 61, 56, 48, 73, 69, 80, 86, 79, 67

Example 6.4.2 *Find a post order and preorder traversal of the following tree.* **GTU : Winter-12, Marks 7**

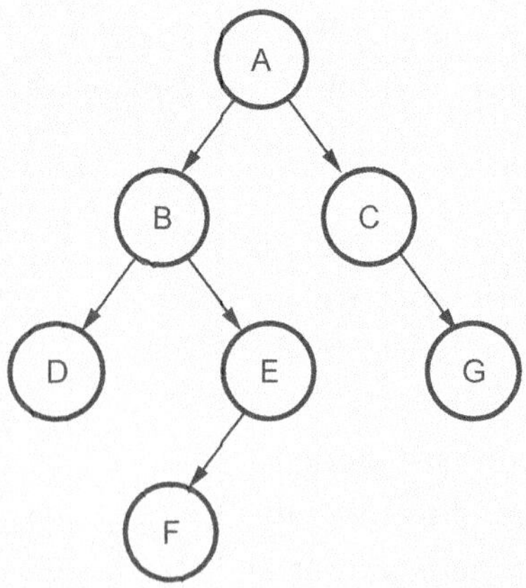

Solution :

1. **Postorder Traversal :** DBFEACG
2. **Preorder Traversal :** ABDEFCG

Example 6.4.3 *Give preorder and inorder traversal of following Fig. 6.4.4*

GTU : Summer-14, Marks 7

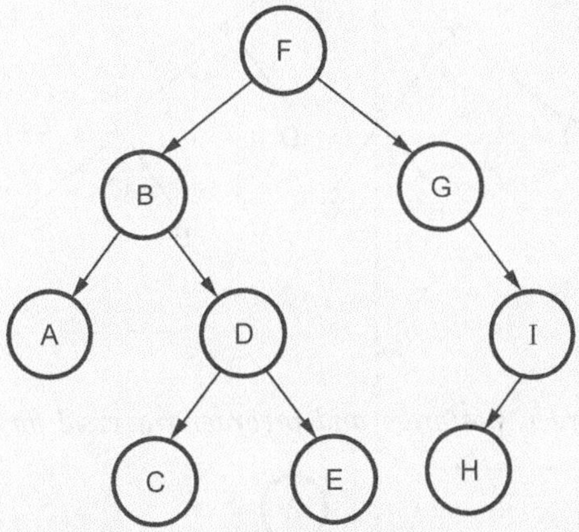

Fig. 6.4.4

Solution :

Preorder : F, B, A, D, C, E, G, I, H

Inorder : A, B, C, D, E, F, G, H, I

Example 6.4.4 *Draw a binary expression tree for the following and perform preorder traversal : (A \$ B \$ C) + (D – E * F).*

GTU : Summer-16, Marks 4

Solution : The binary expression tree will be as follows -

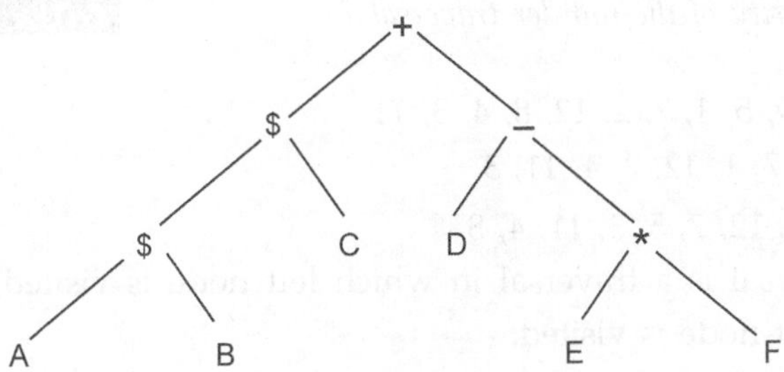

The preorder traversal will be

+ \$ \$ A B C – * E F D

Example 6.4.5 *Draw a binary expression tree for the following and perform preorder traversal for the same :*

*(A + B $ C) + (D + E * F)* **GTU : Winter-16, Marks 3**

Solution : The binary expression tree is

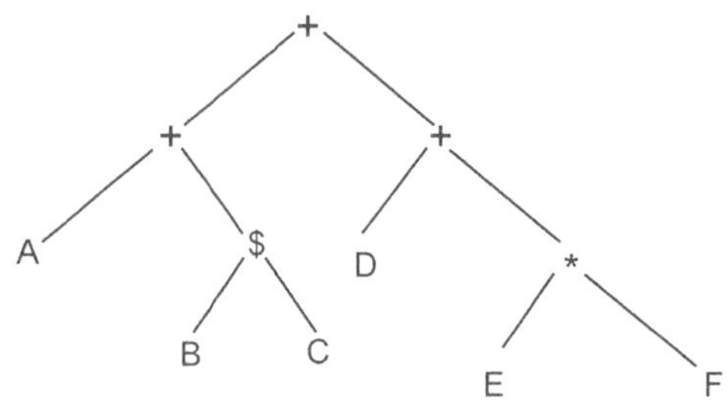

The preorder traversal is :

+ + A $ B C + * E F D

Example 6.4.6 *Perform inorder, postorder and preorder traversal for the following binary tree.*

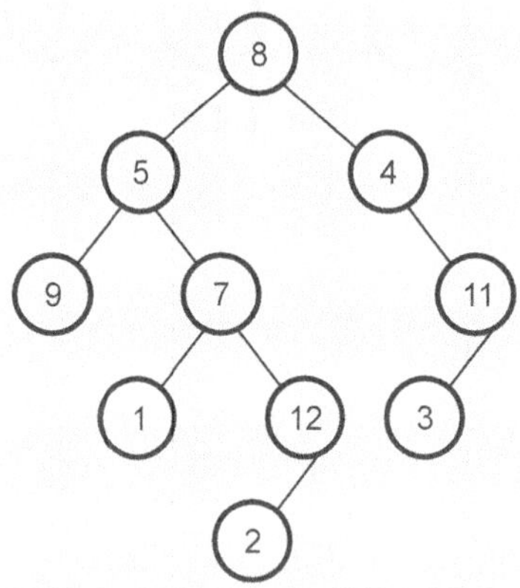

What is the percularity of the inorder traversal ? **GTU : Summer-18, Marks 7**

Solution : Inorder : 9, 5, 1, 7, 2, 12, 8, 4, 3, 11

Preorder : 8, 5, 9, 7, 1, 12, 2, 4, 11, 3

Postorder : 9, 1, 2, 12, 7, 5, 3, 11, 4, 8

The inorder traversal is a traversal in which left node is visited, then parent node is visited and then right node is visited.

Review Questions

1. *What is preorder and postorder traversal of a binary tree ?Explain.* **GTU : Dec.-05, 06, Marks 6**
2. *What is binary tree traversal ? What are the various traversal methods ? Explain any two with suitable example.* **GTU : Winter-15, Marks 7**

6.5 Binary Tree Operations

GTU : Dec.-05, May-11, Winter-14, Summer-15, Marks 7

Various operations that can be performed on the binary trees are

1. Creation of binary tree.
2. Insertion of a node in the tree.
3. Display of a binary tree.

1. Creation of simple binary tree

Now we will understand the concept of binary tree by creating a simple binary tree. When the data will be entered by the user, the first element will form the root node. For all the next elements user has to enter whether that element has to be inserted as a left child or a right child of previous node. For the sake of understanding, let us build the simple binary tree for some elements.

Let us take value 10. Now root node will be formed for 10.

If next element is say 12 then user will be asked for his choice, I mean, he will be asked if 12 is attached to the left or right of 10. If user answers l or L (that means left) then tree will be

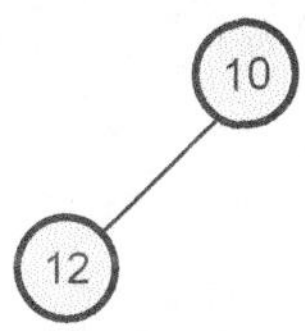

Then if the next element is 8 then again user has to give his choice, whether it is L (left) or R (right). That means first whether user want to attach 8 left or right of 10 will be asked, if user answers L then again whether user want to attach 8 to left or right of 12 will be asked, if he answers R then the node 8 will be attached as a right child of 12.

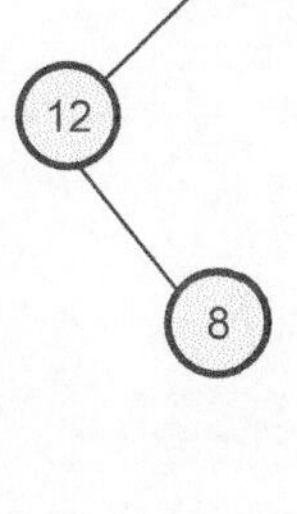

If the next element is 17 and user want to attach it as a right child of 10 then

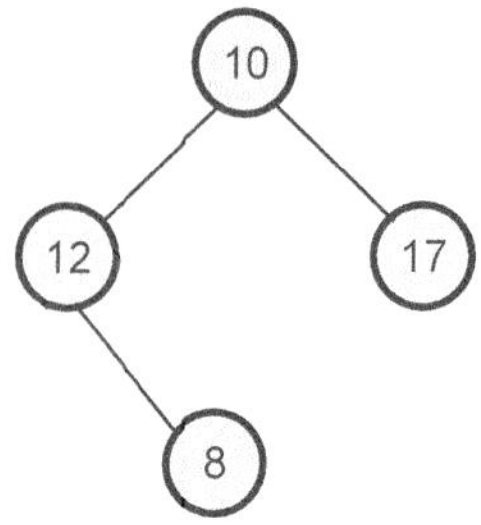

Thus a simple binary tree will be generated. The principle idea behind this creation is always ask the user where he wants to attach the next node and always start scanning the tree from root. Now let us see the C program for it.

The C structure for node of a binary tree can be represented as

```
typedef struct bin
{
 int data;
 struct bin *left;
 struct bin *right;
}node;
```

left	data	right

node

The insertion of a node in the binary tree can be done using following function.

```
void insert(node *root,node *New)
 {
  char ch;
  printf("\n Where to insert left/right of %d: ",
        root->data);
  ch=getche();
  if ((ch=='r')||(ch=='R'))
  {
      if(root->right==NULL)
       {
        root->right=New;
       }
       else
        insert(root->right,New);
   }
   else
       {
        if (root->left==NULL)
  {
               root->left=New;
          }
         else
              insert(root->left,New);
       }
 }
```

Initially root = NULL

Then we will create a node containing a value 10 as follows.

NULL	10	NULL

New

As root = NULL, we will call **New** node as **root**.

NULL	10	NULL

New / root

Now onward if we want to insert any node in the tree we will call **insert** function. Now suppose we want to insert 12 then there are two cases.

i) Insertion of a node as a left child

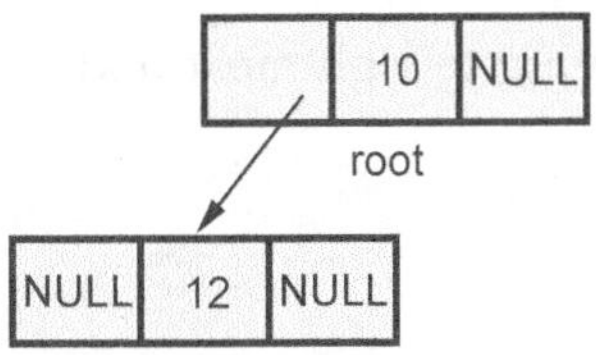


```
if(root→left = = NULL)
  root→left =New
```

ii) Insertion of a node as a right child

Suppose we want to insert 17 as a right child of node 10 then

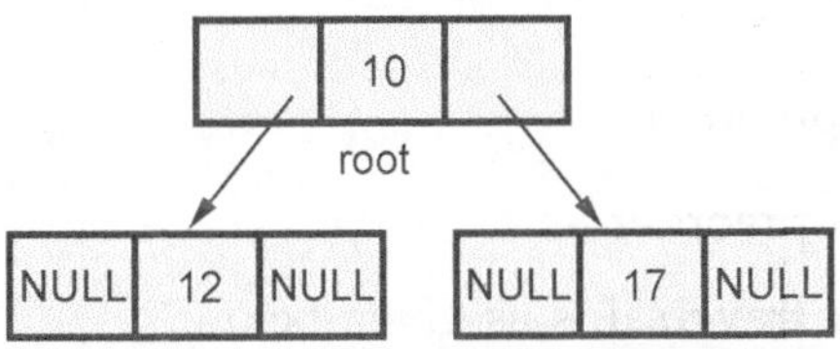


```
if(root→right = = NULL)
  root→right=New
```

Now further if we want to insert node 8 as a right child of node 12 then

insert (root → left, New);

By this we will reach at left node of 10 and then attach 8 as a right child of 12.

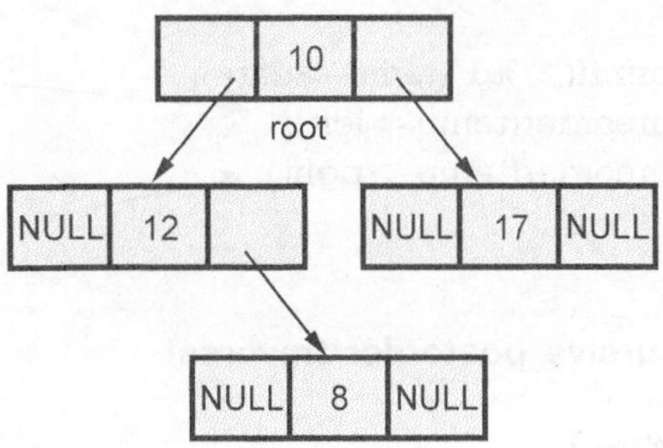

After creation of tree it can be traversed using inorder, preorder and postorder traversals.

1. Recursive inorder traversal

Algorithm :

1. If tree is not empty then

   a. traverse the left subtree in inorder.

   b. visit the root node.

   c. traverse the right subtree in inorder.

The recursive routine for inorder traversal is as given below.

```
void inorder(node *temp)
{
 if(temp!=NULL)
 {
      inorder(temp->left);          <- Moving to leftmost node
      printf(" %d",temp->data);
      inorder(temp->right);         <- Moving to rightmost node
 }
}
```

2. Recursive preorder traversal

Algorithm :

1. If tree is not empty then

   a. visit the root node.

   b. traverse the left subtree in preorder.

   c. traverse the right subtree in preorder

The recursive routine for preorder traversal is as given below.

```
void preorder(node *temp)
{
 if(temp!=NULL)
 {
      printf(" %d",temp->data);
      preorder(temp->left);         <- Moving to leftmost node
      preorder(temp->right);        <- Moving to rightmost node
 }
}
```

3. Recursive postorder traversal

Algorithm :

1. If tree is not empty then

   a. traverse the left subtree in postorder.

b. traverse the right subtree in postorder. c. visit the root node.

The recursive routine for postorder traversal is as given below.

```
void postorder(node *temp)
{
 if(temp!=NULL)
{
	postorder(temp->left);
	postorder(temp->right);
	printf(" %d",temp->data);
 }
}
```

The implementation of above routines is illustrated by following programs -

C Program for Recursive traversals

```
/*****************************************************************
Program for creation of a binary tree and display the tree using recursive inorder, preorder
and post order traversals
*****************************************************************/
#include <stdio.h>
#include<alloc.h>
#include<conio.h>

typedef struct bin
{
  int data;
  struct bin *left;
  struct bin *right;
}node;/*Binary tree structure*/

 void insert(node *, node *);
 void inorder(node *);
 void preorder(node *);
 void postorder(node *);
 node *get_node();

 void main()
 {
	int choice;
	char ans='n';
	node *New,*root;
	root=NULL;
```

```
clrscr();
do
{
 printf("\n Program For Implementing Simple Binary Tree");
    printf("\n 1.Create");
    printf("\n 2.Inorder");
    printf("\n 3.Preorder ");
    printf("\n 4.Postorder");
    printf("\n 5.Exit");
    printf("\n\t Enter Your Choice: ");
    scanf("%d",&choice);
    switch(choice)
    {
    case 1:root=NULL;
        do
        {
            New=get_node();
            printf("\n Enter The Element: ");
            scanf("%d",&New->data);
            if(root==NULL)
            root=New;

         else
            insert(root,New);
         printf("\n Do You want To Enter More
                 elements?(y/n):");
         ans=getche();
        }while(ans=='y'||ans=='Y');
        clrscr();
        break;
     case 2:if(root==NULL)
           printf("Tree Is not Created!");
          else
           inorder(root);
        break;
     case 3:if(root==NULL)
            printf("Tree Is Not Created!");
            else
```

```
            preorder(root);
              break;
           case 4:if(root==NULL)
                      printf("Tree Is Not Created!");
                  else
        postorder(root);
                        break;
        }
          }while(choice!=5);
    }

node *get_node()
{
    node *temp;
    temp = (node *)malloc(sizeof(node));

    temp->left = NULL;
    temp->right= NULL;
    return temp;
}

void insert(node *root,node *New)
{
 char ch;
 printf("\n Where to insert left/right of %d: ", root->data);
 ch=getche();
 if ((ch=='r')||(ch=='R'))
 {
     if(root->right==NULL)
     {
      root->right=New;
     }
     else
      insert(root->right,New);
 }
 else
     {
     if (root->left==NULL)
      {
```

```
            root->left=New;
        }
        else
            insert(root->left,New);
    }
}

void inorder(node *temp)
{
 if(temp!=NULL)
 {
     inorder(temp->left);
     printf(" %d",temp->data);
     inorder(temp->right);

 }
}
void preorder(node *temp)
{
 if(temp!=NULL)
 {
     printf(" %d",temp->data);
     preorder(temp->left);
     preorder(temp->right);
 }
}

void postorder(node *temp)
{
 if(temp!=NULL)
 {
     postorder(temp->left);
     postorder(temp->right);
     printf(" %d",temp->data);
 }
}
```

Output

```
Program For Implementing Simple Binary Tree
     1.Create
     2.Inorder
     3.Preorder
```

```
4.Postorder
5.Exit
Enter Your Choice: 1
Enter The Element: 10
Do You Want To Enter More Elements?(y/n): y
Enter The Element: 12
Where to insert left/right of 10: l
Do You Want To Enter More Elements?(y/n): y
Enter The Element: 17
Where to insert left/right of 10: r
Do You Want To Enter More Elements?(y/n): y
Enter The Element: 8

Where to insert left/right of 10: l
Where to insert left/right of 12: r
Do You Want To Enter More Elements?(y/n):
Program For Implementing Simple Binary Tree
1.Create
2.Inorder
3.Preorder
4.Postorder
5.Exit
Enter Your Choice: 2
12  8  10  17
Program For Implementing Simple Binary Tree
1.Create
2.Inorder
3.Preorder
4.Postorder
5.Exit
Enter Your Choice: 3
10  12  8  17
Program For Implementing Simple Binary Tree
1.Create
2.Inorder
3.Preorder
4.Postorder
5.Exit
Enter Your Choice: 4
8 12 17 10
Program For Implementing Simple Binary Tree
1.    Create
2.    Inorder
3.    Preorder
4.    Postorder
5.    Exit
Enter Your Choice: 5
```

C Program - For Non Recursive Traversals

```
/*******************************************************************
Program For Implementation Of Simple Binary Tree and
Non recursive inorder, preorder and postorder traversals.
*******************************************************************/
#include<stdio.h>
#include<conio.h>
#include <stdlib.h>
typedef struct bst

{
 int data;
 struct bst *left,*right;
}node;
	node *get_node();
	void push(node *item,int *top,node *s[10]);
	int stempty(int);
	void pop(int *top,node *s[10],node **curent);

void main()
{
	int choice;
	char ans='N';
	node  *root,*New;
	void display(node *);
	void insert(node *,node *);


	clrscr();
	printf("\n\t Program For Binary Tree ");
	root=NULL;
	while(1)
	{
		printf("\n\n1.Create\n2.Display \n3. Exit");
		printf("\n\n Enter your choice :");
		scanf("%d",&choice);
		switch(choice)
		{
		 case 1:root=NULL;
			do
			{
				New=get_node();
				printf("\n Enter The Element: ");
				scanf("%d",&New->data);
				if(root==NULL)
				root=New;
			else
```

```
                    insert(root,New);
            printf("\n Do You want To Enter More
                    elements?(y/n):");
            ans=getche();
           }while(ans=='y'||ans=='Y');
           clrscr();
           break;

      case 2:display(root);
             break;
      case 3:exit(0);
      }
   }
}
node *get_node()
{
 node *temp;
 temp=(node *)malloc(sizeof(node));
 temp->left=NULL;
 temp->right=NULL;
 return temp;
}
void insert(node *root,node *New)
{
  char ch;
  printf("\n Where to insert left/right of %d: ",root->data);
  ch=getche();
  if ((ch=='r')||(ch=='R'))
  {
       if(root->right==NULL)
        {
         root->right=New;
        }
       else
         insert(root->right,New);
  }
  else
  {
     if (root->left==NULL)
      {
       root->left=New;
      }
      else
        insert(root->left,New);
  }
}
```

```
/*
      display of binary search tree
*/
void display(node *root)
{
 void inorder(node *);
 void preorder(node *);
 void postorder(node *);
 if(root==NULL)
       printf("Tree Is Not Created");
 else
       {
             printf("\n The Inorder Traversal of Tree is : ");
             inorder(root);
             printf("\n The Preorder Traversal of Tree is : ");
             preorder(root);
             printf("\n The Postorder Traversal of Tree is : ");
             postorder(root);
       }
}
/*
             Inorder display of tree
*/
void inorder(node  *root)
{
 node *current,*s[10];
 int top=-1;
 if(root==NULL)
 {
       printf("\n Tree is empty\n");
       return;
 }
 current=root;
 for(;;)
 {
       while(current!=NULL)
       {
             push(current,&top,s);
             current=current->left;
       }
       if(!stempty(top))
       {
             pop(&top,s,&current);
             printf(" %d",current->data);
             current=current->right;
```

```
        }
        else
                return;
}
}

/*
        Preorder display of tree
*/
void preorder(node *root)
{
 node *current,*s[10];
 int top=-1;
 if(root==NULL)
 {
        printf("\n The Tree is empty\n");
        return;
 }
 current=root; //start from root node
 for(;;)
 {
        while(current!=NULL)
        {
         printf(" %d",current->data); // print the current parent node
         push(current,&top,s);  //push this visited node onto the stack
         current=current->left; //move onto left branch
        }
        if(!stempty(top))
        {
         pop(&top,s,&current); //pop the most recently visited node
         current=current->right; // and move onto right branch
        }
        else
         return;
 }
}
/*
        Postorder display of tree
*/
void postorder(node *root)
{
 struct stack
 {
        node *element;//Here placing the node containing value
        int check;//check 1 means visiting left subtree
                //check 0 means visiting right subtree
 }st[10];
```

```
 int top=-1;
 node *current;
 if(root==NULL)
 {
     printf("\n The Tree is empty\n");
     return;
 }
 current=root;
 for(;;)
 {
      while(current!=NULL)
      {
           top++;
           st[top].element=current;
           st[top].check=1;//visiting the left subbranch
           current=current->left;
      }
      while(st[top].check==0)
      {
           current=st[top].element;
           top--;
           printf(" %d",current->data);
           if(stempty(top))
            return;
      }
      current=st[top].element;//pushing the element onto the stack
      current=current->right;
      st[top].check=0;//visiting right subtree
 }
}
/*
           pushing the element onto the stack
*/
void push(node *item,int *top,node *s[])
{
 *top=*top+1;
 s[*top]=item;
}
/*
     popping the element from the stack

*/
void pop(int *top,node *s[],node **current)
{
```

```
 *current=s[(*top)--];
}
/*
 Checking for stack empty condition
*/
int stempty(int top)
{
 if(top==-1)
        return 1;
 else
        return 0;
}
```

Output

```
        Program For Binary Tree

1.Create
2.Display
3.Exit

 Enter your choice :1

 Enter The Element: 4

 Do You want To Enter More elements?(y/n):y
 Enter The Element: 3

 Where to insert left/right of 4: l
 Do You want To Enter More elements?(y/n):y
 Enter The Element: 6

 Where to insert left/right of 4: r
 Do You want To Enter More elements?(y/n):y
 Enter The Element: 1

 Where to insert left/right of 4: l
 Where to insert left/right of 3: l
 Do You want To Enter More elements?(y/n):y
 Enter The Element: 2

 Where to insert left/right of 4: l
 Where to insert left/right of 3: l
 Where to insert left/right of 1: r
 Do You want To Enter More elements?(y/n):y
```

```
Enter The Element: 5

Where to insert left/right of 4: r
Where to insert left/right of 6: l
Do You want To Enter More elements?(y/n):y
Enter The Element: 7

Where to insert left/right of 4: r
Where to insert left/right of 6: r
Do You want To Enter More elements?(y/n):y

1.Create
2.Display
3. Exit

Enter your choice :2

The Inorder Traversal of Tree is :  1 2 3 4 5 6 7
The Preorder Traversal of Tree is : 4 3 1 2 6 5 7
The Postorder Traversal of Tree is :  2 1 3 5 7 6 4

1.Create
2.Display
3. Exit

Enter your choice :3
```

Review Questions

1. *Write a C program to delete a node in a binary tree* **GTU : Dec.-05, Marks 7, May-11, Marks 6**
2. *List out different traversal way of tree and demonstrate any two with example.* **GTU : Winter-14, Marks 7**
3. *Write an algorithm to delete a node from tree.* **GTU : Winter-14, Marks 7**
4. *Write recursive 'C' functions for (1) in-order (2) pre-order and (3) post-order traversals of binary search tree.* **GTU : Summer-15, Marks 7**

6.6 Binary Search Tree

GTU : May-12, Summer-13,14,15,17,18, Winter-13,15,16,18, Marks 7

In the simple binary tree the nodes are arranged in any fashion. Depending on user's desire the new nodes can be attached as a left or right child of any desired node. In such a case finding for any node is a long cut procedure, because in that case we have to search the entire tree. And thus the searching time complexity will

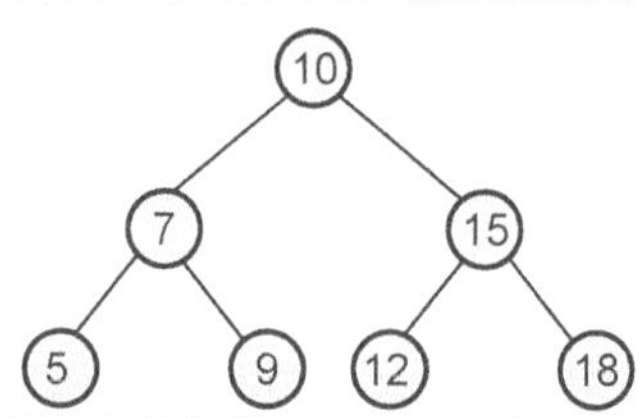

Fig. 6.6.1 Binary search tree

get increased unnecessarily. So to make the searching algorithm faster in a binary tree we will go for building the binary search tree. The binary search tree is based on the binary search algorithm. While creating the binary search tree the data is systematically arranged. That means values at left subtree < root node value < Right subtree values. See the Fig. 6.6.1

If you observe the Fig. 6.6.1 carefully, you will find that the left value < parent value < right value is followed throughout the tree.

Definition of binary search tree : Binary search tree is a binary tree in which left node is < parent node < right node.

Various operations that can be performed on binary search tree are -

1. Insertion of a node in a binary tree.
2. Deletion of some element from the binary search tree.
3. Searching of an element in the binary tree.
4. Display of binary tree.

Let us discuss each operation one by one -

1. Insertion of a node in a binary tree

Algorithm :

1. Read the value for the node which is to be created and store it in a node called **New**.
2. Initially if (root!=**NULL**) then root=**New**.
3. Again read the next value of node created in **New**.
4. If (New–>value < root–>value) then attach **New** node as a left child of root otherwise attach **New** node as a right child of root.
5. Repeat step 3 and 4 for constructing required binary search tree completely.

```
void insert(node *root,node *New)
{
 if(New->data<root->data)
 {
  if(root->left==NULL)
       root->left=New;
  else
       insert(root->left,New);
  }
  if(New->data>root->data)
  {
   if(root->right==NULL)
        root->right=New;
         else
        insert(root->right,New);
  }
}
```

Attaching left node to the current node

If the root node has already some left child, then move on to left - subtree

While inserting any node in binary search tree, first of all we have to look for its appropriate position in the binary search tree. We start comparing this new node with each node of the tree. If the value of the node which is to be inserted is greater than the value of current node we move on to the right subbranch otherwise we move on to the left subbranch. As soon as the appropriate position is found we attach this new node as left or right child appropriately.

In the Fig. 6.6.2 if we want to insert 23. Then we will start comparing 23 with value of root node i.e. 6. As 23 is greater than 10, we will move on right subtree. Now we will compare 23 with 20 and move right, compare 23 with 22 and move right. Now compare 23 with 24 but it is less than 24. We will move on left branch of 24. But as there is NULL node as left child of 24, we can attach 23 as left child of 24.

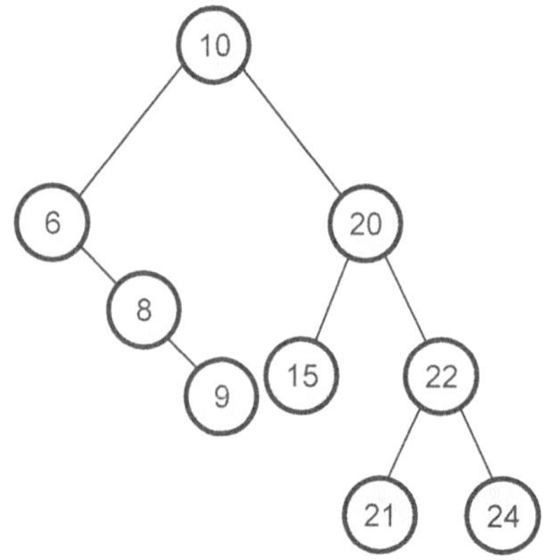

Fig. 6.6.2 Before insertion

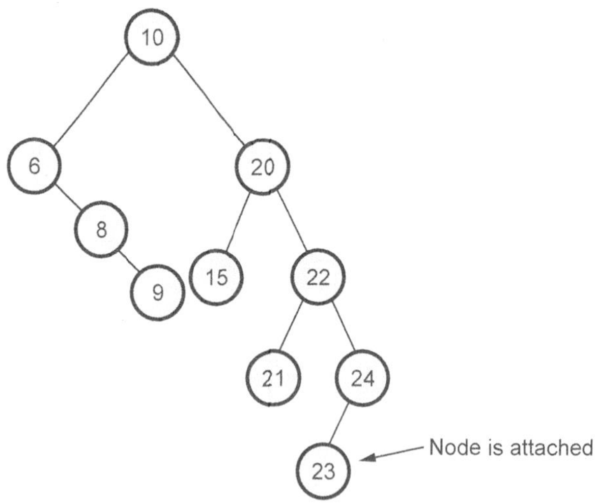

Fig. 6.6.3 After insertion

Example 6.6.1 *Construct the binary search tree from the following set of strings. MAR, MAY, NOV, AUG, APR, JAN, DEC, JUL, FEB, JUN, OCT and SEP. Show all the steps.*

Solution : Consider the set of strings.

as - MAR, MAY, NOV, AUG, APR, JAN, DEC, JUL, FEB, JUN, OCT, SEP.

We will arrange these nodes in their alphabetical order, for building the binary search tree.

Step 1 :

Step 2 :

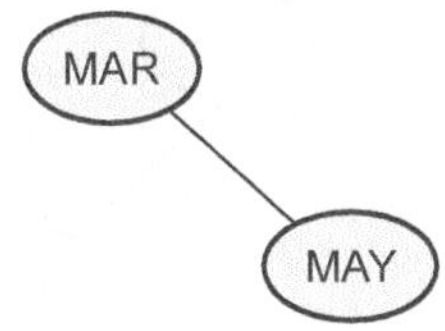

Step 3 :

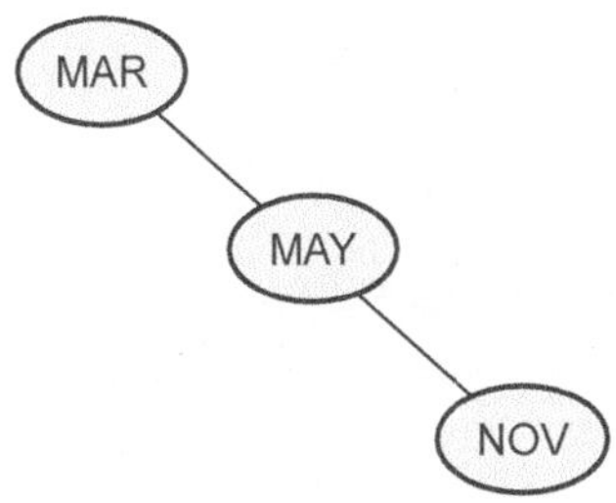

Step 4 :

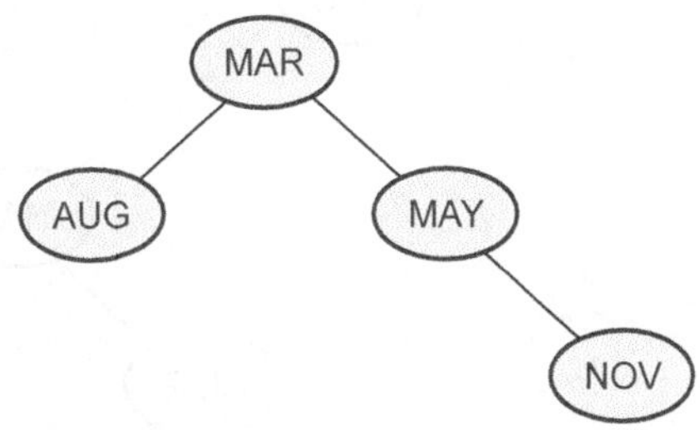

Step 5 :

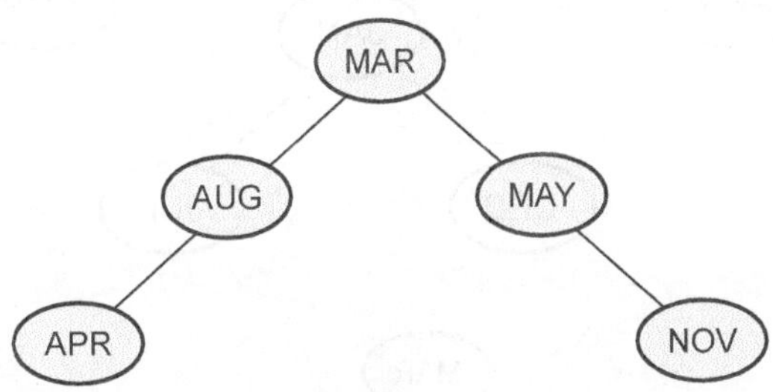

Step 6 :

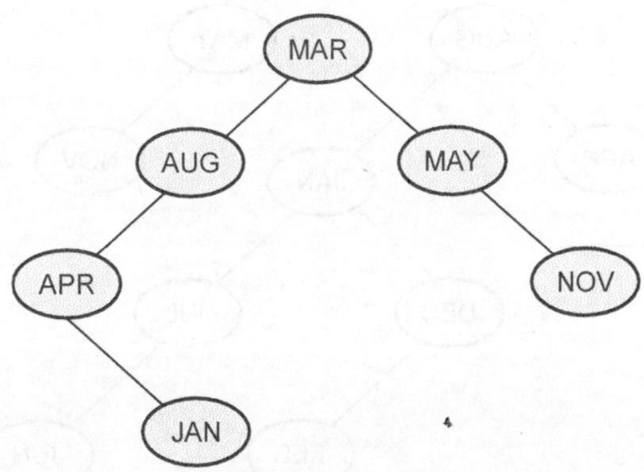

Step 7 :

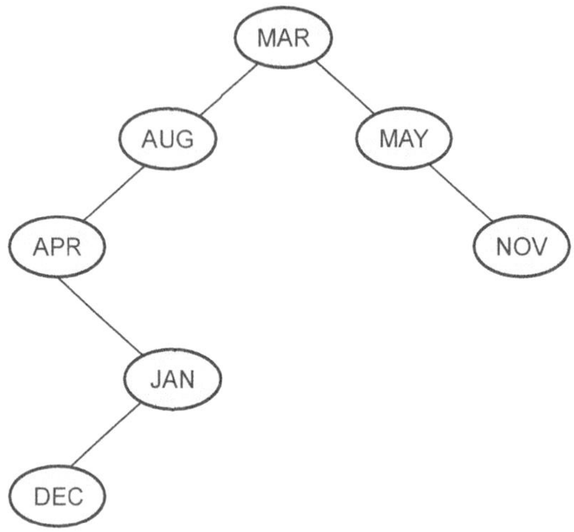

Step 8 :

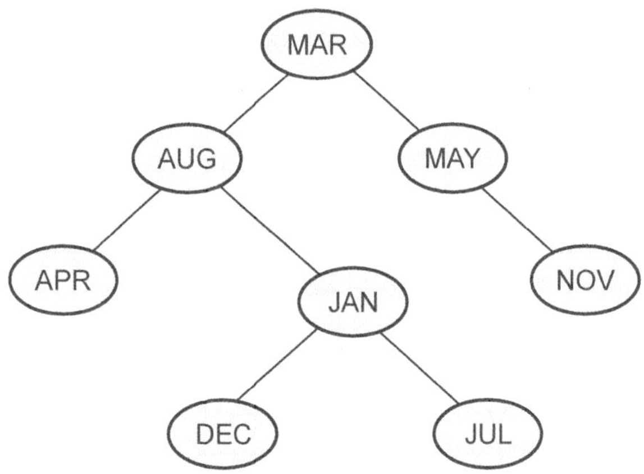

Step 9 :

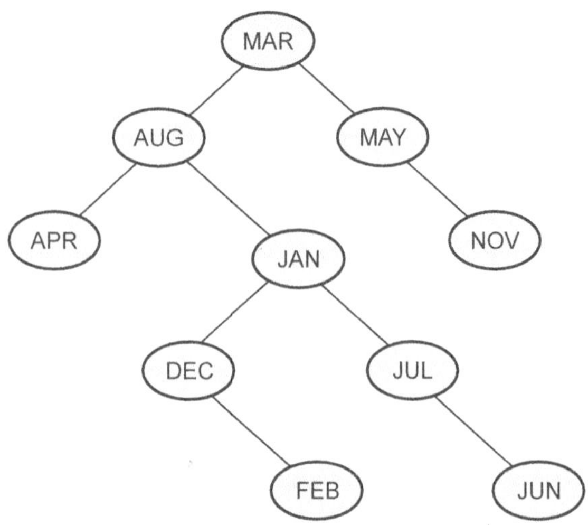

Step 10 :

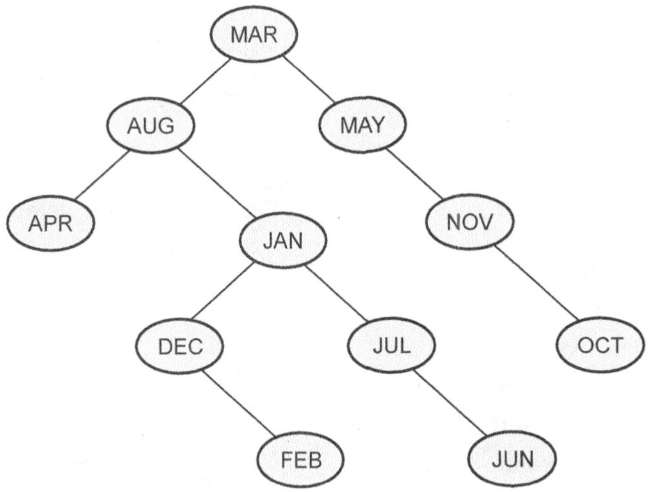

Step 11 :

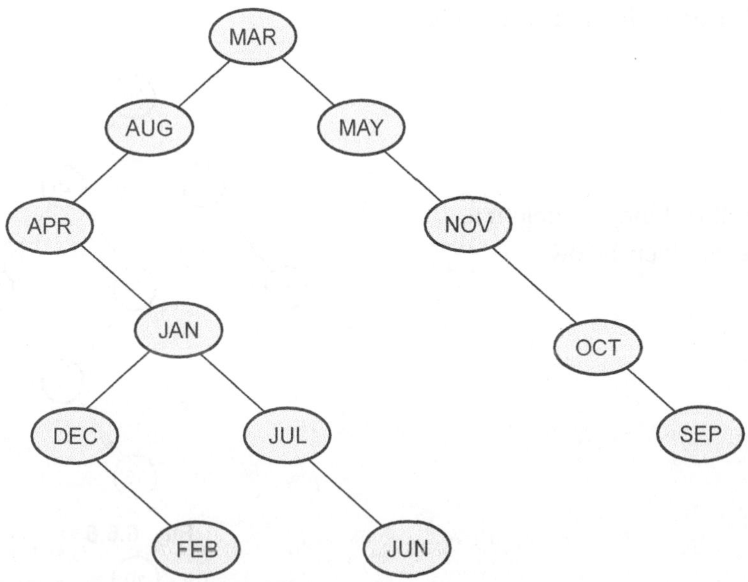

Thus the binary search tree is build.

2. Deletion of an element from the binary tree

For deletion of any node from binary search tree there are three cases which are possible.

i) Deletion of leaf node.

ii) Deletion of a node having one child.

iii) Deletion of a node having two children.

Let us discuss the above cases one by one.

i) Deletion of leaf node.

This is the simplest deletion, in which we set the left or right pointer of parent node as NULL.

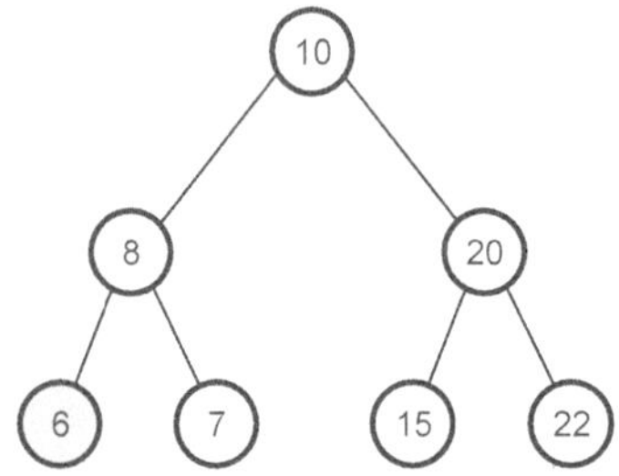

Fig. 6.6.4 Before deletion

From the above tree, we want to delete the node having value 6 then we will set left pointer of its parent node as NULL. That is left pointer of node having value 8 is set to NULL.

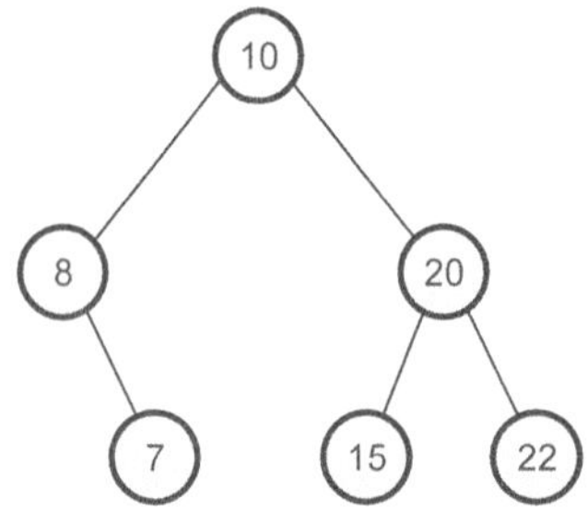

Fig. 6.6.5 After deletion

ii) Deletion of a node having one child.

To explain this kind of deletion, consider a tree as given below.

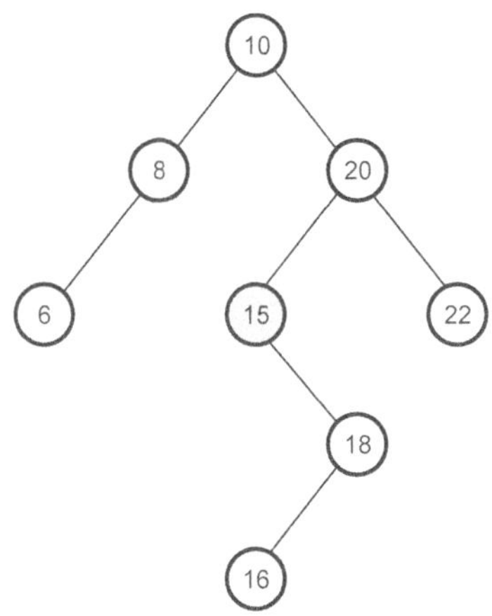

Fig. 6.6.6

If we want to delete the node 15, then we will simply copy node 18 at place of 15 and then set the node free. The inorder successor is always copied at the position of a node being deleted.

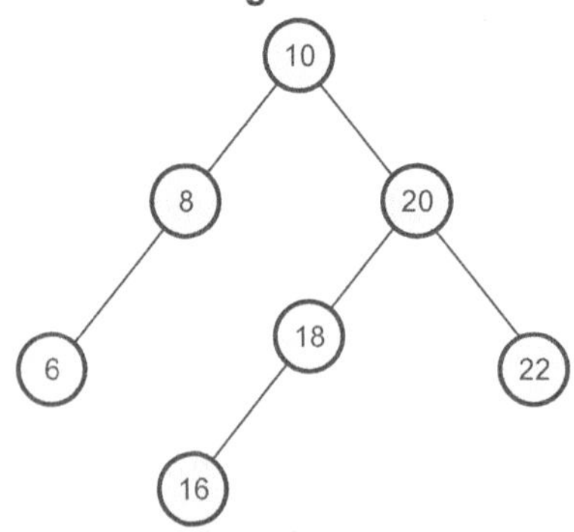

Fig. 6.6.7 After deletion

iii) The node having two children.

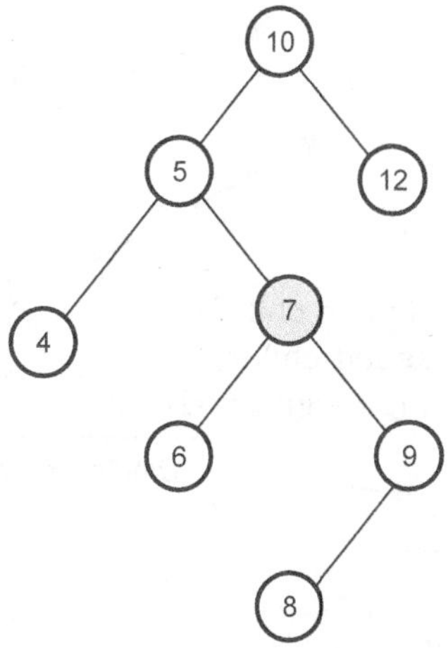

Fig. 6.6.8 Before deletion

Again, let us take some example for discussing this kind of deletion.

Let us consider that we want to delete node having value 7. We will then find out the inorder successor of node 7. The inorder successor will be simply copied at location of node 7. Thats it !

That means copy 8 at the position where value of node is 7. Set left pointer of 9 as NULL. This completes the deletion procedure.

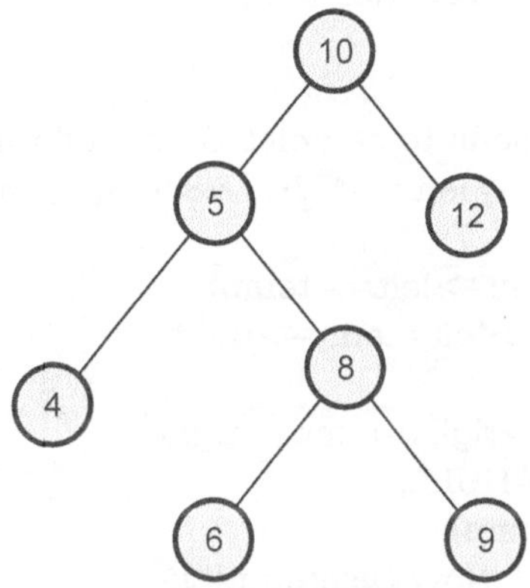

Fig. 6.6.9 After deletion

```
void del(node *root,int key)
 {
      node *temp,*parent,*temp_succ;

      temp=search(root,key,&parent);
      /*deleting a node with two children*/
      if(temp->left!=NULL&&temp->right!=NULL)
      {
       parent=temp;
       temp_succ=temp->right;
       while(temp_succ->left!=NULL)
       {
```

temp is node which is to be deleted. Parent is a node which deeps track of parent of node **temp** and **temp_succ** is for keeping track of success of **temp**.

```
            parent=temp_succ;
            temp_succ=temp_succ->left;
        }
        temp->data=temp_succ->data;
        parent->right=NULL;
        printf(" Now Deleted it!");
        return;
}
```

Moving to leftmost subtree

Copying the successor node's data to temp node. Thus content of temp node gets deleted.

```
    /*deleting a node having only one child*/
    /*The node to be deleted has left child*/
    if(temp->left!=NULL &&temp->right==NULL)
    {
      if(parent->left==temp)
         parent->left=temp->left;
     else
    parent->right=temp->left;
     temp=NULL;
     free(temp);
     printf(" Now Deleted it!");
     return;
    }
```

Dinding parent of temp.

```
    /*The node to be deleted has right child*/
    if(temp->left==NULL &&temp->right!=NULL)
    {
     if(parent->left==temp)
    parent->left=temp->right;
     else
    parent->right=temp->right;
     temp=NULL;
     free(temp);
     printf(" Now Deleted it!");
     return;
}
    /*deleting a node which is having no child*/
    if(temp->left==NULL &&temp->right==NULL)
    {
     if(parent->left==temp)
            parent->left=NULL;
     else
            parent->right=NULL;
     printf(" Now Deleted it!");
     return;
    }
}
```

We are deleting left node of **parent** node means simply set left pointer of **parent** to NULL

Otherwise set right pointer of **parent** to NULL

3. Searching a node from binary search tree.

In searching, the node which we want to search is called a key node. The key node will be compared with each node starting from root node if value of key node is greater than current node then we search for it on right subbranch otherwise on left subbranch. If we reach to leaf node and still we do not get the value of key node then we declare "node is not present in the tree".

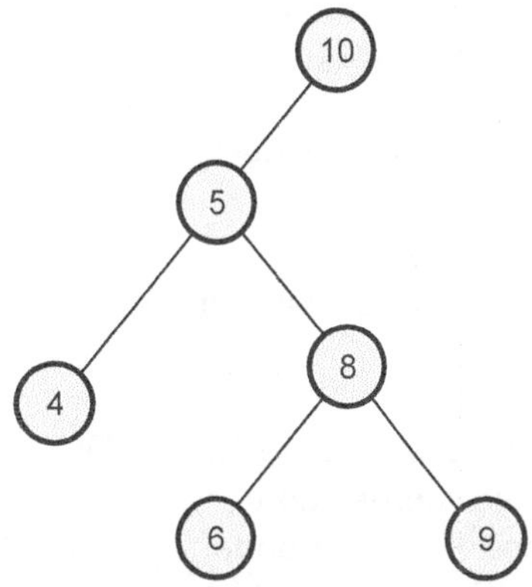

Fig. 6.6.10 Binary search tree

In the above tree, if we want to search for value 9. Then we will compare 9 with root node 10. As 9 is less than 10 we will search on left subbranch. Now compare 9 with 5, but 9 is greater than 5. So we will move on right subbranch. Now compare 9 with 8 but as 9 is greater than 8 we will move on right subbranch. As the node we will get holds the value 9. Thus the desired node can be searched. Let us see the 'C' implementation of it.

The routine is as given below -

```
node *search(node *root,int key,node **parent)
{
 node *temp;
 temp=root;
 while(temp!=NULL)
 {
  if(temp->data==key)
  {
       printf("\n The %d Element is Present",temp->data);
       return temp;
  }
       *parent=temp;          ← Marking the parent node
       if(temp->data>key)     ← If current node is greater than key
            temp=temp->left;  ← Search for the left subtree
       else
       temp=temp->right;
 }
 return NULL;
}
```

We can display a tree in inorder fashion. Hence the complete implementation is given below along with appropriate output.

C Program

```
/*************************************************************
Program For Implementation Of Binary Search Tree and
perform insertion deletion, searching, display of tree.
*************************************************************/
```

```
# include <stdio.h>
# include <conio.h>
# include <stdlib.h>

typedef struct bst
{
      int data;
      struct bst *left,*right;
}node;

void insert(node *,node *);
void inorder(node *);
node *search(node *,int,node **);
void del(node *,int);

void main()
{
 int choice;
 char ans='N';
 int key;
 node *New,*root,*tmp,*parent;
 node *get_node();
 root=NULL;
 clrscr();
 printf("\n\t Program For Binary Search Tree ");
 do
 {
  printf("\n1.Create\n2.Search\n3.Delete\n4.Display");
  printf("\n\n Enter your choice :");
  scanf("%d",&choice);
  switch(choice)
  {
   case 1:do
          {
           New=get_node();
           printf("\n Enter The Element ");
           scanf("%d",&New->data);
           if(root==NULL)   /* Tree is not Created */
               root=New;
           else
             insert(root,New);
           printf("\n Do u Want To enter More
            Elements?(y/n)");
           ans=getch();;
          }while(ans=='y');
          break;
```

```
    case 2:printf("\n Enter The Element Which You Want To
                          Search");
              scanf("%d",&key);
              tmp=search(root,key,&parent);
              printf("\n Parent of node %d is %d",
                          tmp->data,parent->data);
                 break;
     case 3:printf("\n Enter The Element U wish to Delete");
               scanf("%d",&key);
               del(root,key);
               break;
     case 4:if(root==NULL)
                 printf("Tree Is Not Created");
               else
               {
                 printf("\n The Tree is : ");
                 inorder(root);
               }
               break;
      }
 }while(choice!=5);
}
node *get_node()
{
 node *temp;
 temp=(node *)malloc(sizeof(node));
 temp->left=NULL;
 temp->right=NULL;
 return temp;
}

/*This function is for creating a binary search tree */

void insert(node *root,node *New)
{
 if(New->data<root->data)
 {
 if(root->left==NULL)
      root->left=New;
 else
      insert(root->left,New);
 }
 if(New->data>root->data)
 {
  if(root->right==NULL)
       root->right=New;
  else
```

```
        insert(root->right,New);
  }
}


/*
This function is for searching the node from binary Search Tree
*/
node *search(node *root,int key,node **parent)
{
 node *temp;
 temp=root;
 while(temp!=NULL)
 {
  if(temp->data==key)
  {
        printf("\n The %d Element is Present",temp->data);
        return temp;
  }
  *parent=temp;
  if(temp->data>key)
    temp=temp->left;
  else
        temp=temp->right;
 }
 return NULL;
}
/*
This function is for deleting a node from binary search tree There exists three possible
cases for deletion of a node
*/
void del(node *root,int key)
{
       node *temp,*parent,*temp_succ;
       temp=search(root,key,&parent);
       /*deleting a node with two children*/
       if(temp->left!=NULL&&temp->right!=NULL)
       {
        parent=temp;
        temp_succ=temp->right;
        while(temp_succ->left!=NULL)
        {
               parent=temp_succ;
               temp_succ=temp_succ->left;
        }

        temp->data=temp_succ->data;
```

Finding successor node of **temp node**

```
        parent->right=NULL;
        printf(" Now Deleted it!");
        return;
       }
```

Copy the data of successor node to temp node

```
      /*deleting a node having only one child*/
      /*The node to be deleted has left child*/
      if(temp->left!=NULL &&temp->right==NULL)
      {
       if(parent->left==temp)
        parent->left=temp->left;
       else
      parent->right=temp->left;
       temp=NULL;
       free(temp);
       printf(" Now Deleted it!");
       return;
      }
      /*The node to be deleted has right child*/
      if(temp->left==NULL &&temp->right!=NULL)
      {
       if(parent->left==temp)
      parent->left=temp->right;
```

Parent's left child is deleted

```
       else
      parent->right=temp->right;
       temp=NULL;
       free(temp);
       printf(" Now Deleted it!");
       return;
      }
      /*deleting a node which is having no child*/
      if(temp->left==NULL &&temp->right==NULL)
      {
       if(parent->left==temp)
             parent->left=NULL;
```

Simply make parent's left pointer NULL, so that left child of parent is deleted

```
       else
             parent->right=NULL;
       printf(" Now Deleted it!");
       return;
      }
 }
/*
This function displays the tree in inorder fashion
*/
void inorder(node *temp)
{
 if(temp!=NULL)
 {
```

```
        inorder(temp->left);
        printf(" %d",temp->data);
        inorder(temp->right);
    }
}
```

Output

```
Program For Binary Search Tree
 1. Create
 2. Search
 3. Delete
 4. Display

 Enter your choice :1

 Enter The Element 10

 Do u Want To enter More  Elements?(y/n)
 Enter The Element 8

 Do u Want To enter More  Elements?(y/n)
 Enter The Element 9

 Do u Want To enter More  Elements?(y/n)
 Enter The Element 7

 Do u Want To enter More  Elements?(y/n)
 Enter The Element 15

 Do u Want To enter More  Elements?(y/n)
 Enter The Element 13

 Do u Want To enter More  Elements?(y/n)
 Enter The Element 14

 Do u Want To enter More  Elements?(y/n)
 Enter The Element 12

 Do u Want To enter More  Elements?(y/n)
 Enter The Element 16
 Do u Want To enter More  Elements?(y/n)
 1. Create
 2. Search
 3. Delete
 4. Display

 Enter your choice :4
 The Tree is :  7  8  9  10  12  13  14  15  16
```

```
1. Create
2. Search
3. Delete
4. Display

 Enter your choice :2

 Enter The Element Which You Want To Search16

 The 16 Element is Present
 Parent of node 16 is 15
1. Create
2. Search
3. Delete
4. Display

 Enter your choice :3

 Enter The Element U wish to Delete13

 The 13 Element is Present Now Deleted it!
1. Create
2. Search
3. Delete
4. Display

 Enter your choice :4

 The Tree is :   7  8  9  10  12  14  15  16
1. Create
2. Search
3. Delete
4. Display

 Enter your choice :3
 Enter The Element U wish to Delete8


 The 8 Element is Present Now Deleted it!
1. Create
2. Search
3. Delete
4. Display

 Enter your choice :4
 The Tree is :   7  9  10  12  14  15  16
1. Create
```

2. Search
3. Delete
4. Display

Enter your choice : 5

Example 6.6.2 *First insert 10 and then 24. After these insertions, delete 37 and then delete 22 from the following binary search tree. Draw the tree after each operation.*

GTU : May-12, Marks 7

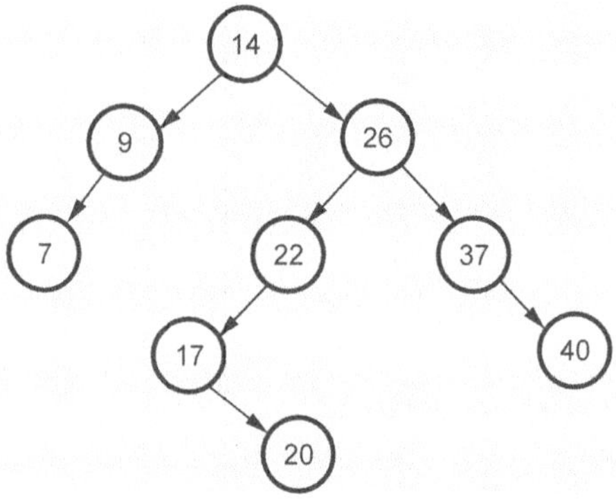

Solution :

Step 1 : Insert 10

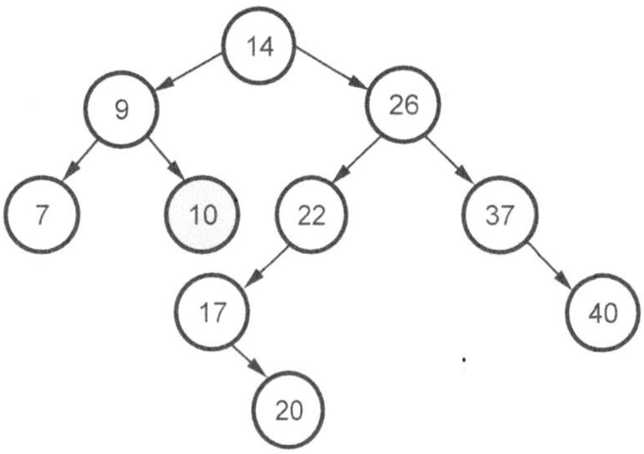

Step 2 : Insert 24

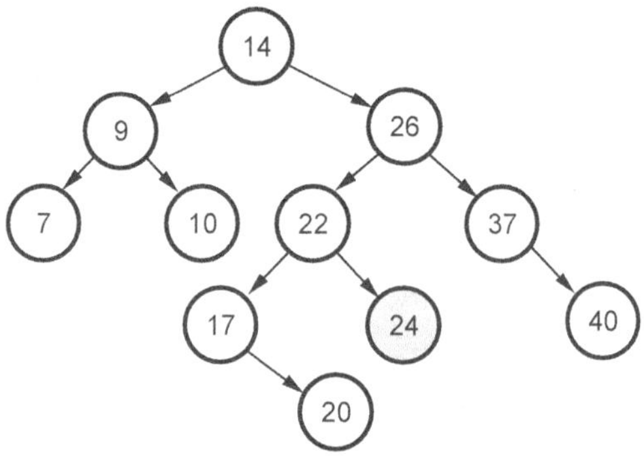

Step 3 : Insert 37

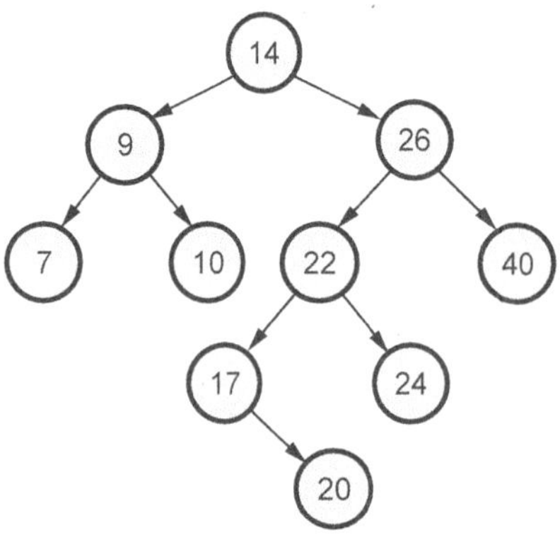

Step 4 : Insert 22

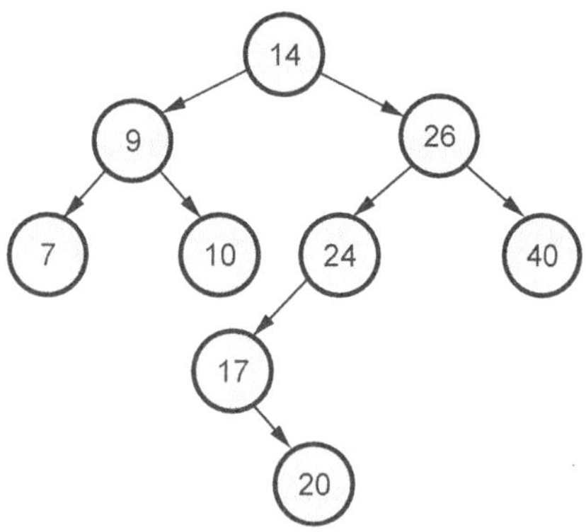

Example 6.6.3 *Briefly explain advantages of binary search tree. Construct binary search tree for the following elements*

8, 3, 11, 5, 9, 12, 13, 4, 6, 20. **GTU : Summer-13, Marks 7**

Solution :

Advantages of BST

1. The nodes are arranged systematically.
2. The insertion and deletion operations are efficient.
3. Searching of any node is efficient.

Step 1 : Insert 8

Step 2 : Insert 3

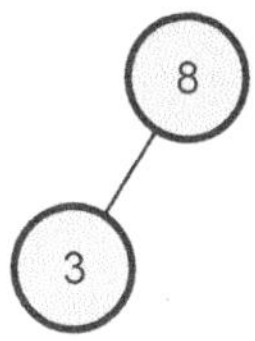

Step 3 : Insert 11

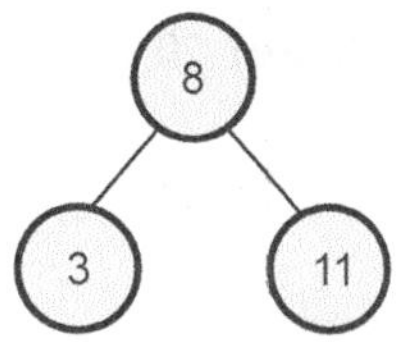

Step 4 : Insert 5

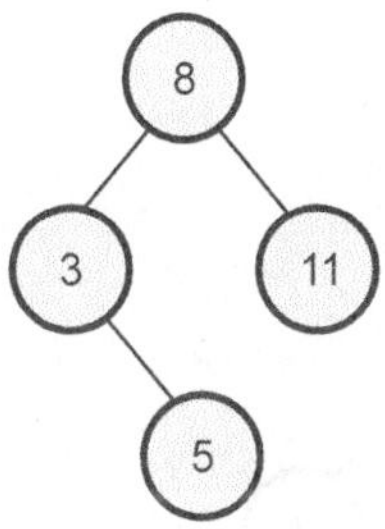

Step 5 : Insert 9

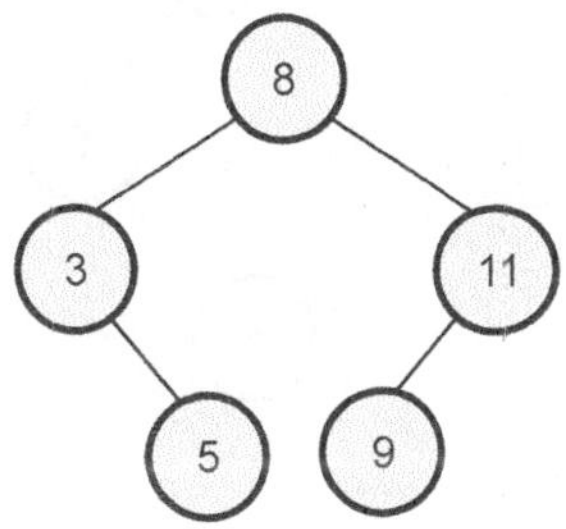

Step 6 : Insert 12

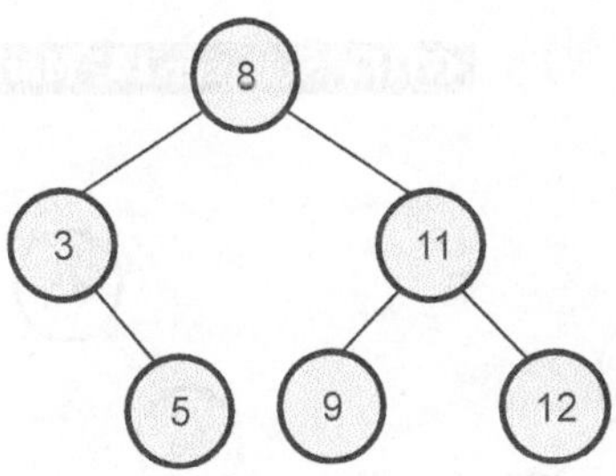

Step 7 : Insert 13

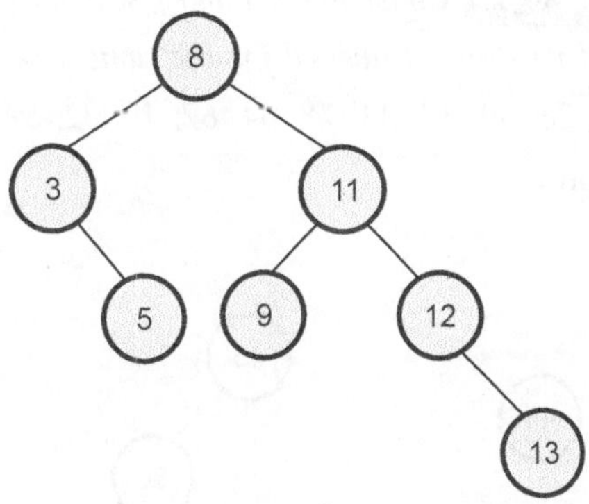

Step 8 : Insert 4

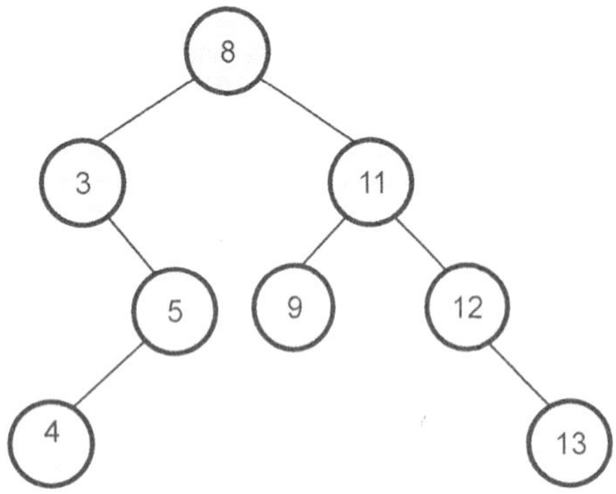

Step 9 : Insert 6

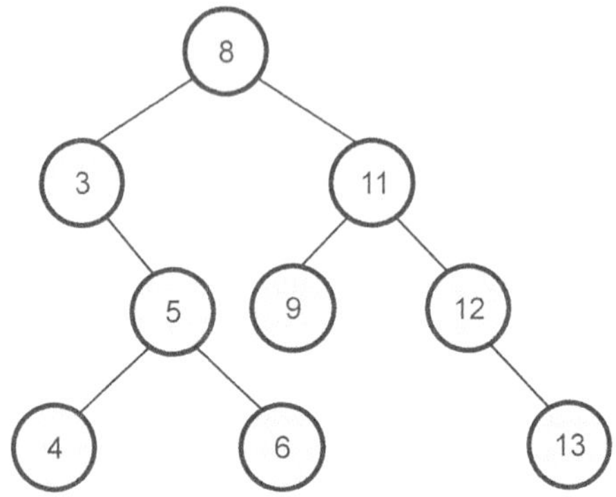

Step 10 : Insert 20

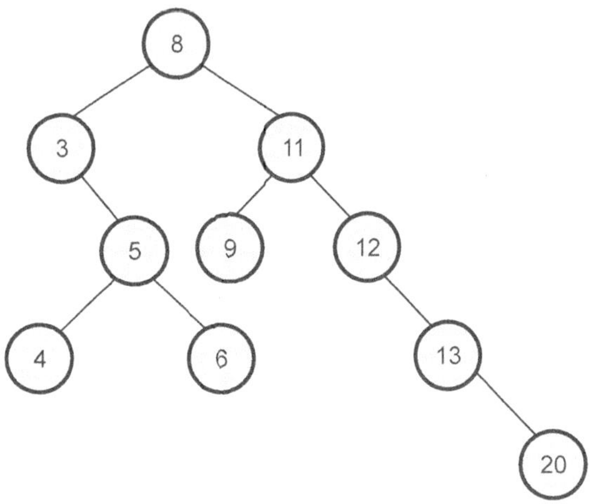

Example 6.6.4 *Construct a binary search tree for the following sequence. Also do the inorder and postorder traversal for the same.*

45, 56, 39, 12, 34, 78, 54, 67, 10, 32, 89, 81 **GTU : Summer-14, Marks 7**

Solution :

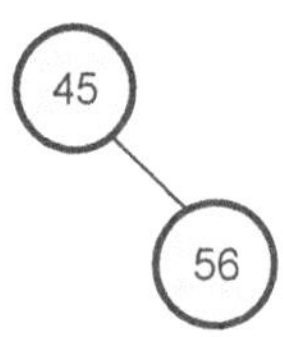

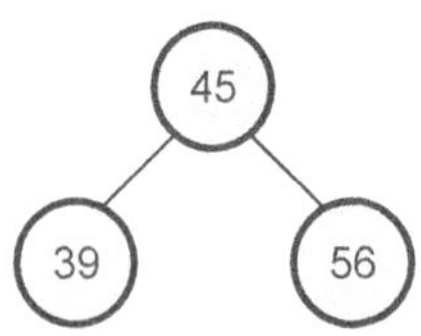

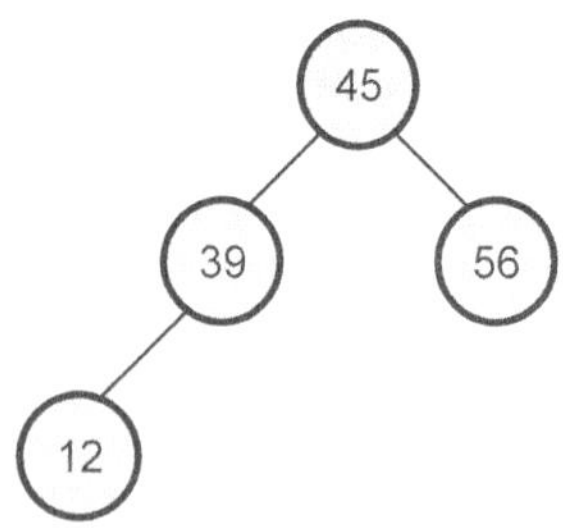

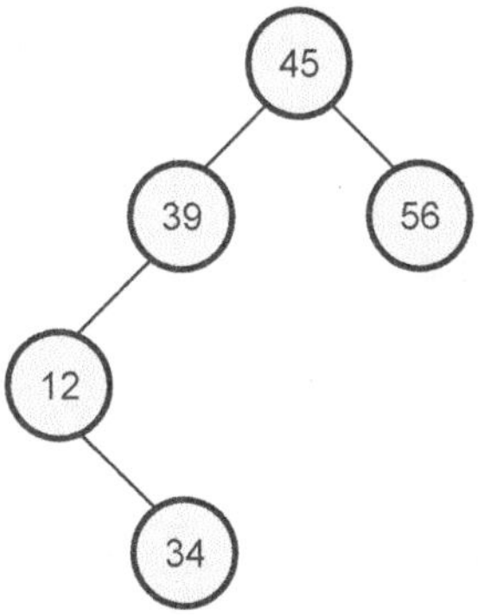
45
39
56
12
34

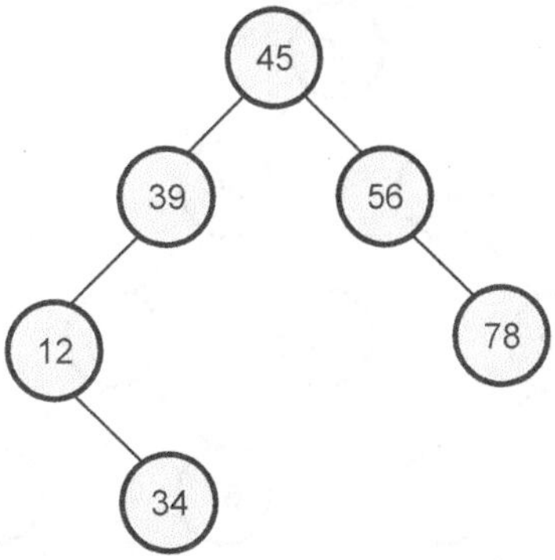
45
39
56
12
78
34

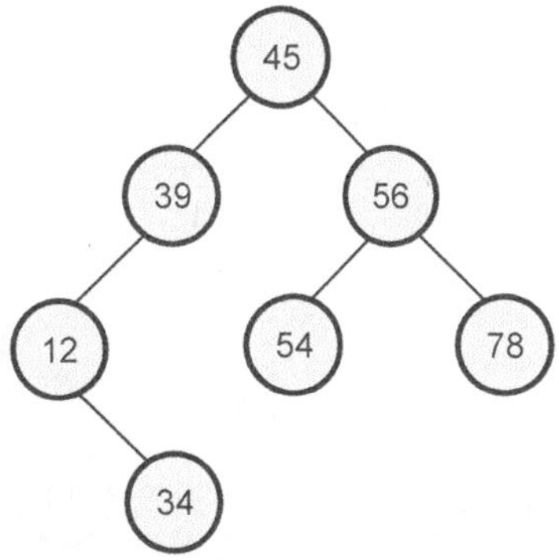
45
39
56
12
54
78
34

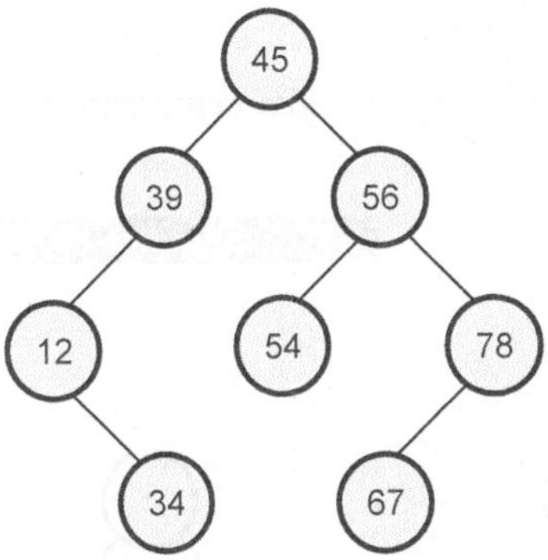
45
39
56
12
54
78
34
67

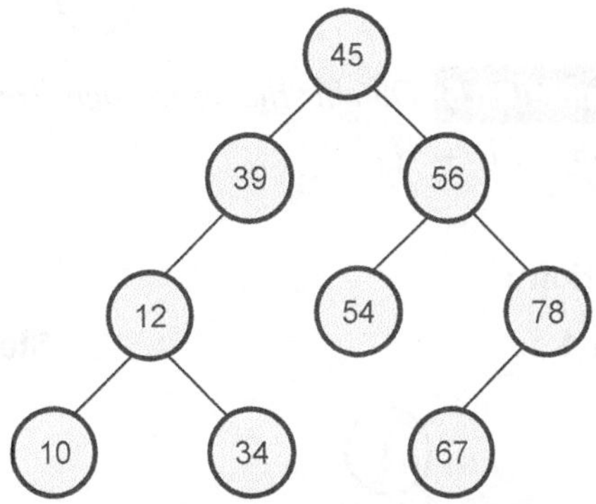
45
39
56
12
54
78
10
34
67

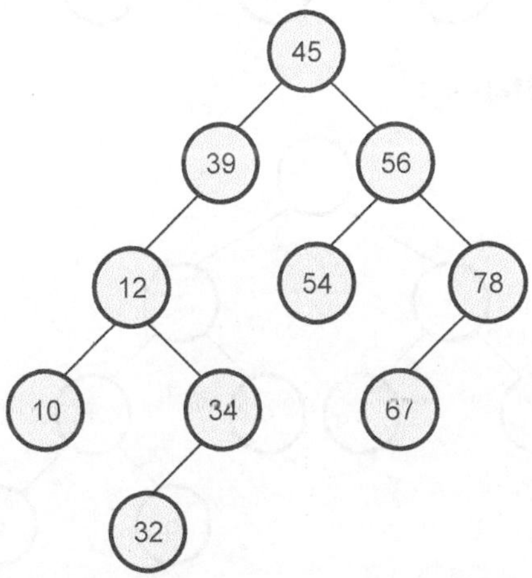
45
39
56
12
54
78
10
34
67
32

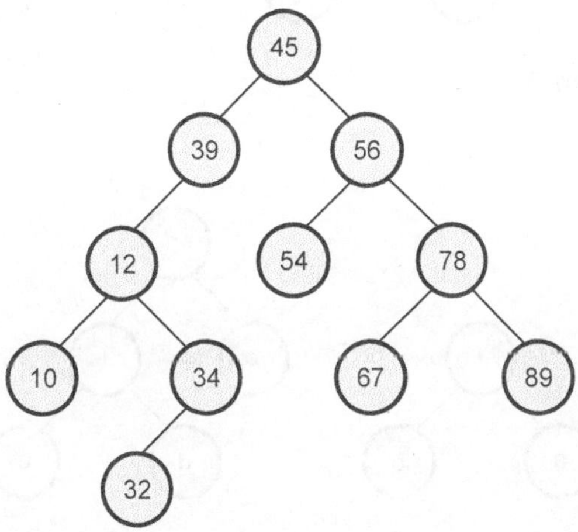
45
39
56
12
54
78
10
34
67
89
32

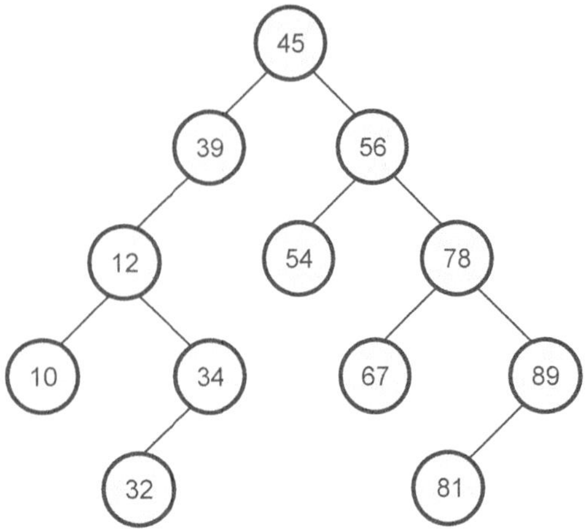

Example 6.6.5 *Obtain the expression tree from the following postfix representation ab + cde + ***

GTU : Summer-14, Marks 2

Solution :

Step 1 :

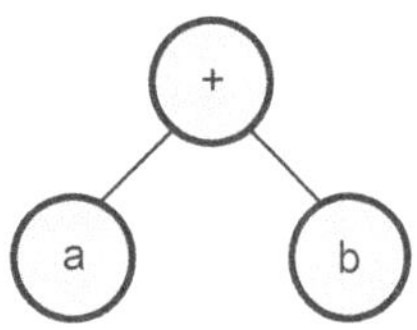

Step 2 :

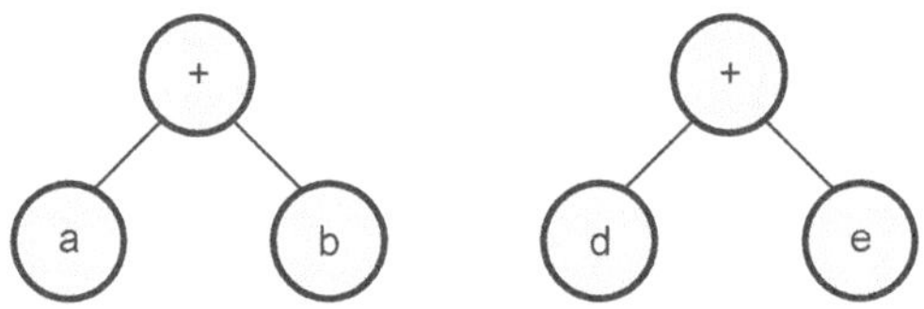

Step 3 :

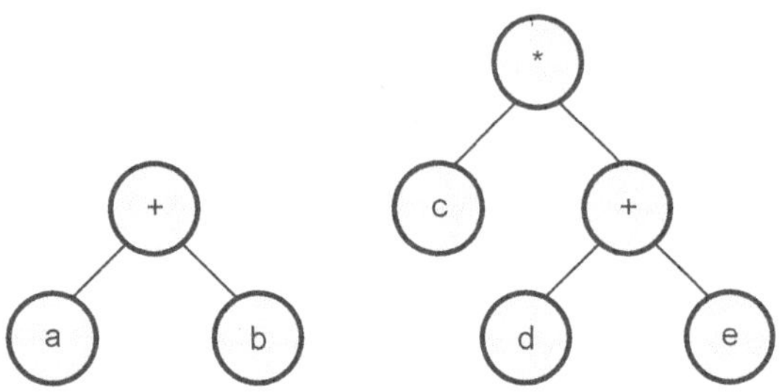

Step 4 :

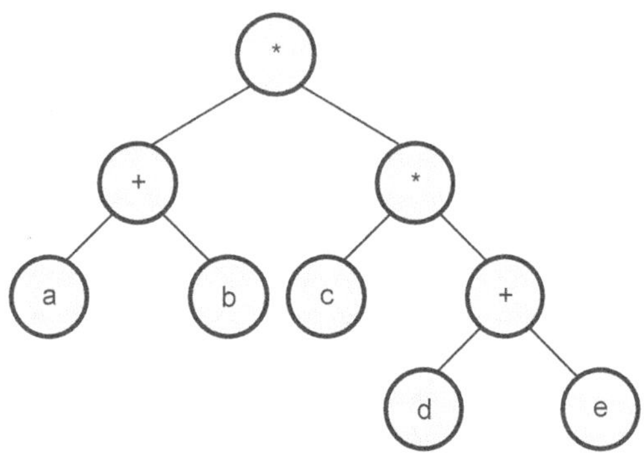

Expression tree

Example 6.6.6 *Generate a binary search tree for following numbers and perform in-order and post-order traversals :*

50, 40, 80, 20, 0, 30, 10, 90, 60, 70

GTU : Summer 2015, Marks 7

Solution :

Step 1 : Insert 50

Step 2 : Insert 40

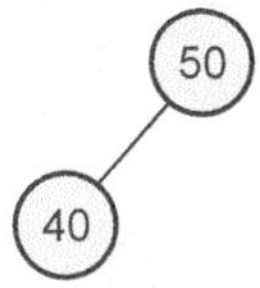

Step 3 : Insert 80

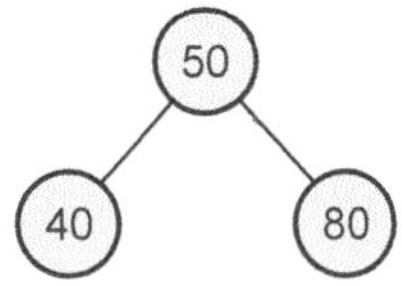

Step 4 : Insert 20

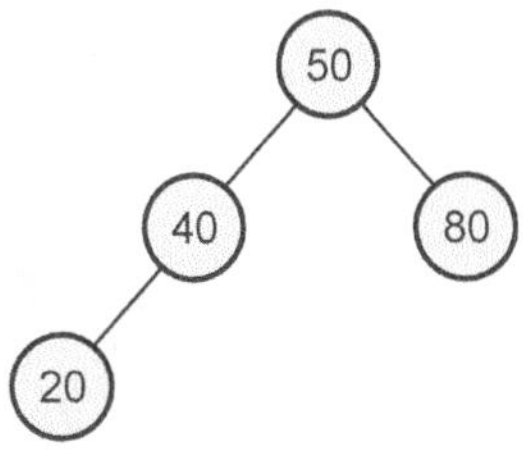

Step 5 : Insert 0

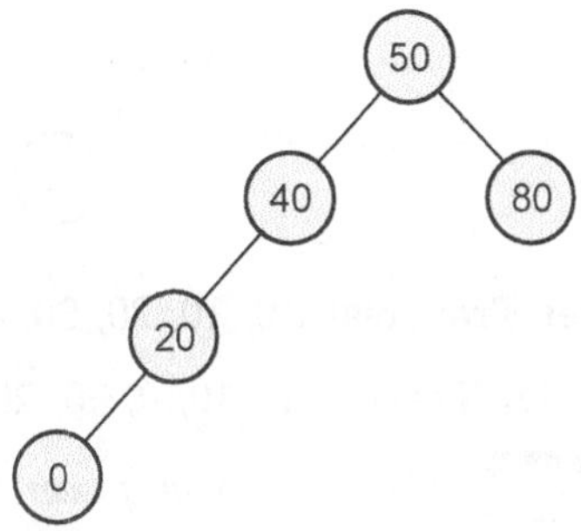

Step 6 : Insert 30

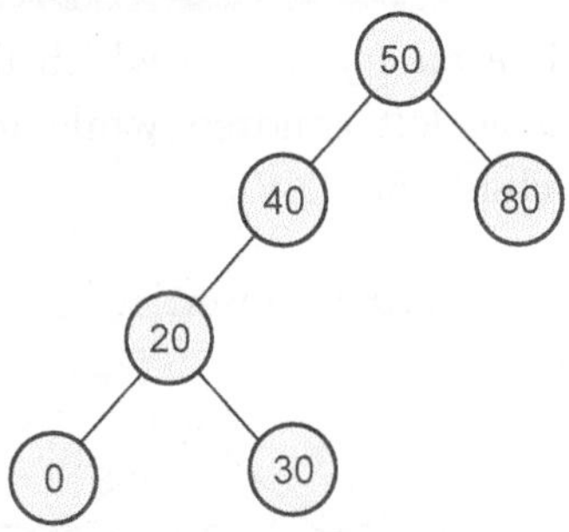

Step 7 : Insert 10

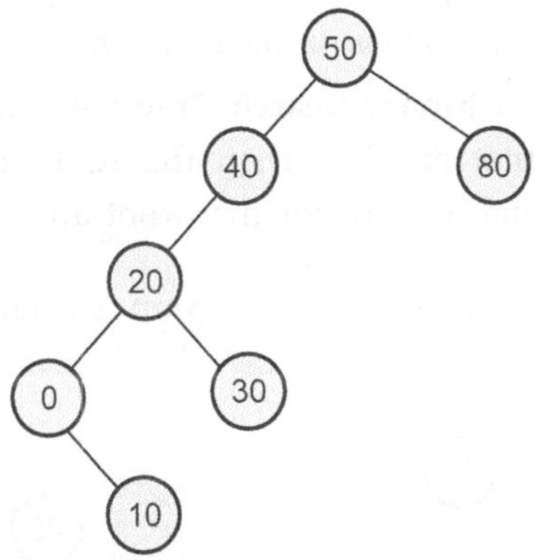

Step 8 : Insert 90

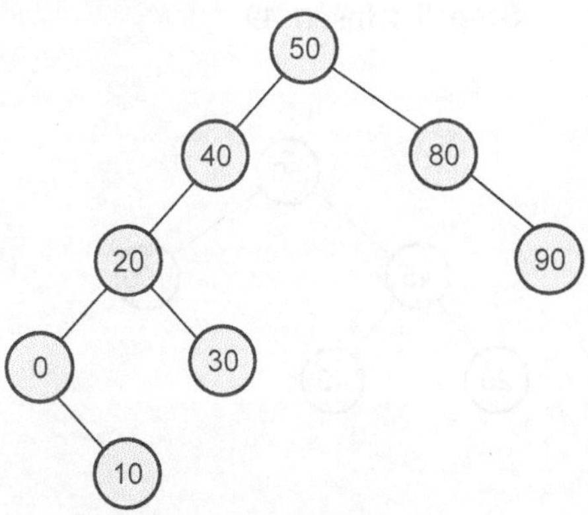

Step 9 : Insert 60

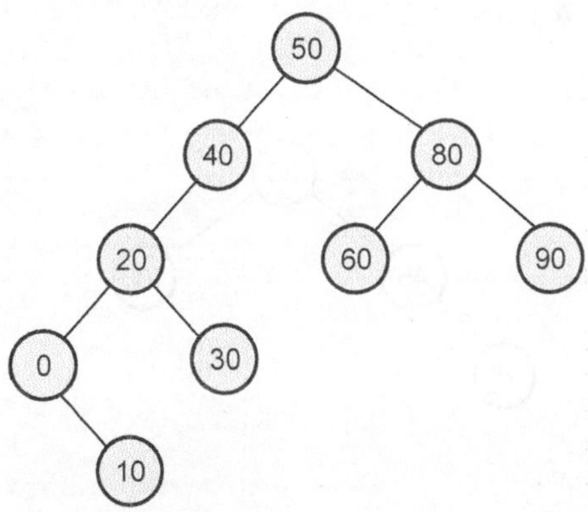

Step 10 : Insert 70

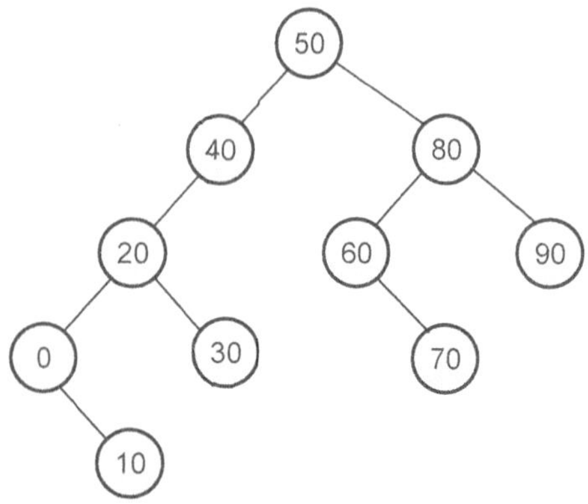

In-order Traversal : 0, 10, 20, 30, 40, 50, 60, 70, 80, 90

Post-order Traversal : 10, 0, 30, 20, 40, 70, 60, 90, 80, 50.

Example 6.6.7 *What is a binary search tree ? Create a binary search tree for inserting the following data :*

50, 45, 100, 25, 49, 120, 105, 46, 90, 95

Explain deletion in the above tree. **GTU : Winter 2015, Marks 7**

Solution : Binary Search Tree : A binary search tree is a binary tree in which the node values that are less than the root node are arranged as left children while the node values that are greater than root are arranged as right children.

Step 1 : Insert 50

Step 2 : Insert 45

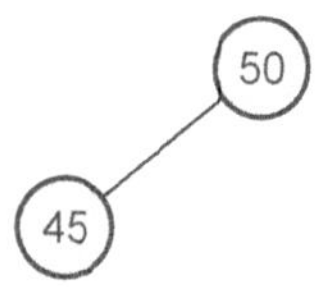

Step 3 : Insert 100

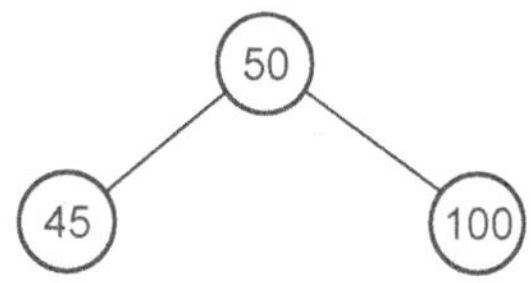

Step 4 : Insert 25

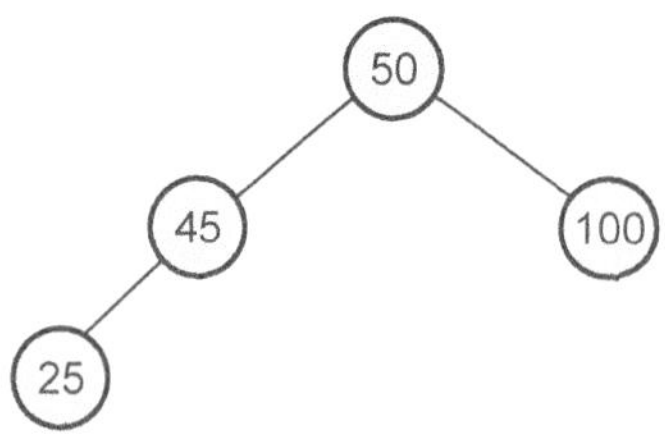

Step 5 : Insert 49

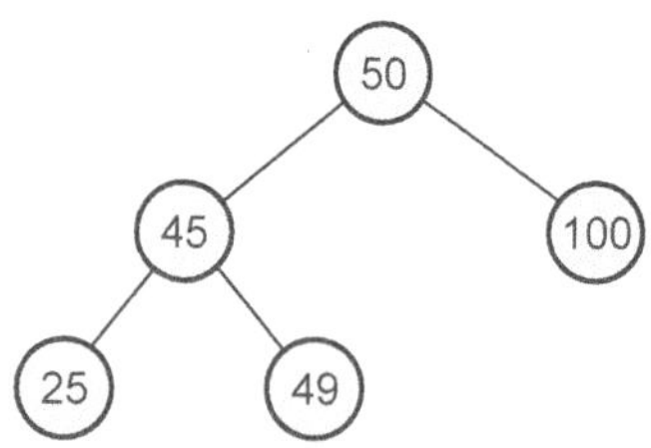

Step 6 : Insert 120

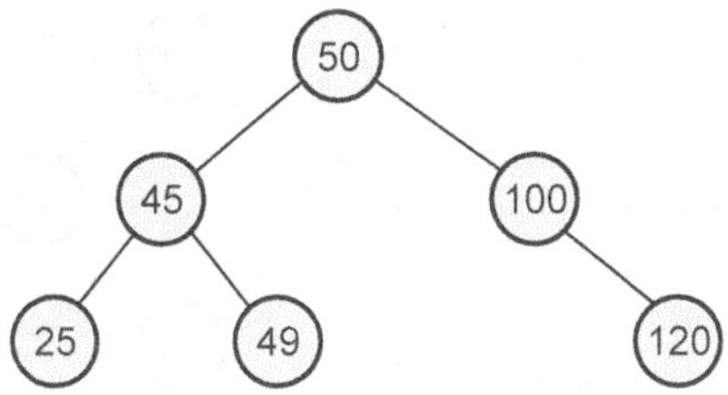

Step 7 : Insert 105

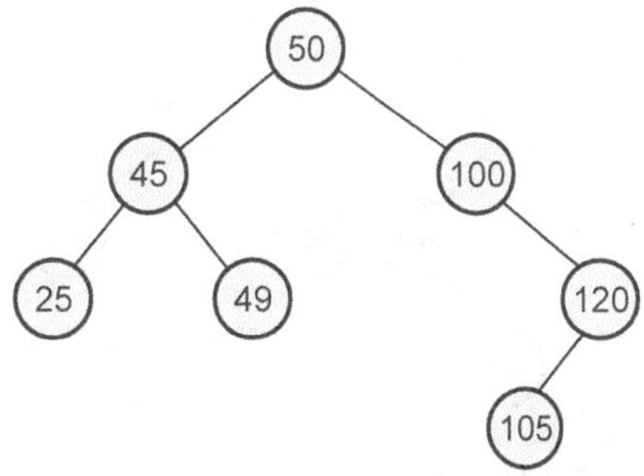

Step 8 : Insert 46

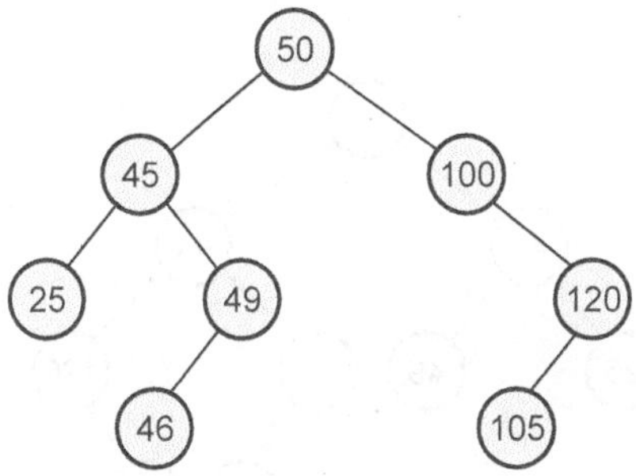

Step 9 : Insert 90

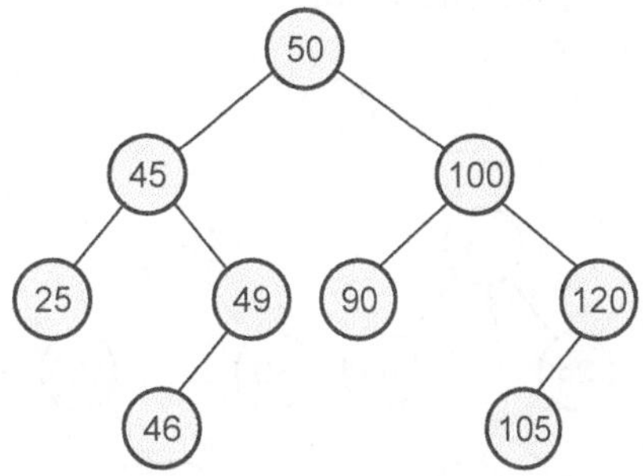

Step 10 : Insert 95

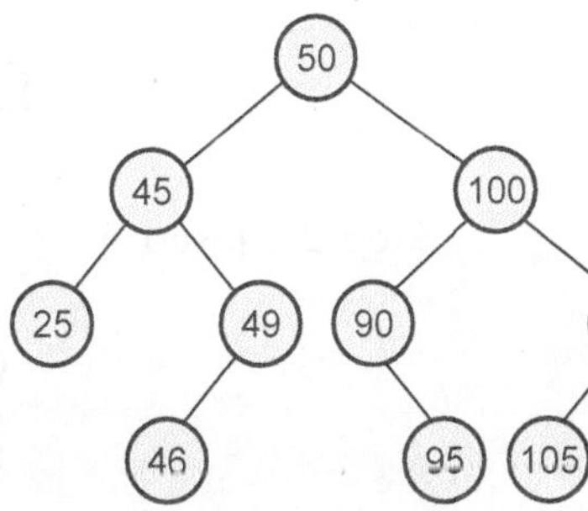

Required BST

Deletion : **Case 1 :** Deletion of leaf Node. Suppose we want to delete 46 then simply set the value of corresponding node to NULL.

Case 2 : Deletion of a node having single child.

Suppose we want to delete node 120 then it is replaced by its in-order predecessor

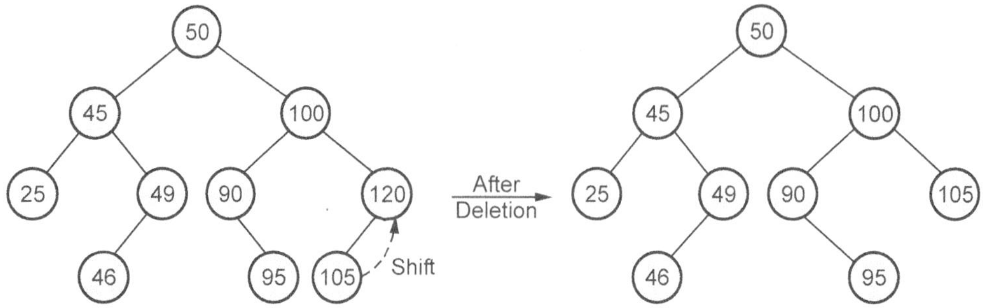

Case 3 : Deletion of node having two children

Suppose we want to delete the node 45 from the binary search tree then it is replaced by its inorder successor.

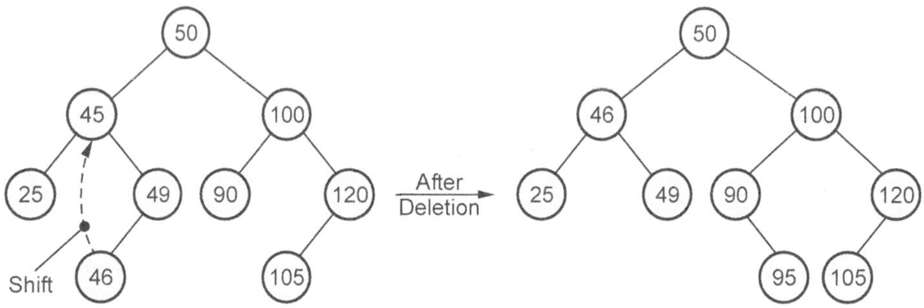

Example 6.6.8 *Construct a binary search tree for the following and perform inorder and postorder traversals :*

5 9 4 8 2 1 3 7 6

GTU : Winter-2016, Marks 4

Solution :

Step 1 : Insert 5

Step 2 : Insert 9

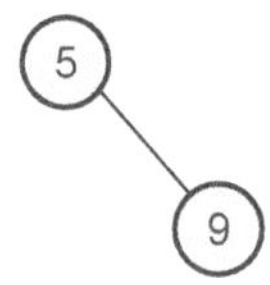

Step 3 : Insert 4

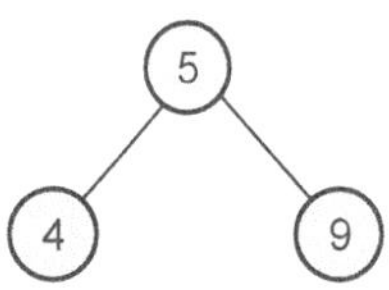

Step 4 : Insert 8

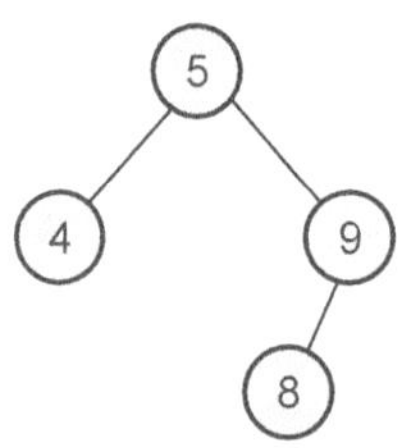

Step 5 : Insert 2

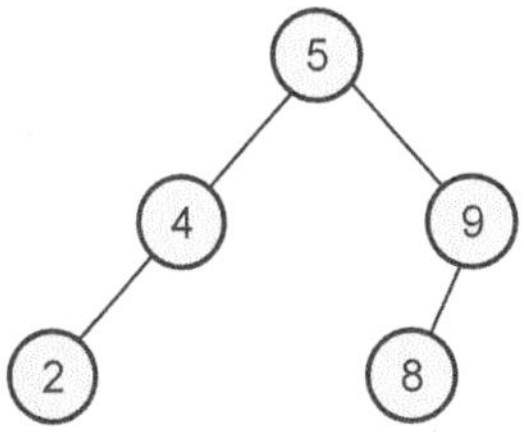

Step 6 : Insert 1

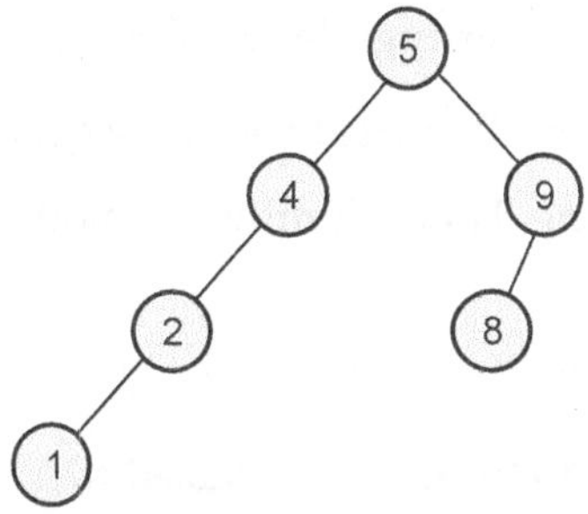

Step 7 : Insert 3

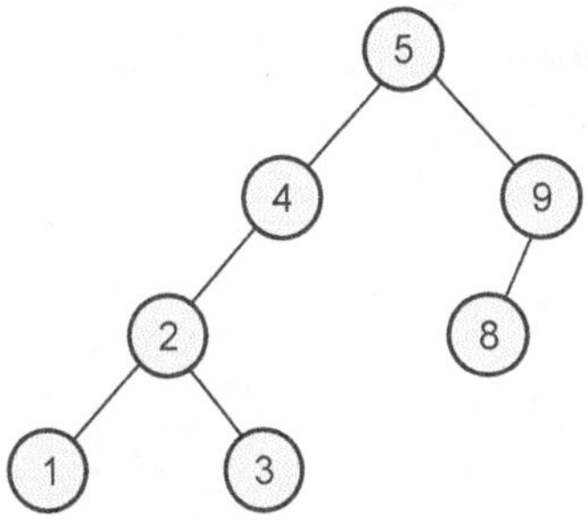

Step 8 : Insert 7

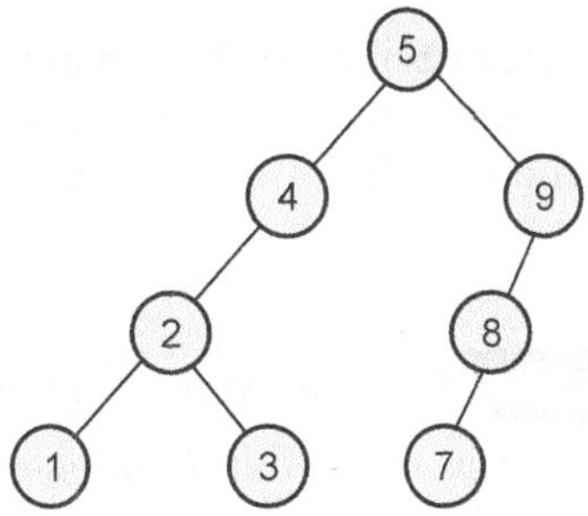

Step 9 : Insert 6

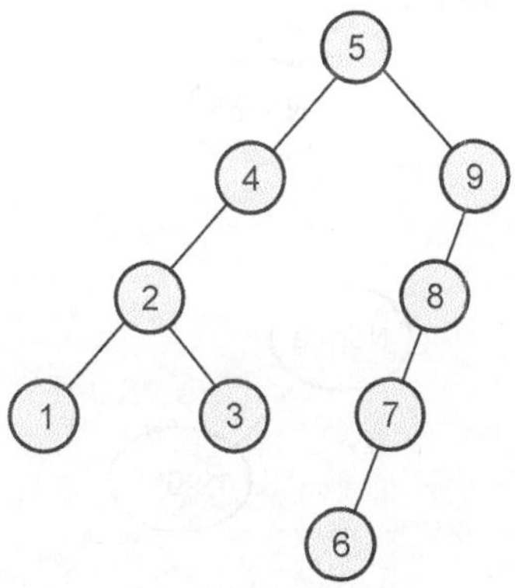

Required binary search tree

Inorder : 1 2 3 4 5 6 7 8 9

Postorder : 1 3 2 4 6 7 8 9 5

Example 6.6.9 *Write 'C' functions for : inserting a node, postorder traversal and counting total number of nodes for binary search tree.* **GTU : Winter-2016, Marks 7**

Solution : Inserting Node : Refer section 6.6

Postorder Traversal : Refer section 6.5

Counting Total Number of Nodes :

```
int count(node *temp)//initially temp is a root node
{
  int c = 1;//count is initialized to 1
   if (temp == NULL)
      return 0;
  else
  {
      c+= count(temp->left);//each time on visiting a node
      c+= count(temp->right);//count is incremented by 1
      return c;//finally return count
   }
}
```

Example 6.6.10 *Insertion sequence of names is :*

Norma, Roger, John, Bill, Leo, Paul, Ken and Maurice

i) Show the behavior of creating a lexically ordered binary tree.

ii) Insert Kirk. Show the binary tree.

iii) Delete John. Show the binary tree. **GTU : Summer-2017, Marks 7**

Solution : i) Step 1 : Insert **Norma**

Step 2 : Insert **Roger**

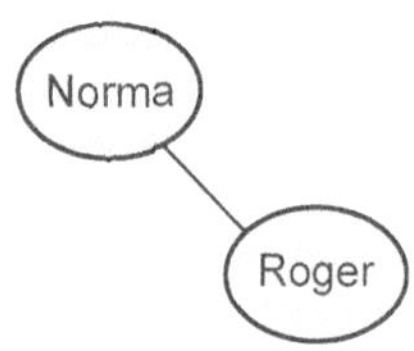

Step 3 : Insert John

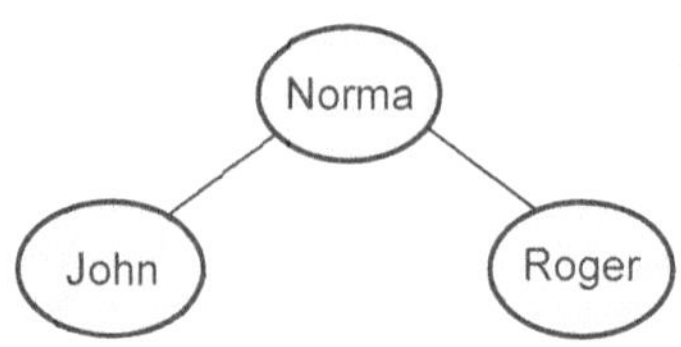

Step 4 : Insert Bill

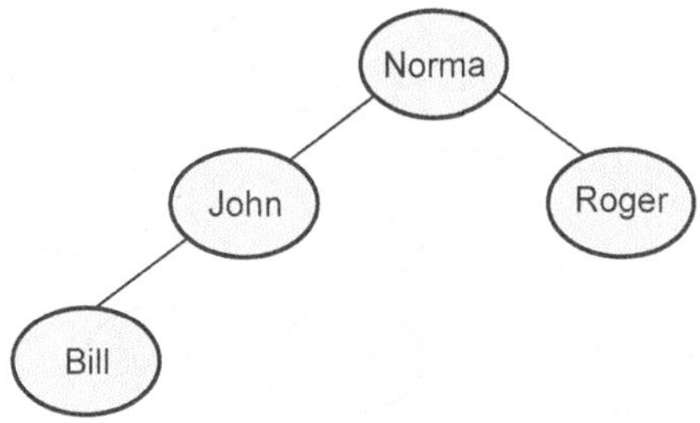

Step 5 : Insert Leo

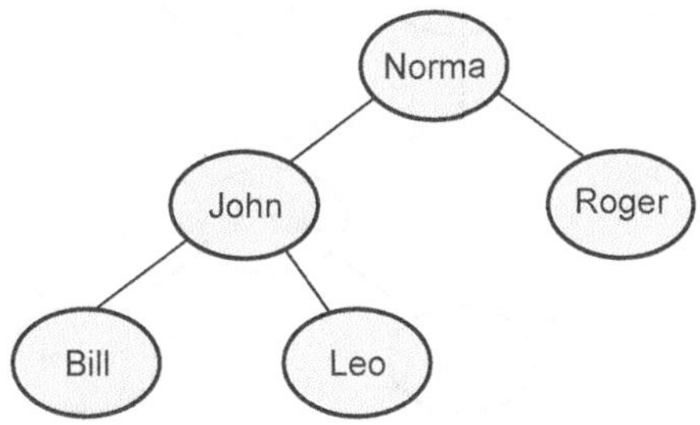

Step 6 : Insert Paul

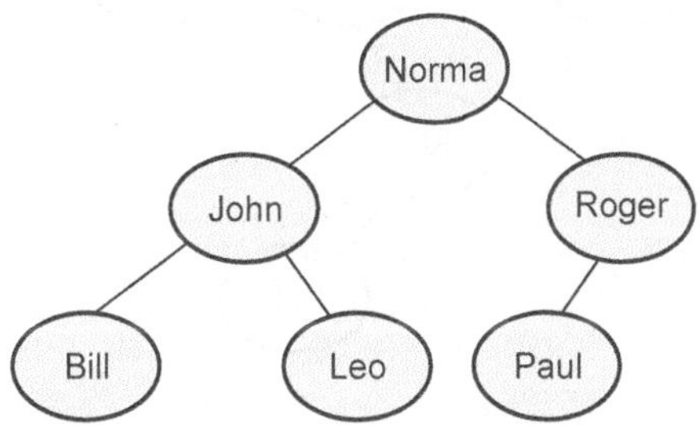

Step 7 : Insert Ken

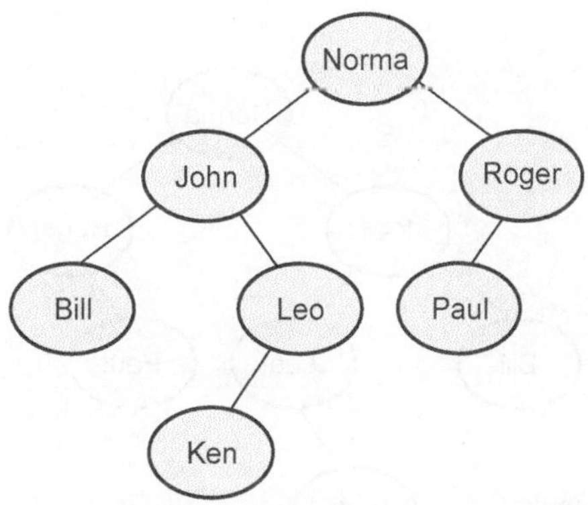

Step 8 : Insert Maurice

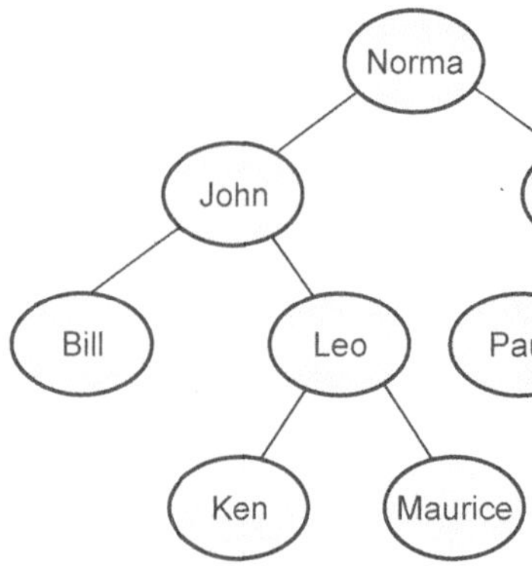

ii) Insert Kirk

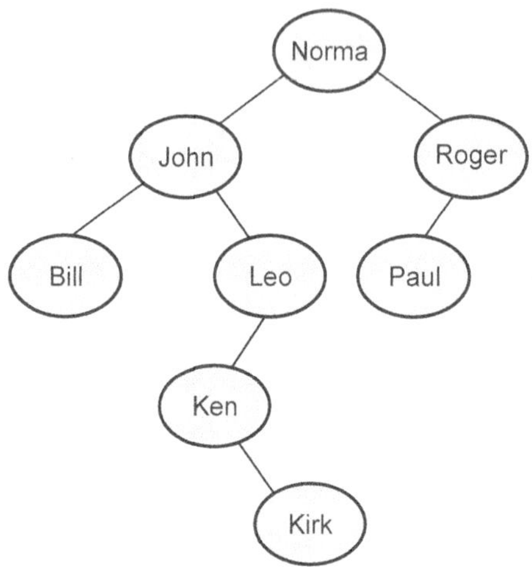

iii) Delete John

On deleting the node John the inorder successor takes the place of John. The tree will become -

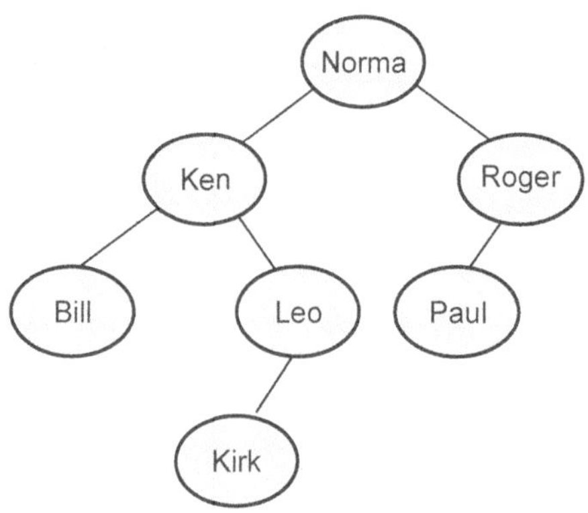

Example 6.6.11 *What is a binary search tree ? Create a binary search tree for following data 14, 10, 17, 12, 10, 11, 20, 12, 18, 25, 20, 8, 22, 11, 23*

Explain deleting node 20 in the resultant binary search tree.

GTU : Summer-18, Marks 7

Solution : Binary Search Tree - Refer section 6.6.

Step 1 : Insert 14

Step 2 : Insert 10

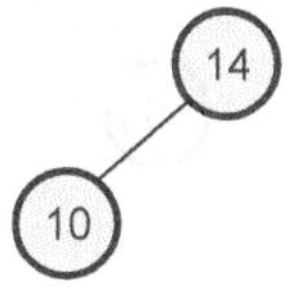

Step 3 : Insert 17

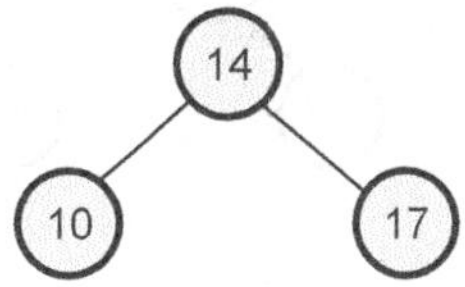

Step 4 : Insert 12

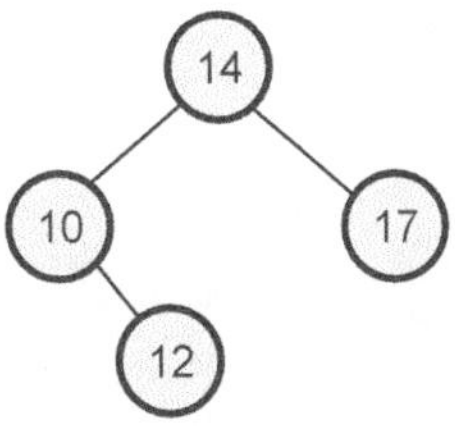

Step 5 : Insert 10

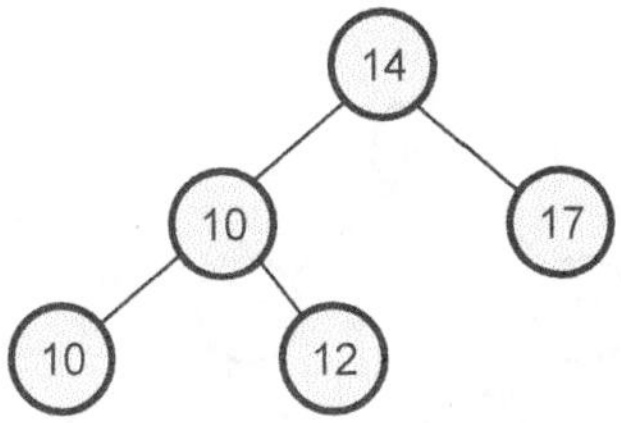

Step 6 : Insert 11

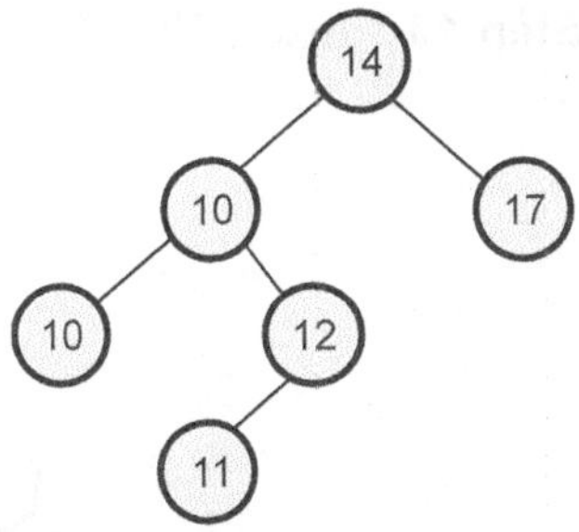

Step 7 : Insert 20

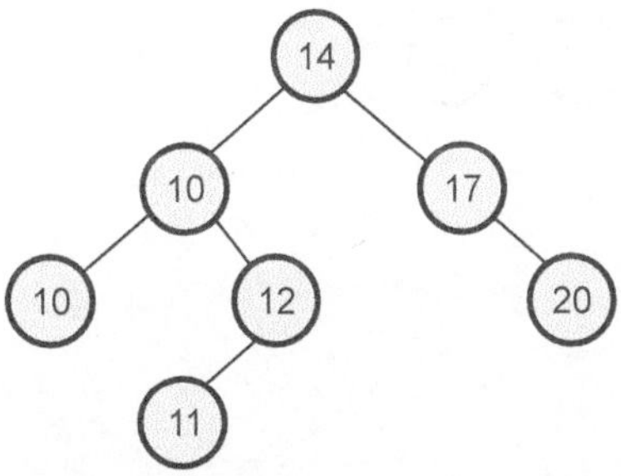

Step 8 : Insert 12

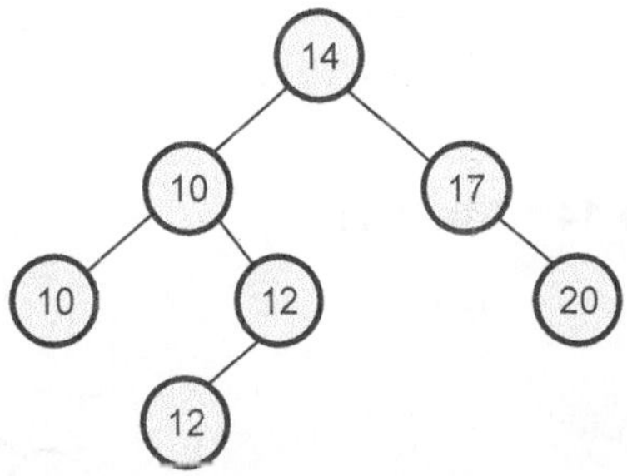

Step 9 : Insert 18

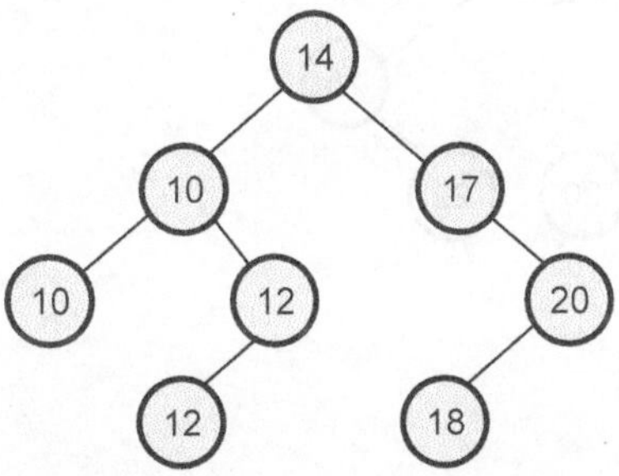

Step 10 : Insert 25

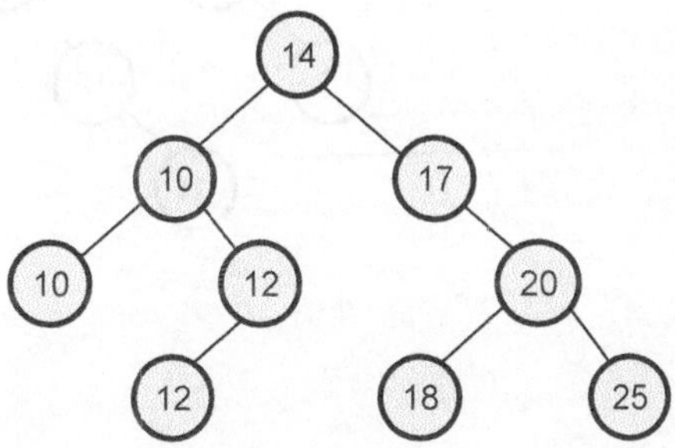

Step 11 : Insert 20

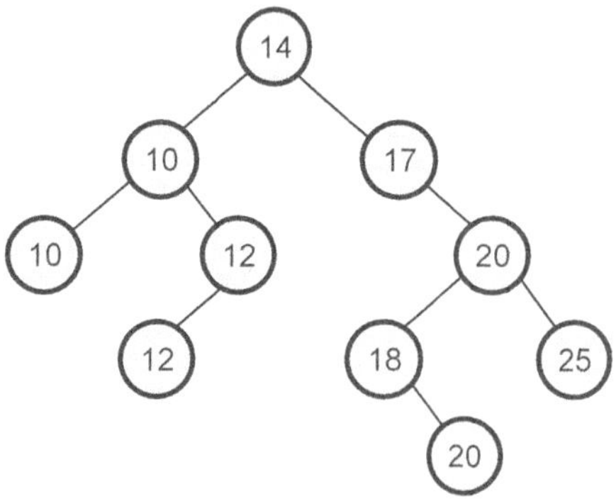

Step 12 : Insert 8

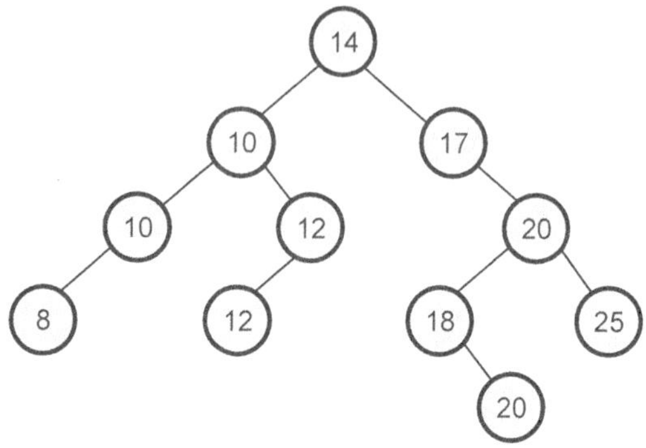

Step 13 : Insert 22

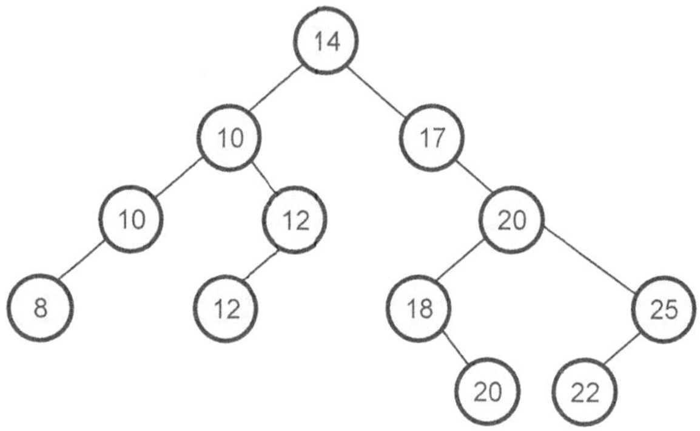

Step 14 : Insert 11

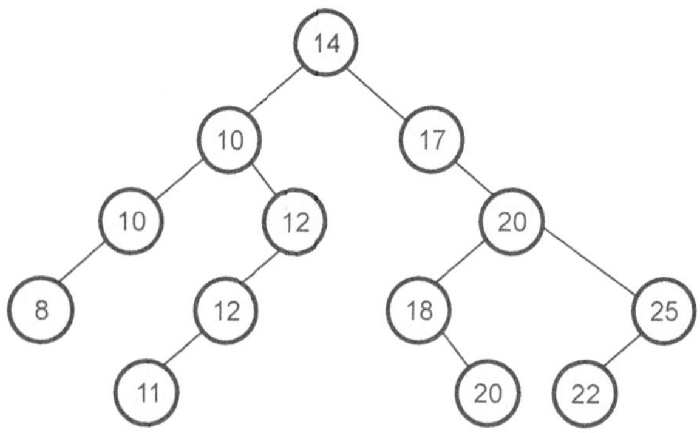

Step 15 : Insert 23

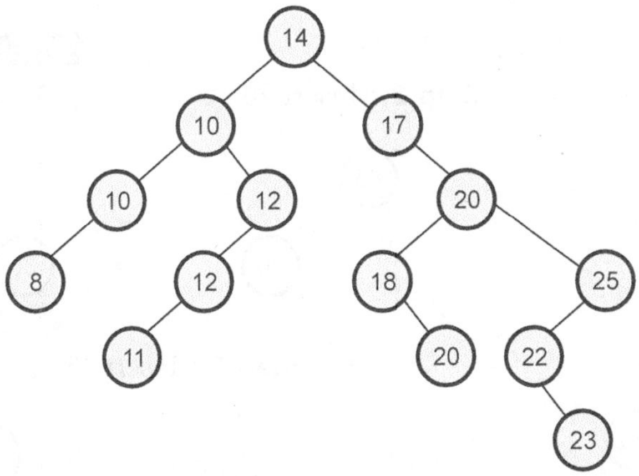

Now there are two 20's in above BST. After deleting 20 (leaf node), we get -

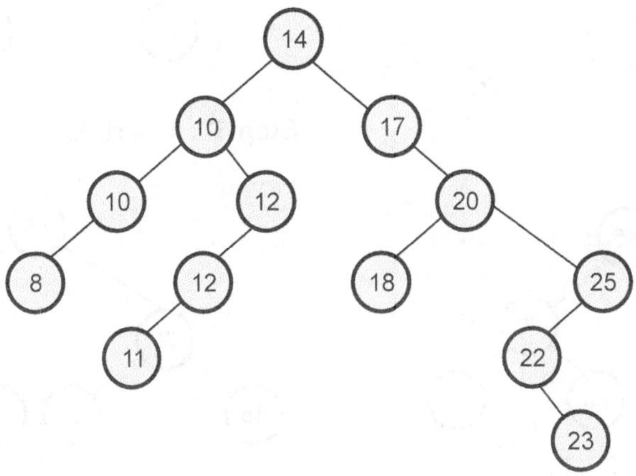

Now deleting 20, having two child nodes

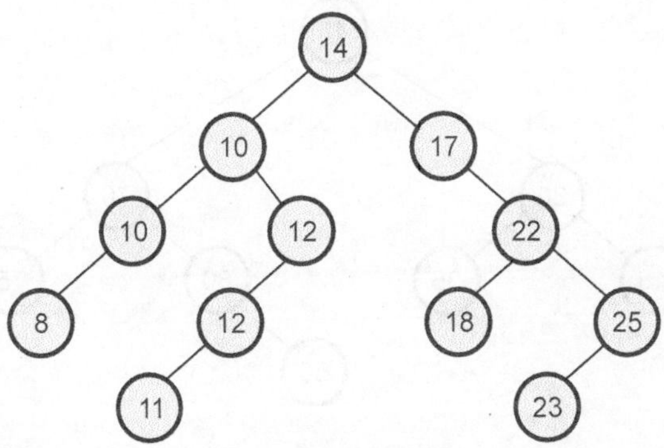

Example 6.6.12 *Create a binary search tree for following data and do inorder, preorder and postorder traversal of the tree*

45, 70, 30, 60, 15, 75, 35, 55, 20, 85, 80

GTU : Winter-18, Marks 7

Solution : Step 1 : Insert 45

Step 2 : Insert 70

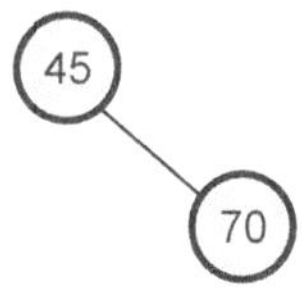

Step 3 : Insert 30

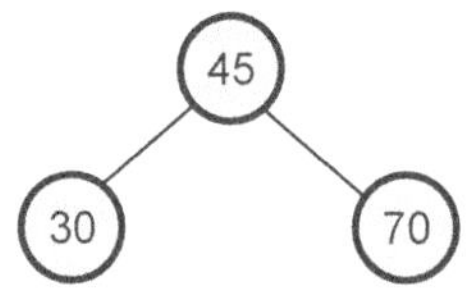

Step 4 : Insert 60

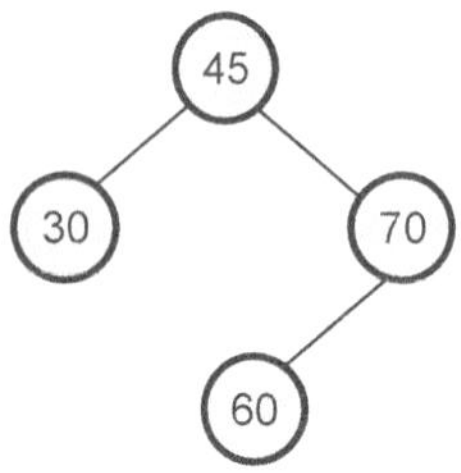

Step 5 : Insert 15

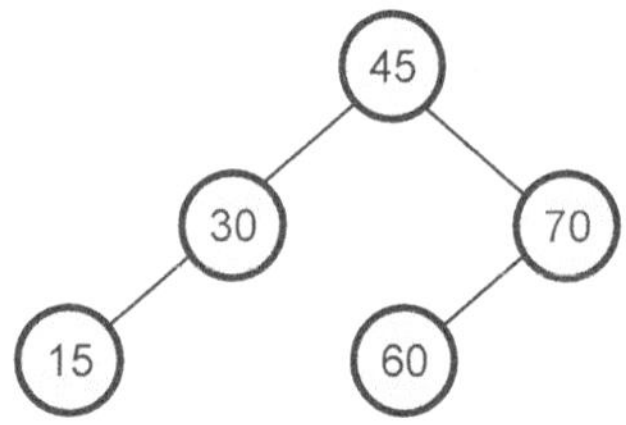

Step 6 : Insert 75

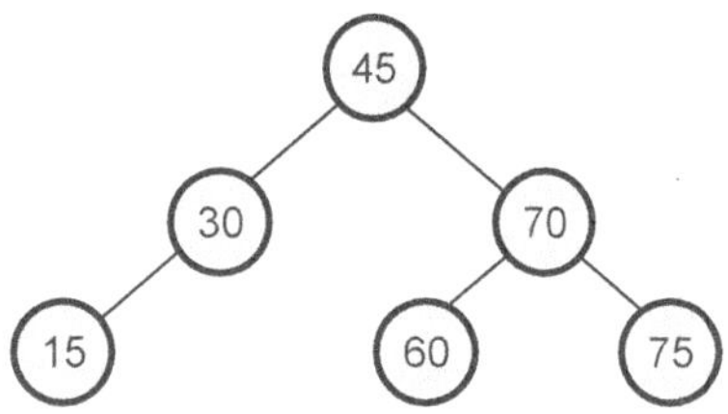

Step 7 : Insert 35

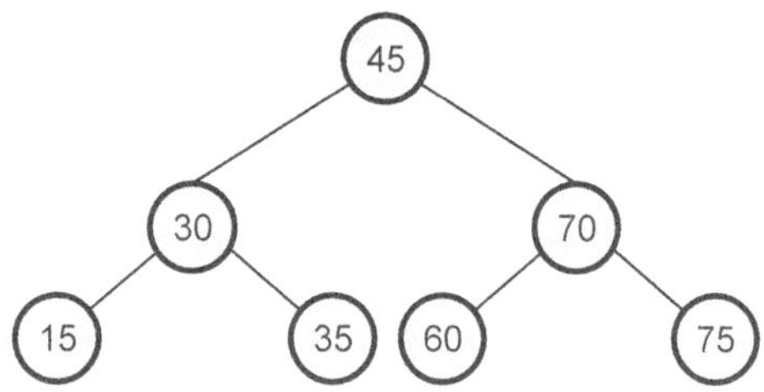

Step 8 : Insert 55

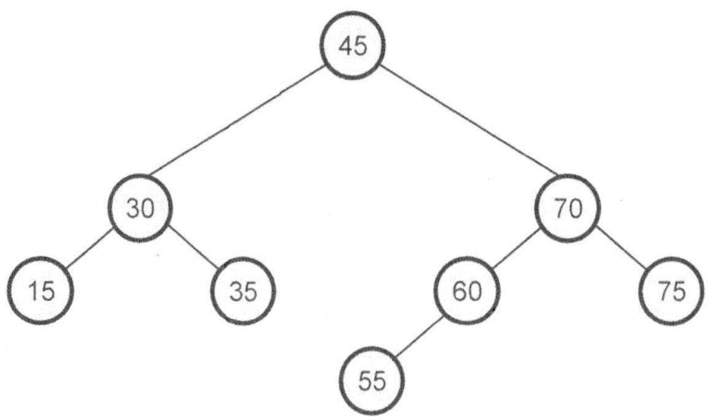

Step 9 : Insert 20

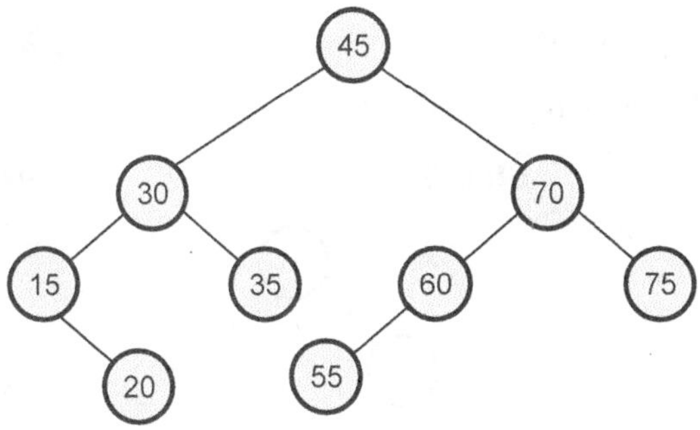

Step 10 : Insert 85

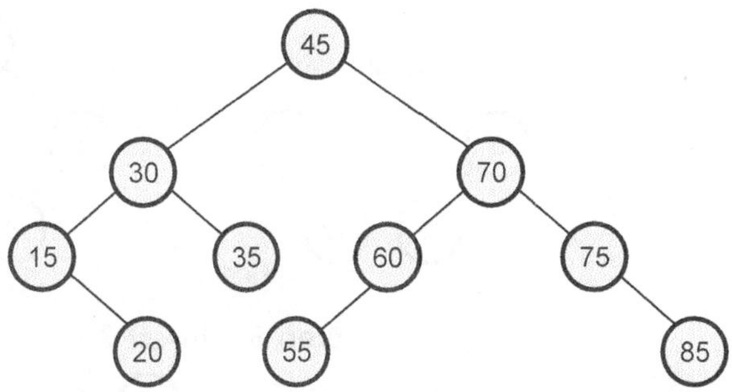

Step 11 : Insert 80

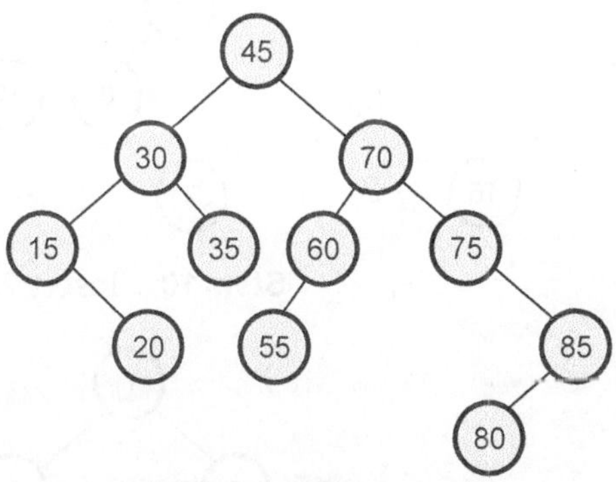

This is required binary search tree

Step 12 :

Inorder traversal : 15, 20, 30, 35, 45, 55, 60, 70, 75, 80, 85

Preorder tréaversal : 45, 30, 15, 20, 35, 70, 60, 55, 75, 85, 80

Postorder traversal : 20, 15, 35, 30, 55, 60, 85, 75, 70, 45

Example 6.6.13 *What is binary search tree ? Construct binary search tree for following elements.*

11, 6, 14, 8, 12, 15, 16, 7, 9, 23 **GTU : Winter-18, Marks 7**

Solution : Binary search tree - Refer section 6.6.

Step 1 : Insert 11

Step 2 : Insert 6

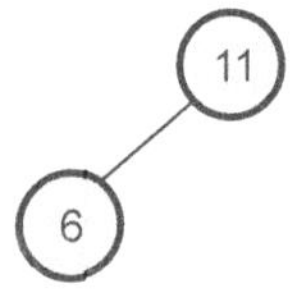

Step 3 : Insert 14

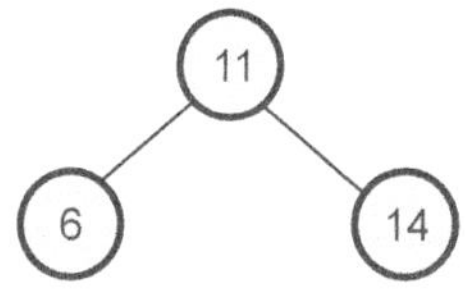

Step 4 : Insert 8

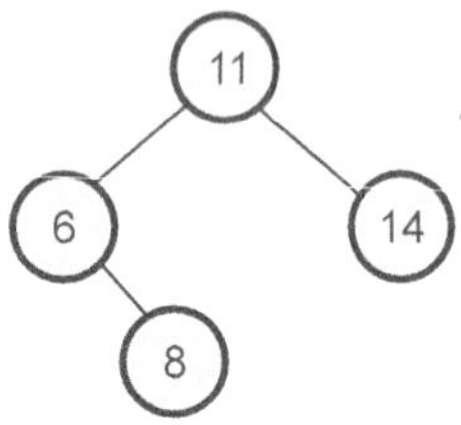

Step 5 : Insert 12

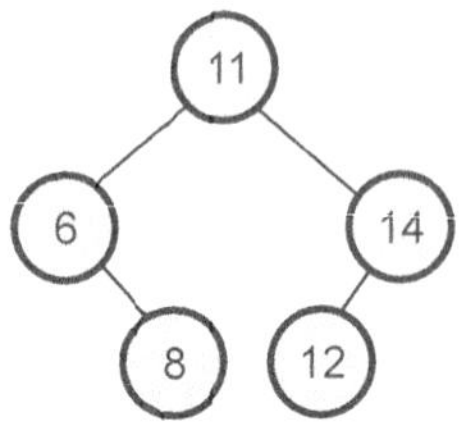

Step 6 : Insert 15

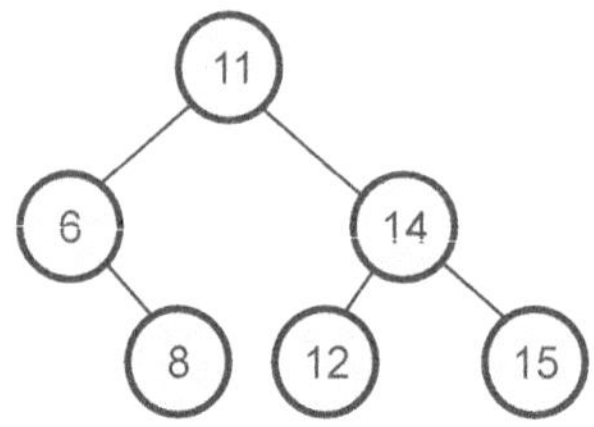

Step 7 : Insert 16

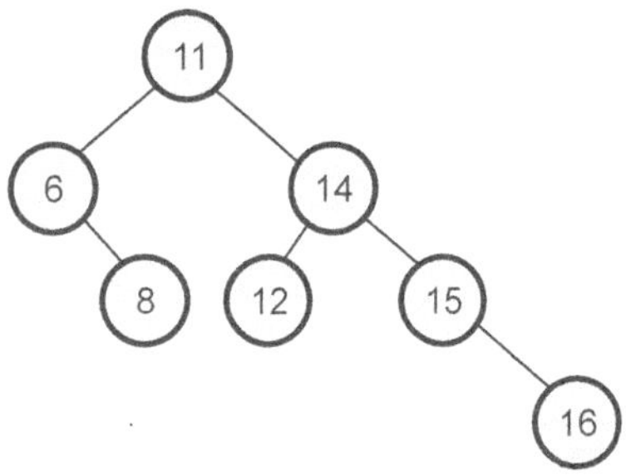

Step 8 : Insert 7

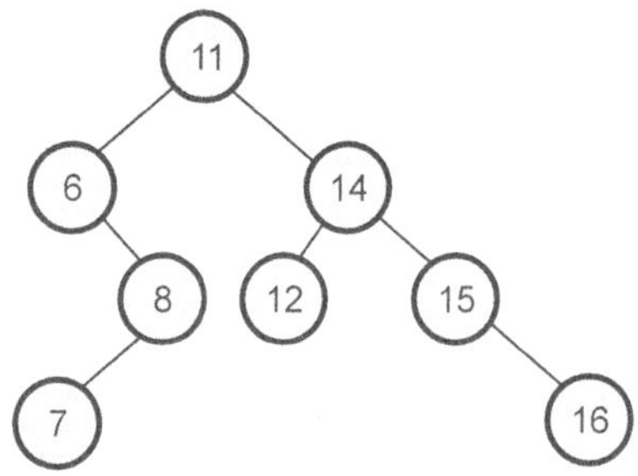

Step 9 : Insert 9

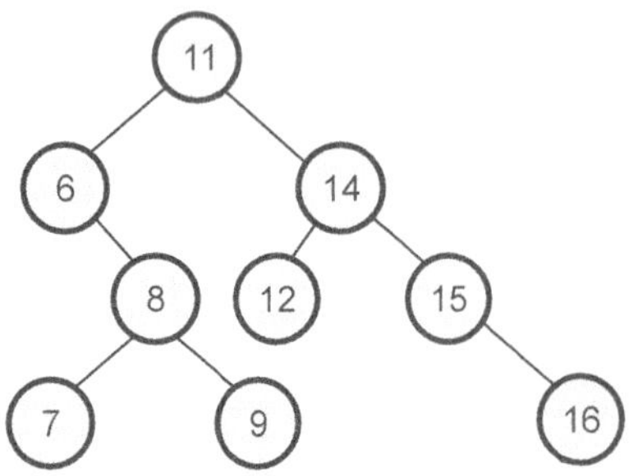

Step 10 : Insert 23

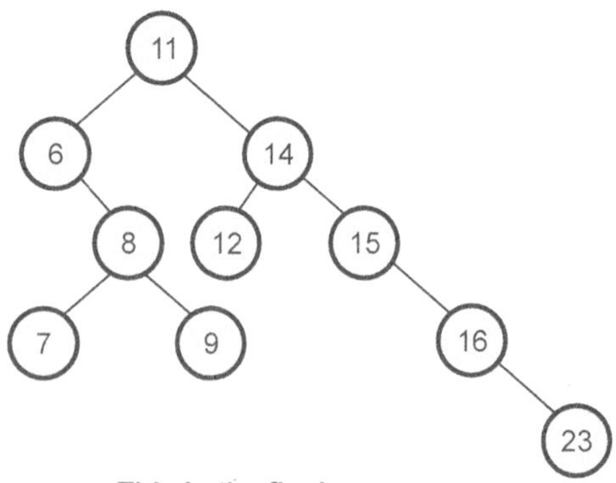

This is the final binary search tree

Review Question

1. *Define tree. Write an algorithm to do in-order and post order traversal of the binary search tree.* **GTU : Winter-13, Marks 7**

6.7 Creation of Binary Tree from Basic Traversal

GTU : Summer-13, 14, 16, 17, Winter-15, 16, 17, Marks 7

We have already seen inorder, preorder and postorder traversals. Now a question may come in your mind that is it possible to predict a tree from any one traversal ? The answer is no ! Surprised ? Yes, because the fact is that one traversal gives the ambiguous result.

For example :

Consider the inorder traversal as ABC the trees could be

Thus the only inorder traversal gives two different trees. So, to predict the exact tree from the tree traversals we require atleast any two traversals.

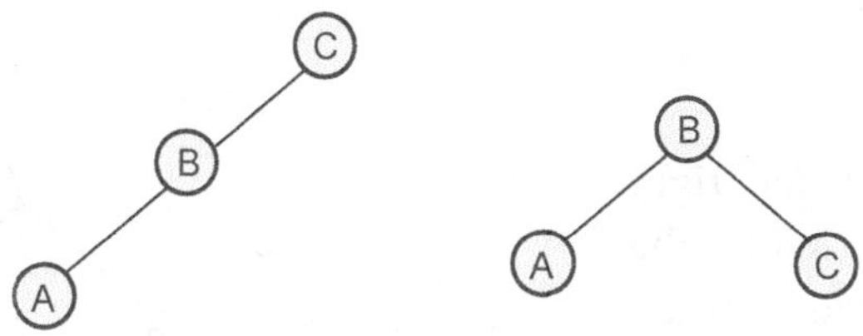

Fig. 6.7.1 Two sample trees for ABC inorder traversal

Example 6.7.1 *Obtain binary tree from -*

Postorder H I D E B F G C A

Inorder H D I B E A F C G

Solution :

Step 1 :

The last node in postorder sequence is the root node. In above example "A" is the root node. Now observe inorder sequence locate the "A". Left sequence to "A" indicates the left subtree and right sequence to "A" indicates the right subtree. i.e. as shown in Fig. 6.7.2.

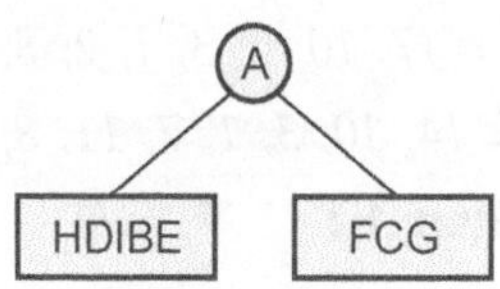

Fig. 6.7.2

Step 2 :

Now, with these alphabets H, D, I, B, E observe the postorder and sequences in inorder

Postorder H I D [E] B

Inorder H D I B [E]

Here B is parent node, therefore pictorically tree will be, as shown in Fig. 6.7.3

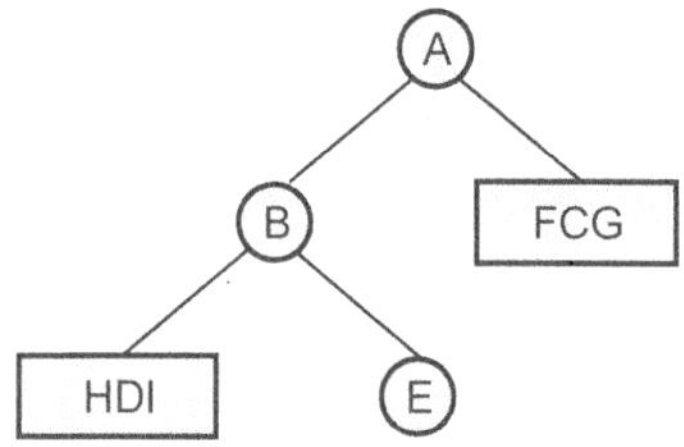

Fig. 6.7.3

Step 3 :

With the alphabets H, D and I observe both the sequences.

Postorder H I [D]

Inorder H [D] I

D is the parent node, H is leftmost node and I is the right child of D node. So tree will be as shown in Fig. 6.7.4

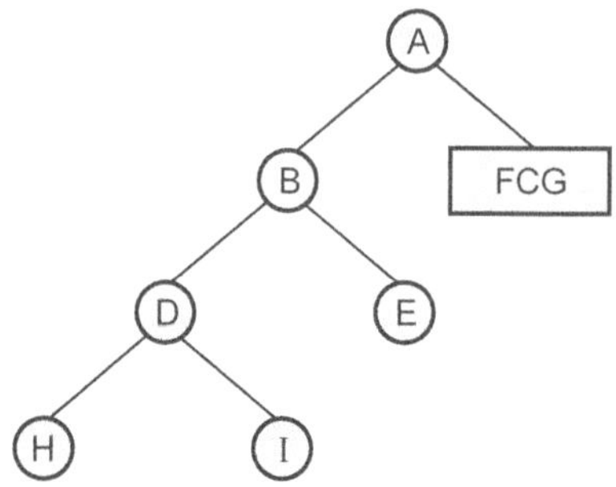

Fig. 6.7.4

Step 4 :

Now we will solve for right subtree of root "A". With the alphabets F, C, G observe both the sequences.

Postorder F G [C]

Inorder F [C] G

'C' is the parent node, F is the left child and G is the right child. So finally the tree will be as shown in Fig. 6.7.5

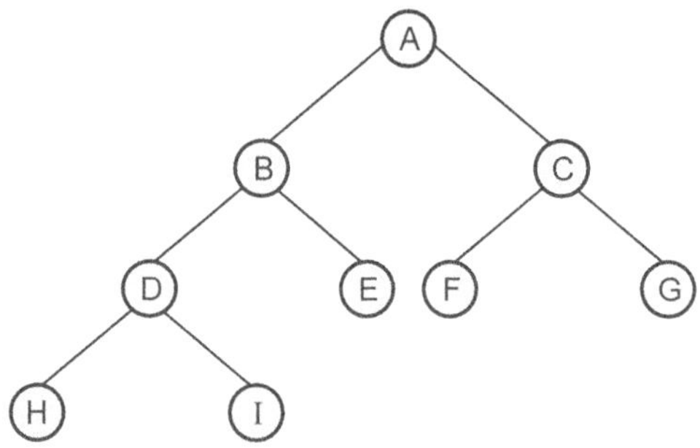

Fig. 6.7.5

Example 6.7.2 *Given the following traversals, create a binary tree from that. Also give the postorder traversal for the same.*

Preorder = {7, 10, 4, 3, 1, 2, 8, 11}

Inorder = {4, 10, 3, 1, 7, 11, 8, 2}

GTU : Summer-14, Marks 7

Solution : Step 1 :

Preorder : [7] 10 4 3 1 2 8 11

Inorder : 4 10 3 1 [7] 11 8 2

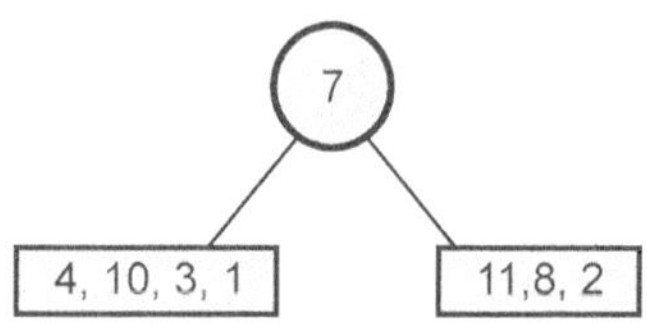

Step 2 : Consider left sub-branch

Preorder : [10] 4 3 1

Inorder : 4 [10] 3 1

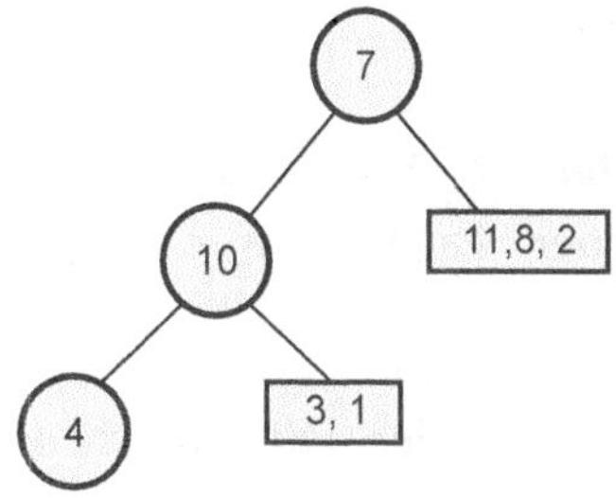

Step 3 :

Preorder : [3] 1

Inorder : [3] 1

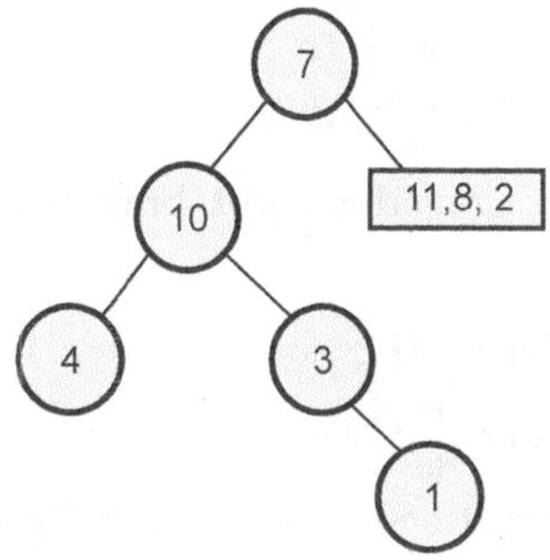

Step 4 : Now consider right sub-branch of the tree created in step 1.

Preorder : [2] 8 11

Inorder : 11 8 [2]

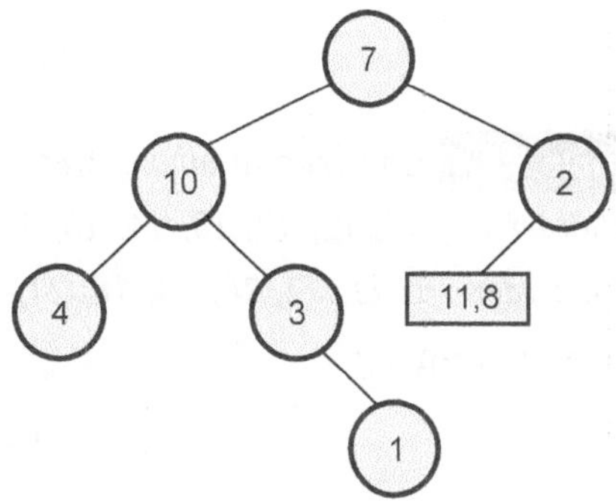

Step 5 :

Preorder : [8] 11

Inorder : [11] 8

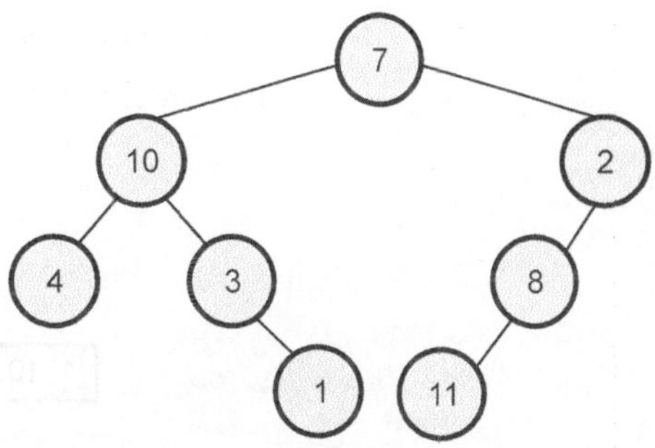

Binary tree

Example 6.7.3 *The inorder and preorder traversal of binary tree are*

d b e a f c g

a b d e c f g respectively construct binary tree and find its postorder traversal.

GTU : Summer-13, Marks 7

Solution :

Step 1 :

Inorder : d b e [a] f c g

Preorder : [a] b d e c f g

↑ root

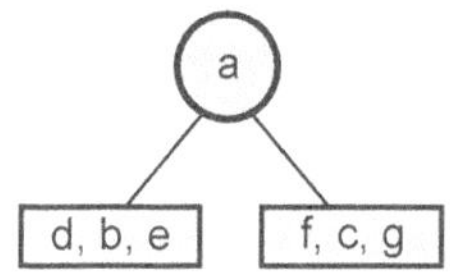

Step 2 : Consider left branch (of tree in step 1)

Inorder : d [b] e

Postorder : [b] d e

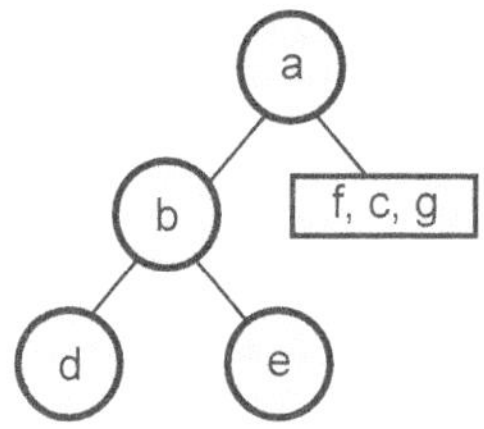

Step 3 : Consider right branch (of tree in step 1)

Inorder : f [c] g

Preorder : [c] f g

Postorder sequence : d e b f g c a

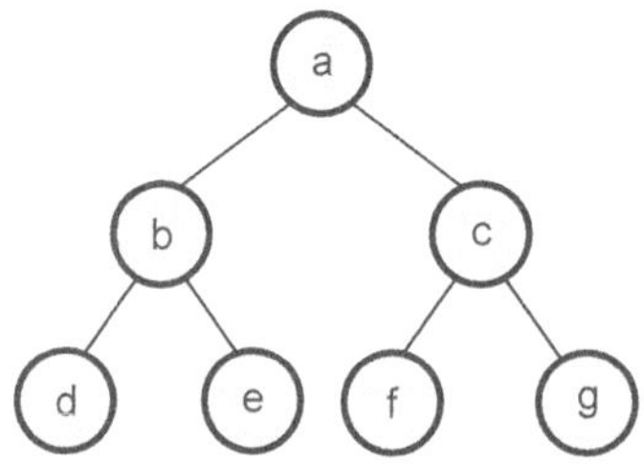

Binary tree

Example 6.7.4 *Construct a binary tree from the traversals given below :*

Inorder : 1, 10, 11, 12, 13, 14, 15, 17, 18, 21

Postorder : 1, 11, 12, 10, 14, 18, 21, 17, 15, 13 **GTU : Winter-2015, Marks 4**

Solution : Step 1 :

Left branch (1, 10, 11, 12) Right branch (14, 15, 17, 18, 21)

Inorder : 1, 10, 11, 12, [13], 14, 15, 17, 18, 21

Postorder : 1, 11, 12, 10, 14, 18, 21, 17, 15, [13]

↑ Root

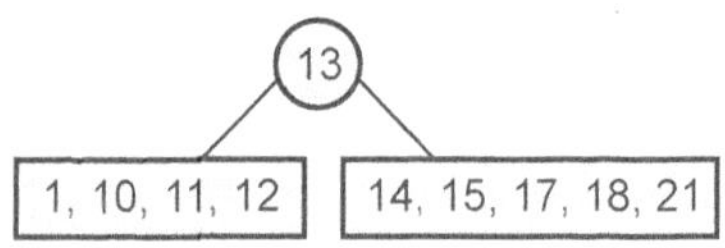

Step 2 : Now we will consider the **left Branch** sequence obtained in step 1.

Left (1) Right (11, 12)

Inorder : 1, [10], 11, 12

Postorder : 1, 11, 12, [10]

↑ Parent

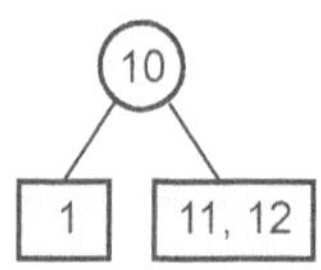

Step 3 : Now consider the right sub branch obtained in step 2.

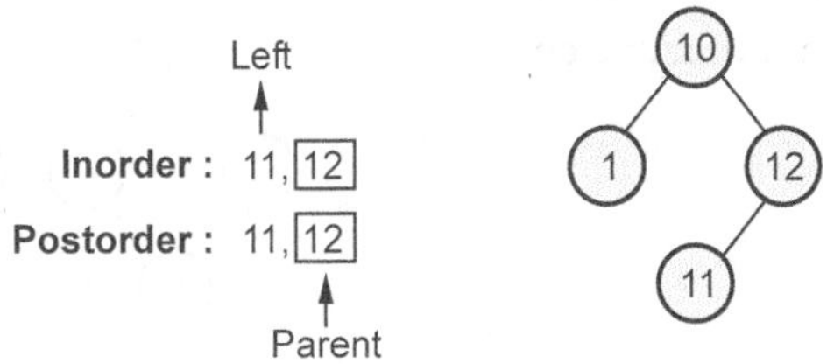

Step 4 : Now consider the **Right Branch** sequence obtained in step 1.

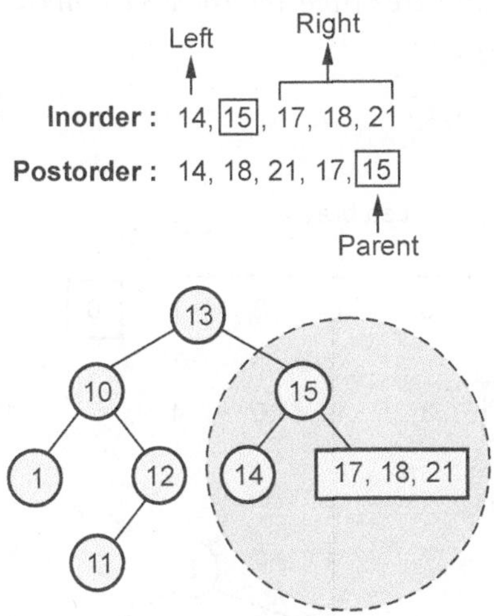

Step 5 : Consider the right sub branch sequence obtained in step 4.

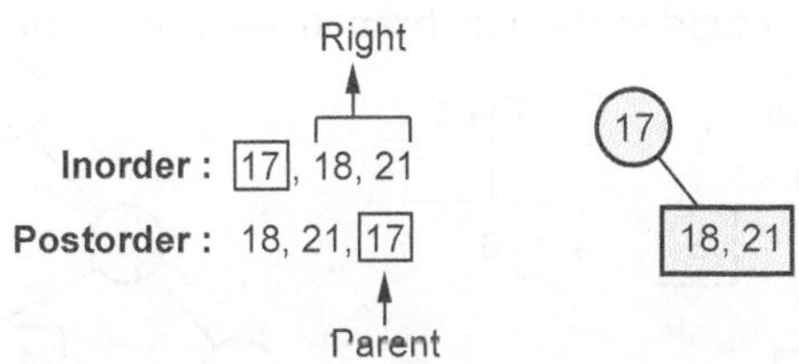

Step 6 : Consider the right sub branch sequence obtained in step 5.

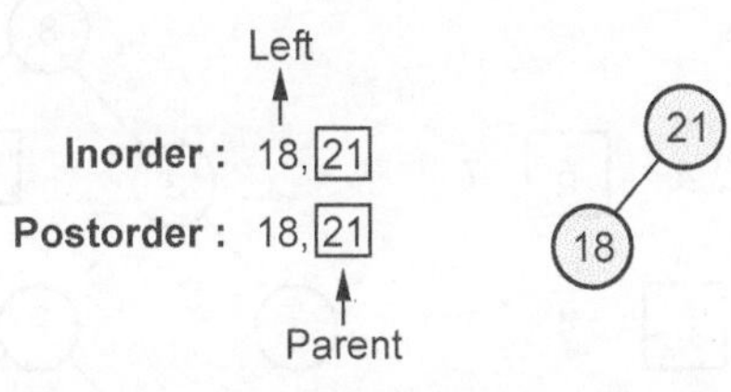

Step 7 : Now consolidating all the sub-branches obtained in above steps we get the final required binary tree as -

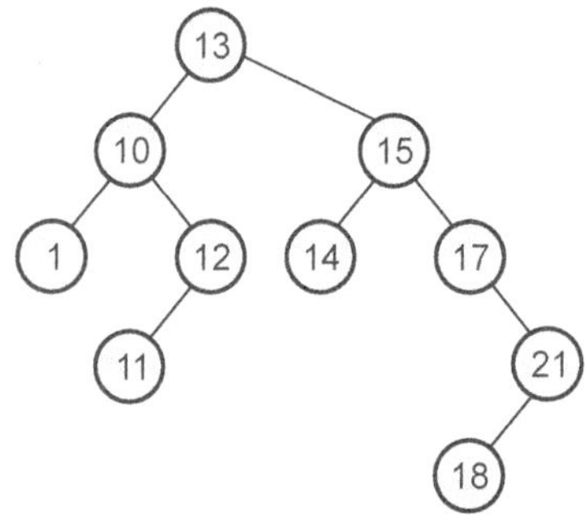

Example 6.7.5 *Construct a binary tree from the traversals given below :*

Inorder : 1 3 4 6 7 8 10 13 14

Preorder : 8 3 1 6 4 7 10 14 13

GTU : Summer-16, Marks 4

Solution : Step 1 :

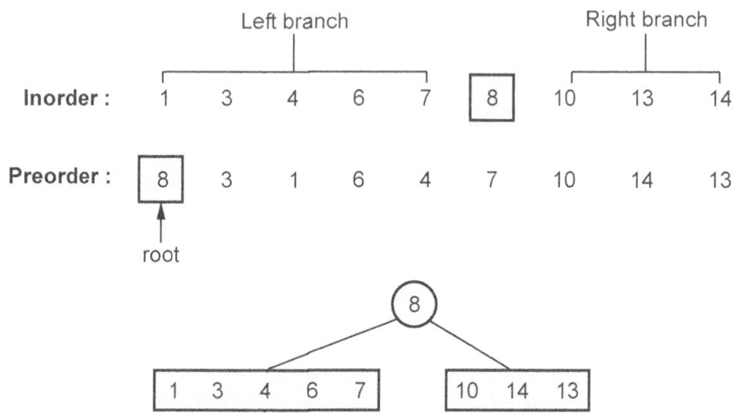

Step 2 : Now we will consider the left branch sequence obtained in step 1 :

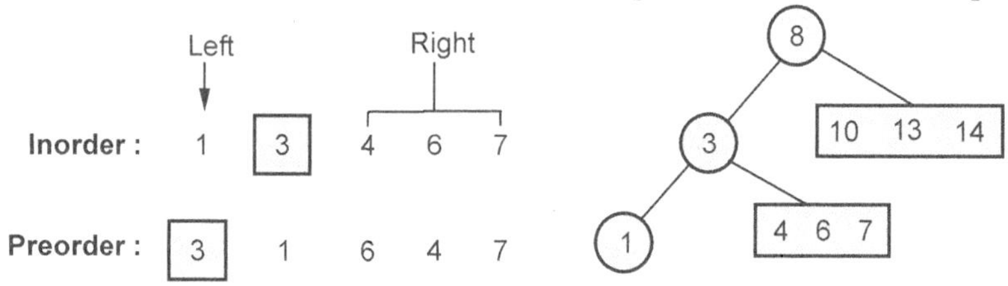

Step 3 : Now we will consider right subbranch obtained in step 2.

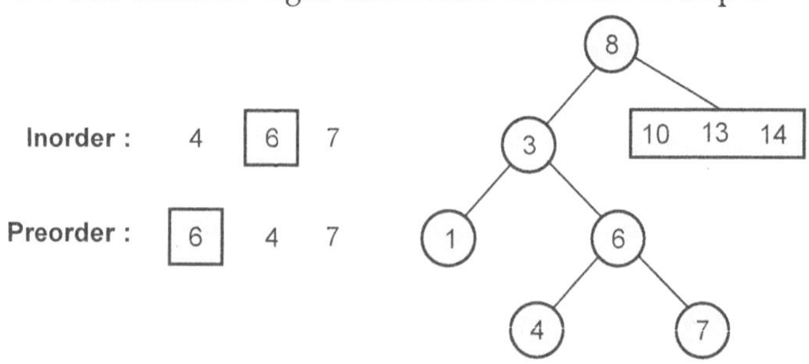

Step 4 : Now we will consider right branch of step 1.

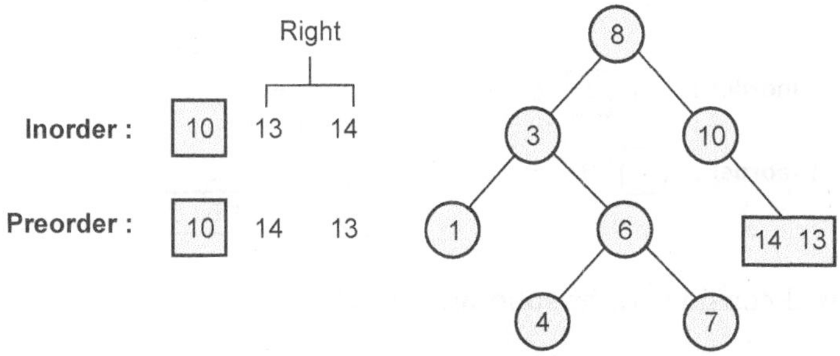

Step 5 : Now we will consider right sub branch obtain in step 4.

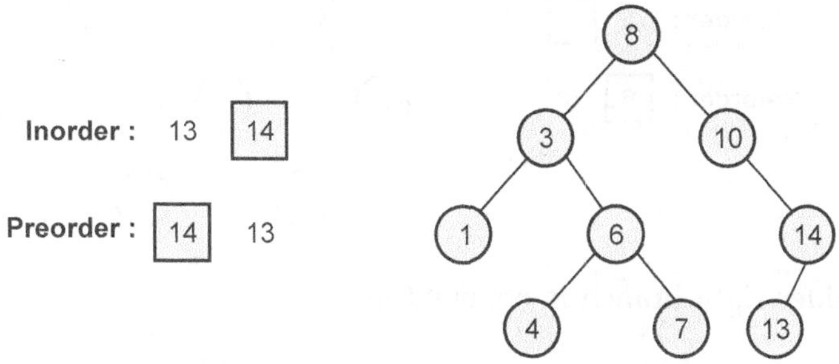

Final binary tree

Example 6.7.6 *Construct a binary search tree from the following traversals :*

Inorder : 3 4 5 6 7 9 17 20 22

Preorder : 9 4 3 6 5 7 17 22 20

GTU : Winter-2016, Marks 4

Solution : Step 1 :

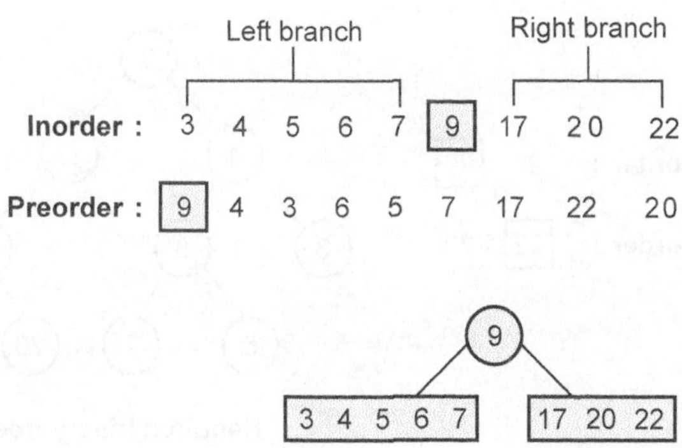

Step 2 : Now we will consider the left branch sequence obtained in step 1.

Inorder : 3 4 5 6 7

Preorder : 4 3 6 5 7

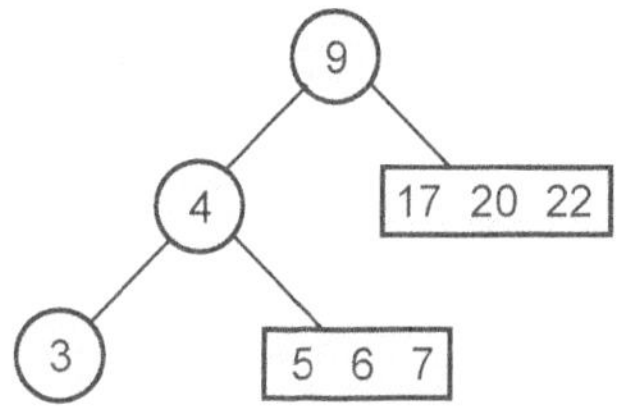

Step 3 : We will consider right subbranch of step 2.

Inorder : 5 6 7

Preorder : 6 5 7

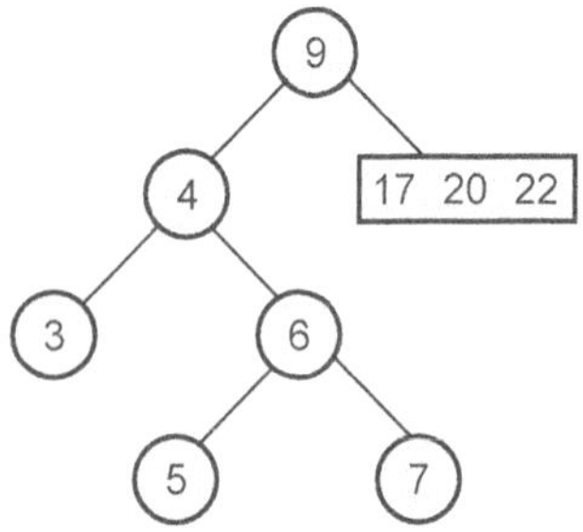

Step 4 : Consider right branch is obtained in step 1.

Inorder : 17 20 22

Preorder : 17 22 20

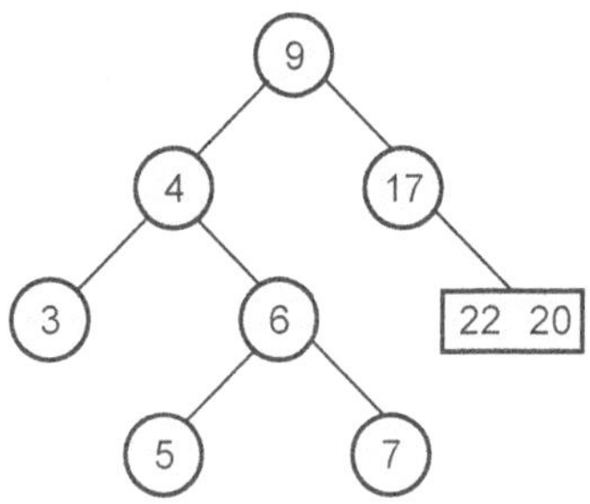

Step 5 : Consider right branch obtained in step 4.

Inorder : 20 22

Preorder : 22 20

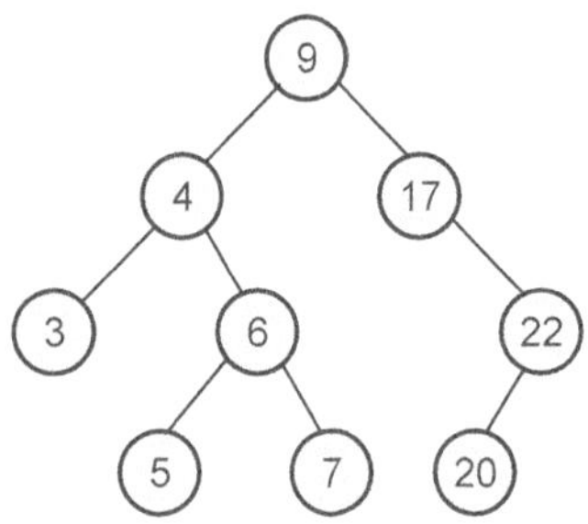

Required binary tree

Example 6.7.7 *Given Inorder and Preorder traversal, find Postorder traversal.*

Inorder traversal = {4, 2, 5, 1, 3, 6}

Preorder traversal = {1, 2, 4, 5, 3, 6} **GTU : Summer-2017, Marks 4**

Solution : We will first build the tree from given traversals.

Inorder Traversal : 4 2 5 [1] 3 6

Preorder Traversal : [1] 2 4 5 3 6

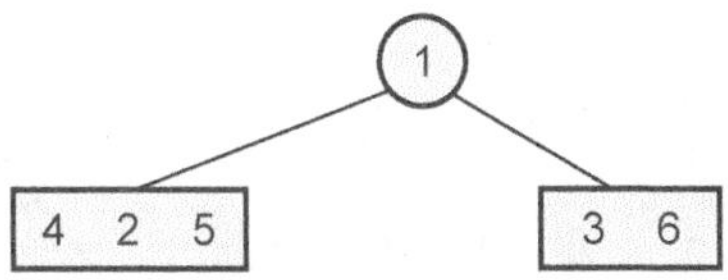

Inorder Travesal : 4 [2] 5

Preorder Traversal : [2] 4 5

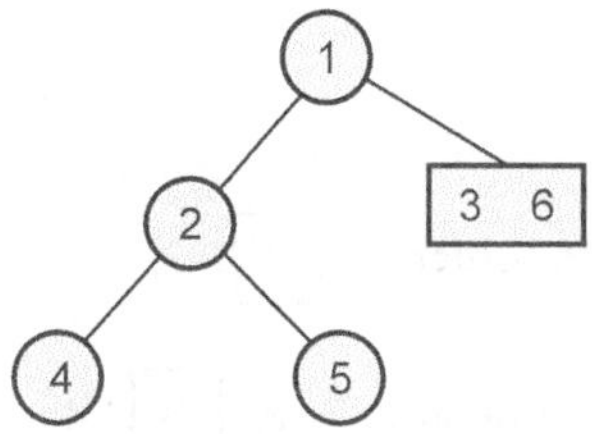

Inorder Traversal : [3] 6

Preorder Traversal : [3] 6

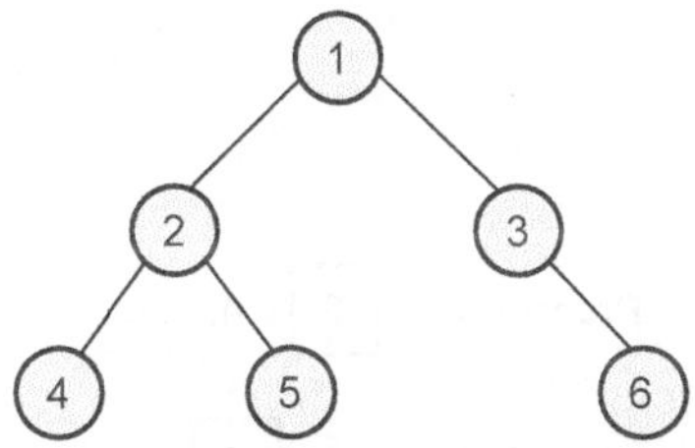

The postorder traversal is :

4, 5, 2, 6, 3, 1

Example 6.7.8 *The preorder traversal of the tree is*

7, 1, 0, 3, 2, 5, 4, 6, 9, 8, 10,

The inorder traversal of the tree is

0, 1, 2, 3, 4, 5, 6, 7, 8, 9, 10.

What is the postorder traversal ?

How a general tree can be converted to binary tree ? **GTU : Winter-2017, Marks 7**

Solution :

Preorder : 7, 1, 0, 3, 2, 5, 4, 6, 9, 8, 10

Inorder : 0, 1, 2, 3, 4, 5, 6, 7, 8, 9, 10

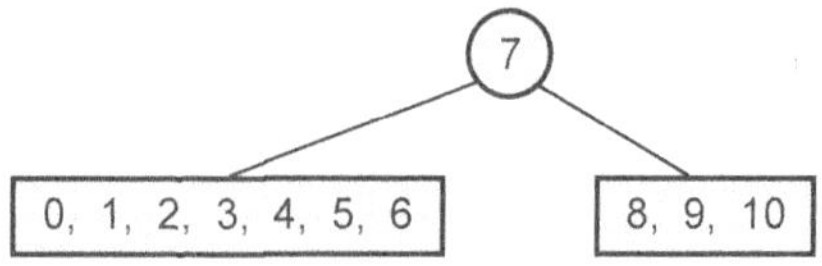

Preorder : 1, 0, 3, 2, 5, 4, 6

Inorder : 0, 1, 2, 3, 4, 5, 6

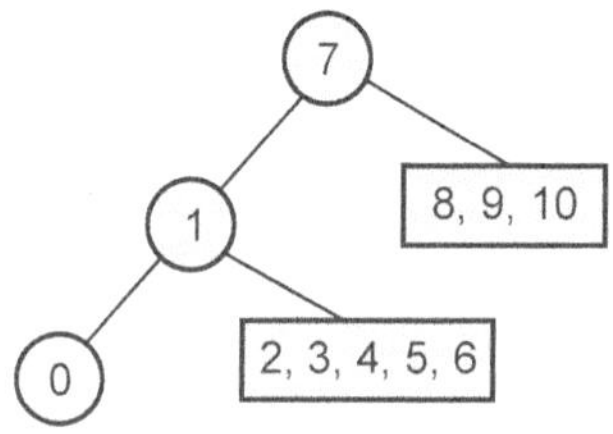

Preorder : 3, 2, 5, 4, 6

Inorder : 2, 3, 4, 5, 6

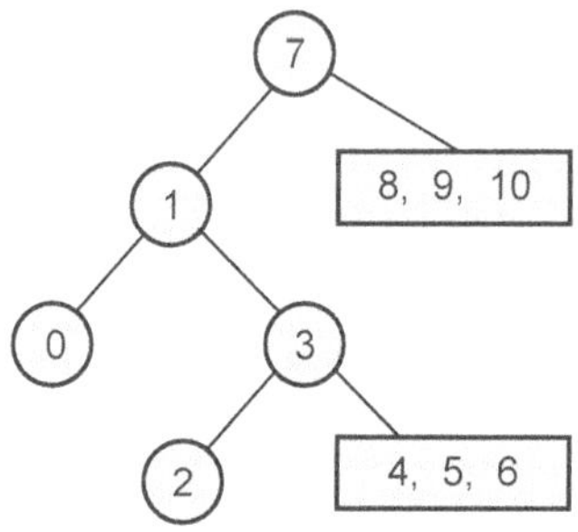

Preorder : 5, 4, 6

Inorder : 4, 5, 6

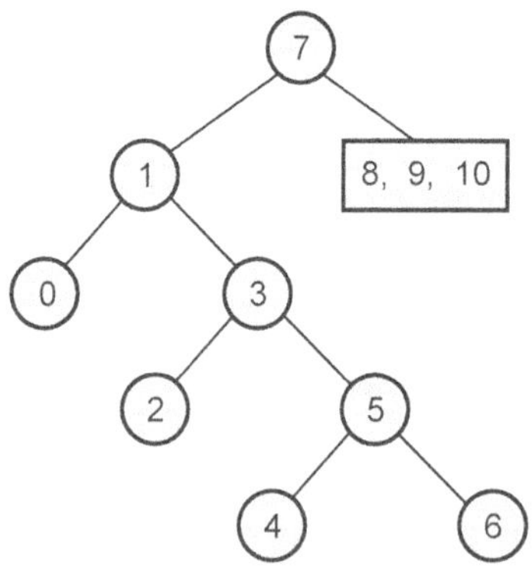

Preorder : 9, 8, 10

Inorder : 8, 9, 10

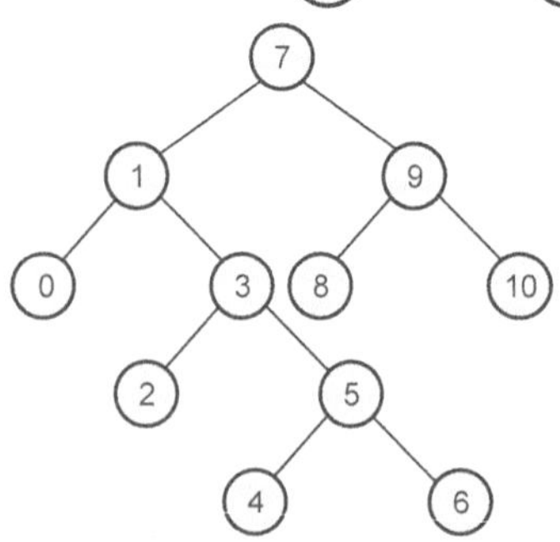

Postorder Traversal : 0, 2, 4, 6, 5, 3, 1, 8, 10, 9, 7

General Tree to Binary Tree - Refer section 6.8

6.8 Conversion of General Trees to Binary Trees

GTU : Winter-12, Summer-16, Marks 7

General trees are those trees in which there could be any number of nodes that can be attached as a child nodes. The number of subtrees for each node may be varying. For example - Following tree is a **General tree**.

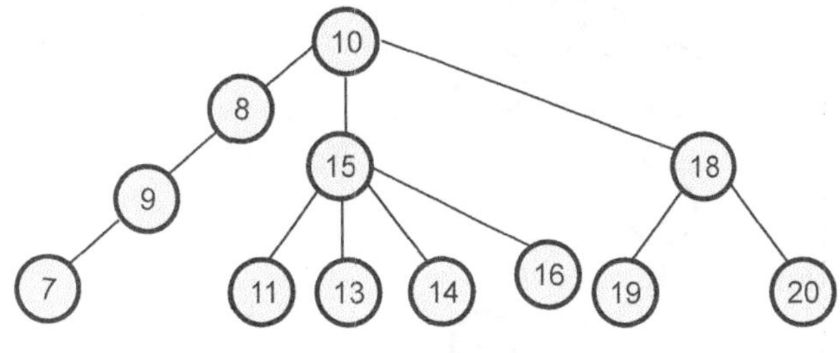

Fig. 6.8.1 General tree

We can convert the given general tree into equivalent binary tree as follows.

Rule 1 : The root of general tree becomes the root of the binary tree.

Rule 2 : Find the first child node of the node attach it as a left child to the current node in binary tree.

Rule 3 : The right sibling can be attached as a right child of that node.

Let us convert the given general tree in Fig 6.8.2 into equivalent binary tree.

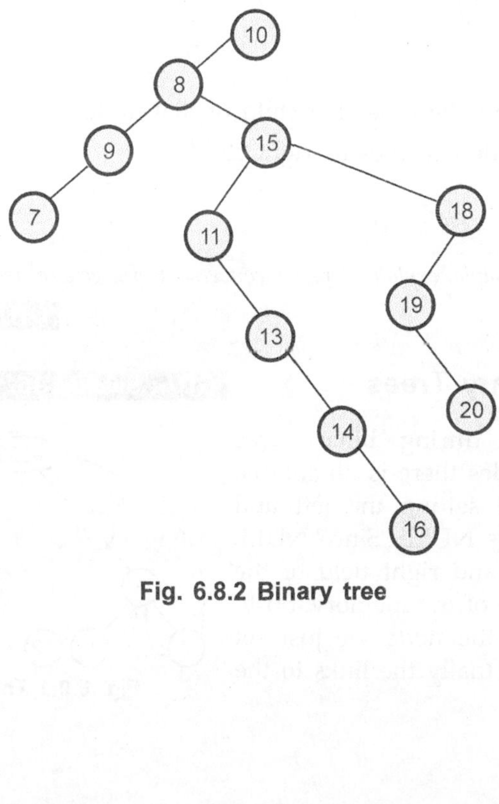

Fig. 6.8.2 Binary tree

Example 6.8.1 *Trace procedure to convert following forest into binary tree.*

GTU : Winter-12, Marks 6

Solution : i)

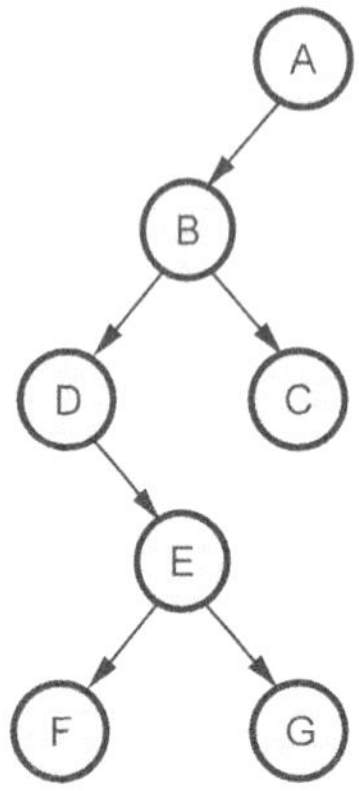

ii)

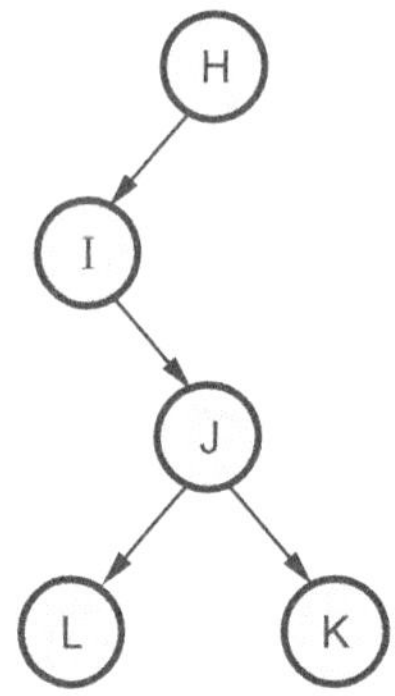

Rules -

1. The left child of node becomes left child of that node.
2. The sibling of a node becomes its right child.

Review Questions

1. *With a suitable example, explain steps for conversion of a general tree into a binary tree.*

GTU : Summer-16, Marks 7

6.9 Threaded Binary Trees

GTU : Summer-15, 16, Winter-17, Marks 7

As we know that during binary tree creation, for the leaf nodes there is no subtree further. So we are just setting the left and right fields of leaf nodes NULL. Since NULL value is put in the left and right field of the node it is just a wastage of the memory. So to avoid NULL values in the node we just set the threads which are actually the links to the

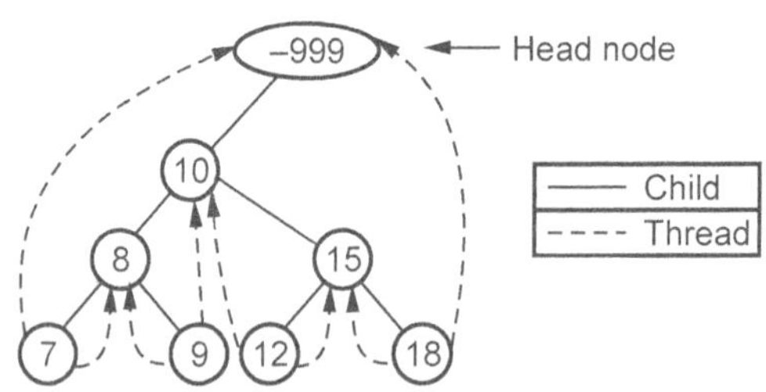

Fig. 6.9.1 Threaded binary tree

predecessor and successor nodes. There are three types of threading possible.

Inorder, preorder and postorder threading. We will discuss the inorder threading technique. The typical threaded binary tree looks as shown in Fig. 6.9.1.

The typical 'C' structure of the node is

```
typedef struct thread
{
 int data;
int lth,rth;
struct thread *left;
struct thread *right;
}Th;
```

The basic idea in inorder threading is that the left thread should point to the predecessor and the right thread points to the successor. Here we are assuming the head node as the starting node and the root node of the tree is attached to left of head node which is as shown in Fig. 6.9.1.

Let us see the 'C' program for the creation of threaded binary tree.

```
/*************************************************************************************
Program for Implementation of Inorder Threaded Binary Search Tree
and perform insertion, deletion and display of tree.
*************************************************************************************/
#include<stdio.h>
#include<conio.h>
#include<alloc.h>
typedef struct bst
 {
   int data;
   int lth, rth;
 struct bst *left,*right;
 }node;
 node *dummy;
/*
-------------------------------------------------------------------------------------
The main function
-------------------------------------------------------------------------------------
*/
void main()
{
  int choice,key;
  char ans='N';
  node *root,*temp,*parent;
  node *create(node *),*search(node*,int,node**);
  void inorder(node *),del(node*,int);
  clrscr();
```

```
do
{
        clrscr();
        printf("\n\t Program For Threaded Binary Tree");
        printf("\n1.Create \n2.Display \n3.Search \n4.Delete");
        scanf("%d",&choice);
        switch(choice)
        {
        case 1:root=NULL;
             do
             {
                  root=create(root);
                  printf("\n Do u Want To enter More Elements?(y/n)");

                  ans=getch();
             }while(ans=='y');
             break;
    case 2:if(root==NULL)
              printf("Tree Is Not Created");
             else
              {
               printf("\n The Tree is : ");
               inorder(root);
              }
             break;
    case 3:printf("\n Enter The Element Which You Want To Search") ;
             scanf("%d",&key);
             temp=search(root,key,&parent);
             if(temp==NULL)
              printf("\nElement is Not Present");
             else
              printf("Its Parent Node is %d",parent->data);
             break;
    case 4:printf("\n Enter The Element U wish to Delete");
             scanf("%d",&key);
             del(root,key);
             break;
     }
     printf("\n\nWant To See Main Menu?(y/n)");
     ans=getche();
    }while(ans=='y');
}
/*
------------------------------------------------------------------------
The create function
------------------------------------------------------------------------
*/
```

```
node *create(node *root)
{
 void insert(node *,node *);
 node *New;
 New=(node*)malloc(sizeof(node));
 New->left=NULL;
 New->right=NULL;
 New->lth=0;
 New->rth=0;
 printf("\n Enter The Element ");
 scanf("%d",&New->data);
 if(root==NULL)
 {                          // Tree is not Created
  root=New;
  dummy=(node*)malloc(sizeof(node));
  dummy->data=-999;
  dummy->left=root;
  root->left=dummy;
  root->right=dummy;
 }
 else
 insert(root,New) ;
 return root;
}

/*
------------------------------------------------------------------------------------------------
This function is for creating a binary search tree
------------------------------------------------------------------------------------------------
*/
void insert(node *root,node *New)
{
 if(New->data<root->data)
 {
      if(root->lth==0)
      {
           New->left=root->left;
           New->right=root;
           root->left=New;
           root->lth=1;
      }
      else
           insert(root->left,New);
 }
 if(New->data>root->data)
 {
      if(root->rth==0)
```

```
        {
            New->right=root->right;
            New->left=root;
            root->rth=1;
            root->right=New;
        }
        else
         insert(root->right,New);
  }
}

/*
------------------------------------------------------------------------
The search function
------------------------------------------------------------------------
*/
node *search(node *root,int key,node **parent)
{
 node *temp;
 temp=root;
 while((temp!=dummy))
 {
  if(temp->data==key)
  {
      printf("\n The %d Element is Present",temp->data);
      return temp;
 }
  *parent=temp;
  if(temp->data>key)
      temp=temp->left;
  else
      temp=temp->right;
 }
return NULL;
}
/*
------------------------------------------------------------------------
This function is for deleting a node from binary search tree
There exists three possible cases for deletion of a node
------------------------------------------------------------------------
*/
void del(node *root,int key)
{
 node *temp,*parent,*temp_succ;
 node *search(node *,int,node **);
 int flag=0;
```

```
temp=search(root,key,&parent);
if(root==temp)
{
 printf("\n Its Root Node Which Can Not Be Deleted!!");
 return;
}
//deleting a node with two children
if(temp->lth==1&&temp->rth==1)
{
 parent=temp;
 temp_succ=temp->right;//Finding Inorder successor
 while(temp_succ->lth==1)
 {
 flag=1;
      parent=temp_succ;
      temp_succ=temp_succ->left;
 }
 if(flag==0)
 {
      temp->data=temp_succ->data;
      parent->right=temp_succ->right;
      parent->rth=0;
      }
 else//inorder successor is on left subbranch.
           // and it has to be traversed
      {
      temp->data=temp_succ->data;
      parent->rth=0;
      parent->lth=0;
      parent->left=temp_succ->left;
 }
 printf(" Now Deleted it!");
 return;
}
//deleting a node having only one child
 //The node to be deleted has left child
 if(temp->lth==1 &&temp->rth==0)
 {
  if(parent->left==temp)
  {
      (temp->left)->right=parent;
       parent->left=temp->left;
  }
  else
  {
      (temp->left)->right=temp->right;
      parent->right=temp->left;
```

```
 }
 temp=NULL;
 delete temp;
 printf(" Now Deleted it!");
 return;
}
//The node to be deleted has right child
if(temp->lth==0 &&temp->rth!=0)
{
 if(parent->left==temp)
 {
      parent->left=temp->right;
      (temp->right)->left=temp->left;
      (temp->right)->right=parent;
 }
 else
 {
      parent->right=temp->right;
      (temp->right)->left=parent;
 }
 temp=NULL;
 free(temp);
 printf(" Now Deleted it!");
 return;
}
//deleting a node which is having no child
if(temp->lth==0 &&temp->rth==0)
{
      if(parent->left==temp)
      {
        parent->left=temp->left;
        parent->lth=0;
      }
      else
       {
         parent->right=temp->right;
         parent->rth=0;
       }
 printf(" Now Deleted it!");
 return;
}
}

/*
------------------------------------------------------------------------
The inorder function
------------------------------------------------------------------------
```

```
*/
void inorder(node *temp)
{
  while(temp!=dummy)
  {
      while(temp->lth==1)
       temp=temp->left;
  printf(" %d",temp->data);
  while(temp->rth==0)
  {
  temp=temp->right;
      if(temp==dummy)
       return;
      printf("  %d",temp->data);
  }
  temp=temp->right;
  }
}
```

Output

```
        Program For Threaded Binary Tree
     1. Create
     2. Display
     3. Search
     4. Delete 1

      Enter The Element 10

      Do u Want To enter More  Elements?(y/n)
      Enter The Element 8

     Do u Want To enter More  Elements?(y/n)
     Enter The Element 7
     Do u Want To enter More  Elements?(y/n)
     Enter The Element 15

     Do u Want To enter More  Elements?(y/n)
     Enter The Element 11

     Do u Want To enter More  Elements?(y/n)
     Enter The Element 17

     Do u Want To enter More  Elements?(y/n)
     Want To See Main Menu?(y/n)

        Program For Threaded Binary Tree
     1. Create
     2. Display
```

```
    3. Search
    4. Delete2
     The Tree is :  7  8  9  10  11  15 17
    Want To See Main Menu?(y/n)

            Program For Threaded Binary Tree
    1. Create
    2. Display
    3. Search
    4. Delete3

     Enter The Element Which You Want To Search11

     The 11 Element is PresentIts Parent Node is 15

    Want To See Main Menu?(y/n)
            Program For Threaded Binary Tree
    1. Create
    2. Display
    3. Search
    4. Delete 4

     Enter The Element U wish to Delete 15

     The 15 Element is Present Now Deleted it!

Want To See Main Menu?(y/n)
            Program For Threaded Binary Tree
    1. Create
    2. Display
    3. Search
    4. Delete2
     The Tree is :  7  8 9  10 11  17
    Want To See Main Menu?(y/n)
```

Logic explanation for threaded binary tree -

In thread binary tree, the NULL pointers are avoided. Instead of left NULL pointer the link points to **inorder predecessor** of that node. Similarly instead of right NULL pointer the link points to **inorder successor** of that node.

There are two additional fields in each node named as l^{th} and r^{th} these fields indicate whether left or right thread is present. Thread present means the NULL link is replaced by a link to inorder predecessor or inorder successor. To represent that there exists thread the lth or r^{th} fields are set to 0. Let us take one example to explain how a threaded binary tree gets created. Suppose we want to create a threaded binary tree for the nodes having values.

10, 8, 6, 12, 9, 11, 14

Initially we will create a dummy node which will act as a header of the tree.

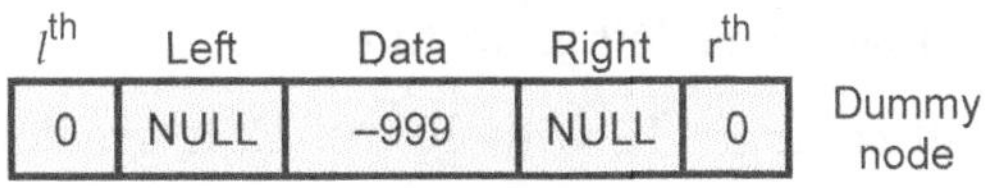

Fig. 6.9.2

Now let us take first value i.e. 10. The node with value 10 will be the root node we will attach this root node as left child of dummy node.

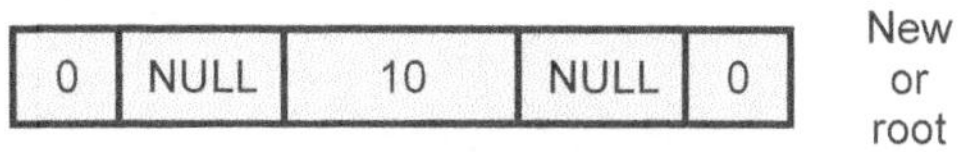

Fig. 6.9.3

The NULL links of root's left and right child will be pointed to dummy.

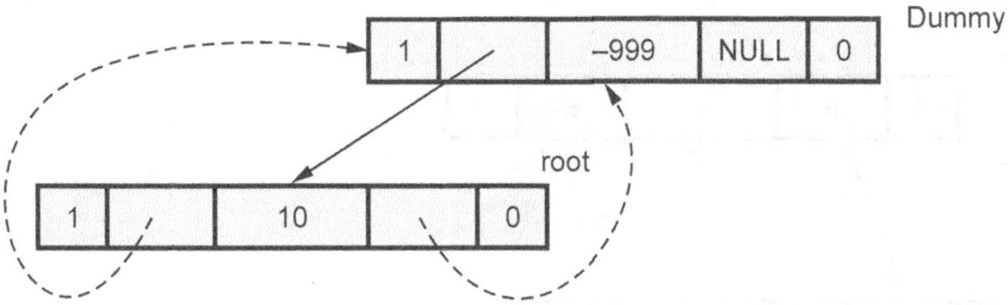

Fig. 6.9.4

Now next comes 8. The 8 will be compared with 10, as the value is less than 10, we will attach 8 as left child of 10 and we will set root's 1th field to 1, indicating that the node 10 is having left child. See then how the links are arranged.

```
New → left = root → left
New → right = root;
root → left = New;
root → lth = 1;
```

Note that the left link of node 8 points to its inorder predecessor and right link of node 8 points to its inorder successor.

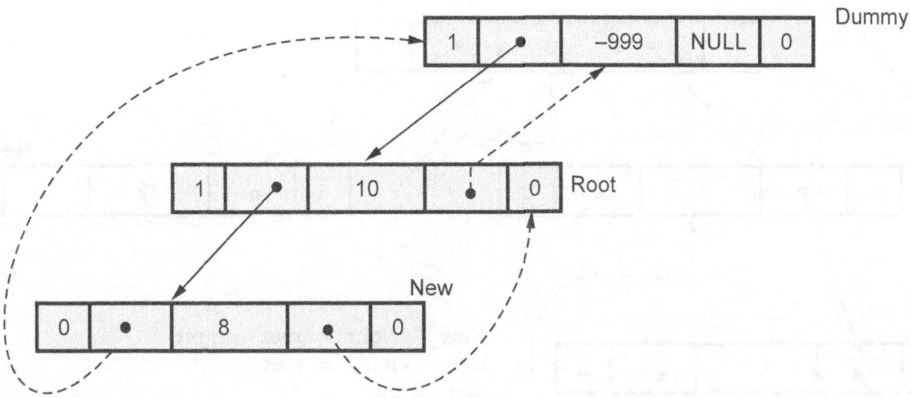

Fig. 6.9.5

Next comes 6. The value 6 will be first compared with root i.e. with 10. As 6 is less than 10, we will move on left subbranch. The 6 will then be compared with 8, so we have to move on left subbranch of 8. But l^{th} of node 8 is 0, indicating that there is no left child to 8, so we will attach 6 as left child to 8.

Then comes 12. We will compare 12 with 10. As 12 is greater than 10, we will attach the node 12 as right child of 10.

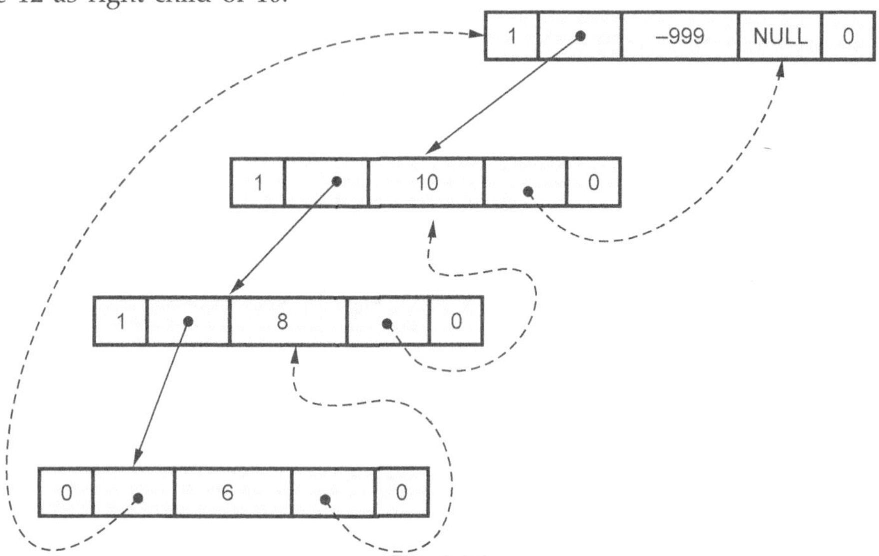

Fig. 6.9.6

Note that the left field of node 12 points to its inorder predecessor and right field of node 12 points to its inorder successor. Thus by attaching 9, 11, 14 as appropriate children, the threaded binary tree will look like this -

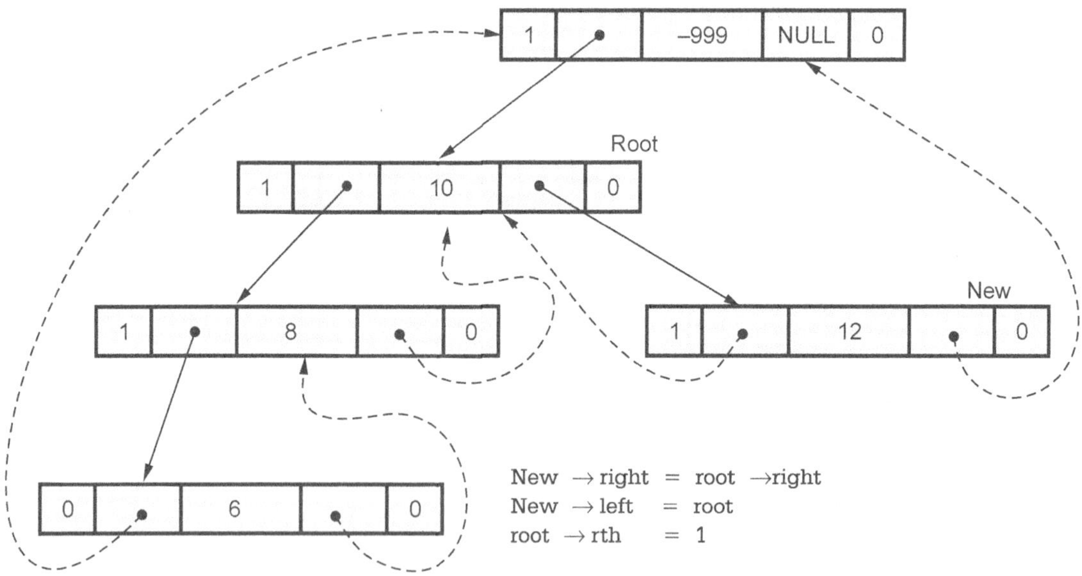

Fig. 6.9.7

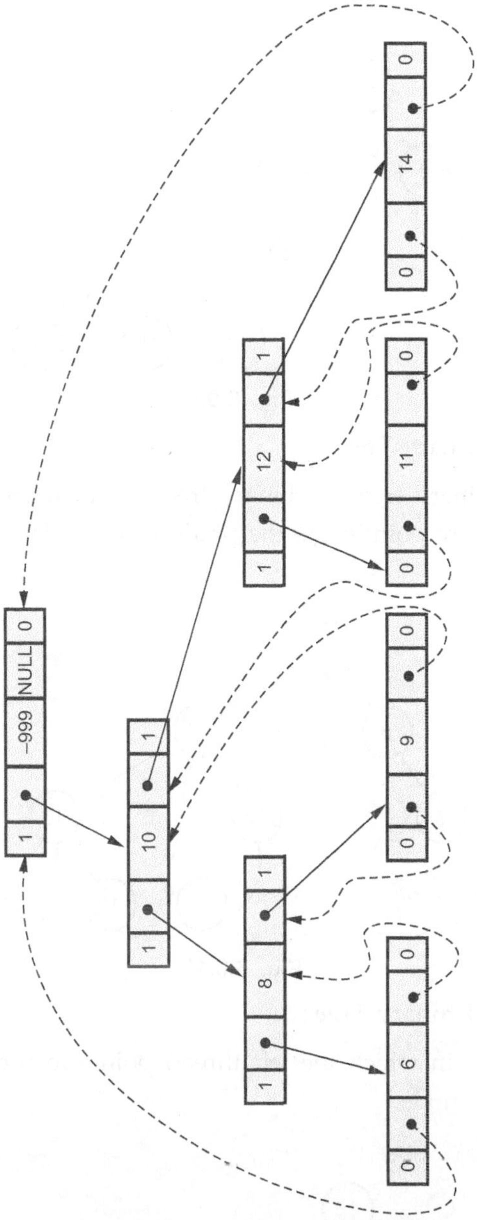

Fig. 6.9.8 Threaded binary tree

Such a threaded tree is called inorder threaded binary tree.

Example 6.9.1 *Explain Right-in, left-in and Full-in threaded binary tree.*

Summer 2015, Marks 7

Solution : (1) Right-in-Threaded Binary Tree

The right-in threaded binary tree is a binary tree in which the threads are only on right side of the node and are pointing to the successor node.

For example :

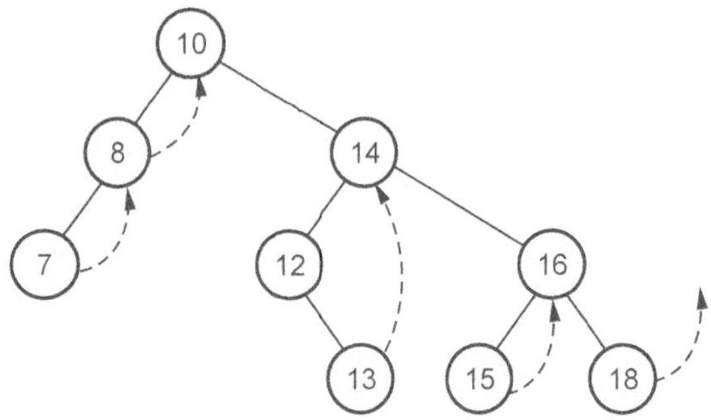

Fig. 6.9.9

(2) Left-in Threaded Binary Tree

The left-in threaded binary tree is a binary tree in which the threads are only on the left side of the node and are pointing to the predecessor node.

For example :

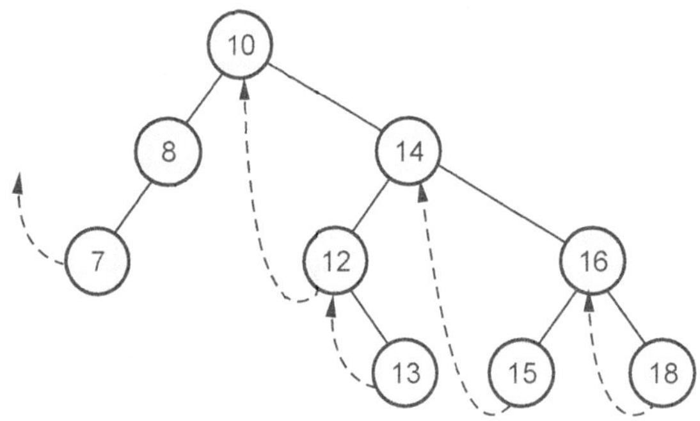

Fig. 6.9.10

(3) Full - in - threaded binary Tree

A threaded binary tree in which the left thread points to predecessor node and right thread points to successor node.

For example :

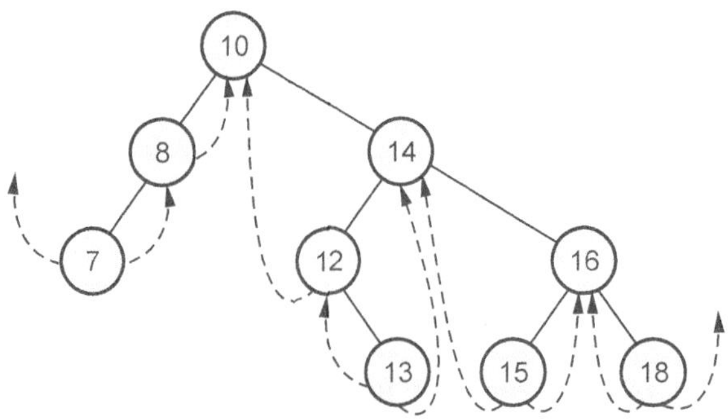

Fig. 6.9.11

Review Questions

1. *Explain threaded binary trees with suitable examples.* **GTU : Summer-16, Marks 4**
2. *Explain the structure of threaded binary tree.* **GTU : Winter-17, Marks 3**

6.10 Applications of Trees

GTU : Summer-15, Marks 7

The purpose of binary tree is to have efficient retrieval of data. It is a useful data structure when we require to take twoway decisions. The use of binary tree is exploited by following data structures.

1. Binary search trees
2. Expression trees
3. Threaded binary trees
4. Game Tree

Review Question

1. *Briefly explain various linear and non-linear data structures along with their applications.* **GTU : Summer-15, Marks 7**

6.11 Concept of Balanced Trees

Balanced trees are useful data structures that are useful to store the data at some specific location. As compared to simple binary tree, the balanced search trees are more efficient because the insertion or deletion of nodes in this data structure requires O(log N) time.

Definition : A balanced tree is a rooted tree where each subtree of the root has equal number of nodes. The height of such binary tree is O(log N).

Various types of balanced trees are -

1. Height balance tree or AVL tree
2. Splay tree
3. Red-black trees
4. B-trees

These balanced structures allow to perform various dictionary operations such as **insertions** and **deletions**. In balanced trees as items are inserted and deleted, the tree is structured to keep the nodes balanced. The search paths in such trees must be uniform. The insert, delete and search operations are performed in O(log n) time for balanced trees.

6.12 AVL Trees

GTU : May-11, Dec.-03, Summer-13,14,16, Winter-14,15,16, Marks 7

Adelsion, Velski and Lendis in 1962 introduced binary tree structure that is balanced with respect to height of subtrees. The tree can be made balanced and because of this retrieval of any node can be done in O(log n) times, where n is total number of nodes. From the name of these Scientists the tree is called **AVL tree**.

Definition

An empty tree is height balanced if T is a non-empty binary tree with T_L and T_R as its left and right subtrees. The T is height balanced if and only if

i) T_L and T_R are height balanced.

ii) $h_L - h_R$ <=1 where h_L and h_R are heights of T_L and T_R.

The idea of balancing a tree is obtained by calculating the balance factor of a tree.

Definition of Balance Factor

The balance factor BF(T) of a node in binary tree is defined to be $\mathbf{h_L - h_R}$ where h_L and h_R are heights of left and right subtrees of T.

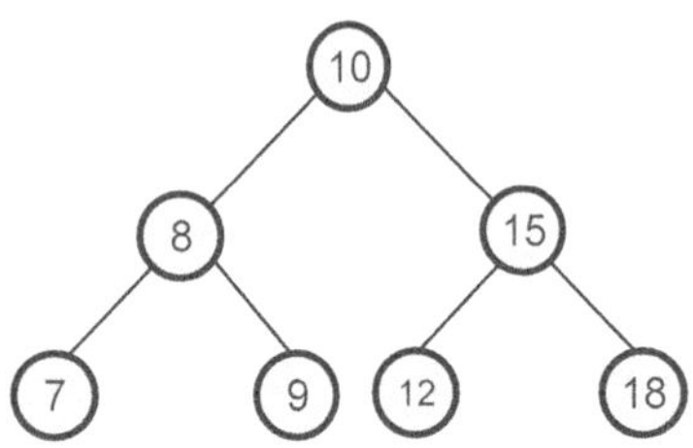

Fig. 6.12.1 AVL tree

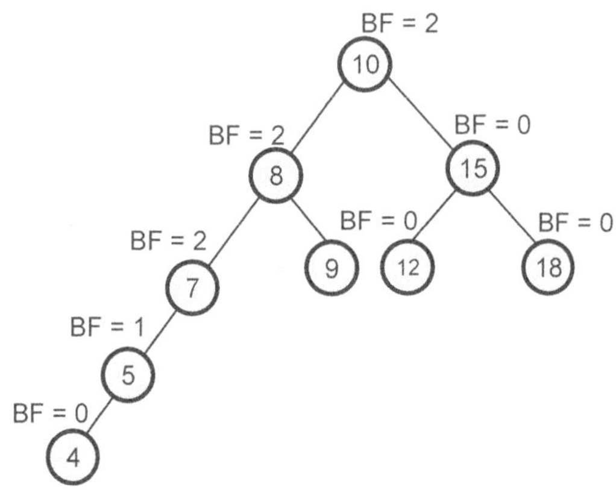

Fig. 6.12.2 Not an AVL tree

For any node in AVL tree the balance factor i.e. BF(T) is **–1, 0 or +1.**

Height of AVL tree

Theorem : The height of AVL tree with n elements (nodes) is O(log n).

Proof : Let an AVL tree with n nodes in it. N_h be the minimum number of nodes in an AVL tree of height h.

In worst case, one subtree may have height h – 1 and other subtree may have height h–2. And both these subtrees are AVL trees. Since for every node in AVL tree the height of left and right subtrees differ by at most 1.

Hence, $N_h = N_{h-1} + N_{h-2} + 1$

where N_h denotes the minimum number of nodes in an AVL tree of height h.

$\therefore \quad N_0 = 0 \qquad N_1 = 2$

We can also write it as

$$
\begin{aligned}
N &> N_h = N_{h-1} + N_{h-2} + 1 \\
&> 2N_{h-2} \\
&> 4N_{h-4} \\
&\vdots \\
&> 2^i N_{h-2^i}
\end{aligned}
$$

If value of h is even, let $i = \frac{h}{2-1}$

Then equation becomes,

$$
\begin{aligned}
N &> 2^{h/2-1} N_2 \\
N &> 2^{h/2-1} \times 4 \quad \because N_2 = 4 \\
&= O(\log N)
\end{aligned}
$$

If value of h is odd, let $i = (h-1)/2$ then equation becomes.

$$
\begin{aligned}
N &> 2^{(h-1)/2} N_1 \\
N &> 2^{(h-1)/2} \times 1 \quad \because N_1 = 1 \\
\therefore \quad h &= O(\log N)
\end{aligned}
$$

This proves that height of AVL tree is always O(log N). Hence search, insertion and deletion can be carried out in logarithmic time.

Theorem : The height of AVL tree h with minimum number of nodes n is 1.44 log n.

Proof : Let F_h be the AVL tree with height h having minimum number of nodes.

The tree can be shown as below.

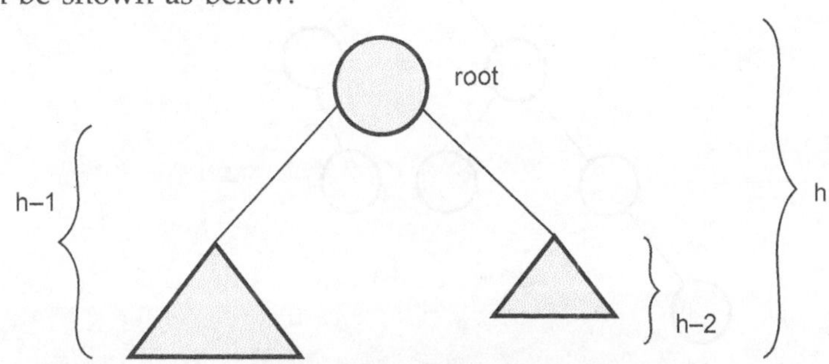

Fig. 6.12.3 AVL tree F_h

Hence minimum number of nodes in AVL tree is

$$= \text{Length of left subtree} + \text{Length of right subtree} + 1$$

$$|F_h| = |F_{h-1}|+|F_{h-2}|+1$$

Also $|F_0| = 1$ and $|F_1| = 2$

This denotes the Fibonacci tree.

Adding 1 to both sides.

$$|F_h|+1 = (|F_{h-1}|+1)+(|F_{h-2}|+1)$$

Thus the numbers $|F_h|+1$ are Fibonacci numbers. Using approximate formula for Fibonacci numbers, we will get an approximate value as :

$$|F_h|+1 \approx \frac{1}{\sqrt{5}}\left(\frac{1+\sqrt{5}}{2}\right)^{h+3}$$

Taking logarithm

$$= h \approx 1.44 \log |F_h|$$

Hence the worst case height of an AVL tree with n nodes is 1.44 log n.

The Fibonacci trees are as shown below.

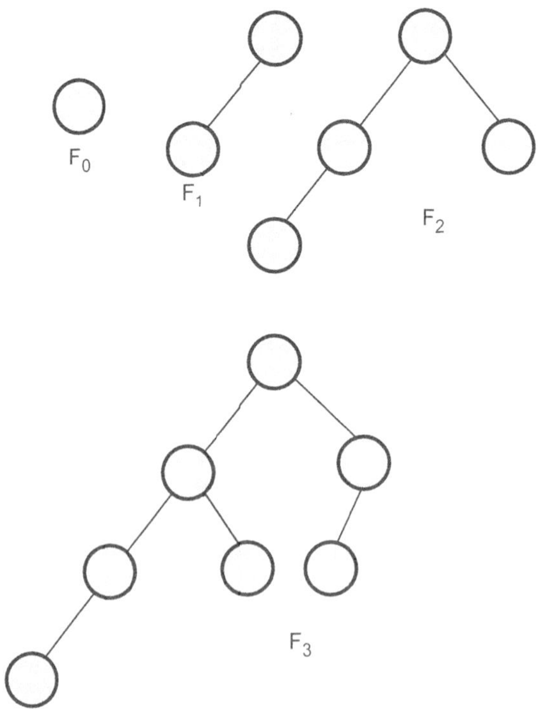

Fig. 6.12.4 Fibonacci trees

$F_0 = 1$

$F_1 = F_0 + 1$ node

$F_2 = F_1 + 2$ nodes

$F_3 = F_2 + 3$ nodes

Thus adding Fibonacci number of nodes each time.

6.12.1 Representation of AVL Tree

- The AVL tree follows the property of binary search tree. Infact AVL trees are basically binary search trees with balance factor as –1, 0 or + 1.
- After insertion of any node in an AVL tree if the balance factor of any node becomes other than –1, 0 or + 1 then it is said that AVL property is violated. Then we have to restore the destroyed balance condition. The balance factor is denoted at right top corner inside the node.

For example :

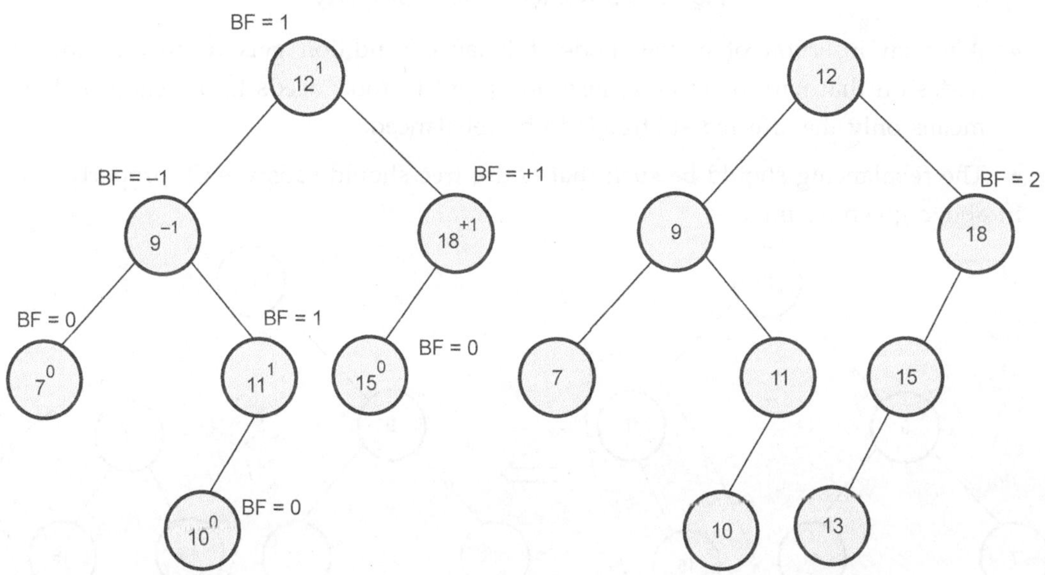

Orignal AVL Tree

Insert 13 Property violated

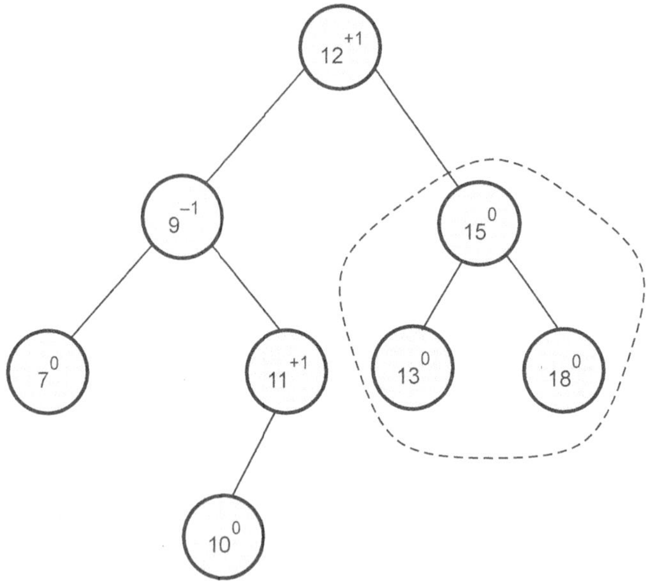

Fig. 6.12.5 Restoring AVL property

- After an insertion of a new node if balance condition gets destroyed, then the nodes on that path (new node insertion point to root) needs to be readjusted. That means only the affected subtree is to be rebalanced.
- The rebalancing should be such that entire tree should satisfy AVL property.

In above given example -

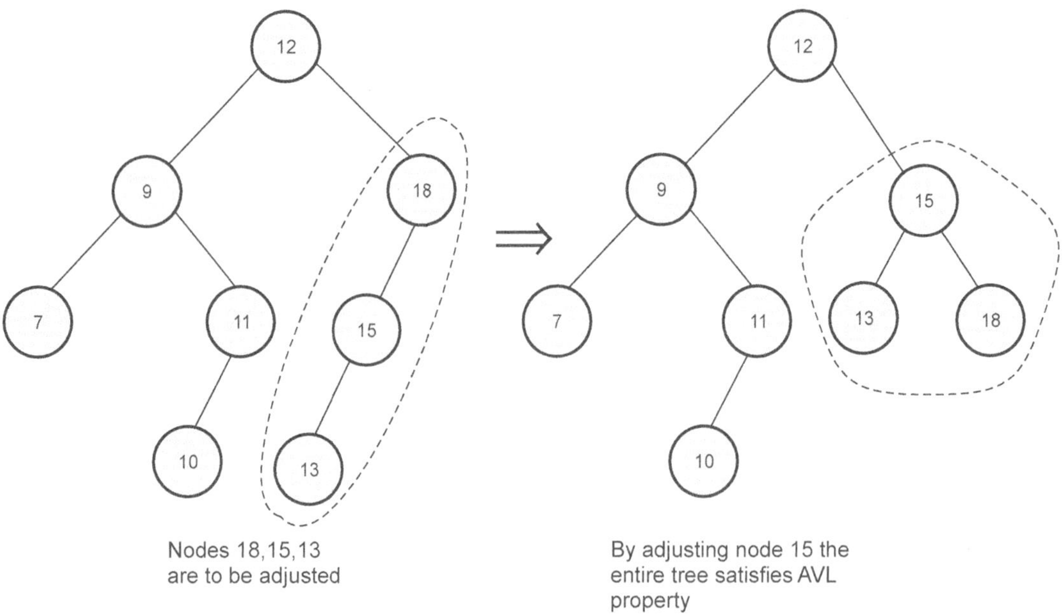

Fig. 6.12.6

6.12.2 Insertion

- There are four different cases when rebalancing is required after insertion of new node.
    1. An insertion of new node into left subtree of left child (LL).
    2. An insertion of new node into right subtree of left child (LR).
    3. An insertion of new node into left subtree of right child (RL).
    4. An insertion of new node into right subtree of right child (RR).

There is a symmetry between case 1 and 4. Similarly symmetry exists between case 2 and 3.

> Some modifications done on AVL tree in order to rebalance it is called rotations of AVL tree.

- There are two types of rotations.

- Single rotation
    - Left-Left (LL rotation)
    - Right-Right (RR rotation)
- Double rotation
    - Left-Right (LR rotation)
    - Right-Left (RL rotation)

Insertion algorithm

1. Insert a new node as new leaf just as in ordinary binary search tree.
2. Now trace the path from insertion point (new node inserted as leaf) towards root. For each node 'n' encountered, check if heights of left (n) and right (n) differ by at most 1.

    a) If yes, move towards parent (n).

    b) Otherwise restructure by doing either a single rotation or a double rotation.

    Thus once we perform a rotation at node 'n' we do not require to perform any rotation at any ancestor on 'n'.

Different rotations in AVL tree

1. LL rotation

When node '1' gets inserted as a left child of node 'C' then AVL property gets destroyed i.e. node A has balance factor + 2.

The LL rotation has to be applied to rebalance the nodes.

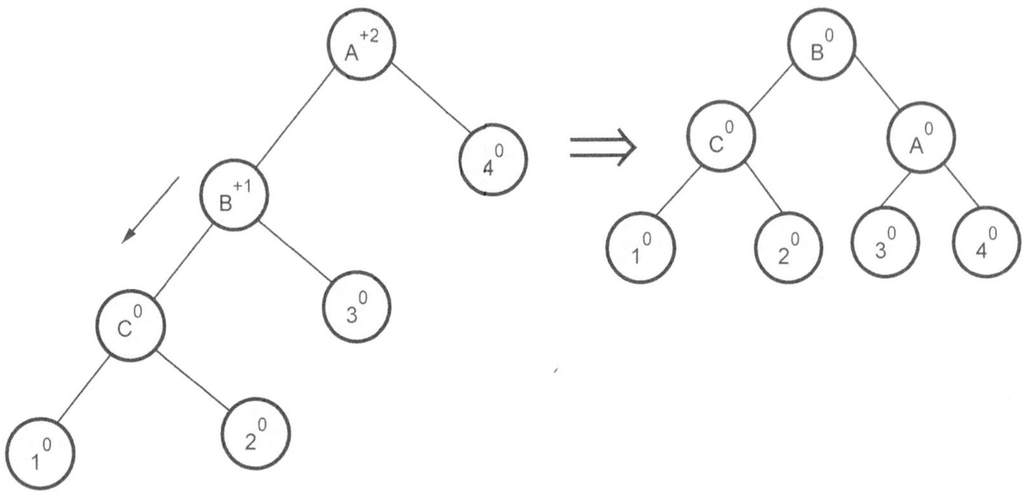

Fig. 6.12.7

2. RR rotation

When node '4' gets attached as right child of node 'C' then node 'A' gets unbalanced. The rotation which needs to be applied is RR rotation as shown in Fig. 6.12.8

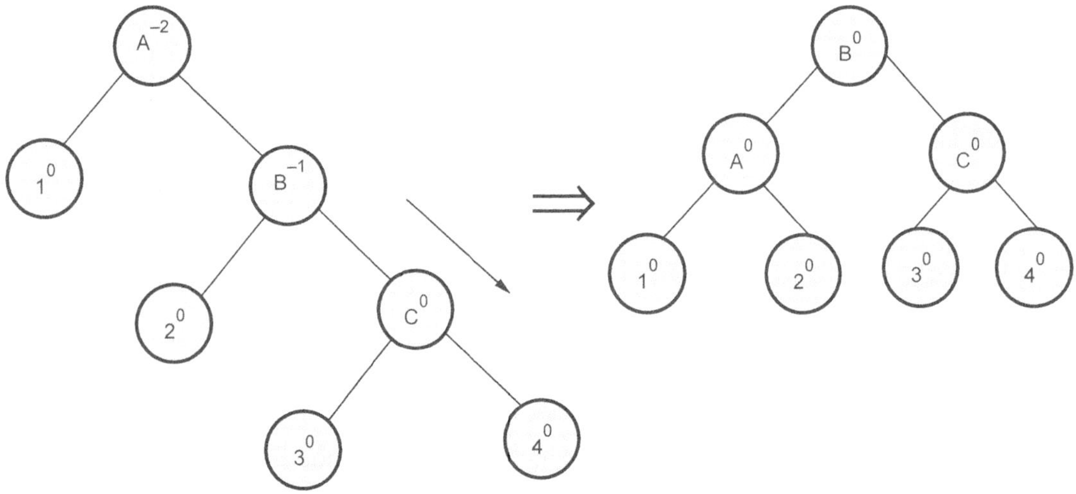

Fig. 6.12.8

3. LR rotation

When node '3' is attached as a right child of node 'C' then unbalancing occurs because of LR. Hence LR rotation needs to be applied.

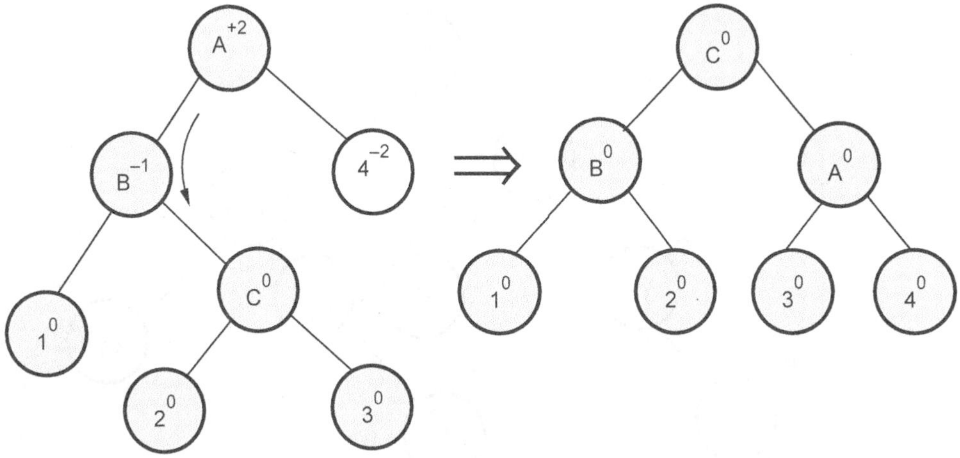

Fig. 6.12.9

4. RL rotation

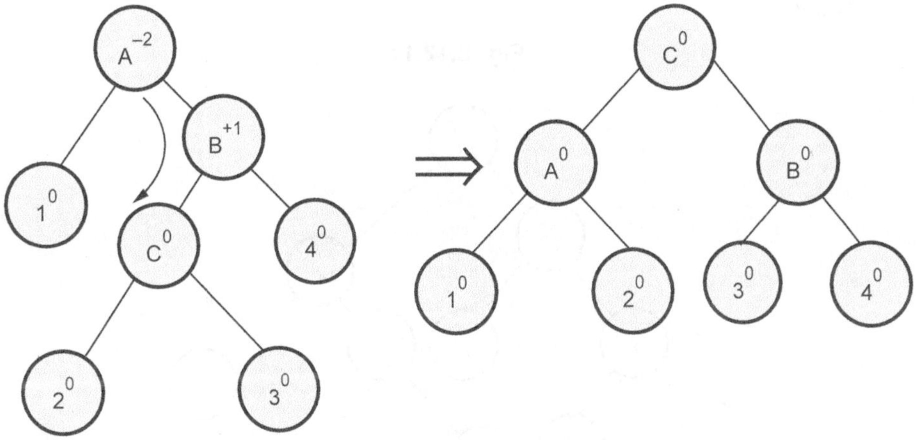

Fig. 6.12.10

When node '2' is attached as a left child of node 'C' then node 'A' gets unbalanced as its balance factor becomes − 2. Then RL rotation needs to be applied to rebalance the AVL tree.

Example 6.12.1 *Insert 1, 25, 28, 12 to build AVL tree.*

Solution :

Insert 1

To insert node '1' we have to attach it as a left child of '2'. This will unbalance the tree as follows. We will apply LL rotation to preserve AVL property of it.

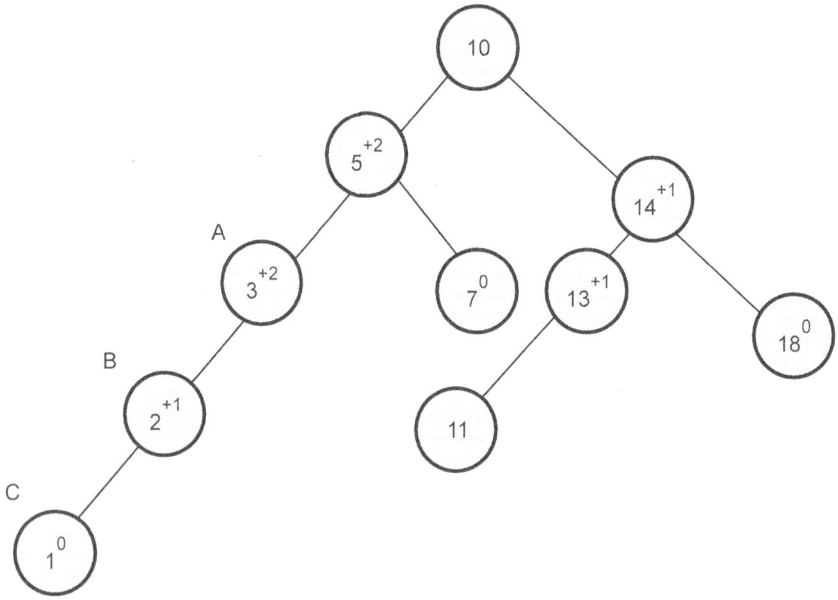

Fig. 6.12.11

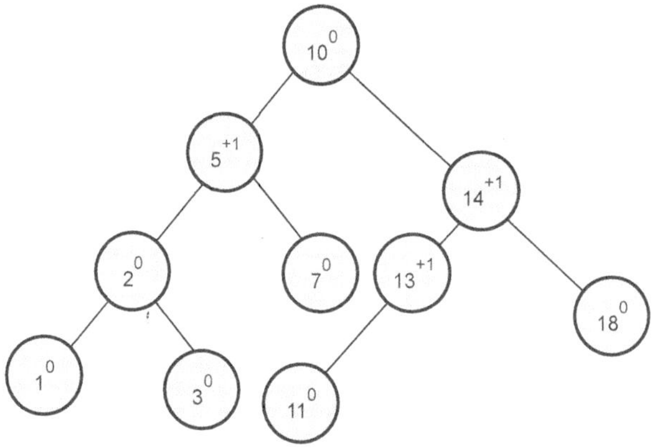

Fig. 6.12.12

Insert 25

We will attach 25 as a right child of 18. No balancing is required as entire tree preserves the AVL property.

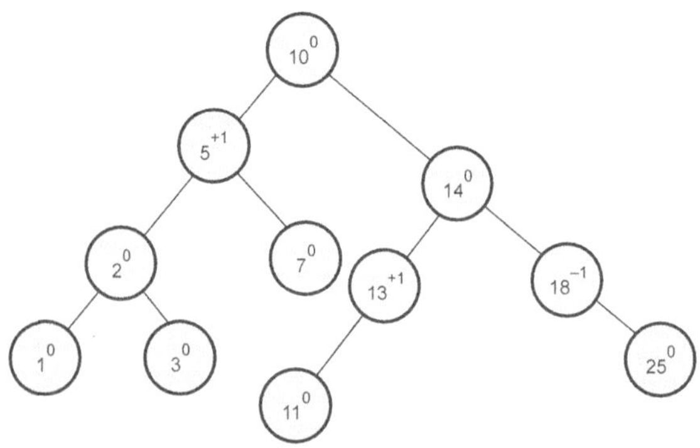

Fig. 6.12.13

Insert 28

The node '28' is attached as a right child of 25. RR rotation is required to rebalance.

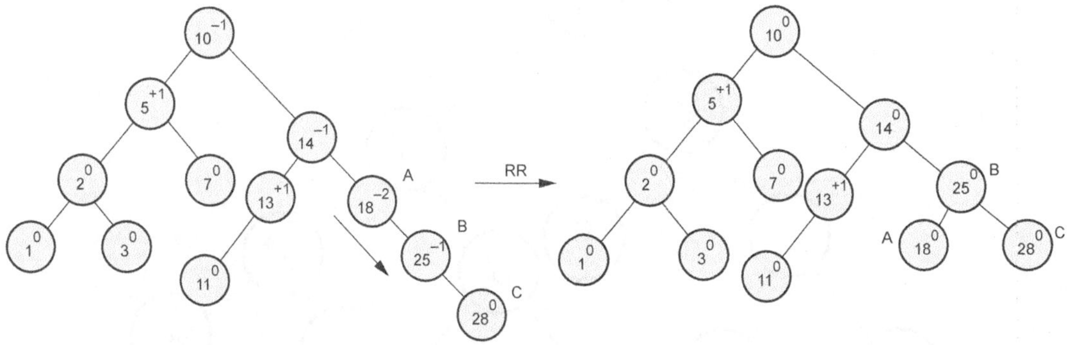

Fig. 6.12.14

Now we will insert 12.

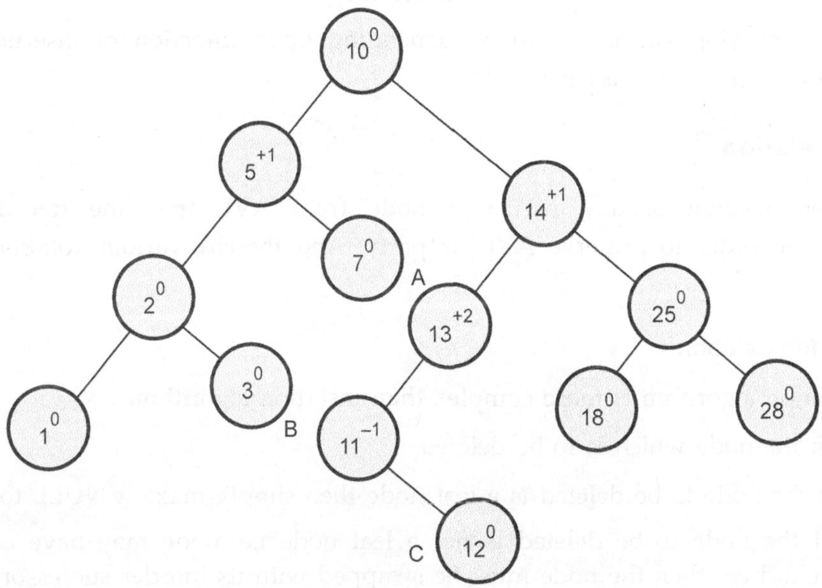

Fig. 6.12.15

To rebalance the tree we have to apply LR rotation.

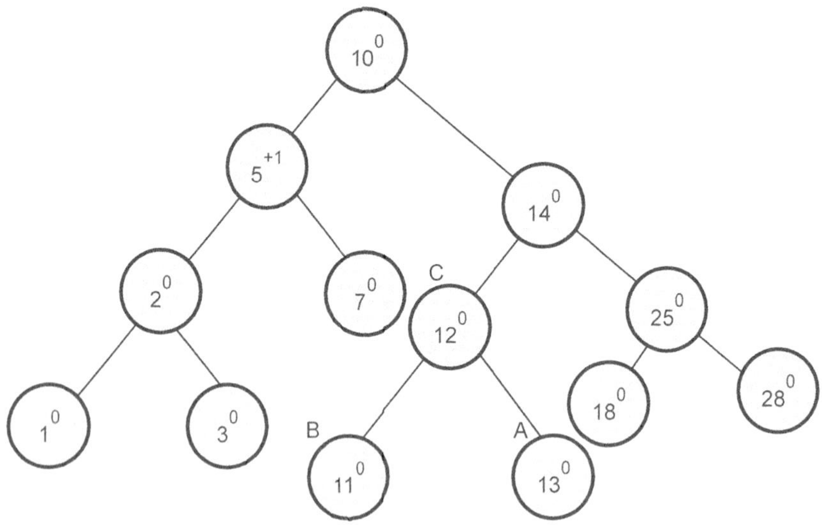

Fig. 6.12.16

Thus by applying various rotations depending upon direction of insertion of new node the AVL tree can be restructured.

6.12.3 Deletion

Evenafter deletion of any particular node from AVL tree, the tree has to be restructured in order to preserve AVL property. And thereby various rotations need to be applied.

Algorithm for deletion

The deletion algorithm is more complex than insertion algorithm.

1. Search the node which is to be deleted.
2. a) If the node to be deleted is a leaf node then simply make it NULL to remove.
   b) If the node to be deleted is not a leaf node i.e. node may have one or two children, then the node must be swapped with its inorder successor. Once the node is swapped, we can remove this node.
3. Now we have to traverse back up the path towards root, checking the balance factor of every node along the path. If we encounter unbalancing in some subtree then balance that subtree using appropriate single or double rotations.

The deletion algorithm takes O(log n) time to delete any node.

Consider an AVL tree.

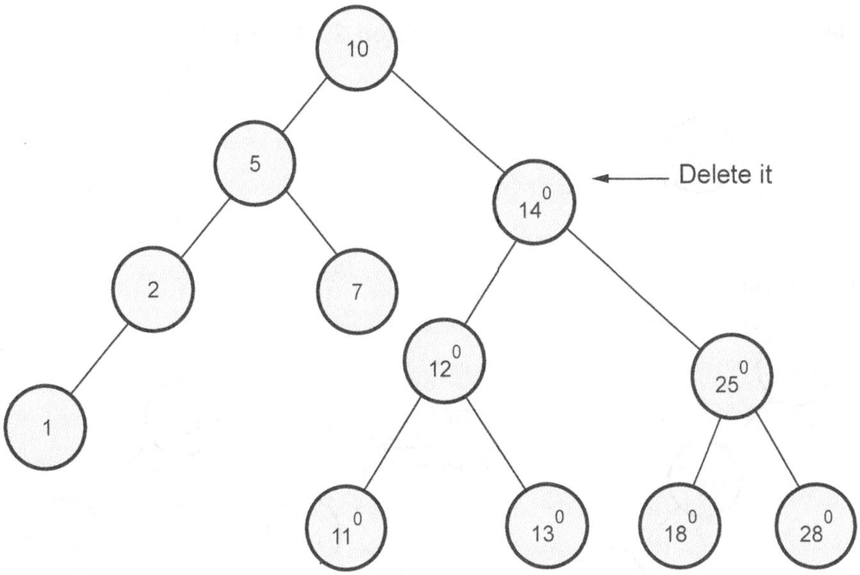

Fig. 6.12.17

The tree becomes

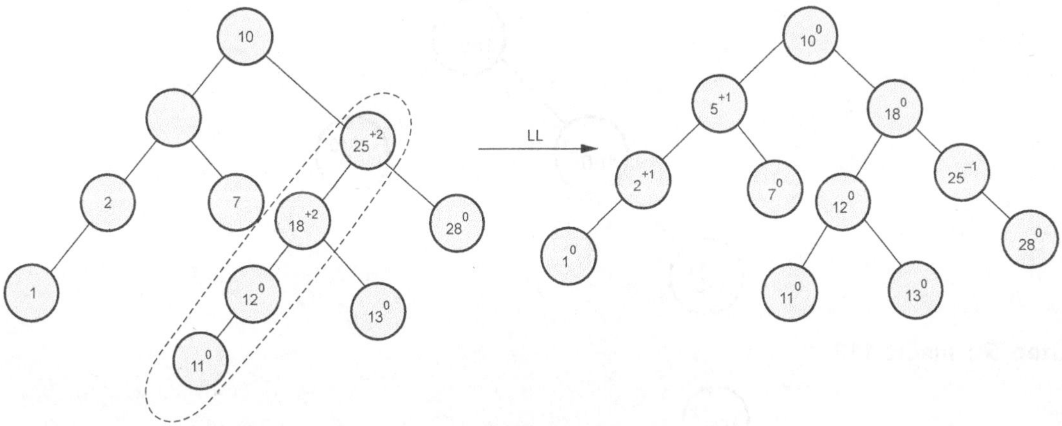

Fig. 6.12.18

Thus the node 14 gets deleted from AVL tree.

Example 6.12.2 *Define an AVL tree. Obtain an AVL tree by inserting one integer at a time in the following sequence.*

150, 155, 160, 115, 110, 140, 120, 145, 130, 147, 170, 180.

Show all the steps. **GTU : May-11, Marks 7**

Solution :

AVL Tree - Refer section 6.12.

Construction of AVL tree

Step 1 : Insert 150

Step 2 : Insert 155

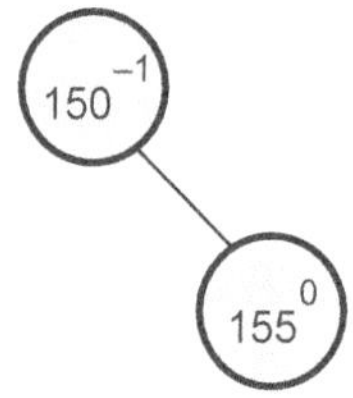

Step 3 : Insert 160

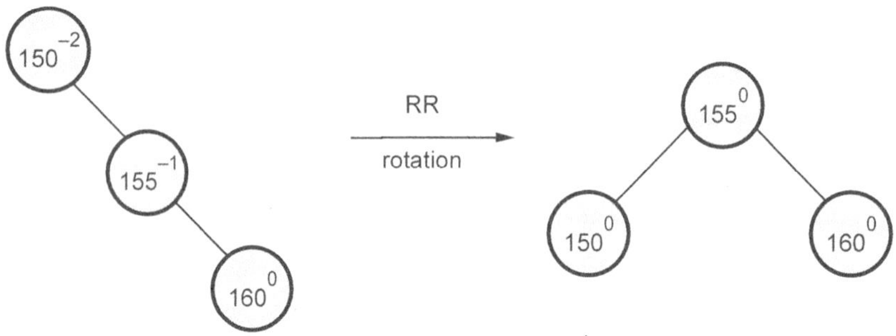

Step 4 : Insert 115

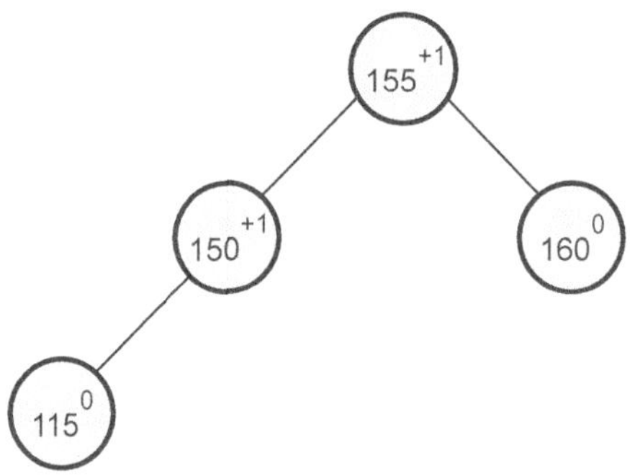

Step 5 : Insert 110

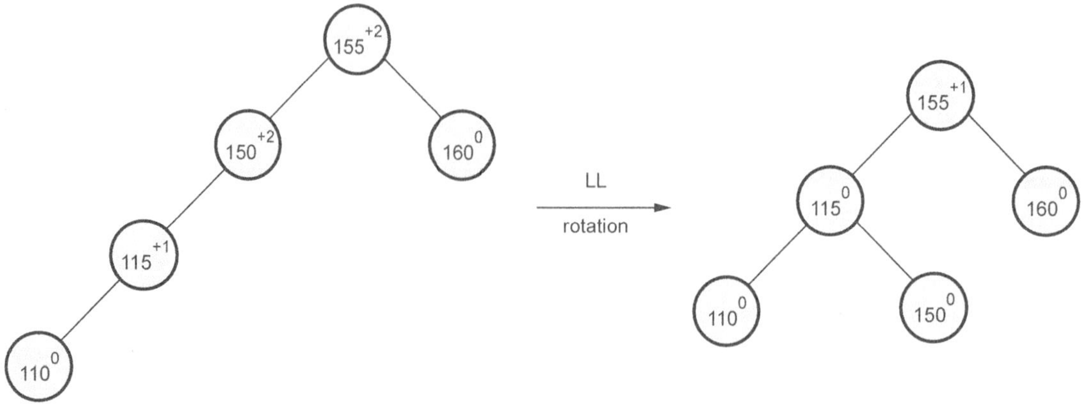

Step 6 : Insert 140

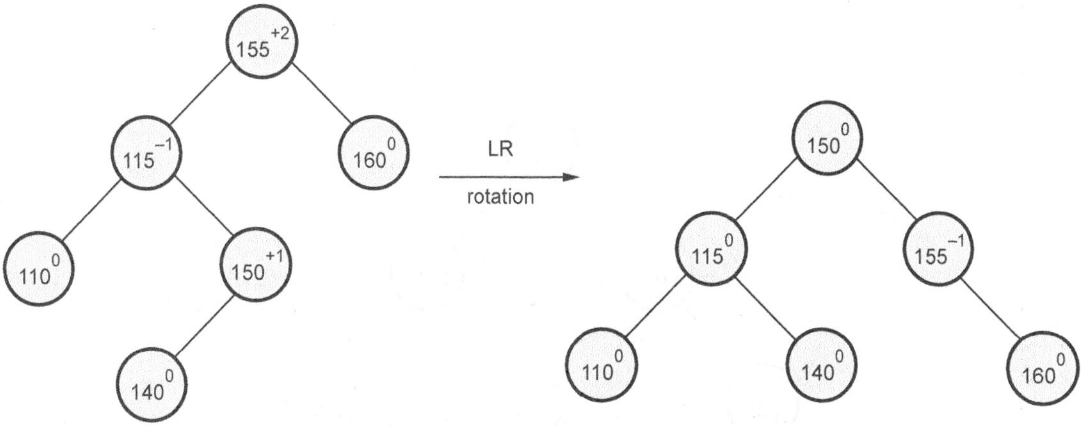

Step 7 : Insert 120

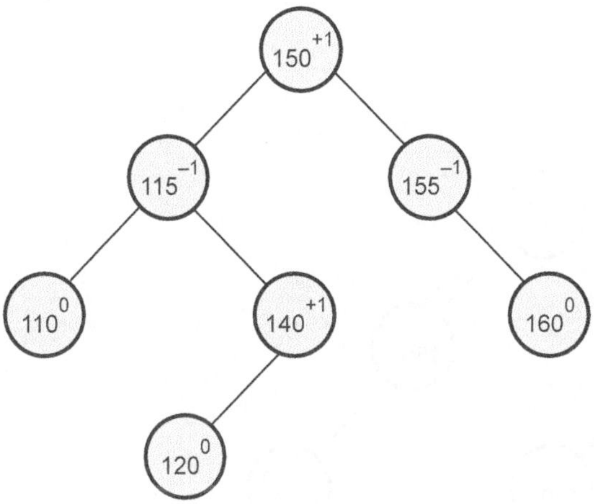

Step 8 : Insert 145

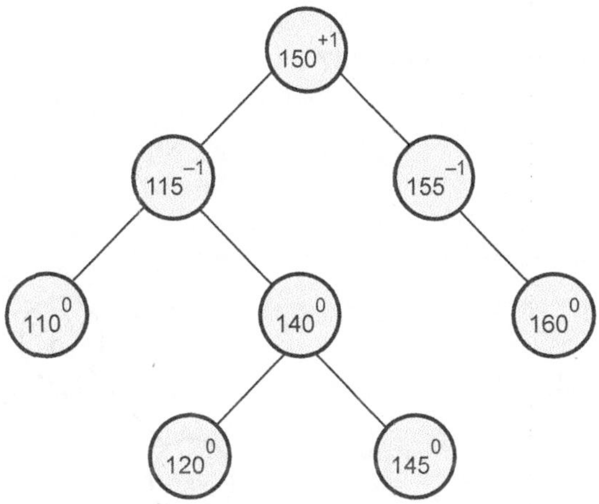

Step 9 : Insert 130

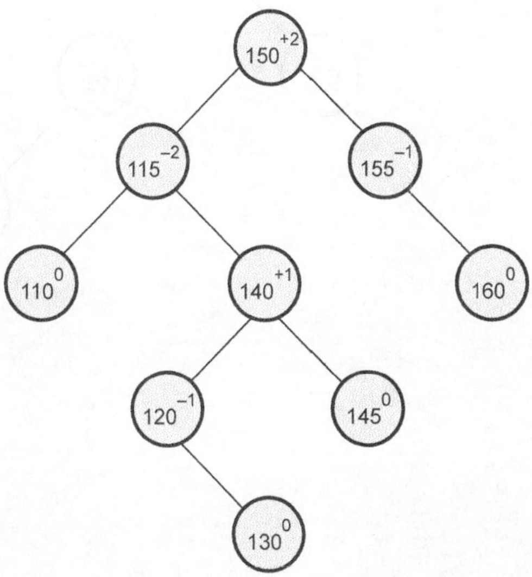

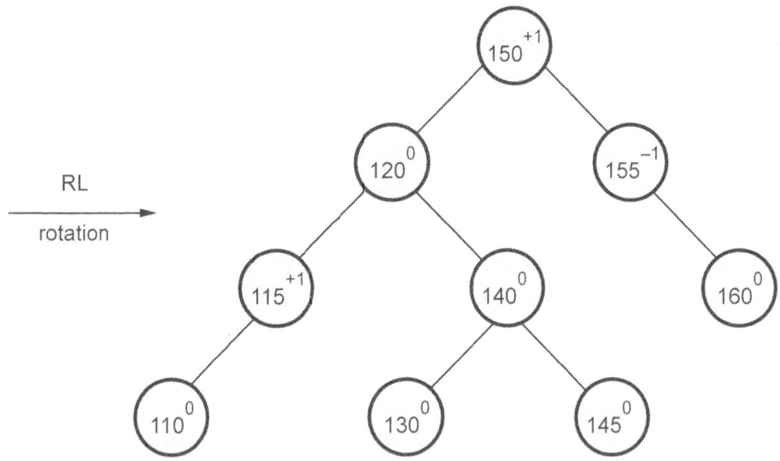

Step 10 : Insert 147

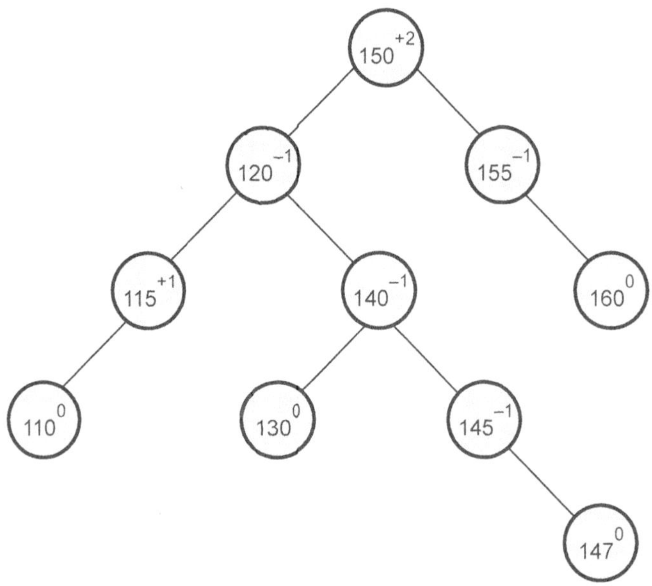

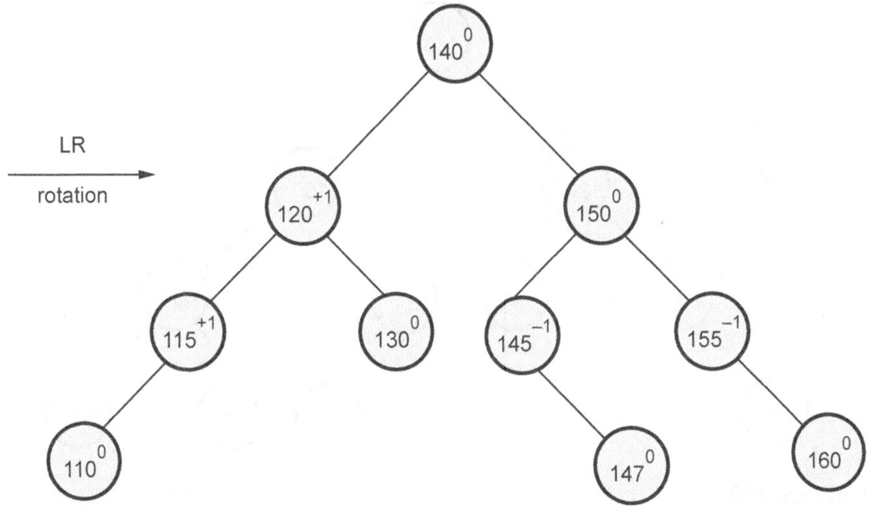

Step 11 : Insert 170

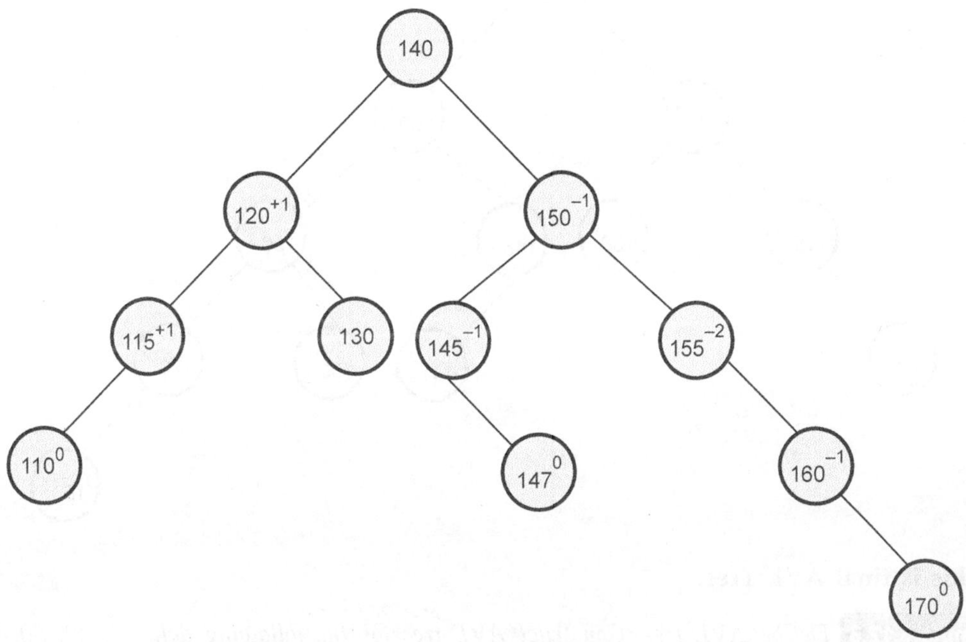

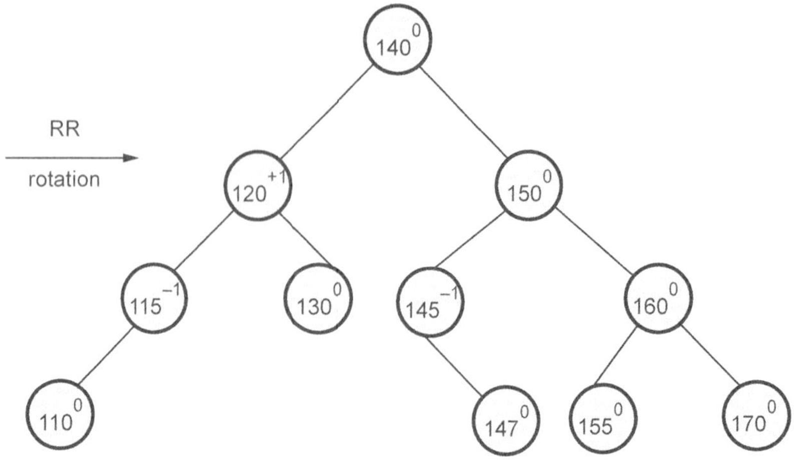

Step 12 : Insert 180

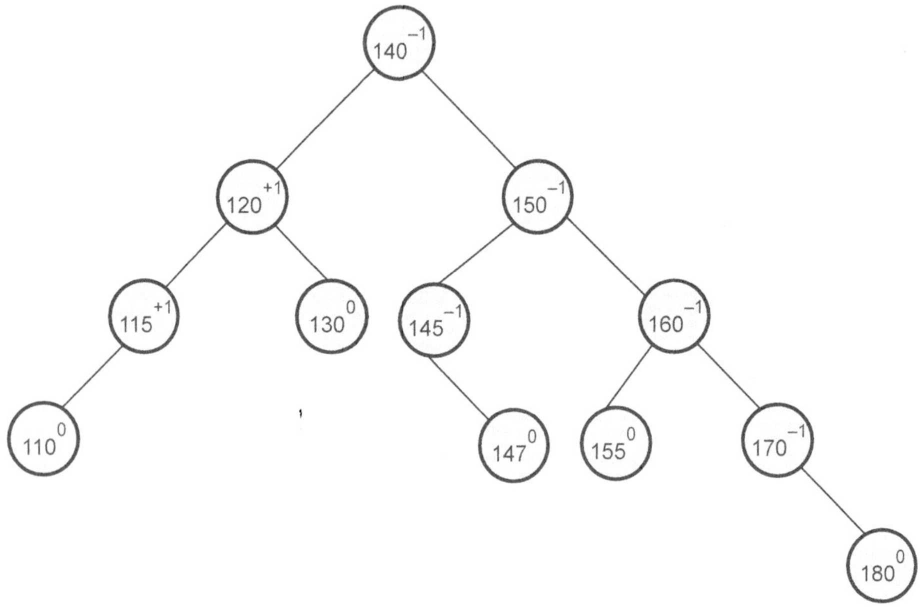

This is final AVL Tree.

Example 6.12.3 *Define AVL tree. Construct AVL tree for the following data 10, 20, 30, 40, 50, 60, 70, 80* **GTU : Summer-13, Marks 7**

Solution :

Step 1 :

Step 2 :

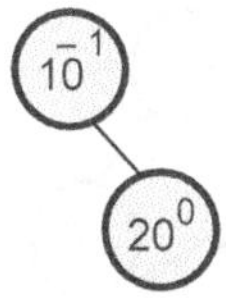

Step 3 :

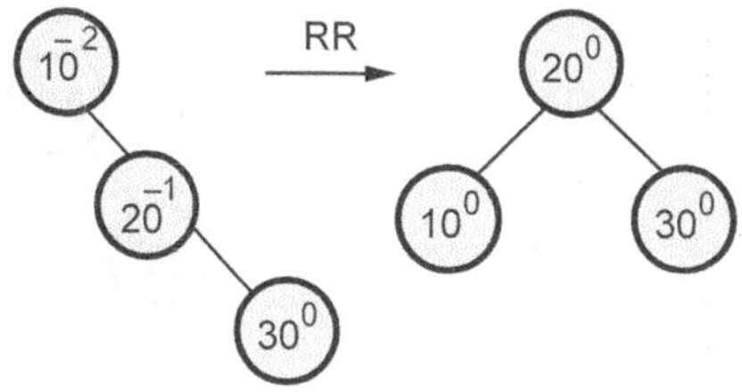

Step 4 :

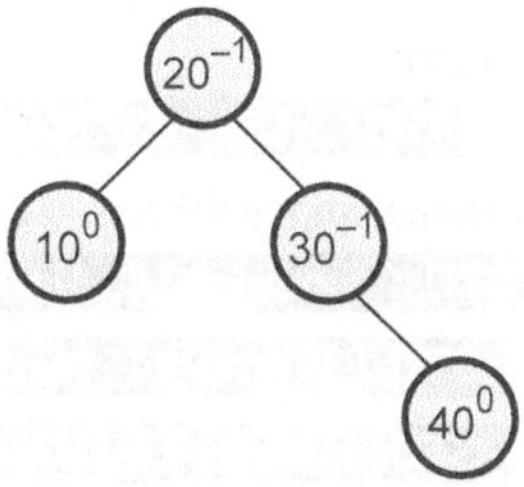

Step 5 :

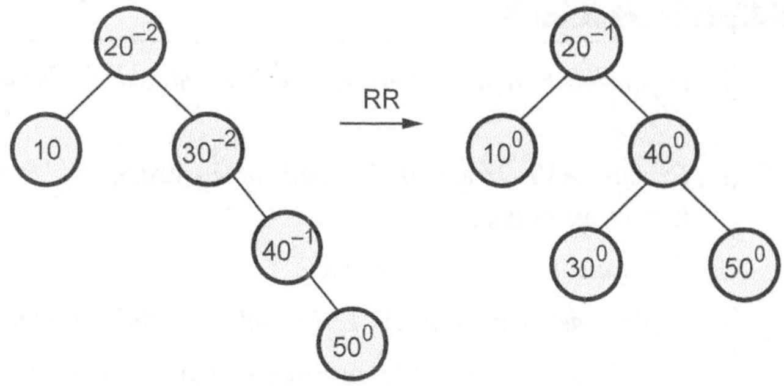

Step 6 :

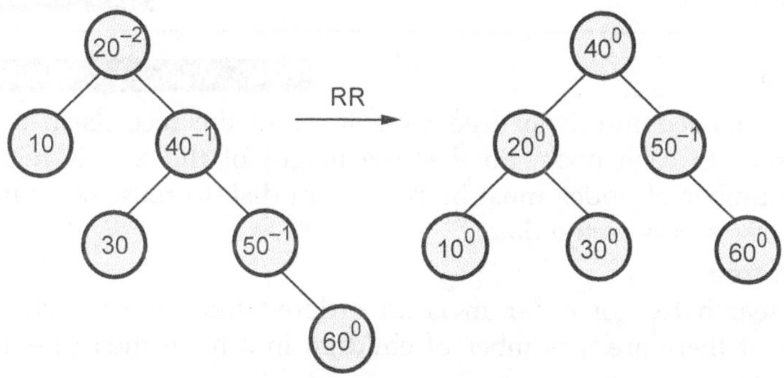

Step 7 :

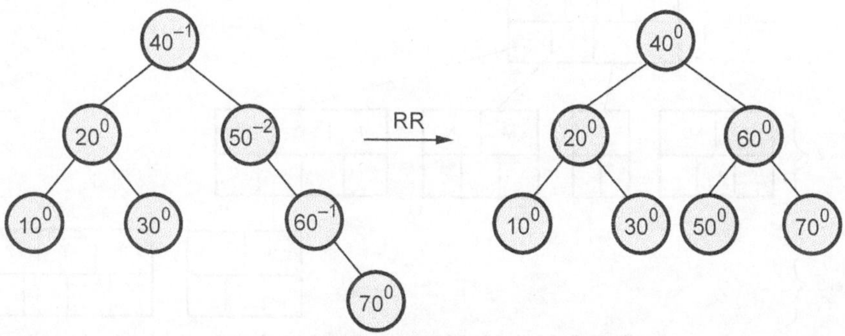

Step 8 :

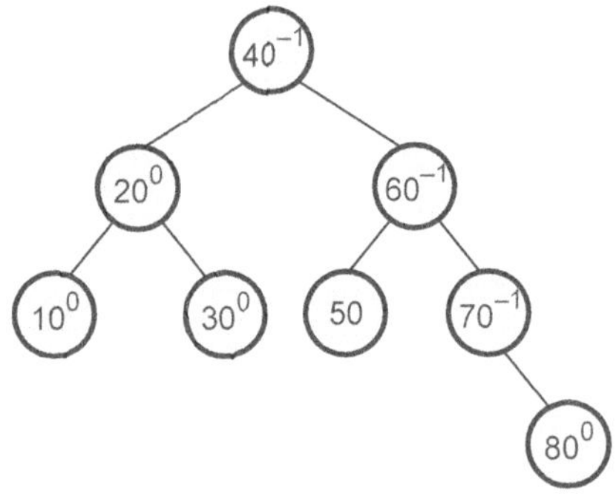

Review Questions

1. *Define left-heavy, right heavy and balanced node for height-balanced tree* **GTU : Dec.-03, Marks 3**
2. *Explain AVL tree with the help of an example also show insertions and deletions with the help of an example* **GTU : Summer-14, Marks 7**
3. *Explain AVL tree with example.* **GTU : Winter-14, Marks 7**
4. *Explain deletion in an AVL tree with a suitable example.* **GTU : Winter-15, Marks 4**
5. *Explain insert and delete operations in AVL trees with suitable examples.* **GTU : Summer-16, Marks 7**
6. *Explain AVL trees.* **GTU : Winter-16, Marks 3**

6.13 B-Trees **GTU : Winter-15, Summer-18, Marks 7**

B-tree is a specialized multiway tree used to store the records in a disk. There are number of subtrees to each node. So that the height of the tree is relatively small. So that only small number of nodes must be read from disk to retrieve an item. The goal of B-trees is to get fast access of the data.

Multiway search tree

A multiway search tree of order m is an ordered tree where each node has at the most m children. If there are n number of children in a node then (n – 1) is the number of keys in the node.

For example : Following is a tree of order 4.

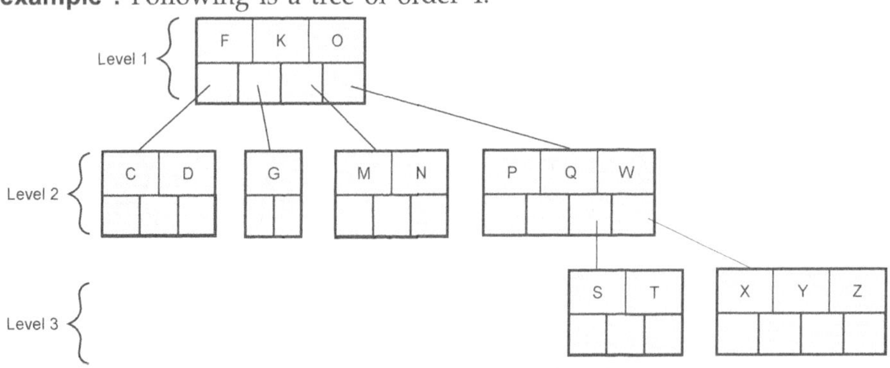

Fig. 6.13.1 Multiway tree of order 4

From above tree following observations can be made.

1. The node which has n children possess (n – 1) keys.

2. The keys in each node are in ascending order.

3. For every node Node. child [0] has only keys which are less than Node. key [0] similarly, Node. child [1] has only keys which are greater than Node. key [0].

In other words, the node at level 1 has F, K and O as keys. At level 2 the node containing keys C and D are arranged as child of key F (the cell before F). Similarly the node containing key G will be child of F but should be attached after F and before K, as G is between F and K. Here the alphabets F, K, O are called keys and branches are called children. The B-tree of order m should be constructed such that -

Rule 1 : All the leaf nodes are on the bottom level.

Rule 2 : The root node should have atleast two children.

Rule 3 : All the internal nodes except root node have atleast ceil (m/2) nonempty children. The ceil is a function such that ceil (3.4) = 4, ceil (9.3) = 10, ceil (2.98) = 3, ceil (7) = 7.

Rule 4 : Each leaf node must contain atleast ceil (m/2) – 1 keys.

6.13.1 Insertion

Thus the B-tree is fairly balanced tree which can be illustrated by following example.

Example of B-tree :

We will consruct a B-tree of order 5 following numbers.

3, 14, 7, 1, 8, 5, 11, 17, 13, 6, 23, 12, 20, 26, 4, 16, 18, 24, 25, 19.

The order 5 means at the most 4 keys are allowed. The internal node should have atleast 3 nonempty children and each leaf node must contain atleast 2 keys.

Step 1 : Insert 3, 14, 7, 1 as follows.

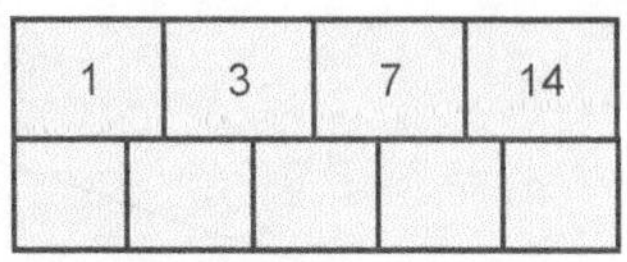

Step 2 : If we insert 8 then we need to split the node 1, 3, 7, 8, 14 at medium.

Hence

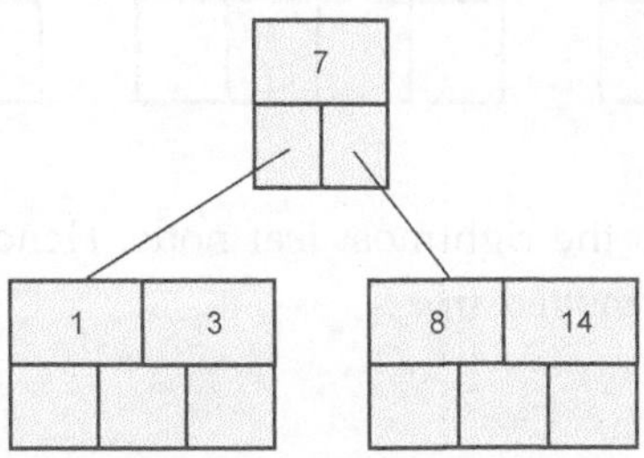

Step 3 : Insert 5, 11, 7 which can be easily inserted in a B-tree.

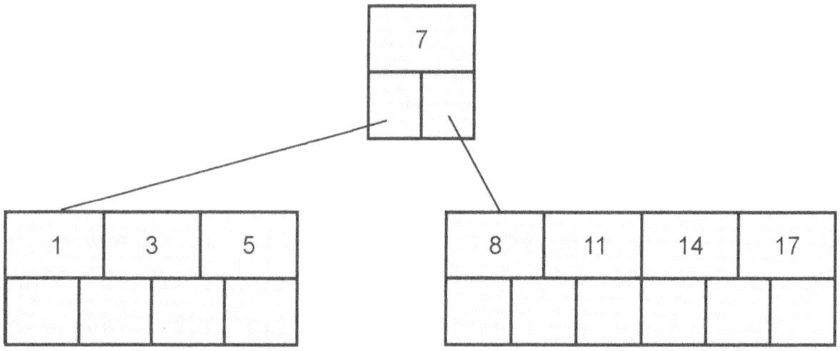

Step 4 : Now insert 13. But if we insert 13 then the leaf node will have 5 keys which is not allowed. Hence 8, 11,(13), 14, 17 is split and medium node 13 is moved up.

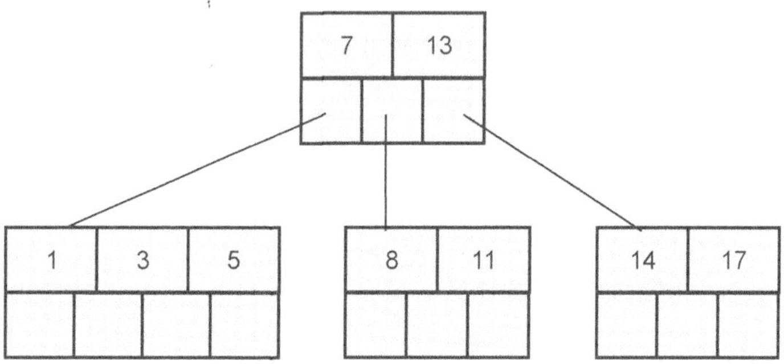

Step 5 : Now insert 6, 23, 12, 20 without any split.

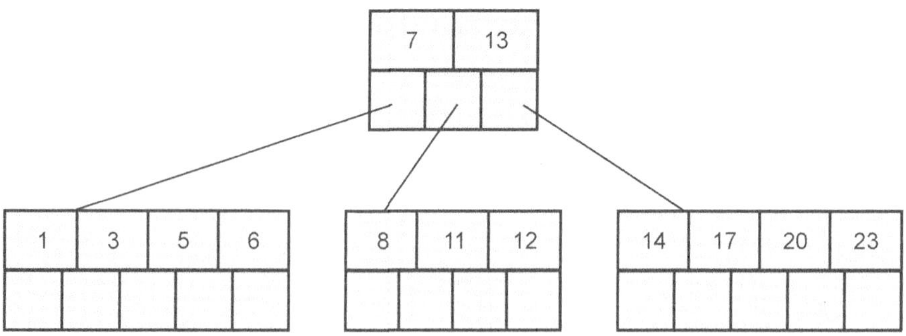

Step 6 : The 26 is inserted to the rightmost leaf node. Hence 14, 17, 20, 23, 26 the node is split and 20 will be moved up.

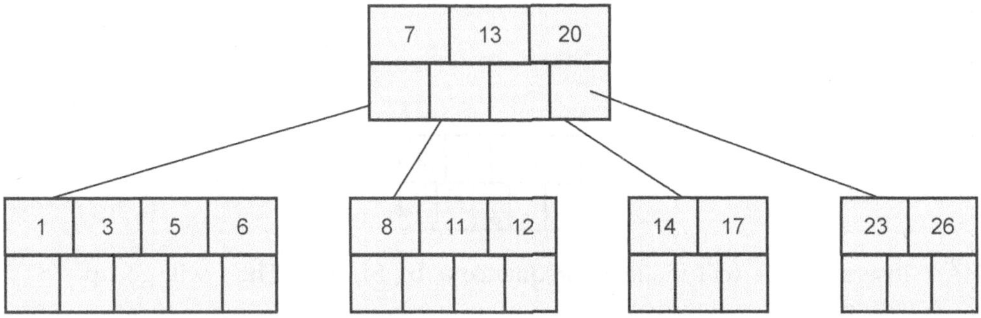

Step 7 : Insertion of node 4 causes leftmost node to split. The 1, 3, 4, 5, 6 causes key 4 to move up. Then insert 16, 18, 24, 25.

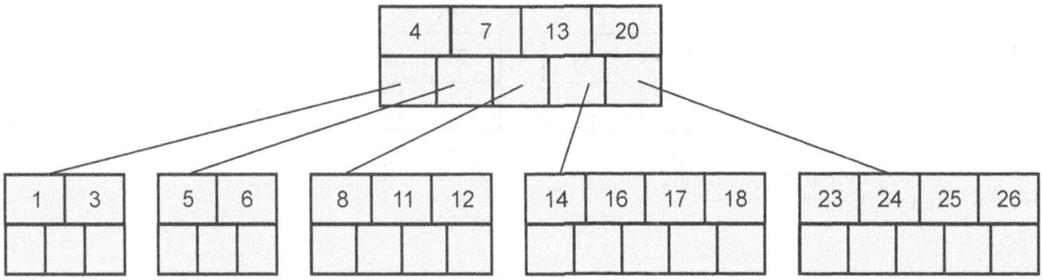

Step 8 : Finally insert 19. Then 4, 7, 13, 19, 20 needs to be split. The median 13 will be moved upto form a root node.

The tree then will be -

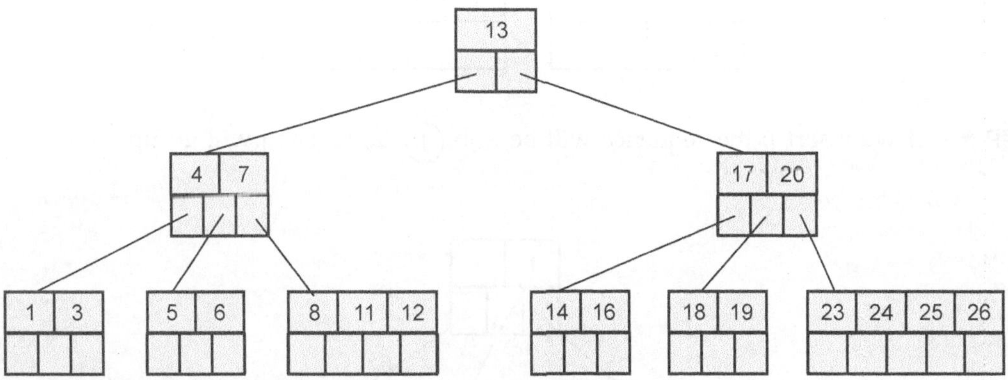

Thus the B-tree is constructed.

Example 6.13.1 *Insert the following elements in B-tree :*

a, g, f, b, k, c, h, n, j

GTU : Winter-15, Marks 3

Solution : We will construct B-tree of order 5. That means 4 keys are allowed in each node.

Step 1 : Insert a, g, f, b

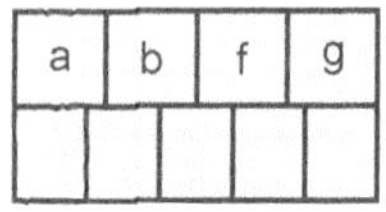

Step 2 : Insert k. This will make the sequence a, b,(f), g, k. The f will go up

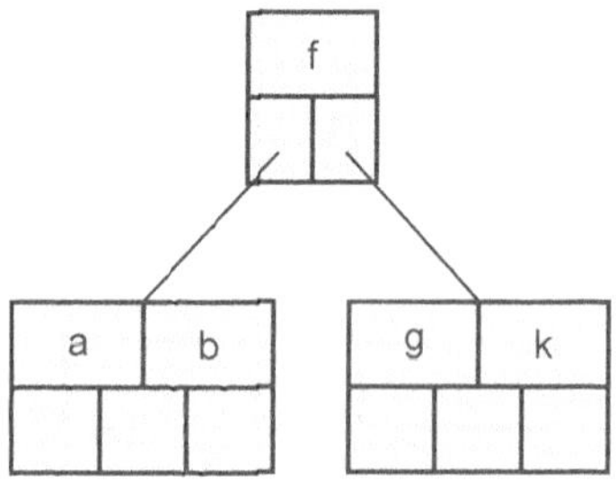

Step 3 : Insert c, h, n

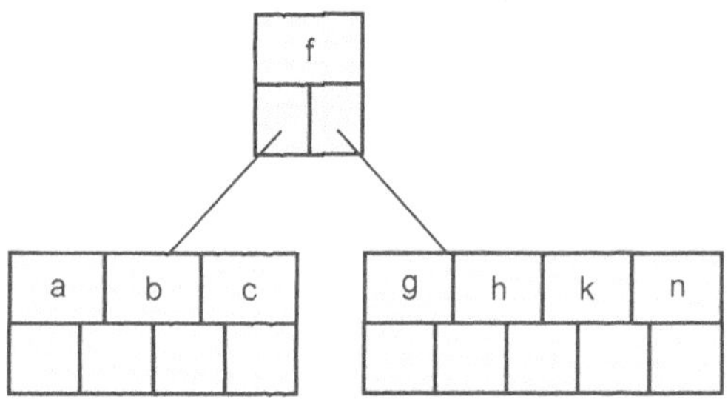

Step 4 : If we insert j, the sequence will be g, h,(j), k, n. The j will go up.

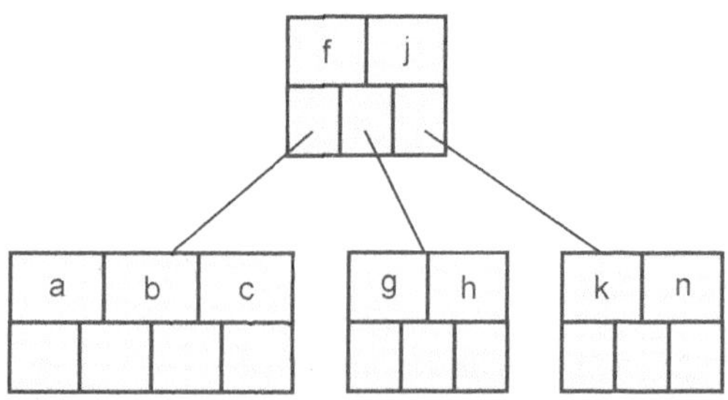

Algorithm for insertion in B-tree

```
Algorithm insert (root, key)
{
    // Problem Description: This algorithm is for
    // inserting key node in B-tree.
    temp ← root
    if (n[temp] = 2t – 1) then
        s ← get_node ( ) // memory is allocated.
    {
        root ← s
        leaf [s] ← FALSE
        n [s] ← 0
        child1[s] ← root
        split_child (s, 1, root)
        Insert_In (s, key)
    }
    else
        Insert_In(s, key)
}
```

Insertion is needed if (2t – 1) key are there.

It is similar to **cutting and pasting** for splitting node.

For inserting the **key** node in a non full root node.

Example 6.13.2 *Insert the following letters into an empty B-tree of order 5 C, N, G, A, H, E, K, Q, M, F, W, L, T, Z, D, P, R, X, Y, S.* **GTU : Summer-18, Marks 7**

Solution : The order 5 means 4 keys are allowed. The internal node should have atleast 3 non empty children.

Step 1 : Insert C, N, G, A

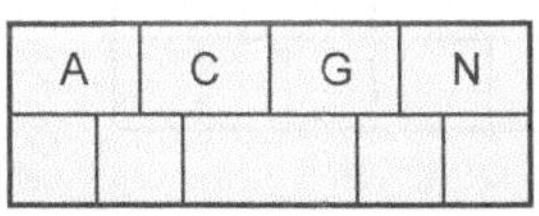

Step 2 : If we insert H then we need to split the node at medium. A, C , (G), H, N

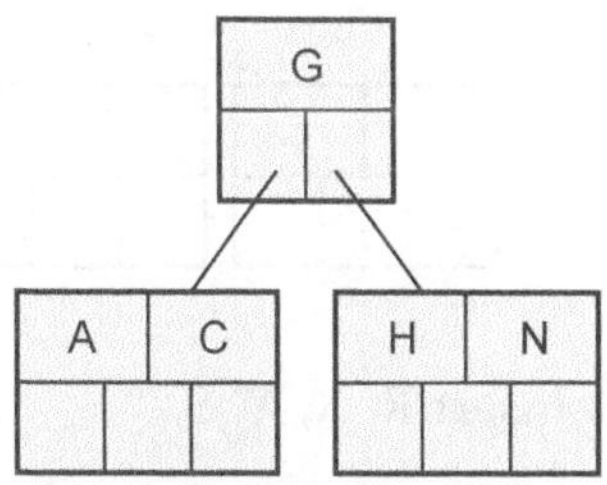

Step 3 : Insert E, K, Q, M

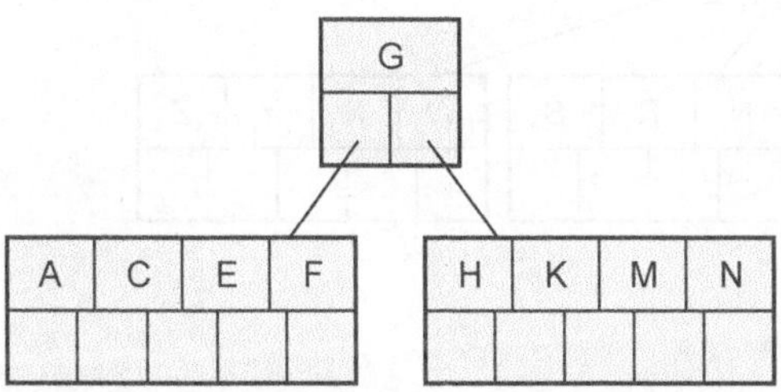

Step 4 : Insert W. The sequence becomes H K (M) N W. The M goes up

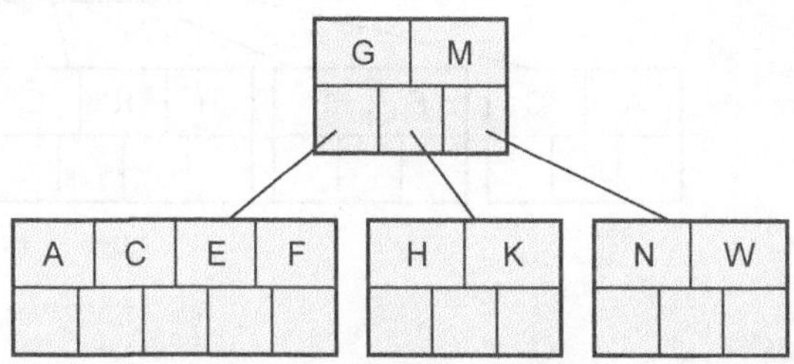

Step 5 : Insert L, T, Z

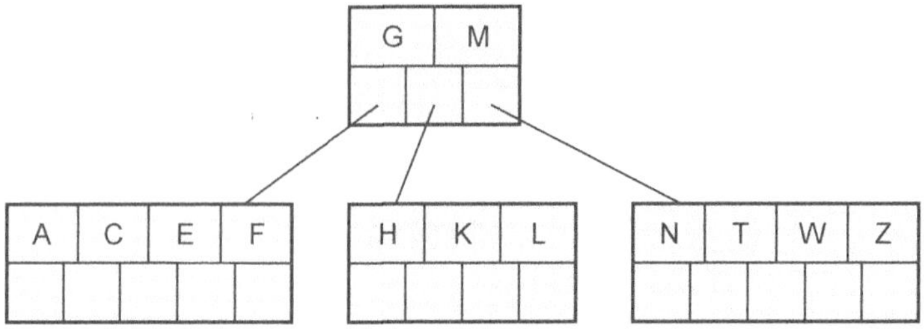

Step 6 : Insert D. The sequence becomes A, C, (D), E, F. The D goes up

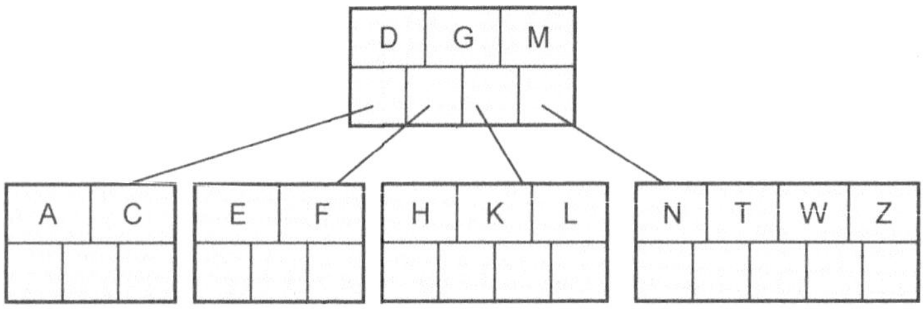

Step 7 : Insert P. The sequence becomes N, P, (T), W, Z. The T goes up

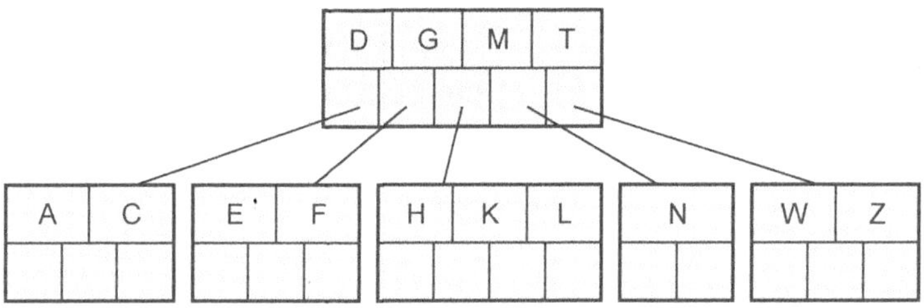

Step 8 : Insert R, X, Y, S

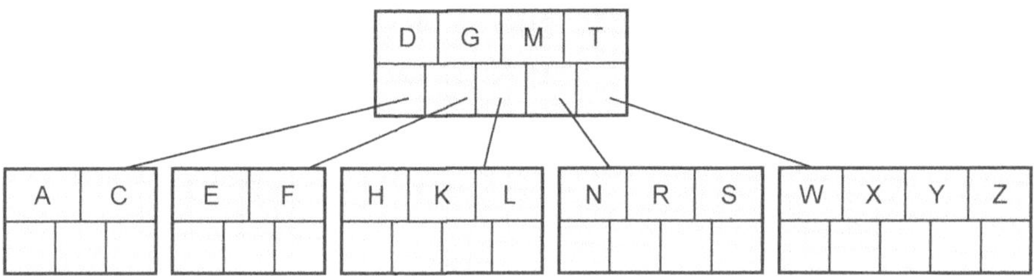

6.13.2 Deletion

Consider a B-tree.

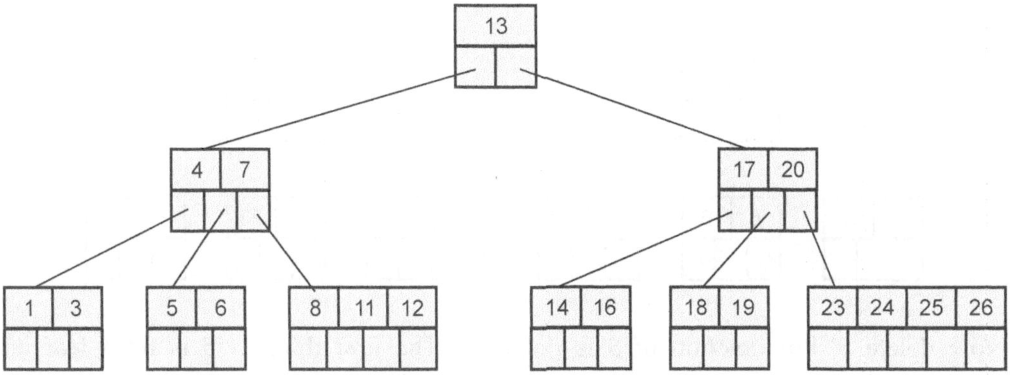

If we want to delete 8 then it is very simple.

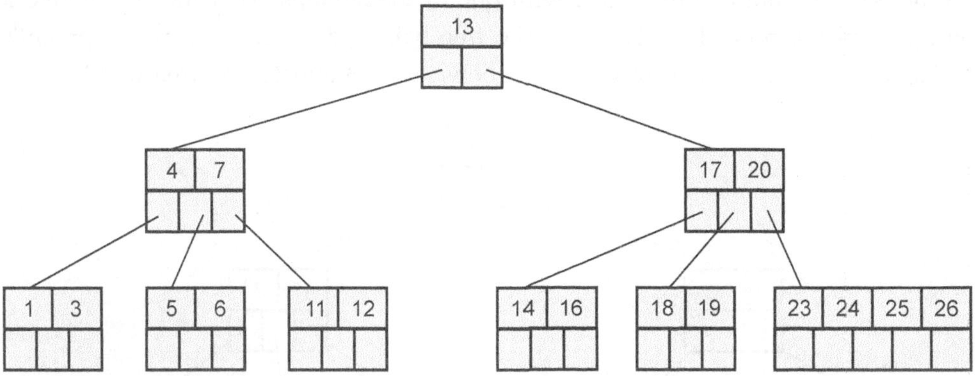

Now we will delete 20, the 20 is not in a leaf node so we will find its successor which is 23. Hence 23 will be moved upto replace 20.

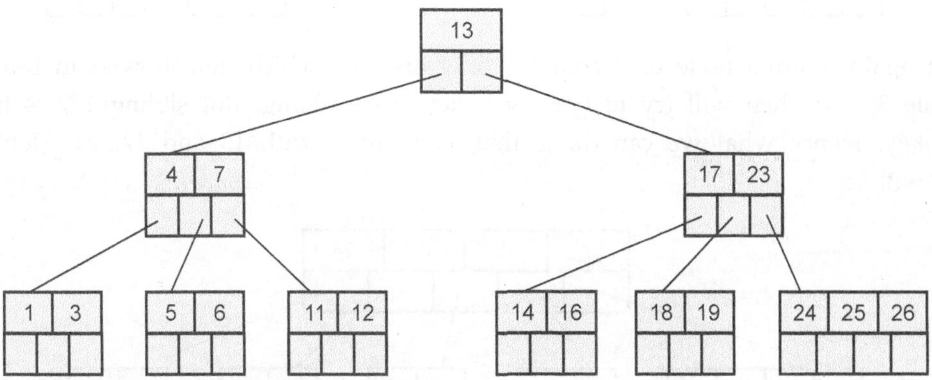

Next we will delete 18. Deletion of 18 from the corresponding node causes the node with only one key, which is not desired (as per rule 4) in B-tree of order 5. The sibling node to immediate right has an extra key. In such a case we can borrow a key from parent and move spare key of sibling to up. See the following figure.

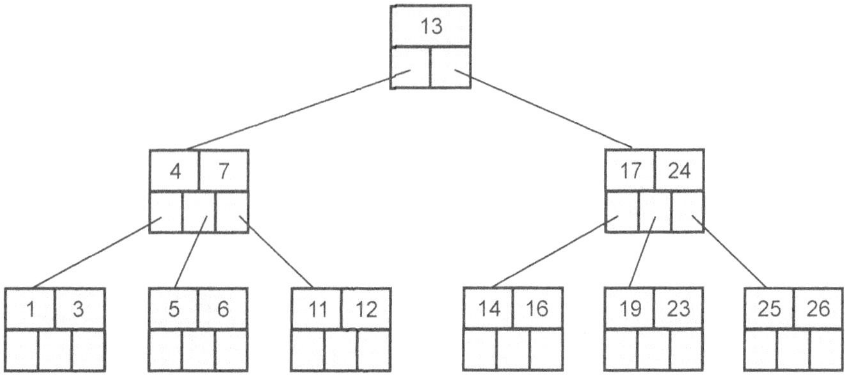

Now delete 5. But deletion of 5 is not easy. The first thing is 5 is from leaf node. Secondly this leaf node has no extra keys nor siblings to immediate left or right. In such a situation we can combine this node with one of the siblings. That means remove 5 and combine 6 with the node 1, 3. To make the tree balanced we have to move parent's key down. Hence we will move 4 down as 4 is between 1, 3 and 6. The tree will be -

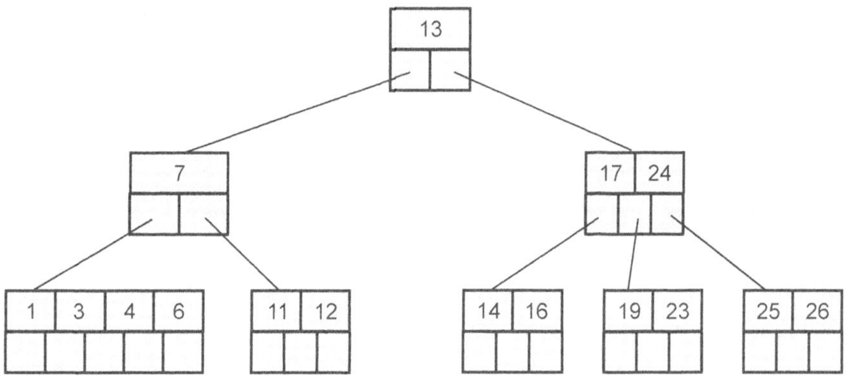

But again internal node of 7 contains only one key which not allowed in B-tree (as per rule 3). We then will try to borrow a key from sibling. But sibling 17, 24 has no spare key. Hence what we can do is that, combine 7 with 13 and 17, 24. Hence the B-tree will be

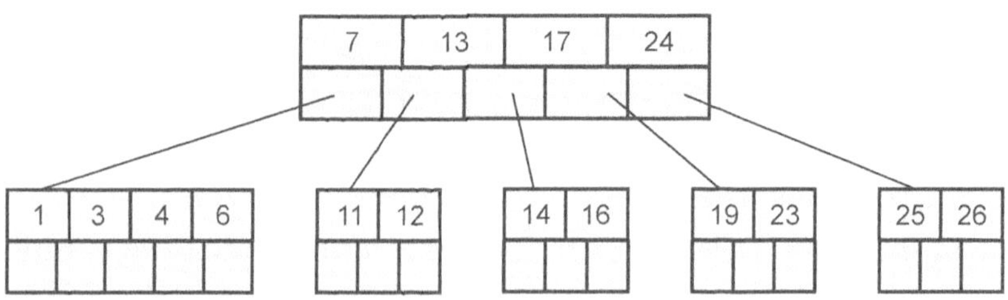

6.13.3 Searching

The search operation on B-tree is similar to a search on binary search tree. Instead of choosing between a left and right child as in binary tree, B-tree makes an m-way choice. Consider a B-tree as given below.

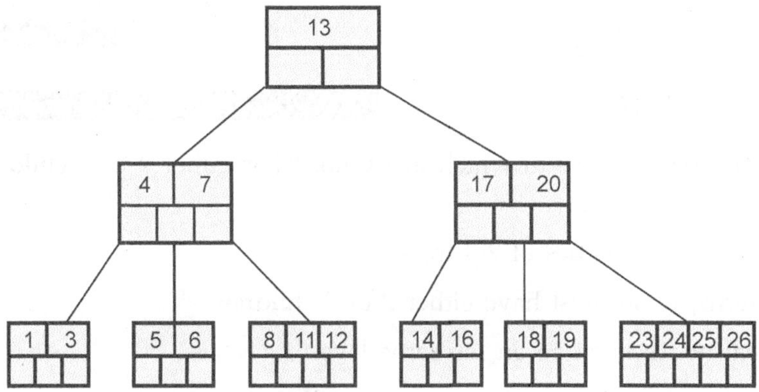

If we want to search node 11 then

i) 11 < 13 : Hence search left node.

ii) 11 > 7 : Hence rightmost node.

iii) 11 > 8 , move in second block.

iv) Node 11 is found.

The running time of search operation depends upon the height of the tree. It is O(log n).

Algorithm

The algorithm for searching a target node is as follows.

```
Algorithm Search (temp, target)
{
    // Problem Description: This algorithm is for
    // searching the 'target' node
        i ← 1
    while i ← i + 1 (( i ≤ n[temp]) AND (target > key_i [temp]))
    if (( i ≤ n[temp]) AND (target == key_i[temp]))
        return (temp, i)
    if (leaf [temp] == TRUE) then
        return NULL
    else READ ( C_i[temp] )
        return search ((C_i [temp], target)
}
```

Desired node is present.

The **search** operation on B-tree is similar to a search operation on a binary tree. The desired child is chosen by performing linear search of values in the node. The running time of this algorithm is O(log n).

Review Question

1. *Mention the properties of a B-Tree.* **GTU : Winter-15, Marks 3**

6.14 The 2-3 Trees

GTU : Dec.-10, May-12, Summer-13, Marks 7

A 2-3 tree is type of B-tree in which every node has either 2 or 3 children except the leaf nodes.

Following are the properties of 2-3 trees.

1. Every internal node must have either 2 or 3 children.
2. All the leaf nodes must be on the same level.
3. The data in each node must be in sorted order.

For example

Creation of 2-3 tree by inserting the nodes

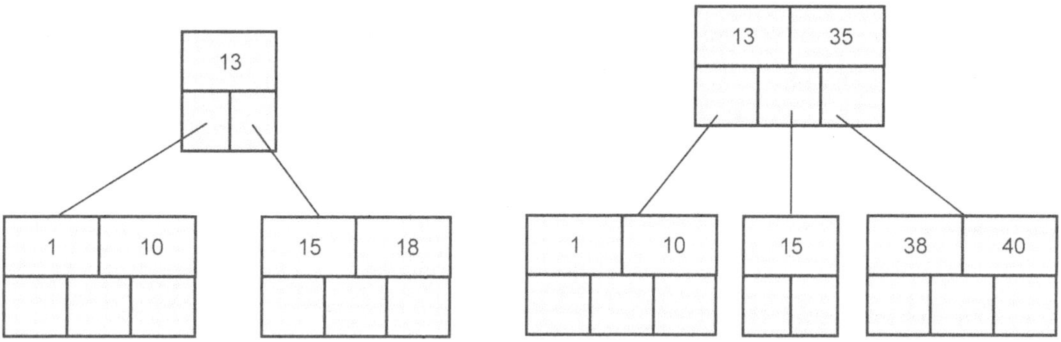

Fig. 6.14.1 2-3 Trees

For creation of 2-3 trees consider 58, 15, 82, 36, 23, 64, 27, 35, 45.

Step 1 : Insert 58

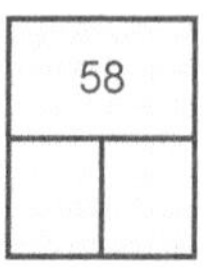

Step 2 : Insert 15

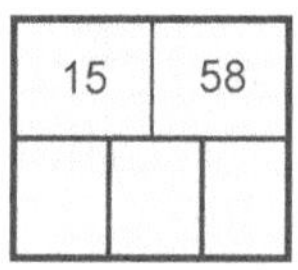

Step 3 : Insert 82

We will arrange it as 15, 58, 82. As only 3 children are allowed the middle element 58

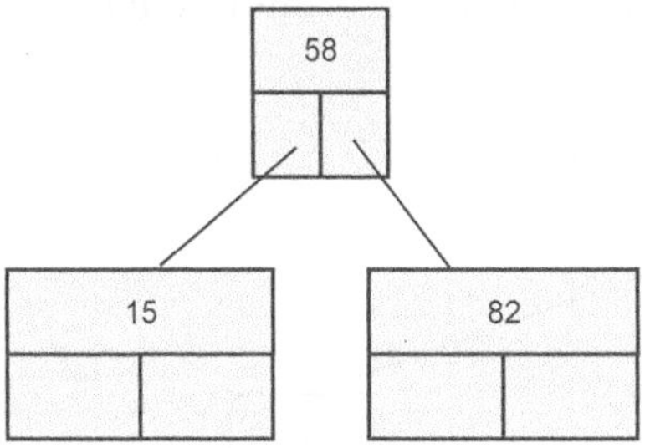

Step 4 : Insert 36

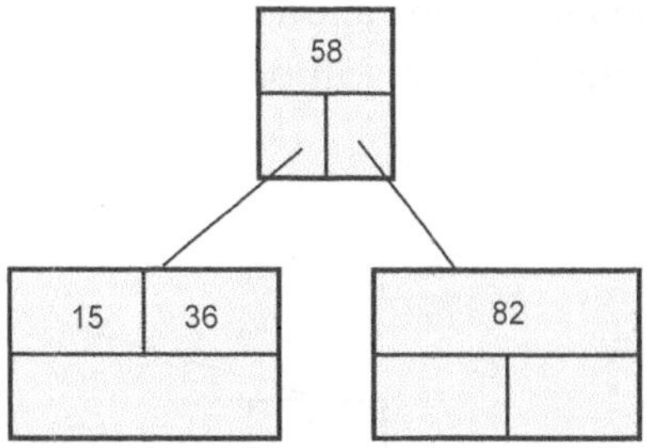

Step 5 : Insert 23

We will arrange 15, 23, 36 in ascending order. The 23 will go up.

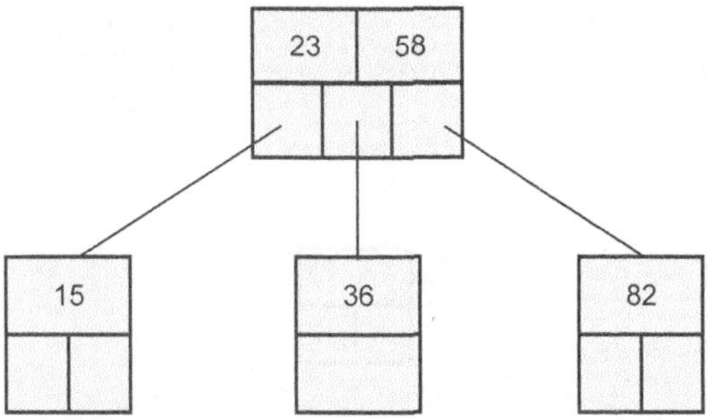

Step 6 : Insert 64

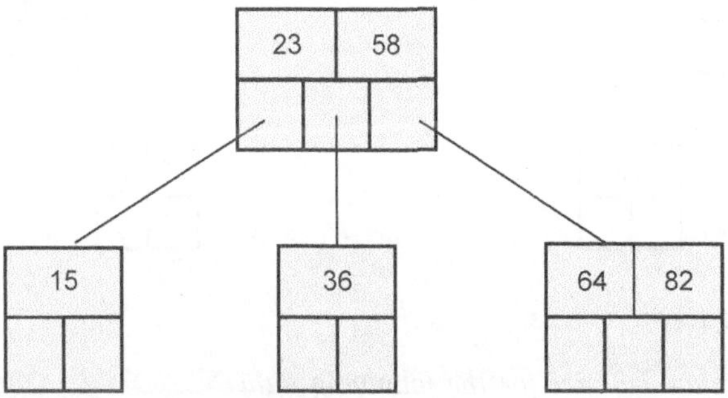

Step 7 : Insert 27

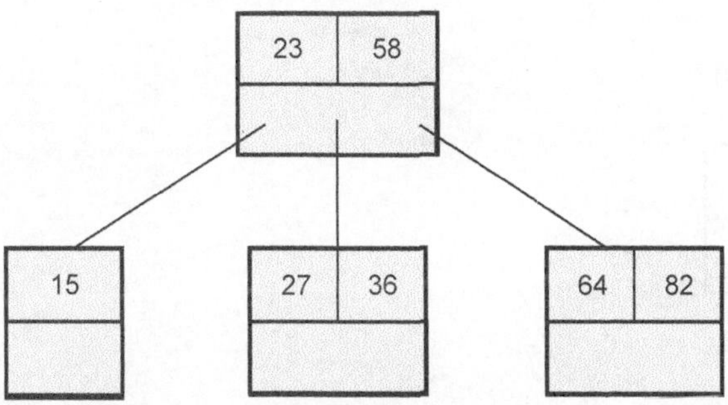

Step 8 : Insert 35

We arrange it as 27, 35, 36. Hence the middle element 35 will go up. But again at the previous level 23 and 58 are there. So we arrange them with 35 as 23, 35, 58. But 3 key elements are not allowed in 2-3 trees. Therefore the 35 will (i.e. middle element) go up. And the 2-3 tree will be

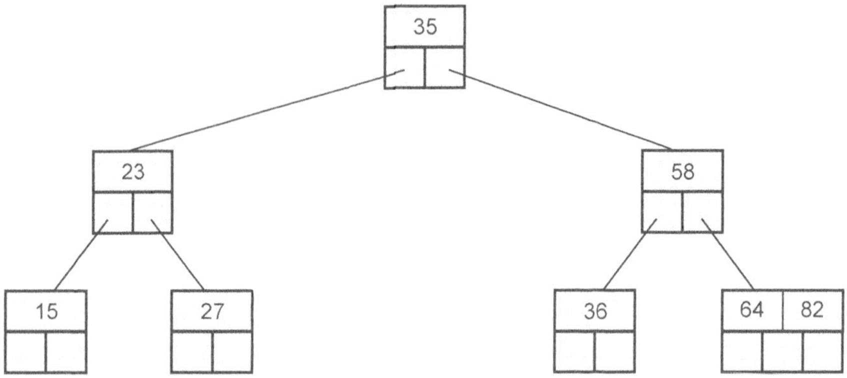

Step 9 : Insert 45

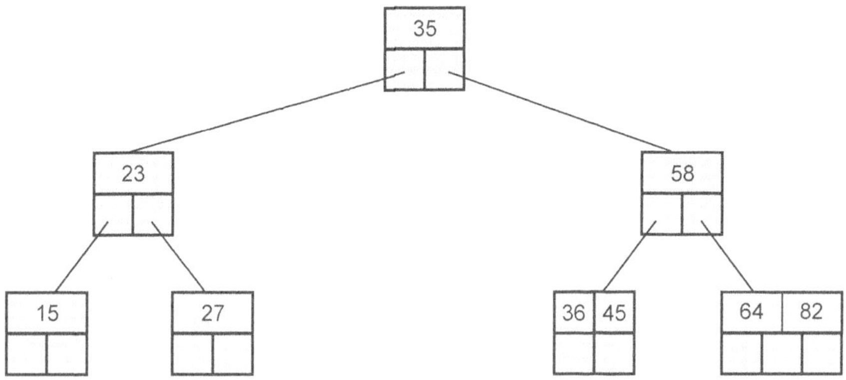

is the required 2-3 tree.

Example 6.14.1 *Construct 2-3 tree for the following data*

12, 50, 85, 6, 10, 37, 100, 120, 25, 70 **GTU : Summer-13, Marks 7**

Solution :

Step 1 : Insert 12, 50

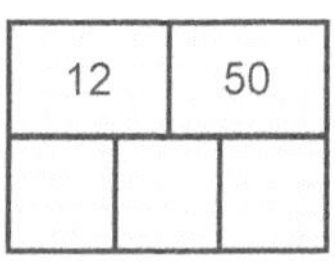

Step 2 : Insert 85

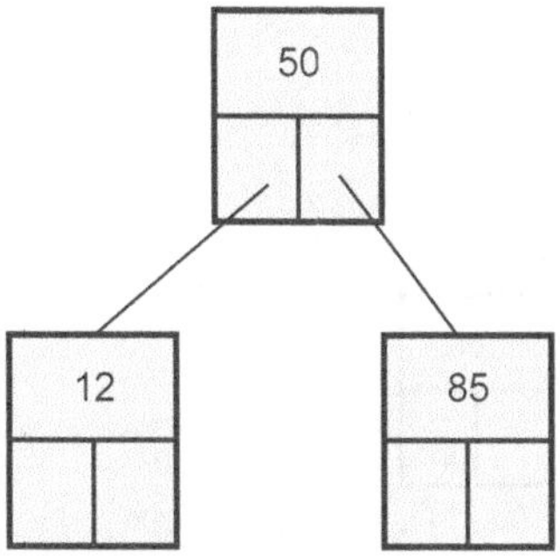

Step 3 : Insert 6

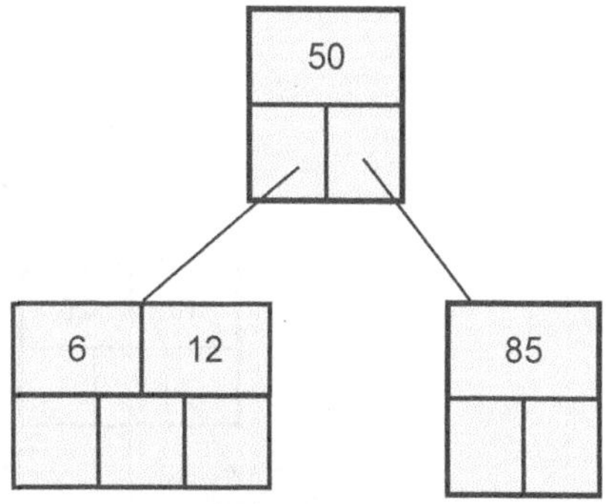

Step 4 : Insert 10

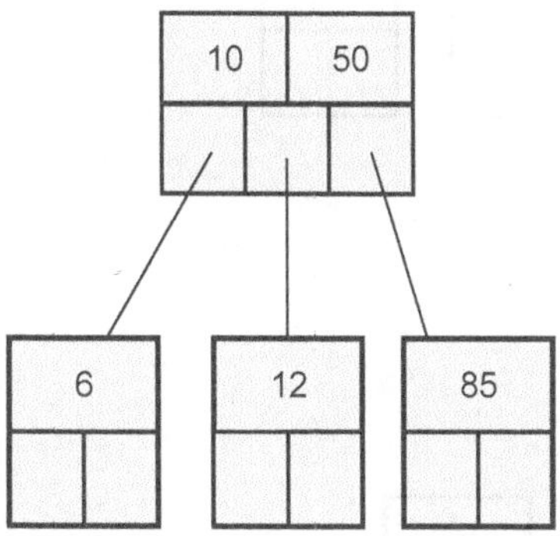

Step 5 : Insert 37, 100

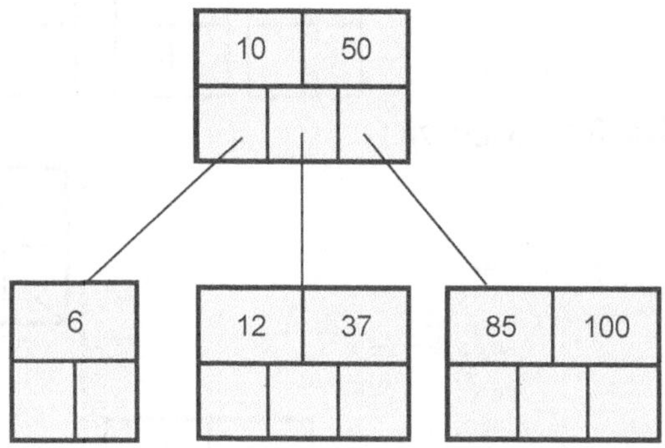

Step 6 : Insert 120

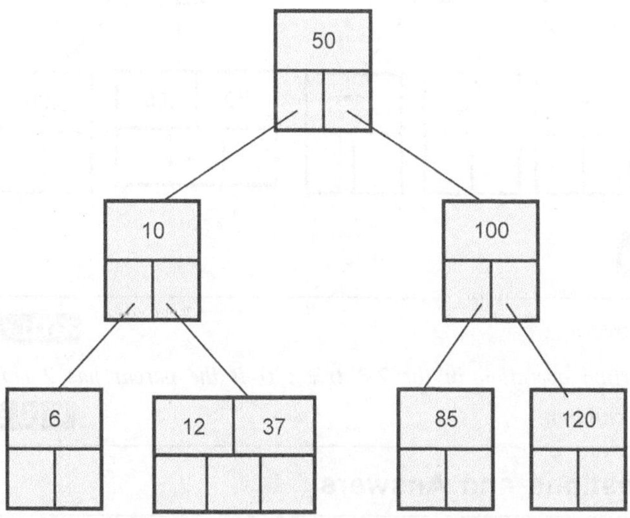

Step 7 : Insert 25

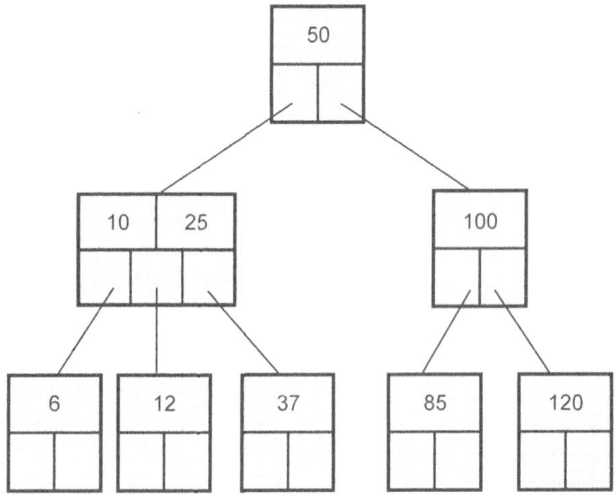

Step 8 : Insert 70

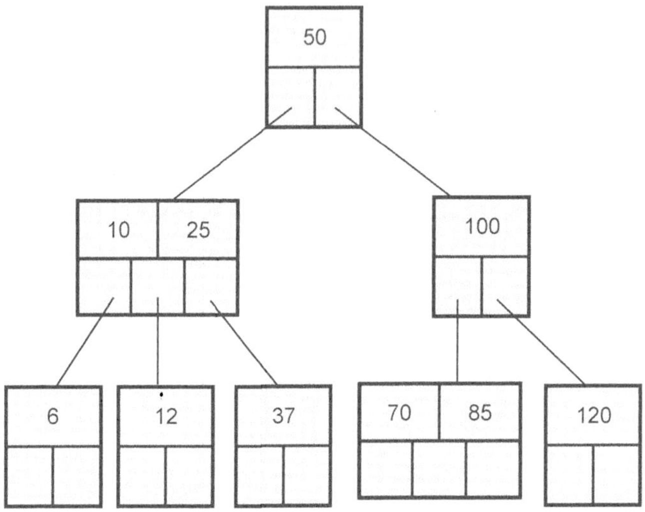

Review Questions

1. *What is 2-3 tree ?* **GTU : Dec.-10, Marks 2**
2. *Explain insertion operation in the 2-3 tree : i) If the parent has 2 children and ii) If the parent has 3 children.* **GTU : May-12, Marks 7**

6.15 Oral Questions and Answers

Q.1 Give various implementation of tree.

Ans. : The tree can be implemented by two ways

1. Sequential implementation : The tree is implemented using arrays in this type of implementation.

2. Linked implementation : The tree is implemented or represented using linked list.

Q.2 Define : binary tree.

Ans. : A binary tree is a finite set of nodes which is either empty or consists of root and two disjoint binary trees called the left subtree and right subtree.

Q.3 Which tree representation is mostly preferred by the developers - sequential or linked ? Justify.

Ans. : There are two ways of representing the binary tree - sequential representation and linked representation. The linked representation is normally preferred by developers because in the linked representation the binary tree is represented using linked list. Hence the tree with any number of nodes can be created. Secondly there is no wastage or shortage of the memory in this representation.

Q.4 List the applications of trees.

Ans. :

1. In computer networking such as Local Area Network (LAN), Wide Area Networking (WAN), internetworking.
2. In telephone cabling graph theory is effectively used.
3. In job scheduling algorithms the graphs are used.

Q.5 In tree construction which is the suitable efficient data structure ?

Ans. : The linked list is the efficient data structure for constructing the trees. Because using linked list there is no wastage of memory or shortage of memory. The nodes can be allocated or deallocated as per the requirements.

Q.6 Write a C structure of binary tree. **GTU : Summer-16**

Ans. :

```
typedef struct node
{
    int data;
    struct node *left;
    struct node *right;
}bin;
```

Q.7 What is meant by equivalent binary tree ?

Ans. : The two binary trees are said to be equivalent if the sequence of there traversal is same.

Q.8 Define complete binary tree. **GTU : Winter-16**

Ans. : A complete binary tree is a tree in which every node except the root node should have exactly two children not necessarily on the same level.

Q.9 Define binary search tree.

Ans. : Bianry search tree is a binary tree in which nodes are systematically arranged. That means the left child has less value than its parent node and the right child has the greater value than its parent node.

Q.10 Threaded binary tree can be used to avoid recursive routines for preorder and post order traversal. Justify.

Ans. : In the threaded binary tree each node maintains a field for storing left and right threads. These threads point to inorder predecessor and successor respectively. Hence there is no need to have recursive calls.

Q.11 What is level of a tree ?

Ans. : The root node is always considered at level zero. The adjacent nodes to root are supposed to be at level 1 and so on.

Q.12 What are internal and external nodes in a tree ?

Ans. : Leaf node means a node having no child node. As leaf nodes are not having further links, we call leaf nodes external nodes and non-leaf nodes are called internal nodes.

Q.13 What is sibling node in a tree ?

Ans. : The nodes with common parent are called siblings or brothers.

Q.14 What is forest ?

Ans. : Forest is a collection of disjoint trees. From a given tree if we remove its root then we get a forest.

Q.15 What is full binary tree ?

Ans. : A full binary tree is a tree in which every node has zero or two children.

Q.16 List out the traversal techniques used in tree.

Ans. : 1. Preorder 2. Postorder 3. Inorder Traversal

Q.17 Which traversal results in elements in sorted order ?

Ans. : The inorder traversal results in elements in sorted order.

Q.18 Define B-tree. **GTU : Summer-16**

Ans. : The B tree is a multiway search tree of order m where each node has at the most m children. If there are n number of children in a node then (n-1) is the number of keys in this node.

Q.19 Describe the time complexity of binary search algorithm. **GTU : Summer-16**

Ans. : The worst and average case time complexity is O(logn). The best case time complexity is O(1).

Q.20 List the applications of binary tree. **GTU : Summer-16**

Ans. : 1) For evaluating the expression, the expression tree is created.

2) In searching and indexing

3) For obtaining shortest path

4) Network routing.

Q.21 What is the height of a complete binary with n nodes ? GTU : Winter-15

Ans. : The height of complete binary tree with n nodes is log(n+1).

Q.22 Explain the term : 2-3 tree. GTU : Winter-16

Ans. : A 2-3 tree is type of B-tree in which every node has either 2 or 3 children except the leaf nodes.

Q.23 In which type of tree, each leaf node is kept at the same distance from root ? GTU : Summer-17

Ans. : Perfect Binary Tree

Q.24 Which of the traversal technique outputs the data in sorted order in a Binary Search Tree ? GTU : Summer-17

Ans. : Inorder Traversal

Q.25 What is common in inorder, preorder and postorder traversal ? GTU : Summer-17

Ans. : Left sub-tree is always visited first before right sub-tree.

Q.26 In 2-3 trees, what do leaves contain and what do nonleaf nodes indicate ? GTU : Summer-17

Ans. : In 2 - 3 trees, each leaf node contains data value. Whereas, each non - leaf node contains two values - first value is largest value in left sub-tree while second value is the largest value in middle sub-tree.

Q.27 Draw tree whose postorder traversal is C B F E G D A GTU : Summer-17

Ans. : It is not possible to draw a tree with only one traversal. We assume inorder traversal gives ascending ordered list. Hence the two traversals are :

Inorder : A B C D E F G

Postorder : C B F E G D A

The last node in postorder sequence indicates the root node. Just locate root node in inorder sequence.

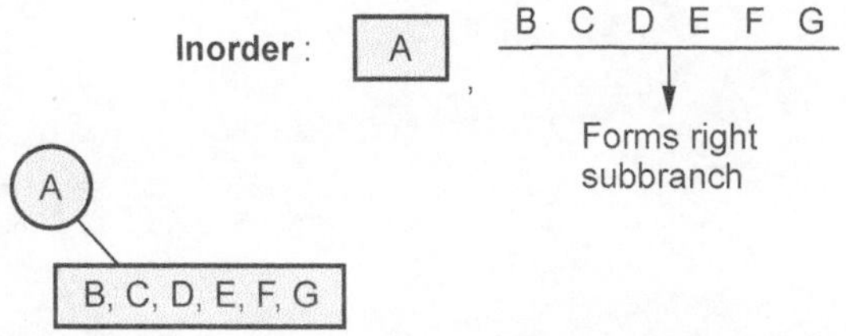

Step 2 : Now search the postorder sequence, the last node indicates parent node. Find this node in inorder sequence, mark appropriate left and right sub-branches.

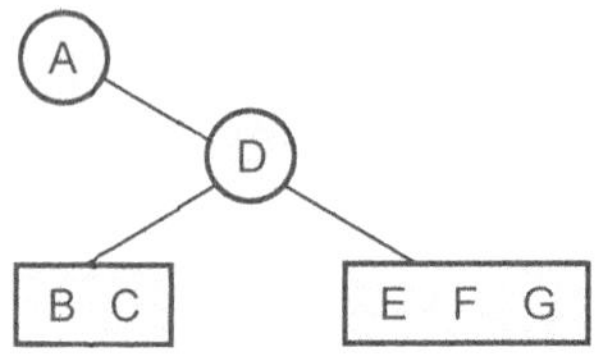

Step 3 :

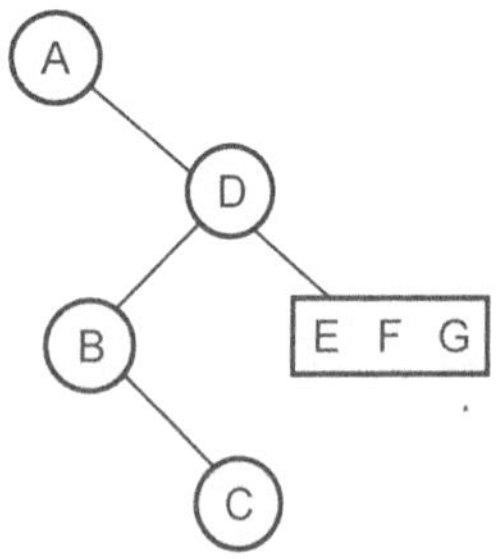

Step 4 :

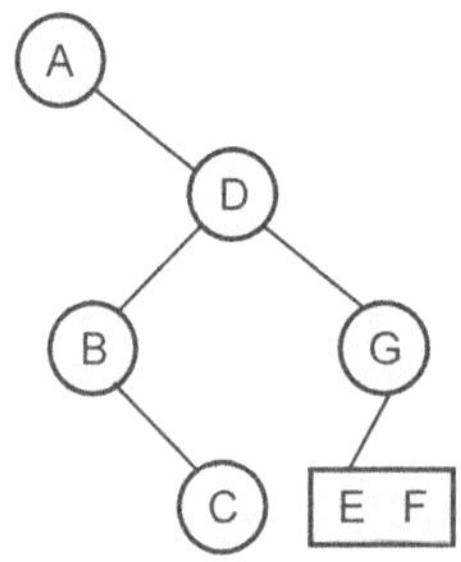

Step 5 :

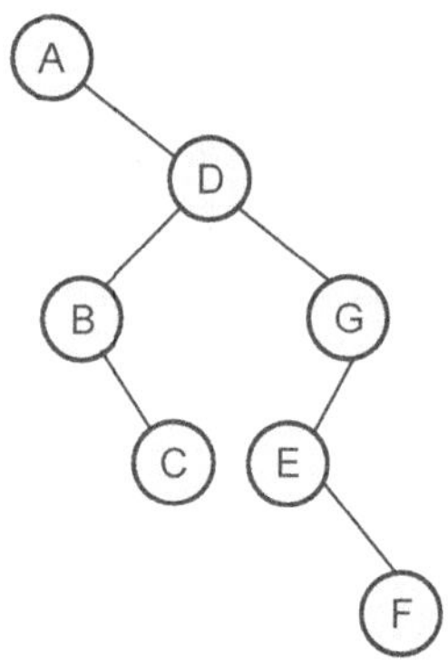

Q.28 How many full branches a binary tree possesses ? **GTU : Winter-17**

Ans. : A binary tree with n nodes has exactly n + 1 null nodes.

❑❑❑

7 Non Linear Data Structures : Graphs

Syllabus

Graph-matrix representation of graphs, Elementary graph operations, (Breadth first search, Depth first search, Spanning trees, Shortest path, Minimal spanning tree.)

Contents

7.1 Concept of Graph

GTU : Summer-15,17, Marks 2

A graph is a collection of two sets **V** and **E** where V is a finite non-empty set of **vertices** and E is a finite non-empty set of **edges**.

- **Vertices** are nothing but the nodes in the graph.
- Two adjacent vertices are joined by **edges**.
- Any graph is denoted as G = {V, E}.
- **For example :**

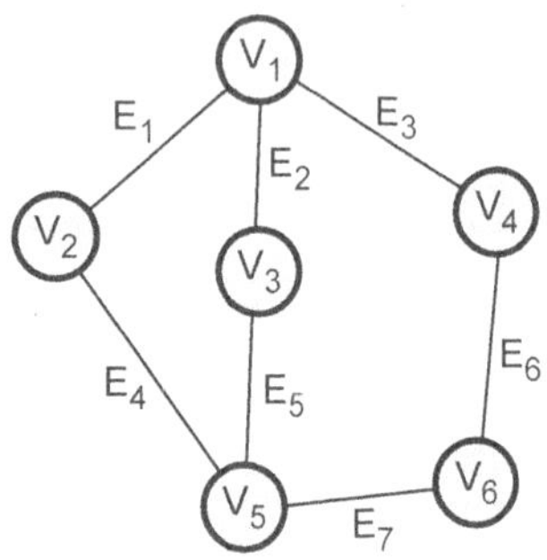

$$G = \{\{V_1, V_2, V_3, V_4, V_5, V_6\}, \{E_1, E_2, E_3, E_4, E_5, E_6, E_7\}\}$$

Fig. 7.1.1 Graph G

7.1.1 Comparison between Graph and Trees

Sr.No.	Graph	Tree
1.	Graph is a **non-linear data** structure.	Tree is a **non-linear data structure.**
2.	It is a collection of **vertices / nodes and edges.**	It is a collection of **nodes and edges.**
3.	Each node can have any number of edges.	General trees consist of the nodes having any number of child nodes. But in case of binary trees every node can have at the most two child nodes.
4.	There is no unique node called root in graph.	There is a unique node called **root** in trees.
5.	A **cycle** can be formed.	There will **not** be any **cycle**.
6.	**Applications** : For finding shortest path in networking graph is used.	**Applications** : For game trees, decision trees, the tree is used.

7.1.2 Types of Graph

Basically graphs are of two types - 1. Directed graphs 2. Undirected graphs.

In the directed graph the directions are shown on the edges. As shown in the Fig. 7.1.2, the edges between the vertices are ordered. In this type of graph, the edge E_1 is in between the vertices V_1 and V_2. The V_1 is called head and the V_2 is called the tail. Similarly for V_1 head the tail is V_3 and so on.

We can say E_1 is the set of (V_1, V_2) and not of (V_2, V_1).

Similarly, in an undirected graph, the edges are not ordered. Please see the Fig. 7.1.3 for clear understanding of undirected graph. In this type of graph the edge E_1 is set of (V_1, V_2) or (V_2, V_1).

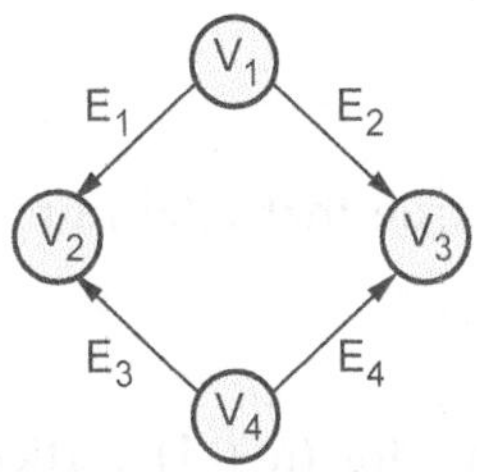

Fig. 7.1.2 Directed graph

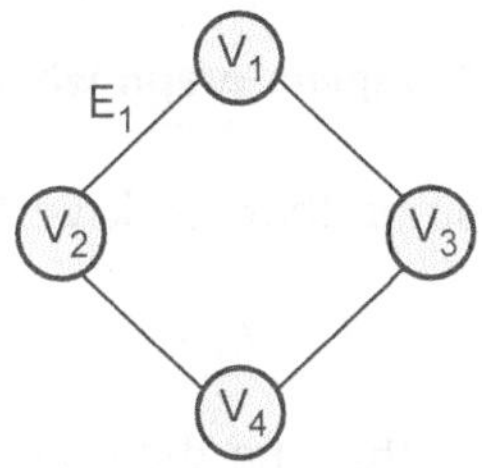

Fig. 7.1.3 Undirected graph

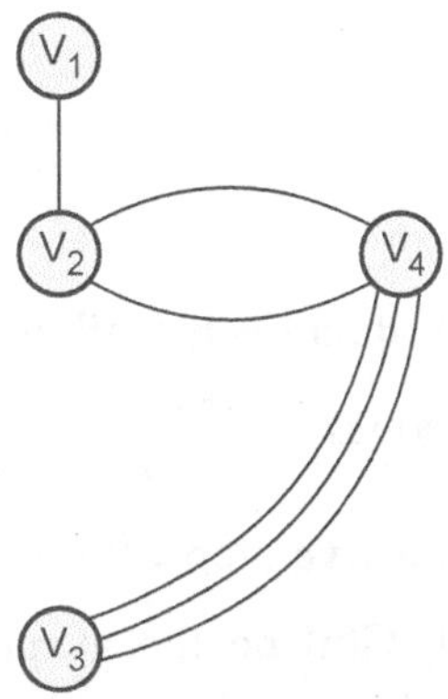

Fig. 7.1.4 A multi-graph

Similarly the object shown in the Fig. 7.1.4 is a multi-graph.

Review Question

1. *Give definition : Graph* **GTU : Summer-17, Marks 2**

7.2 Basic Terminologies **GTU : May-11, Winter-13, Summer-14, 15,17, Marks 7**

1. **Complete graph :** If an undirected graph of n vertices consists of $\frac{n(n-1)}{2}$ number of edges then that graph is called a complete graph.

For example : The graph shown in Fig 7.2.1 is a complete graph.

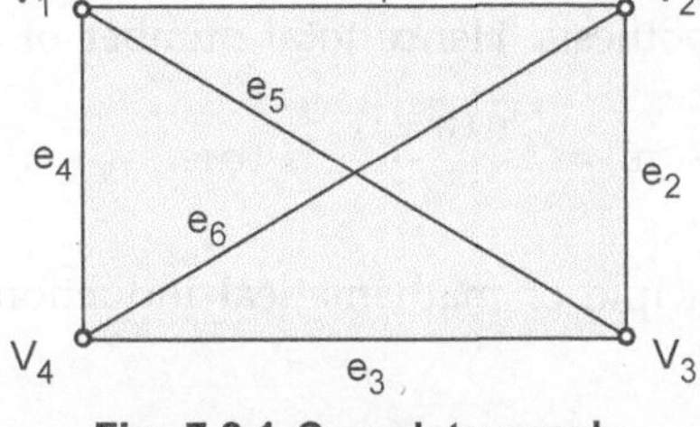

Fig. 7.2.1 Complete graph

Here $n = 4$

$$\therefore e = \frac{n(n-1)}{2} = \frac{4(3)}{2} = 6$$

Theorem : A complete graph with n vertices has $\frac{n(n-1)}{2}$ number of edges.

Proof : This can be proved by principle of mathematical induction.

Basis of induction : This theorem is true for n = 1 i.e. a graph with single node because when n = 1, total number of edges = 1(1 – 1)/2 = 0.

For instance :

Fig. 7.2.2 Complete graph when n = 1

Induction hypothesis : We assume that for k vertices it is true that total number of edges $= \frac{k(k-1)}{2}$.

Inductive step : We have to show that the theorem is also true for (n + 1) vertices.

Let, G(n) be the graph with n vertices. If we add one more vertex to G(n) then to make this graph complete, we need to add edges to this newly added vertex from all the previous n vertices then total number of edges in G(n+1) will be

$$\text{Edges} = \text{Edges in } G(n) + n = \frac{n(n-1)}{2} + n = \frac{n(n-1)+2n}{2}$$

$$= \frac{n^2 - n + 2n}{2} = \frac{n^2 + n}{2}$$

$$\text{Total edges in } G(n+1) = \frac{n(n+1)}{2} \qquad \text{...(7.2.1)}$$

If we put n + 1 = k then n = k – 1. Hence we can rewrite equation (7.2.1) as

$$= \frac{(k-1)k}{2} \quad \text{i.e.} \quad \frac{k(k-1)}{2}$$

This is true by induction hypothesis. Hence total number of edges in G(n+1) graph is

$$= \frac{n(n-1)}{2} + n = \frac{n(n+1)}{2} \text{ is true.}$$

Thus it is proved by principle of mathematical induction that total number of edges in complete graph is $\frac{n(n-1)}{2}$.

2. Subgraph : A subgraph G' of graph G is a graph such that the set of vertices and set of edges of G' are proper subset of the set of edges of G.

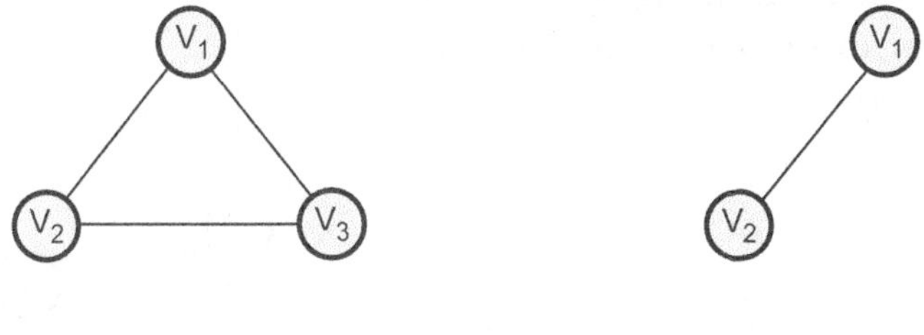

Graph G Graph G'

Fig. 7.2.3 Subgraph

3. Connected graph : An undirected graph is said to be connected if for every pair of distinct vertices V_i and V_j in V(G) there is an edge V_i to V_j in G.

Note that there is path from any two vertices.

For example :

- $V_1 - V_2$ • $V_2 - V_1$ • $V_3 - V_1$ • $V_4 - V_3 - V_1$
- $V_1 - V_3$ • $V_2 - V_1 - V_3$ • $V_3 - V_1 - V_2$ • $V_4 - V_2$
- $V_1 - V_4$ • $V_2 - V_4$ • $V_3 - V_4$ • $V_4 - V_3$

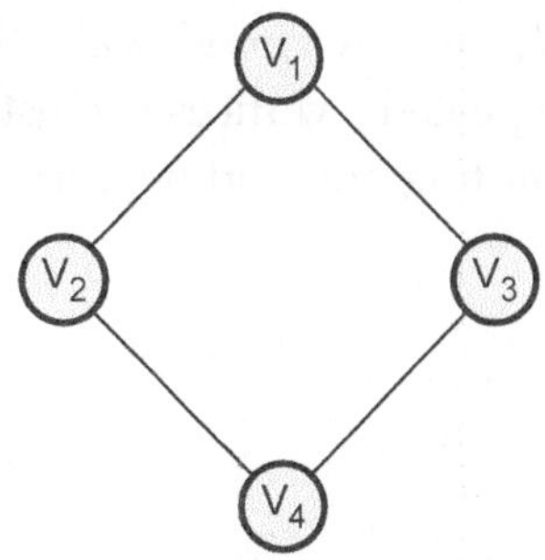

Fig. 7.2.4 Connected graph

Weighted graph

A weighted graph is a graph which consists of weights along its edges.

For example :

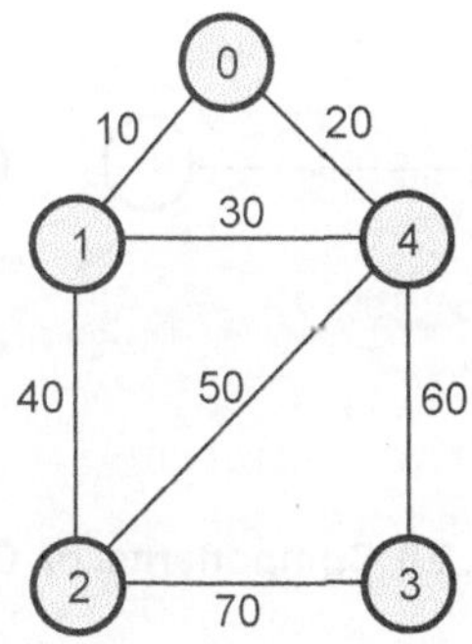

Fig. 7.2.5 Weighted graph

Path : A path is denoted using sequence of vertices and there exists an edge from one vertex to the next vertex.

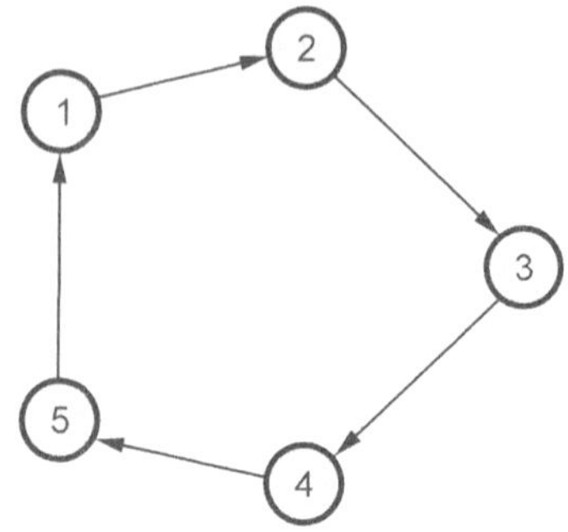

Fig. 7.2.6 Path of G is 1-2-3-4-5

Cycle : A closed walk through the graph with repeated vertices, mostly having the same starting and ending vertex is called a cycle.

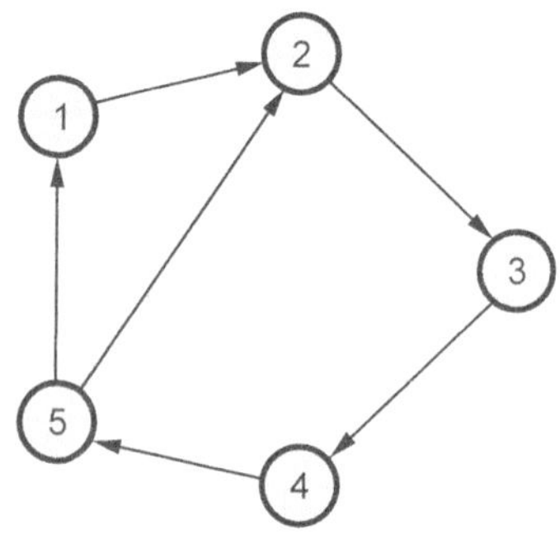

Fig. 7.2.7 Cycle 2-3-4-5-2 or 1-2-3-4-5-1

Component : The maximal connected subgraph of a graph is called component of a graph.

For example : Following are 3 components of a graph.

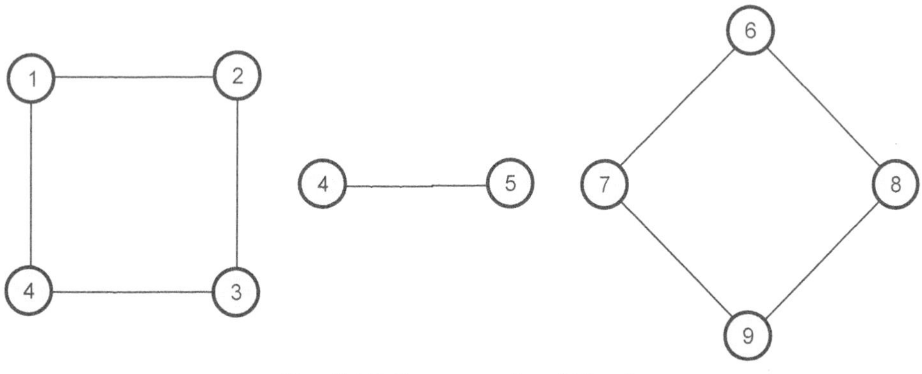

Fig. 7.2.8 Components of Graph

In-degree and out-degree

GTU : Summer-15, Mark 1

The degree of vertex is the number of edges associated with the vertex.

In-degree of a vertex is the number of edges that incident to that vertex. Out-degree of the vertex is total number of edges that are going away from the vertex.

Vertices	In-degree	Out-degree
V_1	1	1
V_2	2	1
V_3	1	1
V_4	1	2

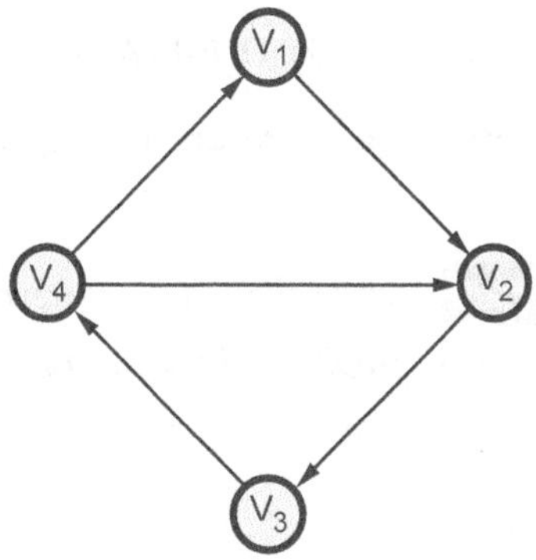

Self loop : Self loop is an edge that connects the same vertex, to itself.

Fig. 7.2.9 Self loop

Difference between cycle and Hamiltonian cycle

Cycle is a closed walk through the graph with repeated vertices having the same starting and ending vertex called a cycle.

Hamiltonian cycle is also a cycle having a closed walk through the graph but the vertices in the cycle **are not repeated at all**. In other words a cycle having all the vertices with same starting and ending vertex in which every vertex appears only once.

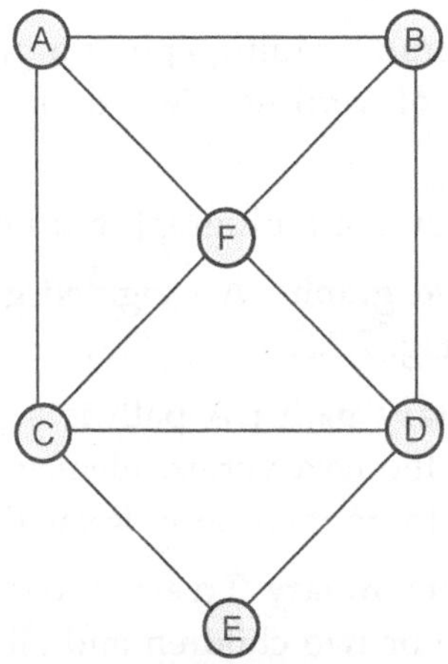

Graph G

For example - Consider Graph G.

Hamiltonian cycle is A - B - D - E - C - F - A.

Example 7.2.1 *Answer the following for the below given Graph.*

1. *What is the outdegree of node B ?*
2. *Write down a path from node D to node A.*
3. *Is the above graph a multigraph ? Give a reason for your answer.*
4. *What is the total degree of node A ?*

GTU : May-11, Marks 4

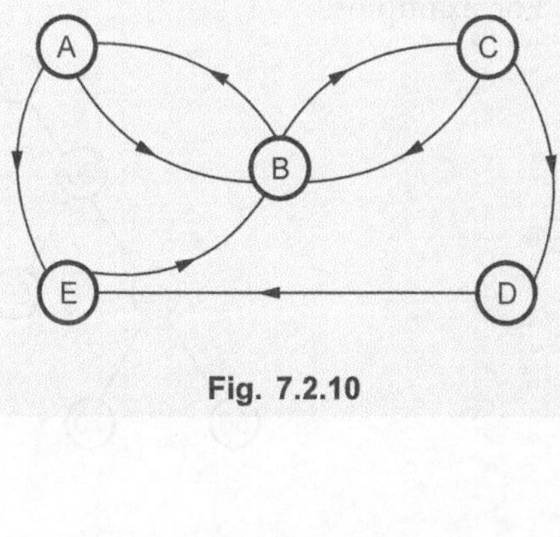

Fig. 7.2.10

Solution : 1) **2** 2) **D-E-B-A**

3) **Yes. Because there are multiple edges between some vertices**

4) **1**

Example 7.2.2 *Define the following terms 1) Graph 2) Tree 3) Multigraph 4) Weighted graph 5) Elementary path 6) Complete Binary Tree 7) Descendent node*

GTU : Winter-14, Marks 7

Solution :

1) Graph : A graph is a collection of two sets V and E where V is a finite non-empty set of **vertices** and E is a finite non-empty set of **edges**. Refer Fig. 7.1.1.

2) Tree : A tree is a finite set of one or more nodes such that -

i) There is a specially designated node called **root**.

ii) The remaining nodes are partitioned into n > = 0 disjoint sets $T_1, T_2, T_3, \ldots T_n$ Refer Fig. 6.1.1.

3) Multigraph : Multigraph is a graph in which there can be more than one edge to join the pair of vertices. Two or more edges that join the pair of vertices are called parallel edges.

Every graph is a multigraph but not all multigraphs are graph. Refer Fig. 7.1.4.

4) Weighted graph : A weighted graph is a graph which consists of weights along its edges. Refer Fig. 7.2.5.

5) Elementary path : A path is a sequence of vertices and there exists an edge from one vertex to the next vertex. Elementary path is basically a path of a graph in which no vertex occurs more than once. Refer Fig. 7.2.6 along with given path.

6) Complete Binary Tree : A complete binary tree is a binary tree in which every node has zero or two children and all leaves are at the same depth. Refer Fig. 6.2.4.

7) Descendant node : The node X is descendant of Y if -

i) X is a child of Y or

ii) X is a descendant of a child of Y

For example

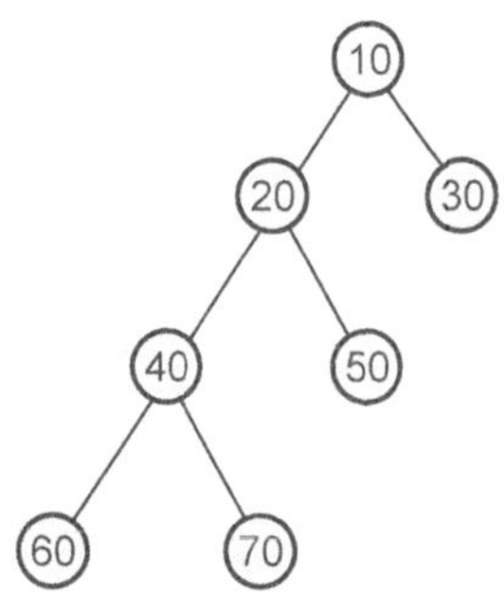

The descendant of node 20 are 40, 50, 60, 70.

Review Questions

1. *Define : Path, Cycle, Degree of vertex, Sibling* **GTU : Winter-13, Marks 7**
2. *Define the following terms : Node, Sibling, Path, Indegree and Outdegree of a vertex, connected graph* **GTU : Summer-14, Marks 7**
3. *Explain outdegree and indegree.* **GTU : Summer-17, Marks 3**
4. *Define the following terms with respect to a graph : Node, Edge, Path.* **GTU : Summer-18, Marks 3**

7.3 Representation of Graphs

GTU : Summer-18, Marks 4

Normally a graph can be represented by two representations and those are

1. Adjacency matrix : In this representation, matrix or 2 dimensional array is used to represent the graph.

2. Adjacency list : In this representation a **linked list** is used to represent the graph.

7.3.1 Adjacency Matrix Representation

Let us first discuss adjacency matrix representation.

Consider a graph G of n vertices and the matrix M. If there is an edge present between vertices V_i and V_j then M[i][j] = 1 else M[i][j] = 0. Note that for an undirected graph if M[i][j] = 1 then for M[j][i] is also 1. Here are some graphs shown by adjacency matrix.

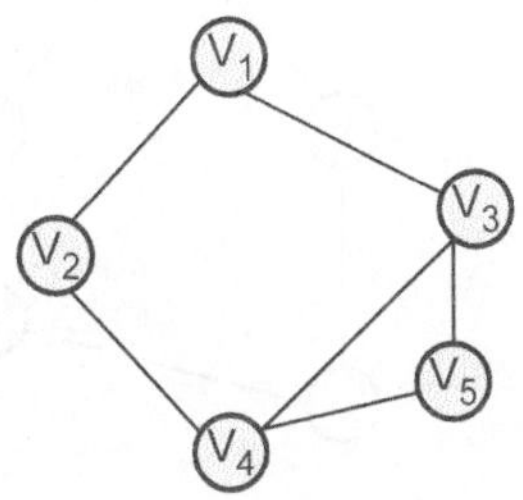

	1	2	3	4	5
1	0	1	1	0	0
2	1	0	0	1	0
3	1	0	0	1	1
4	0	1	1	0	1
5	0	0	1	1	0

Fig. 7.3.1 An adjacency matrix representation

Adjacency matrix for weighted graph

- In the weighted graph, weights or distances are given along every edge. Hence in an adjacency matrix representation any edge which is present between vertices V_i and V_j is denoted by its weight. Hence M[i][j] = Weight of edge.

- If there is no edge between V_i and V_j then, M[i][j] = 0.

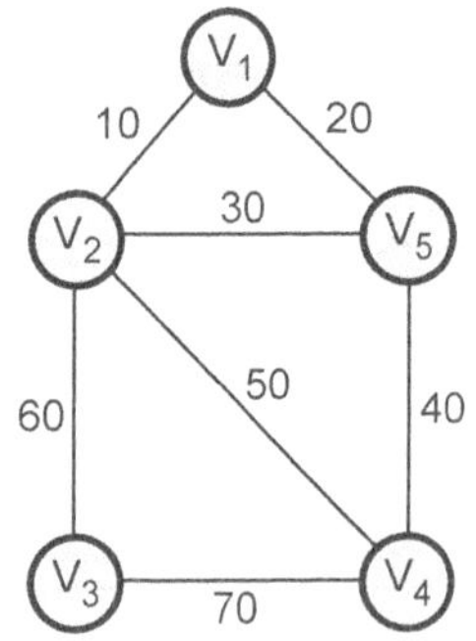

Weighted graph

	1	2	3	4	5
1	0	10	0	0	20
2	10	0	60	50	30
3	0	60	0	70	0
4	0	50	70	0	40
5	20	30	0	40	0

Adjacency matrix

Fig. 7.3.2 Adjacency matrix representation for weighted graph

7.3.2 Adjacency List Representation

In the previous sections we have seen how a graph can be represented using adjacency matrix. Mainly we have used array data structure over there. But the problems associated with array are still there in the adjacency matrix. So somewhere we feel that there should be some flexible data structure and so we go for a linked data structure for creation of a graph. The type in which a graph is created with the linked list is called adjacency list. So all the advantages of linked list can be obtained in this type of graph. We need not have a prior knowledge of maximum number of nodes. Actually there are many ways to create a adjacency matrix but we will discuss the two methods of adjacency list -

Method 1 :

As we know the graph is a set of vertices and edges, we will maintain the two structures, for vertices and edges respectively.

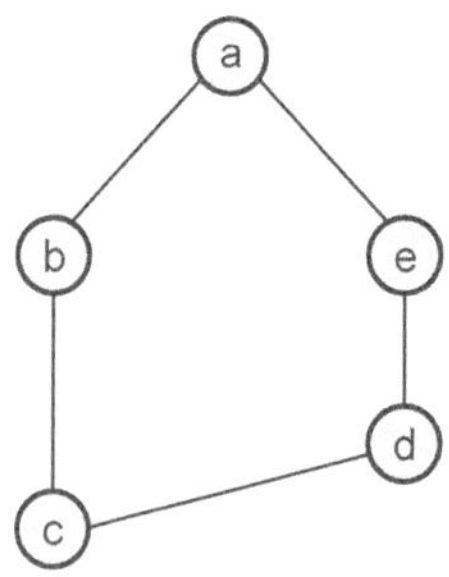

Fig. 7.3.3 Graph G

For example :

Now the above graph have the nodes as a, b, c, d, e so we will maintain the linked list of these head nodes as well as the adjacent nodes. The 'C' structure will be

```
typedef struct head
{
  char data;
  struct head *down;
 struct head *next;
```

```
}
typedef struct node
{
 int ver;
struct node *link;
}
```

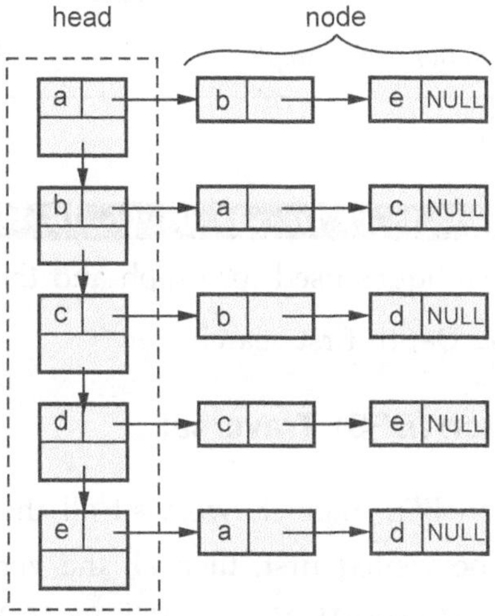

Fig. 7.3.4 Adjacency list

Explanation :

This is purely the adjacency list graph. The down pointer helps us to go to each node in the graph where as the next node is for going to adjacent node of each of the head node.

Method 2 : In this method of representing the adjacency list, We take mixed data structure. That means instead of taking the head list as a linked list we will take an array of head nodes. So only one 'C' structure will be there representing the adjacent nodes. See the Fig. 7.3.5 representing the adjacency list for the above graph. First let us see the 'C' structure.

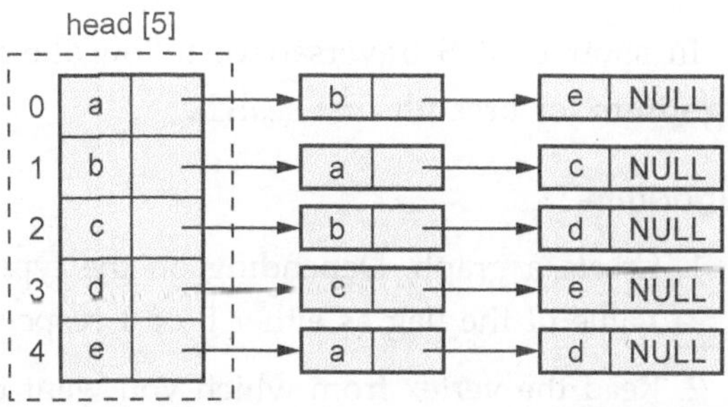

Fig. 7.3.5 Representing adjacency list (Method 2)

```
typedef struct node1
{
        char vertex;
        struct node1 *next;
}node
node * head [5]
```

Explanation : This is the graph which can be represented with the array and linked list data structures. Array is used to store the head nodes. The node structure will be the same through out.

Review Question

1. *Discuss different representations of a graph.*	**GTU : Summer-18, Marks 4**

7.4 Display of Graph

GTU : May-11, 12, Summer-13,16,17, Dec.-03, 05, 06, 10, Winter-11, 14, 15,16, Marks 7

There are two traversal techniques used for graph and those are -

1. Breadth first search 2. Depth first search

7.4.1 Breadth First Search (BFS) Traversal

For traversing the graph in BFS manner, we visit all the nodes on each level. Say a vertex V_1 in the graph will be visited first, then all the vertices adjacent to V_1 will be traversed suppose adjacent to V_1 are $(V_2, V_3, V_4, \ldots V_n)$. So $V_2, V_3, \ldots V_n$ will be printed first. Then again from V_2 the adjacent vertices will be printed. This process will be continued for all the vertices to get encounterd. To keep track of all the vertices and their adjacent vertices we will make use of queue data structure. Also we will make use of an array for visited nodes. The nodes which are get visited are set to 1. Thus we can keep track of visited nodes.

In short in BFS traversal we follow the path in **breadthwise** fashion. Let us see the algorithm for breadth first search.

Algorithm :

1. Create a graph. Depending on the type of graph i.e. directed or undirected set the value of the flag as either 0 or 1 respectively.
2. Read the vertex from which you want to traverse the graph say V_i.
3. Initialize the visited array to 1 at the index of V_i.
4. Insert the visited vertex V_i in the queue.
5. Visit the vertex which is at the front of the queue. Delete it from the queue and place its adjacent nodes in the queue.
6. Repeat the step 5, till the queue is not empty.
7. Stop.

'C' program

```
/*****************************************************************
    Program to create a Graph. The graph is represented using
    Adjacency Matrix.
*****************************************************************/
#include<stdio.h>
#include<conio.h>
#include<stdlib.h>
#define size     20
#define TRUE     1
#define FALSE 0
int g[size][size];
int visit[size];
int   Q[size];
int   front, rear;
int n;
    /*
______________________________________________________________
  The main Function
  Calls:create,bfs
  Called By:O.S.
--------------------------------------------------------------
*/
void main ( )
{
    int v1, v2;
    char ans ='y';
    void create(),bfs();;
    clrscr();
    create();
    clrscr();
    printf("The Adjacency Matrix for the graph is \n");
    for ( v1 = 0; v1 < n; v1++)
    {
        for ( v2 = 0; v2 < n; v2++)
            printf(" %d ", g[v1][v2]);
        printf("\n");
    }
        getch();
    do
    {
        for ( v1 = 0; v1 < n; v1++)
            visit[v1] = FALSE;
        clrscr();
        printf("Enter the Vertex from which you want to traverse ");
        scanf("%d", &v1);
        if ( v1 >= n )
```

```
                printf("Invalid Vertex\n");
            else
            {
            printf("The Breadth First Search of the Graph is \n");
            bfs(v1);
            getch();
            }
            printf("\nDo you want to traverse from any other node?");
            ans=getche();
        }while(ans=='y');
        exit(0);
}
/*
----------------------------------------------------------------------------
        The create function
        g :None
        Output:None, creates graph and stores in Adj. Matrix
        Parameter Passing Method :None
        Called By : main()
----------------------------------------------------------------------------
*/
void create()
{
        int    v1, v2
        char ans='y';
        printf("\n\t\t This is a Program To Create a Graph");
        printf("\n\t\t The Display Is In Breadth First Manner");
        printf("\nEnter no. of nodes");
        scanf("%d",&n);
        for ( v1 = 0; v1 < n; v1++)
            for ( v2 = 0; v2 < n; v2++)
                g[v1][v2] = FALSE;
        printf("\nEnter the vertices no. starting from 0");
        do
        {
            printf("\nEnter the vertices v1 & v2");
            scanf("%d%d", &v1, &v2);
            if ( v1 >= n || v2 >= n)
                printf("Invalid Vertex Value\n" );
            else
            {
                g[v1][v2] = TRUE;
                g[v2][v1] = TRUE;
            }
            printf("\n\nAdd more edges??(y/n)");
            ans=getche();
        }while(ans=='y');
```

```
}
/*
-----------------------------------------------------------------------------------------
        The bfs function
        g :Pointer to a vertex of a graph
        Output: Displays data in breadth First Search order
        Parameter Passing Method : By Value
        Called By : main()
        Calls : None
-----------------------------------------------------------------------------------------
*/
void bfs(int v1)
{
        int v2;

        visit[v1] = TRUE;
        front = rear = -1;
        Q[++rear] = v1;
        while ( front != rear )
        {
                v1 = Q[++front];
                printf("%d\n", v1);
                for ( v2 = 0; v2 < n; v2++)
                {
                        if ( g[v1][v2] == TRUE &&  visit[v2] == FALSE )
                        {
                                Q[++rear] = v2;
                                visit[v2] = TRUE;
                        }
                }
        }
}
```

Output

```
        This is a Program To Create a Graph
        The Display Is In Breadth First Manner
Enter no. of nodes 4
Enter the vertices no. starting from 0
Enter the vertices v1 & v2
0 1
Add more edges??(y/n)y
Enter the vertices v1 & v2
0 2
Add more edges??(y/n)y
Enter the vertices v1 & v2
1 3
Add more edges??(y/n)y
Enter the vertices v1 & v2
```

```
2 3
Add more edges??(y/n)
The Adjacency Matrix for the graph is
 0 1 1 0
 1 0 0 1
 1 0 0 1
 0 1 1 0
Enter the Vertex from which you want to traverse 0
The Breadth First Search of the Graph is
0
1
2
3
Do you want to traverse from any other node?
Enter the Vertex from which you want to traverse 1
The Breadth First Search of the Graph is
1
0
3
2
Do you want to traverse from any other node?
```

Explanation of logic of BFS

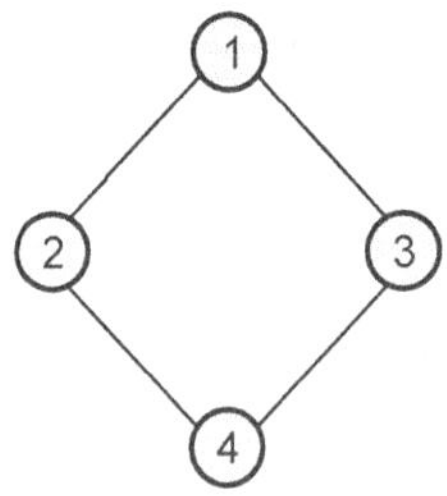

Fig. 7.4.1

In BFS the queue is maintained for storing the adjacent nodes and an array 'visited' is maintained for keeping the track of visited nodes. i.e. once a particular node is visited it should not be revisited again. Let us see how our program works :

Step 1 : Start with vertex 1

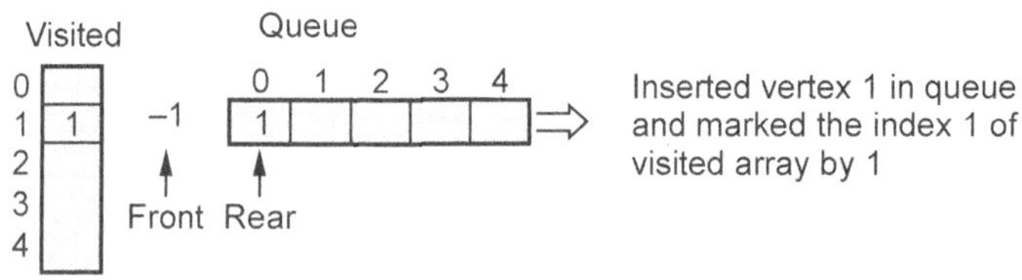

Step 2 :

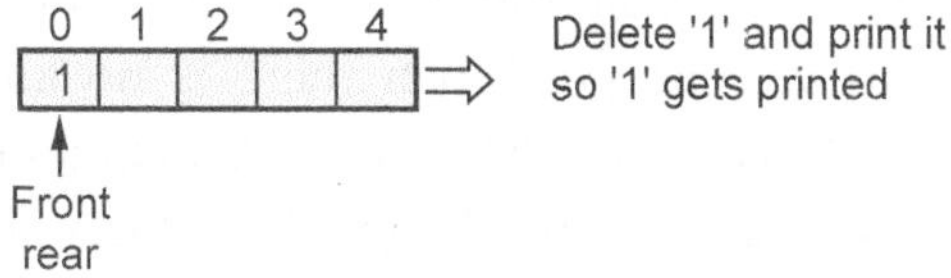

Step 3 : Find adjacent vertices of vertex 1 and mark them as visited, insert those in queue.

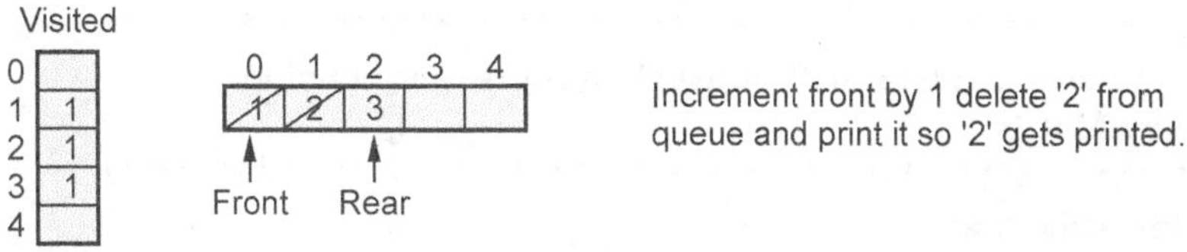

Step 4 : Find adjacent to '2' and insert those nodes in queue as well as mark them as visited.

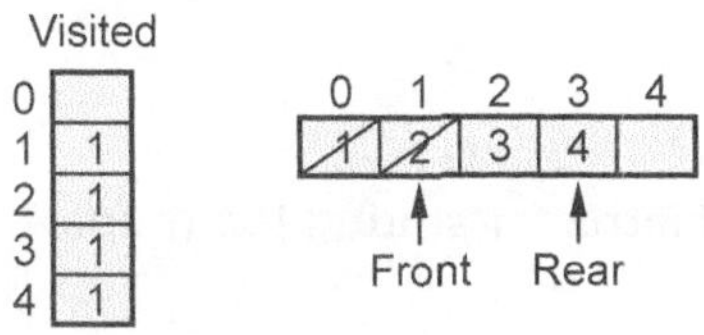

Step 5 : Increment front and delete the node print it.

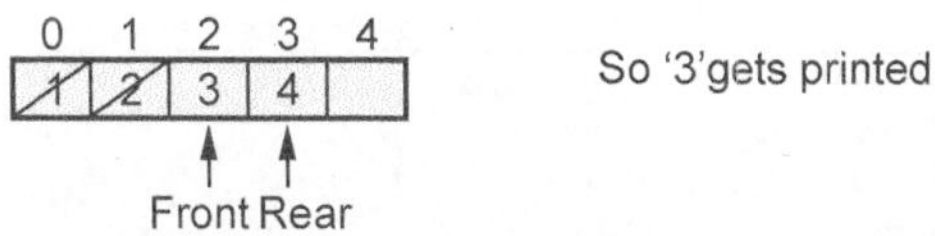

Step 6 : Find adjacent to '3' i.e. 4 check whether it is marked as visited. If it is marked as visited do not insert in the queue.

Increment front, delete the node from queue and print it.

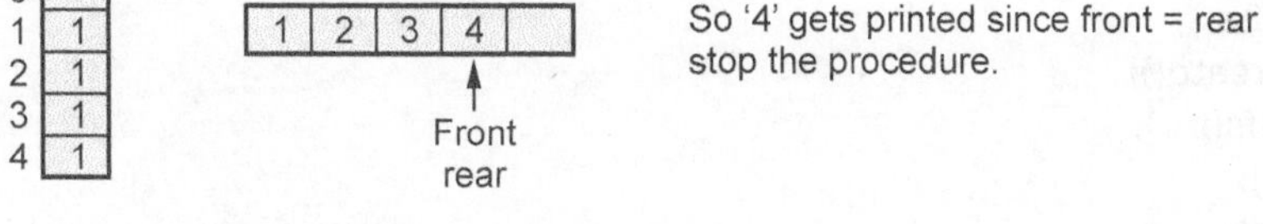

So output will be - BFS for above graph as

1 2 3 4

7.4.2 Depth First Search (DFS) Traversal

Now, we will discuss the another algorithm for traversal of the graph.In this case we follow the path as deeply as we can go. When there is no adjacent vertex present we traverse back and search for unvisited vertex. We will maintain a visited array to mark all the visited vertices. In case of DFS the depth of a graph should be known. Let see one example of a graph to traverse it by DFS.

'C' program

```
/****************************************************************
Program to create a Graph. The graph is represented using
Adjacency Matrix.
****************************************************************/
#include<stdio.h>
#include<conio.h>
#include<stdlib.h>

/* List of defined constants */
#define MAX 20
#define TRUE 1
#define FALSE 0

/* Declare an adjacency matrix for storing the graph */

int g[MAX][MAX];
int v[MAX];
int n;
/*
--------------------------------------------------------------------
The main function
Called By : The O.S.
Calls : create(), Dfs()
--------------------------------------------------------------------
*/
void main ( )
{
 /* Local declarations */
        int v1, v2;
  char ans;
  void create();
  void Dfs(int);
  clrscr();
  create();
  clrscr();
  printf("The Adjacency Matrix for the graph is \n");
```

```
   for ( v1 = 0; v1 < n; v1++)
   {
        for ( v2 = 0; v2 < n; v2++)
             printf(" %d ", g[v1][v2]);
        printf("\n");
  }
  getch();
  do
  {
   for ( v1 = 0; v1 < n; v1++)
        v[v1] = FALSE;
   clrscr();
   printf("Enter the Vertex from which you want to traverse :");
   scanf("%d", &v1);
   if ( v1 >= MAX )
   printf("Invalid Vertex\n");
   else
   {
       printf("The Depth First Search of the Graph is \n");
       Dfs(v1);
   }
   printf("\n Do U want To Taverse By any Other Node?");
   ans=getch();
  }while(ans=='y');
  }
  /*
  ---------------------------------------------------------------------------------
  The Create function
  Output:None, creates graph and stores in Adj. Matrix
  Parameter Passing Method :None
  Called By : main()
  ---------------------------------------------------------------------------------
  */

  void  create()
  {
        int ch,v1, v2, flag;
        char ans='y';
        printf("\n\t\t This is a Progrm To Create a Graph");
        printf("\n\t\t The Display Is In Depth First Manner");
        getch();
        clrscr();
        flushall();
        for ( v1 = 0; v1 < n; v1++)
             for ( v2 = 0; v2 < n; v2++)
                  g[v1][v2] = FALSE;
        printf("\nEnter no. of nodes");
```

```
        scanf("%d",&n);
        printf("\nEnter the vertices no. starting from 0");
        do
        {
                printf("\nEnter the vertices v1 & v2");
                scanf("%d%d", &v1, &v2);
                if ( v1 >= n || v2 >= n)
                        printf("Invalid Vertex Value\n" );
                else
                {
                        g[v1][v2] = TRUE;
                        g[v2][v1] = TRUE;

                }
                printf("\n\nAdd more edges??(y/n)");
                ans=getche();
        }while(ans=='y');
}
/*
----------------------------------------------------------------------------------------
The Dfs function
Input :Pointer to a vertex of a graph
Output: Displays data in Depth First Search order
Parameter Passing Method : By Value
Called By : main()
Calls : Dfs() itself(recursive call)
----------------------------------------------------------------------------------------
*/
void Dfs(int v1)
{
  int v2;
  printf("%d\n", v1);
  v[v1] = TRUE;
  for ( v2 = 0; v2 < MAX; v2++)
    if ( g[v1][v2] == TRUE &&  v[v2] == FALSE )
      Dfs(v2);
}
```

Output

```
This is a Program To Create a Graph
The Display Is In Depth First Manner
Enter no. of nodes 4
Enter the vertices no. starting from 0
Enter the vertices v1 & v2 0 1
Add more edges??(y/n)y
Enter the vertices v1 & v2 0 2
Add more edges??(y/n)y
Enter the vertices v1 & v2 1 3
```

```
Add more edges??(y/n)y
Enter the vertices v1 & v2 2 3
Add more edges??(y/n)
The Adjacency Matrix for the graph is
 0 1 1 0
 1 0 0 1
 1 0 0 1
 0 1 1 0
Enter the Vertex from which you want to traverse : 1
The Depth First Search of the Graph is
1
0
2
3
 Do U want To Traverse By any Other Node?
```

Expalnation of logic for depth first traversal

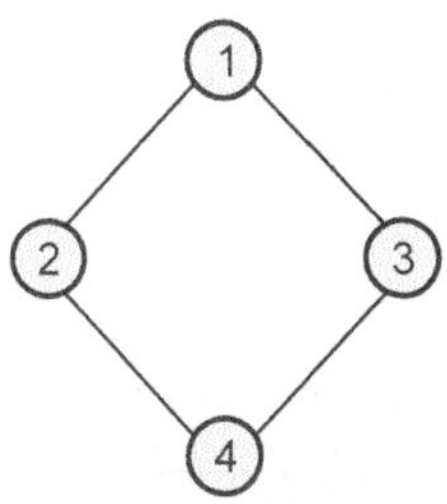

Fig. 7.4.2 Graph

In DFS the basic data structure for storing the adjacent nodes is stack. In our program we have used a recursive call to DFS function. When a recursive call is invoked actually push operation gets performed. When we exit from the loop pop operation will be performed. Let us see how our program works.

Step 1 : Start with vertex 1, print it so '1' gets printed. Mark 1 as visited.

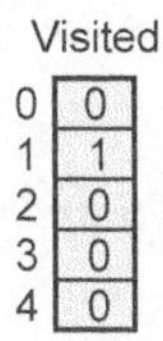

Step 2 : Find adjacent vertex to 1, say i.e. 2 if it is not visited, call DFS(2) i.e. 2 will get inserted in the stack, mark is as visited.

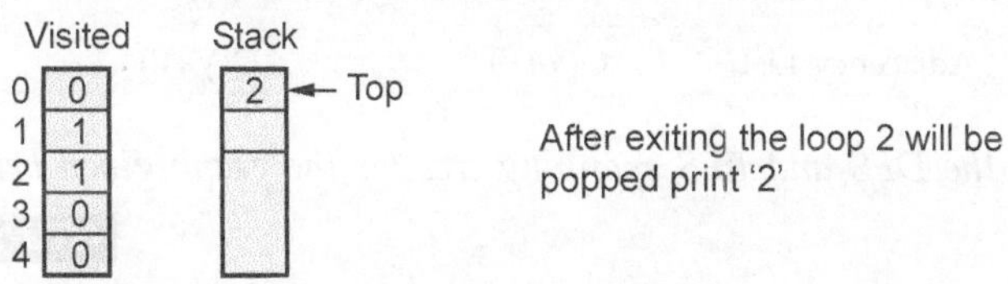

Step 3 : Find adjacent to '2' i.e. vertex 4 if it is not visited call DFS(4) i.e., 4 will get pushed on to the stack mark it as visited.

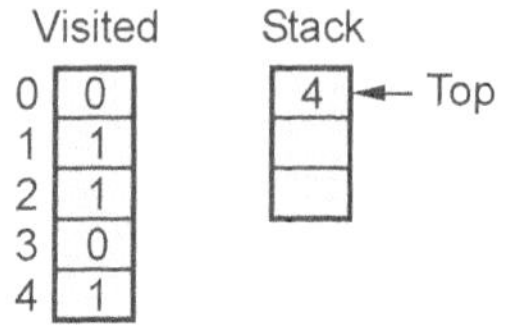

After exiting the loop 4 will be popped print '4'

Step 4 : Find adjacent to '4' i.e. vertex 3 if it is not visited call DFS(3) i.e. 3 will be pushed onto the stack mark it visited.

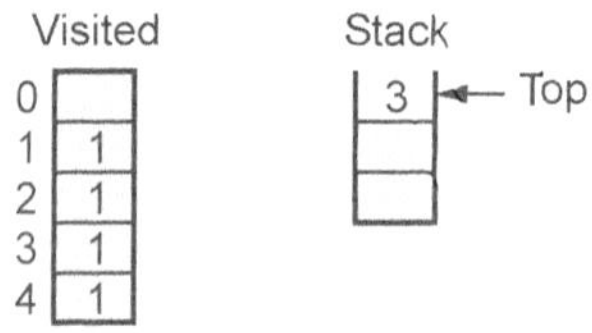

After exiting the loop 3 will be popped print '3'

Since all the nodes are covered stop the procedure.

So output of DFS is

1 2 4 3

7.4.3 BFS Vs. DFS

Sr. No.	Depth first search	Breadth first search
1.	This type of search is done with the help of **stack**.	This type of search is done with the help of queue.
2.	This algorithm works in **two stages** - In the first stage the visited vertices are pushed onto the stack and later on when there is no vertex further to visit, those are popped off.	This algorithm works in **single stage**. - The visited vertices are removed from the queue and then displayed at once.

Example 7.4.1 *Compare the efficiencies of BFS and DFS.* **GTU : May-11, Marks 3,**

Solution :

	BFS	DFS
Adjacency matrix	$O(V^2)$	$O(V^2)$
Adjacency List	O(V+E)	O(V+E)

Example 7.4.2 *Give the DFS and BFS spanning tree for the graph given below.*

GTU : May-11, Marks 4

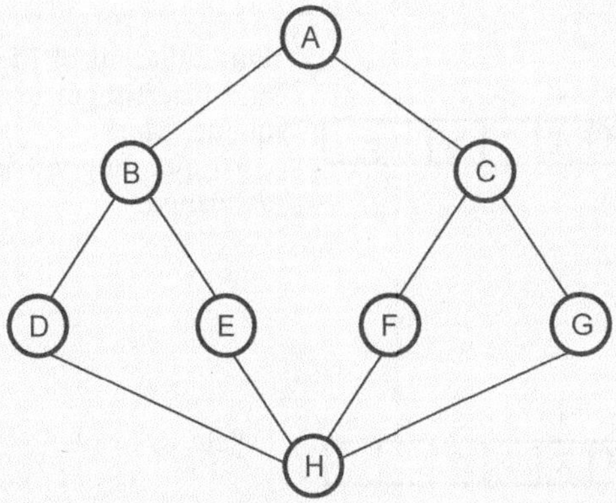

Fig. 7.4.3

Solution : DFS : The DFS sequence will be ABDHECFG.

BFS : The BFS sequence will be ABCDEFGH.

Example 7.4.3 *The breadth first search algorithm has beem implemented using the queue data structure. Find breadth first search for graph shown in Fig. 7.4.4 starting node M.*

GTU : Summer-13, Marks 7

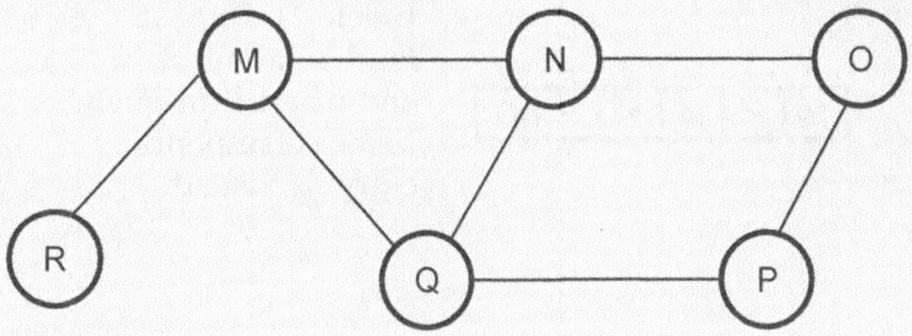

Fig. 7.4.4

Solution :

Step 1 : visited	**Queue**	**Action**	**Output**
M 1 R Q N O P	0 1 2 3 4 5 M	Insert M in queue Mark visited (M) = 1	-
Step 2 :	0 1 2 3 4 5 ~~M~~	Delete M and print	M

Visited array	Queue (0 1 2 3 4 5)	Action	Output
M 1, R 1, Q 1, N 1, O, P	~~M~~ R Q N _ _	Find adjacent of M and insert them in queue. Mark corresponding entries as visited.	M
	~~M~~ ~~R~~ Q N _ _	Delete R, Print	M R
M 1, R 1, Q 1, N 1, O, P 1	~~M~~ ~~R~~ ~~Q~~ N P _	Delete Q, Print it. Find adjacent of Q, which is P. Insert P in queue. Mark corresponding vertices as visited.	M R Q
M 1, R 1, Q 1, N 1, O 1, P 1	~~M~~ ~~R~~ ~~Q~~ ~~N~~ P O	Delete N, Print it. Find adjacent of N and insert it in queue. Mark corresponding entry as visited.	M R Q, N
		Delete remaing entries from queue and print them.	M, R, Q, N, P, O. This is BFS sequence.

Review Questions

1. *Write an algorithm for BFS.* **GTU : Dec.-03, Marks 6**
2. *Explain BFS and DFS with example.*
   GTU : Dec.-05, Marks 4, Dec.-06, 10, Marks 6, May-12, Marks 5, Winter-14, Marks 7
3. *List advantages and disadvantages of Breadth First Search and Depth First Search.*
   GTU : Winter-15, Marks 3
4. *Explain depth first search in graphs with an example.* **GTU : Summer-16, Marks 3**
5. *Explain breadth first search in graphs with an example.* **GTU : Summer-16, Marks 3**
6. *Explain depth first search and breadth first search in graphs with an example.*
   GTU : Winter-16, Marks 7

7. *Explain Depth First Search operation.* **GTU : Summer-17, Marks 4**
8. *Explain Breadth First Search operation.* **GTU : Summer-17, Marks 4**

7.5 Applications of Graphs

GTU : Dec.-06, Summer-15, Marks 6

The graph theory is used in the computer science very widely. There are many interesting applications of graph. We will list out few applications -

1. In computer networking such as Local Area Network (LAN), Wide Area Networking(WAN), internetworking.
2. In telephone cabling graph theory is effectively used.
3. In job scheduling algorithms.

Review Questions

1. *Attempt: Graph Applications.* **GTU : Dec.-06, Marks 6**
2. *Briefly explain various linear and non-linear data structures along with their applications.* **GTU : Summer-15, Marks 7**

[Hint : Linear data structures are stack, queue and nonlinear data structures are trees and graphs.]

7.6 Spanning Trees

A spanning tree S is a subset of a tree T in which all the vertices of tree T are present but it may not contain all the edges.

7.7 Minimum Spanning Tree

GTU : Summer-14,15,16,18, Nov.-06, Winter-12,15,16,18, Marks 7

The minimum spanning tree of a weighted connected graph G is called minimum spanning tree if its **weight is minimum**.

7.7.1 Prim's Algorithm

The Prim's algorithm can be given as follows -

Step 1 : Select the pair with minimum weight.

Step 2 : Select the adjacent vertex and select the minimum weighted edge using this adjacent vertex. The selected adjacent vertex should not form the circuit.

Step 3 : Repeat step 1 and 2 until all the vertices are getting covered.

Following are some examples that illustrate how to obtain minimum cost spanning tree using Prim's algorithm.

Example 7.7.1 *Define the spanning tree. Write the Prim's algorithm to find the minimum cost spanning tree of the following.* **UPTU : 2010-11**

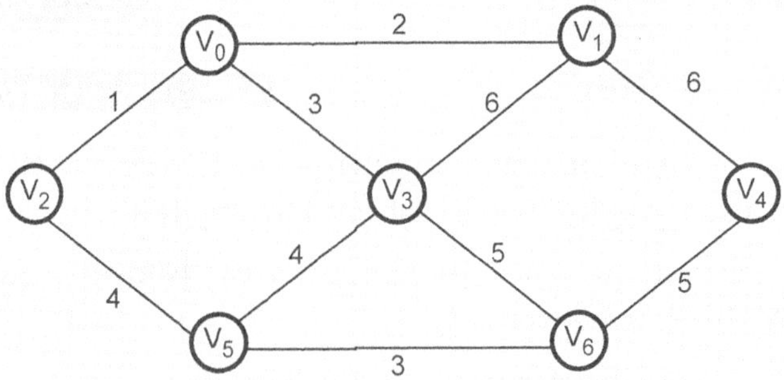

Solution : Spanning tree : Refer section 7.6

Example

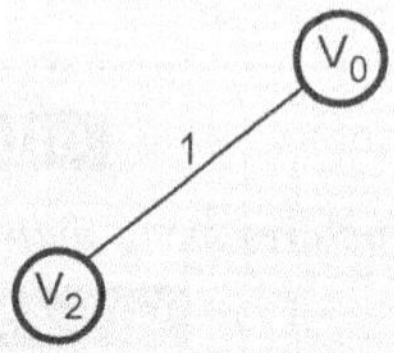	Path length = 1
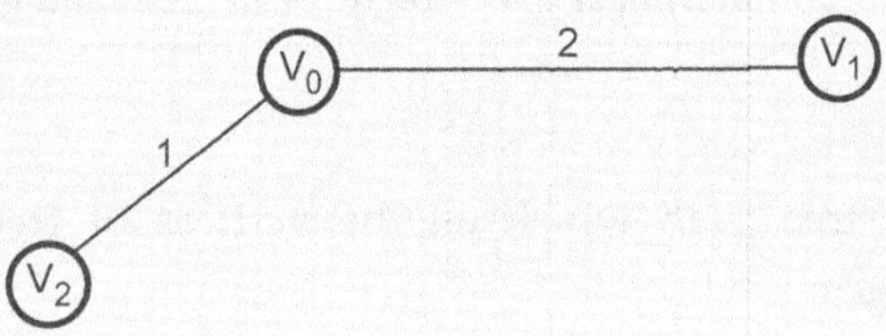	Path length = 3
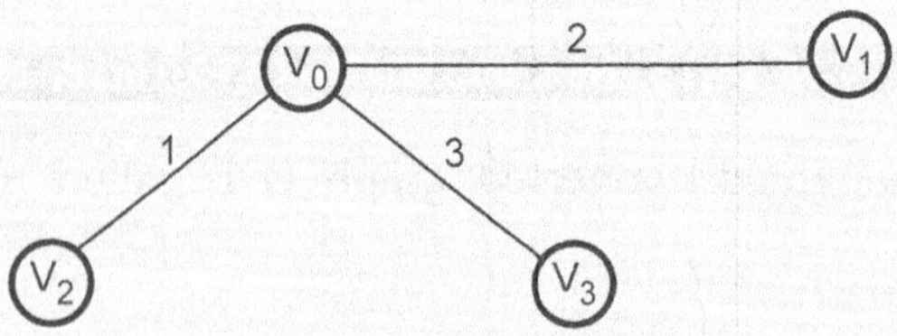	Path length = 6
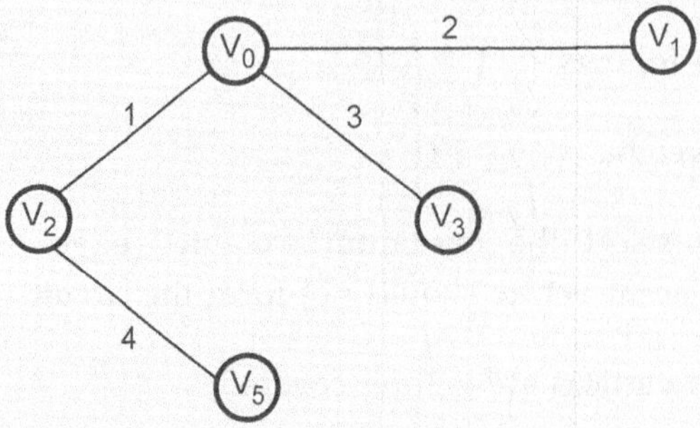	Path length = 10

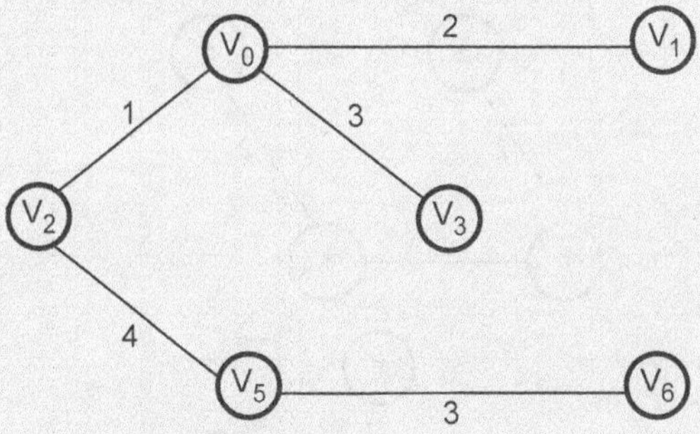	Path length = 13
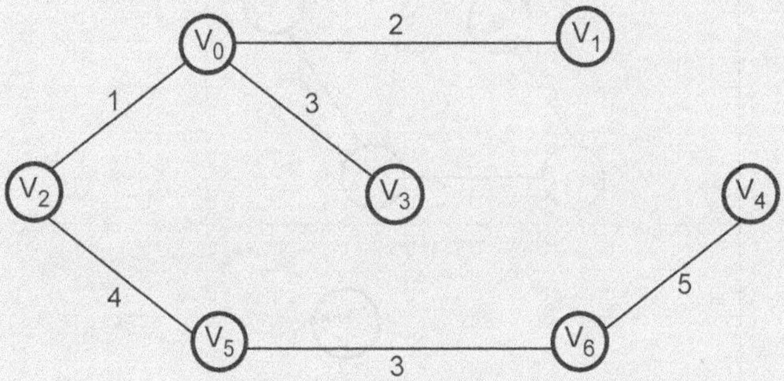 This is required MST	Path length = 18

Example 7.7.2 *Find the minimum spanning tree for the graph shown below*

GTU : Summer-14, Marks 7

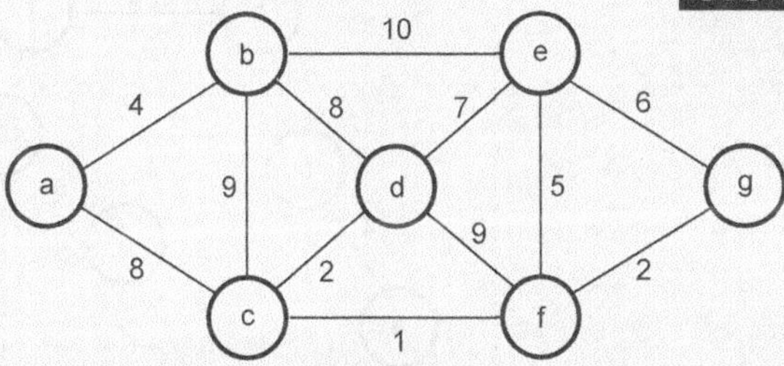

Fig. 7.7.1

Solution : We will obtain minimum spanning tree using Prim's algorithm.

Select edge c - f Path length = 1	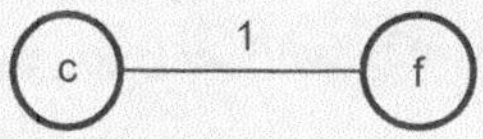
Select an edge f - g Path length = 3	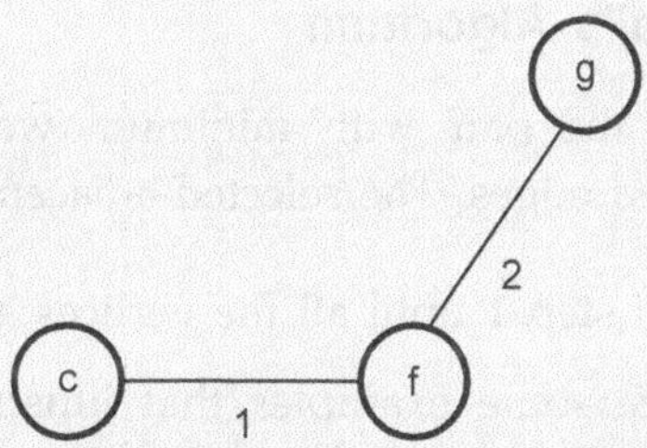

Select an edge c - d
Path length = 5

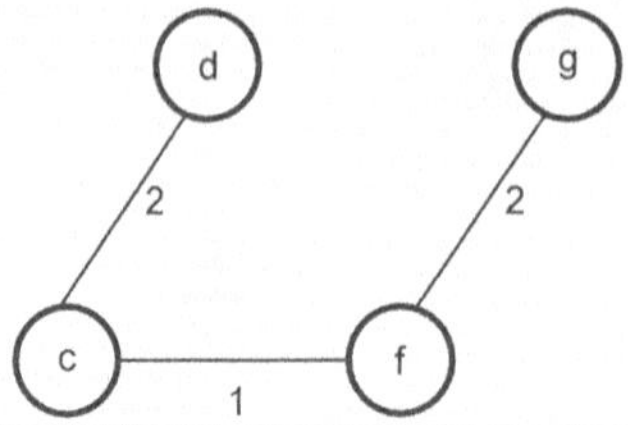

Select an edge f - e
Path length = 10

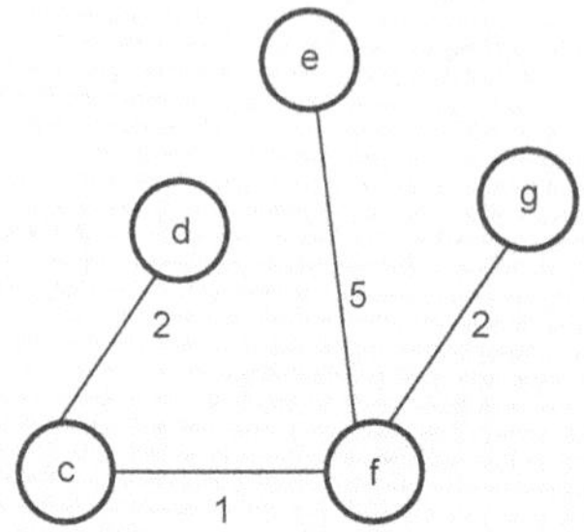

Select an edge a - c
Path length = 18

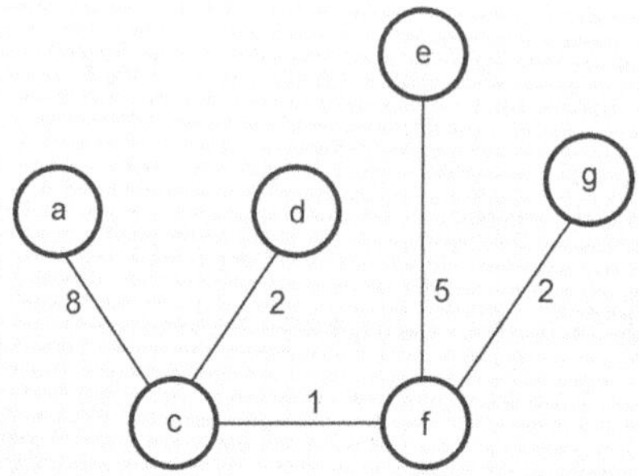

Select an edge a - b
Path length = 22

As all the vertices are visited, we obtain the minimum spanning tree with path length 22

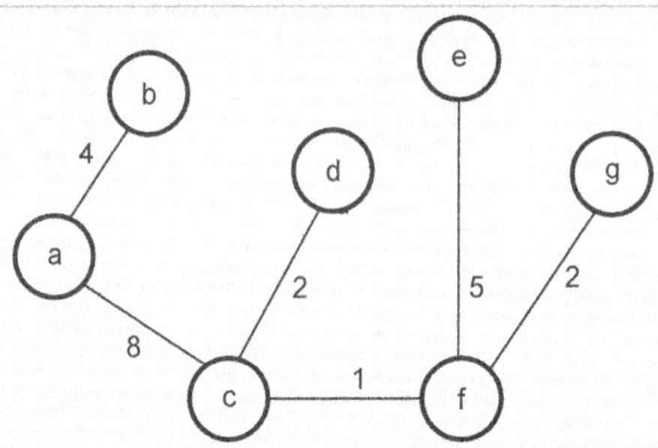

Minimum spanning tree

7.7.2 Kruskal's Algorithm

Step 1 : Select the pair with minimum weight each time and make the union of the selected edges. The selected adjacent vertex should not form the circuit.

Step 2 : Repeat step 1 until all the vertices are getting covered.

Following are some examples that illustrate how to obtain minimum cost spanning tree using Kruskal's algorithm.

Example 7.7.3 *Find a minimum spanning tree of the following graph using Kruskal's algorithm :*

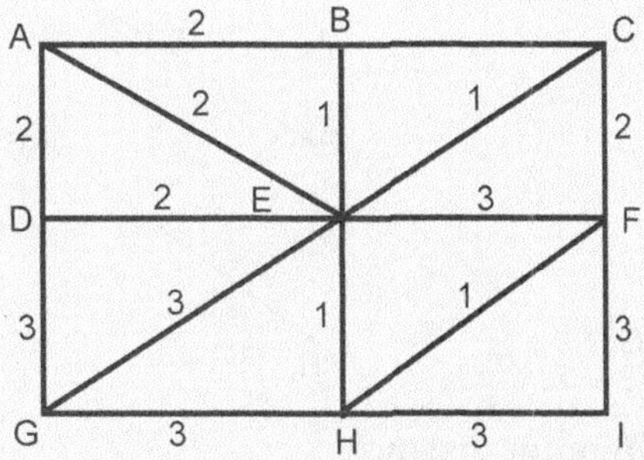

UPTU : 2006-07, 2008-09

Solution : Step 1 :

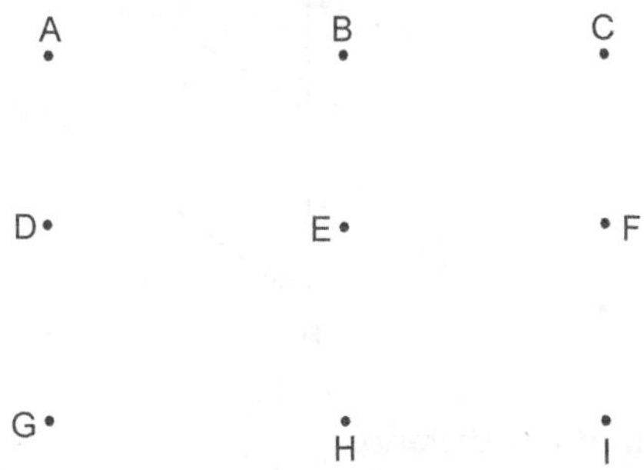

Step 2 : We will now select an edge with minimum distance.

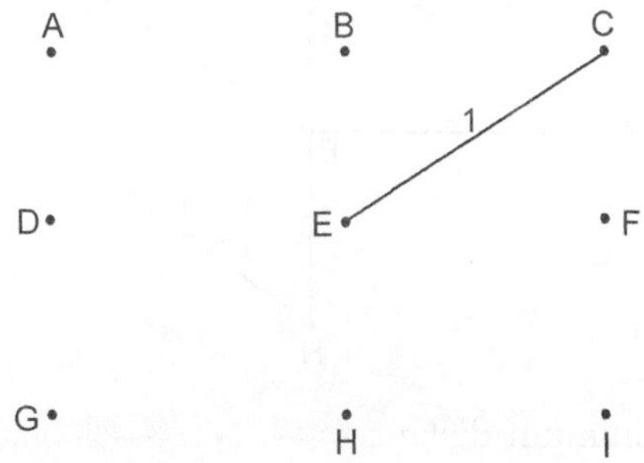

Step 3 : Then select **next** minimum distance

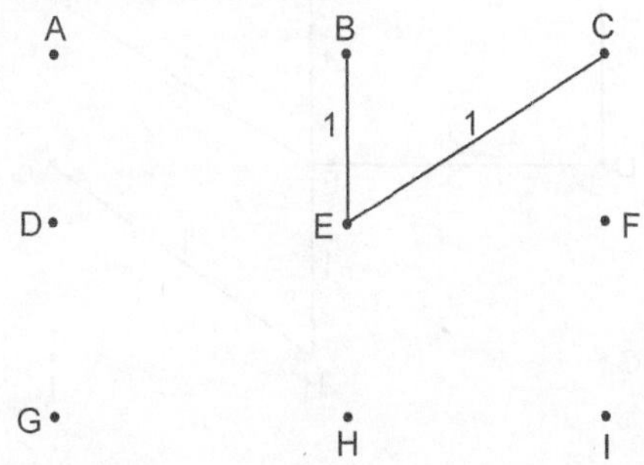

Step 4 : Then select next minimum distance

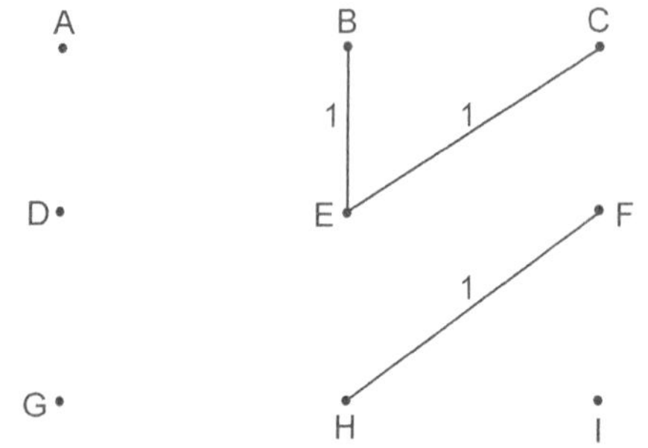

Step 5 : Then select next minimum distance

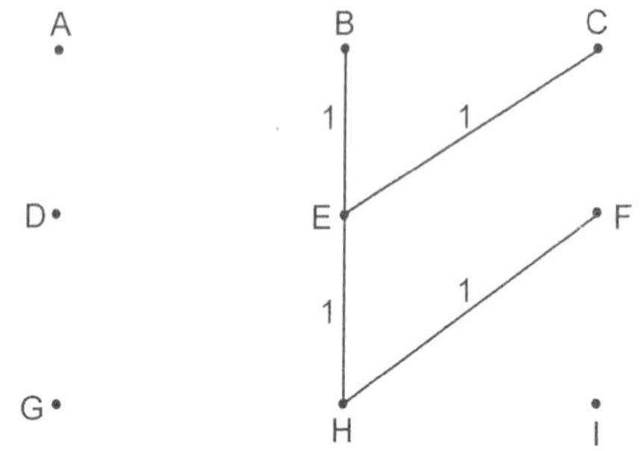

Step 6 : Then select next minimum distance

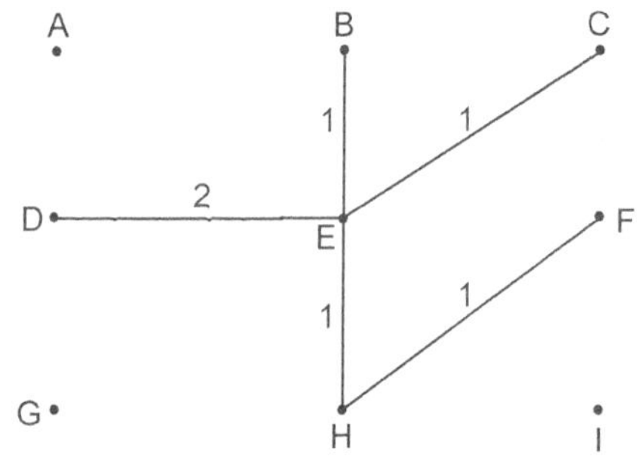

Step 7 : Then select next minimum distance

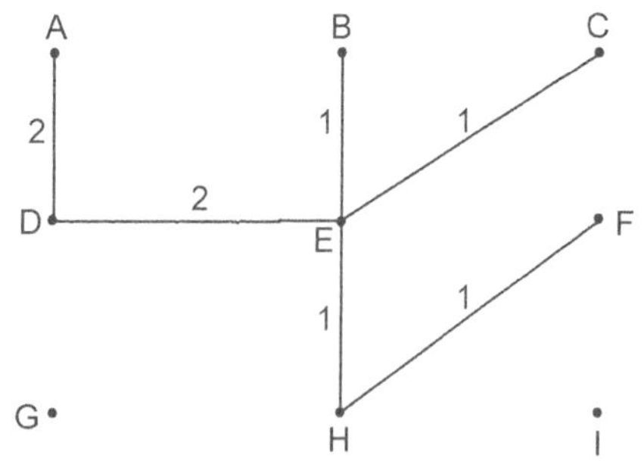

Step 8 :

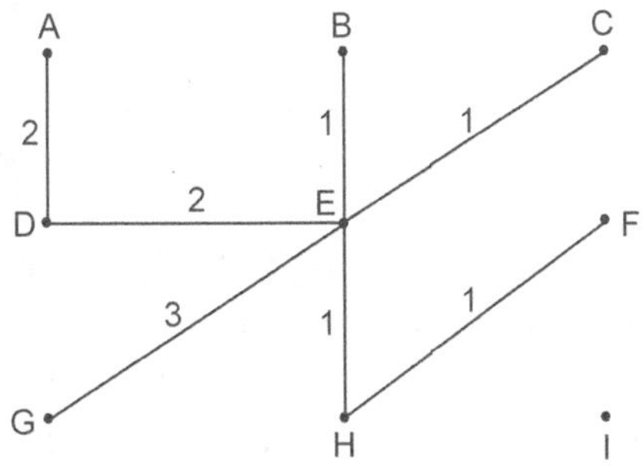

Step 9 :

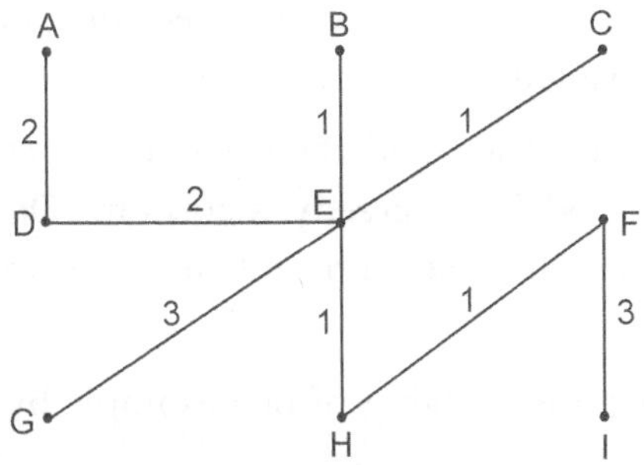

7.7.3 Difference between Prim's and Kruskal's Algorithm

Prim's algorithm	Kruskal's algorithm
This algorithm is for obtaining minimum spanning tree by selecting the adjacent vertices of already selected vertices.	This algorithm is for obtaining minimum spanning tree but it is not necessary to choose adjacent vertices of already selected vertices.

Review Questions

1. *Explain Kruskal's algorithm for minimum cost spanning tree.* **GTU : Nov.-06, Marks 4**
2. *Write short note on spanning tree.* **GTU : Winter-12, Marks 7**
3. *Compare Prim's and Kruskal's algorithm with the help of an example.* **GTU : Summer-14, Marks 7**
4. *Write Kruskal's algorithm for minimum spanning tree and explain with an example.* **GTU : Summer-15, Marks 7**
5. *What is a minimum spanning tree ? Explain Kruskal's algorithm for finding a minimum spanning tree.* **GTU : Winter-15, Marks 4**
6. *Write Prim's algorithm for minimum spanning tree with an example.* **GTU : Summer-16, Marks 7**
7. *Write Kruskal's algorithm for minimum spanning tree with an example.* **GTU : Winter-16, Marks 7**

8. *Explain the working of the Kruskal's algorithm.* **GTU : Summer-18, Marks 3**
9. *Explain spanning tree with example.* **GTU : Winter-18, Marks 3**

7.8 Shortest Path

GTU : Summer-18, Marks 7

The Dijkstra's shortest path algorithm suggests the shortest path from some source node to the some other destination node. The source node or the node from we start measuring the distance is called the start node and the destination node is called the end node. In this algorithm we start finding the distance from the start node and find all the paths from it to neighbouring nodes. Among those which ever is the nearest node that path is selected. This process of finding the nearest node is repeated till the end node. Then whichever is the path that path is called the shortest path.

Since in this algorithm all the paths are tried and then we are choosing the shortest path among them, this algorithm is solved by a greedy algorithm. One more thing is that we are having all the vertices in the shortest path and therefore the graph doesn't give the spanning tree.

For clear understanding let us see stepwise solving of one example by this algorithm.

Example :

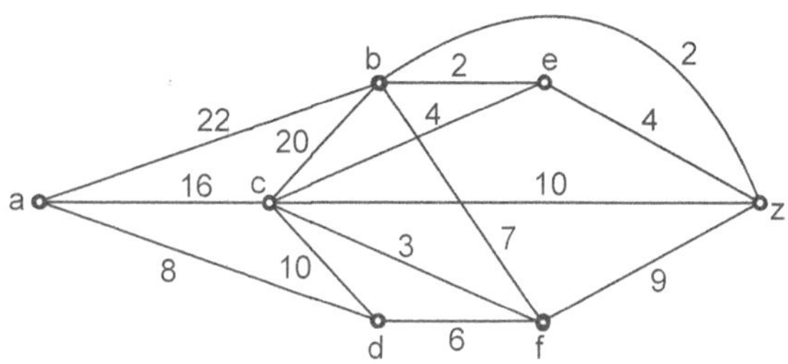

Fig. 7.8.1

P = Set which is for nodes which have already selected

T = Remaining node

Step 1 : v = a

P={a}, T={b,c,d,e,f,z}

dist(b) = min{old dist(b),dist(a)+w(a,b)}

dist(b) = min{∞,0+22}

dist(b) = 22

dist(c) = 16

dist(d) = 8 ← minimum node

dist(e) = ∞

dist(f) = ∞

dist(z) = ∞

So minimum node is selected in P i.e. node d

Step 2 : v = d

P={a,d} T = {b,c,e,f,z}

dist(b) = min{old dist(b),dist(d)+w(b,d)}

dist(b) = min{22,8+∞}

dist(b) = 22

dist(c) = min{16,8+10} = 16

dist(e) = min{∞,8+∞} = 8

dist(f) = min{∞,8+6} = 14

dist(z) = min{∞,8+∞} = ∞

Step 3 : v = f

P={a,d,f} T = {b,c,e,z}

dist(b) = min{22,14+7} = 21

dist(c) = min{16,14+3} = 16

dist(e) = min{∞ ,14 +∞ } = ∞

dist(z) = min{∞, 14+9} = 23

Step 4 : v = c

P={a,d,f,c} T = {b,e,z}

dist(b) = min{21,16+20} = 21

dist(e) = min{∞ ,16+4} = 20

dist(z) = min{23,16+10} = 23

Step 5 : v = e

P ={a,d,f,c,e} T = {b,z}

dist(b) =min{21,20+2} = 21

dist(z) =min{23,20+4} = 23

Step 6 : v = b

P={a,d,f,c,e,b} T = {z}

dist(z) = min{23,21+2} = 23.

Now the target vertex for finding the shortest path is z. Hence the length of the shortest path from the vertex a to z is 23.

The shortest path is as shown below :

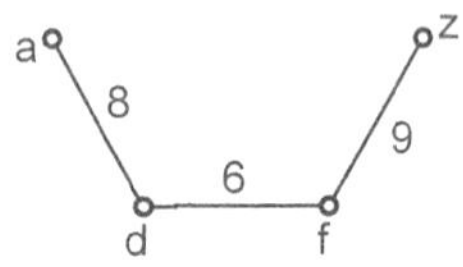

Fig. 7.8.2

Example 7.8.1 *Apply Dijkstra's algorithm for the following graph with Node S as the starting node.* **GTU : Summer-18, Marks 7**

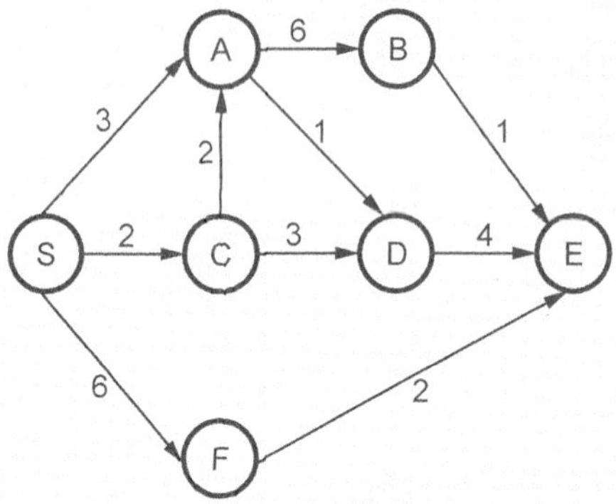

Fig. 7.8.1

Sol. :

Step 1 :

Source = { S }, **Target** = {A, B, C, D, E, F}

d(S, A) = 3

d(S, B) = ∞

d(S, C) = 2 ← Min distance

d(S, D) = 4

d(S, E) = ∞

d(S, F) = 6

The minimum distance is 2. Hence select C.

Step 2 :

Source = { S, C }, **Target** = {A, B, D, E, F}

d(S, A) = 3 ← Min distance

d(S, B) = ∞

d(S, D) = 2 + 3 = 5

d(S, E) = ∞

d(S, F) = 6

The minimum distance is 3. Hence select A.

Step 3 :

Source = { S, C, A }, **Target** = {B, D, E, F}

d(S, B) = 6 + 3 = 9

d(S, D) = 3 + 1 = 4 ← **Min distance**

d(S, E) = ∞

d(S, F) = 6

Step 4 :

Source = { S, C, A, D }, **Target** = {B, E, F}

d(S, B) = 9

d(S, E) = d(S, A) + d(A, D) + d(D, E)

= 3 + 1 + 4 = 8

d(S, F) = 6 ← **Min distance**

Step 5 :

Source = { S, C, A, D, F },

Target = {B, E}

d(S, B) = 9

d(S, E) = 8 ← **Min distance**

Step 6 :

Source = { S, C, A, D, F, E },

Target = { B }

d(S, B) = 9

Step 7 : Thus we obtain the shortest paths from single source to all other vertices.

d(S, A) = 3 d(S, E) = 8

d(S, B) = 9 d(S, F) = 6

d(S, C) = 2

d(S, D) = 4

'C' program

```
#include<stdio.h>
#include<conio.h>
#define member 1
#define nomember 0
#define infinity 999

typedef struct edge
{
int wt;
}edge;
int n;
edge g[10][10];
/*
      The main function
      Parameter Passing Method :None
      Called By : The O.S.
      Calls :get(),shrt()
*/
void main()
{
 int src,dest;
 void get();
 int shrt(int,int);
 clrscr();
 printf("\n Program For Shortest Path Algorithm\n");
 printf("enter no of vertices: ");
 scanf("%d",&n);
 get();
 printf("\nEnter The Source");
 scanf("%d",&src);
 printf("\nEnter The  Destination: ");
 scanf("%d",&dest);
 printf("\nshortest path:%d",shrt(src,dest));
 getch();
}
/*
      The get function
      Parameter Passing Method :None
      Called By : main
      Calls : none
*/
void get()
{
int i,j,v1,v2;
for(i=1;i<=n;i++)
{
```

```
for(j=1;j<=n;j++)
{
 printf("enter The  edge Of V%d TO V%d:",i,j);
 scanf("%d",&g[i][j].wt);
 }
 printf("\n");
 }
}
/*
      The shrt function
      Input Parameter:source and destination
      Parameter Passing Method :By value
      Called By : main
      Calls : none
*/
int shrt(int src,int dest)
{
 int small,perm[10],dist[10],current,start,new1;
 int k=1,temp,i;
 for(i=0;i<=n;i++)
 {
  perm[i]=0;
  dist[i]=infinity;
 }

 perm[src]=1;
 dist[src]=0;
 current=src;
 while(current!=dest)
 {
      small=infinity;
      start=dist[current];
      for(i=1;i<=n;i++)
      {
       if(perm[i]==0)
       {
      new1=start+g[current][i].wt;
      if(new1<dist[i])
        dist[i]=new1;
      if(dist[i]<small)
      {
        small=dist[i];
        temp=i;
      }
       }
 }
  current=temp;
```

```
  perm[current]=1;
  k++;
  printf("%d",current);
  }

 return(small);
}
```

Output

```
Program For Shortest Path Algorithm

enter no of vertices : 5
enter The  edge Of V1 TO V1:999
enter The  edge Of V1 TO V2:9
enter The  edge Of V1 TO V3:4
enter The  edge Of V1 TO V4:999
enter The  edge Of V1 TO V5:999

enter The  edge Of V2 TO V1:9
enter The  edge Of V2 TO V2:999
enter The  edge Of V2 TO V3:999
enter The  edge Of V2 TO V4:3
enter The  edge Of V2 TO V5:999

enter The  edge Of V3 TO V1:4
enter The  edge Of V3 TO V2:999
enter The  edge Of V3 TO V3:999
enter The  edge Of V3 TO V4:999
enter The  edge Of V3 TO V5:1

enter The  edge Of V4 TO V1:999
enter The  edge Of V4 TO V2:3
enter The  edge Of V4 TO V3:999
enter The  edge Of V4 TO V4:999
enter The  edge Of V4 TO V5:1

enter The  edge Of V5 TO V1:999
enter The  edge Of V5 TO V2:999
enter The  edge Of V5 TO V3:1
enter The  edge Of V5 TO V4:1
enter The  edge Of V5 TO V5:999

Enter The Source1

Enter The  Destination: 5

Shortest path : 1 3  5
```

Review Questions

1. *Describe Dijkstra's algorithm for finding shortest path with the help of suitable example.*
2. *Write Warshall algorithm to find shortest path between any two vertices of a graph. Explain the algorithm briefly.*
3. *How can you find shortest path between two nodes in a graph by Dijkstra's algorithm ? Explain by suitable diagram and algorithm.*
4. *Describe the Dijikstra's algorithm for finding shortest path with help of suitable example.*
5. *Write and explain an algorithm for finding shortest path between any two nodes of a given graph.*

7.9 Oral Questions and Answers

Q.1 Define graph. **GTU : Summer-16**

Ans. : A graph is a collection of two sets of V and E where V is finite non empty set of vertices and E is a finite non empty set of edges.

Vertices are nothing but the nodes in the graph and two adjacent vertices are joined by edges.

The graph is denoted by G = {V,E}

Q.2 What are the storage representation of the graph ?

Ans. : The graph can be represented by using arrays or linked list.

1. The adjacency matrix is a storage representation of the graph by which the graph is stored in two dimensional arrays.
2. The adjacency list is a storage representation of a graph by which the graph is stored in linked list.

Q.3 What are the applications of graph ? **GTU : Summer-16**

Ans. : The graph theory is used widely in the computer science very widely. The applications of graph theory are -

1. In computer networking such as Local Area Network (LAN), Wide Area Networking (WAN) internetworking the graph is used.
2. In telephone cabling graph theory is effectively used.
3. In job scheduling algorithms the graph is used.

Q.4 What is the major difference between graph and tree ?

Ans. : Tree has a special node called root while graph does not have root node.

Q.5 When does a graph becomes a tree ?

Ans. : A graph becomes a tree when it contains an unique node which has no incoming(incident) edge but have all the outgoing edges. This node will become the root of the tree.

Remaining nodes of the graph have at the most one incoming edges(these will become the internal nodes).

There must be some nodes in the graph having no outgoing edge at all(these will then become the leaf nodes).

The graph should be connected.

Q.6 Explain degree of a vertex in a graph. GTU : Summer-16

Ans. : The degree of vertex is number of edges associated with the vertex.

Q.7 What is meant by adjacency matrix ?

Ans. : Adjacency matrix is a method of representation of a graph using two dimensional matrix. For example - If the edge is present between two vertices then the value in adjacency matrix is set to 1 otherwise 0.

Q.8 Define digraph.

Ans. : Digraph is a directed graph in which the directions are represented along the edges.

Q.9 What is depth first search in a graph ?

Ans : Depth first search is a traversal method of a graph in which the graph is visited in depth wise manner. The data structure stack is used for this type of traversal.

Q.10 How breadth depth first search and depth first search is implemented on a computer.

Ans. : The breadth first and depth first search is implemented using adjacency matrix or adjacency list.

Q.11 What is meant by minimum spanning tree ? GTU : Winter-16

Ans. : A minimum spanning tree is a spanning tree which has minimum weight and all the vertices of tree T are present in it but it may not contain all the edges.

Q.12 What do you mean by shortest path in a graph? What is the practical application ?

Ans. : The shortest path is the shortest distance between source and destination node of a graph. Shortest path is required to obtain Local Area Network (LAN) or Wide Area Network (WAN) wherein two computers are connected to each other.

Q.13 What is complete graph ?

Ans. : If an undirected graph of n vertices consists of n(n–1)/2 number of edges then that graph is called a complete graph.

Q.14 What is connected graph ?

Ans. : An undirected graph is said to be connected if for every pair of distinct vertices Vi and Vj in V(G) there is an edge Vi to Vj in G.

Q.15 What is cycle in graph ?

Ans. : A closed walk through the graph with repeated vertices mostly having same starting and ending vertex is called cycle.

Q.16 Give two applications of graphs. GTU : Winter-15

Ans. : Applications of graph - i) In computer networking for LAN, WAN design.
ii) In job scheduling algorithms.

Q.17 Degree of vertex. GTU : Winter-16

Ans. : The degree of vertex is the number of edges associated with the vertex.

Q.18 A graph containing only isolated nodes is called a ___. GTU : Summer-17

Ans. : Null Graph

❑❑❑

Notes

8 Hashing

Syllabus

The symbol table, Hashing functions, Collision - Resolution techniques.

Contents

8.1 The Symbol Table

- **Definition**

> The symbol table is defined as the set of **Name** and **Value** pairs.

For example

	Name	Value
0	a	10
1	b	0
2	c	0
3		
4		
5		
6		

Fig. 8.1.1 Symbol table storing 3 identifiers

- **Use of Symbol Table**

The symbol tables are typically used in **compilers**. Basically compiler is a program which scans the application program (for instance : your C program) and produces machine code. During this scan compiler stores the identifiers of that application program in the symbol table. These identifiers are stored in the form of name, value address, type. Here the name represents the name of identifier, value represents the value stored in an identifier, the address represents memory location of that identifier and type represents the data type of identifier. Thus compiler can keep track of all the identifiers with all the necessary information.

- **Types of Symbol Tables**

There are two types of symbol tables.

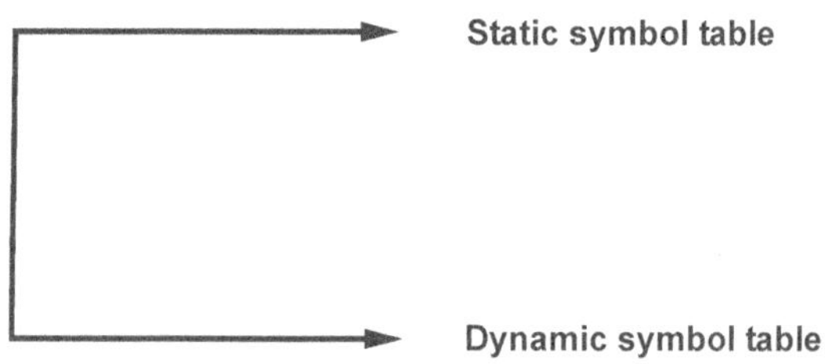

The static symbol table stores the fixed amount of information whereas dynamic symbol table stores the dynamic information.

These symbol tables are normally used to implement static and dynamic data structures. Hence there can be static tree tables or dynamic tree tables, which are implemented using static and dynamic symbol tables respectively.

Examples of static symbol table : Optimal Binary Search Tree (OBST), Huffman's coding can be implemented using static symbol table.

Example of dynamic symbol table : An AVL tree is implemented using dynamic symbol table.

- **Advantages of using Symbol Tables**

Following are some advantages of using symbol tables. As symbol table is normally used in compiler, these advantages are relevant to compilers -

1. During compilation of source program, **fast look up** for the required identifiers is possible due to use of symbol table.
2. The runtime allocation for the identifiers is managed using symbol tables.
3. Use of symbol table allows to handle certain issues like scope of identifiers, and implicit declarations.

- **Operations on Symbol Table**

Following operations can be performed on symbol table -

1. Insertion of an item in the symbol table.
2. Deletion of any item from the symbol table.
3. Searching of desired item from symbol table.

8.2 Concept of Hashing

GTU : Summer-13 Marks 2

- **Hash Table** is a data structure used for storing and retrieving data very quickly. Insertion of data in the hash table is based on the key value. Hence every entry in the hash table is associated with some key. For example for storing an employee record in the hash table the employee ID will work as a key.
- Using the **hash key** the required piece of data can be searched in the hash table by few or more key comparisons. The searching time is then dependant upon the size of the hash table.
- The effective representation of dictionary can be done using hash table. We can place the dictionary entries (key and value pair) in the hash table using hash function.

Review Question

1. *Define Hashing.* **GTU : Summer-13, Marks 2**

8.3 Hashing Functions

GTU : Dec.-10, Winter-12, 13, 14, 15, 17, 18, Summer-14, 18, Marks 7

- Hash function is a function which is used to put the data in the hash table. Hence one can use the same hash function to retrieve the data from the hash table. Thus hash function is used to implement the hash table.

- The integer returned by the hash function is called hash key.

For example : Consider that we want place some employee records in the hash table. The record of employee is placed with the help of key : employee ID. The employee ID is a 7 digit number for placing the record in the hash table. To place the record, the key 7 digit number is converted into 3 digits by taking only last three digits of the key.

If the key is 496700 it can be stored at 0th position. The second key is 8421002, the record of this key is placed at 2nd position in the array.

Hence the hash function will be –

H(key)=key%1000.

Where key%1000 is a hash function and key obtained by hash function is called hash key. The hash table will be –

	Employee ID	Record
0	4968000	
1		
2	7421002	
	•	•
	•	•
	•	•
	•	•
396	4618396	
397	4957397	
399	7886399	
	•	•
	•	•
	•	•
998	7886998	
999	0001999	

- **Bucket and Home bucket :** The hash function H(key) is used to map several dictionary entries in the hash table. Each position of the hash table is called bucket.

  The function H(key) is home bucket for the dictionary with pair whose value is *key*.

Types of Hash function –

There are various types of hash functions that are used to place the record in the hash table –

1. Division method : The hash function depends upon the remainder of division.

Typically the divisor is table length. For example :-

If the record 54, 72, 89, 37 is to be placed in the hash table and if the table size is 10 then

h(key) = record%table size

4 = 54 % 10

2 = 72 % 10

9 = 89 % 10

7 = 37 % 10

Index	Record
0	
1	
2	72
3	
4	54
5	
6	
7	37
8	
9	89

2. Mid square : In the mid square method, the key is squared and the middle or mid part of the result is used as the index.

If the key is a string, it has to be preprocessed to produce a number.

Consider that if we want to place a record 3111 then

$$3111^2 = 9678321$$

For the hash table of size 1000

H(3111) = 783 (the middle 3 digits)

3. Multiplicative hash function : The given record is multiplied by some constant value. The formula for computing the hash key is –

H(key)=floor(p *(fractional part of key*A)) where p is integer constant and A is constant real number.

Donald Knuth suggested to use constant A =0.61803398987

If key 107 and p=50 then

$$\begin{aligned} H(key) &= floor(50*(107*0.61803398987) \\ &= floor(3306.4818458045) \\ &= 3306 \end{aligned}$$

At 3306 location in the hash table the record 107 will be placed.

4. **Digit folding :** The key is divided into separate parts and using some simple operation these parts are combined to produce the hash key.

For example, consider a record 12365412 then it is divided into separate parts as 123 654 12 and these are added together

$$\begin{aligned} H(key) &= 123+654+12 \\ &= 789 \end{aligned}$$

The record will be placed at location 789 in the hash table.

5. **Digit analysis :** The digit analysis is used in a situation when all the identifiers are known in advance. We first transform the identifiers into numbers using some radix, r. Then we examine the digits of each identifier. Some digits having most skewed distributions are deleted. This deleting of digits is continued until the number of remaining digits is small enough to give an address in the range of the hash table. Then these digits are used to calculate the hash address.

Review Questions

1. *What do you mean by hashing ? What are various hash functions ? Explain each one in brief.* **GTU : Dec.-10, Marks 7**
2. *Explain different Hash function methods.* **GTU : Winter-12, Marks 7**
3. *What do you mean by Hashing ? Explain any FOUR hashing techniques.* **GTU : Winter-13, Summer-14, Marks 7**
4. *List out different hash methods and explain any three.* **GTU : Winter-14, Marks 7**
5. *What is hashing ? What are the qualities of a good hash function ? Explain any two hash functions in detail.* **GTU : Winter-15, Marks 7**
6. *How following has functions work ?*
   i) The midsquare method ii) Digit analysis **GTU : Winter-17, Marks 4**
7. *Explain two hash functions.* **GTU : Summer-18, Marks 4**
8. *What is hashing ? Explain different hashing techniques in brief.* **GTU : Winter-18, Marks 7**

8.4 Collision

GTU : Winter-15, Summer-18, Marks 7

Definition : *The situation in which the hash function returns the same hash key(home bucket) for more than one record is called collision and two same hash keys returned for different records is called synonym.*

Similarly when there is no room for a new pair in the hash table then such a situation is called overflow. Sometimes when we handle collision it may lead to overflow conditions. Collision and overflow show the poor hash functions.

For example :

Consider a hash function.

H(key) = recordkey%10 having the hash table of size 10.

The recordkeys to be placed are

131, 44, 43, 78, 19, 36, 57 and 77

0	
1	131
2	
3	43
4	44
5	
6	36
7	57
8	78
9	19

Now if we try to place 77 in the hash table then we get the hash key to be 7 and at index 7 already the recordkey 57 is place. This situation is called collision. From the index 7 if we look for next vacant passion at subsequent indices 8,9 then we find that there is no room to place 77 in the hash table. This situation is called overflow.

Characteristics of Good Hashing Function –

1. The hash function should be simple to compute.
2. Number of collisions should be less while placing the record in the hash table. Ideally no collision should occur. Such a function is called perfect hash function.
3. Hash functions should produce such a keys(buckets) which will get distributed uniformly over an array.
4. The hash function should depend upon every bit of the key. Thus the hash function that simply extracts the portion of a key is not suitable.

Review Questions

1. *What is hashing ? What are the qualities of a good hash function ? Explain any two hash functions in detail.* **GTU : Winter-15, Marks 7**
2. *Discuss various methods to resolve hash collision with suitable examples.* **GTU : Winter-15, Marks 7**
3. *List the qualities of a good has function.* **GTU : Summer-18, Marks 3**

8.5 Collision Resolution Techniques

GTU : May-11, 12, Summer-13, 15, 16, 17, 18, Winter-16, 17, 18, Marks 7

If collision occurs then it should be handled by applying some techniques. Such a technique is called **collision handling technique**.

There are two methods for detecting collisions and overflows in the hash table :

1. Chaining
2. Open addressing (linear probing)

Two more difficult collision handling techniques are –

1. Quadratic probing
2. Double hashing

8.5.1 Chaining

In collision handling method chaining is a concept which introduces an additional field with data i.e. chain. A separate chain table is maintained for colliding data. When collision occurs then a linked list(chain) is maintained at the home bucket.

For example :

Consider the keys to be placed in their home buckets are

131, 3, 4, 21, 61, 24, 7, 97, 8, 9

Then we will apply a hash function as

H(key) = key%D

where D is the size of table. The hash table will be -

Here D = 10.

A chain is maintained for colliding elements. For instace 131 has a home bucket (key) 1. Similarly keys 21 and 61 demand for home bucket 1. Hence a chain is maintained at index 1. Similarly the chain at index 4 and 7 is maintained.

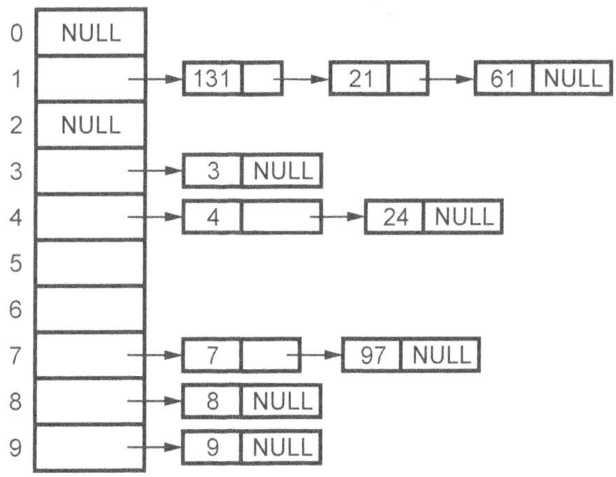

Fig. 8.5.1 Chaining

8.5.2 Open Addressing-Linear Probing

This is the easiest method of handling collision. When collision occurs i.e. when two records demand for the same home bucket in the hash table then collision can be solved by placing the second record linearly down whenever the empty bucket is found. When use linear probing(open addressing), the hash table is represented as a one-dimensional array with indices that range from 0 to the desired table size-1. Before inserting any elements into this table, we must initialize the table to represent the situation where all slots are empty. This allows us to detect overflows and collisions when we insert elements into the table. Then using some suitable hash function the element can be inserted into the hash table.

For example :

Consider that following keys are to be inserted in the hash table.

131, 4, 8, 7, 21, 5, 31, 61, 9, 29

Initially, we will put the following keys in the hash table.

131, 4, 8, 7.

We will use Division hash function. That means the keys are placed using the formula

H(key) = key%tablesize

H(key) = key%10

For instance the element 131 can be placed at

H(key) = 131%10

= 1

Index 1 will be the home bucket for 131. Continuing in this fashion we will place 4, 8 and 7.

Index	Key
0	NULL
1	131
2	NULL
3	NULL
4	4
5	NULL
6	NULL
7	7
8	8
9	NULL

Now the next key to be inserted is 21. According to the hash function

H(key) = 21%10

H(key) = 1.

But the index 1 location is already occupied by 131 i.e. collision occurs. To resolve this collision we will linearly move down and at the next empty location we will prob the element. Therefore 21 will be placed at the index 2. If the next element is 5 then we get the home bucket for 5 as index 5 and this bucket is empty so we will put the element 5 at index 5.

Index	Key
0	NULL
1	131
2	21
3	NULL
4	4
5	5
6	NULL
7	7
8	NULL
9	NULL

After placing record keys 31, 61 the hash table will be

Index	Key
0	NULL
1	131
2	21
3	31
4	4
5	5
6	61
7	7
8	8
9	NULL

The next recordkey that comes is 9. According to decision hash function it demands for the home bucket 9. Hence we will place 9 at index 9. Now the next final recordkey is 29 and it hashes a key 9. But home bucket 9 is already occupied. And there is no next empty bucket as the table size is limited to index 9. The overflow occurs. To handle it we move back to bucket 0 and is the location over there is empty 29 will be placed at 0th index.

Problem with linear probing

One major problem with linear probing is primary clustering. Primary clustering is a process in which a block of data is formed in the hash table when collision is resolved.

For example :

19 % 10 = 9

18 % 10 = 8

39 % 10 = 9

29 % 10 = 9

8 % 10 = 8

Index	Value	
0	39	cluster is formed
1	29	
2	8	
3		rest of the table is empty
4		
5		
6		
7		
8	18	
9	19	

This clustering problem can be solved by quadratic probing.

```
/*************************************************************
    Program to create hash table and handle the collision using linear probing. In this
Program hash function is (number %10)
*************************************************************/
#include<stdio.h>
#include<conio.h>
#include<stdlib.h>
#define MAX 10
void main()
{
 int a[MAX],num,key,i;
 char ans;
 int create(int);
 void linear_prob(int [],int,int),display(int []);
 clrscr();
 printf("\nCollision Handling By Linear Probing");
 for(i=0;i<MAX;i++)
  a[i]= -1;
 do
 {
  printf("\n Enter The Number");
  scanf("%d",&num);
  key=create(num);/*returns hash key*/
  linear_prob(a,key,num);/*collision handled by linear probing*/
```

```
 printf("\n Do U Wish To Continue?(y/n)");
 ans=getche();
}while(ans=='y');
display(a);/*displays hash table*/
getch();
}
int create(int num)
{
int key;
key=num%10;
return key;
}
void linear_prob(int a[MAX],int key,int num)
{
int flag,i,count=0;
void display(int a[]);
flag=0;
if(a[key]==-1)/*if the location indicated by hash key is empty*/
 a[key]=num;/*place the number in the hash table*/
else
{
 i=0;
 while(i<MAX)
 {
      if(a[i]!= -1)
           count++;
      i++;
 }
      if(count==MAX)        /*checking for the hash full*/
      {
       printf("\nHash Table Is Full");
       display(a);
       getch();
       exit(1);
       }
      for(i=key+1;i<MAX;i++)/*moving linearly down*/
       if(a[i]== -1)    /*searching for empty location*/
       {
        a[i]=num;  /*placing the number at empty location*/
        flag=1;
        break;
       }
/*From key position to the end of array we have searched empty location and now we
want to check empty location in the upper part of the array*/
      for(i=0;i<key&&flag==0;i++)/*array from 0th to keyth location will be scanned*/
      if(a[i]== -1)
      {
```

```
        a[i]=num;
        flag=1;
        break;
        }
 } /*outer else*/
} /*end*/
void display(int a[MAX])
{
 int i;
 printf("\n The Hash Table is...\n");
 for(i=0;i<MAX;i++)
  printf("\n %d   %d",i,a[i]);
}
```

Output

```
Collision Handling By Linear Probing
Enter The Number131
Do U Wish To Continue?(y/n)y
Enter The Number21
Do U Wish To Continue?(y/n)y
Enter The Number3
Do U Wish To Continue?(y/n)y
Enter The Number4
Do U Wish To Continue?(y/n)y
Enter The Number5
Do U Wish To Continue?(y/n)y
Enter The Number8
Do U Wish To Continue?(y/n)y
Enter The Number9
Do U Wish To Continue?(y/n)y
Enter The Number18
Do U Wish To Continue?(y/n)n
The Hash Table is...

 0  18
 1  131
 2  21
 3  3
 4  4
 5  5
 6  -1
 7  -1
 8  8
 9  9
```

8.5.3 Chaining without Replacement

In collision handling method chaining is a concept which introduces an additional field with data i.e. chain. A separate chain table is maintained for colliding data. When collision occurs we store the second colliding data by linear probing method. The address of this colliding data can be stored with the first colliding element in the chain table, without replacement.

For example consider elements,

131, 3, 4, 21, 61, 6, 71, 8, 9

Index	Data	Chain
0	–1	–1
1	131	2
2	21	5
3	3	–1
4	4	–1
5	61	7
6	6	–1
7	71	–1
8	8	–1
9	9	–1

Fig. 8.5.2 Chaining without replacement

From the example, you can see that the chain is maintained the number who demands for location 1. First number 131 comes we will place at index 1. Next comes 21 but collision occurs so by linear probing we will place 21 at index 2, and chain is maintained by writing 2 in chain table at index 1 similarly next comes 61 by linear probing we can place 61 at index 5 and chain will be maintained at index 2. Thus any element which gives hash key as 1 will be stored by linear probing at empty location but a chain is maintained so that traversing the hash table will be efficient.

The drawback of this method is in finding the next empty location. We are least bothered about the fact that when the element which actually belonging to that empty location cannot obtain its location. This means logic of hash function gets disturbed. Let us now see a 'C' program which implements chaining without replacement.

```
/*************************************************************
        Program to create hash table and handle the collision using chaining Without
replacement. In this Program hash function is (number%10)
*************************************************************/
#include<stdio.h>
#include<conio.h>
#include<stdlib.h>
#define MAX 10

void main()
{
 int a[MAX][2],num,key,i;
 char ans;
 int create(int);
 void chain(int [][2],int,int),display(int [][2]);

 clrscr();
 printf("\nChaining Without Replacement");
 for(i=0;i<MAX;i++)
 {
  a[i][0]= -1;
  a[i][1]= -1;
 }
 do
 {
  printf("\n Enter The Number");
  scanf("%d",&num);
  key=create(num); /*create hash key*/
  chain(a,key,num);
  printf("\n Do U Wish To Continue?(y/n)");
  ans=getche();
 }while(ans=='y');
 display(a);
 getch();
}

int create(int num)
{
 int key;
 key=num%10;
 return key;
}
void chain(int a[MAX][2],int key,int num)
{
 int flag,i,count=0,ch;
 void display(int a[][2]);
 flag=0;
```

```
 if(a[key][0]==-1)/*no collision case*/
  a[key][0]=num;
 else /*if collision occurs*/
 {
  ch=a[key][1];/*taking the chain*/
  /*If only one number in hash table with current obtained key*/
  if(ch== -1)
  {
        for(i=key+1;i<MAX;i++)/*performing linear probing*/
        {
         if(a[i][0]==-1) /*at immediate empty slot*/
         {
          a[i][0]=num;/*placing number*/
          a[key][1]=i; /*setting the chain*/
          flag=1;
          break;
         }
        }
  }
  /*if many numbers are already in the hash table
  we will find the next empty slot to place number*/
  else
  {
        while((a[ch][0]!=-1)&&(a[ch][1]!=-1))/*traversing
        through chain till empty slot is found*/
         ch=a[ch][1];
        for(i=ch+1;i<MAX;i++)
        {
         if(a[i][0]== -1)
         {
          a[i][0]=num;/*placing the number*/
          a[ch][1]=i; /*setting chain*/
          flag=1;
          break;
         }
        }
  }
/*      If the numbers are occupied somewhere from middle and are stored upto the MAX
then we will search for the empty slot upper half of the array
*/
if(flag!=1)
{
if(ch== -1)
  {
       for(i=0;i<key;i++)/*performing linear probing*/
       {
        if(a[i][0]==-1) /*at immediate empty slot*/
```

```
    {
     a[i][0]=num;/*placing number*/
     a[key][1]=i; /*setting the chain*/
     flag=1;
     break;
    }
   }
 }
 /*if many numbers are already in the hash table
 we will find the next empty slot to place number*/
 else
 {
   while((a[ch][0]!=-1)&&(a[ch][1]!=-1))/*traversing through chain till empty slot is
found*/
    ch=a[ch][1];
   for(i=ch+1;i<key;i++)
   {
    if(a[i][0]==-1)
    {
     a[i][0]=num;/*placing the number*/
     a[ch][1]=i; /*setting chain*/
     flag=1;
     break;
    }
   }
  }
 }
}
}
void display(int a[MAX][2])
{
 int i;
 printf("\n The Hash Table is...\n");
 for(i=0;i<MAX;i++)
   printf("\n %d   %d  %d",i,a[i][0],a[i][1]);
}
```

Output

```
Chaining Without Replacement
 Enter The Number 232

 Do U Wish To Continue?(y/n)y
 Enter The Number1

 Do U Wish To Continue?(y/n)y
 Enter The Number3

 Do U Wish To Continue?(y/n)y
 Enter The Number2
```

```
Do U Wish To Continue?(y/n)n
The Hash Table is...
                              0      - 1      - 1
                              1      1        - 1
                              2      232      4
                              3      3        - 1
                              4      2        - 1
                              5      - 1      - 1
                              6      - 1      - 1
                              7      - 1      - 1
                              8      - 1      - 1
                              9      - 1      - 1
```

8.5.4 Chaining with Replacement

As previous method has a drawback of loosing the meaning of the hash function, to overcome this drawback the method known as changing with replacement is introduced. Let us discuss the example to understand the method. Suppose we have to store following elements :

131, 21, 31, 4, 5

0	– 1	– 1
1	131	2
2	21	3
3	31	– 1
4	4	– 1
5	5	– 1
6		
7		
8		
9		

Now next element is 2. As hash function will indicate hash key as 2 but already at index 2. We have stored element 21. But we also know that 21 is not of that position at which currently it is placed.

Hence we will replace 21 by 2 and accordingly chain table will be updated. See the table :

Index	data	chain
0	– 1	– 1
1	131	6
2	2	– 1
3	31	– 1
4	4	– 1
5	5	– 1
6	21	3
7	– 1	– 1
8	– 1	– 1
9	– 1	– 1

The value –1 in the hash table and chain table indicate the empty location.

The advantage of this method is that the meaning of hash function is preserved. But each time some logic is needed to test the element, whether it is at its proper position.

```
/*************************************************************
    Program to create hash table and handle the collision using chaining With
replacement. In this Program hash function is (number%10)
*************************************************************/
#include<stdio.h>
#include<conio.h>
#include<stdlib.h>
#define MAX 10
int a[MAX][2];

void main()
{
 int num,key,i;
 char ans;
 int create(int);
 void chain(int,int),display();

 clrscr();
 printf("\nChaining With Replacement");
 for(i=0;i<MAX;i++)
 {
  a[i][0]= -1;
  a[i][1]= -1;
 }
 do
 {
  printf("\n Enter The Number");
```

```
  scanf("%d",&num);
  key=create(num); /*create hash key*/
  chain(key,num);
  printf("\n Do U Wish To Continue?(y/n)");
  ans=getche();
 }while(ans=='y');
 display();
 getch();
}

int create(int num)
{
 int key;
 key=num%10;
 return key;
}

void chain(int key,int num)
{
 int flag,i,count=0,ch,temp,j,prev_ch;
 void display();
 int match(int,int);
 flag=0;
/*checking full condition*/
  i=0;
  while(i<MAX)
  {
        if(a[i][0]!= -1)
                count++;
        i++;
  }
        if(count==MAX)
        {
         printf("\nHash Table Is Full");
         display();
         getch();
         exit(1);
         }
/*placing number otherwise*/
 if(a[key][0]== -1)/*no collision case*/
  a[key][0]=num;
 else
 {
  ch=a[key][1];
  if(match(a[key][0],num))
  {
        if(ch==-1)/*no chain*/
```

```
{
 for(i=key+1;i<MAX;i++)
      if(a[i][0]== -1)
      {
       a[i][0]=num;
       a[key][1]=i;
       flag=1;
       break;
      }
}
else
{
 while((a[ch][0]!= -1)&&(a[ch][1]!= -1))
 ch=a[ch][1];
for(i=ch+1;i<MAX;i++)
{
 if(a[i][0]==-1)
      {
       a[i][0]=num;
       a[ch][1]=i;
       flag=1;
       break;
      }
}
}
}
else                    /*unmatched*/
{
 if(ch== -1)
 {
  temp =a[key][0];
  for(i=key+1;i<MAX;i++)
      if(a[i][0]== -1)
      {
       a[key][0]=num;/*replacement is done*/
       a[i][0]=temp;
       for(j=0;j<MAX;j++)
        if(key==a[j][1])
                    a[j][1]=i;
                    flag=1;
       break;
      }
 }
 else /*chain exists*/
 {
  for(j=0;j<MAX;j++)
      if(key==a[j][1])
```

```
            prev_ch=j;
            temp=a[key][0];
            ch=key;
            while(a[ch][1]!=-1) /*traversal for continuos chain*/
            ch=a[ch][1];
            for(i=ch+1;i<MAX;i++)
             if(a[i][0]==-1)/*actual replacement*/
             {
                        a[i][0]=temp;
                        a[ch][1]=i;
                        a[key][0]=num;
                        a[prev_ch][1]=a[key][1];
                        a[key][1]=-1;
                        flag=1;
                        break;
             }
            }
        }
 if(flag!=1)
 {
    if(match(a[key][0],num))
 {
     if(ch==-1)/*no chain*/
     {
      for(i=0;i<key;i++)
        if(a[i][0]==-1)
        {
         a[i][0]=num;
         a[key][1]=i;
         flag=1;
         break;
        }
     }
     else
     {
      while((a[ch][0]!=-1)&&(a[ch][1]!=-1))
      ch=a[ch][1];
     for(i=0;i<key;i++)
     {
      if(a[i][0]==-1)
        {
         a[i][0]=num;
         a[ch][1]=i;
         flag=1;
         break;
        }
     }
```

```
        }
        }
        else                    /*unmatched*/
        {
         if(ch==-1)
         {
          temp =a[key][0];
          for(i=0;i<key;i++)
                if(a[i][0]==-1)
                {
                 a[key][0]=num;/*replacement is done*/
                 a[i][0]=temp;
                 for(j=0;j<MAX;j++)
                  if(key==a[j][1])
                                a[j][1]=i;
                                flag=1;
                 break;
                }
         }
         else /*chain exists*/
         {
          for(j=0;j<MAX;j++)
        if(key==a[j][1])
        prev_ch=j;
        temp=a[key][0];
        ch=key;
        while(a[ch][1]!=-1) /*traversal for continuos chain*/
                ch=a[ch][1];
                for(i=0;i<key;i++)
                 if(a[i][0]==-1)/*actual replacement*/
                  {
                                a[i][0]=temp;
                                a[ch][1]=i;
                                a[key][0]=num;
                                a[prev_ch][1]=a[key][1];
                                a[key][1]=-1;
                                flag=1;
                                break;



                }
                                        }
                                }
                        }
                    }
                }
```

```
int match(int prev,int num)
{
 if(create(num)==create(prev))
       return 1;
 return 0;
}
void display()
{
 int i;
 printf("\n The Hash Table is...\n");
 for(i=0;i<MAX;i++)
       printf("\n %d   %d  %d",i,a[i][0],a[i][1]);
}
```

Output

```
Chaining With Replacement
Enter The Number232

Do U Wish To Continue?(y/n)y
Enter The Number21

Do U Wish To Continue?(y/n)y
Enter The Number31

Do U Wish To Continue?(y/n)y
Enter The Number41

Do U Wish To Continue?(y/n)y
Enter The Number3

Do U Wish To Continue?(y/n)n
The Hash Table is...
                    0     -1     -1
                    1     21      4
                    2    232     -1
                    3      3     -1
                    4     41      5
                    5     31     -1
                    6     -1     -1
                    7     -1     -1
                    8     -1     -1
                    9     -1     -1
```

8.5.5 Quadratic Probing

Quadratic probing operates by taking the original hash value and adding successive values of an arbitrary quadratic polynomial to the starting value. This method uses following formula –

$$H_i(key) = (Hash(key)+i^2)\%m$$

where m can be a table size or any prime number.

For example : If we have to insert following elements in the hash table with table size 10 :

37, 90, 55, 22, 17, 49, 87.

We will fill the hash table step by step

37 % 10 = 7

90 % 10 = 0

55 % 10 = 5

22 % 10 = 2

11 % 10 = 1

Index	Value
0	90
1	11
2	22
3	
4	
5	55
6	
7	37
8	
9	

Now if we want to place 17 a collision will occur as 17 % 10 = 7 and bucket 7 has already an element 37. Hence we will apply quadratic probing to insert this record in the hash table.

$$H_i(key) = (Hash(key) + i^2)\%\ m$$

Consider $i = 0$ then

$(17+0^2)\ \%\ 10 = 7$

$(17+1^2)\ \%\ 10 = 8$, When $i = 1$

The bucket 8 is empty hence we will place the element at index 8.

Then comes 49 which will be placed at index 9.

49 % 10 = 9

Index	Value
0	90
1	
2	22
3	
4	
5	55
6	
7	37
8	17
9	49

Fig. 8.5.3

Now to place 87 we will use quadratic probing.

Index	Value
0	90
1	11
2	22
3	
4	
5	55
6	87
7	37
8	17
9	49

Fig. 8.5.4

$(87 + 0)\%10 = 7$

$(87 + 1)\%10 = 8$ ... but already occupied

$(87 + 2^2)\%10 = 1$ ... already occupied

$(87 + 3^2)\%10 = 6$

It is observed that if we want to place all the necessary elements in the hash table the size of divisor (m) should be twice as large as total number of elements.

8.5.6 Double Hashing

Double hashing is technique in which a second hash function is applied to the key when a collision occurs. By applying the second hash function we will get the number of positions from the point of collision to insert.

There are two important rules to be followed for the second function :

- It must never evaluate to zero.
- Must make sure that all cells can be probed.

The formula to be used for double hashing is

$$H_1(\text{key}) = \text{key mod tablesize}$$

$$H_2(\text{ key }) = M - (\text{ key mod } M)$$

where M is a prime number smaller than the size of the table.

Consider the following elements to be placed in the hash table of size 10.

37, 90, 45, 22, 17, 49, 55

Initially insert the elements using the formula for $H_1(\text{key})$.

Insert 37, 90, 45, 22.

$H_1(37) = 37 \% 10 = 7$

$H_1(90) = 90 \% 10 = 0$

$H_1(45) = 45 \% 10 = 5$

$H_1(22) = 22 \% 10 = 2$

$H_1(49) = 49 \% 10 = 9$

0	90
1	
2	22
3	
4	
5	45
6	
7	37
8	
9	49

Now if 17 is to be inserted then

$$H_1(17) = 37 \% 10 = 7$$

$$H_2(\text{key}) = M - (\text{key} \% M)$$

0	90
1	17
2	22
3	
4	
5	45
6	
7	37
8	
9	49

Fig. 8.5.5

Here M is a prime number smaller than the size of the table. Prime number smaller than table size 10 is 7.

$$\text{Hence } M = 7$$

$$H_2(17) = 7 - (17\%7) = 7 - 3 = 4$$

That means we have to insert the element 17 at 4 places from 37. In short we have to take 4 jumps. Therefore the 17 will be placed at index 1.

Now to insert number 55.

$$H_1(55) = 55\%10=5 \quad \text{... collision}$$

$$H_2(55) = 7 - (55\%7) = 7 - 6 = 1$$

That means we have to take one jump from index 5 to place 55. Finally the hash table will be –

0	90
1	17
2	22
3	
4	
5	45
6	55
7	37
8	
9	49

Comparison of quadratic probing and double hashing

The double hashing requires another hash function whose probing efficiency is same as some another hash function required when handling random collision.

The double hashing is more complex to implement than quadratic probing. The quadratic probing is fast technique than double hashing.

8.5.7 Rehashing

Rehashing is a technique in which the table is resized, i.e., the size of table is doubled by creating a new table. It is preferable if the total size of table is a prime number. There are situations in which the rehashing is required-

- When table is completely full.
- With quadratic probing when the table is filled half.
- When insertions fail due to overflow.

In such situations, we have to transfer entries from old table to the new table by recomputing their positions using suitable hash functions.

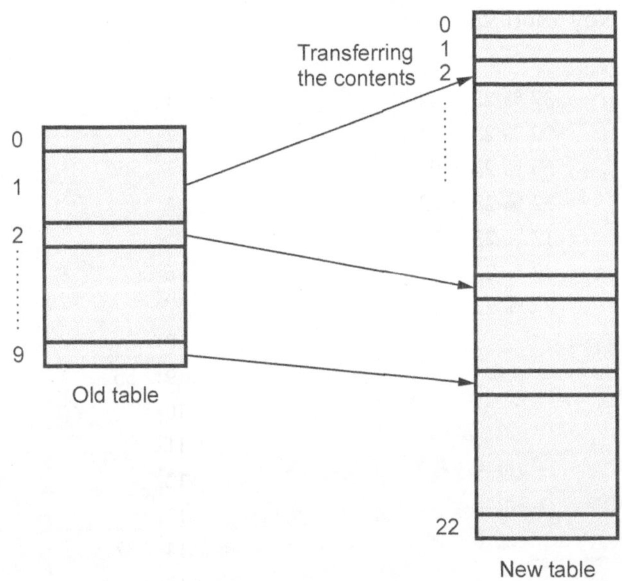

Fig. 8.5.6 Rehashing

Consider we have to insert the elements 37, 90, 55, 22, 17, 49 and 87. The table size is 10 and will use hash function,

$$H(key) = key \bmod tablesize$$

37 % 10 = 7

90 % 10 = 0

55 % 10 = 5

22 % 10 = 2

17 % 10 = 7 Collision solved by linear probing, by placing it at 8

49 % 10 = 9

Index	Value
0	90
1	
2	22
3	
4	
5	55
6	
7	37
8	17
9	49

Now this table is almost full and if we try to insert more elements collisions will occur and eventually further insertions will fail. Hence we will rehash by doubling the table size. The old table size is 10 then we should double this size for new table, that becomes 20. But 20 is not a prime number, we will prefer to make the table size as 23. And new hash function will be

H(key) = key mod 23

37 % 23 = 14

90 % 23 = 21

55 % 23 = 9

22 % 23 = 22

17 % 23 = 17

49 % 23 = 3

87 % 23 = 18

Index	Value
0	
1	
2	
3	49
4	
5	
6	
7	
8	
9	55
10	
11	
12	
13	
14	37
15	
16	
17	17
18	87
19	
20	
21	90
22	22

Now the hash table is sufficiently large to accommodate new insertions.

Advantages

1. This technique provides the programmer a flexibility to enlarge the table size if required.
2. Only the space gets doubled with simple hash function which avoids occurrence of collisions.

Example 8.5.1 *The keys 12, 18, 13, 2, 3, 23, 5 and 15 are inserted into an initially empty hash table of length 10 using open addressing with hash function h(k) = k mod 10 and linear probing. What is the resultant hash table ?* **GTU : Summer-13, Marks 7**

Solution : Given data :

The hash function is h(k) = k mod 10

Hash table length = 10

12 % 10 = 2
18 % 10 = 8
13 % 10 = 3
2 % 10 = 2
Collision occurs
∴ By linear probing
Move down and place 2 at index 4.
3 % 10 = 3 ← Collision
23 % 10 = 3 ← Collision
5 % 10 = 5 ← Collision
15 % 10 = 5 ← Collision

Index	Hash Table
0	
1	
2	12
3	13
4	2
5	3
6	23
7	5
8	18
9	15

Hash Table

Review Questions

1. *What is hashing ? Explain hash clash and its resolving techniques.* **GTU : May-11, Marks 7**
2. *Define hash clash. Explain primary clustering, secondary clustering, rehashing, and double hashing.* **GTU : May-11, Marks 7**
3. *Explain the basic two techniques for Collision-resolution in Hashing with example. Also explain primary clustering.* **GTU : May-12, Marks 5**
4. *Describe various collision resolution techniques in hashing.* **GTU : Summer-15, Marks 7**
5. *Explain various hash collision resolution techniques with examples.* **GTU : Summer-16, Marks 7**
6. *Discuss variou rehashing techniques.* **GTU : Winter-16, Marks 4**

7. *How open addressing can be used for collision resolution ?* **GTU : Summer-17, Marks 4**

8. *Hash function map several keys into same address called collision. How collision resolution techniques work ?* **GTU : Winter-17, Marks 7**

9. *What is hashing ? Explain hash collision and any one collision resolution technique.* **GTU : Summer-18, Marks 4**

10. *What is hashing ? Explain hash clash and its resolving techniques.* **GTU : Winter-18, Marks 7**

8.6 Applications of Hashing

1. In compilers to keep track of declared variables.
2. For online spelling checking the hashing functions are used.
3. Hashing helps in Game playing programs to store the moves made.
4. For browser program while caching the web pages, hashing is used.

8.7 Oral Questions and Answers

Q.1 What is symbol table ?

Ans. : The symbol table is defined as the set of Name and Value pairs.

Q.2 What is the use of symbol table ?

Ans. : The symbol tables are typically used in compilers. During the complete scan of program the compiler stores the identifiers of that application program in the symbol table.

Q.3 What are the types of symbol table ?

Ans. : There are two types of symbol tables -1. Static symbol table 2. Dynamic symbol table.

The static symbol table stores the fixed amount of information whereas dynamic symbol table stores the dynamic information.

Q.4 Give examples of static symbol table and dynamic symbol table.

Ans. : Examples of static symbol table : Optimal Binary Search Tree (OBST), Huffman's coding can be implemented using static symbol table.

Example of dynamic symbol table : An AVL tree is implemented using dynamic symbol table.

Q.5 What are the advantages of using symbol table ?

Ans. :

1. During compilation of source program, fast look up for the required identifiers is possible due to use of symbol table.

2. The runtime allocation for the identifiers is managed using symbol tables.
3. Use of symbol table allows to handle certain issues like scope of identifiers, and implicit declarations.

Q.6 What are the operations that can be performed on symbol table ?

Ans. : Following operations can be performed on symbol table -

1. Insertion of an item in the symbol table.
2. Deletion of any item from the symbol table.
3. Searching of desired item from symbol table.

Q.7 What is hash table ?

Ans. : Hash Table is a data structure used for storing and retrieving data very quickly. Insertion of data in the hash table is based on the key value.

Q.8 What is hash function ?

Ans. : Hash function is a function which is used to put the data in the hash table. Hence one can use the same hash function to retrieve the data from the hash table. Thus hash function is used to implement the hash table.

Q.9 What is hash key ?

Ans. : The integer returned by the hash function is called hash key.

Q.10 Enlist various hash functions used.

Ans. : 1. Division Method 2. Mid Square Method 3. Multiplicative Hash Function 4. Digit Folding

Q.11 What is hash collision ? **GTU : Summer-16, Winter-16**

Ans. : The situation in which the hash function returns the same hash key(home bucket) for more than one record is called collision.

Q.12 State any two characteristics of good hash function.

Ans. :

1. The hash function should be simple to compute.
2. Number of collisions should be less while placing the record in the hash table. Ideally no collision should occur. Such a function is called perfect hash function.
3. Hash functions should produce such a keys(buckets) which will get distributed uniformly over an array.

Q.13 Enlist the commonly used collision handling techniques.

Ans. : 1. Chaining 2. Open addressing (linear probing) 3. Quadratic probing 4. Double hashing

Q.14 What is linear probing ?

Ans. : When collision occurs i.e. when two records demand for the same home bucket in the hash table then collision can be solved by placing the second record linearly down whenever the empty bucket is found.This technique is called linear probing

Q.15 What is double hashing ?

Ans. : Double hashing is technique in which a second hash function is applied to the key when a collision occurs. By applying the second hash function we will get the number of positions from the point of collision to insert.

Q.16 What is rehashing ?

Ans. : Rehashing is a technique in which the table is resized, i.e., the size of table is doubled by creating a new table. It is preferable if the total size of table is a prime number.

Q.17 List out the applications of hashing.

Ans. :

1. In compilers to keep track of declared variables.
2. For online spelling checking the hashing functions are used.
3. For browser program while caching the web pages, hashing is used.

Q.18 Write two simple hash functions. **GTU : Winter-15**

Ans. : (1) Mid Square Function (2) Division Method

Q.19 What is the 2's complement representation for integer 5 in modulo 16 ? **GTU : Summer-17**

Ans. : We will express integer 5 as modulo 16 number. It is as follows.

Step 1 : 16 mod 5 = 5

Step 2 : 16 + (16 mod 5) = 16 + 5 = 21

Step 3 : 21 = $(10101)_2$

Q.20 What is the result of 7 + 7 using 2's complement representation and modulo 16 arithmetic ? **GTU : Summer-17**

Ans. : $7 + 7 = (0111)_2 + (0111)_2 = (1110)_2 = -2$

Q.21 What is the problem with sign and magnitude representation if addition of +7 with – 6 is performed ? Evaluate 7 + 7 using 2's complement representation and modulo 16 arithmetic. **GTU : Winter-17**

Ans. : The major disadvantages of sign an magnitude representation is that operation to be performed may often depend on the signs of the operands. The sign and magnitude representation requires to frequently compare both the signs and magnitudes of the operands.

Evaluation of 7 + 7 - Refer Q.1 (5) of Summer 2017.

❑❑❑

9 File Structure

Syllabus

Concepts of fields, Records and files, Sequential, Indexed and relative/random file organization, Indexing structure for index files, Hashing for direct files, Multi-key file organization and access methods.

Contents

9.1 Concepts of Fields, Records and File

GTU : Winter-14, Marks 7

A **file** is a collection of records. **Record** is nothing but the source of information. It typically stored in rows in the file structure. **Field** is a piece of data which is associated with the entire record. It is refered as column.

For example : Assume that we have a file "Student.dat" having the contents as follows -

Roll No.	Name	Marks
1	John	66
2	Mathew	70
3	Steve	60

So by observing above file, we can say that this file is a collection of 3 records. These records can be written in File with the associated fields such as Roll_No, Name and Marks. To identify each record, a unique key is associated with it. In above file **Roll_No** can be thought of as a **key**. Using a key we can access information from file. We must choose unique field as a key. This key is called the primary key of file.

University Question

1. *Explain file in terms of fields, records and database.* **GTU : Winter-14, Marks 7**

9.2 Operations on File

1. Declaration of file Pointer :

Syntax: - FILE *filepointer;

Example : FILE *fp;

FILE is a structure which is defined in "stdio.h". Each file we open will have its own FILE structure. The structure contains information like usage of the file, its size, memory location and so on. The fp is a pointer variable which contains the address of the structure FILE.

2. Creating a file / Opening a file :

Syntax : filepointer = fopen("filename","mode");

where filename is the name of file you want to create or open

mode can be – read - "r"

write - "w"

append - "a"

Depending on the type of file we want to open/create we use –"rb", "wb", or just "r", "w", "a".

Using "r" opens the file in read mode. If the file does not exist, it will create a new file, but such a file created is of no use as you cannot write to any file in read mode.

Using "r+" allows to read from file as well as write to the file.

Using "w" opens a file in write mode. If the file does not exist, it will create a new file.

Using "w+" allows you to write contents to file, read them as well as modify existing contents.

Using "a" opens the file in append mode. If the file does not exist, then it creates a new file. Opening a file in append mode allows you to append new contents at the end of the file.

Using "a+" allows to append a file, read existing records, cannot modify existing records.

Example :

```
fp = fopen("Student.dat","w");
```

3. Closing the file :

Syntax : fclose(filepointer);

Example :

```
fclose(fp);  /* closes the file pointed by the fp */
```

4. Setting the pointer to start of file :

Syntax : rewind(filepointer);

Example :

```
rewind(fp);  /* places pointer at the start of the file */
```

5. Writing a character to file :

Syntax: fputc(character, filepointer);

Example :

Suppose we have

```
char ch='a';
```

To write the character to the file, we use

```
fputc(ch,fp);
```

Note If the file is opened in "w" mode, it will overwrite the contents of the entire file and write the only character we want to write. To write it at the end of the file, open the file in "a+" mode.

6. Reading a character from file :

Syntax : fgetc(filepointer);

Example :

```
char ch;  /* ch is the character where you are going to get the char
  from file*/
          ch = fgetc(fp);
```

7. Writing string to file:

Syntax : fputs(string, filepointer);

Example :

Suppose you have a string

```
char s[] ="abcd";
```

then we write as

```
fputs(s,fp);
```

The above operation writes the string "abcd" to the file pointed by fp.

8. Reading string from file:

Syntax: fgets(stringaddress, length, filepointer);

Example :

```
char s[80]; /* declared a string into which we want  to read the
               string from file */
fgets(s,79,fp);  /* Will read the 78, (79–1) characters of string from
               file into s */
```

9. Writing of characters, strings, integers,floats to file :

Syntax:

fprintf(filepointer, "format string", list of variables);

We are already aware of the printf function. fprintf has the same arguments as that of printf, addition to which filepointer is added. The variables included in the fprintf are written to the file. But how can we write the data without knowing their values, so we need to have a scanf function before it and then can write the data to file. You will understand this better by following example.

'C' Program

```
/****************************************************************
    Program for introducing the file premitives such as
    fopen,fclose,fprintf.
****************************************************************/
#include<stdio.h>
/*
The main Function
Input:none
Output:none
Called By:O.S.
*/
main()
{
FILE *fp;
int rno;
char name[20];
clrscr();

fp = fopen("Student.dat","w");
if(fp==NULL)
{
printf("File opening error");
exit(1);
}
printf("Enter the rollno and name:");
scanf("%d %s",&rno,&name);        /* asking user to enter data */
fprintf(fp,"%d %s",&rno,&name);  /* writing data to file */

fclose(fp);
getch();
return;
}
/**********************End Of Program**********************/
```

Output

```
Enter the rollno and name:
1
aaa
                  student.dat
1 aaa
```

10. Reading of variables from file :

Syntax:

fscanf(filepointer,"format string",list of addresses of variables);

Having similar arguments as that of the fprintf statement, the fscanf reads the contents of the file into the variables specified.

Example :

fscanf(fp,"%d %s",&rno,&name);

printf("Read data is: %d %s",rno,name);

Note *The fprintf and fscanf statements are useful only when the data we want to enter is less, or rather they have disadvantage that when the number of variables increase, writing them or reading them becomes clumsy.*

11. Writing contents to file through structure :

Syntax : fwrite(pointer to struct,sizeof struct,no.of data items,filepointer);

'C' Program

```
/*****************************************************************
Program for file primitives such as fopen,fwrite.This program writes the string to the file.

*****************************************************************/
#include<stdio.h>
#define MAX 20
struct stud  /* structure declaration */
{
 int rno;
 char name[MAX];
};
/*
The main Function
Input :none
Output:none
*/
main()
{
struct stud s;
FILE *fp;
clrscr();
s.rno=1;            /* fill the structure contents*/
strcpy(s.name,"Sachin");
fp = fopen("Student.dat","w");
if(fp==NULL)
{
printf("File opening error");
exit(1);
}

fwrite(&s,sizeof(s),1,fp);  /* write the structure contents to file*/
fclose(fp);
```

```
return;
}
/********************End of Program*************************/
```

Output –student.dat

Sachin 0 ≅ + ÛI□2

Thus we can see from the output of the program that fwrite writes the data in the file in binary mode.

12. Reading contents of file through structure :

Syntax : fread(pointer to struct,sizeof struct, no.of data items, filepointer);

Example :

To read the contents written in file we can have:-

fread(&s,sizeof(s),1,fp);

Note *Prior to this statement it is necessary that the pointer is located at the proper position from where we want to read the file. Here you can use the rewind(filepointer) function.*

An fread or fwrite function moves the pointer to the beginning of the next record in that file.

13. Moving the pointer from one record to another :

Syntax: fseek(filepointer, offset, whence);

where

offset is difference in bytes between offset and whence position.

whence can be:

1) SEEK_SET move the pointer with reference to beginning of the file.
2) SEEK_CUR move the pointer with reference to its current position in file.
3) SEEK_SET move the pointer from end of file.

Example :

Let us take the example where we have written a record in file. Suppose we want to read that record, we have two options :

1) To use rewind function. 2) To use fseek.

We can use fseek in following fashion:

prior to the fclose(fp), we can have

fseek(fp,-sizeof(s),SEEK_CUR);

This will place the pointer to the beginning of the record we have currently written.Then we can make use of fread(...) to read that record again.

9.3 Types of Files

There are three types of file organizations -

1. Sequential file
2. Indexed file
3. Random file

Let us discuss them in detail.

9.4 Sequential Files

GTU : Summer-16,17, Marks 7

To understand the sequential files, lets start with an example. Consider the example of a tape or rather a cassette where the songs are stored sequentially. Whenever we want to play any song from it, we read it sequentially. Storing data sequentially is the simplest form of file, but a tedious one. Reading data to a file or writing data from it takes a lot of time as the data is not sorted. The data is stored on FCFS basis. Taking example where we want to retrieve a record which is unfortunately stored at the last position in the file requires to search the entire file. Hence the time required is very large in this case.

'C' Program

```
/*********************************************************************
Implementation of various file operations such as create, display, search and modification
on student database with USN,Name and marks of three subjects
*********************************************************************/
#include<stdio.h>
#include<stdlib.h>
#include<string.h>
#include<conio.h>
struct record
{
 int USN;
 char name[20];
 int marks1,marks2,marks3;
};
struct record r;
FILE *fp;
void main()
{
 int n,choice;
 char ch;
 void Create_file(int);
```

```
void Display_file(int);
void Modify_file();
struct record *Search_file();
clrscr();
printf("\n How many Records are there in the file?");
scanf("%d",&n);
do
{
 clrscr();
 printf("\n\t Main Menu");
 printf("\n1. Create a file");
 printf("\n2. Display a file");
 printf("\n3. Search a file");
 printf("\n4. Modify a file");
 printf("\n5. Exit");
 printf("\n Enter Your Choice ");
 scanf("%d",&choice);
 switch(choice)
 {
     case 1:Create_file(n);
            break;
     case 2:Display_file(n);
            break;
     case 3:r=*Search_file();
          printf("\n USN      Name      marks1  marks2   marks3\n");
          printf("\n-------------------------------------------\n");
          flushall();
     printf(" %d    %s       %d    %d   %d \n",r.USN,r.name,r.marks1, r.marks2,r.marks3);
          printf("\n-------------------------------------------\n");
        break;
     case 4:Modify_file();
            break;
     case 5:exit(0);
 }
 printf("\n Do You want To Continue?");
 ch=getch();
}while(ch=='y'||ch=='Y');
getch();
}
void Create_file(int n)
{
      int i;
      fp=fopen("stud.dat","a+");
      for (i=0;i<n; i++)
      {
            printf("\n Enter The name of the student ");
            flushall();
```

```
            gets(r.name);
            printf("\n Enter University Seat Number ");
            scanf("%d",&r.USN);
            printf("\n Enter marks for First Subject ");
            scanf("%d",&r.marks1);
            printf("\n Enter marks for second Subject ");
            scanf("%d",&r.marks2);
            printf("\n Enter marks for Third Subject ");
            scanf("%d",&r.marks3);
            fwrite(&r,sizeof(struct record),1,fp);
      }
      fclose(fp);
}

void Display_file(int n)
{
 int i;
 printf("\nReading all the records sequentially\n");
 fp=fopen("stud.dat","r");
 printf("\n USN       Name       marks1   marks2  marks3\n");
 printf("\n-------------------------------------------------\n");
 for (i=0;i<n; i++)
 {
      fread(&r,sizeof(struct record),1,fp);
      flushall();
      printf(" %d       %s          %d       %d       %d
      \n",r.USN,r.name,r.marks1,r.marks2,r.marks3);
 }
 printf("\n-------------------------------------------------\n");
 fclose(fp);
}

void Modify_file()
{
 int i;
 int key,new_USN,new_marks1,new_marks2,new_marks3;
 char new_name[20];
 printf("Modifying the desired record");
 printf("\n Enter the University Seat Number for modification of
 record ");
 scanf("%d",&key);
 fp=fopen("stud.dat","r+");
 i=0;
 while(!feof(fp))
 {
      fread(&r,sizeof(struct record),1,fp);
      if(r.USN==key)
```

```
      {
            fseek(fp,sizeof(struct record)*i,SEEK_SET);
            printf("\n Enter the new record");
            printf("\n Enter new name ");
            flushall();
            gets(new_name);
            printf("\n Enter New USN ");
            scanf("%d",&new_USN);
            printf("\n Enter new marks1 ");
            scanf("%d",&new_marks1);
            printf("\n Enter new marks2 ");
            scanf("%d",&new_marks2);
            printf("\n Enter new marks3 ");
            scanf("%d",&new_marks3);
            r.USN=new_USN;
            strcpy(r.name,new_name);
            r.marks1=new_marks1;
            r.marks2=new_marks2;
            r.marks3=new_marks3;
            fseek(fp,sizeof(struct record)*i,SEEK_SET);
            fwrite(&r,sizeof(struct record),1,fp);
      }
      i++;
 }
 fclose(fp);
}

struct record *Search_file()
{
 int key,i;
 printf("\n Enter the University Seat Number for Searching the record ");
 scanf("%d",&key);
 fp=fopen("stud.dat","r+");
 i=0;
 while(!feof(fp))
 {
      fread(&r,sizeof(struct record),1,fp);
      if(r.USN==key)
      {
            fseek(fp,sizeof(struct record)*i,SEEK_SET);
            fclose(fp);
            return &r;
      }
      i++;
 }
 printf("\n The Record is not present ");
```

```
return NULL;
}
```

Output

```
How many Records are there in the file?5
        Main Menu
1. Create a file
2. Display a file
3. Search a file
4. Modify a file
5. Exit

Enter Your Choice 1
Enter The name of the student aaa
Enter University Seat Number 1
Enter marks for First Subject 40
Enter marks for second Subject 50
Enter marks for Third Subject 60
Enter The name of the student bbb
Enter University Seat Number 2
Enter marks for First Subject 55
Enter marks for second Subject 66
Enter marks for Third Subject 77
Enter The name of the student ccc
Enter University Seat Number 3
Enter marks for First Subject 99
Enter marks for second Subject 44
Enter marks for Third Subject 70
Enter The name of the student ddd
Enter University Seat Number 4
Enter marks for First Subject 45
Enter marks for second Subject 65
Enter marks for Third Subject 76
Enter The name of the student eee
Enter University Seat Number 5
Enter marks for First Subject 32
Enter marks for second Subject 43
Enter marks for Third Subject 40
Do You want To Continue?

        Main Menu
        1. Create a file
        2. Display a file
        3. Search a file
        4. Modify a file
        5. Exit
         Enter Your Choice 2
```

```
Reading all the records sequentially

USN Name       marks1    marks2    marks3
-----------------------------------------------------------
1    aaa     40        50        60
2    bbb     55        66        77
3    ccc     99        44        70
4    ddd     45        65        76
5    eee     32        43        40
-----------------------------------------------------------
Do You want To Continue?
    Main Menu
1. Create a file
2. Display a file
3. Search a file
4. Modify a file
5. Exit
Enter Your Choice 3

Enter the University Seat Number for Searching the record 4

USN   Name    marks1  marks2  marks3
-----------------------------------------------------------
4    ddd    45     65    76
-----------------------------------------------------------
Do You want To Continue?
    Main Menu
1. Create a file
2. Display a file
3. Search a file
4. Modify a file
5. Exit
Enter Your Choice 4
Modifying the desired record
Enter the University Seat Number for modification of record 3
Enter the new record
Enter new name XYZ
Enter New USN 50
Enter new marks1 55
Enter new marks2 66
Enter new marks3 77
Do You want To Continue?
    Main Menu
1. Create a file
2. Display a file
3. Search a file
4. Modify a file
```

```
        5. Exit
         Enter Your Choice 2
        Reading all the records sequentially
         USN       Name          marks1    marks2    marks3
-------------------------------------------------------------------------------
         1          aaa   40      50        60
         2          bbb   55      66        77
         50         XYZ   55      66        77
         4          ddd   45      65        76
         5          eee   32      43        40
-------------------------------------------------------------------------------
 Do You want To Continue?
        Main Menu
        1. Create a file
        2. Display a file
        3. Search a file
        4. Modify a file
        5. Exit
         Enter Your Choice 5
```

Advantage of sequential file:

Sequential files are very simple to manage.

Disadvantages of sequential file:

1. Time required to retrieve any record is more as the entire file is searched.
2. Efficiency is less.

Owing to these drawbacks let us start with other file which will overcome these drawbacks.

Review Questions

1. *Explain the sequential file organization.*
2. *Write a C program for implementing the sequential file organization.*
3. *Explain sequential file organizations and list its advantages and disadvantages.*

   GTU : Summer-16, Marks 3

4. *Explain structure of sequential file. Explain processing in sequential file.*

   GTU : Summer-17, Marks 7

9.5 Indexed Sequential File

GTU : May-12, Winter-12,17, Summer-13,14,17, Marks 7

Since we are clear with sequential files, lets now got to other type which is 'Indexed Sequential' file format. There are many advantages of using an 'indexed sequential' over a normal sequential. Firstly, in an indexed sequential format, we maintain two files - 1. Normal sequential file and 2. An sorted index file.

What ever is our data we store it in the sequential file and in the index file we have the id or say the primary key of the sequential file along with the offset of that particular record in the sequential file.

To be more precise lets take the following example:

We have to maintain grossery details, where in the sequential file we have

itemno. name price type

To refer to any item if we were using normal sequential file, we would have to scan the entire file to find that particular item details. But with the indexed sequential we have another index file which will in this case contain

itemno.offset

Another example is of students database the main file will have **Roll, Name, Age, Marks,** and the index file will have **Roll offset.**

This will be in sorted format for the index file. Hence whenever we are referring to any record, first the index file will be searched. From that search the offset is retrieved and the required record can be seek from the sequential file. See Fig. 9.5.1.

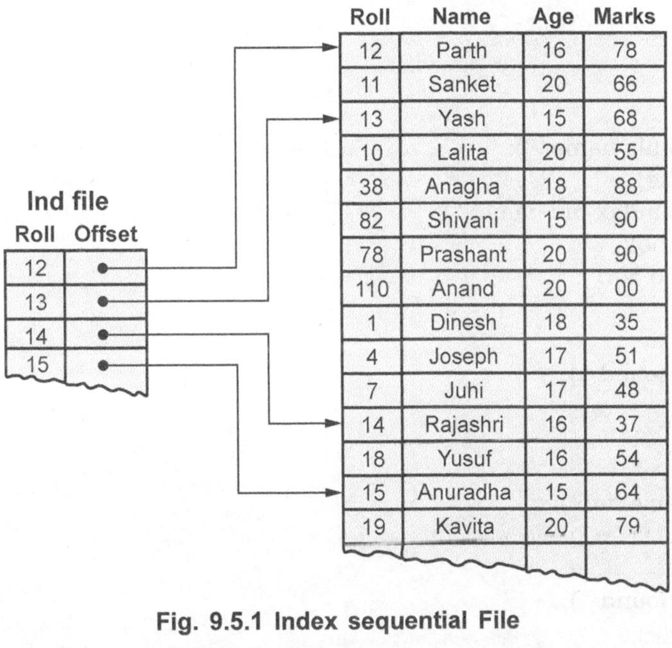

Fig. 9.5.1 Index sequential File

You will be more clear from the following sample figure and sample program.

Here we are storing various functions in function.cpp and structure in includes.h

'C' Program

```
/*****************************************************************
    Program for the indexed sequential file.We have assumed the student database for
this type of file organization.
*****************************************************************/
```

```
/*include Files*/
#include<stdio.h>
#include<conio.h>
#include<stdlib.h>
#include"c:\includes.h"
        /*stores the structures of
         master and index file*/
#include"c:\function.cpp" /*stores all the functions for file primitives*/

/* The main Function
  input:none
  Output:none
  called by:OS.
  Calls: ADD_RECORD,DELETE_RECORD,MODIFY_RECORD,SEARCH_RECORD,
              DISPLAY_ALL_RECORD
*/
void main(void)
{
 int choice;
 int status;
 int roll_no;
 char ch;
 clrscr();
 printf("Enter the file name: ");
 scanf("%s",f_name);
 printf("Enter the index file name: ");
 scanf("%s",if_name);
 ptr=fopen(f_name,"wb");
 if(ptr == NULL)
 {
  printf("File not found ");
  getch();
  exit(0);
 }
  iptr=fopen(if_name,"wb");
  if(iptr == NULL)
  {
  printf("File not found ");
  getch();
  exit(0);
  }
  fclose(ptr);
  fclose(iptr);
  while(1)
  {
              clrscr();
              printf("\n1.add");
```

```
            printf("\n2.delete");
            printf("\n3.modify");
            printf("\n4.search");
            printf("\n5.Display");
            printf("\n6.exit");
            printf("\nEnter the choice :");
            scanf("%d",&choice);
            switch(choice)
  {
  case 1:
       status=ADD_RECORD();
       if(status==1)

      printf("The record has been successfully added");

      else
      printf("The record could not be added");
      break;

   case 2:

      printf("Enter the roll_no of the record to
                   delete : ");
      scanf("%d",&roll_no);
      status=DELETE_RECORD(roll_no);
      if(status==1)
      printf("The record has been successfully deleted");
  else
      printf("The record could not be found");

      break;

 case 3:
      printf("Enter the roll_no of the record to
                   modify: ");
      scanf("%d",&roll_no);
      status=MODIFY_RECORD(roll_no);
      if(status==1)

      printf("The record has been successfully
                          modified");
   else
             printf("The record could not be found");

         break;
```

```
     case 4:
          printf("Enter the roll_no of the record to
                         searched: ");
          scanf("%d",&roll_no);
          status=SEARCH_RECORD(roll_no);
          if(status==1)

               printf("The record has been found");

            else
               printf("The record could not be found");
            getch();

            break;

     case 5:
               DISPLAY_ALL_RECORD();
               getch();
               break;

     case 6:
               getch();
               exit(0);

          }
          printf("Do u want to continue : ");
          ch=getchar();
          if(ch == 'n' || ch =='N')

          break;
     }
          getch();
     }
/************************************************************
                         function.cpp
************************************************************/
/*
 The SORT_FILE Function
 Input:none
 Output:1 or -1
 Called By:ADD_RECORD
 Calls:none

*/
int SORT_FILE()
{
  int size;
```

```
int i,j;
is ind, ind_temp;
ss stud;
int flag = 0;

iptr=fopen(if_name,"rb+");
if(iptr == NULL)
{
            printf("File not opened");
            return -1;
}
ptr=fopen(f_name,"rb+");
if(ptr == NULL)
{
            printf("File not opened");
            return -1;
}
size = 0;
       while(fread(&ind, sizeof(is), 1, iptr))
            size++;
fclose(iptr);
iptr=fopen(if_name,"rb+");
if(iptr == NULL)
{
            printf("File not opened");
            return -1;
}
for(i = 0; i < size; i++)
{
            flag = 0;
            for(j = 0; j < size - (i+1); j++)
   {
        fseek(iptr, j*sizeof(is), SEEK_SET);
        fread(&ind, sizeof(is), 1, iptr);
        //fseek(iptr, (j+1)*sizeof(is), SEEK_SET);
        fread(&ind_temp, sizeof(is), 1, iptr);
        if(ind.iroll_no > ind_temp.iroll_no)
        {
        fseek(iptr, j*sizeof(is), SEEK_SET);
        fwrite(&ind_temp, sizeof(is), 1, iptr);
        fseek(iptr, (j+1)*sizeof(is), SEEK_SET);
        fwrite(&ind, sizeof(is), 1, iptr);
        flag = 1;
        }
   }
   if(flag == 0)
       break;
```

```
  }
  fclose(iptr);
  return 1;
}
/*
 The ADD_RECORD Function
 Input:none
 Output:1 or -1
 Called By:main
 Calls:SORT_FILE
*/
int ADD_RECORD()
{
  ss stud;
  is ind;
  long offset;
  ptr=fopen(f_name,"rb+");
  if(ptr == NULL)
  {
                printf("File not opened");
                return -1;
  }
  while(fread(&stud, sizeof(stud), 1, ptr));
  offset=ftell(ptr);
  printf("Enter the name of the student :   ");
  fflush(stdin);
  scanf("%s",&stud.name);
  printf("Enter the roll no. of the student :   ");
  fflush(stdin);
  scanf("%d",&stud.roll_no);
  printf("Enter the age of the student :   ");
  fflush(stdin);
  scanf("%d",&stud.age);
  printf("Enter the marks of the student :   ");
  fflush(stdin);
  scanf("%d",&stud.mark);
  fwrite(&stud, sizeof(stud), 1, ptr);
  fclose(ptr);
  iptr=fopen(if_name,"ab+");
  if(iptr == NULL)
  {
                printf("File not opened");
                return -1;
  }
  ind.iroll_no=stud.roll_no;
  ind.offset=offset;
  ind.flag=1;
```

```
  fwrite(&ind, sizeof(ind), 1,iptr);
  fclose(iptr);
  SORT_FILE();
  return 1;
}
/*
 The DELETE_RECORD Function
 Input:roll_no
 Output:either -1 or 1
 Called By:main
 Calls:none
*/
int DELETE_RECORD(int roll_no)
{
  is ind;
  int flag = 0;
  iptr=fopen(if_name,"rb+");
  if(iptr == NULL)
  {
                printf("File not opened");
                return -1;
  }
  while(fread(&ind, sizeof(is), 1, iptr))
  {
      if(ind.iroll_no == roll_no)
      {
              flag = 1;
              break;
      }
  }
  if(flag == 1 )
  {
                ind.flag = -1;
                fseek(iptr,-(long)sizeof(is), SEEK_CUR);
                fwrite(&ind,sizeof(is), 1, iptr);
                fclose(iptr);
                return 1;
  }
  fclose(iptr);
  return -1;
}
/*
 The MODIFY_RECORD Function
 Input:roll_no
 Output:1
 Called By: main
 Calls:none
```

```
*/
int MODIFY_RECORD(int roll_no)
{
  is ind;
  ss stud;
  int flag = 0;
  iptr=fopen(if_name,"rb+");
  if(iptr == NULL)
  {
                printf("File not opened");
                return -1;
  }
  while(fread(&ind, sizeof(is), 1, iptr))
  {
      if(ind.iroll_no == roll_no)
      {
            flag = 1;
            break;
      }
  }
  fclose(iptr);
  if(flag == 1 )
  {
                ptr=fopen(f_name,"rb+");
                if(ptr == NULL)
      {
            printf("File not opened");
            return -1;
      }
      fseek(ptr, ind.offset, SEEK_SET);
      fread(&stud, sizeof(stud), 1, ptr);

                printf("Enter the name of the student :   ");
                fflush(stdin);
      scanf("%s",stud.name);
      printf("Enter the age of the student :   ");
      fflush(stdin);
      scanf("%d",&stud.age);
      printf("Enter the marks of the student :   ");
      fflush(stdin);
      scanf("%d",&stud.mark);
      fseek(ptr, -(long)sizeof(stud), SEEK_CUR);
      fwrite(&stud, sizeof(stud), 1, ptr);
      fclose(ptr);
      return 1;
  }
  return -1;
```

```
}

/*
 The SEARCH_RECORD Function
 Input:roll_no
 Output:if record found then 1
 Called By:main
 Calls:none
*/
int SEARCH_RECORD(int roll_no)
{
  is ind;
  ss stud;
  iptr=fopen(if_name,"rb+");
  if(iptr == NULL)
  {
              printf("File not opened");
              return -1;
  }
  while(fread(&ind, sizeof(is), 1, iptr))
  {
      if(ind.iroll_no == roll_no && ind.flag == 1)
      {
          fclose(iptr);
          return 1;
      }

  }
  fclose(iptr);
  return -1;
}
/*
 The DISPLAY_ALL_RECORD Function
 Input:none
 Output:-1 if no record present otherwise 1
 Called By:main
 Calls:none
*/
int DISPLAY_ALL_RECORD()
{
  is ind;
  ss stud;
  iptr=fopen(if_name,"rb+");
  if(iptr == NULL)
  {
              printf("File not opened");
              return -1;
```

```
  }
  ptr=fopen(f_name,"rb+");
  if(ptr == NULL)
  {
          printf("File not opened");
          return -1;
  }
  while(fread(&ind, sizeof(is), 1, iptr))
  {
     if(ind.flag == 1)
     {
        fseek(ptr, ind.offset, SEEK_SET);
        fread(&stud, sizeof(stud), 1, ptr);
        printf("\n\n\nRoll     :     %d ", stud.roll_no);
        printf("\nName     :     %s", stud.name);
        printf("\nAge      :     %d", stud.age);
        printf("\nMarks  : %d", stud.mark);
     }
  }
  fclose(iptr);
  fclose(ptr);
  return 1;
}
/**************************************************************
                    include.h
**************************************************************/
typedef struct student
  {
     int roll_no;
     char name[20];
     int age;
     int mark;
  }ss;
  typedef struct index
  {
     int iroll_no;
     long offset;
     int flag;
  }is;
  FILE *ptr=NULL;
  FILE *iptr=NULL;
  char f_name[20];     /*master file*/
  char if_name[20];    /*index file*/
```

Output

```
Enter the file name: main
Enter the index file name: ind
```

```
1. add
2. delete
3. modify
4. search
5. display
6. exit
Enter the choice : 1
Enter the name of the student : babu
Enter the roll no. of the student : 12
Enter the age of the student : 10
Enter the marks of the student : 98
1. add
2. delete
3. modify
4. search
5. display
6. exit
Enter the choice :1
Enter the name of the student : anand
Enter the roll no. of the student : 11
Enter the age of the student : 32
Enter the marks of the student : 0

1. add
2. delete
3. modify
4. search
5. display
6. exit

Enter the choice :1
Enter the name of the student : anuradha
Enter the roll no. of the student : 13
Enter the age of the student : 27
Enter the marks of the student : 100
1. add
2. delete
3. modify
4. search
5. display
6. exit

Enter the choice :5

Roll   : 11
Name        : anand
Age         : 32
```

```
Marks     : 0

Roll  :  12
Name      : babu
Age       : 10
Marks     : 98

Roll      : 13
Name      : anuradha
Age       : 27
Marks     : 100

1. add
2. delete
3. modify
4. search
5. display
6. exit
Enter the choice : 2

Enter the roll_no of the record to deleted: 13
1. add
2. delete
3. modify
4. search
5. display
6. exit
Enter the choice : 5

Roll      : 11
Name      : anand
Age       : 32
Marks     : 0
Roll      : 12
Name      : babu
Age       : 10
Marks     : 98

1. add
2. delete
3. modify
4. search
5. display
6. exit
Enter the choice : 4
Enter the roll_no of the record to searched : 11
The record has been found
```

```
1. add
2. delete
3. modify
4. search
5. display
6. exit
Enter the choice :3
Enter the roll_no of the record to modify: 12
Enter the name of the student :  Parth
Enter the age of the student :  10
Enter the marks of the student :  100

1.add
2.delete
3.modify
4.search
5.display
6.exit
Enter the choice :5

Roll      : 11
Name      : anand
Age       : 32
Marks     : 0

Roll      : 12
Name      : Parth
Age       : 10
Marks     : 100
1. add
2. delete
3. modify
4. search
5. display
6. exit
Enter the choice : 4
Enter the roll_no of the record to searched : 5
The record could not be found
```

Advantages of Indexed Sequential File:

1. More efficient than sequential file.
2. Time required is relatively less than sequential files.

Disadvantage:

Maintaining two files relatively increases the overhead.

Review Questions

1. *Write a short note on - Indexed sequential file.* **GTU : May-12, Summer-13, 14, Marks 4, Winter-12, Marks 7**
2. *Explain the structure of indexed sequential file.* **GTU : Summer-17, Marks 7**
3. *Explain indexing structure for index file.* **GTU : Winter-17, Marks 3**

9.6 Random File

GTU : Summer-15, Winter-18, Marks 7

Random organization is a kind of file organization in which records are stored at random locations on the disks.

There are three techniques used in random organization and those are given in following Fig. 9.6.1.

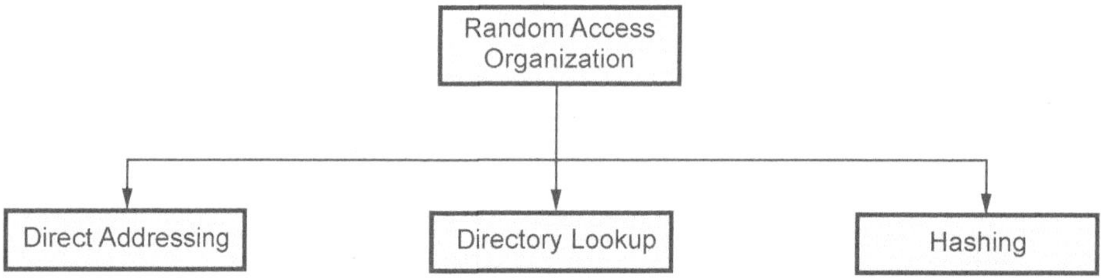

Fig. 9.6.1 Random access organization

Let us discuss each of them -

1. Direct Addressing

- In direct addressing two types of records are handled: fixed length record and variable length record.
- For storing the fixed length records the disk space is divided into the nodes. These nodes are large enough to hold individual record.
- Every fixed length record is stored in node number # which is equal to the primary key value. For example: If a primary key value is 185 then the record must be present in the node number 185.

For example

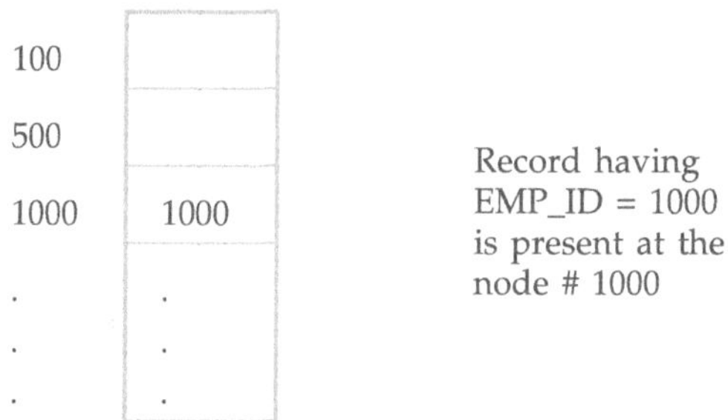

Fig. 9.6.2 Storing of fixed length record

- If we consider that the records are stored on the external storage devices then **deletion** and **searching** of the record requires one disk access. If we want to **update** a record then it requires two disk access, one for reading the record and one for writing the updated data back to the disk.
- For storing the **variable length records** on the disk, the address (pointer) of each individual record is stored in the file at specific index. We can locate the variable length record using the index of the pointer. This pointer will point to desired record which is present on the disk.

Variable length records make the storage management more **complex**.

2. Directory Lookup

- In this scheme the index for the pointers to the records is maintained.
- For retrieving the desired record first of all the index for the record address is searched and then using this record address the actual record is accessed.

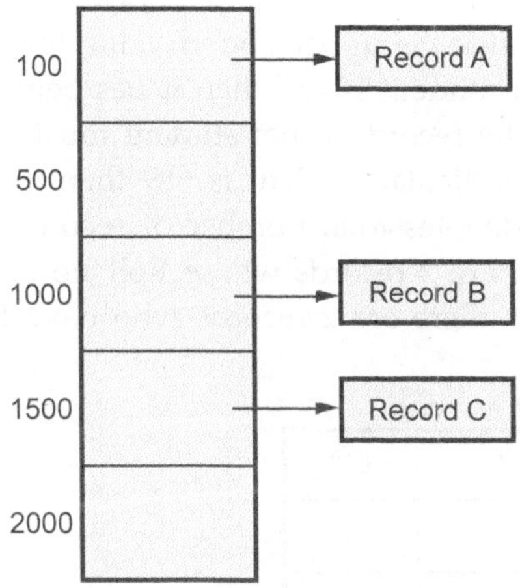

Fig. 9.6.3 Directory lookup

- The **drawback** of this method is that it requires more disk access than direct address method.
- **Advantage** of this method is that effective disk space utilization in it as compared to direct addressing method.

3. Hashing

- Hashing is a technique in which hash key is obtained using some suitable **hash function** and record is placed in the hash table with the help of this **hash key**.
- Thus in this random organization, the record can be quickly searched with the help of hash function being used.

- For creation of hash table the available file space is divided into **buckets** and **slots**.
- Some file space is left aside for handling the overflow situation.
- The total number of slots per bucket is equal to the total number of records each bucket can hold.

Review Questions

1. *Explain sequential, indexed sequential and random file organizations.*
   GTU : Summer-15, Marks 7
   [Hint : For sequential file - Refer section 9.4, for index sequential - Refer section 9.5]
2. *Explain different types of file organizations and discuss the advantages and disadvantages of each of them.* **GTU : Winter-18, Marks 7**
3. *Explain sequential files and indexed sequential files structures.* **GTU : Winter-18, Marks 7**

9.7 Multi-Key File Organization

GTU : Winter-13, 17, Marks 7

For understanding multiple key access file organization consider the Roll_no record. In the Roll_no record structure, there are 3 fields - **value, length** and **pointer to the first record**. The value field indicates the upper bound value for the Roll_no. For instance : If the roll number of particular student is 437 then it lies between 0 to 500. Note that here upper bound is 500. Hence the record of that student must be associated with value 500. Similarly if roll_number of particular student is 689 then it must be associated with the value 700. The length field denotes total number of records. From Fig. 9.7.1 length 2 in the value of 500 means there are 2 records whose Roll_no lie between 0 to 500. Similarly length 2 for value 700 means there are 2 records who have Roll_no that lie between 500 to 700.

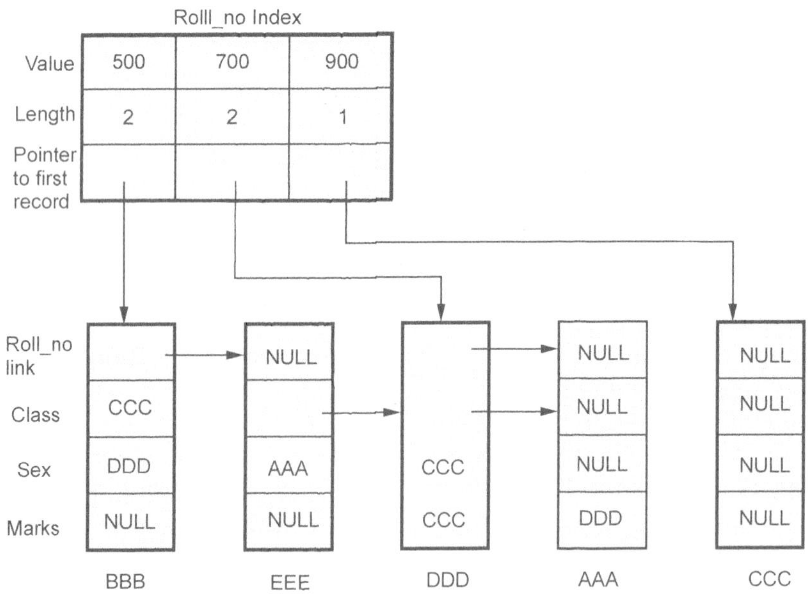

Fig. 9.7.1 Multi-list structure

The third field is the pointer or a link field which points to the first record. For instance in Fig. 9.7.1. For **value 500** the pointer field points to record BBB and in the record BBB there is a field Roll_no link which points to record EEE. Thus there are total 2 records BBB and EEE with value 500.

Similarly for **value 700** there are 2 records the pointer field points to the first record DDD. The record DDD shows the next record of it by pointing to AAA (Refer the Roll_no link of record DDD).

And for **value 900** there is only one record i.e. CCC which is pointed by pointer field. The index for each key field is maintained which is useful for executing any query. Observe Fig. 9.7.1 of class index. This figure tells us that there are two records for fifth standard and 3 records for tenth standard. The first student of fifth standard class is BBB and second student is CCC. (Just refer the class field of record BBB from Fig. 9.7.1)

Thus we can solve the query "select * from stud_table where class = fifth" and the answer will be BBB and CCC. If we observe Fig. 9.7.1 of Marks index, the column of **second class** value shows that there are 3 records, out of which first record is AAA. Now from Fig. 9.7.1 record AAA has a Marks field which denotes next record as DDD and Marks field of record DDD denotes CCC as the next record. And for record CCC the Marks field denotes the value NULL. This all indicates the second class holder students are AAA, CCC and DDD.

Advantages

1) The multi-list structure provides satisfactory solution to simple and range queries. For instance : "Select * from dept_table where salary > 10000"
   Such queries can be executed efficiently using multi-list structure.

2) Quick access to every individual record is possible.

Disadvantage

1) Some amount of memory gets consumed in maintaining the link or address field.

Review Questions

1. *Explain various multiple key access file organization in brief with advantages and disadvantages of each method.* **GTU : Winter-13, Marks 7**
2. *How access of record is performed in multi key file organization.* **GTU : Winter-17, Marks 4**

9.8 Access Methods

GTU : Winter-12

The method by which records can be retrieved or updated from the file is called access method. Records within the file can be organized in variety of ways. Fig. 9.8.1 shows various types by which a file can be organized -

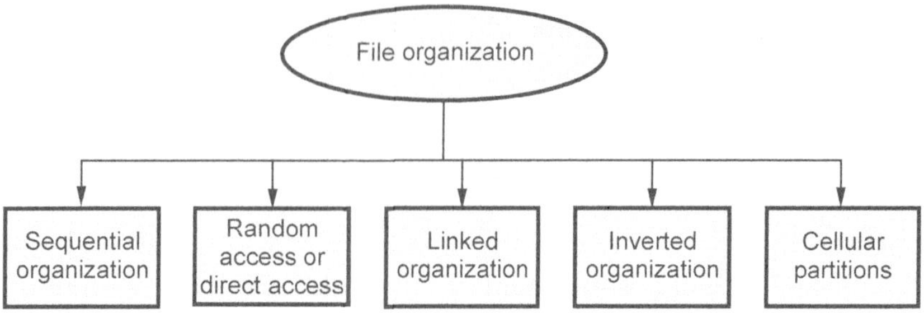

Fig. 9.8.1

9.8.1 Linked Organization

- In linked organization the logical sequence of the records is different than the physical sequence. In any sequential organization if we are accessing n^{th} node at Loc_i then $(n+1)^{th}$ record may be located at (Loc_i+c) where c is the constant which represents the length of the record or it may be some inter-record spacing.
- In linked organization we can access next logical record by following the **link-value** pair. The link-value pair denotes each individual record.
- The typical structure of every record is as follows -

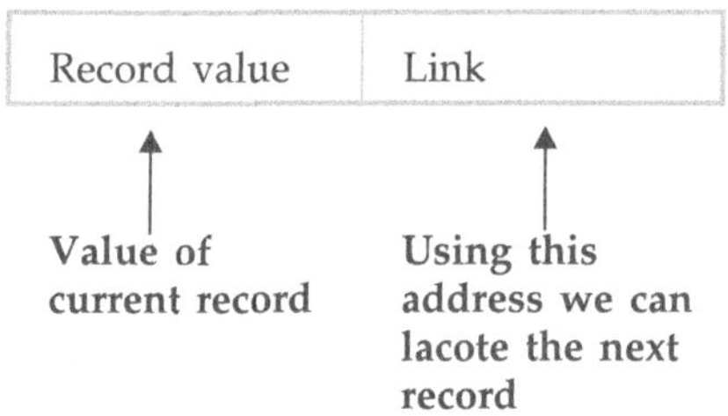

Thus records in the linked organization can be stored as follows -

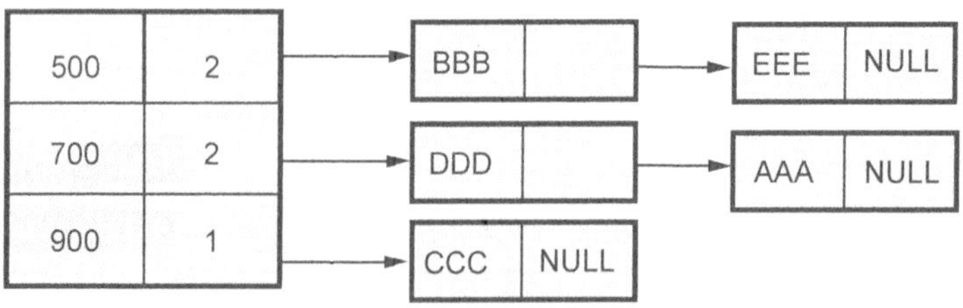

Fig. 9.8.2 Roll_No index

9.8.2 Inverted File Organization

- Inverted files are similar to multi-lists.

- The difference between multi-list and inverted files is that in multi-lists records with the same key value are linked together along with the **link information** being kept in **individual record**. But in case of inverted files this **link information** is kept in the **index itself**.

For example

437	BBB
488	EEE
689	DDD
695	AAA
778	CCC

Fig. 9.8.3 (a) Roll_No index

Fifth	BBB, CCC
Tenth	EEE, DDD, AAA

Fig. 9.8.3 (b) Class index

Female	BBB, DDD, CCC
Male	EEE, AAA

Fig. 9.8.3 (c) Sex index

First class	EEE
Second class	AAA, DDD, CCC
Pass class	BBB

Fig. 9.8.3 (d) Marks index

Consider Fig. 9.8.3 (a) of Roll-no index which shows records BBB, EEE, DDD, AAA and CCC. In Fig. 9.8.3 (b) of class index two class are there fifth and tenth and we can observe that in the link information is stored in the index itself. Hence for fifth class records are BBB and CCC. And for tenth class records are EEE, DDD and AAA .

Similarly from sex index Fig. 9.8.3 (c), it is clear that BBB, DDD and CCC are females and EEE and AAA are males.

- The above index structure is a dense index structure **Dense Indexing**. The dense index is a kind of indexing in which record appers for every search key value in the file.

For example

- Thus in inverted files the index entries is of variable length. Hence inverted files structure is **more complex** than multi-list file structure.

- Following are the two steps that are adopted while searching a record from inverted files -

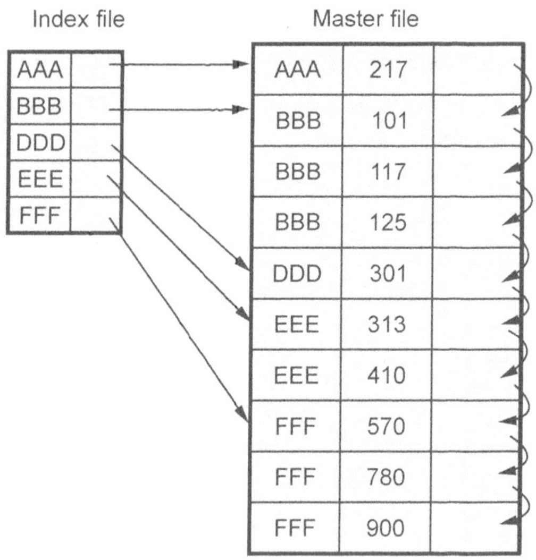

Fig. 9.8.4 Dense indexing

i) Index of required record is searched first of all.

ii) Then actual record is retrieved.

- In inverted files the index structure is important. The records can be arranged sequentially, randomly or linked depending on primary key.
- The number of disk accesses required = Number of records being retrieved + Processing for indexes.

Advantages

1) Inverted files are space saving as compared to other file structures when record retrieval does not require retrieval does not require retrieval of key fields.

Disadvantages

1) Insertion and deletion of records is complex because it requires the ability to insert and delete within indexes.

2) Index maintainance is complicated as compared to multi-list.

9.8.3 Cellular Partitions

- For reducing the searching time during file operations, the storage media (e.g. secondary memory, magnetic disk, magnetic tape etc.) may be divided into cells.
- The cells can be of two types -

  i) Entire disk pack can be a cell

  ii) A cylinder can be a cell.

- A list of records can occupy either entire disk pack or it may lie on particular cylinder.
- If all the records lie on the same cylinder then without moving the read/write head the records can be accessed.
- If the cell is nothing but entire disk pack then the disk is partitioned into different partitions. Such partitions are called **cellular partitions**. Then these different cells can be searched in parallel.

Advantages of cellular partitions

1) Various read operations can be performed parallely in order to reduce the search time.
2) Faster execution of any query.

Disadvantage

1) If multiple records lie in the same cell then reading a single cell becomes a time consuming process.

Review Questions

1. *Write a short note on inverted key file organization.* **GTU : Winter-12, Marks 7**
2. *Write a short note on Cellular Partitions.*

9.9 Oral Questions and Answers

Q.1 Define the terms - file, Record and Field.

Ans. : A file is a collection of records. Record is nothing but the source of information. It typically stored in rows in the file structure. Field is a piece of data which is associated with the entire record. It is referred as column.

Q.2 What are various operations that can be performed in file ?

Ans. : Various operations that can be performed on file are 1. Creation of file 2. Insertion of record in file 3. Updation of some record 4. Deletion of desired record.

Q.3 What are various modes ?

Ans. : Various modes in which file can be opened are -

read - "r" write - "w" append - "a"

Q.4 Explain file close operation.

Ans. : The file close operation used for closing the file.

Syntax : fclose(filepointer);

Example : fclose(fp); /* closes the file pointed by the fp */

Q.5 What is the purpose of putc or getc functions ?

Ans. : For writing the character fputc is used and reading from the character from the file fgetc function is used.

Q.6 What are different types of files ?

Ans. : There are three types of files 1. Sequential file 2. Index file 3. Random file

Q.7 What are advantages of index sequential file over sequential file ?

Ans. : Various advantages of index sequential file are

1. More efficient than sequential file.
2. Time required is relatively less than sequential files.

❑❑❑

10 Sorting and Searching

Syllabus

Sorting - bubble sort, Selection sort, Quick sort, Merge sort searching - Sequential search and binary search.

Contents

10.1 Concept of Sorting

GTU : Winter-14, 15,16,17,18, Summer-15,16,17,18, Marks 7

- **Definition of sorting :** Sorting is a process of arranging the data in some specific order.
- **Ascending order :** If the elements are arranged in increasing order then it is called ascending order.
- **Descending order :** If the elements are arranged in decreasing order then it is called descending order.
- There are two types of sorting techniques - Internal sorting and External sorting.
  1. **Internal sorting :** This is a sorting technique in which data resides on the main memory of computer.
  2. **External sorting :** This is a sorting technique in which there is huge amount of data and it resides.
- The internal sorting techniques are - 1. Bubble sort 2. Selection sort 3. Quick sort 4. Merge sort.

We will discuss these methods with the help of illustrative examples.

10.1.1 Bubble Sort

This is the simplest kind of sorting method in this method. We do this bubble sort procedure in several iterations, which are called passes.

Example :

Consider 5 unsorted elements are

45 – 40 190 99 11

First store those elements in the array a

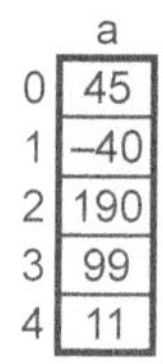

Pass 1

Compare 45 and – 40

Is 45 > – 40 ∴ Interchange

i.e. compare a[0] and a[1], after interchange

∴ a[0] = – 40

a[1] = 45

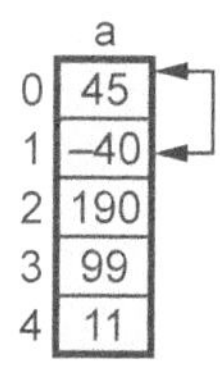

Compare a[1] and a[2]

Is 45 > 190 ∴ No interchange

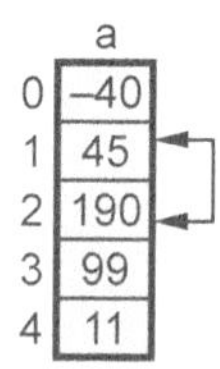

Compare a[2] and a[3]

Is 190 > 99 ∴interchange

a[2] = 99

a[3] = 190

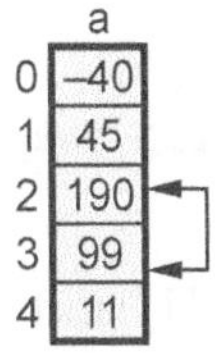

Compare a[3] and a[4]

Is 190 > 11 ∴Interchange

a[3] = 11

a[4] = 190

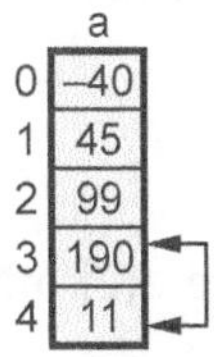

After first pass the array will hold the elements which are sorted to some extent.

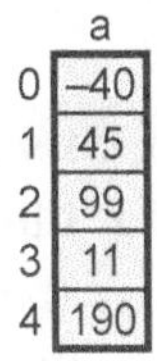

Pass 2

Compare a[0] and a[1]

no interchange

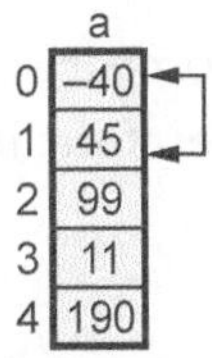

ompare a[0] and a[1]

no interchange.

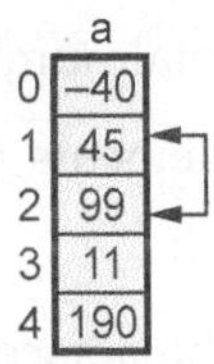

Compare a[2] and a[3]

Since 99 > 11 interchange

∴a[2] = 11

a[3] = 99

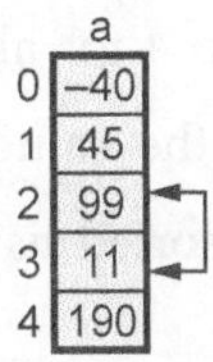

No interchange

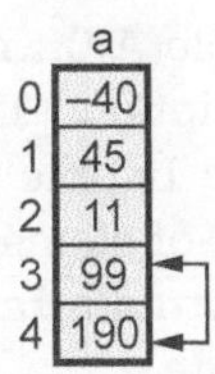

Pass 3

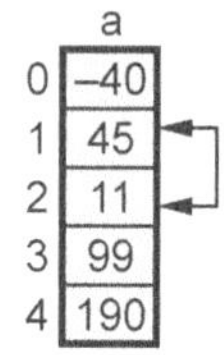

First compare a[0] and a[1], no interchange

∴ Compare a[1] and a[2]

45 > 11 ∴ Interchange

a[1] = 11

a[2] = 45

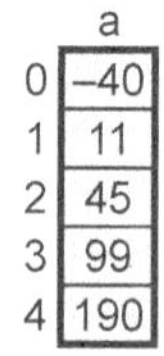

Next compare a[2] and a[3] similarly

a[3] and a[4]

No interchange.

This is end of pass 3. This process will be thus continued till pass 4. Finally at the end of last pass the array will hold all the sorted elements like this,

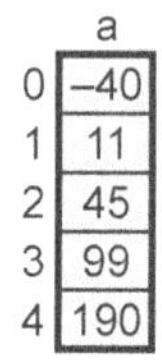

Since the comparison positions look like bubbles, therefore it is called **bubble sort**.

Algorithm :

1. Read the total number of elements say n
2. Store the elements in the array
3. Set the i = 0 .
4. Compare the adjacent elements.
5. Repeat step 4 for all n elements.
6. Increment the value of i by 1 and repeat step 4, 5 for i< n
7. Printf the sorted list of elements.
8. Stop.

```
Algorithm Bubble(A[0...n-1])
//Problem Description : This algorithm is for sorting the
//elements using bubble sort method
//Input:An array of elements A[0...n-1] that is to be sorted
//Output: The sorted array A[0...n-1]
for i ← 0 to n-2 do
{
   for j ← 0 to n-2-i do
   {
```

```
            if(A[j]>A[j+1])then
            {
            temp ← A[j]
            A[j] ← A[j+1]
            A[j+1] ← temp
            }
    }//end of inner for loop
}//end of outer for loop
```

'C' Function

```
void bubblesort (int a[20], int n)
{
        int i, j, m,temp;
        for (i = 0; i < n – 1; i ++)
        {
                for (j= 0; j < n; j ++)
                {
                        if (a[j] > a [j + 1])
                        {
                                temp = a[j];
                                a[j] = a[j+1];
                                a[j + 1] = temp;
                        }
                }
        }
```

'C' Program

```
/*****************************************************************
 Program for sorting the elements by bubble sort method
*****************************************************************/
/* Header Files*/
#include<stdio.h>
#include<conio.h>
#include<process.h>
 /*Declaration*/
void bubblesort(int a[20],int n);
/*
 Name:Bubblesort
 Input Parameter:array a,total elements n
 Output Parameter:none
 Called By:main()
 Calls:none
 */
void bubblesort(int a[20],int n)
        {
        int i,j,m,temp;
```

```
        for(i=0;i<n-1;i++)
        {
            for(j=0;j<n;j++)
             { if(a[j]>a[j+1])
            { temp=a[j];
              a[j]=a[j+1];
              a[j+1]=temp;
            }
             }
        }
        //Printing the sorted array//
        for(i=0;i<n;i++)
            printf("\n\t%d",a[i]);
        }
/*
 Name:main()
 Input Parameter:none
 Output:none
 Called By O.S.
 Calls:bubblesort()
 */
void main()
{
  int a[20],i,n;
  int ch;
  clrscr();
  printf("\nEnter the number of elements
            in the sorting array: ");
  scanf("%d",&n);
   //Accepting n number of elements in the array
  printf("\nEnter the elements for the array\n");
  for(i=0;i<n;i++)
    scanf("%d",&a[i]);
  bubblesort(a,n);
  getch();
}
/*********************End Of Program *********************/
```

Output

```
Enter the number of elements in the sorting array: 5
Enter the elements for the array
30
20
50
40
10
        10
        20
```

30
40
50

Analysis : In above algorithm basic operation if (a[j] > a[j +1]) which is executed within nested for loops. Hence time complexity of bubble sort is $\Theta(\mathbf{n})^2$.

Example 10.1.1 *Sort the following list of numbers using bubble sort technique*
52, 1, 27, 85, 66, 23, 13, 57.

Solution : Pass 1 :

0	1	2	3	4	5	6	7
52	1	27	85	66	23	13	57

As 1 < 52
∴ Interchange

0	1	2	3	4	5	6	7
1	52	27	85	66	23	13	57

As 27 < 52
∴ Interchange

0	1	2	3	4	5	6	7
1	27	52	85	66	23	13	57

As 52 < 85
∴ No Interchange

0	1	2	3	4	5	6	7
1	27	52	85	66	23	13	57

As 66 < 85
∴ Interchange

0	1	2	3	4	5	6	7
1	27	52	66	85	23	13	57

As 23 < 85
∴ Interchange

0	1	2	3	4	5	6	7
1	27	52	66	23	85	13	57

As 13 < 85
∴ Interchange

0	1	2	3	4	5	6	7
1	27	52	66	23	13	85	57

As 57 < 85
∴ Interchange

0	1	2	3	4	5	6	7
1	27	52	66	23	13	57	85

Pass 2 :

0	1	2	3	4	5	6	7
1	27	52	66	23	13	57	85

As 23 < 66
∴ Interchange

0	1	2	3	4	5	6	7
1	27	52	23	66	13	57	85

As 13 < 66
∴ Interchange

0	1	2	3	4	5	6	7
1	27	52	23	13	66	57	85

As 57 < 66
∴ Interchange

0	1	2	3	4	5	6	7
1	27	52	23	13	57	66	85

No Interchange

Pass 3 :

0	1	2	3	4	5	6	7
1	27	52	23	13	57	66	85

As 23 < 52
∴ Interchange

0	1	2	3	4	5	6	7
1	27	23	52	13	57	66	85

As 13 < 52
∴ Interchange

0	1	2	3	4	5	6	7
1	27	23	13	52	57	66	85

Pass 4 :

0	1	2	3	4	5	6	7
1	27	23	13	52	57	66	85

As 23 < 27
∴ Interchange

0	1	2	3	4	5	6	7
1	23	27	13	52	57	66	85

As 13 < 27
∴ Interchange

0	1	2	3	4	5	6	7
1	23	13	27	52	57	66	85

Pass 5 :

0	1	2	3	4	5	6	7
1	23	13	27	52	57	66	85

As 13 < 23
∴ Interchange

0	1	2	3	4	5	6	7
1	13	23	27	52	57	66	85

Pass 6 :

0	1	2	3	4	5	6	7
1	13	23	27	52	57	66	85

No interchange takes place. Hence the sorted list is -

1	13	23	27	52	57	66	85

Example 10.1.2 *"If no interchanges occurred, then the table must be sorted and no further passes are required". Which sorting method works on this principal ?*

Apply above sorting technique on the following data

5 1 4 2 8

GTU : Winter -17, Marks 7

Solution : The bubble sort method is used on given principal.

Pass 1 :

0	1	2	3	4
5	1	4	2	8

As 5 > 1
Interchange

0	1	2	3	4
1	5	4	2	8

Interchange

0	1	2	3	4
1	4	5	2	8

Interchange

0	1	2	3	4
1	4	2	5	8

No interchange

Pass 2 :

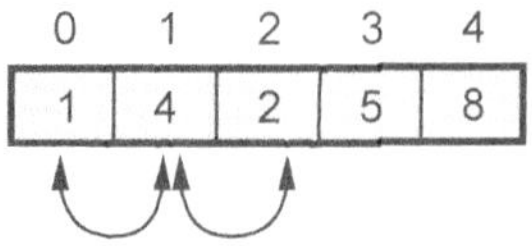

Interchange

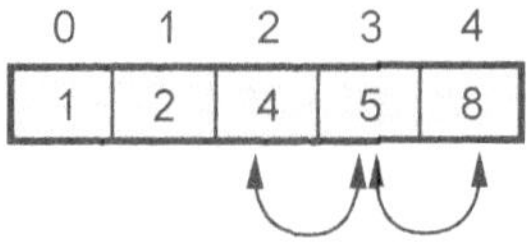

No interchange

Pass 3 :

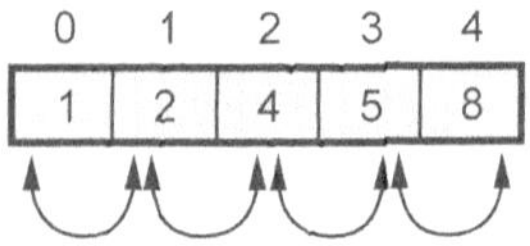

No interchange

Thus we get sorted list as **1, 2, 4, 5, 8**

Review Questions

1. *Write a function in C to perform bubble sort. Also find out its worst case time complexity.*
2. *Write a 'C' program for Bubble sort.* **GTU : Winter-16, Marks 4**
3. *Explain the trace of bubble sort on following data.*
   42, 23, 74, 11, 65, 58, 94, 36, 99, 87 **GTU : Summer-17, Marks 7**
4. *Write an algorithm for Bubble sort.* **GTU : Winter-18, Marks 3**

10.1.2 Selection Sort

GTU : Winter-14, Marks 7

Scan the array to find its smallest element and swap it with the first element. Then, starting with the second element scan the entire list to find the smallest element and swap it with the second element. Then starting from the third element the entire list is scanned in order to find the next smallest element. Continuing in this fashion we can sort the entire list.

Generally, on pass *i* $(0 \le i \le n-2)$, the smallest element is searched among last $n-i$ elements and is swapped with A[i]

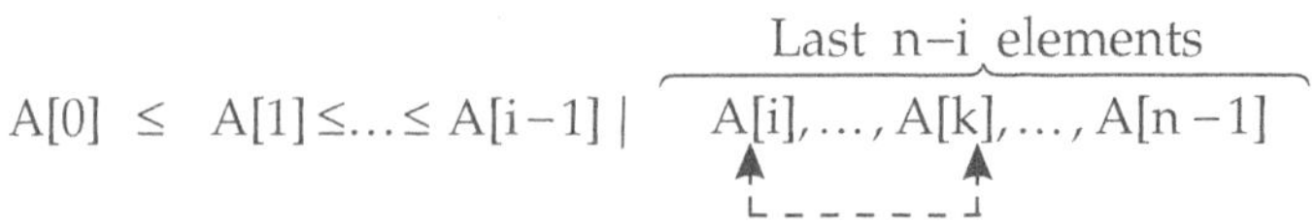

A[k] is smallest element

so swap A[i] and A[k]

The list gets sorted after n–1 passes.

Example :

Consider the elements

70, 30, 20, 50, 60, 10, 40

We can store these elements in array A as :

70	30	20	50	60	10	40
A[0]	A[1]	A[2]	A[3]	A[4]	A[5]	A[6]
↑	↑					
Min	j					

Initially set Min j

1st pass :

A[0]	A[1]	A[2]	A[3]	A[4]	A[5]	A[6]
70	30	20	50	60	10	40

↑ Min — Scan the array for finding smallest element

70	30	20	50	60	10	40
↑					↑	
i					Smallest element found	

Now swap A[i] with smallest element. Then we get,

10	30	20	50	60	70	40

2nd pass :

A[0]	A[1]	A[2]	A[3]	A[4]	A[5]	A[6]
10	30	20	50s	60	70	40

↑ i, Min — Scan the array for finding smallest element

10	30	20	50	60	70	40
	↑	↑				
	i	Smallest element				

Swap A[i] with smallest element. The array becomes,

10	20	30	50	60	70	40

3rd pass :

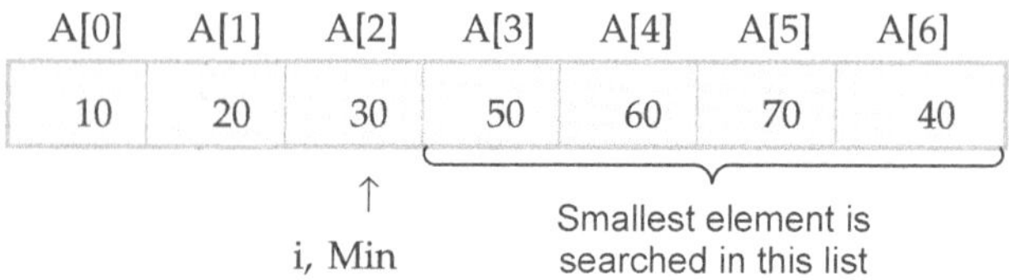

As there is no smallest element than 30 we will increment i pointer.

4th pass :

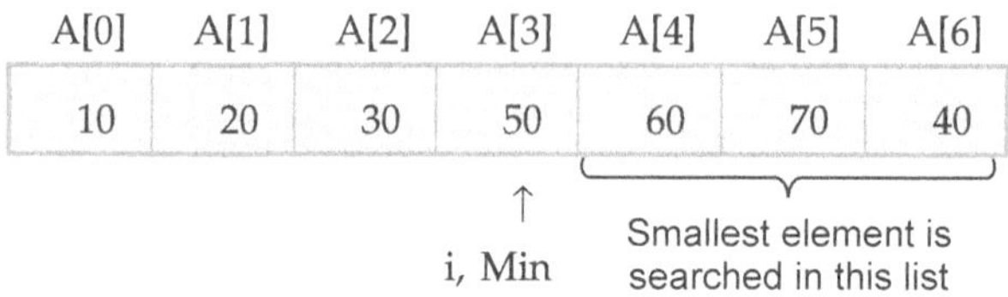

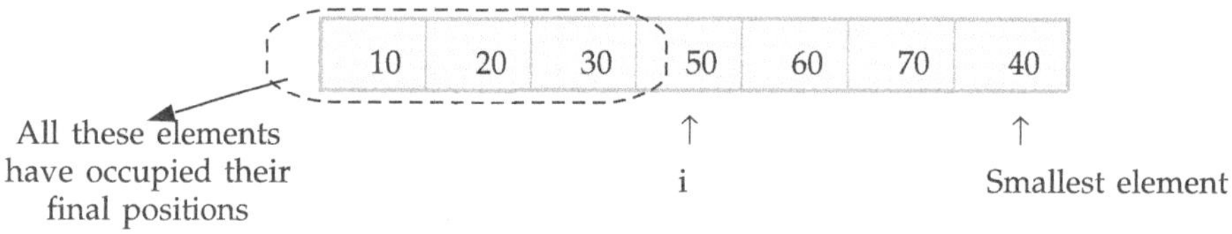

Swap A[i] with smallest element. The array then becomes,

10	20	30	40	60	70	50

5th pass :

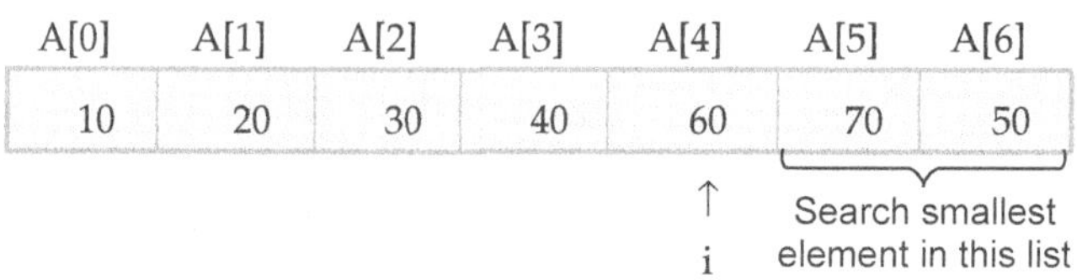

10	20	30	40	60	70	50
				↑ i		↑ Smallest element

Swap A[i] with smallest element. The array then becomes,

10	20	30	40	50	70	60

All these elements have got their positions (10, 20, 30, 40, 50)

6 th **pass :**

10	20	30	40	50	70	60
					↑ i	↑ Smallest element

Swap A[i] with smallest element. The array then becomes,

A[0]	A[1]	A[2]	A[3]	A[4]	A[5]	A[6]
10	20	30	40	50	60	70

This is a sorted array.

C Function

```
void selection (int A[10])
{
        int i,j,Min,temp;
        for (i=0;i<=n-2;i++)
        {
              Min=i;
              for(j=i+1;j<=n-1;j++)
              {
                     if(A[j]<A[Min])
                     Min=j;
              }
              temp=A[i];
              A[i]=A[Min];
              A[Min]=temp;
        }
        printf("\n The sorted List is ...\n");
        for(i=0;i<n;i++)
                     printf(" %d,A[i]);
}
```

Anaysis : The algorithm can be analysed mathematically. We will apply a general plan for non recursive mathematical analysis.

Step 1 : The **input size** is n i.e. total number of elements in the list.

Step 2 : In the algorithm the **basic operation** is key comparison.

if A[j] < A[min]

Step 3 : This basic operation depends only on array size n. Hence we can find **sum** as

$$C(n) = \underset{\text{with variable i}}{\text{Outer for loop}} \times \underset{\text{with variable j}}{\text{Inner for loop}} \times \text{Basic operation}$$

$$\therefore \quad C(n) = \sum_{i=0}^{n-2} \times \sum_{j=i+1}^{n-1} 1$$

$$C(n) = \sum_{i=0}^{n-2} (n-1-i)$$

> $\sum_{i=0}^{n} 1 = (n-0+1)$ using this formula we get,
>
> $\sum_{j=i+1}^{n-1} 1 = [(n-1)-(i+1)+1]$
>
> $= (n-1-i)$

Step 4 : Simplifying sum we get,

$$C(n) = \sum_{i=0}^{n-2} (n-1-i)$$

$$= \sum_{i=0}^{n-2} (n-1) - \sum_{i=0}^{n-2} i$$

> $\sum_{i=1}^{n} i = \frac{n(n+1)}{2}$ using this formula
>
> $\sum_{i=0}^{n-2} i = \frac{(n-2)(n-2+1)}{2}$
>
> $= \frac{(n-2)(n-1)}{2}$

$$= \sum_{i=0}^{n-2} (n-1) - \frac{(n-2)(n-1)}{2}$$

Now taking (n – 1) as common factor we get,

$$C(n) = (n-1)\sum_{i=0}^{n-2} 1 - \frac{(n-2)(n-1)}{2}$$

> As $\sum_{i=1}^{n} 1 = (n-1+1)$, we get,
>
> $\sum_{i=0}^{n-2} 1 = (n-2-0+1) = (n-1)$

$$= (n-1)(n-1) - \frac{(n-2)(n-1)}{2} = (n-1)^2 - \frac{(n-2)(n-1)}{2}$$

Solving this equation we will get,

$$= \frac{2(n-1)(n-1) - (n-2)(n-1)}{2} = \frac{2(n^2-2n+1) - (n^2-3n+2)}{2}$$

$$= \frac{n^2-n}{2} = \frac{n(n-1)}{2}$$

$$\approx \frac{1}{2}(n^2)$$
$$\in \Theta(n^2)$$

Thus time complexity of selection sort is $\Theta(\mathbf{n}^2)$ for all input. But total number of key swaps is only $\Theta(n)$.

Let us see the complete implementation of selection sort.

C Program

```
#include<stdio.h>
#include<conio.h>
int n;
void main()
{
 int i,A[10];
 void selection(int A[10]);
 clrscr();
 printf("\n\t\t Selection Sort\n");
 printf("\n How many elements are there?");
 scanf("%d",&n);
 printf("\n Enter the elements\n");
 for(i=0;i<n;i++)
            scanf("%d",&A[i]);
            selection(A);
 getch();
}
void selection(int A[10])
{
 int i,j,Min,temp;
 for(i=0;i<=n-2;i++)
 {
            Min=i;
            for(j=i+1;j<=n-1;j++)
            {
            if(A[j]<A[Min])
                    Min=j;

            }
            temp=A[i];
            A[i]=A[Min];
            A[Min]=temp;
 }
 printf("\n The sorted List is ...\n");
 for(i=0;i<n;i++)
            printf(" %d",A[i]);
}
```

Output

```
Selection Sort

How many elements are there?7
Enter the elements
70
```

```
30
20
50
60
10
40
The sorted List is ...
10 20 30 40 50 60 70
```

Review Question

1. *Write a selection sort algorithm and also discuss its efficiency.* **GTU : Winter-14, Marks 7**
2. *Write an algorithm for selection sort method. Explain each step with an example.* **GTU : Summer-16, Marks 7**
3. *Write a 'C' function for selection sort.* **GTU : Winter-16, Marks 3**
4. *Explain the trace of selection sort on following data :*
   42, 23, 74, 11, 65, 58, 94, 36, 99, 87 **GTU : Summer-17, Marks 7**
5. *Write an algorithm for selection sort.* **GTU : Winter-18, Marks 3**

10.1.3 Quick Sort

Quick sort is a sorting algorithm that uses the divide and conquer strategy. In this method division is dynamically carried out. The three steps of quick sort are as follows :

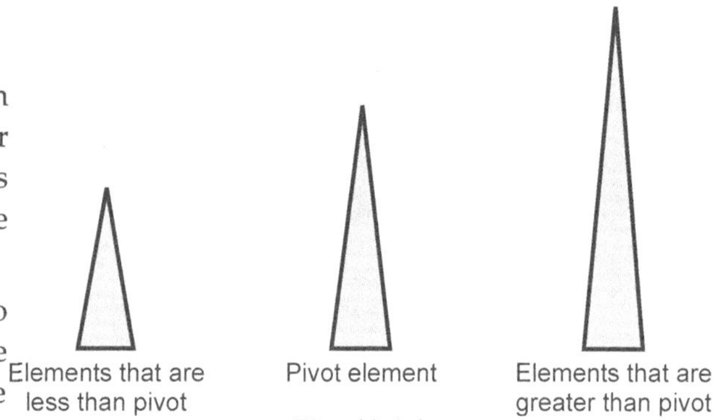

Fig. 10.1.1

Divide : Split the array into two sub arrays that each element in the left sub array is less than or equal the middle element and each element in the right sub array is greater than the middle element. The splitting of the array into two sub arrays is based on pivot element. All the elements that are less than pivot should be in left sub array and all the elements that are more than pivot should be in right sub array.

Conquer : Recursively sort the two sub arrays.

Combine : Combine all the sorted elements in a group to form a list of sorted elements.

Consider an array A[i] where is ranging from 0 to n – 1 then we can formulize the division of array elements as

A[0] ... A[m–1],A[m],A[m+1]...A[n–1]

These elements are less than A[m] | Mid | These elements are greater than A[m]

Let us understand this algorithm with the help of some example.

Example

Step 1 :

Low						High	
50	30	10	90	80	20	40	70
i / Pivot						j	

We will now split the array in two parts.

The left sublist will contain the elements less than Pivot (i.e. 50) and right sublist contains elements greater than pivot.

Step 2 :

Low							
50	30	10	90	80	20	40	70
Pivot	i						j

We will increment i. If A[i] ≤ Pivot, we will continue to increment it until the element pointed by i is greater than A[Low].

Step 3 :

Low							
50	30	10	90	80	20	40	70
Pivot		i					j

Increment i as A[i] ≤ A [Low].

Step 4 :

Low							
50	30	10	90	80	20	40	70
Pivot			i				j

As A[i] > A [Low], we will stop incrementing i.

Step 5 :

Low							High
50	30	10	90	80	20	40	70
Pivot			i			j	

As A[j] > Pivot (i.e. 70 > 50). We will decrement j. We will continue to decrement j until the element pointed by j is less than A [Low].

Step 6 :

Low							High
50	30	10	90	80	20	40	70
Pivot			i			j	

Now we can not decrement j because 40 < 50. Hence we will swap A[i] and A[j] i.e. 90 and 40.

Step 7 :

Low							
50	30	10	40	80	20	90	70
Pivot			i			j	

As A[i] is less than A[Low] and A[j] is greater than A[Low] we will continue incrementing i and decrementing j, until the false conditions are obtained.

Step 8 :

Low							
50	30	10	40	80	20	90	70
Pivot				i	j		

We will stop incrementing i and stop decrementing j. As i is smaller than j we will swap 80 and 20.

Step 9 :

Low							High
50	30	10	40	20	80	90	70
Pivot				i	j		

As A[i] < A[Low] and A[j] > A[Low], we will continue incrementing i and decrementing j.

Step 10 :

Low							High
50	30	10	40	20	80	90	70
Pivot					i, j		

Low							High
50	30	10	40	20	80	90	70
Pivot				j	i		

As A[j] < A[Low] and j has crossed i. That is j < i, we will swap A[Low] and A[j].

Step 11 :

Low							High
20	30	10	40	50	80	90	70
				j	i		
	Now we have left sublist			Pivot is shifted at its position	Now we have right sublist		

We will now start sorting left sublist, assuming the first element of left sublist as pivot element. Thus now new pivot = 20.

Step 12 :

Low							High
20	30	10	40	50	80	90	70
Pivot	i		j	Occupied its position			

Now we will set i and j pointer and then we will start comparing A[i] with A[Low] or A[Pivot]. Similarly comparison with A[j] and A[Pivot].

Step 13 :

Low							
20	30	10	40	50	80	90	70
Pivot	i		j				

As A[i] > A[Pivot], hence stop incrementing i. Now as A[j] > A[Pivot], hence decrement j.

Step 14 :

Low							
20	30	10	40	50	80	90	70
Pivot	i	j					

Now j can not be decremented because 10 < 20. Hence we will swap A[i] and A[j].

Step 15 :

Low							
20	10	30	40	50	80	90	70
Pivot	i	j					

As A[i] < A[Low], increment i.

Step 16 :

Low							
20	10	30	40	50	80	90	70
Pivot		i, j					

Now as A[i] > A[Low], or A[j] > A[Pivot] decrement j.

Step 17 :

Low							
20	10	30	40	50	80	90	70
Pivot	j	i					

As A[j] < A[Low] we cannot decrement j now. We will now swap A[Low] and A[j] as j has crossed i and i > j.

Step 18 :

Low							
10	20	30	40	50	80	90	70
Left sublist	↑ Pivot	Right sublist					

As there is only one element in left sublist hence we will sort right sublist.

Step 19 :

Low							
10	20	30	40	50	80	90	70
					Now consider this sublist for sorting		

As left sublist is sorted completely we will sort right sublist, assuming first element of right sublist as pivot.

Step 20 :

10	20	30	40	50	80	90	70
					Pivot	i	j

As A[i] > A[Pivot], hence we will stop incrementing i. Similarly A[j] < A[Pivot]. Hence we stop decrementing j. Swap A[i] and A[j].

Step 21 :

10	20	30	40	50	80	70	90
					Pivot	i	j

As A[i] < A[Pivot], increment i.

Step 22 :

10	20	30	40	50	80	70	90
					Pivot		i, j

As A[i] > A[Pivot], decrement j.

Step 23 :

10	20	30	40	50	80	70	90
					Pivot	j	i

Now swap A[Pivot] and A[j].

Step 24 :

10	20	30	40	50	70	80	90
						Pivot	

The left sublist now contains 70 and right sublist contains only 90. We can not further subdivide the list.

Hence list is

10	20	30	40	50	70	80	90

This is a sorted list.

Algorithm

The quick sort algorithm is performed using following two important functions - *Quick* and *partition.* Let us see them -

```
Algorithm Quick(A[0...n-1],low,high)
//Problem Description : This algorithm performs sorting of
//the elements given in Array A[0...n-1]
//Input: An array A[0...n-1] in which unsorted elements are
//given. The low indicates the leftmost element in the list
//and high indicates the rightmost element in the list
//Output: Creates a sub array which is sorted in ascending
//order
if(low<high)then
//split the array into two sub arrays
m ← partition(A[low...high])// m is mid of the array
Quick(A[low...m-1])
Quick(A[mid+1...high] )
```

In above algorithm call to partition algorithm is given. The *partition* performs arrangement of the elements in ascending order. The recursive *quick* routine is for dividing the list in two sub lists. The pseudo code for *Partition* is as given below -

```
Algorithm Partition (A[low...high])
//Problem Description: This algorithm partitions the
//subarray using the first element as pivot element
//Input: A subarray A with low as left most index of the
//array and high as the rightmost index of the array.
//Output: The partitioning of array A is done and pivot
//occupies its proper position. And the rightmost index of
//the list is returned
pivot ← A[low]
i ← low
j ← high+1
while(i<=j) do
{
 while(A[i]<=pivot) do
  i ← i+1
 while(A[j]>=pivot) do
  j ← j-1;
if(i<=j) then
```

```
            swap(A[i],A[j])//swaps A[i] and A[j]
}
swap(A[low],A[j])//when i crosses j swap A[low] and A[j]
return j//rightmost index of the list
```

The partition function is called to arrange the elements such that all the elements that are less than pivot are at the left side of pivot and all the elements that are greater than pivot are all at the right of pivot. In other words pivot is occupying its proper position and the partitioned list is obtained in an ordered manner.

Analysis

When pivot is chosen such that the array gets divided at the mid then it gives the best case time complexity. The best case time complexity of quick sort is $O(n\log_2 n)$.

The worst case for quick sort occurs when the pivot is minimum or maximum of all the elements in the list. This can be graphically represented as -

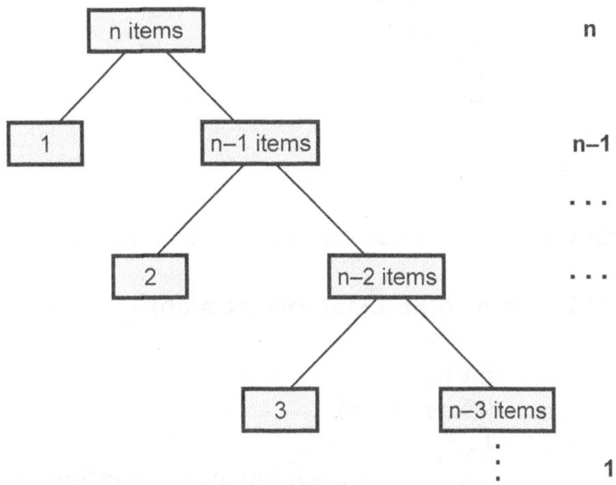

Fig. 10.1.2

This ultimately results in $O(n^2)$ time complexity. When array elements are randomly distributed then it results in average case time complexity, and it is $O(n\log_2 n)$.

C Program

```
/*****************************************************************
    Program to sort the elements in ascending order using Quick Sort.
*****************************************************************/
#include<stdio.h>
#include<conio.h>
#include<stdlib.h>
#define SIZE 10
void Quick(int A[SIZE],int,int);
int partition(int A[SIZE],int,int);
void swap(int A[SIZE],int *,int *);
int n;
int main()
{
        int i;
        int A[SIZE];
```

```
        clrscr();
        printf("\n\t\t Quick Sort Method \n");
        printf("\n Enter Total numbers to sort : ");
        scanf("%d",&n);
        for(i=0;i<n;i++)
        {
         printf("\nEnter %dth number : ",i+1);
         scanf("%d",&A[i]);
        }
        Quick(A,0,n-1);
        printf("\n\n\t Sorted Array Is: \n");
        for(i=0;i<n;i++)
         printf("\t%d ",A[i]);
        getch();
        return 0;
}

/*
This function is to sort the elements in a sublist
*/
void Quick(int A[SIZE],int low,int high)
{
        int m,i;
        if(low<high)
        {
          m=Partition(A,low,high);//setting pivot element
          Quick(A,low,m-1);//splitting of list
          Quick(A,m+1,high);//splitting  of list
        }

}
/*
This function is to partition a list and decide the pivot
element
*/
int Partition(int A[SIZE],int low,int high)
{
        int pivot=A[low],i=low,j=high;
        while(i<=j)
        {
         while(A[i]<=pivot)
                i++;
         while(A[j]>pivot)
                j--;
         if(i<j)
                swap(A,&i,&j);
        }
```

```
        swap(A,&low,&j);
        return j;
}

void swap(int A[SIZE],int *i,int *j)
{
        int temp;

        temp=A[*i];
        A[*i]=A[*j];
        A[*j]=temp;
}
```

Output

```
                Quick Sort Method

Enter Total numbers to sort : 8

Enter 1th number : 50

Enter 2th number : 30

Enter 3th number : 10

Enter 4th number : 90

Enter 5th number : 80

Enter 6th number : 20

Enter 7th number : 40

Enter 8th number : 70

   Sorted Array Is:
10  20  30  40  50  70  80  90
```

Example 10.1.3 *Trace the Quick sort algorithm for the following list of numbers : 90, 77, 60, 99, 55, 88, 62.*

Solution : Let us arrange the given numbers in an array.

Step 1 :

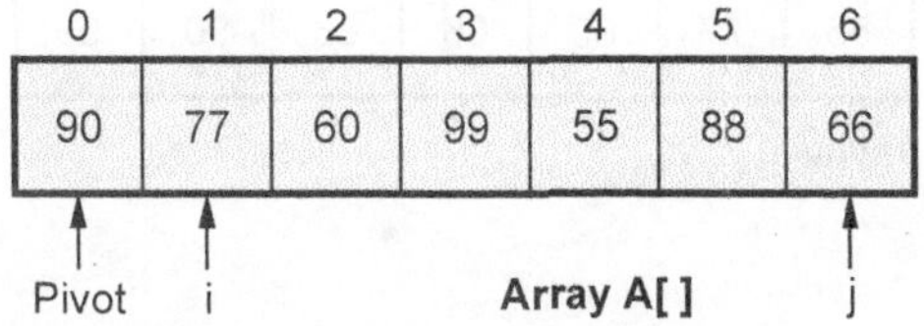

Assume A [0] = 90 as pivot element. Set A [1] = 77 as i^{th} and A [6] as j^{th} element.

If A [pivot] > A [i] increment i and if A [j] > A [pivot] then decrement j. Otherwise swap A [i] and A [j] element.

Step 2 :

90	77	60	99	55	88	66
↑ Pivot			i			j

Swap A [i] and A [j]. Then if A [pivot] > A [i] then increment i and if A [pivot] < A [j] then decrements j.

90	77	60	66	55	88	99
					i/j	

As i = j Swap A [pivot] and A [j].

88	77	60	66	55	90	99
Left sublist						Right sublist

Step 3 :

88	77	60	66	55	90	99
Pivot	i			j		

88	77	60	66	55	90	99
				i/j		

55	77	60	66	88	90	99
Pivot	i		j			

Step 4 :

55	77	60	66	88	90	99
Pivot/i j						

Step 5 :

55	77	60	66	88	90	99
	Pivot	i	j			

55	77	60	66	88	90	99
	Pivot		i/j			

As i = j Swap A [j] and A [pivot]

Step 6 :

55	66	60	77	88	90	99
	Pivot		i/j			

55	66	60	77	88	90	99
	Pivot	i/j				

Swap A [j] and A [pivot]

Step 7 :

55	60	66	77	88	90	99

This is the sorted list.

Example 10.1.4 *Apply quicksort algorithm to sort the following data.*

Justify the steps

42, 29, 74, 11, 65, 58. **GTU : Winter-15, Marks 4**

Solution :

Step 1 : Arrange the elements in array.

42	29	74	11	65	58
pivot	i				j

i) If A [i] < A [pivot] increment i.

ii) If A [j] > A [pivot] decrement j

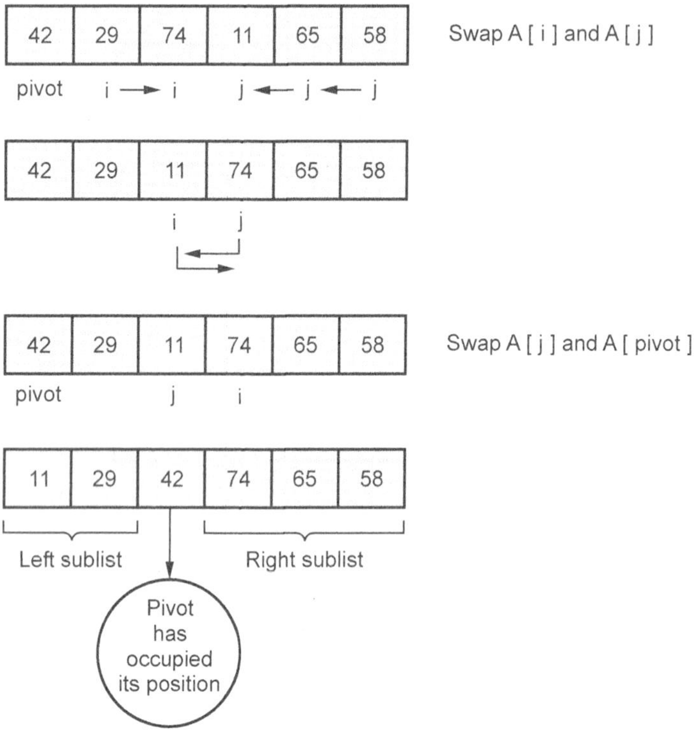

Step 2 : Now we will handle left sub-list obtained in step 1.

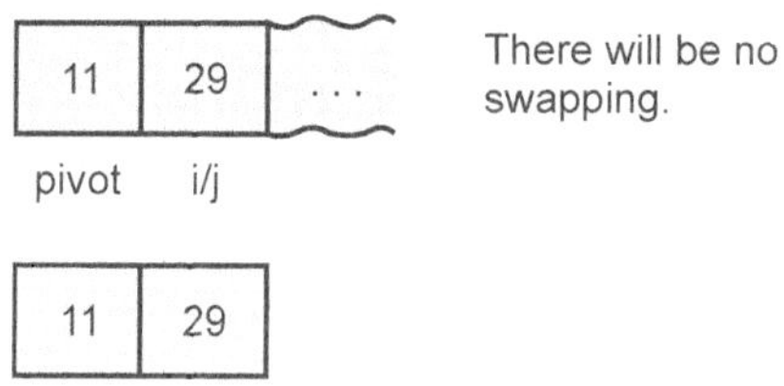

Step 3 : We will handle right sub-list obtained in step 2.

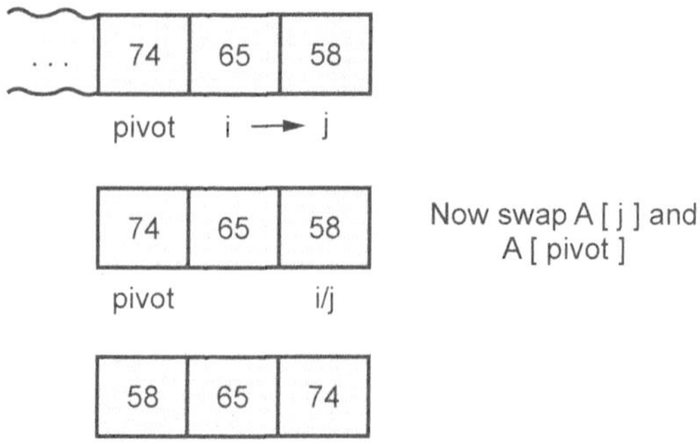

Step 4 : Finally after combining all the sublists we get -

11	29	42	58	65	74

This is sorted list.

Example 10.1.5 *Sort the following numbers using (i) Selection sort (ii) Quick sort.*

10 50 0 20 30 10

GTU : Winter-16, Marks 7

Solution : i) Selection sort :

Step 1 :

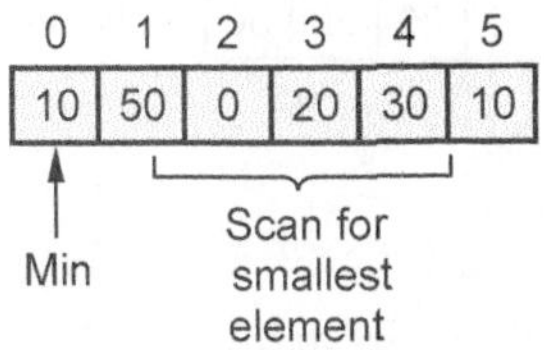

Swap A[0] and A[2]

0	1	2	3	4	5
0	50	10	20	30	10

Step 2 :

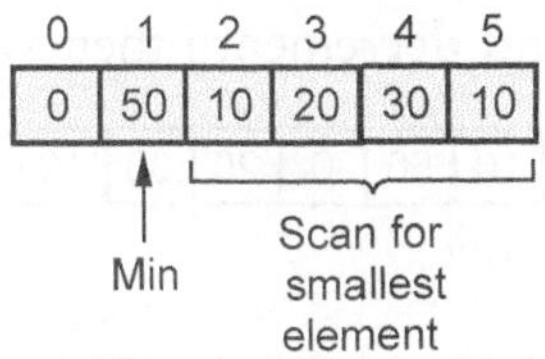

Swap A[1] and A[2]

0	1	2	3	4	5
0	10	50	20	30	10

Step 3 :

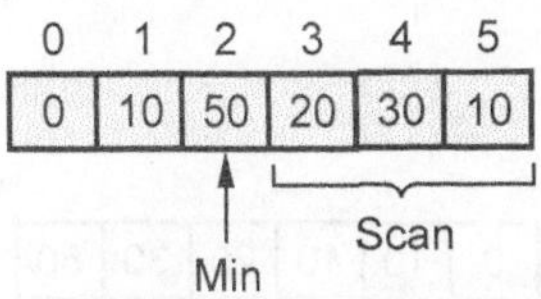

Swap A[2] and A[5]

0	1	2	3	4	5
0	10	10	20	30	50

Step 4 :

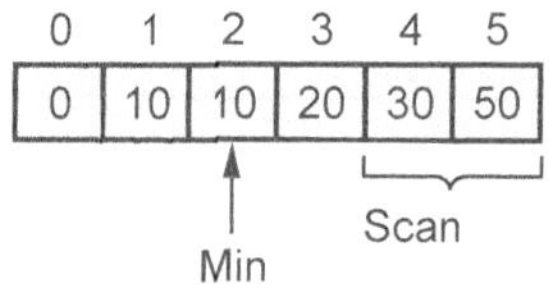

No swapping take place.

Step 5 :

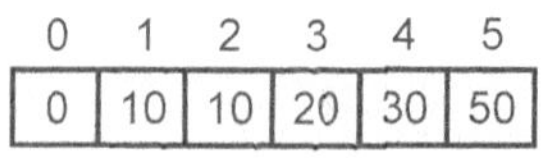

No swappings

This a final sorted list.

ii) Quick sort :

Step 1 : Consider list of elements in an array

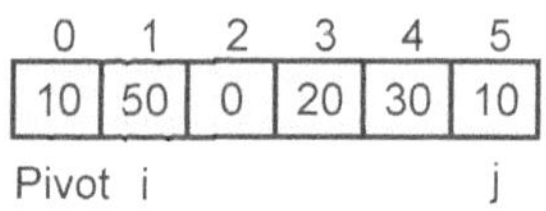

i) If A[i] < A [pivot] increment i.

ii) If A[j] > A [pivot] decrement j.

iii) If we can not increment i and decrement j then swap A[i] and A[j].

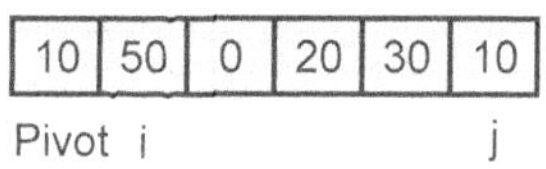

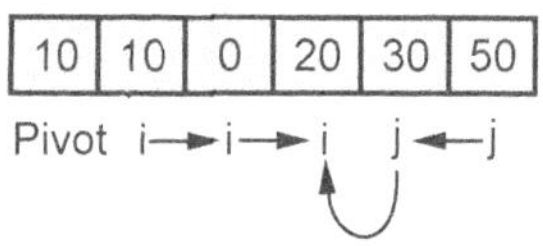

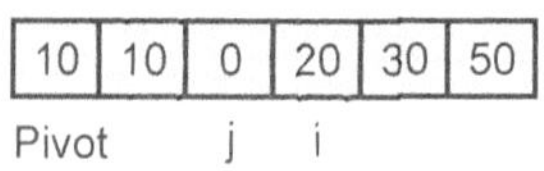

Swap A[Pivot] and A[j]

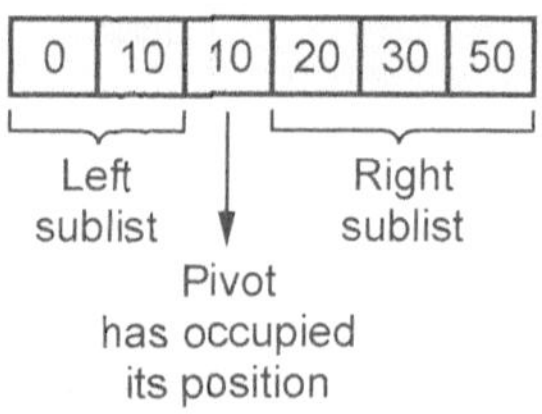

Step 2 : Now we will handle left sublist obtained in step 1.

Hence we get

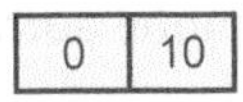

Step 3 : We will handle right sublist obtained in step 1.

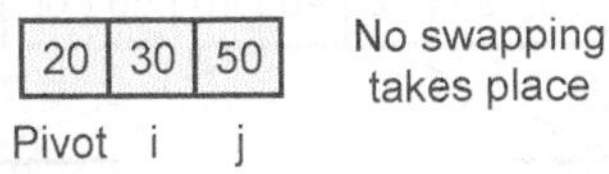

Hence we get

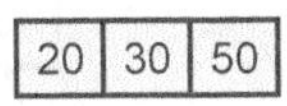

Step 4 : Combining all sublists from above steps we get -

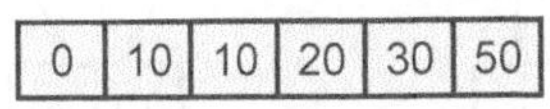

This is sorted list

Review Questions

1. *Write down the algorithm for bubble sort and explain how you can sort an unsorted array of integers by using quick-sort. Find out the time complexity of your algorithm.*
2. *Write the algorithm for bubble sort and insertion sort. Explain their best case and worst case complexities.*
3. *Explain quick sort method and determine its complexities.*
4. *Write an algorithm for quick sort.* **GTU : Winter-16, Marks 4**
5. *Apply quick sort on following data*
   42 23 74 11 65 58 94 36 99 87. **GTU : Winter-17, Marks 7**
6. *What is the complexity of the quick sort algorithm on sorted data ? Justify your answer.* **GTU : Summer-18, Marks 3**

10.1.4 Merge Sort

The merge sort is a sorting algorithm that uses the divide and conquer strategy. In this method division is dynamically carried out.

Merge sort on an input array with n elements consists of three steps :

Divide : partition array into two sub lists s1 and s2 with n/2 elements each.

Conquer : Then sort sub list s1 and sub list s2.

Combine : Merge s1 and s2 into a unique sorted group.

Example 1 : Consider the elements as

70, 20, 30, 40, 10, 50, 60

Now we will split this list into two sublists.

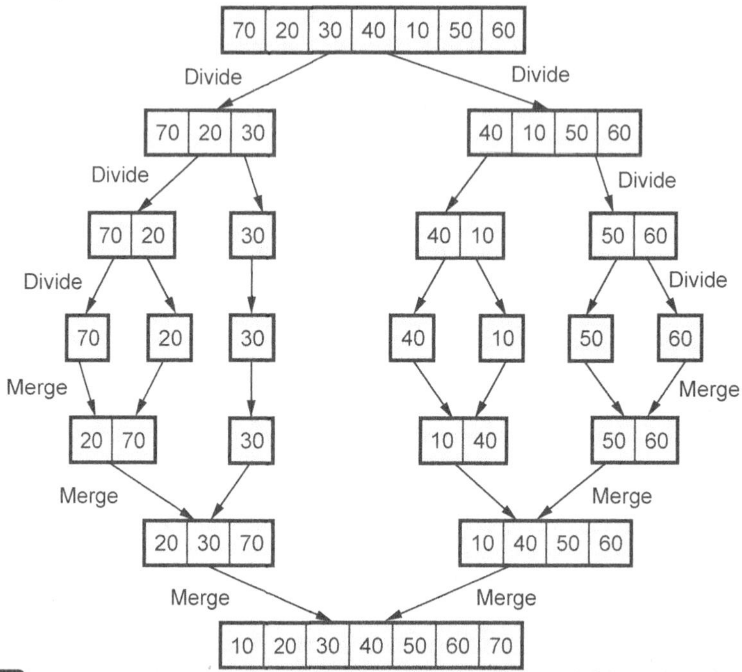

Example 10.1.6 *Use merge-sort algorithm to sort the following elements 15, 10, 5, 20, 25, 30, 40, 35.*

Solution :

15	10	5	20	25	30	40	35

Divide the list, recursively

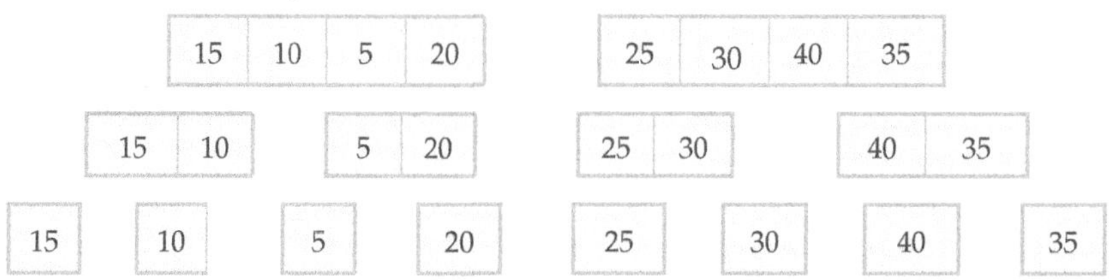

Now combine each group

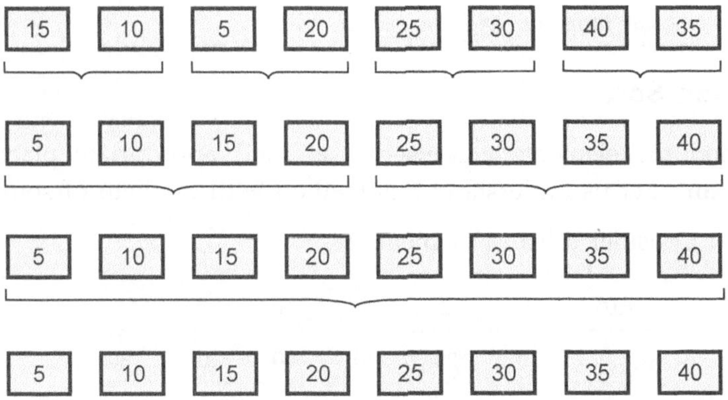

This is a sorted list

Example 10.1.7 *Apply merge sort algorithm for the following data and show the steps.*
66, 33, 40, 22, 55, 88, 11, 80, 20, 50, 44, 77, 30. **GTU : Summer-18, Marks 7**

Solution :

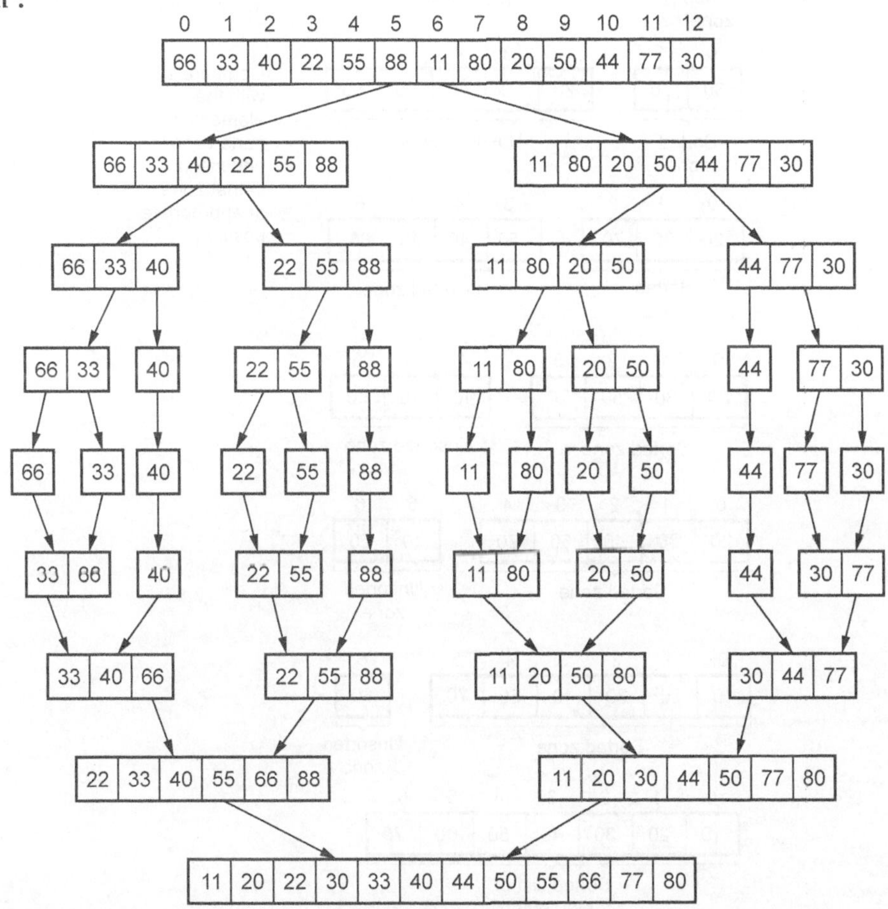

This is sorted list

Review Question

1. *Explain Merge sort technique with the help of example.*

10.1.5 Insertion Sort

In this method the elements are inserted at their appropriate place. Hence is the name **insertion sort**. Let us understand this method with the help of some example -

For Example : Consider a list of elements as,

0	1	2	3	4	5	6
30	70	20	50	40	10	60

The process starts with first element

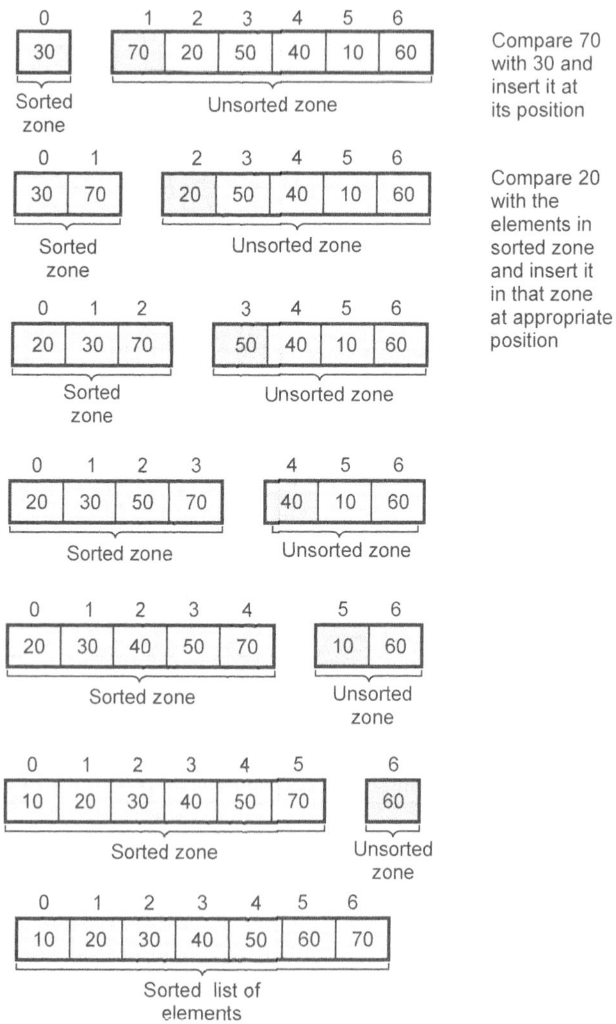

Algorithm

Although it is very natural to implement insertion using recursive(top down) algorithm but it is very efficient to implement it using bottom up(iterative) approach.

```
Algorithm Insert_sort(A[0...n−1])
//Problem Description: This algorithm is for sorting the
//elements using insertion sort
//Input: An array of n elements
//Output: Sorted array A[0...n−1] in ascending order
 for i ← 1 to n-1 do
{
        temp ← A[i]//mark A[i]th element
        j ← i−1//set j at previous element of A[i]
        while(j>=0)AND(A[j]>temp)do
        {
    //comparing all the previous elements of A[i] with
    //A[i].If any greater element is found then insert
    //it at proper position
        A[j+1] ← A[j]
        j ← j−1
        }
        A[j+1] ← temp //copy A[i] element at A[j+1]
}
```

Analysis

When an array of elements is almost sorted then it is **best case** complexity. The best case time complexity of insertion sort is **O(n).**

If an array is randomly distributed then it results in **average case** time complexity which is $O(n^2)$.

If the list of elements is arranged in descending order and if we want to sort the elements in ascending order then it results in **worst case** time complexity which is $O(n^2)$.

C Program

```
/*****************************************************************
    Implementation of insertion sort
*****************************************************************/
#include<stdio.h>
#include<conio.h>
void main()
{
 int A[10],n,i;
 void Insert_sort(int A[10],int n);
 clrscr();
 printf("\n\t\t Insertion Sort");
```

```
 printf("\n How many elements are there?");
 scanf("%d",&n);
 printf("\n Enter the elements\n");
 for(i=0;i<n;i++)
          scanf("%d",&A[i]);
 Insert_sort(A,n);
 getch();

}
void Insert_sort(int A[10],int n)
{
 int i,j,temp;
 for(i=1;i<=n-1;i++)
 {
          temp=A[i];
          j=i-1;
          while((j>=0)&&(A[j]>temp))
          {
           A[j+1]=A[j];
           j=j-1;
          }
          A[j+1]=temp;
 }
 printf("\n The sorted list of elements is...\n");
 for(i=0;i<n;i++)
          printf("\n%d",A[i]);
}
```

Output

```
                         Insertion Sort
     How many elements are there?5

     Enter the elements
30
20
10
40
50

     The sorted list of elements is...
10
20
30
40
50
```

Logic Explanation

For understanding the logic of above C program consider a list of unsorted elements as,

Then the control moves to **while loop**. As j >= 0 and A[j] > temp is **True**, the while loop will be executed.

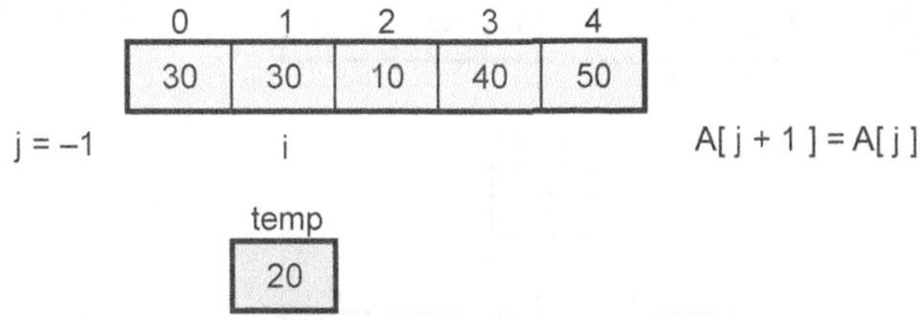

Now since j >= 0 is false, control comes out of while loop.

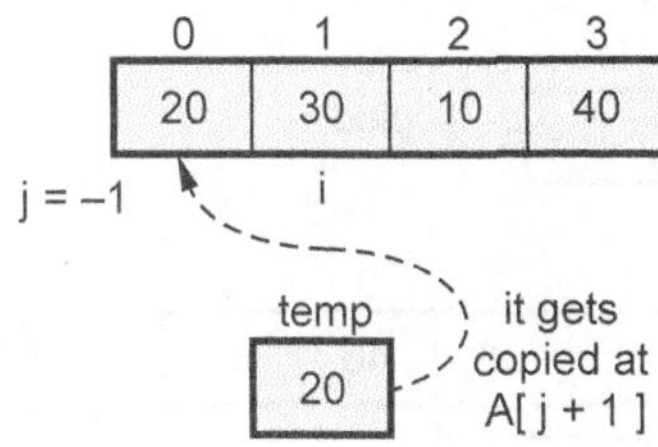

Then list becomes,

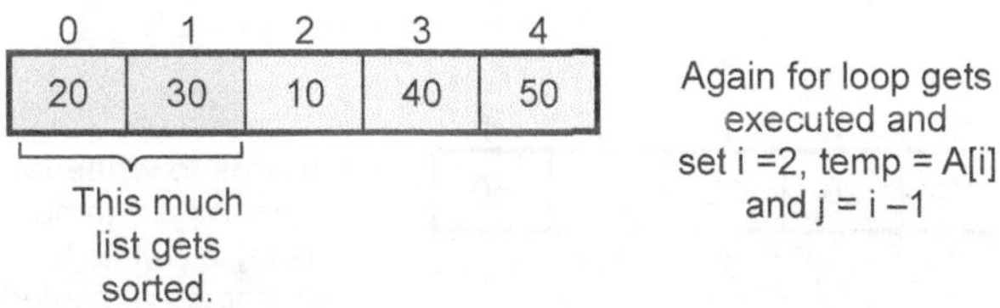

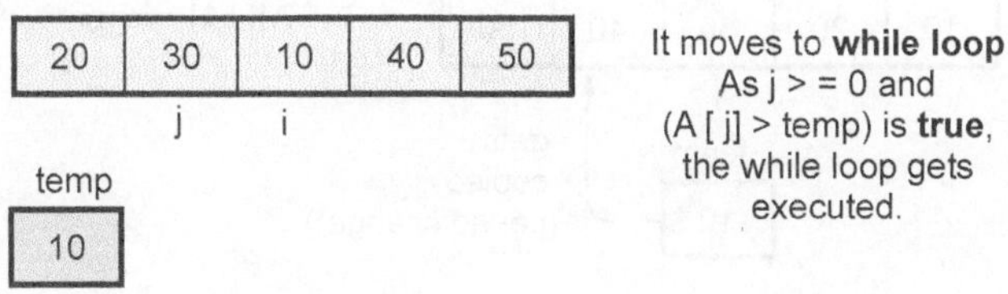

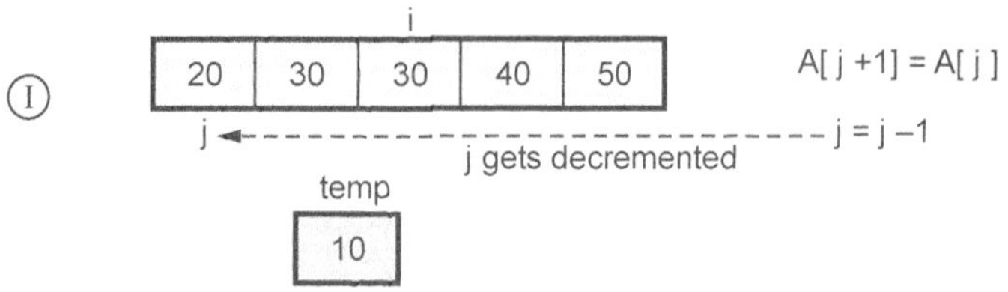
I
i
20 30 30 40 50
A[j +1] = A[j]
j
j = j –1
j gets decremented
temp
10

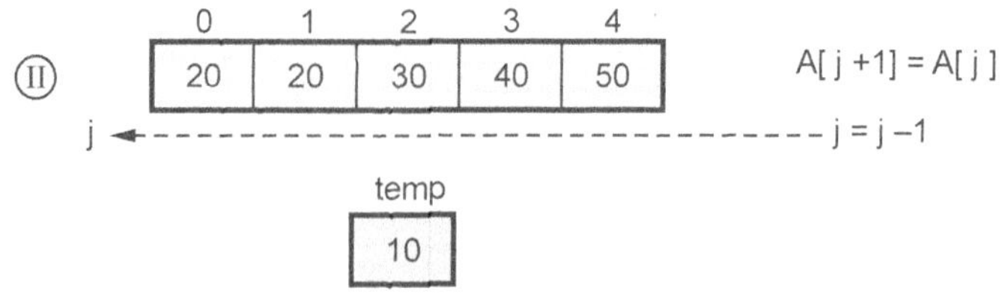
II
0 1 2 3 4
20 20 30 40 50
A[j +1] = A[j]
j
j = j –1
temp
10

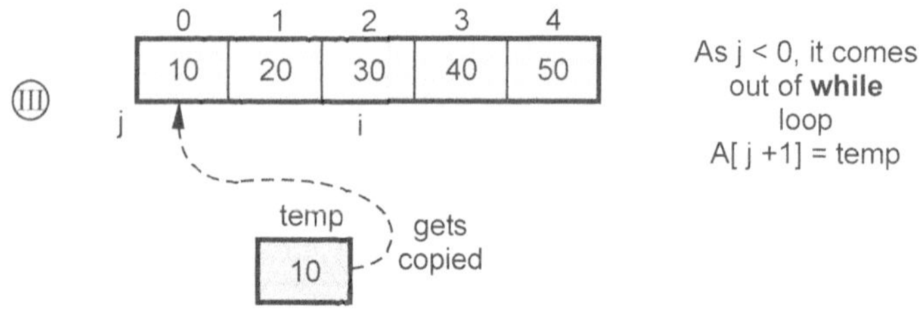
III
0 1 2 3 4
10 20 30 40 50
As j < 0, it comes out of while loop
A[j +1] = temp
j
i
temp
10
gets copied

Thus,

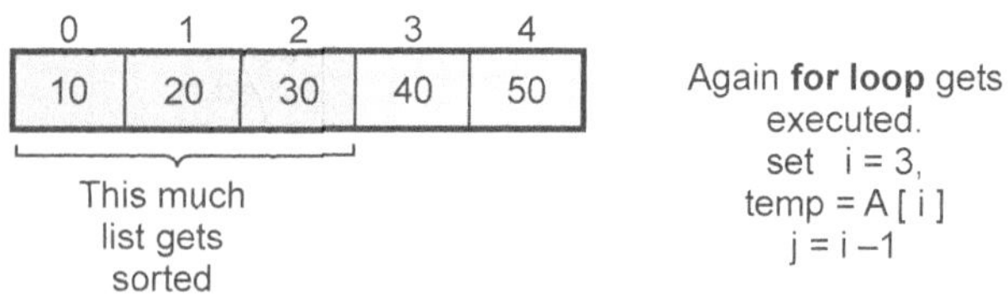
0 1 2 3 4
10 20 30 40 50
This much list gets sorted
Again for loop gets executed.
set i = 3,
temp = A [i]
j = i –1

Then,

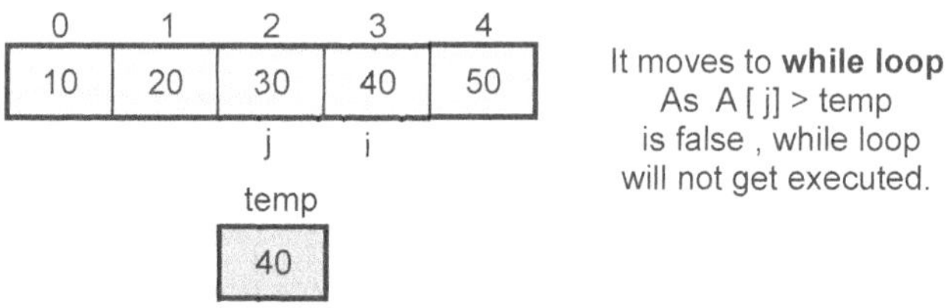
0 1 2 3 4
10 20 30 40 50
j
i
temp
40
It moves to while loop
As A [j] > temp
is false , while loop
will not get executed.

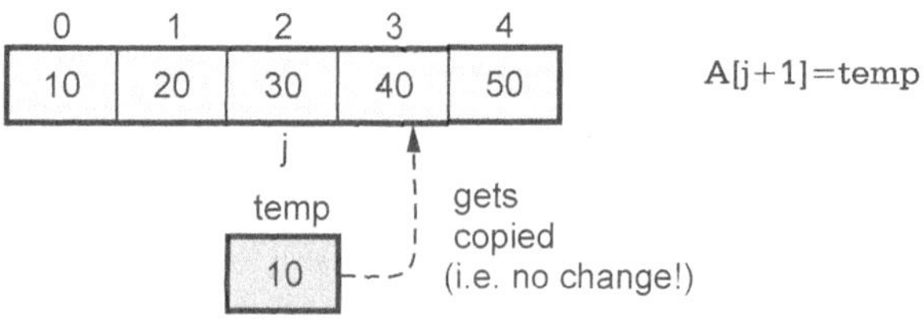
0 1 2 3 4
10 20 30 40 50
A[j+1]=temp
j
temp
10
gets copied
(i.e. no change!)

Then,

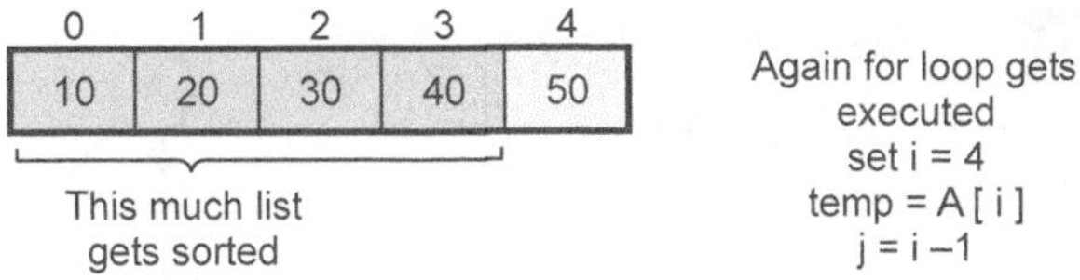

Then,

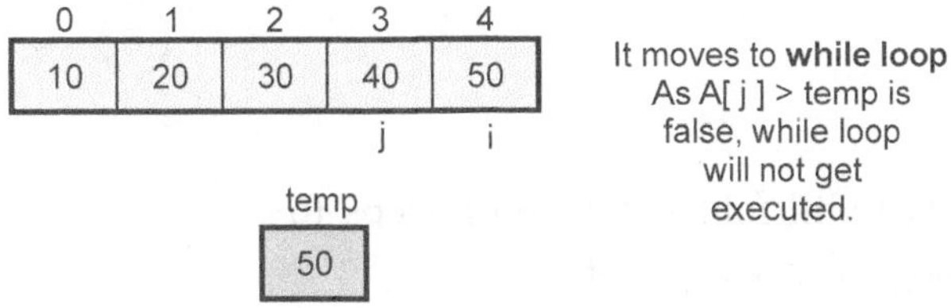

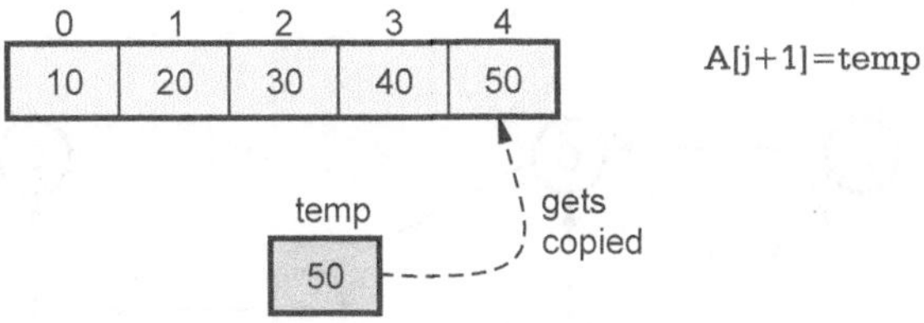

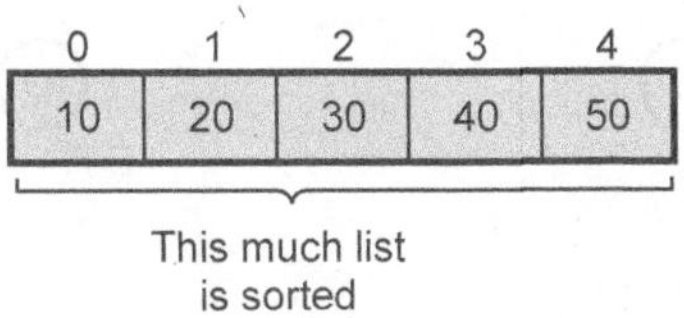

Thus we have scanned the entire list and inserted the elements at corresponding locations. Thus we get the sorted list by insertion sort.

10.1.6 Topological Sorting

Following are the steps to be followed in topological sorting algorithm -

1. From a given graph find a vertex with no incoming edges. Delete it along with all the edges outgoing from it. If there are more than one such vertices then break the tie randomly.
2. Note the vertices that are deleted.
3. All these recorded vertices give topologically sorted list.

Let us understand this algorithm with some examples -

Example 10.1.8 *Sort the digraph for topological sort using source removal algorithm.*

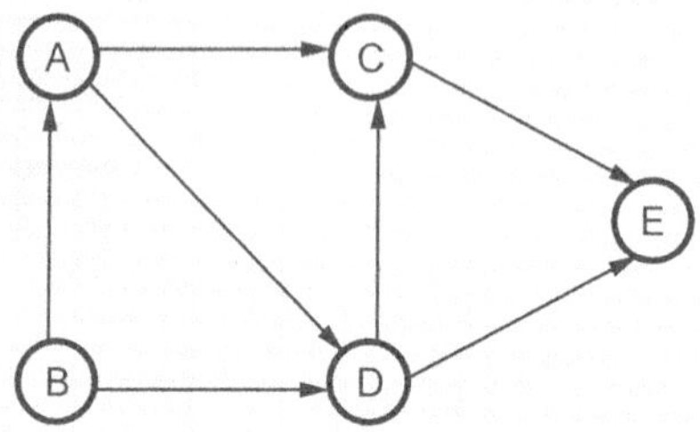

Solution : We will follow following steps to obtain topologically sorted list.

Choose vertex B, because it has no incoming edge, delete it along with its adjacent edges.

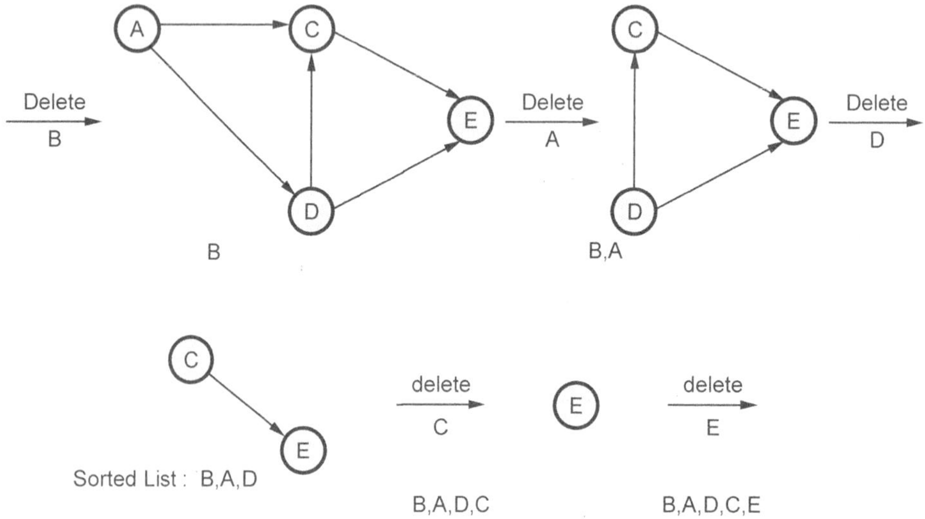

Hence the list after topological sorting will be B, A, D, C, E.

Review Question

1. *Write a 'C' program for insertion sort and discuss its efficiency.* **GTU : Summer-15, Marks 7**
1. *Write an algorithm for insertion sort method. Explain each step with an example.* **GTU : Summer-16, Marks 7**
2. *Explain the difference between insertion sort and selection sort with an example. What is the time complexity of these algorithms ? How ?* **GTU : Summer-18, Marks 7**

10.2 Searching

GTU : Winter-14, 16,17,18, Summer-15,16,18

Searching is a technique of finding particular record with the help of some key value. The most desirable characteristic of searching technique is that - it should be efficient.

Searching can be performed by various methods, but the most popularly used methods are -

1. Sequential Search
2. Binary Search

Let us discuss them with the help of examples and C programs.

10.2.1 Sequential Search

- In this technique, **each record is visited sequentially** from the beginning of the list and compared with the key element. The key element represents the element to be searched from the list.
- Although this is a **simple searching technique, unnecessary comparisons** are performed.
- This method does not give the satisfactory solution for the system for large number of elements.
- The time complexity of this searching technique is **O(n)**
- The time complexity will increase linearly with the value of n. For higher value of n the linear search is not the satisfactory solution.

Array

	Roll no.	Name	Marks
0	15	Parth	96
1	2	Anand	40
2	13	Lalita	81
3	1	Madhav	50
4	12	Arun	78
5	3	Jaya	94

Fig. 10.2.1 Represents students database for sequential search

From the above Fig. 10.2.1 the array is maintained to store the students record. The record is not sorted at all. If we want to search the student's record whose roll number is 12 then with the key-roll number we will see the every record whether it is of roll number = 12. We can obtain such a record at array [4] location.

Let us implement the sequential search using C program

'C' program :

```
/**********************************************************
Program to perform the linear search operation on some number of elements.
**********************************************************/
#include<stdio.h>
#include<conio.h>
#define MAX 10
int a[MAX],n,i;

/*
The create Function
Input :none
Output:none
Called By: main
Calls:none
*/
void create()
{
 printf("\n How Many Elements");
 scanf("%d",&n);
 printf("\n Enter The Elements");
 for(i=0;i<n;i++)
  scanf("%d",&a[i]);
}
/*

 The display Function
 Input:none
 Output:none
 Called By:main
 Calls:none
*/
void display()
{
 printf("\n The Elements Are");
 for(i=0;i<n;i++)
  printf("\n%d",a[i]);

}
/*
The search function
Input:key element- which is to be searched
Output:the status
Called By:main
Calls:none
*/
search(int k)
```

```
{
 for(i=0;i<n;i++)
 {
  if(a[i]==k)
  return 1;
 }
return 0;
}
void main()
{
 int status,key;
 clrscr();
 create();
 display();
 printf("\n Enter the Element Which You wish to Search ");
 scanf("%d",&key);
 status=search(key);
 if (status ==1)
  printf("\n The Element is Present");
 else
  printf("\n The Element Is Not Found");
 getch();
}
/******************End Of Program*********************/
 How Many Elements 5
 Enter The Elements 10
1
100
1000
10000
 The Elements Are
10
1
100
1000
10000
 Enter the Element Which You wish to Search 99
 The Element Is Not Found
 How Many Elements 5
 Enter The Elements 10
1
100
1000
10000
 The Elements Are
10
1
```

```
100
1000
10000
 Enter the Element Which You wish to Search 100
 The Element is Present
```

Advantages of linear searching

1. It is simple to implement.
2. It does not require specific ordering before applying the method.

Disadvantage of linear searching

1. It is less efficient.

Review Question

1. *Explain sequential search method.* **GTU : Summer-16, Marks 3**
2. *Write an algorithm for sequential search.* **GTU : Winter-18, Marks 4**

10.2.2 Binary Search

GTU : Winter-14, Marks 7

Precondition :

The prerequisite for this searching technique is that the list should be sorted.

Example :

As mentioned earlier the necessity of this method is that all the elements should be sorted. So let us take an array of sorted elements.

Array

0	1	2	3	4	5	6	7
– 40	11	33	37	42	45	99	100

Step 1 : Now the key element which is to be searched is = 99 ∴ key = 99.

Step 2 : Find the middle element of the array. Compare it with the key

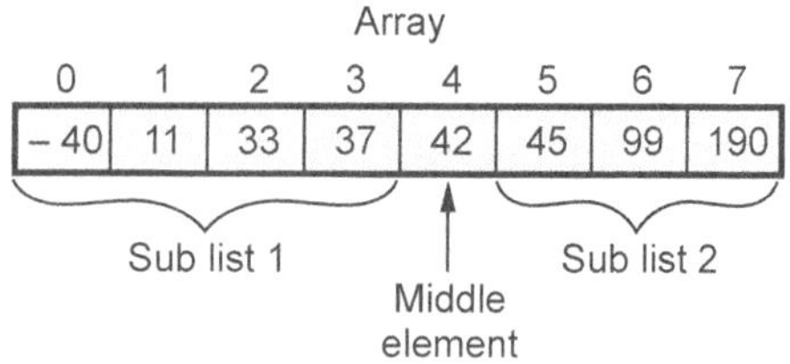

if middle $\overset{?}{=}$ key

i.e. if 42 $\overset{?}{=}$ 99

if 42 < 99 search the sublist 2

Now handle only sublist 2. Again divide it, find mid of sublist 2 if middle $\overset{?}{==}$ key

i.e. if 99 $\overset{?}{==}$ 99

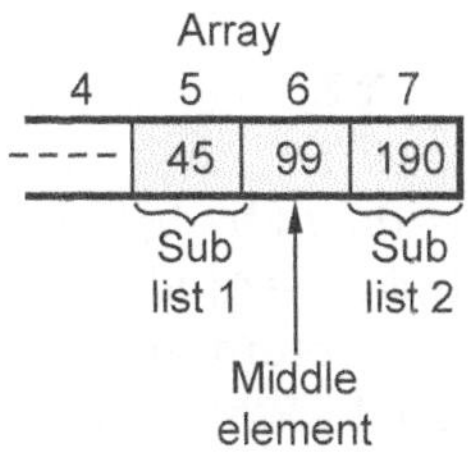

So match is found at 7th position of array i.e. at array [6]

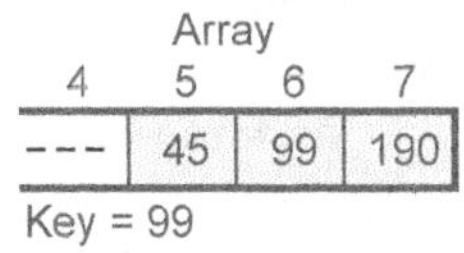

Thus by binary search method we can find the element 99 present in the given list at array $[6]^{th}$ location.

Non recursive binary search program

```
/*******************************************************************
Implementation of non recursive Binary Search algorithm
*******************************************************************/
#include<stdio.h>
#include<conio.h>
#define SIZE 10
int n;
void main()
{
 int A[SIZE],KEY,i,flag;
 int BinSearch(int A[SIZE],int KEY);
 clrscr();
 printf("\n How Many elements in an array?");
 scanf("%d",&n);
 printf("\n Enter The Elements");
 for(i=0;i<n;i++)
      scanf("%d",&A[i]);
 printf("\n Enter the element which is to be searched");
 scanf("%d",&KEY);
 flag=BinSearch(A,KEY);
 if(flag==-1)
      printf("\n The Element is not present");
 else
      printf("\n The element is at A[%d] location",flag);
 getch();
}
int BinSearch(int A[SIZE],int KEY)
{
 int low,high,m;
 low=0;
```

```
 high=n-1;
 while(low<=high)
 {
          m=(low+high)/2;//mid of the array is obtained
          if(KEY==A[m])
                 return m;
          else if(KEY<A[m])
                 high=m-1;        //search the left sub list
          else
                 low=m+1;         //search the right sub list
     }
     return-1; //if element is not present in the list
}
```

Output (Run 1)

```
How Many elements in an array? 6

Enter The Elements
10
20
30
40
50
60

     Enter the element which is to be searched 50

     The element is at A[4] location
```

(Run 2)

```
     How Many elements in an array? 5

     Enter The Elements
     10
     20
     30
     40
     50
     Enter the element which is to be searched 80

     The Element is not present
```

Algorithm for binary search using recursive definition :

1. if(low > high)
2. return;

3. mid = (low + high)/2;
4. if(x==a[mid])
5. return (mid);
6. if(x < a[mid])
7. search for x in a[low] to a[mid-1];
8. else
9. search for x in a[mid + 1] to a[high];

Recursive binary search program

```
/************************************************************
Program for searching the number by Binary Search. The list of
numbers should be in ascending order. The program also shows the
location at which the number is present(if at all)
*************************************************************/
#include<stdio.h>
#include<conio.h>
#include<stdlib.h>
#define size 10
/*
 The binsearch Function
 Input:array of elements,key element,
        starting and ending element of the list
        i.e.a,x,low and high.
 Output:loaction at which the numebr can be present
 Called By:main
 Calls:itself
*/
int binsearch(int a[],int x,int low,int high)
{
 int mid;
 if(low>high)
  return(-1);
 mid = (low+high)/2;
 if(x ==a[mid])
  return(mid);
 else if(x<a[mid])
  binsearch(a,x,low,mid-1);
 else
  binsearch(a,x,mid+1,high);
}
/*
 The main Function
 Input:none
 Output:none
```

```
 Called By:O.S.
 Calls:binsearch
*/
void main(void)
{
 int n,i,low,high,a[size],key,ans;
 clrscr();
 printf("\n\t\t\t Binary Search Method ");
 printf("\n Enter the total number of elements");
 scanf("%d",&n);
 printf("\nEnter the list of elements");
 for(i=0;i<n;i++)
  scanf("%d",&a[i]);
  low = 0;
  high = n-1;
 printf("\n Enter the element which you want to search");
 scanf("%d",&key);
 ans=binsearch(a,key,low,high);
 if(ans!= -1)
 printf("\n The number %d is present in the list at
                  location %d",key,ans+1);
 else
  printf("\n The number is not present in the list");
 getch();
}
/****************** End Of Program ********************/
```

Output

```
                  Binary Search Method
Enter the total number of elements 5
Enter the list of elements
10
20
30
40
50
Enter the element which you want to search 40
The number 40 is present in the list at location 4
```

Advantage of binary searching

1. It is an efficient technique.

Disadvantages of binary searching

1. It requires specific ordering before the applying the method.
2. It is complex to implement.

Review Question

1. *Write down precondition and algorithm of binary search method.* **GTU : Winter-14, Marks 7**
2. *Write an algorithm for binary search method and discuss its efficiency.* **GTU : Summer-15, Marks 7**
3. *Explain binary search method.* **GTU : Summer-16,18, Marks 4**
4. *Write an algorithm for binary search method.* **GTU : Winter-16,18, Marks 3**
5. *How binary search technique can be applied to search for a particular item with a certain key ?* **GTU : Winter-17, Marks 4**
6. *Write the algorithm for binary search and find its complexity.* **GTU : Summer-18, Marks 4**

10.2.3 Difference between Sequential Search and Binary Search

Sr. No.	Sequential search	Binary search
1.	For searching the element by using sequential search method it is not required to arrange the elements in some specific order.	The elements need to be arranged either in ascending or descending order.
2.	Each and every element is compared with the key element from the beginning of the list.	The list is subdivided into two sublists. The key element is searched in the sublist.
3.	Less efficient method.	Efficient method.
4.	Simple to implement.	Additional computation is required for computing mid element.

Review Questions

1. *Explain sequential search. Write a C function for implementing sequential search.*
2. *Explain binary search with the help of illustrative example.*
3. *Give the difference between sequential search and binary search.*

10.3 Oral Questions and Answers

Q.1 What do you understand by the term sorting ?

Ans. : Sorting is a mechanism of arranging the data in particular order.

Q.2 What is the need for sorting ?

Ans. : The sorting is useful for - 1. Searching the desired data efficiently. 2. Responding to the queries.

Q.3 What is the meaning of sort key ?

Ans. : Sort key is a field in the record based on which the sorting is conducted.

Q.4 Name the slowest and fastest sorting technique.

Ans. : Bubble sort is a slowest sorting technique and quick sort is the fastest sorting technique.

Q.5 Differentiate between internal and external sorting.

Ans. : Internal sorting : This is a type of sorting technique in which data resides on main memory of computer.

External sorting : This is a sorting technique in which there is huge amount of data and it resides on secondary storage devices while sorting.

Q.6 Explain the meaning of the term passes in context with sorting.

Ans. : While sorting the elements in some specific order, there is lot of arrangement of elements. The phases in which the elements are moving to acquire their proper position is called passes.

Q.7 What is ascending and descending order ?

Ans. : Ascending order is the sorting order in which the elements are arranged from low value to high value. In other words it is called increasing order.
For example : 10, 20, 30, 40.

Descending order is the sorting order in which the elements are arranged from high value to low value. In other words it is called decreasing order.
For example : 40, 30, 20, 10.

Q.8 What is the basic principle behind the quick sort ?

Ans. : The division of the list into two sublists(which is called partition) and then sorting each sublist independently. This is the basic principle used in quick sort. Based on the value of pivot element, the list is subdivided.

Q.9 Enlist four internal sorting techniques.

Ans. : Following are some internal sorting techniques -

1. Insertion sort
2. Selection sort
3. Merge sort
4. Bubble sort.

Q.10 The way a card game player arranges his cards as he picks them one by one , is an example of ______.

Ans. : insertion sort.

Q.11 What are the advantages of binary search over the linear search ?

Ans. : Binary search is an efficient searching method than the linear search. Using this method, the list is subdivided each time and only sublist is scanned for locating the key value.

Q.12 List the sorting algorithms which uses logarithmic time complexity.

Ans. : The sorting algorithms which use the logarithmic time complexity are - Quick sort and merge sort.

Q.13 What is the worst case time complexity of searching an element in a list ? How ? GTU : Winter-15

Ans. : The O(n) is the worst case time complexity where n denotes number of elements in the list. In this case the complete list is searched for the key but it is not present in the list.

Q.14 What is the complexity of binary search algorithm ? GTU : Winter-15

Ans. : The complexity of binary search algorithm is O(log n).

Q.15 Name two divide and conquer algorithms for sorting. GTU : Winter-15

Ans. : The merge sort and quick sort algorithms make use of divide and conquer algorithm.

Q.16 For sorting 1 GB of data with only 100 MB of available main memory. Which sorting technique will be most appropriate ? GTU : Summer-17

Ans. : Merge Sort

Q.17 Consider a situation where swap operation is very costly. Which of the sorting algorithms should be preferred so that the number of swap operations are minimized in general ? GTU : Summer-17

Ans. : Selection sort

Q.18 What is time complexity of quick sort algorithm in the worst case ? GTU : Summer-16

Ans. : $O(N^2)$

❑❑❑

Notes

Data Structures Laboratory

Experiment 1 : Introduction to pointers. Call by Value and Call by reference.

- **Definition of Pointer :** A pointer is a variable that represents the memory location of some other variable. The purpose of pointer is to hold the memory location and not the actual value.
- In C declaration if the variable name is preceded by **asterisk** or * then such a variable is called **pointer variable**.

  For example,

  ```
  int *a;
  ```

  Here the variable **a** is preceded by an asterisk and it is called **pointer variable**.
- **Declaration :** Consider the variable declaration

  ```
  int *ptr;
  ```

  ptr is the name of our variable. The * informs the compiler that we want a pointer variable, the **int** says that we are using our pointer variable which will actually store the address of an integer. Such a pointer is said to be **integer pointer**.

  Thus **ptr** is now ready to store an address of the value which is of integer type.
- **Initialization :** Once the pointer variable is declared then it can be used further. In the sense we can assign some value to it. But note that the pointer variable is basically used to store some address of the variable which is holding some value.

Program to access variable using pointer

```
#include<stdio.h>
#include<conio.h>
void main()
{
    int *ptr;
    int a,b;
    clrscr();
    a=10; /*storing some value in a*/
    ptr=&a;/*storing address of a in ptr*/
    b=*ptr;/*getting value at ptr in b*/
    printf("\n a= %d",a);/*printing value stored at a*/
    printf("\n ptr= %u",ptr);/*printing address stored at ptr*/
    printf("\n ptr=%d",*ptr);/*Level of indirection at ptr*/
    printf("\n b= %d",b);/*printing the value stored at b*/
    getch();
}
```

Output

```
a= 10
ptr= 65524
ptr=10
b= 10
```

Call by Value and Call by Reference

Call By Value	Call By Reference
When a function is called, then in that function actual values of the parameters are passed.	When a function is called, then in that function addresses of the parameters are passed.
The parameters are simple variables.	The parameters are pointer variables.
If the values of the parameters get changed in the function then that change is not permanent. That means the values of the parameter get restored when the control returns back to the caller function.	If the values of the parameters get changed in the function then that change is permanent. That means the values of the parameter get changed when the control returns back to the caller function.

For example :
main()
{
x=10;
fun(x);
printf("%d",x);
}
 	
void fun(x)
{
x=15;
}
Output will be 10 and not 15
	For example :
	main()
	{
	*x=10;
	fun(x);
	printf("%d",*x);
	}
	
	void fun(x)
	{
	x=15;
	}
	Output will be 15 and not 10

Compiler executes this type function slowly as values get copied to formal parameters.	Compiler executes this type of function faster as addresses get copied to the formal parameters

Experiment 2 : Introduction to Dynamic Memory Allocation. DMA functions malloc(), calloc(), free() etc.

- C supports with memory management using some functions. These functions can be used to allocate and free memory during the program execution.
- The following functions are used in C for purpose of memory management.

Function	Purpose
malloc	Allocates memory of desired size and returns a pointer to the 1st byte of allocated space.
calloc	Allocates space for an array of elements initializes them to zero and returns a pointer to the memory.
free	Frees previously allocated space.
realloc	Modifies the size of previously allocated space.

- The malloc function is used to allocate the memory of desired size.
- By default the malloc returns the void pointer.
- The **syntax** for malloc is

```
void *malloc(size)
```

- **For example**

```
int *i;
i=(int*)malloc(sizeof(int)
```

Program to demonstrate use of malloc function

```
// This program is for sorting the list of elements using malloc function
#include <stdio.h>
#include <conio.h>
#include <stdlib.h>
int main()
{
	int n,*p,i,j,temp;
	printf("\nHow many numbers are there?: ");
	scanf("%d",&n); //for 10 numbers enter value of n as 10
	p=(int *) malloc(n*2);
	if(p==NULL)
	{
		printf("\nMEMORY ALLOCATION UNSUCCESSFUL");
		return 0;
	}
	for(i=0;i<n;i++)
	{
		printf("\nENTER NUMBER %d: ",i+1);
		scanf("%d",p+i);
	}
	for(i=0;i<n;i++)
	{
		for(j=0;j<n;j++)
		{
			if(*(p+i)<*(p+j))
			{
				temp=*(p+i);
				*(p+i)=*(p+j);
				*(p+j)=temp;
			}
		}
	}
	printf("\nThe sorted numbers are...\n");
	for(i=0;i<n;i++)
		printf("%d ",*(p+i));
	getch();
```

```
    return 0;
}
```

Output

```
How many numbers are there?: 5
ENTER NUMBER 1: 30
ENTER NUMBER 2: 10
ENTER NUMBER 3: 50
ENTER NUMBER 4: 20
ENTER NUMBER 5: 40
The sorted numbers are...
10 20 30 40 50
```

- The **calloc** function allocates memory and then initializes it.
- Its **syntax** is

```
void *calloc(number of elements, size of single element);
```

- **For example -**

```
int *i;
```

- i=calloc(10,sizeof(int));
- The allocated block of memory can be deleted using the **free** function.
- The syntax of free is

```
void free(void *pointer)
```

For example

```
int *i;
i=(int*)malloc(sizeof(int));
free(i);
```

- The **realloc()** is a function that takes a chunk of memory. This memory is allocated with malloc() or calloc(). Then the size of the specified memory is altered.
- The syntax for relloc is

```
relloc(void *ptr, size)
```

Program to demonstrate calloc and realloc functions

```
#include<stdio.h>
#include<conio.h>
#include<alloc.h>
void main()
{
 int i,*ptr,*m,n;
 int val;
 clrscr();
 printf("\n Enter the total number of data items ");
 scanf("%d",&n);
```

```
ptr=(int*)calloc(n,sizeof(n));
for(i=0;i<n;i++)
{
 printf("\n%dth memory block contains %d",i,*ptr);
 *ptr++;
}
printf("\n Enter the new size ");
scanf("%d",&n);
realloc(ptr,n);
m=ptr;
for(i=0;i<n;i++)
{
 printf("\n Enter the data ");
 scanf("%d",&val);
 *m=val;
  *m++;
}
for(i=0;i<n;i++)
{
 printf("\n%dth memory block contains %d",i,*ptr);
 *ptr++;
}
getch();
}
```

Output

```
Enter the total number of data items 3

0th memory block contains 0
1th memory block contains 0
2th memory block contains 0
Enter the new size 5

Enter the data 11
Enter the data 22
Enter the data 33

Enter the data 44

Enter the data 55

0th memory block contains 11
1th memory block contains 22
2th memory block contains 33
```

```
3th memory block contains 44
4th memory block contains 55
```

Experiment 3 : Implement a program for stack that performs following operations using array.

(a) PUSH (b) POP (c) PEEP (d) CHANGE (e) DISPLAY

(Refer section 3.3)

Experiment 4 : Implement a program to convert infix notation to postfix notation using stack. **(Refer section 3.5.1)**

Experiment 5 : Write a program to implement QUEUE using arrays that performs following operations (a) INSERT (b) DELETE (c) DISPLAY

(Refer section 4.2)

Experiment 6 : Write a program to implement Circular Queue using arrays that performs following operations. (a) INSERT (b) DELETE (c) DISPLAY

(Refer section 4.3)

Experiment 7 : Write a menu driven program to implement following operations on the singly linked list. **(Refer section 5.2)**

(a) Insert a node at the front of the linked list.

(b) Insert a node at the end of the linked list.

(c) Insert a node such that linked list is in ascending order.(according to info. Field)

(d) Delete a first node of the linked list.

(e) Delete a node before specified position.

(f) Delete a node after specified position.

Experiment 8 : Write a program to implement stack using linked list.

(Refer section 5.5)

Experiment 9 : Write a program to implement queue using linked list.

(Refer section 5.6)

Experiment 10 : Write a program to implement following operations on the doubly linked list. **(Refer section 5.3)**

(a) Insert a node at the front of the linked list.

(b) Insert a node at the end of the linked list.

(c) Delete a last node of the linked list.

(d) Delete a node before specified position.

Experiment 11 : Write a program to implement following operations on the circular linked list. **(Refer section 5.4)**

(a) Insert a node at the end of the linked list.

(b) Insert a node before specified position.

(c) Delete a first node of the linked list.

(d) Delete a node after specified position.

Experiment 12 : Write a program which create binary search tree. **(Refer section 6.6)**

Experiment 13 : Implement recursive and non-recursive tree traversing methods inorder, preorder and post-order traversal. **(Refer section 6.5)**

Experiment 14 : Write a program to implement Queue Sort **(Refer section 10.1.3)**

Experiment 15 : Write a program to implement Merge Sort **(Refer section 10.1.4)**

Experiment 16 : Write a program to implement Bubble Sort **(Refer section 10.1.1)**

Experiment 17 : Write a program to implement Binary Search. **(Refer section 10.2.2)**

❑❑❑

Notes

Winter-2015 **Data Structures** Semester - III (CE/IT/ICT)	**Gujarat Technological University** **Solved Paper**

Time : $2\frac{1}{2}$ Hours] **[Maximum Marks : 70**

Instructions :

1) **Attempt all questions.**
2) **Make suitable assumptions wherever necessary.**
3) **Figures to the right indicate full marks.**

Q.1 *Short Questions* **[14]**

1. *Define data structure.*
(Refer Q.3 from oral questions and answers of Chapter - 1) **[1]**

2. *List operations performed on a stack.*
(Refer Q.21 from oral questions and answers of Chapter - 3) **[1]**

3. *Mention variations of the queue data structure.*
(Refer Q.17 from oral questions and answers of Chapter - 4) **[1]**

4. *What is the worst case time complexity of searching an element in a list ? How ?*
(Refer Q.13 from oral questions and answers of Chapter - 10) **[1]**

5. *Mention one operation for which use of doubly linked list is preferred over the singly linked list.*
(Refer Q.19 from oral questions and answers of Chapter - 5) **[1]**

6. *Write an algorithm/steps to traverse a singly linked list.*
(Refer Q.20 from oral questions and answers of Chapter - 5) **[1]**

7. *Define : Height of a tree.* **(Refer section 6.1.1(8))** **[1]**

8. *What is the height of a complete binary with n nodes ?*
(Refer Q.21 from oral questions and answers of Chapter - 6) **[1]**

9. *Write two simple hash functions.* **(Refer section 8.3)** **[1]**

10. *What is a header node and what is its use ?*
(Refer Q.21 from oral questions and answers of Chapter - 5) **[1]**

11. *Is Queue a priority queue ? Justify.*
(Refer Q.18 from oral questions and answers of Chapter - 4) [1]

12. *What is the complexity of binary search algorithm ?*
(Refer Q.14 from oral questions and answers of Chapter - 10) [1]

13. *Name two divide and conquer algorithms for sorting.*
(Refer Q.15 from oral questions and answers of Chapter - 10) [1]

14. *Give two applications of graphs.*
(Refer Q.16 from oral questions and answers of Chapter - 7) [1]

Q.2 a) *Write an algorithm to check if an expression has balanced parenthesis using stack.* **(Refer example 3.4.2)** [3]

b) *What is postfix notation ? What are its advantages ? Convert the following infix expression to postfix.*
A$B–C*D+E$F/G **(Refer example 3.6.5)** [4]

c) *Write a C program to implement a stack with all necessary overflow and underflow checks using array.* **(Refer section 3.3.4)** [7]

OR

c) *Write a C program to implement a circular queue using array with all necessary overflow and underflow checks.* **(Refer section 4.3)** [7]

Q.3 a) *Evaluate the following postfix expression using a stack.*
Show the stack contents.
*AB*CD$-EF/G/+*
A = 5, B = 2, C = 3, D = 2, E = 8, F = 2, G = 2 **(Refer example 3.6.6)** [3]

b) *Perform following operations in a circular queue of length 4 and give the Front, Rear and Size of the queue after each operation.*
1) Insert A, B 2) Insert C
3) Delete 4) Insert D
5) Insert E 6) Insert F
7) Delete **(Refer example 4.3.2)** [4]

c) *Write a program to insert and delete an element after a given node in a singly linked list.* **(Refer section 5.2)** [7]

OR

Q.3 a) *Explain various applications of queue.* **(Refer section 4.7)** [3]

b) *Differentiate between arrays and linked list.* **(Refer section 5.2.2)** [4]

c) *Create a doubly circularly linked list and write a function to traverse it.* **(Refer section 5.3)** [7]

Q.4 a) *Define complete binary tree and almost complete binary tree.* **(Refer section 6.2.2)** [3]

b) *Explain deletion in an AVL tree with a suitable example.* **(Refer section 6.12.3)** [4]

c) *What is binary tree traversal ? What are the various traversal methods ? Explain any two with suitable example.* **(Refer section 6.4)** [7]

OR

Q.4 a) *Mention the properties of a B-Tree.* **(Refer section 6.13)** [3]

b) *Construct a binary tree from the traversals given below :*
Inorder : 1, 10, 11, 12, 13, 14, 15, 17, 18, 21
Postorder : 1, 11, 12, 10, 14, 18, 21, 17,15, 13 **(Refer example 6.7.4)** [4]

c) *What is a binary search tree ? Create a binary search tree for inserting the following data.*
50, 45, 100, 25, 49, 120, 105, 46, 90, 95
Explain deletion in the above tree. **(Refer example 6.6.7)** [7]

Q.5 a) *Insert the following elements in a B-Tree.*
a, g, f, b, k, c, h, n, j **(Refer example 6.13.1)** [3]

b) *Apply quicksort algorithm to sort the following data. Justify the steps.*
42, 29, 74, 11, 65, 58 **(Refer example 10.1.3)** [4]

c) *What is hashing ? What are the qualities of a good hash function ? Explain any two hash functions in detail.* **(Refer sections 8.3 and 8.4)** [7]

OR

Q.5 a) *List advantages and disadvantages of Breadth First Search and Depth First Search.* **(Refer section 7.4)** [3]

b) *What is a minimum spanning tree ? Explain Kruskal's algorithm for finding a minimum spanning tree.* **(Refer section 7.7)** [4]

c) *Discuss various methods to resolve hash collision with suitable examples.* **(Refer section 8.4)** [7]

❑❑❑

Summer-2016 **Data Structures** Semester - III (CE/IT/ICT)	**Gujarat Technological University** **Solved Paper**

Time : 2 $\frac{1}{2}$ Hours] [Maximum Marks : 70

Instructions :

1) Attempt all questions.
2) Make suitable assumptions wherever necessary.
3) Figures to the right indicate full marks.

Q.1 *Short Questions* [14]

1. *Define primitive data structure.*
(Refer Q.13 from oral questions and answers of chapter 1)

2. *Explain space and time complexity.*
(Refer Q.10 and Q.11 from oral questions and answers of chapter 1)

3. *What is the time complexity of quicksort algorithm in the worst case ?*
(Refer Q.18 from oral questions and answers of chapter 10)

4. *List the applications of stack.*
(Refer Q.13 from oral questions and answers of chapter 3)

5. *Define graph.* **(Refer Q.1 from oral questions and answers of chapter 7)**

6. *Explain degree of a vertex in a graph.*
(Refer Q.6 from oral questions and answers of chapter 7)

7. *List the applications of graphs.*
(Refer Q.3 from oral questions and answers of chapter 7)

8. *List the applications of Binary trees.*
(Refer Q.4 from oral questions and answers of chapter 6)

9. *Define B-tree.* **(Refer Q.18 from oral questions and answers of chapter 6)**

10. *Describe the time complexity of binary search algorithm.*
(Refer Q.14 from oral questions and answers of chapter 10)

11. *What is hash collision ?*
(Refer Q.11 from oral questions and answers of chapter 8)

12. *Write 'C' structure of binary tree.*
(Refer Q.6 from oral questions and answers of chapter 6)

13. *Write 'C' structure of singly linked list.* **(Refer section 5.1.1)**

14. *Define priority queue.*
(Refer Q.19 from oral questions and answers of chapter 4)

Q.2 a) *Write an algorithm for simple queue with ENQUEUE operations.*
(Refer example 4.2) [3]

b) *Write an algorithm to reverse a string using stack.* **(Refer example 3.4.1)** [4]

c) *Write a program to implement stack using linked list.* **(Refer section 5.5)** [7]

OR

c) *Write a program to implement circular queue using array.* **(Refer section 4.3)**[7]

Q.3 a) *Evaluate the following postfix expression using a stack.*
*a) 9 3 4 * 8 + 4 / - b) 5 6 2 + * 1 2 4 / - +* **(Refer example 3.6.7)** [3]

b) *Explain the concept of circular queue. Compare circular queue with simple queue.*
(Refer example 4.3) [4]

c) *Explain insert and delete operations in AVL trees with suitable examples.*
(Refer section 6.12) [7]

OR

Q.3 a) *Explain double ended queue.* **(Refer section 4.6)** [3]

b) *Write 'C' functions to implement DELETE_FIRST_NODE and TRAVERSE operations in doubly linked list.* **(Refer section 5.3)** [4]

c) *With a suitable example, explain steps for conversion of a general tree into a binary tree.* **(Refer section 6.8)** [7]

Q.4 a) *Explain sequential search method.* **(Refer section 10.2.1)** [3]

b) *Explain threaded binary trees with suitable examples.*
(Refer section 6.9) [4]

c) *Write an algorithm for selection sort method. Explain each step with an example.*
(Refer section 10.1.2) [7]

OR

Q.4 a) *Explain depth first search in graphs with an example.* **(Refer section 7.4.2)** **[3]**

b) *Explain binary search method.* **(Refer section 10.2.2)** **[4]**

c) *Write an algorithm for insertion sort method. Explain each step with an example.* **(Refer section 10.1.5)** **[7]**

Q.5 a) *Explain breadth first search in graphs with an example.*
a, g, f, b, k, c, h, n, j **(Refer section 7.4.1)** **[3]**

b) *Construct a binary tree from the traversals given below :*
Inorder : 1 3 4 6 7 8 10 13 14
Preorder : 8 3 1 6 4 7 10 14 13 **(Refer example 6.7.5)** **[4]**

c) *Explain various hash collision resolution techniques with examples.* **(Refer section 8.5)** **[7]**

OR

Q.5 a) *Explain sequential file organizations and list its advantages and disadvantages.* **(Refer section 9.4)** **[3]**

b) *Draw a binary expression tree for the following and perform preorder traversal :* *(A $ B $ C) + (D – E * F).* **(Refer example 6.2.4)** **[4]**

c) *Write Prim's algorithm for minimum spanning tree with an example.* **(Refer section 7.7.1)** **[7]**

❑❑❑

Winter-2016 **Data Structures** Semester - III (CE/IT/ICT)	**Gujarat Technological University** **Solved Paper**

Time : 2 $\frac{1}{2}$ Hours] **[Maximum Marks : 70**

Instructions :

1) **Attempt all questions.**
2) **Make suitable assumptions wherever necessary.**
3) **Figures to the right indicate full marks.**

Q.1 *Explain the following terms in brief.* **[14]**

1. *Primitive data structure.*
(Refer Q.13 from oral questions and answers of chapter 1)

2. *Non-primitive data structure.*
(Refer Q.16 from oral questions and answers of chapter 1)

3. *Linear data structure.*
(Refer Q.17 from oral questions and answers of chapter 1)

4. *Non-linear data structure.*
(Refer Q.18 from oral questions and answers of chapter 1)

5. *Recursion.* **(Refer Q.22 from oral questions and answers of chapter 3)**

6. *Time complexity of an algorithm.*
(Refer Q.10 from oral questions and answers of chapter 1)

7. *Double-ended queue.*
(Refer Q.20 from oral questions and answers of chapter 4)

8. *Priority queue.*
(Refer Q.19 from oral questions and answers of chapter 4)

9. *Circular linked list.*
(Refer Q.23 from oral questions and answers of chapter 5)

10. *Complete binary tree.*
(Refer Q.8 from oral questions and answers of chapter 6)

11. *2-3 tree.* **(Refer Q.22 from oral questions and answers of chapter 6)**

12. *Minimum spanning tree.*
(Refer Q.11 from oral questions and answers of chapter 7)

13. *Degree of vertex.*
(Refer Q.17 from oral questions and answers of chapter 7)

14. *Hash collision.*
(Refer Q.11 from oral questions and answers of chapter 8)

Q.2 a) *Write a pseudo-code for PUSH and POP operations of stack.*
(Refer section 3.3.3) **[3]**

b) *What is prefix notation ? Convert the following infix expression into prefix.*
*A + B – C * D * E $ F $ G* **(Refer example 3.5.10)** **[4]**

c) *Write an algorithm to perform various operations (insert, delete and display) for simple queue.* **(Refer section 4.2)** **[7]**

OR

c) *Write differences between simple queue and circular queue. Write an algorithm for insert and delete operations for circular queue.* **(Refer section 4.3)** **[7]**

Q.3 a) *Convert the following infix expression into postfix.*
*A + B – C * D * E $ F $ G* **(Refer example 3.5.5)** **[3]**

b) *Write algorithm(s) to perform INSERT_FIRST (to insert a node at the first position) and REVERSE_TRAVERSE (to display the data in nodes in reverse order) operations in doubly linked list.* **(Refer section 5.3)** **[4]**

c) *Write a 'C' program to implement stack using linked list.*
(Refer section 5.5) **[7]**

OR

Q.3 a) *Enlist and briefly explain various applications of stack.* **(Refer section 3.4)** **[3]**

b) *Discuss various rehashing techniques.* **(Refer section 8.5.7)** **[4]**

c) *Write 'C' functions to implement INSERT_FIRST (to insert a node at the first position), DELETE_FIRST (to delete a node from the first position), DELETE_LAST (delete a node from the last position) and TRAVERSE (to display the data in nodes) operations in circular linked list.*
(Refer section 5.4) **[7]**

Q.4 a) *Write an algorithm for binary search method.* **(Refer section 10.2.2)** **[3]**

b) *Write a 'C' program for Bubble sort.* **(Refer section 10.1.1)** [4]

c) *Sort the following numbers using (i) Selection sort (ii) Quick sort.*
10 50 0 20 30 10 **(Refer example 10.1.5)** [7]

OR

Q.4 a) *Write a 'C' function for selection sort.* **(Refer section 10.1.2)** [3]

b) *Write an algorithm for quick sort.* **(Refer section 10.1.3)** [4]

c) *Explain depth first search and breadth first search in graphs with an example.* **(Refer section 7.4)** [7]

Q.5 a) *Draw a binary expression tree for the following and perform preorder traversal for the same :*
*(A + B $ C) + (D + E * F)* **(Refer example 6.4.5)** [3]

b) *Construct a binary search tree for the following and perform inorder and postorder traversals :*
5 9 4 8 2 1 3 7 6 **(Refer example 6.6.8)** [4]

c) *Write 'C' functions for : inserting a node, postorder traversal and counting total number of nodes for binary search tree.* **(Refer example 6.6.9)** [7]

OR

Q.5 a) *Explain AVL trees.* **(Refer section 6.12)** [3]

b) *Construct a binary search tree from the following traversals :*
Inorder : 3 4 5 6 7 9 17 20 22
Preorder : 9 4 3 6 5 7 17 22 20 **(Refer example 6.7.6)** [4]

c) *Write Kruskal's algorithm for minimum spanning tree with an example.* **(Refer section 7.7.2)** [7]

❑❑❑

Summer-2017 **Data Structures** Semester - III (CE/IT/ICT)	**Gujarat Technological University** **Solved Paper**

Time : 2 $\frac{1}{2}$ Hours] **[Maximum Marks : 70**

Instructions :

1) **Attempt all questions.**
2) **Make suitable assumptions wherever necessary.**
3) **Figures to the right indicate full marks.**

Q.1 *Short Questions* **[14]**

1. *Arithmetic expression evaluation is an explanation of which data structure ?*
(Refer Q.19 from oral questions and answers of chapter 1) **[1]**

2. *How many stacks are needed to implement a queue. Consider the situation where no other data structure like arrays, linked list is available.*
(Refer Q.21 from oral questions and answers of chapter 4) **[1]**

3. *A graph containing only isolated nodes is called a ___.*
(Refer Q.18 from oral questions and answers of chapter 7) **[1]**

4. *What is the 2's complement representation for integer 5 in modulo 16 ?*
(Refer Q.19 from oral questions and answers of chapter 8) **[1]**

5. *What is the result of 7 + 7 using 2's complement representation and modulo 16 arithmetic.*
(Refer Q.20 from oral questions and answers of chapter 8) **[1]**

6. *In which type of tree, each leaf node is kept at the same distance from root ?*
(Refer Q.23 from oral questions and answers of chapter 6) **[1]**

7. *What is the reverse polish notation for infix expression a/b*c ?*
(Refer Q.23 from oral questions and answers of chapter 3) **[1]**

8. *What does the following function do for a given Linked List with first node as head ?*

```
void fun1 (struct node* head)
{
if (head == NULL)
```

return;
fun1(head->next);
printf("%d", head->data);
} **(Refer Q.24 from oral questions and answers of chapter 5)**

9. *Which of the traversal technique outputs the data in sorted order in a Binary Search Tree ?*
(Refer Q.24 from oral questions and answers of chapter 6) **[1]**

10. *What is common in inorder, preorder and postorder traversal ?*
(Refer Q.25 from oral questions and answers of chapter 6) **[1]**

11. *For sorting 1 GB of data with only 100 MB of available main memory. Which sorting technique will be most appropriate ?*
(Refer Q.16 from oral questions and answers of chapter 10) **[1]**

12. *In 2-3 trees, what do leaves contain and what do nonleaf nodes indicate ?*
(Refer Q.26 from oral questions and answers of chapter 6) **[1]**

13. *Consider a situation where swap operation is very costly. Which of the sorting algorithms should be preferred so that the number of swap operations are minimized in general ?*
(Refer Q.17 from oral questions and answers of chapter 10) **[1]**

14. *Draw tree whose postorder traversal is C B F E G D A*
(Refer Q.27 from oral questions and answers of chapter 6) **[1]**

Q.2 a) *Write an algorithm for finding average of given numbers. Calculate time complexity.* **(Refer example 1.4.6)** **[3]**

b) *Given Inorder and Preorder traversal, find Postorder traversal.*
Inorder traversal = {4, 2, 5, 1, 3, 6}
Preorder traversal = {1, 2, 4, 5, 3, 6} **(Refer example 6.7.7)** **[4]**

c) *Consider an example where the size of the queue is four elements. Initially the queue is empty. It is required to insert symbols 'A', 'B' and 'C'. Delete 'A' and 'B' and insert 'D' and 'E'. Show the trace of the contents of the queue.*
(Refer example 4.3.5) **[7]**

OR

c) *Insertion sequence of names is :*
Norma, Roger, John, Bill, Leo, Paul, Ken and Maurice
i) Show the behavior of creating a lexically ordered binary tree.
ii) Insert Kirk. Show the binary tree.
iii) Delete John. Show the binary tree. **(Refer example 6.6.10)** **[7]**

Q.3 a) *Write an algorithm to return the value of ith element from top of the stack.* **(Refer example 3.3.2)** **[3]**

b) *Write an algorithm for inserting an element in a stack, removing an element from stack.* **(Refer section 3.3.3)** **[4]**

c) *Write an algorithm for inserting and deleting an element in a circular queue.* **(Refer section 4.3)** **[7]**

OR

Q.3 a) *Consider the expression v1*v2 – (v3 + v4 ^ v5). Show the tree corresponding to the expression.* **[3]**

Ans. :

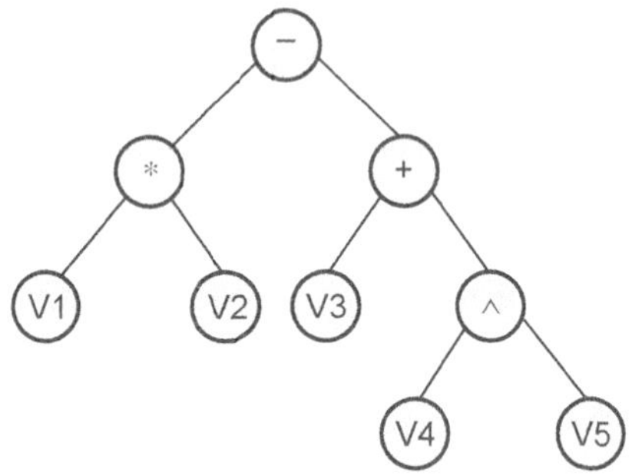

Expression Tree

b) *What is an ordered tree ? What is forest ?* **[4]**

Ans. : Ordered Tree : An ordered tree contains nodes which can be ordered according to particular criteria.

Binary Search Tree is said to be an ordered tree in which left node is always less than parent node while right node is greater than parent node value.

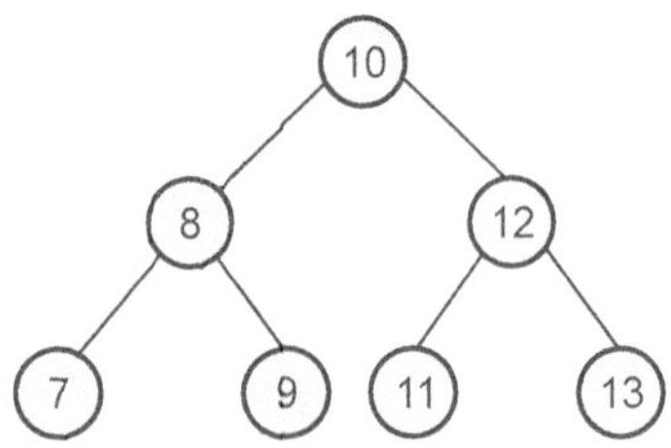

Ordered Tree

Forest : Refer section 6.1.1 (13).

c) *Explain the structure of indexed sequential file.* **(Refer section 9.5)** **[7]**

Q.4 a) *Consider singly linked storage structures. Write an algorithm which inserts a node into a linked linear list in a stack like manner.* **(Refer section 5.5)** [3]

b) *How open addressing can be used for collision resolution ?* **(Refer section 8.5.2)** [4]

c) *Explain structure of sequential file. Explain processing in sequential file.* **(Refer section 9.4)** [7]

OR

Q.4 a) *Consider singly linked storage structures. Write an algorithm which performs an insertion at the end of a linked linear list.* **(Refer section 5.2 (3))** [3]

b) *Give definitions : i) Graph* **(Refer section 7.1)**
ii) Adjacent nodes [4]

c) *What is priority queue ? Explain the array representation of priority queue.* **(Refer section 4.5)** [7]

Q.5 a) *Explain outdegree and indegree.* **(Refer section 7.2)** [3]

b) *Explain Depth First Search operation.* **(Refer section 7.4.2)** [4]

c) *Explain the trace of selection sort on following data :*
42, 23, 74, 11, 65, 58, 94, 36, 99, 87 **(Refer section 10.1.2)** [7]

OR

Q.5 a) *Write and explain application of queue.* **(Refer section 4.7)** [3]

b) *Explain Breadth First Search operation.* **(Refer section 7.4.1)** [4]

c) *Explain the trace of bubble sort on following data.*
42, 23, 74, 11, 65, 58, 94, 36, 99, 87 **(Refer similar example 10.1.1)** [7]

❑❑❑

# Winter-2017 ## Data Structures Semester - III (CE/IT/ICT)	Gujarat Technological University **Solved Paper**

Time : $2\frac{1}{2}$ Hours] **[Maximum Marks : 70**

Instructions :

1) **Attempt all questions.**
2) **Make suitable assumptions wherever necessary.**
3) **Figures to the right indicate full marks.**

Q.1 a) *A two dimensional array is stored row by row, then what is the address of matrix element A[i, j] for n row and m column matrix ? How array representation of polynomial $2x^2 + 5xy + y^2$ can be done ?* **[3]**

Ans. : Refer section 2.2

Polynomial $2x^2 + 5xy + y^2$ using arrays.

coeff	exp_x	exp_y
2	2	0
5	1	1
1	0	2

b) *Which data structure is used in a time sharing single central processing unit and one main memory computer system where many users share the system simultaneously ? How users are added for use of the system ?*
(Refer section 4.7) **[4]**

c) *The preorder traversal of the tree is*
7, 1, 0, 3, 2, 5, 4, 6, 9, 8, 10,
The inorder traversal of the tree is
0, 1, 2, 3, 4, 5, 6, 7, 8, 9, 10.
What is the postorder traversal ?
How a general tree can be converted to binary tree ? **(Refer example 6.7.8)** **[7]**

Q.2 a) *What is the problem with sign and magnitude representation if addition of +7 with –6 is performed ? Evaluate 7 + 7 using 2's complement representation and modulo 16 arithmetic.*
(Refer Q.21 from oral questions and answers of chapter 8) **[3]**

b) *Write an algorithm for calculating square of the number for all the prime numbers ranging between 1 to n. Perform time and space analysis.*
(Refer example 1.4.7) **[4]**

c) *Given a linked list whose typical node consists of an INFO and LINK field. Formulate an algorithm which will count the number of nodes in the list.*
(Refer section 5.2.1) **[7]**

OR

c) *What is the need of doubly linked linear list to the left of a specified node whose address is given by variable M. Give details of algorithm.* **(Refer section 5.3)** **[7]**

Q.3 a) *How directed tree can be represented ?* **(Refer section 6.3)** **[3]**

b) *How following has functions work ?*
i) The midsquare method ii) Digit analysis **(Refer section 8.3)** **[4]**

c) *i) In which case insertion and delection cannot be performed in stack ?*
ii) How stack can be used to recognize strings aca, bcb, abcba, bacab, abbcbba ? Show the trace of contents of stack for recognizing the string abcba.
(Refer example 3.3.2) **[7]**

OR

Q.3 a) *How primitive data type floating point is stored in computer ?* **[3]**

Ans. : The floating point number is stored in computer system using Mantissa and an exponent. This form is brought in $M \times 10^E$ format. The value of M and E are converted to equivalent binary form, to store in computer system.

b) *A communications network is represented by graph. Each node represents a communication line and each edge indicate the presence of interconnection between the lines. Which traversal technique can be used to find breakdown in line ? Explain.* **(Refer example 1.2.1)** **[4]**

c) *i) Convert a+b*c-d/e*h to postfix.*
ii) Convert ((a+b^c^d)(e+f/d)) to postfix.*
iii) Which stack operations are needed for performing conversion from infix to postfix ? Write the algorithm. **(Refer example 3.5.6)** **[7]**

Q.4 a) *How many full branches a binary tree possesses ?*
(Refer Q.28 from oral questions and answers of chapter 6) [3]

b) *What is the difference between serial and sequential processing ? How a record can be deleted in sequential file ?* [4]

Ans. : The difference between a sequential file and serial file is that - the sequential file is ordered in a logical sequence based on a key field. While in serial files, records are entered in the order of their creation.

The record can be deleted from sequential file, using logical deletion. That means simply change the values of records to some negative or null values.

c) *What is the advantage of circular queue ? Write an algorithm for inserting 'A', 'B', 'C', delete 'A' and 'B' and insert 'D' and 'E' in circular queue.*
(Refer Q.2 (c) of summer 2017) [7]

OR

Q.4 a) *Explain indexing structure for index file.* **(Refer section 9.5)** [3]

b) *Write recursive algorithm for computing factorial. Which data structure can be used to implement this algorithm ?* **(Refer section 3.10)** [4]

c) *"If no interchanges occurred, then the table must be sorted and no further passes are required". Which sorting method works on this principal ?*
Apply above sorting technique on the following data
5 1 4 2 8 **(Refer example 10.1.2)** [7]

Q.5 a) *How does priority queue work ?* **(Refer section 4.5)** [3]

b) *How binary search technique can be applied to search for a particular item with a certain key ?* **(Refer section 10.2.2)** [4]

c) *Apply quick sort on following data*
42 23 74 11 65 58 94 36 99 87. **(Refer similar example 10.1.3)** [7]

OR

Q.5 a) *Explain the structure of threaded binary tree.* **(Refer section 6.9)** [3]

b) *How access of record is performed in multi key file organization ?*
(Refer section 9.7) [4]

c) *Hash function map several keys into same address called collision. How collision resolution techniques work ?* **(Refer section 8.5)** [7]

❑❑❑

Summer-2018 **Data Structures** Semester - III (CE/IT)	**Gujarat Technological University** **Solved Paper**

Time : 2 $\frac{1}{2}$ Hours] **[Total Marks : 70**

Instructions :

1) **Attempt all questions.**
2) **Make suitable assumptions wherever necessary.**
3) **Figures to the right indicate full marks.**

Q.1 a) *Differentiate between linear and non-linear data structures.* **(Refer section 1.6)** [3]

b) *Discuss the variations of a queue.* **(Refer section 4.6)** [4]

c) *Write an algorithm to convert an infix expression to postfix expression. Show the working of the algorithm for the following expression.*
*A+B*C/D$E – (F*G)* **(Refer example 3.5.7)** [7]

Q.2 a) *Evaluate the following postfix expression using a stack. Show the steps.*
*2 $ 3 + 5 * 2 $ 2 – 12 $ 6* **(Refer example 3.6.8)** [3]

b) *Consider the stack S of characters, where S is allocated 18 memory cells.*
S : A, C, D, F, K,_, _, _
Describe the stack as the following operations take place.
Pop(), Pop(), Push(L), Push(P), Pop(), Push(R), Push(S), Pop()
(Refer example 3.3.4) [4]

c) *Write a program to implement queue and check for boundary conditions.* **(Refer section 4.2)** [7]

OR

c) *Write a program to implement a circularly linked list.* **(Refer section 5.4)** [7]

Q.3 a) *List the advantages of a doubly linked list over singly linked list.* **(Refer section 5.3)** [3]

b) *Write an algorithm to swap two nodes, n and n+1, in a singly linked list.* **(Refer example 5.2.3)** [4]

c) *Perform inorder, postorder and preorder traversals for the following binary tree.*

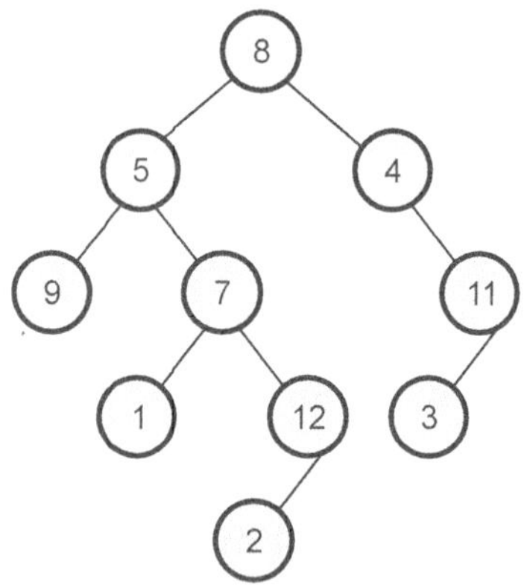

Fig. 1

What is the peculiarity of the inorder traversal ? **(Refer example 6.4.6)** **[7]**

OR

Q.3 a) *What is a header node ? Explain is importance.*
(Refer Q.11 from oral questions and answers of chapter 5) **[3]**

b) *Write an algorithm to count the number of nodes in a singly circularly linked list.* **(Refer example 5.4.2)** **[4]**

c) *What is a binary search tree ? Create a binary search tree for the following data.*
14, 10, 17, 12, 10, 11, 20, 12, 18, 25, 20, 8, 22, 11, 23
Explain deleting node 20 in the resultant binary search tree.
(Refer example 6.6.11) **[7]**

Q.4 a) *Explain the working of the Kruskal's algorithm.* **(Refer section 7.7)** **[3]**

b) *Write the algorithm for binary search and find its complexity.*
(Refer section 10.2) **[4]**

c) *Insert the following letters into an empty B-tree of order 5 :*
C N G A H E K Q M F W L T Z D P R X Y S **(Refer example 6.13.2)** **[7]**

OR

Q.4 a) *Define the following terms with respect to a graph : Node, Edge, Path.*
(Refer section 7.2) **[3]**

b) *Discuss different representations of a graph.* **(Refer section 7.3)** **[4]**

c) *Apply Dikstra's algorithm for the following graph with Node S as the starting node.* **(Refer example 7.8.1)** **[7]**

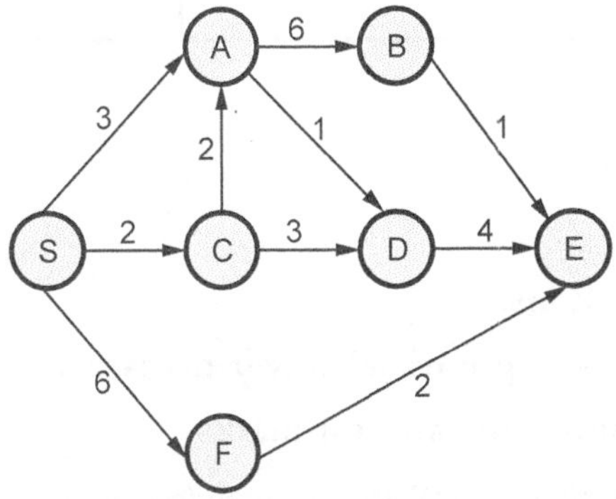

Fig. 3

Q.5 a) *What is the complexity of the quick sort algorithm on sorted data ? Justify your answer.* **(Refer section 10.1.3)** **[3]**

b) *What is hashing ? Explain hash collision and any one collision resolution technique.* **(Refer section 8.5)** **[4]**

c) *Explain the difference between insertion sort and selection sort with an example. What is the time complexity of these algorithms ? How ?*
(Refer section 10.1.5) **[7]**

OR

Q.5 a) *List the qualities of a good hash function.* **(Refer section 8.4)** **[3]**

b) *Explain two hash functions.* **(Refer section 8.3)** **[4]**

c) *Apply merge sort algorithm for the following data and show the steps.*
66, 33, 40, 22, 55, 88, 11, 80, 20, 50, 44, 77, 30.
(Refer example 10.1.7) **[7]**

❑❑❑

Winter-2018 **Data Structures** Semester - III (CE/IT)	**Gujarat Technological University** **Solved Paper**

Time : 2 $\frac{1}{2}$ Hours] **[Total Marks : 70**

Instructions :

1) **Attempt all questions.**
2) **Make suitable assumptions wherever necessary.**
3) **Figures to the right indicate full marks.**

Q.1 a) *What is Recursion ? Write a pseudocode in 'C' language to find the multiplication of two natural numbers.* **(Refer example 3.7.1)** **[3]**

b) *Differentiate between Stack and Queue.* **(Refer section 4.1)** **[4]**

c) *Write algorithm for Push and Pop operations on a stack.* **(Refer section 3.3)** **[7]**

Q.2 a) *Convert Infix Expression A ^ B * C – D + E / F / (G + H) into Postfix expression using stack.* **(Refer example 3.5.8)** **[3]**

b) *Explain average case timing analysis for Search Algorithm.* **(Refer section 1.5)** **[4]**

c) *Write an algorithms to convert Infix Expression (without parenthesis) into Postfix Expression.* **(Refer section 3.5)** **[7]**

OR

c) *Write algorithms for Insert and Delete operation in Circular Queue.* **(Refer section 4.3)** **[7]**

Q.3 a) *Evaluate the Postfix Expression 6 2 3 + – 3 8 2 / + * 2 $ 3 + using Stack.* **(Refer example 3.6.8)** **[3]**

b) *Write an algorithm for insertion of node at last position in Liner Linked List.* **(Refer section 5.2)** **[4]**

c) *Create a Binary Search Tree for the following data and do Inorder, Preorder and Postorder traversal of the tree.* **[7]**

45, 70, 30, 60, 15, 75, 35, 55, 20, 85, 80 **(Refer example 6.6.12)**

OR

Q.3 a) *Explain Priority Queue ?* **(Refer section 4.4)** [3]

b) *Write an algorithm for deletion of node in Liner Linked List.* **(Refer section 5.2)** [4]

c) *What is Binary Search Tree ? Construct a binary search tree for the following elements 11, 6, 14, 8, 12, 15, 16, 7, 9, 23.* **(Refer example 6.6.13)** [7]

Q.4 a) *Write an algorithm for Bubble sort.* **(Refer section 10.1.1)** [3]

b) *Write an algorithm for insertion of a node in Doubly Linked List.* **(Refer section 5.3)** [4]

c) *What is hashing ? Explain Different Hashing techniques in brief.* **(Refer section 8.3)** [7]

OR

Q.4 a) *Write an algorithm for Selection sort.* **(Refer section 10.1.2)** [3]

b) *Write an algorithm for deletion of a node in Doubly Linked List.* **(Refer section 5.3)** [4]

c) *What is hashing ? Explain hash clash and its resolving techniques.* **(Refer section 8.5)** [7]

Q.5 a) *Explain spanning tree with example.* **(Refer section 7.7)** [3]

b) *Write an algorithm for Sequential Search.* **(Refer section 10.2)** [4]

c) *Explain different types of File Organizations and discuss the advantages and disadvantages of each of them.* **(Refer section 9.6)** [7]

OR

Q.5 a) *What is Topological sorting ?* **(Refer section 10.1.6)** [3]

b) *Write an algorithm for Binary Search.* **(Refer section 10.2)** [4]

c) *Explain Sequential Files and Indexed Sequential Files Structures.* **(Refer section 9.6)** [7]

□□□

SOLVED MODEL QUESTION PAPER

Data Structures

Semester - III (CE/IT)

Time : $2\frac{1}{2}$ Hours] [Total Marks : 70

Instructions :

1) Attempt all questions.
2) Make suitable assumptions wherever necessary.
3) Figures to the right indicate full marks.

Q.1 a) *Define data type. Narrate importance of abstract datatype with suitable example.* **(Refer section 1.2)** **(3)**

b) *Write an algorithm for finding average of given numbers. Calculate time complexity.* **(Refer example 1.4.6)** **(4)**

c) *What is sparse matrix? Give the algorithm for addition of two sparse matrices* **(Refer section 2.5)** **(7)**

Q. 2 a) *Write an algorithm to return the value of element from top of the stack.* **(Refer example 3.3.2)** **(3)**

b) *Explain push and pop operations on a stack.* **(Refer section 3.3.3)** **(4)**

c) *Perform following operations in a circular queue of length 4 and give the front, Rear and size of the queue after each operation*
1) Insert A, B 2) Insert C
3) Delete 4) Insert D.
5) Insert E 6) Insert F 7) Delete **(Refer example 4.3.4)** **(7)**

OR

c) *Explain insert and delete operation in simple queue.* **(Refer section 4.2)** **(7)**

Q.3 a) *Give C representation of Linked list* **(Refer section 5.1.1)** **(3)**

b) *Consider singly linked storage structures. Write an algorithm which performs an insertion at the end of a linked linear list.* **(Refer section 5.2)** **(4)**

c) *Write C program for concatenation of two linked lists* **(Refer section 5.2.1(3)** **(7)**

OR

Q.3 a) *Explain terms in terms of tree: height, degree, forest.* **(Refer section 6.1)** **(3)**

b) *Write an algorithm for deletion of a node in doubly linked list.* **(Refer section 5.3)** **(4)**

c) *What is binary tree traversal ? What are the various traversal methods ? Explain any two with suitable example.* **(Refer section 6.4)** **(7)**

Q.4 a) *Make comparison between Graph and Tree.* **(Refer section 7.1.1)** **(3)**

b) *Explain types of graph with suitable examples* **(Refer section 7.1.2)** **(4)**

c) *Define the following terms*
1) Graph 2) Tree 3) Multigraph 4) Weighted graph
5) Elementary path 6) Complete Binary Tree
7) Descendent node **(Refer example 7.2.2)** **(7)**

OR

Q.4 a) *What is symbol table? Give advantages of symbol table* **(Refer section 8.1)** **(3)**

b) *Explain two hash functions.* **(Refer section 8.3)** **(4)**

c) *The keys 12, 18, 13, 2, 3, 23, 5 and 15 are inserted into an initially empty hash table of length 10 using open addressing with hash function h(k) = k mod 10 and linear probing. What is the resultant hash table ?* **(Refer example 8.5.1)** **(7)**

Q.5 a) *Explain the terms - File, Records and Fields.* **(Refer section 9.1)** **(3)**

b) *Give advantages and disadvantages of sequential file* **(Refer section 9.4)** **(4)**

c) *Explain Multi-key File organization with suitable example.* **(Refer section 9.7)** **(7)**

OR

Q.5 a) *Explain the terms - (1) Sorting order (2) Internal Sorting (3) External Sorting* **(Refer section 10.1)** **(3)**

b) *Sort the following list of numbers using bubble sort technique 52, 1, 27, 85, 66, 23, 13, 57.* **(Refer example 10.1.1)** **(4)**

c) *Explain binary search algorithm with suitable example.* **(Refer section 10.2.2)** **(7)**

❑❑❑

Notes

Winter-2019 Data Structures Semester - III (CE/IT)	Gujarat Technological University Solved Paper

Time : $2\frac{1}{2}$ Hours] [Total Marks : 70

Instructions :

1) Attempt all questions.

2) Make suitable assumptions wherever necessary.

3) Figures to the right indicate full marks.

Q.1 a) *Discuss various types of data structures with example.* **(Refer section 1.6)** [3]

b) *What is hash function used for ? Give one example of a hash function.* **(Refer section 8.3)** [4]

c) *What is time and space analysis ? State and explain time analysis for linear search and binary search method.* **(Refer section 10.2)** [7]

Q.2 a) *Compare array and link list.* **(Refer section 5.2.2)** [3]

b) *State disadvantages of simple queue. How to overcome it ?* **(Refer section 4.3)** [4]

c) *Write an algorithm for INSERT, DELETE and DISPLAY function of circular queue.* **(Refer section 4.3)** [7]

OR

c) *Write an algorithm for INSERT operation to insert a node at a given position in a link list.* **(Refer section 5.2(3))** [7]

Q.3 a) *Discuss height balance tree.* **(Refer section 6.12)** [3]

b) *Discuss minimal spanning tree.* **(Refer section 7.7)** [4]

c) *Write a recursive function to compute factorial of a number. Show usage of STACK in recursion for this function.* **(Refer section 3.7.2)** [7]

OR

Q.3 a) *Write an algorithm to find length of a simple link list.* **(Refer section 5.2.1(1))** [3]

b) *Write an algorithm to insert a node in a circular link list at the FIRST position.* **(Refer section 5.4(3))** **[4]**

c) *Write an algorithm for DELETE operation in a binary search tree.* **(Refer section 6.6(2))** **[7]**

Q.4 a) *Discuss threaded binary tree.* **(Refer section 6.9)** **[3]**

b) *Write an algorithm for a non recursive (Iterative) pre order traversal of binary search tree.* **(Refer section 6.5 (C program for non-recursive traversal))** **[4]**

c) *Create an AVL tree for the following sentence of numbers. Also mention name of action taken.* **[7]**

200, 400, 800, 900, 850, 700, 950, 100, 150
(Refer similar example 6.12.2)

OR

Q.4 a) *Define following with respect to Tree :* **[3]**

i) M-ary tree **(Refer section 6.13)**

ii) Out degree **(Refer section 6.1.1)**

iii) Leaf **(Refer section 6.1.1)**

b) *State at least one efficient representation of a ...***(insufficient data)** **[4]**

c) *Discuss algorithm of Breadth First Search (BFS) traversal for a graph. Explain with an example.* **(Refer section 7.4.1)** **[7]**

Q.5 a) *Write algorithm for bubble sort method.* **(Refer section 10.1.1)** **[3]**

b) *Write algorithm for merge sort method.* **(Refer section 10.1.4)** **[4]**

c) *Explain sequential files and indexed sequential files structures.* **(Refer sections 9.4 and 9.5)** **[7]**

OR

Q.5 a) *Create 2-3 tree for the following sequence : 50, 100, 150, 200.* **[3]**

Ans. :

Step 1 : Insert 50

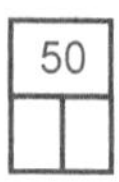

Step 2 : Insert 100

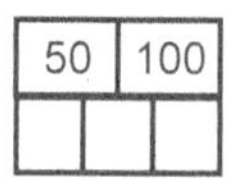

Step 3 : Insert 150

We will arrange 50, 100, 150. The middle element 100 will go up.

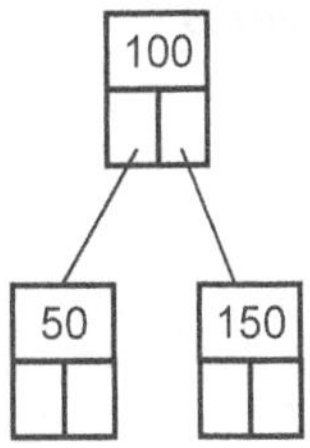

Step 4 : Insert 200

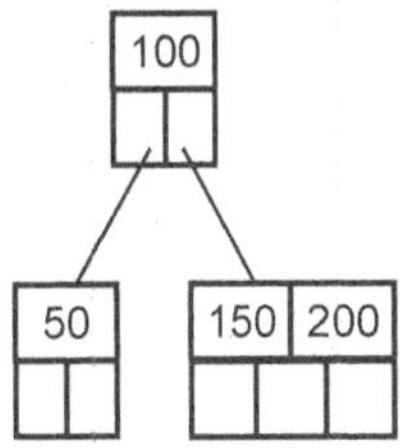

b) *Represent following in form of an expression tree :* $A + B^{*}(C + D)$ **[4]**

Ans. :

Step 1 :

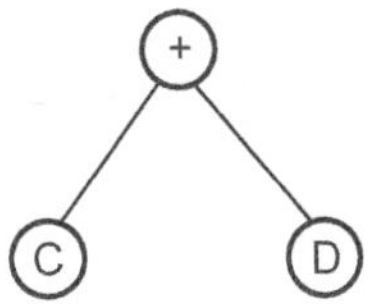

Step 2 :

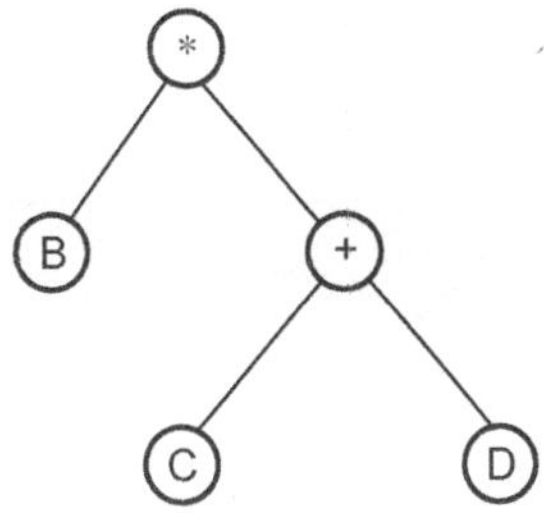

Step 3 :

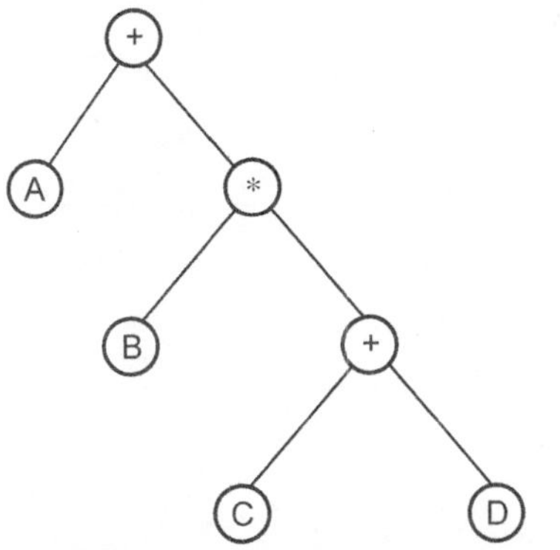

c) *State and explain collision resolution techniques in hashing.*
(Refer section 8.5) **[7]**

❑❑❑

Notes